THE GREAT BEYOND
Scientific Evidence of Life after Death

"If the world is rationally constructed, there must be an afterlife."

Kurt Gödel

THE GREAT BEYOND

Scientific Evidence of Life after Death

Sudipta Kumar De

KALPAZ

First Published, 2020

Published by

Kalpaz Publications
C-30, Satyawati Nagar,
Delhi – 110052
Ph.: 011-47034999, 9811692060
www.kalpazpublications.com
E-mail: kalpaz@hotmail.com

Printed at: G. Print Process, Delhi

Cataloging in Publication Data—DK
Courtesy: D.K. Agencies (P) Ltd. <docinfo@dkagencies.com>

De, Sudipta Kumar, author.
The great beyond: scientific evidence of life after death / Sudipta Kumar De.
pages cm
ISBN 9789353241919

1. Future life. 2. Religion and science. 3. Evidence. I. Title.

LCC BF1311.F8D47 2019 | DDC 202.3 23

Contents

Introduction 7

CHAPTER 1
Life and death are illusions of mind 13

CHAPTER 2
Otherworld journeys - strange cases of OBE and NDE 47

CHAPTER 3
Deathbed phenomena 133

CHAPTER 4
Ghosts, apparitions and after-death contacts 173

CHAPTER 5
Demon possession 237

CHAPTER 6
Psychical unfoldment through mediumship and channeling 257

CHAPTER 7
Reincarnation 303

CHAPTER 8
The law of Karma 381

CHAPTER 9
The spirit world 405

References 439

Introduction

"*Death is not extinguishing the light; it is putting out the lamp because dawn has come.*"

Nobel Laureate Poet Rabindranath Tagore

"*When one door closes another door opens; but we often look so long and so regretfully upon the closed door, that we do not see the ones which open for us.*"

Alexander Graham Bell, inventor and educator, b. 1847

The universal criterion of humanity is to seek the meaning of life and understanding its purpose. The earthly life of every conscious individual should have two important concerns – the origin (from where I came?) and the destination (where will I go after death?), and these two concerns have too much importance to the meaning the individual gives to his life. Our faculty has shown enormous interest in our origins with evolutionary theory exploring many aspects of human origin, but we express so little scientific interest in our destination in spite of the obvious fact that every life on Earth must end with death. How many people have ever asked themselves whether their ideas about death are actually correct until they are confronted with their own mortality after a death, serious accident, or life-threatening illness in their family or friends? Of course, no one is qualified to discuss something that can only be proven by death but at least we can show some scientific curiosity if death is really 'death' or it is another form of life.

Sigmund Freud viewed the belief in immortality as a denial of death and a refusal to face annihilation, and Carl Jung took the position that the concept of immortality is universally present in the individual's unconscious. If death represents ultimate ego annihilation, it is no wonder that people have an aversion to thinking and talking about death as seventeenth century French writer and moralist La Rouchefoucauld (Feifel, 1959, p. xi) commented, "*One can no more look steadily at death than at the sun*". A number of psychologists, including Freud, have considered death to be the root source of all human anxiety, but oddly, nonexistence before one's conception and birth does not cause frustration or anxiety. Many unanswered questions about death come flooding into our consciousness when we are shocked and severely grief-stricken. This is the time we feel a need to analyze the phenomenon of death in order to answer these questions. As Cavendish (1977, p. 7) stated, "*the human solution to this grim dilemma is a life in some different world after death*", often the philosophy of afterlife comes in our mind.

For many years there has been strong opposition towards afterlife research in the mainstream media, in universities and in some of the churches. The discoveries of dedicated scientists working to prove the afterlife have been ridiculed, misreported, distorted and censored with the result that general public knows very little about the great body of scientific research that has been accumulated. Many of these afterlife researchers are highly practical people whose major discoveries in other areas fundamentally changed the way people work and live. Many of them are the most educated people, rationalists and humanists, and they appeal to the authority of knowledge and science. None have motives to fabricate evidence; they just describe the clear findings of their research. But they face intense opposition from both traditional Christian clergy and from materialist scientists who joined together to try to suppress their findings. Why is there lack of reason?

Psychologists have agreed that 'judgment after death', a common feature of most major religions, can be a terrifying factor. Where there is wickedness and illogic in daily life, the afterlife is a powerful reminder of possible judgment and punishment. Yet much of modern society is based on disregard for morality along with unrestrained materialism. Could it be that this global pursuit of materialism leads to a denial of an afterlife and of the judgment that may await in the life hereafter? Although the widespread belief is that science (a method of exploration) and materialistic ideology (a worldview) are inseparable, "*it is not written anywhere that the rest of us who appreciate science have to believe that. In fact, most of the great founders of modern science did not.*" (Haught, 2005, p. 367). Put simply, when one acknowledges the presence of afterlife and the judgment of self that it entails, it powerfully challenges the materialist worldview. Hence, we have to move science well beyond the bounds of strict materialism and demystify the phenomena of death and afterlife by a systematic scientific study.

This book, based upon scientific facts and evidence, starts where all the so-called religious books, ancestral beliefs and practices, godman, fortune-tellers and the prophets of various gods fail. Later conclusions may sound audacious but they are all based on verifiable data and rooted in the evidence and facts in earlier chapters. The religionists deal with matters of faith. Its main basis is often revelation from a deity – either orally transmitted from generation to generation or recorded in a sacred text or revealed to individuals through prayer. On the other hand, science is based on the analysis of evidence. It uses its own method and aims to different goals than the theologians, as Jerry A. Coyne (Kurtz, 2003, p. 13) agrees that "*[Science] requires an open mind, free inquiry, critical thinking, the willingness to question assumptions...*" Theology has answers that need be questioned whereas science has questions that need to be answered. Scientific facts can be beautiful or ugly, while religious faiths are immune to ugly facts. Through the eyes of a religionist, everything should look beautiful and conform to his faith. While researching for this book, I did not bind myself to any such restrictions. Unscientific and illogical – that I would never be. According to me there is nothing called inexplicable phenomenon. If anyone pursues the scientific method – using laboratory protocol and research – most of the unanswered questions of the Universe would eventually be answered in one form or another. Hence, all the 'inexplicable phenomena' are actually 'scientific facts' waiting to be discovered. Throughout this book I have strongly embraced this basic logic. Also, just because we cannot explain something does not mean it is not real. As Jung (1998, p. 57) said, "*I shall not commit the fashionable stupidity of regarding everything I cannot explain as a fraud.*"

Often people ask if it is safe to do afterlife study. I understand it – whenever we face the unknown, it scares us. However, we cannot approach truth with fear. Early European sailors believed the earth was flat and they could sail off the edge. Because of their fear of the unknown they concluded it was dangerous to sail too far west, as example, on October 10, 1492, Columbus' crew grew mutinous after fearing sailing off a flat earth and demanded Columbus turn around to avert disaster (De, 2016, p. 29). When they conquered their fear and went bravely ahead, not only did they discover a completely new world but also made the transition from two-dimensional thinking to three-dimensional thinking about their reality. Likewise, if we can conquer our fears, we will also discover a completely new world and we will make the transition from three-dimensional thinking to four-or-more-dimensional thinking about our reality. It is actually much more efficient and practical to accept this fact that there is more to reality than what the physical senses can show. All the great pioneers have set aside their fears, at least temporarily, and went ahead despite the dangers. If we can solve the mystery of afterlife it will add a whole new dimension to our lives.

Physical death, far from being the ultimate end, is like a second birth, a necessary step in our evolution. Death is not a denial of our significance, rather it teaches us the significance of life. The old Latin saying is literally true – *Mors janua vitae* – death is the gateway of life (Davey, 2007, p. 175). This is exactly what it is – a gate into a fuller and higher life. The ancients knew much more about death in those days, and since they knew more they mourned less. Except the burdensome physical body, meaningless worldly possessions and selfish gratification nothing is lost in death. Hence, terminally ill or dying people should not see themselves as losers. The baseless and foolish hellfire theory of the Muslim faith is not only a defective teaching but also an insult to human faculty. It has done more harm than even its promoters know, for it has worked evil beyond the grave as well as on this side. Love, brotherhood and forgiveness are three mightiest powers of the Universe whether it be in life or in death. Ultimately, we all share a common source and destination regardless of race, religion, or gender. John Donne, priest, poet, and preacher of sixteenth century (Black, 2011, p. 928) puts it this way.

> "*All mankind is of one author, and is one volume; when one man dies, one chapter is not torn out of the book, but translated into a better language and every chapter must be so translated.*"

Since death is our inevitable, inescapable fate, and because billions and billions of people have died since the beginning of time, the new world must be quite safe for human 'existence' and not as frightening as many of us think. In addition, fear wears off over time. After we confront the unknown a hundred times, it is no longer as frightening. Therefore, we must explore and try to understand it to demystify it. Also, when we die, we will be forced out of this physical world (just as an infant is cast into our physical world), and we will have to deal with the afterlife issue then. Is not it logical, if we learn the rules before our death we can handle it better when our time is up? Perhaps our transition to the strange new world – the world of non-material reality – will be smoother.

In writing this book, it is not my intention to try to change anybody's beliefs, philosophy, or religion. I am an open-minded skeptic. Whatever you will read in this book is pure scientific enquiry, not science fiction story to amuse you. I will give you access to some very important objective information about the afterlife. Much of it consists of carefully researched case studies and evidential reports of instances of unusual human capacities witnessed and investigated by researchers with reputations for high intelligence, high competence, and high integrity.

However, ultimately, given all the information, you – the reader – will have to decide what you accept or reject because some of my findings may oppose your cherished religious faith. Mainstream science led us to believe that there were only three basic dimensions of experience (plus time) and five senses. Everything else was labeled superstition, nonsense, hallucination, or theology. However, for a true scientific enquirer, heavy questions nag in his heart because science had been too deeply ingrained in him, that in search for the truth he can even distrust science itself while still using the scientific method as a tool!

The largest enemy of scientific progress is not human ignorance but human arrogance – the willful rejection and purposeful refusal to study seeming incomprehensible, strange and unknown facts. In the past, the clergy refused to accept science because it conflicted with his personal religious beliefs.

When Galileo showed the Pope the telescope and told him that it would prove his view of the Universe, the Pope called the telescope "*the work of the devil*" and refused to look through it (West, 2014, p. 193). Many of the 'Learned Doctors' of those days felt no need to look through Galileo's telescope – after all, the idea of planets having moons was simply too preposterous to be entertained.

Giordano Bruno was burned at the stake over one hundred years before Galileo because of his belief (and undoubtedly, his attempts to convince others) that the Earth was not the center of the Universe, that Earth and the other planets revolved around the sun (Auerbach, 1993, p. 250). Since such beliefs were contrary to the teachings of the Church at that time, such men were heretics, heathens, and subject to (often fatal) censure by the Church. However, the clergy had to eventually accept that science prevailed over personal, subjective religious beliefs. The academic establishment is in the same position today as was the Pope who refused to look through Galileo's telescope. It can never be any other way. Today people with scientific views that may be contrary to the 'accepted, known laws' are no longer burned at the stake; they are branded 'crackpots' and ridiculed openly. Galileo is reported to have said after his conviction by the Inquisition, "*And yet, it moves*". (Livio, 2010, p. 83). The members of the clergy still don't have courage to face the scientific people. Our experience had repeatedly shown us that once people feel comfortable with a set of beliefs, they do not want to change them even if new, objective and scientific information shows they are completely invalid.

Examining and conquering age-old beliefs is not easy because many beliefs become part of the emotional makeup and are hard-wired into the nervous system. Even if information is scientific, we initially tend to reject it if it is too far advanced – if it challenges our "boggle threshold" (the level above which the mind boggles when faced with some new fact or report or idea – a term coined by writer and psychical researcher Renee Haynes – Wainer, 2016, p. 2) by being too far ahead of our existing knowledge, especially if the information is not consistent with our secular or religious beliefs, history, culture, values, and traditions. I am writing this book to try to dispel some of these myths, and to offer a new perspective on the afterlife mystery. This is the challenge I take up in this book.

In writing this book, I am acutely conscious that I will have to face a lot of criticism, mainly from four areas – first, from deeply religious people (particularly those people who include with their name a title identifying them as functionaries in a religious organization) who will be upset by anyone who dares to do research in an area which is supposed to be taboo (as example, John Calvin, the famous French theologian never wanted to discuss on the nature of the afterlife because the Bible says so little about it); second, those who simply felt that the question of life after death should not be questioned by anyone as it should be shrouded in mystery; third, the scientists and physicians who regard this kind of study as 'unscientific'; and fourth the uninformed and biased skeptics who come to the investigation with rigid, prejudicial viewpoints, looking to proselytize you to their belief system or prove you're wrong without regard for evidence.

In the past few decades, science has begun a sudden but timely review of ancient divine wisdom. Though the general trend of science since the seventeenth century has been to evolve toward a material focus, science had now begun to explore the previously marginalized spiritual arena. Eventually, the weight of evidence begins to set in, and as a result, public interest in afterlife is growing; the latest demographic surveys continue to show a rising interest in afterlife studies. Newton (2016b, p. 398) wrote,

> "*It is not a bad thing to accept life as it is, asking no questions and assuming that in the end what is supposed to happen will happen. However, for those with a longing to know more, simple acceptance of life is totally unsatisfying. For some travelers, life's mysteries cry out for attention, if being alive is to have any meaning.*"

This book will no doubt serve to push this interest even higher. And as we will open our minds to universal questions about life, death, and consciousness, our view of humanity will undergo a profound transformation. I sincerely hope that this book will make a positive contribution to this process.

I will show you in this book that afterlife studies are not only compatible with modern science but can actually help to explain certain phenomena with which post-modern science is struggling. This research has changed my life, and if you read this book with an open mind, the evidence will speak to you compellingly, and probably you will come away with a new attitude toward life and death. This book will also help connecting you to your real self – the immortal soul inside you.

This book is heavy reading and lengthy. I ask for the readers' patience on this.

Chapter 1

Life and death are illusions of mind

"*Reality is merely an illusion, although a very persistent one.*"

Albert Einstein

"*As the world is perceived through the images formed and stored in the minds of individuals, the question is whether these images, which are just pictorial representations of objects and not the actual objects, truly represent reality and how they influence the perception and interpretation of reality. The important issue is how to free the mind from preconceived ideas, and look at every image from a fresh perspective, without any influence of prior semantic context.*"

Ben G. Yacobi (2013, p. 205)

"*Along with philosophers' reduction of all objective reality to a shadow-world of perceptions, scientists have become aware of the alarming limitation of man's senses.*"

Lincoln Barnett

Why we are born on this Planet Earth? Why we grow with time and ultimately die? Do we actually belong to some other place, and come to Earth – voluntarily or involuntarily – to be able to use our five senses and enjoy the unique atmosphere only available here? Our body is made up of earthly material – the flesh, bones, body fluids etc. – all deteriorate and perish and return back to Earth when they cease to function. So, if the end result is zero what purpose does it serve? Today, these questions do not belong to philosophy alone but science also.

We live our lives believing that we are important individuals – the things we do are important, the jobs we do are important, our lives are important.

We are often proud of our successes. We like to feel special and unique. Out of the more than seven billion people on Earth right now (according to the UN, world population reached seven billion on October 31, 2011 – De, 2016, p. 10), every individual on Earth is unique and different from others. If there were one grain of rice for every human on the planet, an individual would be one grain in one of the 61,000 gallon (231,000 liter) containers filled with rice (Champlain, 2013, p. 100). And, what if we consider that the Earth has been spinning well over 3,00,000 years with human beings living on it? In 2011, scholar and demographer Carl Haub published the article 'How Many People Have Ever Lived on Earth?' where he approached a guesstimate of 107,602,707,791 (Murdock, 2014, p. 123). It means about 6.5% of all people ever born are alive today. Each one of the one hundred and seven billion of us has felt special and unique in our lifetimes.

Planet Earth is home to 8.74 million species of plants and animals (Deza and Deza, 2013, p. 388). This is absolutely an incredible amount of life on our planet. We think we control the world but the exact opposite is the truth. The average physical human body is a group of over 60 trillion living cells that do what they do by themselves. Every second, trillions of things are happening inside our bodies that keep us alive, and we have no control over it. Blood is being pumped, cells are being created, hormones distributed, the nails and hair grow without our authorization. An average size and mass of a human body could contain at most about 300 billion billion billion billion (four times) megabytes of information (Tipler, 1994, p. 407). It means, a trillion things out of our control have to happen just for us to digest food, and we are not even aware that it is happening right now. We also do not control what is going on outside of our physical body either. Hence, control is an illusion, a deception created by the mind. Many people believe in an all-powerful God, but they also want to believe that they are in control of the world. This is another mind game.

There is no definitive answer to the question of what reality is. In broadest terms, reality is all that exists irrespective of whether or not it can be observed or understood. As human being, we are 'taught' to live our lives like everything around us is very real. Our five senses tell us what is real and what is not, and lead us to perceive the reality that we experience. So, when we perceive something through our senses, it must be true.

Now, let us turn to science. The amount of information in the visible Universe is at the most 10^{116} megabytes (Tipler, 1994, p. 221). Every waking second, 400 billion bits of information approach the brain through sensory input channels, but the brain processes only 2,000 of these bits per second (Willis, 2007, p. 66; Cameron, 2007, p. 100). Since the brain can never catch up, what is the 'real' reality? How much of reality is completely unknown or inaccessible to human reason and understanding? Where did it originally come from? Ultimate reality cannot be defined by concepts or words. While nothing in the Universe is truly permanent, is the ultimate reality unchangeable? Will the physical laws and constants remain the same with cosmic evolution? Our search for reality is a lifelong endless struggle against the unknown. The limits of existence, cognitive biases, and the boundaries of understanding can result in illusions that can be perceived as reality. It means, we may not actually be what we think we are. This is the mysterious nature of reality. In our struggle we are not sure whether we arrive at a deeper understanding of reality or just move from one illusion to another. Moreover, no two minds pick up the same 2,000 bits. When two persons have observed the same exact event by their five senses, the descriptions do not exactly match to one another because of this reason. Also, we do not just perceive the bits. The mind plays a trick with us – it takes the bits, passes them through our past memories of those bits, and subconsciously tells us how to think and how to feel about what we observe as per one's needs and desires.

Hence our brains cannot accurately tell what is real or not real. As example, schizophrenia – the visions and sounds schizophrenic patients 'see' and 'hear' are just as real to them as this book you are reading, or the chair on which you now sit. The brain has the capacity to construct a spatio-temporal reality (existing in both space and time) as real as the one you are experiencing now. Another example is when we are having a pleasant dream or a nightmare. If I am a non-swimmer, and in my dream I find myself in the ocean I get scared. This is because, in that particular moment, my brain tells me that the ocean is real, the water is real, and my life is in grave danger.

Now, what do we understand from this example? My body is like a robot that is controlled by the mind. What the mind tells the robot is real, the robot will experience. Thus, in my dream I have experienced the water and the fear. The illusion was in the mind, and bodily sensation was produced to support the illusion. Although nothing was real, my body (robot) thought it was. If the brain can generate a world and populate that world with various objects and the expressions of other seemingly human and non-human personalities, then how can we know whether or not our waking worlds are merely unusually coherent dreams? And if we can't tell the difference between waking and dreaming, then how can we know whether or not other people are merely figments of our brains? Where is the surety that we living beings are not in a 'dream condition' produced by the illusion of some higher and stronger mental power? If so, all of our activities, emotions, fears etc. are unreal, and at the moment of our death we actually wake up from our dreams and experience the 'reality'. Life is as unreal as a bad or pleasant dream.

Let me take another practical example. I pick up a book from the table. But, is this book real? Everyone will reply in the affirmative because the object is within our five sensory perceptions. But the real answer may be no because even the things we can sense may have no substance at all. Physicists say that everything we can touch, see, hear, feel, or taste is all made up of energy. Atoms are 99.99% empty space (Rutherford's nuclear model of atom). The matter, the 'stuff' we seem to touch and feel, is actually mostly empty space. Our senses deceive us.

In the past, the scientists thought that atoms were unbreakable, so the hydrogen atom was considered the smallest particle. But at the beginning of the 20th century, it was discovered that atoms are made up of protons, neutrons and electrons. The electron is indivisible and fundamental, but protons and neutrons appear to be built out of much smaller particles called quarks. Quarks are believed to be made of energy, 'strings' of light energy.

Human eye cannot see these strings. For argument's sake, if we put a tiny camera inside an atom, still we will see nothing. It would be invisible because all that is in there is vibrating loops of energy. Anything we see around us becomes invisible when we break it down to its smallest size. Strings of energy cannot be seen, but we know they exist because we can see things that exist around us. The living body of a giant animal, or a bacterium, or a virus, or a lifeless rock – all is nothing more than vibrating strings of light. Also, there are many things that exist in reality such as, radio waves, television signals, wireless connection, cell phone frequencies, microwaves, infra-red, visible light (which really isn't visible at all), ultraviolet light, X-rays, and gamma rays etc. that we do not see. These are also a form of energy. Since the human senses are limited and they determine the boundaries of the world, we confuse 'reality' with 'appearances' which is a partial representation of the ultimate reality. How can we know with certainty that our brain is not giving us the illusion of a physical world?

Next, I will show that at the subatomic level energy responds to our mindful attention and becomes matter. It means mind and matter are no longer separate but intrinsically related.

1.1: Quantum physics and consciousness

"*If quantum physics hasn't profoundly shocked you, you haven't understood it yet.*"

Niels Bohr

"*The more success the quantum theory has, the sillier it looks.*"

Albert Einstein (from a letter to Heinrich Zangger, May 20, 1912)

How can we discern illusion from reality in the physical world? In this scientific era, the most logical place to turn for an answer is quantum physics, the extremely successful theory physicists use to describe our world. This undoubtedly correct but still somewhat mysterious theory implies there are two layers of illusion in our perceptions of the world around us.

The first illusion has to do with what matter is made of. The universally held view is that the physical Universe is made up of particles – electrons, protons, atoms, and so on. But in quantum physics, the world is made from wave functions (similar to water waves, sound waves etc.) which has created the illusion that matter is made from particles! Particles don't really exist, but the wave function just behaves like particles under certain circumstances. The second illusion is even more astonishing. When we look at any physical object, it appears solid, objective, actually there. There appears to be a single version of the world in general and of each of us in particular. But that is not true in quantum physics; instead its mathematics implies there are many versions of the physical world – and of each of us.

Quantum physics is the study of matter and energy. The word quantum means "a discrete quantity" such as a quantum of light (i.e., a photon), is an isolated, indivisible amount of energy (Goswami, 2013, p. 12). When the physicists study matter at the subatomic level, they find that matter does not exist until it is observed by a conscious being – "*Before matter can peep forth – as a pebble, a snowflake, or even a subatomic particle – it has to be observed by a living creature*" (Lanza, 2009, p. 54). Conscious mind cannot be replaced with an inanimate device in its role of observer (Thompson, 2003, p. 62). It means, the effect of the observer on the physical system being observed must be understood as a part of that system.

The logic-defying double-slit experiment demonstrates that a conscious observer is required to collapse a probability wave into a particle. Thus, consciousness is necessary first before matter can exist, and it is impossible for consciousness to have been produced by matter. Hence, the brain, which is composed of matter, cannot produce consciousness. Founders of quantum physics, including Nobel Prize winners in physics, such as Max Planck and Erwin Schrodinger have recognized this fact.

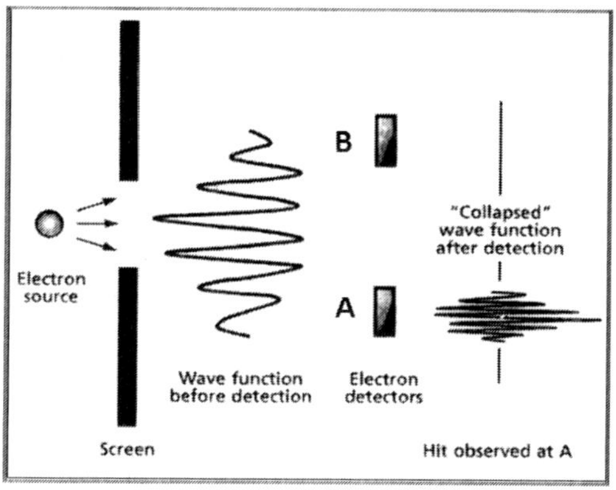

Wave function collapse in
conventional quantum physics

In the above figure, an electron is localized by passing through an aperture. The probability that it will then be found at the particular position is determined by the wave function illustrated to the right of the aperture. When the electron is then detected at A, the wave function instantaneously collapses so that it is zero at B.

Furthermore, if something in an unstable quantum state is observed continuously by a conscious observer, it will never decay. This is called the Quantum Zeno Effect (also known as the Turing Paradox) (Fisica, 2012, p. 423). The name comes from Zeno's Arrow Paradox. Zeno of Elea (490 to 430 BC) was one of the first proponents of the rhetorical technique of 'reductio ad absurdum', in which he would derive impossible conclusions from the opinions of his philosophical opponents. He is best known for four apparent paradoxes that have been adequately explained only in this century through sophisticated applications of the concepts of space and time. One of his most famous paradoxes involves a flying arrow. Because an object cannot occupy two places at the same time, he argued, the arrow is at only one place at any given moment during its flight. But to be in one place is to be at rest. Therefore, the arrow is at rest during every moment of its flight, he concluded, and motion is impossible.

One can 'freeze' the evolution of the system by measuring it frequently enough in its known initial state. Continuous observation of unstable radioactive isotopes can prevent them from disintegrating radioactively. Theoretically, by the tenets of the Zeno effect, if a nuclear bomb were watched intently enough, it could not explode. The effect cannot be produced by matter alone which indicates that consciousness cannot be produced by any physical process. In the 1970s, theoretical physicist Ennackal Sudarshan and his colleagues at the University of Texas in Austin showed in theory that "*a continuously observed quantum state cannot decay*" (Runsheng, 2018, p. 52), i.e., an atom in one energy state cannot change its energy as long as it is being observed.

It means, consciousness is an independent, causal factor in the real world, and we do not live in a pre-determined world. This truly radical and paradigm-shattering (a paradigm shift is a change in the basic explanatory concepts of a science) discovery is not just a philosophical statement. It is exactly what quantum physics tells us, too. With this move, the relationship between matter, life, and sentience can be approached in an entirely new light. Moreover, with further research, I believe, one day the scientists will be able to show that the molecules within a living cell move in different ways than they do outside the cells.

Quantum physics, which falls under the category of post-modern science, has pushed traditional science beyond the narrow and excessively abstract position of earlier centuries. Consciousness of the 'observer' not only enables us to observe the outcome of experiments, but makes decisions among otherwise merely probable outcomes, and thus causes them to actualize. In sum, this factor of existence – consciousness – has real effects in the physical world, but its decisions are not determined by anything in the physical world at all. Consciousness is that which feels and makes choices. Life and intelligence are independent of physical matter for their existence. Jahn (2001, p. 456) argues that in relation to consciousness,

> "*as yet we do not really know how to define it, how to characterize it, how to model it, or how to measure its properties. We do not understand its relationship with the physical world, including those with its own physiological mechanics... in studying consciousness, we are doing nothing less than studying our own vital essence: our minds; our spirits; our lives; and our eternal presence and purpose in the cosmic plan.*"

Traditionally, physicists have treated consciousness as non-existent or beyond the scope of their discipline. For those who recognized its existence, the general premise within the discipline was that consciousness emerged from the physical, and fundamentally it was not any different from it. Stapp (1989, p. 208), when explaining this stance, asserts that for these physicists,

> "*classical physics has no natural place for consciousness. According to the classical precepts, the sole ingredients of the physical universe are particles and local fields, and every system is completely described by specifying the disposition over space and time of these kinds of localized fields*".

In response to the understanding that the simple act of observation alters the nature of a physical system, the founders of modern physics, Heisenberg, Schrodinger and Einstein pondered deeply on the nature of human consciousness.

Max Planck the founder of quantum physics and winner of the Nobel physics prize in 1918 said,

> "*I regard consciousness as fundamental. I regard matter as derivative from consciousness. We cannot get behind consciousness. Everything that we talk about, everything that we regard as existing, postulates consciousness*". (Fredriksson, 2015, p. 5) (quoted in 'The Observer' on January 25, 1931)

> "*As a man who has devoted his whole life to the most clear-headed science, to the study of matter, I can tell you as a result of my research about atoms this much: There is no matter as such. All matter originates and exists only by virtue of a force which brings the particle of an atom to vibration and holds this most minute solar system of the atom together.*

> *We must assume behind this force the existence of a conscious and intelligent mind. This mind is the matrix of all matter.*" (Pickover, 2008, p. 417)

We are part of a vast, invisible field of energy that contains all possible realities. This responds to our thought and feeling. Haldane (1927, p. 209) expressed,

> "*It seems immensely unlikely that mind is a mere byproduct of matter. For if my mental processes are determined wholly by the motions of atoms in my brain I have no reason to suppose that my beliefs are true. They may be sound chemically, but that does not make them sound logically. And hence I have no reason for supposing my brain to be composed of atoms.*"

Erwin Schrodinger, winner of the Nobel physics prize in 1933 wrote,

> "*Consciousness cannot be accounted for in physical terms. For consciousness is absolutely fundamental, it cannot be accounted for in terms of anything else.*" (Wuppuluri and Ghirardi, 2017, p. 364)

Quantum theory still isn't taught in high schools because who can teach what makes no sense? How can we even have an understanding of physics when what we call 'matter' isn't even real? How can we understand it if when we observe an atom at its tiniest level the behavior of that atom changes? The quantum world is definitely a weird one, but we do recognize the significance and potential it has to help transform our world.

Proponents would argue that the findings within quantum physics are significant at the subatomic level. But are we not all existing at the subatomic level? When we observe ourselves and our physical environment at the smallest level, we are made up of atoms and subatomic particles. We are also what we observe. If our consciousness makes sense of the world, then what we perceive by five senses cannot be present without our consciousness. Quantum behavior is not limited to the microscopic world. New experiments carried out in the laboratories around the world with huge molecules called buckyballs show that quantum reality extends into the macroscopic world we live in. In 2005, Potassium Hydrogen Carbonate crystals exhibited quantum entanglement ridges one-half inch high – visible signs of behavior nudging into everyday levels of discernment (Lanza, 2009, p. 59). Various new experiments have furnished the most powerful evidence to date that the quantum point of view of the world is correct at the level of living organisms. Thus, the actual 'reality' is different. Philosophers of our ancient past were right; our senses really do deceive us. Now, we have some serious questions.

1. Who was the 'Observer' for the entire Universe to display particle-like properties? Was there a cosmic conscious moment at a particular

instant during or before the Big Bang? I will discuss on this issue later.

2. Since conscious awareness is independent of brain function, it exists after bodily death. Then what happens to the consciousness after physical death? If awareness is the ultimate reality, paramount and limitless, it cannot be lost into nothingness.
3. Do memories and awareness transfer after death to other lifetimes – reincarnation? How this transfer takes place?
4. Since the human beings are atoms and made up of subatomic particles, we are actually a bunch of energy vibrating at a certain frequency. These vibrational beings of energy exhibit consciousness that can manifest, create and correlate to our material world. What level of consciousness / state of being do we individually, and more importantly, collectively operate from?
5. At our subatomic level how the manifestation of physical reality changes?
6. Sometimes we suffer from severe depression, or traumatic psychological events seemingly without cause. Does our consciousness have an active role to play, or our consciousness is just a "helpless spectator"?
7. Do we occupy uncertain or even multiple positions in the invisible realm of possibilities? Is it possible that when one quantum system is measured or observed we somehow choose definite states? Do multiple worlds (a multitude of coexisting Universes) exist?

By looking at the Universe from this point of view, this also means space and time do not behave in the hard and fast ways our consciousness tells us it does. In summary, space and time are 'simply tools of our mind'. Then death and the idea of immortality exist in a world without spatial or linear boundaries.

1.2: Biocentrism – a new worldview of consciousness

"*To be conscious that we are perceiving ...is to be conscious of our own existence*".

Aristotle (384 - 322 BC)

"*Science no longer identifies reality with the physical universe, for mind and consciousness belong to the unseen world.*"

Sir Arthur Eddington, 'Science and the Unseen World'

Biocentrism (also known as Biocentric Universe) is a revolutionary view of the Universe. According to this theory, life creates the Universe instead of the other way around. In this paradigm, life is not an accidental byproduct of the laws of physics. The living beings on Earth are not merely the activity of an admixture of carbon and a few other elements, and there is an exhilarating possibility that life is fundamentally immortal.

Biocentrism states that biology is the central driving science in the Universe, and other sciences are reliant on a deeper understanding of biology. Life and biology are central to being, reality, and the cosmos. It asserts that "*our current theories of the physical world don't work, and can never be made to work, until they account for life and consciousness.*" (Lanza, 2009, p. 2). While physics is considered fundamental to the study of the Universe, and chemistry fundamental to the study of life, biocentrism claims that scientists will need to place biology before the other sciences to produce a theory of everything.

> "*Biocentrism is the only humanly comprehensible explanation for how the world can be like that, and we are unlikely to shed any tears when we leave the conventional ways of thinking.*" (Lanza, 2009, p. 48)

There are seven principles that form the core of biocentrism (Lanza, 2009, pp. 159-60). These principles clearly show that biocentrism is a well thought out theory that gives bold and straightforward explanations. A brief explanation is as follows,

1. The reality that we perceive is just a perception. What we experience is a translation of energy interactions. The objects of our lives, such as the book in front of you for example, do not exist as such outside of conscious perception.
2. Our experience with reality happens within our brains; there is no 'out there'. What we perceive as objective reality is our interpretation of energy interactions. The 'outside' reality does not exist in any recognizable form without the intervention of consciousness.
3. Consciousness collapses the probability cloud of subatomic particles.
4. Since consciousness collapses the probability clouds, a Universe without consciousness necessarily only exists in an undetermined state of probability.
5. The physical Universe is fine-tuned for life.
6. Our sense of the forward motion of time in a smooth, continuous path is actually a false impression. Time is not an absolute reality, but a feature of our mind.
7. Like five senses and time, space does not exist without consciousness. As example, quantum entanglement – entangled particles, no matter how great their apparent separation, remain connected. It means, distance is not a fundamental property. It shrinks as an object approaches the speed of light.

In sum, all the seven principles support the view that life is a key part of our understanding of the Universe, and there is no independent external Universe outside of biological existence. Lanza (2009, p. 4) commented "*[The Universe is] not a lifeless collection of particles bouncing against each other, obeying predetermined rules that were mysterious in their origin*". These principles, built on established science, demand a rethinking of our current theories of the physical Universe.

> "*There is no separate physical universe outside of life and consciousness. Nothing is real that is not perceived. There was never a time when an external, dumb, physical universe existed, or that life sprang randomly from it at a later date. Space and time exist only as constructs of the mind, as tools of perception. Experiments in which the observer influences the outcome are easily explainable by the interrelatedness of consciousness and the physical universe. Neither nature nor mind is unreal; both are correlative.*" (Lanza, 2009, p. 159)

Deepak Chopra believes that illness and aging are illusions and we can achieve what he calls 'ageless body, timeless mind' (also the name of his book) by the sheer force of consciousness. His profound conclusion is drawn from quantum physics.

> "*The physical world, including our bodies, is a response of the observer. We create our bodies as we create the experience of our world... beliefs, thoughts, and emotions create the chemical reactions that uphold life in every cell ...the world you live in, including the experience of your body, is completely dictated by how you learn to perceive it*". (Chopra, 1993, pp. 5, 6)

Fritjof Capra accepts that quantum theory has confirmed the traditional teaching of the mystics of eastern religions, that human consciousness and the Universe form an interconnected, irreducible whole (Capra, 1975, p. 305). Lama Govinda (1974, p. 225) commented,

> "*To the enlightened man ...whose consciousness embraces the universe, to him the universe becomes his 'body', while the physical body becomes a manifestation of the Universal Mind, his inner vision an expression of the highest reality, and his speech an expression of eternal truth and mantric [mantra – a sacred utterance] power.*"

All the physical parameters within the Universe are so exact that it is seen as more probable that they are that way in order to allow for existence of life and consciousness, rather than coming about at random. By allowing the observer into the equation, biocentrism purports to offer a way to unify the laws of the Universe and helps us to understand the Universe as a whole. Lanza (2009, p. 161) wrote,

> "*One issue that can arise with biocentrism is solipsism [from Latin solus, meaning 'alone', and ipse, meaning 'self'] – the notion that all is one, that a single consciousness pervades everything, and that appearances of individuality are real only on a relative level but are not true fundamentally.*"

The theory of biocentrism suggests that life is immortal, and what we know as 'death' is actually a continuation of consciousness in another form. Intelligence existed prior to matter because the laws, forces, and constants of the Universe appear to be fine-tuned for life. As Lanza said, we carry space and time around with us "*like turtles with shells*", our existence does not depend on space and time. If we think of the world of many quantum theorists that shows linear time to be a creation of the sentient mind, then time becomes simultaneous, which is also embraced by many regressionists (hypnotic regressions to past-lives), yielding a past, present and future that is all occurring in an expansive now, a time that radiates out in all directions. Albert Einstein himself expressed this when he wrote a letter to the widow of Michele Besso, after learning of his death in March 1955 (as quoted in 'Science and the Search for God Disturbing the Universe' by Freeman Dyson).

> "*Now he has departed from this strange world a little ahead of me. That means nothing. People like us, who believe in physics, know that the distinction between past, present, and future is only a stubbornly persistent illusion.*" (Ryals, 2006, p. 79; Prigogine, 1980, p. 203)

In Einstein's view, the entire sequence of physical events exists timelessly in four-dimensional space-time (Thompson, 2003, p. 52). Hence everything is actually timeless, and a life exists in its entirety with all of its moments. Since the consciousness of a particular moment includes memories of previous moments, there is an illusion of the passage of time. This is what Einstein said to Besso's widow. As humans we believe in death because "*we have been taught we die*".

If some of the readers still have doubt, let me explain farther. Death only exists as a thought because a human identifies himself with his body. If the body is going to perish, we think that their consciousness will disappear too. If the body generates consciousness, then consciousness dies when the body dies. But if the body receives consciousness in the same way that a television receives satellite signals, then of course consciousness does not end at the death of the physical vehicle. It continues to exist outside the constraints of time and space. It is able to be anywhere – in the human body and outside of it. In other words, it is nonlocal in the same sense that quantum objects are nonlocal.

1.3: Space and time are illusions of mind

"*To me every hour of the light and dark is a miracle, every cubic inch of space is a miracle.*"

Walt Whitman

"*If you try to get your hands on time, it's always slipping through your fingers. People are sure time is there, but they can't get hold of it. My feeling is that they can't get hold of it because it isn't there at all.*"

Julian Barbour

An intelligent mind often asks questions related to space and time. This is a great journey of inquiry as we can read in many religious scriptures that narrate the story of creation including a description of how space and time came into being. The ancients in this respect were more imaginative than we. However, the mystery of space and especially time had thickened in the beginning of the 20th century with Einstein's discovery of relativity. Einstein first discovered that time and space are not at all universal but relative to the observer. Now we will try to understand this with the help of quantum physics, more specifically, the quantum entanglement phenomenon.

Quantum entanglement is a phenomenon in which pairs or groups of particles that have been in contact with each other (they share a wave-function according to quantum theory) seem to remain connected over vast distances. When actions are performed on one of the particles, corresponding changes are observed on the others. They can fly apart – even across the width of the galaxy – and yet they still retain this connection, this knowledge of each other. If one is interfered so that it loses its 'anything is possible' nature and has to decide instantly to materialize with, say, a horizontal polarization, its twin will then instantly materialize too, and with a vertical polarity. If one becomes an electron with an up spin, the twin will too, but with a down spin, as if endowed with a kind of ESP. They are eternally linked in a complementary way that acts as if there's no space between them, and no time influencing their behavior. The quantum entanglement phenomenon authenticates the sixth and seventh principles of biocentrism.

In 1997, a team led by Swiss researcher Nicolas Gisin created entangled photons (bits of light) and sent them flying seven miles apart along optical fibers. One encountered an interferometer where it could take one of two paths, always chosen randomly. Gisin found that whichever option a photon took, its twin would always make the other choice 'instantaneously' – faster than the speed of light. The second photon's reaction was not even delayed by the time light could have traversed those seven miles (about 26 milliseconds) but instead occurred less than three ten-billionths (limit of the testing apparatus's accuracy) of a second later (Lanza, 2009, p. 52). Repeated experiments have produced same result. It means, Einstein's insistence on 'locality', means, nothing can influence anything else at superluminal speeds is wrong.

All the greatest minds of the past century have failed to explain this logic-defying behavior. Can either be real if the twins act on information across distances instantly as if there is no separation between them? Einstein's special theory of relativity, claimed to explain how light moves at a constant speed relative to all observers (known as "invariance of the speed of light" – when we talk about 'the speed of light' in a general context, we usually mean the speed in a vacuum), can best be expressed in four dimensions. Instead of considering space and time independently, he proposed a unified vision of spacetime. The nature of time and space is at the heart of the theory of relativity.

For a better understanding, let us start with the time dilation (the faster you go, slower your time gets) formula. In the theory of relativity, time dilation is a difference of elapsed time between two events as measured by observers either moving relative to each other. An accurate clock at rest with respect to one observer may be measured to tick at a different rate when compared to a second observer's own equally accurate clock. Einstein gave an exact formula for calculating this which forms the backbone of relativity, and shows us the fickle nature of space, distance, and time.

$$\Delta T = t.\ \sqrt{\,}(1 - {}^{v^2}/_{c^2})$$

ΔT is the change in your passage of time – what you yourself perceive. Small 't' represents the time passing for those you left behind on Earth, 'v' is your speed, and 'c' is the speed of light (186,282.4 miles per second). In physics the term '$({}^{v}/_{c})$' is called 'beta' – the Greek letter β (which looks like a B with a tail).

Time dilation is so small that it's difficult even to measure unless the velocity is near the speed of light. For airplanes moving at 675 miles per hour, the effect is about 5×10^{-13}. That means that if a person traveled at this speed for one day, he would lose 43 nanoseconds (time taken by light to travel about 43 feet). We get this number by multiplying 5×10^{-13} by the number of seconds (24 x 60 x 60 = 86,400) in a day. If he flies for a year without stoppage, he would experience 16 microseconds less time than the other person who was stationary.

This unnoticeably small effect becomes large if the velocity approaches the speed of light. Let's consider, an astronaut is traveling at a very high speed. At 99.999999999 percent of speed of light (perfectly allowable by the laws of physics), he will experience a dilation effect of 22,360. It means when he spent one year on his spaceship, on Earth 22,360 years have passed for everyone else. We can insert any number for 'v' and the formula will yield how much time passes for the astronaut while a given time passes on Earth. If the astronaut travels at the speed of light, 'v' becomes equal to 'c' and ΔT equals to zero, means time has been frozen for him. Therefore, when a person travels at the speed of light he takes "NO TIME" to travel from any point of the Universe to another. This also means that he will find himself everywhere in the Universe at the same time. Light consists of photon particles, and if a photon were sentient, it would have experienced the same.

Therefore, if a person can overcome the barrier of time, he will immediately feel oneness with the Universe. He will not be thinking about space same as we earthbound people. To a traveler moving at exactly the speed of light, the distance between the center of our Milky Way galaxy and the center of the Andromeda galaxy would look like zero.

One of the consequences of time dilation is that in principle it is possible to travel to the future (but not the past) because, according to stationary observers, moving observers age more slowly than static ones. Hafele and Keating (1972, p. 166) had conducted an experiment that involved flying planes around the world with atomic clocks on board. Upon the trips' completion the clocks were compared to a static, ground based atomic clock. It was found that 273 plus/minus seven nanoseconds had been gained on the planes' clocks. It means, even at the 'slow' velocity of airplanes, the equation works. Even radioactive atoms, when they move, experience less time than the stationary clocks and their radioactive decays slow down. Super-accurate atomic clocks, onboard the earth-orbiting satellites, are 'pre-corrected' as per the above time dilation formula prior to launch so that it will run at exactly the same frequency as an identical clock left behind on the Earth's surface. Neither time is a fixed arrow (always moving from past to present to future) nor do we live at the edge of the time. My wristwatch does not measure time; it is actually used for a simple comparison of events by which we perceive changes. All of nature's reliably recurring events, such as, tides, sun's rotation, phases of moon etc. could be employed to keep track of events. We mistakenly accept that time exists because we have invented clocks which are no way better than the nature's recurring events.

Along with time, space is also a human construct as Einstein said, "*Actually space and time are modes by which we think and not the conditions in which we live.*" (Eijck and Roth, 2013, p. 147). In this space-time premise, space contraction is the counterpart of time dilation. As example,

Suppose an astronaut wants to travel from Earth to a destination one light year away. If he travels close to the speed of light, his time will slow down significantly compared to someone who remained on Earth. For an earth-clock he still takes a year to reach, but his clock having slowed down might show only one day has passed. Knowing that he was traveling close to the speed of light, he will infer that the distance was one light day. If he travels even closer to the speed of light, his clock may record passage of only a minute by the time he reaches which will infer the distance was one light minute. So, depending on the velocity at which he travels, he will infer the distance to be shorter accordingly. The faster he travels, the shorter the distance will be. This is called 'space contraction'. Now, if he travels at a speed extremely close to that of light, he could even cross the Universe in a few seconds, or even less than a second. So, the Universe itself could be just a few meters wide for him in that kind of extreme velocity situation. This is hard to digest at first.

Despite the malleability of space and time, the speed of light is fixed, e.g., light shone from a spaceship going at nearly the speed of light still leaves it at the speed of light. None of this makes much common sense but the experiments have been done.

If we travel outbound at a high speed, the distant stars would lie at an entirely different distance. By mathematical calculation it can be shown that if we head toward the star Sirius at 99% of light's speed of 186,282.4 miles per second, we would find that it was barely more than one light-year away, and not the 8.6 light-years. If we cross a living room 21 feet in length at that speed, every instrument and perception would show that it was actually now three feet in length. The amazing thing is that the living room, or the intervening space from Earth to Sirius, is now not artificially shrunk by some illusion. The star is REALLY that far away. The living room is REALLY only three feet across. And if we could move at 99.9999999 percent of speed of light, which is perfectly allowable by the laws of physics, the living room would now be 1/22,361th of its original size or just a hundredth of an inch across (Lanza, 2009, p. 115). All items, furniture, or people in the room would be likewise Lilliputian, and yet we'd notice nothing amiss.

Earth's 18 miles per second motion around the sun causes stars to shift position by several seconds of arc from their actual locations. If we increase our speed, this effect will become more dramatic. At very close to speed of light,

> "*the entire contents of the cosmos appear to hover in a single blindingly bright ball, dead ahead. If one is looking out any other window, there appears nothing but a strange, absolute blackness*" (Lanza, 2009, p. 126).

If we remove space and time as actual entities rather than subjective, relative, and observer-created phenomena, we will find that the entire Universe has no inherent external structure. Every single particle of this Universe, living or non-living, is connected even if they are billion light years apart. The mysterious quantum entanglement phenomenon is explained.

Quantum entanglement theory has a philosophical aspect. Two particles are mysteriously linked that they will always remain bonded together beyond space and time, means that since we are too made of particles, we are also connected beyond space and time, so quite literally what we do unto others we do unto ourselves.

We doubt the existence of time and space for another reason. Various laws of traditional physics depend on many factors, but there is not a single law that depends on time factor. The laws of physics are not only same for all observers, but also remain unchanged with time, or are symmetric as time 'passes'. These laws also remain unchanged with space. It indicates that space and time – as we understand them with common sense – are actually illusions. This fact has profound implication and unleashed a flood of papers from the academic world.

From survival point of view these explanations are important. Time is a subjective ordering device used by humans to make sense of their world. There is no distinction between past, present and future because all moments of time exist together. In other words, the life of any human being can be regarded as the consequence of some mechanism which picks out sets of events for him to experience. A birth and death experience in such a scenario is merely a phase change. Death, as a terminal event, doesn't exist in a timeless, spaceless world.

1.4: The quantum consciousness

"*Nothing in science is as mysterious as quantum physics – except, perhaps, the mechanics of the mind. In fact, the two are intimately connected*".

Sir Roger Penrose

"*It is almost an absurd prejudice to suppose that existence can only be physical. As a matter of fact, the only form of existence of which we have immediate knowledge is psychic (i.e. in the mind). We might as well say, on the contrary, that physical existence is a mere inference, since we know of matter only in so far as we perceive psychic images mediated by the senses*".

Carl Jung, Psychology and Religion: West and East

The consciousness, also referred to as 'soul' is independent of a physical body and not bound by time and space (Chapter 2: Otherworld journeys: strange cases of OBE and NDE). The soul does not need any support for survival and growth, rather it governs the matter and influence events. Conventional science does not accept its presence but quantum physics does. Hence we call it the 'quantum consciousness' or 'quantum soul'. From a scientific standpoint, the quantum soul is a life force that connects to everything that exists in the Universe from distant stars and galaxies to microscopic atoms within our body. There also exists an eternal (no beginning and no end) consciousness that predates matter. With the understanding of quantum physics, we can now define this concept in scientific terms. Pulitzer Prize-winning author Prof. John E. Mack pointed out that many of us felt uncomfortable when someone attempted to define the soul scientifically,

"*We are now witnessing a coming together of science, psychology and spirituality after centuries of ideological and disciplinary fragmentation. Both modern physics and depth psychology are revealing to us a universe in which ... all that we can perceive around us is connected by resonances, both physical and non-physical, that can make the possibility of universal justice, truth and love more than just a utopian fantasy.*" (Weiss, 2004, p. 17)

Only quantum soul is real. Physicist and astronomer Victor J. Stenger commented, "*The physical universe is the product of a cosmic mind to which the human mind is linked. This interpretation has provided an ostensibly scientific basis for various mind-over-matter claims, from ESP to alternative medicine.*" (Oakley, 2011, p. 93). Some new age scientists and modern mystical literature writers call it "Quantum Mysticism" (Leane, 2007, p. 33). For example, Deepak Chopra (1989) has successfully promoted a notion he calls quantum healing, which suggests we can cure all our ills by the application of sufficient mental power.

After bodily death the quantum soul exists in a state of full consciousness and continues evolving towards truth. It carries with its memories and knowledge which is transferred to other lifetimes with a new identity (Chapter 7: Reincarnation). The soul is responsible and accountable for its actions and inactions while in an earthly life (Chapter 8: The law of Karma). After physical death, the soul either remains earth-bound (Chapter 4: Ghosts, apparitions and after-death contacts) for some reasons, or enters a mysterious world (Chapter 9: The spirit world) much superior and organized than our known materialistic world. After death, animal souls exist in a different abode separated from human soul. Throughout this book I will present plenty rock-hard evidence suggesting the existence of a non-material, non-physical Universe that has a reality even though it may not as yet be clearly perceptible to our senses and scientific instrumentation. The rules by which success is measured in the next world are quite different from the rules of materialistic world.

Many departed souls come back to physical world for specific reasons, such as visiting terminally ill patients (Chapter 3: Deathbed phenomena) with whom they were emotionally attached before death. The departed souls are also responsive to living human beings through those who have psychic powers (Chapter 6: Psychical unfoldment through mediumship and channeling). These qualities are same for all the souls irrespective of their religion, sex, geographical position, social status, upbringing, etc.

The quantum soul obeys the laws of the astral world. It can travel by mere wishing, is weightless and can pass through solid matter. The force of gravity has no effect on it. It is not bound by the laws of the physical world. While a million years pass for Earth plane, the time that passes for the quantum soul may be zero. Quantum soul never ages or undergoes decay. R. Craig Hogan commented,

> "*The evidence from corroborated testimonies, carefully recorded observation, and meticulously controlled studies provides a firm roadway to the conclusion that we are eternal spiritual beings having a physical experience. We are not the temporary, disease-ridden bags of flesh that we see when we look at each other. Instead, we are eternal selves temporarily using bodies.*" (Hogan, 2008, p. xi)

Since consciousness defines our existence and reality, what is the interrelation between the brain and consciousness and how or why human beings have self-aware minds? Human brain is "*just a collection of fat and protein made of 85% water squeezed into the dark enclosure of the skull.*" (Hogan, 2008, p. 1). The learned professors of materialistic science teach us that the human mind is in the three to five pounds of fat and protein compressed inside the skull, but in spite of extensive brain-mapping they can neither locate the mind nor locate the memories. When there is a thought, who is thinking and who regulates the thought – the mind or the brain? When a person is having a conscious experience, what neurological mechanisms are causing such consciousness? How decisions are made or how imagination is set free? Despite the marvelous success of neuroscience in the past 50 years, the neuroscientists acknowledge that they don't know how the brain produces consciousness.

Death has no effect on the quantum soul. In medical science we have enough evidence for the suggestion that the mind and memory function perfectly well when half the brain is removed or the brain doesn't develop fully. I will explain this more in details with suitable cases while discussing terminal lucidity. Scientists focused solely on matter and energy can't understand the quantum soul – it's beyond their reach because they aren't open to studying it. The conventional science rejects even the possibility of an external existence of soul by deriding evidence as unscientific folly. However, in the past few decades we have seen significant unconventional but scientifically valid approaches to the survival of consciousness after physical death. Such approaches explore strata of nature at an even finer scale seeking convincing answers at the quantum level instead – far away from every day 'classical' world.

1.5: Fine-tuning of the Universe proves consciousness predates matter

"*I believe the universe has a purpose, and our greatest intellectual challenge as human beings is to glimpse what this purpose might be.*"

Owen Gingerich

"The more I examine the universe, and the details of its architecture, the more evidence I find that the Universe in some sense must have known we were coming."

Freeman Dyson (Collins, 2007, p. 75)

Fine-tuning refers to the surprising exactness of nature's physical constants at the beginning state of the Universe. Both of these features converge as potential pointers to an eternal consciousness. The slightest variation from their actual values results in an early Universe that never becomes capable of hosting life. For this reason, the Universe seems finely-tuned for life. There is an age-old question in natural theology, first formulated perhaps 1,600 years ago by the great thinker St. Augustine of Hippo, and 800 years ago by St. Thomas Aquinas – *Can God's signature be seen in the universe He created?* This topic has been extensively discussed by philosophers, theologians, and scientists, especially since the early 1970s, with hundreds of articles and dozens of books written on the topic.

It's no accident the cosmos is so ideally suited for us. Theoretical physicist and popular science writer Paul Davies whose early writings were not particularly sympathetic to theism claims that with regard to basic structure of the Universe, "*the impression of design is overwhelming*" (Davies, 1988, p. 203). Eric Weiss made a bold conclusion "*If there wasn't a reason to exist, existence wouldn't happen.*" (Weiss, 2012, p. 151). Six of the most finely-tuned numbers are listed below. Even a small degree of fluctuation in one way or the other wouldn't allow humanity to live on Earth.

1. If the initial explosion of the Big Bang had differed in strength by as little as one part in 10^{60}, the Universe would have either quickly collapsed back on itself, or expanded too rapidly for stars to form. (Davies, 1982, pp. 90-91). In either case, life would be impossible. But how much accurate is this 'lucky accident'? An accuracy of one part in 10^{60} can be compared to firing a bullet at a one-inch target on the other side of the observable Universe, 20 billion light years away, and hitting the target (Davies, 1983, p. 179; Davis, 1987, p. 140).
2. Calculations show that if the strong nuclear force (the force that binds protons and neutrons together in an atom) had been stronger or weaker by as little as 5%, life would be impossible. (Leslie, 1989, pp. 4, 35; Barrow and Tipler, 1986, p. 322)
3. Calculations show that if gravity had been stronger or weaker by one part in 10^{40}, then life-sustaining stars like the sun could not exist. This would most likely make life impossible. (Davies, 1984, p. 242)
4. If the neutron was not about 1.001 times the mass of the proton, all protons would have decayed into neutrons or all neutrons would have decayed into protons, and thus life would not be possible. (Leslie, 1989, pp. 39-40)

5. If the electromagnetic force were slightly stronger or weaker, life would be impossible, for a variety of different reasons. (Leslie, 1988, p. 299)
6. If the mass of neutrinos (subatomic particles similar to electron but electrically neutral) were $5x10^{-34}$ kg instead of $5x10^{-35}$ kg, because of their great abundance in the Universe, the additional gravitational mass would result in a contracting rather than expanding Universe (Davies, 1982, p. 61; Davis, 1987, pp. 140-41; Overman, 1997, p. 141). Hence the figure is fine-tuned by one part in 10^{35}.

Simply, the laws of nature seem to have been designed so as to move the Universe towards the emergence and sustenance of life. This is known as 'Anthropic Principle' (Brandon Carter, famous Australian theoretical physicist, coined this term in 1970 – Anthropic means "relating to human beings or their existence." Principle means "law." The Anthropic Principle is the Law of Human Existence) which had been popularized by great thinkers, such as Martin Rees, John Barrow, and John Leslie (Flew, 2008, p. 115). In his book '*Infinite Minds*', John Leslie, a leading anthropic theorist, argues that fine-tuning is best explained by divine design.

> "*If, then, there were aspects of nature's workings that appeared very fortunate and also entirely fundamental, then these might well be seen as evidence specially favoring belief in God.*" (Leslie, 2001, p. 213).

Famous astrophysicist Sir Fred Hoyle declares,

> "*I do not believe that any scientists who examined the evidence would fail to draw the inference that the laws of nuclear physics have been deliberately designed with regard to the consequences they produce inside stars. If this is so, then my apparently random quirks have become part of a deep-laid scheme. If not then we are back again at a monstrous sequence of accidents.*" (Barrow and Tipler, 1986, p. 22).

> "*A commonsense interpretation of the facts suggests that a superintellect has monkeyed with physics, as well as with chemistry and biology, and that there are no blind forces worth speaking about in nature. The numbers one calculates from the facts seem to me so overwhelming as to put this conclusion almost beyond question.*" (Hoyle, 1981, p. 12)

The question a logical mind should ask is how nature came packaged in this fashion? As the English philosopher Antony Flew commented, "*This is certainly the question that scientists from Newton to Einstein to Heisenberg have asked – and answered. Their answer was the Mind of God*" (Flew, 2008, p. 96). Flew renounced his atheism due to the argument for intelligent design. American philosopher Robin Collins commented,

"*Imaginatively, one could think of each instance of fine-tuning as a radio dial: unless all the dials are set exactly right, life would be impossible. Or, one could think of the initial conditions of the universe and the fundamental parameters of physics as a dart board that fills the whole galaxy, and the conditions necessary for life to exist as a small one-foot wide target: unless the dart hits the target, life would be impossible. The fact that the dials are perfectly set, or the dart has hit the target, strongly suggests that someone set the dials or aimed the dart, for it seems enormously improbable that such a coincidence could have happened by chance.*" (Murray, 1999, p. 49)

Following table shows extreme fine-tuning of five physical parameters that are balanced on a razor's edge for life to occur. (Moreland et al., 2013, p. 50).

Parameters	*Maximum deviation*
Ratio of electrons: protons	$1:10^{37}$
Ratio of electromagnetic force: gravity	$1:10^{40}$
Expansion rate of the Universe	$1:10^{55}$
Mass density of the Universe	$1:10^{59}$
Cosmological constant	$1:10^{120}$

These numbers represent the maximum deviation from the accepted values, that would either prevent the Universe from existing now, not having matter, or be unsuitable for any form of life. As example, ratio of electrons to protons = $1:10^{37}$. This perfect balance establishes the role of gravity in relation to the electromagnetic force. A certain number of protons and electrons were able to survive the primordial annihilation between matter and antimatter at the Big Bang. Strangely the number of protons and electrons that were left unscathed were equivalent to with one part in 10^{37} (Corey, 1993, p. 62). Had this primordial balance between protons and electrons been any different, the electromagnetic force would have so completely dominated the gravitational force that stars and planets could never have evolved. Even a staunch atheist like Stephen Hawking expressed his doubt,

"*The more we discover about the universe, the more we find that it is governed by rational laws... You still have the question: why does the universe bother to exist? If you like, you can define God to be the answer to that question.... If we find the answer to that, it would be the ultimate triumph of human reason – for then we should know the mind of God.*" (Flew, 2008, p. 97)

"*It would be very difficult to explain why the universe should have begun in just this way, except as the act of a God who intended to create beings like us.*" (Hawking, 1998, p. 144)

The degree of fine-tuning is sometimes even difficult to imagine. Hugh Ross gives an example of the least fine-tuned of the above examples,

> "*One part in 10^{37} is such an incredibly sensitive balance that it is hard to visualize. The following analogy might help: Cover the entire North American continent in dimes all the way up to the moon, a height of about 239,000 miles (In comparison, the money to pay for the U.S. federal government debt would cover one square mile less than two feet deep with dimes). Next, pile dimes from here to the moon on a billion other continents the same size as North America. Paint one dime red and mix it into the billions of piles of dimes. Blindfold a friend and ask him to pick out one dime. The odds that he will pick the red dime are one in 10^{37}.*" (Ross, 1995, p. 115)

Michael Turner, astrophysicist at the University of Chicago Fermi Lab wrote (Prager, 2013, p. 6), "*The precision is as if one could throw a dart across the entire universe and hit a bull's eye one millimeter in diameter on the other side*".

In view of the above understanding, the finest accuracy of the Einstein's cosmological constant (1:10^{120}) baffles us completely because without considering fine-tuning it cannot be explained. Cosmological constant is the value of the energy density of the vacuum of space, originally introduced by Einstein in 1917 (usually denoted by the Greek capital letter lambda 'Λ'). Nobel Laureate Physicist Paul Dirac (1933, shared with Erwin Schrodinger) commented, "*God is a mathematician of a very high order and He used advanced mathematics in constructing the universe*" (Dirac, 1963, p. 53). God must be a mathematician, otherwise why there is the mysterious sophistication of the laws of physics? Davies (1984, p. 243) has observed, the laws of physics "*seem themselves to be the product of exceedingly ingenious design*".

Oxford physicist Roger Penrose has noted that a single parameter, the so-called "original phase-space volume", require such precise ne tuning that the "*Creator's aim must have been [precise] to an accuracy of one part in $10^{10^{123}}$ [ten to the power ten to the power 123, which is ten billion multiplied by itself 123 times!]*". Penrose goes on to remark that, "*one could not possibly even write the number down in full ...[since] it would be '1' followed by 10^{123} successive '0's!" – more zeros than the number of elementary particles in the entire universe.* (Penrose, 1989, p. 344). This is more than the total number of atoms believed to exist in the whole Universe. Such is, Penrose concludes, the precision required to set the Universe on its course. It takes far more "faith" to believe that this happened by chance than to believe that it was instigated by an incredibly powerful mind. The latter inference does not require blind faith!

The laws of physics that govern a major part of the natural world are simple enough for a mediocre graduate student to grasp, and the mathematical concepts of these laws can be fully explained in a few ordinary textbooks. But why they are so simple? These laws could be formidably complex so that they would require millions of textbooks or a super computer to define. They might even be an indigestible chaos of special cases and exceptions that could not be reduced to a rational system. This particular fact has led many prominent scientists to conclude that God must be a mathematician. The elegance of the laws of physics is also one of the conditions for the existence of life as we know it.

Another example, we know that all electrons and all protons have exactly the same charge but opposite. This is why the atoms and molecules are stable. If these charges varied randomly from one particle to another, neutral atoms would not be possible, and biological molecules such as DNA could not function. This is such a staggering accuracy that properties of subatomic particles are exactly same. It seems, the elegance of physics goes beyond what would be required for life.

Can we dismiss these coincidences as "lucky incidences", or do they confirm the presence of an eternal consciousness even before the Big Bang? Though the individual calculations of fine-tuning figures may vary slightly, the fact that the Universe is fine-tuned for life is almost beyond question.

> "*There are more than two hundred physical parameters within the solar system and universe so exact that it strains credulity to propose that they are random – even if that is exactly what standard contemporary physics boldly suggests. These fundamental constants of the universe – constants that are not predicted by any theory – all seem to be carefully chosen, often with great precision, to allow for the existence of life and consciousness.*" (Lanza, 2009, p. 7)

Philosopher John Leslie has pointed out, "*clues heaped upon clues can constitute weighty evidence despite doubts about each element in the pile.*" (Leslie, 1988, p. 300). One finely tuned constant is the strong nuclear force (the force that holds atoms together). The Sun 'burns' by fusing hydrogen (and higher elements) atoms together. When two hydrogen atoms fuse, 0.7% of the mass of the hydrogen is converted into energy. If the amount of matter converted was slightly smaller, i.e., 0.6% instead of 0.7%, a proton could not bond to a neutron, and the Universe would consist only of hydrogen. With no heavy elements, there would be no rocky planets and no life. If the amount of matter converted were slightly larger 0.8%, fusion would happen so readily and rapidly that no hydrogen would have survived from the Big Bang. Again, there would be no solar systems and no life. The number must lie exactly between 0.6% and 0.8%.

If the electrical charge of an electron had not been perfectly offset by the charge of the photon, our world would never have the chance to form at all. Since the molecules and atoms would have been so unstable that they never would have been able to endure the test of time. Calculations indicate that if this perfect degree of electrical balance were to be altered by as little as one part in one hundred billion, our bodies would instantaneously explode (Corey, 1993, p. 62). How to explain this perfect degree of electrical balance?

The combination of matter and energy in the Universe accurately fits the future needs of the lives to survive and grow both intellectually and spiritually. This means that the initial state of the Universe must have been very carefully chosen. The second law of thermodynamics concerns about 'Entropy' (the measure of the level of disorder in a closed but changing system). Things disintegrate – they fall apart over time. But that means our Universe began with order and is gradually becoming less orderly. No one knows why there was order at the beginning and not chaos.

There are many remarkable pieces of engineering around us, e.g., the gravitational pull of the Sun and Moon perfectly stabilizes the Earth's tilt of the rotation axis that results in a stable climate, and Moon has the perfect size to cause ocean tides that mix nutrients from the land and oceans to make life possible. Also, Earth is at the perfect distance from the Sun so water can stay liquid with temperature ranges such that human beings can live, and a size sufficient to have an atmosphere. The Earth is also set up remarkably precisely to provide the water and oxygen the planet needs to support life. It has what amounts to an 'oxygen machine' as explained by researchers in the journal 'Nature'.

Our Earth is uniquely situated with distinct properties that allow conscious beings to discover how the Universe works. This is explained in the book 'The Privileged Planet: How Our Place in the Cosmos is Designed for Discovery' (Gonzalez and Richards, 2004). Our Universe is set up not only to allow us to exist but also to allow us to have maximum opportunities to make discoveries about it. As example, the moon is just the right size and just the right distance from the Earth moving in just the right orbit to cover the sun precisely so we can have perfect solar eclipses – the moon exactly covers the sun from where we are standing. As a result, we have made discoveries about the sun's corona and the warping of light by gravity that couldn't have been made without this incredible set of matched conditions. Hogan (2008, pp. 149-50) explains,

> *"We're also situated perfectly so we can observe and make discoveries about the universe. We have front-row seats. There's very little dust where we're located to absorb light from nearby stars and distant galaxies so we can see the remarkable images such as the Hubble image .... We're far enough from the center of the Milky Way Galaxy and the galaxy disk is flat enough that it doesn't excessively obscure our view of the distant universe. We can see a wonderful diversity of nearby stars and other galaxy structures. ... Our position in our own galaxy allows us to see them. And because of where we're situated, we can see the unique cosmic*

microwave background radiation that led us to realize the fact the universe is expanding and finite in age.

All of that is engineered with such precision that it would be impossible for it to occur by chance as a result of an explosive expansion 13.7 billion years ago. These precise placements are within a universe with vast expanses of space where the Sun, Earth, and Moon could have been formed anywhere by chance when the solar system was born 4.5 billion years ago. One analogy is that expecting to get our uniquely designed living environment out of an accidental explosive expansion in the universe is like expecting to get a dictionary out of an explosion in a printing shop".

Stephen Hawking commented to a reporter during 1983,

"*The odds against a universe like ours emerging out of something like the Big Bang are enormous. I think there are clearly religious implications whenever you start to discuss the origins of the Universe. There must be religious overtones. But I think most scientists prefer to shy away from the religious side of it*". (Harriger, 2009, pp. 49-50)

The impossibility of all of these factors coming together accurately but accidentally has led many scientists to suggest 'intelligent design', means that some intelligent power is necessary for the Universe to exist as it does to support human beings. The fine-tuning argument is probably the most powerful argument for the existence of an eternal consciousness which is a critical component of the cosmos even before Big Bang.

1.6: Extra dimensions in space and time

"*Not only is the Universe stranger than we imagine, it is stranger than we can imagine.*"

Sir Arthur Eddington

"*Extra dimensions can have implications for the world we see, and they can explain phenomena that seem utterly mysterious when viewed from the perspective of a three-dimensional observer.*"

Lisa Randall

In recent years, one dramatic possibility is proposed concerning gravitational force, its relation with quantum structure of spacetime, and the unification of electromagnetism and gravitational force as a single force. Gravity dominates the Universe only by default. The entire motion of the solar system from the planets to the moons to the comets can be explained with a single law of gravity. Gravity is by far the weakest force known in nature (gravity might appear to be strong when you are hiking up a mountain but bear in mind that the gravitational force of the entire Earth is working on you). Since it is extravagantly feeble, the question is, where does this outlandish disparity come from? Perhaps the most unusual thing about gravity we know about is that, unlike the other forces of nature, gravity is intimately related to space and time. Why is it so different from the other interactions? Why has it not been able to unify it with the rest? Lisa Randall, professor of physics at Harvard University commented,

> "*Gravity can be very strong in one region of a fourth-dimension of space but very weak everywhere else... The weakness of gravity is the biggest gaping hole in our understanding of the physics of elementary particles, and extra dimensions might naturally provide an answer...another idea for accommodating the hierarchy is very large extra dimensions, in which case gravity would be diluted because it is dispersed over a large region of extra-dimensional space.*" (Randall, 2007, p. 81)

If somehow all the other forces were restricted to our 4D (four-dimensional space-time: x, y, z, and t) manifold, and only gravity could propagate in extra dimensions then once again these dimensions could have been thus far undetected. Moreover, the size of the other dimensions would no longer be restricted to be small. They could be infinitely big!

> "*Physicists speculate about such a possibility for several reasons. One is that we don't know any reason such dimensions cannot exist, whereas we do know how they might be hidden. No theory, even Albert Einstein's general theory of relativity, stipulates a particular number of dimensions. People have often made the mistake of believing only in what they could see. We don't perceive extra dimensions, but that does not mean those dimensions aren't there*".

The nineteenth-century German physicist Johann Zollner first proposed that 'apports' could be explained if objects could be moved in a fourth spatial dimension. In many poltergeist cases (Chapter 4) we have witnessed sudden appearance and disappearance of solid objects within closed areas. These are generally called 'apports', and their apparent paranormal transportation is called 'teleportation'. Fontana (1991, pp. 393-94) described many such cases,

1. When a poltergeist was invited to 'bring a pen', a pen seemed to mysteriously appear in a place that he had previously seen to be clear.
2. When a woman was inside a closed toilet with the door locked stones were thrown at her from inside.
3. Mysterious appearance of various keys. "*These would appear in positions on a work-bench which moments before had been seen to be clear. The majority of the keys were of unknown origin*".

4. A man saw 12 small engineering bolts fall from the ceiling when he was alone in the shop. Fontana relates that "*From his position behind the counter he saw them, some 12 feet away and in his direct line of vision and in good light, apparently 'materialize' just below the ceiling, then fall normally to the floor*".

In paranormal research, such logic-defying occurrences are abundant. And they can only be explained by higher-dimensional movement of objects. Thompson (2003, p. 176) wrote,

> "*Individually, mysterious appearances and disappearances can easily be put down to misperception. However, when they are consistently mentioned in case after case, they suggest that something real might be happening.*"

Teleportation strongly violates the known laws of physics. Seemingly, an apported object has been created out of nothing, thus drastically violating the principle of conservation of energy. But on closer examination, we can see that the appearing objects were already in existence and were simply moved from one location to another, apparently without passing through the intervening space. This is not actually creation of matter, but it is nearly so.

Therefore, we should ask for new scientific explanation. This idea should not upset us because much revolutions had taken place in physical science for last 200 years. Paranormal investigators have repeatedly observed that, "*apports seem to be connected with some intelligent agency. This agency is somehow able to modify an object so that it retains its shape, but is able to move without interacting with its surroundings.*" (Thompson, 2003, p. 177). The 'intelligent agent' is a discarnate entity who is capable of teleportation. Zollner (1976, pp. 41-42) took the assistance of a spirit medium named Henry Slade and proposed a number of interesting tests to verify this hypothesis, and he reported positive results, including the tying of knots in unbroken loops of cord.

Psychical researcher Berthold Schwarz has conducted a number of experiments involving the linking and unlinking of rubber bands and unbroken rings made of different substances. No evidence of cutting and splicing was found while inspected visually and with X-rays. Once a brass nut was linked with a gold fraternity ring. A policeman witnessed the action and remarked, "*I examined them, the solid nut and ring ... no way they should be linked together and yet they are*". They were later unlinked, but they remained solid and unbroken. (Schwarz, 1994, p. 98). Psychic researchers have observed these effects many times. Hence, undetected hoax, delusion and fakery must be overruled. Then how to explain this?

Any point inside a three-dimensional object has three coordinates – x, y, and z. For argument's sake we add a fourth coordinate, w, and assume that all the four coordinates can interact. Now what will happen if the w coordinate of the points making up an object shift slightly while their x, y, z coordinates remain the same? The object will then cease to interact with other nearby objects that have not undergone a w shift, but it will retain the same three-dimensional shape. In other words, the solid object will vanish into thin air in front of our watchful eyes. Now, if we move the solid object to a new location in three-dimensional space and its w coordinate is restored to original values, it will seem that the object disappeared at one location and reappeared at another. Living creatures can be teleported in the same way. This is simply a dimensional shift – mysterious phenomena of apport, teleportation and linking/ unlinking of unbroken rings, mystical powers of the yogi are explained.

Johann Zollner could not establish his theory, and his findings were cast into doubt. In 1914, Gunnar Nordstrom brought the idea of extra spatial dimension into physics by unifying gravity and electromagnetism as a single force. Polish physicist Theodore Kaluza and Swedish physicist Oskar Klein introduced the idea of a fifth dimension in 1919, which led to the Kaluza-Klein theory in 1921.

> "*A string theorist doesn't ask whether extra dimensions exist; instead two of the most important questions are, where are they? and Why haven't physicists seen them?*" (Randall, 2007, p. 80)

Many critics doubted about the extra dimensions, since otherwise why don't we see it? In 1926, Oskar Klein proposed that the fifth dimension was real, but too tiny to see. Further developments in modern physics, such as string theory makes a firm prediction that there are (many) extra dimensions of space. Braneworld theory confirms that the extra dimensions are infinitely large.

Some critics argue that if a fourth coordinate really exists, then all objects would continually tend to drift off into another dimension and vanish from our three-dimensional world. However, scientists have seriously considered theories that add extra dimensions to space, and they have some explanation for this. Physicist Ronald Bryan has proposed that the extra dimensions needed to unify the forces of physics may extend to infinity – "*What keeps quarks and leptons (and us) from drifting off into the higher dimensions may be a local 'well' in space (a soliton) generated by the particles' field equations*". (Bryan, 2000, p. 257). Apports and teleportation might involve intelligent manipulation of this 'well' by a discarnate entity as indicative in the next case summary from Stevenson's file.

A woman named Radhika from an obscure village of India had the reputation among her neighbors of being a sorceress. Mysterious disappearances of food were noted in the village, and people found that the missing food was turning up in Radhika's dwelling. They took it that she was stealing food by mystical means. One of Stevenson's informant decided to put Radhika's abilities to the test. He pointed to a 'lota' (a small container) which he held in his hand and to a man who was milking a cow some distance away, and asked to have some of the milk put into the lota. Instantly the lota became filled with milk and at the same time the milking man noticed that his own vessel had less, rather than more, milk in it. He looked up astonished (Stevenson, 1972, p. 243). On another occasion, Radhika was asked to bring him some 'puran puris' (a sweet, beadlike food) that were being cooked in a neighboring house about 100 feet away. "*He then heard her mutter a few words and almost immediately saw two puran puris come flying through the air and land at his feet.*" (Stevenson, 1972, p. 242). This was first done outside his hut, and then in its interior, which the puris could reach only by following a torturous flight plan. Radhika believed that these effects were due to a discarnate spirit that was allied with her, and Stevenson also had a similar opinion.

The search for extra dimensions has generated tremendous excitement in the physics community. This subject has become a huge research area and I have hardly scratched the surface in the present discussion.

> "*Recent research has provided perhaps the most compelling argument for extra dimensions. A universe with those dimensions might contain answers to physics puzzles that have no convincing solutions without them. That alone makes extra dimensions worthy of investigation.*" (Randall, 2007, p. 80)

The next few decades will bring a wealth of results from new experiments in this fascinating subject. Today, the idea may be 'funny' to think about, but farther research will certainly lead to surprising and unanticipated results. There may be various reasons why we cannot detect the extra dimensions in spite of them being infinitely large.

1. Since we know life only in three dimensions, 4-D or any other dimension beyond that would be impossible to comprehend. Many physicists work under the assumption that there are at least 10 dimensions. Since we only know life in 3-D, our brains don't understand how to look for anything more.
2. Ordinary particles are trapped on a membrane and can't move in the extra dimensions.
3. Extra dimensions are forbidden for us to experience as they are unobservable on presently accessible energy scales.
4. The fifth dimension is absorbed into ordinary four-dimensional spacetime.
5. The extra dimensions may not necessarily be spacelike that we can perceive.

6. According to Richard L. Thompson, we live in a three-dimensional simulated world that appears real to us. Hence, any virtual sense apparatus within this environment can pick up only information included within it. It means, we can't use our virtual senses to see out of the virtual environment. (Thompson, 2003, p. 23).

Extra spatial dimensions are a prediction of string theory, whose discovery would dramatically change our view of space and time. String theory predicts the existence of new particles called 'moduli', associated with extra dimensions and other exotic features of string interactions. String theory confirms that each point in space would have additional spatial dimensions attached to it which can be either too tiny to observe or hidden from view. One leading string theorist David Gross commented,

> "*The real change that's around the corner is in the way we think about space and time. We haven't come to grips with what Einstein taught us. But that's coming. And that will make the world around us stranger than any of us can imagine.*" (Gross, 2005, p. 2039)

It will be an exciting scenario to observe large (at least large enough to be observable) extra dimensions. It will not only bring a revolution in our understanding of space and time, but probably we will be able to see the deities, guiding angels, demons in higher dimensions. Many of these supernatural creatures are more intelligent than human beings confined in a three-dimensional space. We may also interact with the dead people if their soul is still earth-bound. Sometimes we sense their strong presence within our three-dimensional model, but we doubt their existence. If we can look through the higher spatial dimensions, it will help us to understand the paranormal science and psychic phenomena in a better way. This will help us in our afterlife studies.

1.7: Conclusion

> "*I believe there are two sides to the phenomenon known as death, this side where we live, and the other side where we shall continue to live. Eternity does not start with death. We are in eternity now.*"
>
> Norman Vincent Peale

> "*I have absolutely no fear of death. From my near-death research and my personal experiences, death is, in my judgment, simply a transition into another kind of reality.*"
>
> Raymond Moody

With the advent of post-modern science, death, it seems, is no longer Shakespeare's undiscovered country, the one "*from whose bourn no traveller returns*." Leadbeater (1952, p. 3) commented,

> *"Death is no darksome king of terrors, no skeleton with a scythe to cut short the thread of life, but rather an angel bearing a golden key, with which he unlocks for us the door into a fuller and higher life than this."*

The natural skeptics will obviously ask – how can we certainly know that it is really so? Yes, there is plenty of evidence ready to the hand of anyone who will take the trouble to gather it together. With due respect to Shakespeare, travelers sometimes return back from the other side of death and tell us fascinating stories. There are apparitions of the dead that haunt us. We know a lot about various psychic phenomena, reincarnation cases, channeling and mediumship etc. Therefore, at one time it was fashionable to ridicule such stories, but now it is no longer so, because there are great truths behind, which may be discovered by anyone who is willing to devote the necessary time and patience to their unfolding. Those who have paranormal beliefs and experiences are not necessarily associated with psychological ill health. In fact, some people seemed to be healthy not only despite of their paranormal experiences but also because of them.

Hard skeptics may not be willing to take that trouble to investigate the evidence, but I am absolutely fine with them because it is their affair. My only objection is that unless they will examine without any bias using reason and common sense, they have no right to mock at those who have seen, and therefore know that these things are true.

Though the traditional science still doesn't accept the existence of an independent consciousness beyond physical body – a monumental failure of curiosity on the part of academia – the modern and post-modern science is not at war with the soul hypothesis.

Science is the search for explaining new mysteries rather than to stick with old ideas. Hence, the concept of an afterlife is very much scientific against all odd and traditional opinions. In fact, the soul hypothesis is more scientific than many such critics think. The critics have difficulty accepting that something can be real but not physical. Yes, it is possible. Magnetism and gravity are two well-researched areas of scientific study where there is demonstrable existence of something that is real, and yet not solid or tangible. Magnetic fields can fill space and move in time, and though it is neither solid nor tangible nor can be seen, it can exert strong power on iron and move it. Similarly, the quantum soul which is invisible, non-material, super-intelligent, is an animating force that similarly acts on the human body and through the Universe. The visible brain is the instrument of invisible soul, and the soul empowers the instrument just as electricity powers up the light bulb. While the magnetism and gravity are well-researched areas, the power of the soul – the most superior driving force of the Universe beyond the realm of Newtonian physics – is, sadly, under-researched.

The field of psychology has undertaken excellent research since last 50 years. But what is psychology? The word itself is the combination of two

Greek words – "psyche" which means soul and "logia" which means discourse, or studies like all "logies". Hence psychology is "the science of the soul" (Nee, 1972, p. 18). The research engaged in by modern scientists is actually a probing into the soul part of our being.

Since souls are non-physical entities, a soul has no mass, no extension (it does not take up space) and no location. And if we remember the famous quote of Pierre Teilhard de Chardin, "*We are not human beings having a spiritual experience. We are spiritual beings having a human experience*" (Leveille, 2014, p. 4), then at fundamental level we are immortal. The physical body acts as a damper on the soul's inherent intelligence, weighing it down such that the soul is not able to manifest its full intelligence. Famous quantum physicist, Fred Alan Wolf theorized that the soul emerged at the same time that all the matter in the Universe emerged – at the time of the Big Bang 13.5 billion years ago. According to our present scientific model, the Universe and the soul will continue to exist for another several billion years until a time that is referred by scientists as the Big Crunch (Rosen, 1998, p. 248). Wolf commented next,

> "*Many quantum physicists, including myself, believe that the entire universe, the entire creation, was created out of the 'absolute nothingness of the vacuum of space'. It appears this 'vacuum of nothingness' is intelligent, active, and has a consciousness. The source of the soul proceeds from, and is present in this vacuum. Admittedly, the very notion that 'something' can be created from 'nothing' is a very difficult concept for the mind to grasp.*
>
> *Between those two points, from the Big Bang, at the beginning of time – to the Big Crunch, at the end of time – all the matter in the Universe appears, expands to a maximum point, and then contracts again into nothing. And through it all, an ultimate intelligence, call it what you will, guides and directs the various activities of everything in the Universe – including all living life forms, in an unfathomable, unseen way.*
>
> *I don't see the soul and consciousness as an epiphenomenon, or product of matter. It's just the other way around: I see matter as an epiphenomenon of soul and consciousness. The material world has evolved from the absolute vacuum of space – the home of the soul.*"

Quantum Physicist Amit Goswami argues that quantum physics supports the theory of nonlocality of consciousness.

> "*...psychic phenomena, such as distant viewing and out-of-body experiences, are examples of the nonlocal operation of consciousness.... Quantum physics undergirds such a theory by providing crucial support for the case of nonlocality of consciousness.*" (Goswami, 1993, p. 136)

According to Sigmund Freud, the human soul functions on different levels. One of the levels is the unconscious mind. By definition we are not aware of this level, but it stores all our experience and directs us to act, think, respond and feel as we do. Only by accessing the unconscious, we can learn who we are.

The soul has certain powers, and if one can activate the latent power of his own soul (psychic power), others will see manifestations of supranational ability in him. This is not manifested in every person because not all can break through the 'barriers' of the physical body. The man who attains to this power is called an adept. In quoting from 'Wild's Spiritual Dynamics', Pember (1975, pp. 154-55) has recorded that an adept,

> "*[An adept] can consciously see the minds of others. He can act by his soul-force on external spirits. He can accelerate the growth of plants and quench fire; and, like Daniel, subdue ferocious wild beasts. He can send his soul to a distance, and there not only read the thoughts of others, but speak to and touch those distant objects; and not only so, but he can exhibit to his distant friends his spiritual body in the exact likeness of that of the flesh. Moreover ...the adept can command physical objects to come into his presence*".

These are only the manifestations of the latent power of the soul. The soul hypothesis can explain many paranormal happenings, such as OBEs and NDEs, ghostly phenomena, possession, reincarnation, mediumship and channeling etc. Unless we admit the existence of soul as a separate and immortal entity, we cannot explain these phenomena.

The skeptics often ask a question – where do the souls come from since there are so many more people now than when the world started? (Almeder, 1997, pp. 513-15). It is logical to say that not everyone can be the reincarnation of someone who lived on the Earth previously. According to Brian Weiss, well-known psychiatrist and afterlife researcher, this is not the only place where there are souls. There is a reservoir of souls capable of bodily incarnation. There are many dimensions, many different levels of consciousness where there are souls. Our souls are all the same age, which is ageless, but some souls advance more quickly than others (Weiss, 2004, pp. 8, 16). With our present understanding of science, we still cannot apprehend this. We should not feel that the Earth is the only place where there is growth of intelligent lives. There are many inhabited planets. If with modern technology we vaporize the world our souls will nevertheless endure.

Chapter 2

Otherworld journeys - strange cases of OBE and NDE

"*We have clearly identified a phenomenon that threatens to cast a dark shadow on the house of conventional science.*"

Kenneth Ring

An out-of-body experience (OBE), also called 'astral projection' is "*an experience in which a person seems to perceive the world from a location outside his physical body.*" (Blackmore, 1982, p. 1). Most OBEs have common features, for instance, the subjects often see their own physical body during the experience like any other object in the room. They usually report having 'ghostly' astral bodies that cannot carry out any physical task but can pass through solid objects during the experience. Sometimes others can see their ghostly bodies. (Thompson, 2003, p. 148) They often report seeing places or events that were out of eyesight. Hence, OBEs seem to constitute a challenge to the experienced spatial unity of self and body under normal conditions, i.e., the feeling that there is a 'real me' that resides in my physical body and is both the subject and agent of my experiences (Blackmore, 2003). OBEs have attracted the attention of philosophers, psychologists and neurologists alike, and many have conceptualized OBEs as an extreme example of deviant bodily self-consciousness arising from abnormal brain processes.

For most people there is no control over the OBE – it just happens spontaneously. It is estimated that as many as 10% of the general population had these experiences at least once in a lifetime (Kelly et al., 2007, p. 396). OBEs are therefore difficult to study because they generally are of short duration and rare. A person who experiences an OBE does not have to be ill or in a near death situation.

Many researchers are of the opinion that OBEs occur normally during sleep and while practicing meditation. After leaving the body, the consciousness may hover near the body or float below the ceiling of the room. Occasionally it may travel to the far-off places like the planets of the solar system or even beyond (Shrikhande, 2009, p. 52). Only a few travels into the outer space. Many people experience subtle OBEs without realizing that they do so. Twitches and jerks that precede sleep may be due to the partial separation of the astral body from the physical.

The near-death experiences (NDEs) are closely associated with OBEs. Many NDEs are reported to begin with OBEs, and then move into scenarios that are more elaborate. Otherwise in a broader sense, the term 'out of body' could apply to all portions of NDE. NDE is "*an intense awareness, sense, or experience of 'otherworldliness,' whether pleasant or unpleasant, that happens to people who are at the edge of death*" (Atwater, 2007, p. 1). From a broader perspective,

> "*[NDEs are] generally understood to be the unusual, often vivid and realistic, and sometimes profoundly life-changing experiences occurring to people who have been either physiologically close to death, as in cardiac arrest or other life-threatening conditions, or psychologically close to death, as in accidents or illnesses in which they feared they would die.*" (Kelly et al., 2007, p. 369)

Raymond Moody coined the term near-death experience in 1975, and defined them as "*profound spiritual events that happen, uninvited, to some individuals at the point of death*" (Moody, 1975, p. 14). NDEs are mostly triggered by a life-threatening situation, under conditions of intense medical monitoring, and it can be shown that while they are happening, the electrical activity of the brain is entirely flat-lined. The experience is of such magnitude that most experiencers are deeply affected. They often report a subsequently increased sense of spirituality and a connection with their inner self and the world around them.

OBEs and NDEs have fascinated humankind from time immemorial. Reports on such experiences are known from pre-Christian history, ranging from Sumerian to classical Greek culture (Moraldi, 1987, p. 20f). Once regarded as bizarre hallucinations, OBEs and NDEs have become the subject of serious study by medical and other researchers in recent years. The number of NDEs has remarkably increased over the past few decades due to the advances in defibrillation and CPR techniques. Today reports on NDEs have become almost a cultural fashion. Television shows, magazines, newspaper and other media frequently present people who talk about experiences of this kind.

These experiences do not signal any psychopathology; people with mental diseases do not experience them more frequently than normal human beings.

On the contrary, NDErs and OBErs are possibly mentally healthier as a group (Schroeter-Kunhardt, 1993, p. 222). Although some drugs may on occasion induce experiences that bear superficial similarities to an OBE and NDE, comparative studies show that patients who receive medications in fact report fewer OBEs and NDEs than do those who receive no medication. In this chapter, we will analyze OBEs and NDEs and their relevance with the afterlife studies, providing definitions, incidences, key phenomenological features, and reviewing some relevant skeptic literature.

2.1: Out-of-body experiences

In this experience, people have veridical perceptions from a position outside and above their 'lifeless' body – "*highly realistic conscious experience of leaving his or her physical body, usually in the form of an ethereal double, and moving outside of it*" (Metzinger, 2005, p. 59). The range of vision can extend to 360 degrees with simultaneous detailed and bird's-eye views. During OBE, blind people too have the faculty of sight while deaf people can hear perfectly. All it takes to be near someone is to think of that person.

The OBErs have the feeling that they have apparently taken off their body like an old coat and to their surprise they appear to have retained their own identity with the possibility of perception, emotions, and a very clear consciousness. Following is the report of a nurse of a coronary care unit (Van Lommel et al., 2001, p. 2041),

> "*During a night shift an ambulance brings in a 44-year-old cyanotic, comatose man into the coronary care unit... After admission, he receives artificial respiration.... When we want to intubate the patient, he turns out to have dentures in his mouth. I remove these upper dentures and put them onto the 'crash car'. Meanwhile, we continue extensive CPR. After about an hour and a half the patient has sufficient heart rhythm and blood pressure, but he is still ventilated and intubated, and he is still comatose. He is transferred to the intensive care unit. Only after more than a week do I meet again with the patient, who is by now back in the cardiac ward. I distribute his medication. The moment he sees me he says: 'Oh, that nurse knows where my dentures are'. I am very surprised. Then he elucidates: 'Yes, you were there when I was brought into hospital and you took my dentures out of my mouth and put them onto that car, it had all these bottles on it and there was this sliding drawer underneath and there you put my teeth.' I was especially amazed because I remembered this happening while the man was in deep coma and in the process of CPR. When I asked further, it appeared the man had seen himself lying in bed, that he had perceived from above how nurses and doctors had been busy with CPR. He was also able to describe correctly and in detail the small room in which he had been resuscitated as well as*

the appearance of those present like myself. At the time that he observed the situation he had been very much afraid that we would stop CPR and that he would die. And it is true that we had been very negative about the patient's prognosis due to his very poor medical condition when admitted. The patient tells me that he desperately and unsuccessfully tried to make it clear to us that he was still alive and that we should continue CPR. He is deeply impressed by his experience and says he is no longer afraid of death."

Some OBE subjects see or feel themselves in a weightless replica of their original body, others experience themselves as being in no physical body at all or in a kind of indeterminate form, such as a ball of light or an energy pattern (Alvarado, 1997, p. 18; Green, 1968) or even as "pure consciousness" (Alvarado, 2000, p. 186). The physical body viewed from an external perspective is very rarely distorted or changed in shape and size. Schizophrenia patients have maximum OBEs, about 42% (Banerjee and Chakrabarti, 2008, p. 229). But no one should assume that OBEs typically occur in people suffering from severe psychiatric disorders or neurological deficits. Quite the contrary, most OBE-reports come from ordinary people in everyday life situations. One experiencer put it this way (Sabom, 1982, pp. 32-33),

"*I know it was real. I know that I was up there. I know that. And I know that I seen [sic] me down there. I could swear on a Bible that I was there. I seen [sic] things just like I see them now.*"

Melvin Morse and Psychologist Kim Clark reported that a woman had knowledge of a shoe on a window ledge outside the hospital (not near the room where the patient was resuscitated, but next to a fifth-floor office where she was being interviewed). Kim Clark, who interviewed her, crawled along the ledge outside her window and found that the shoe was indeed there (Morse and Perry, 1990, p. 20). Other investigators also reported similar veridical OBEs the most frequent of which are people who leave the operating room (after seeing the resuscitation efforts going on) and visit their relatives and friends in hospital waiting rooms (literally moving through walls). One patient reported seeing her young daughter wearing mismatched plaids (highly unusual and only knowable if she had actually been in the waiting room). Another woman overheard her brother-in-law talking to a business associate in the hospital waiting room in a very derogatory manner, and was able to report this back to him later. A 26-year-old woman described the following experience, dominated by paranormal features that occurred during a pulmonary embolism.

"*I (the real me, the soul, the spirit, or whatever) drifted out of the body and hovered near the ceiling. I viewed the activity in the room from this vantage point. The hospital room was to my right and below me. It confused me that the doctors and nurses were so concerned about the*

> *body they had lifted to the bed. I looked at my body and it meant nothing to me. I tried to tell them I was not in the body. Obviously, they did not hear me. One of the most outstanding things about this experience is that my hearing became extremely acute. I heard many things about the gravity of my situation, some of these from the nurses' station many yards away. I watched the hospital personnel work. I listened to their comments, and I began to feel sorry that they were working so hard, when I felt so happy and feeling no pain where I was".* (Greyson, 1985, p. 393)

The OBE is scientifically important because doctors, nurses, and relatives can verify the reported perceptions, and they can also corroborate the precise moment the OBE occurred. OBE cannot be a hallucination because this means experiencing a perception that has no basis in 'reality', neither can it be a delusion, which is an incorrect assessment of a correct perception. Hence, should we consider an OBE as a kind of non-sensory perception? Greyson (2010, p. 161) wrote the experience of a 56 years old truck-driver during his open-heart surgery who,

> "... *although fully anesthetized, claimed he left his body during the operation and watched from above, where he was surprised to see the surgeon 'flapping his elbows as if trying to fly'. When he later asked the surgeon why he had engaged in this strange behavior, the surgeon explained that he had permitted his assistants to start the surgery, and then he entered the operating suite to supervise them. Having 'scrubbed in' and having been gloved and gowned, and not wanting to risk touching anything that was not in the sterile surgical field until he was ready to do the surgery, he placed his hands securely on his chest and motioned with his elbows to emphasize his instructions to the assistants.*"

Cook et al. (1998, p. 399) also had recorded this incident. How the truck-driver reported accurate out-of-body observations that he could not have known about by normal means? OBE can happen in normal health condition – an ordinary nonpathological context. Waelti (1983, p. 25, English translation by Metzinger, 2005, pp. 62-3) narrated one such incident.

> "*I awoke at night ... about 3 a.m. and realized that I was completely unable to move. I was absolutely certain I was not dreaming, as I was enjoying full consciousness. Filled with fear about my current condition I had only one desire, namely to be able to move my body again. I concentrated all my will-power and tried to roll over to one side: Something rolled, but not my body – something that was me, my whole consciousness including all of its sensations. I rolled onto the floor beside the bed. While this happened, I did not feel bodiless, but I felt as if my body consisted of a substance constituted of a mixture of gas and liquid.... the expected hard bounce never happened. Actually, had the movement*

unfolded in my normal body, my head would have had to collide with the edge of my bedside table. Lying on the floor, I was seized by terrible fear and panic. I knew that I possessed a body, and I only had one great desire – to be able to control it again. With a sudden jolt I regained control, without knowing how I managed to get back to it."

Muldoon and Carrington (1969, pp. 83-84) described the case of Mr. Laufmann, a traveling salesman, who had been hospitalized with an unspecified, but apparently grave, illness while in Omaha (USA). While on the bed, Mr. Laufmann became "*conscious of something like a fleecy ball releasing itself from his physical form*", and then, he described his own experience as this,

"*I was standing there in the middle of the room and distinctly saw my dead body lying upon the bed.... I started to leave the room and met one of the physicians, and was surprised that he said nothing to me, but since he made no effort to stop me, I walked out into the street where I met an acquaintance of mine, Mr. Milton Blose.*

I tried to greet Mr. Blose by hitting him on the back, but my arm went through him.... It was impossible for me to attract his attention.... I saw that he went across the street and looked into a shop window where a miniature 'Ferris wheel' was on display".

Mr. Laufmann then returned to his hospital room and saw the doctors standing over his physical body, discussing his condition. Soon he was back in his body. Mr. Blose later verified that he actually had been in Omaha at the time, and while walking down the street he stopped to look at a 'Ferris wheel' in a shop window.

Following is the experience of a person who is color-blind.

"*I saw the most dazzling colors, which was all the more surprising because I'm color-blind. I can distinguish the primary colors, but pastels all look the same to me. But suddenly I could see them, all kinds of different shades. Don't ask me to name them because I lack the necessary experience for that.*" (Burke, 2015, p. 127)

British Writer Celia Elizabeth Green recorded a case with details that could not have been detected by auditory means by the experiencer.

"*I was in the hospital ... and was very ill. The ward was 'L' shaped; so that anyone in bed at one part of the ward, could not see around the corner.*

One morning I felt myself floating upwards, and found I was looking down on the rest of the patients. I could see myself; propped up against pillows, very white and ill. I saw the sister and nurse rush to my bed with oxygen. Then everything went blank. The next I remember was opening my eyes to see the sister bending over me.

I told her what had happened; but at first she thought I was rambling. Then I said, 'There is a big woman sitting up in bed with her head wrapped in bandages; and she is knitting something with blue wool. She has a very red face. This certainly shook her; as apparently the lady concerned had a mastoid operation and was just as I described.

She was not allowed out of bed; and of course I hadn't been up at all. After several other details; such as the time by the clock on the wall (which had broken down) I convinced her that at least something strange had happened to me." (Green, 1968, p. 121)

Crookall (1972, p. 76) documented the experience of a married woman who was very ill in the hospital.

"*I looked down at my body. I thought I was dead. I went out into the corridor and saw my husband. I wondered where my daughter was and the next instant I was standing beside her in a gift shop. She was looking at some 'Get Well' cards. I could 'hear' her read the verse. She decided it would be disrespectful and bought another. Then I was back in my body. When my daughter came with the card, I repeated the verse she had read*".

Myers (1892, pp. 194-200) recorded the strange case of Mr. L. J. Bertrand, an experienced mountain-climber. On one occasion, he took several students to climb the Titlis in the Alps. When he was exhausted by his efforts, he suggested that his companions go on to the summit without him while he would rest and wait for them. He gave explicit instructions that they climb the peak on its left side and come down on its right side, since there was a dangerous cut on the left side that was more easily seen from below than from above. He also instructed his strongest student to take the position at the end of the rope.

While waiting for the return of his companions, Bertrand apparently began to freeze to death such that he was unable to move. After a brief moment of acute pain, he suddenly found himself,

"*[as] a ball of air in the air, a captive balloon still attached to earth by a kind of elastic string and going up and always up. How strange! I see better than ever, and I am dead.... Looking down, I was astounded to recognize my own envelope*".

Soon Bertrand saw that the students took the wrong path deliberately, the student who was told to be on the end of the rope was neither at the beginning nor at the end but away from it altogether and the guide drinking out of Bertrand's bottle of madeira and eating a piece of Bertrand's chicken. Finally, he saw his wife, with a party of four other people, at a hotel en route to meet him in Lucerne, although she had told him that she would not be traveling until at least a day later.

When the students returned and found him, they rescued and revived him. Bertrand confronted the guide, who seems to have confirmed by his reactions to Bertrand's statements that they had gone up the right slope rather than the left, that two of the students had left their appointed places on the rope, and that the guide had pilfered some of his madeira and chicken. Bertrand also confirmed the next day that his wife had set off for Lucerne earlier than she had planned, with four traveling companions, and that she had stayed at the hotel at which Bertrand had seen her.

Morse (1992, p. 95) recorded the story of a man who 'died' of a road accident. One night he was waiting at a bus stop when a car that had gone out of control hit him. Though everybody thought that he was dead, he came back to life after three days and narrated his OBE. During his OBE, he found himself 'bathed in brightness'. Then he realized that he could 'fly' so he went home to visit his family, where he saw his grieving wife and two small sons. Then he 'visited' the family next door that had a child, born a couple of days before the accident. The couple was deeply distressed by the continuous crying of the baby, who would not stop no matter how he was comforted.

In this disembodied state, the man found that he could talk to the baby. As he put it, "*No words were exchanged but I asked [the baby] maybe through telepathy what was wrong. He told me that his arm hurt. And when he told me that, I was able to see that the bone was twisted and broken*". He told his family what had happened but no one believed him until he provided details of his out-of-body travels and his knowledge of the baby's fracture. After X-ray, the baby was indeed found to have a greenstick fracture of the arm, almost certainly a birth injury.

On May 26, 1935, Sunday Express (London) had published a narration of W. Martin, who at the age of 16 had a strange OBE (Stokes, 2007, pp. 123-4). The narration is lengthy but worth a careful reading.

> "*In 1911, at the age of sixteen, ... a high wall was blown down by a sudden gust of wind as I was passing.... A huge coping stone hit me on top of the head. It then seemed as if I could see myself lying on the ground, huddled up, with one corner of the stone resting on my head and quite a number of people rushing towards me.*
>
> *I watched them move the stone and someone took off his coat and put it under my head, and I heard all their comments, 'Fetch a doctor', 'His neck is broken', 'Skull smashed like an eggshell'.*
>
> *He [apparently a doctor] then wanted to know if anyone knew where I lived, and on being told that I was lodging just around the corner he instructed them to carry me there.*

Now all this time it appeared as though I was disembodied from the form lying on the ground and suspended in midair in the center of the group, and could hear everything that was said.

As they started to carry me it was remarked that it would come as a blow to my people, and I was immediately conscious of a desire to be with my mother. Instantly I was at home, and father and mother were just sitting down to their midday meal. On my entrance mother sat bolt upright in her chair and said, 'Bert, something has happened to our boy'.

'Nonsense', he said, 'whatever has put such an idea into your head?'

There followed an argument, but mother refused to be pacified, and said that if she caught the 2 p.m. train she could be with me before three and satisfy herself.

She had hardly left the room when there came a knock on the front door. It was a porter from the railway station with a telegram saying I was badly hurt.

Then suddenly I was again transported – this time it seemed to be against my wish – to a bed-room, where a woman whom I recognized was in bed, and two other women were quietly bustling around, and a doctor was leaning over the bed.

Then the doctor had a baby in his hands. At once I became aware of an almost irresistible impulse to press my face through the back of the baby's head so that my face would come into the same place as the child's.

The doctor said, 'It looks as though we have lost them both'. And again I felt the urge to take the baby's place in order to show him he was wrong, but the thought of my mother crying turned my thoughts in her direction, when straightway I was in a railway carriage with both her and father.

He [Martin's father] was looking at his watch, and she [Martin's mother] was saying that trains always crawled when you were in a hurry, and dad's reply was that the train was right on time.

I was still with them when they arrived at my lodgings and were shown into my room where I had been put to bed.

Mother sat beside the bed and I longed to comfort her, and the realization came that I ought to do the same thing as I felt impelled to do in the case of the baby and climb into the body in the bed.

At last I succeeded, and the effort caused the real me to sit up in bed fully conscious. Mother made me lie down again, but I said I was all right, and remarked that it was odd she knew something was wrong before the porter had brought the telegram.

Both she and dad were amazed at my knowledge. Their astonishment further increased when I repeated almost word for word some of the conversation they had had at home and in the train.

> *Mother remarked that she supposed that when some people came close to death they were gifted with second sight. I replied by saying I had also been close to birth as well, and told them that Mrs. Wilson, who lived close to us at home, had a baby that day, but it was dead because I would not get into its body.*
>
> *We subsequently learned that Mrs. Wilson died on the same day at 2:05 p.m. after delivering a stillborn girl.*
>
> *I am convinced that if I had willed myself into that baby's body, today I would be a Miss Wilson, instead of still being.*"

The detail of seeming on the verge of being reborn in a baby's body has a parallel in some cases of NDEs among the Druses of Lebanon. Stevenson (1980, p. 12) had investigated three such cases in which the subject, while near death, found himself suddenly at a place where a baby was being born and died or was stillborn. These experiences accord with the Druse belief that rebirth occurs immediately after death.

OBEs frequently occur during extreme sports, for instance in high-altitude climbers or marathon runners. A 32 years old Scottish woman had an OBE while training for a marathon. After running approximately 12-13 miles,

> "*I started to feel as if I wasn't looking through my eyes but from somewhere else. ...I felt as if something was leaving my body, and although I was still running along looking at the scenery, I was looking at myself running as well. My 'soul' or whatever, was floating somewhere above my body high enough up to see the tops of the trees and the small hills.*" (Alvarado, 2000, p. 184)

Devinsky et al. (1989, p. 1082) observed that OBEs can also develop from untypical etiologies like epileptic seizures. While working in a department store a 29 years old woman suddenly fell, and then,

> "*the next thing I knew I was floating just below the ceiling. I could see myself lying there. I wasn't scared; it was too interesting. I saw myself jerking and overheard my boss telling someone to 'punch the timecard out' and that she was going with me to the hospital. Next thing, I was in space and could see Earth. I felt a hand on my left shoulder, and when I went to turn around, I couldn't. Then I looked down and I had no legs; I just saw stars. I stayed there for a while until some inner voice told me to go back to the body. I didn't want to go because it was gorgeous up there, it was warm – not like heat, but security. Next thing, I woke up in the emergency room'. No abnormalities were found on the neurological examination. Skull CT scan was normal.*"

Most of the early views of OBEs emphasized the idea that 'something' (the spirit or the soul) exteriorized from the body and either stays close to the physical body or visit distant locations or dimensions. As early as 1887, Gustav

Fechner, (pseudonym Dr. Mises) wrote that there is an eternal waking for human beings after bodily death (Siegel, 1980, p. 915). Obviously, these views were intimately related to ancient concepts of subtle bodies in religious and occult literatures. One unknown author wrote more than one and a half century ago,

> "*While the soul is normally connected with the body, and is in a great degree dependent upon it, it still may exist as a separate entity, entirely independent of the physical organism.*" (Anonymous, 1854, p. 81).

Owen (1860, p. 347) and many other authors (Brittan, 1864; Cahagnet, 1850; Crowe, 1848; Jung-Stilling, 1851) had presented similar ideas, i.e., the projection of a "spiritual portion" of the body. Some researchers had used the concept of the 'double' or subtle body to explain the spontaneous psychic phenomena. Edmund Gurney and his associates (Gurney et al., 1886) had a different view. They regarded OBE as a hallucination of the pathological type and proposed the concept of telepathically induced hallucinations to explain diverse types of spontaneous ESP experiences, particularly apparitions of the living and "reciprocal apparitions". These are the cases,

> "*in which a person who is undergoing an OBE, and finds himself at or 'projects' himself to a particular spot distant from his physical body, has been seen at that very spot by some person present there.*" (Gauld, 1982, p. 222).

Podmore (1894) and Sidgwick (1891) also supported telepathic hallucinatory explanations. Most of these researchers were the members of the Society for Physical Research (founded in London in 1882) to study anomalous psychological and physical phenomena. Some researchers also tried "traveling clairvoyance" – the subjects were instructed to visit a distant location and report events occurring there. Edmund Gurney's case collections and the attempts of others to induce traveling clairvoyance by hypnosis present the first efforts towards research on OBEs. Early studies in hypnosis showed a lot of promise in inducing OBEs. However, there have been very few experiments in this area and the literature is scarce.

During the first half of last century, numerous case collections, and discussions of cases were published. There was an interesting paper published by Hart and Hart (1933, pp. 205-49). They presented previously published cases of OBE apparitions and compared them to cases of apparitions of diseased persons, and concluded,

> "*Some apparitions of living persons seem to have been self-conscious personalities, while others seem to have retained only vague memories, or no memories whatever, of their having appeared*". (Hart and Hart, 1933, p. 247)

As per another researcher Isaac Kaufmann Funk, OBE apparitions indicated the "*power of the human ego to manifest itself objectively at a distance.*" (Funk, 1907, p. 179). Hyslop (1912, pp. 435-72) accepted the ESP component of the experience, suggesting that the subconscious mind dramatizes images of the locality giving impression that the subject is in a different physical location. Others considered OBE as mere dream (Richet, 1922), and a hallucination or imagination (Osty, 1930, pp. 185-97). Osty's views were criticized because he ignored the aspects of OBEs suggestive of the action of an objective subtle body. Bret (1939) accepted the idea of the subtle body to explain some OBEs, but conceded that some specific cases were dreams or fantasies. Watters (1935, pp. 101-110) also accepted the projection of the subtle body (or, as he called it "the intra-atomic quantity"), but argued that it can occur only at death. In 1938, Italian psychologist and psychical researcher Ernesto Bozzano put forward his argument in a series of publications (1911, 1934 and 1938) which was of particular interest. His hypothesis was a classification of aspects of the phenomena of "bilocation" (the supposed phenomenon of being in two places simultaneously). Bozzano (1938, p. 101) wrote,

> "*The phenomena of 'bilocation' demonstrate that within the 'somatic body' there exists an indwelling 'etheric body', which in rare circumstances is able to release itself temporarily from the 'somatic body'. The inevitable inference follows that if the etheric body is able to separate temporarily preserving its consciousness intact, we must end by recognizing that when it separates definitively at the crisis of death, the individual spirit will continue to exist.*"

Bozzano had made much contributions to the study of psychic phenomena. He presented 20 published cases of out-of-body experiences, reasoning that veridical perceptions showed these were not mere hallucinations. He was a strong defender of spiritualist interpretations and survival theory. He had contributed in many areas of traditional parapsychological research. Long overlooked in the English-speaking world, his work is now being reassessed by paranormal researchers.

Some researchers have gone as far as to suggest that we are not even 'in' a body at all. Perhaps our physical body is just a focus for our consciousness, and when we learn how to change our focus, we can leave the body at will.

Except Gurney's case collections and Bozzano's detailed studies, the early researchers had presented little systematic research. But later the trend towards more systematic study increased. In depth discussions of specific cases or groups of cases was also an important development. The new concepts were somewhat more detailed in their propositions, particularly regarding supposed psychological aspects of the phenomena. An important methodological development was the use of a scale to measure the level of evidentiality of the reports. American sociologist Hornell Hart and English geologist Robert Crookall were pioneers to develop the scale, and in Hart's (1954, p. 125) words,

> *"The scale developed rules out at the start all cases which do not present evidence that the individual who had the psychic experience reported its details before receiving evidence of their veridicality"*.

Robert Crookall had analyzed over 700 reports of OBEs, that include veridical perceptions of events that could not have been sensed by the body, communication with other individuals who are at the time of the contact asleep and in a dream-like condition, and communication with deceased individuals. He found that 81% of those who had experienced them had a firm conviction of life after death owing to their personal experience (Crookall, 1970). What astounded Crookall, a meticulous scientist, was the consistency of the reports of OBEs coming from all over the world with NDEs and with the communications coming from high-level mediums.

These studies represented a transition from older and simpler to newer and more sophisticated approach. Many researchers speculated on OBEs implications for survival research. While Hart (1967, pp. 121-46) and Whiteman (1965, pp. 160-66) argued for the OBEs importance as an indication of survival, others like Ducasse (1961) and Rhine (1960, pp. 279-309) argued that the experience was inconclusive evidence of survival due to the fact that the reports came from living persons underscoring the idea that the phenomenon was dependent on the physical body for its manifestation. Ehrenwald (1974, pp. 227-33) proposed that the OBE is a defence mechanism designed to deal with the threat of death.

Dean Sheils analyzed over a thousand studies of OBEs in 70 non-Western cultures. The results showed that except minor variations in the experiences, there was absolute consistency, and the results were so universal that the phenomenon had to be genuine (Lazarus, 1993, p. 167). During the 1980s, there was also an increased interest in another paranormal phenomenon, i.e., Near Death Experiences (NDEs) and its relationship with OBEs. With this, the amount of serious and organized research and theory building combining both the NDE and OBE phenomena was remarkable.

In recent years, the OBE incidents have received considerable attention. This is evident in a variety of books, and articles in psychiatry and parapsychology journals (Gabberd and Twemlow, 1984; Irwin, 1985; Tobacyk and Mitchell, 1987; Twemlow et al., 1982; Blackmore, 1984; Stanford, 1987). Several studies confirm that OBErs report more claims of ESP and other psychic phenomena than those who are not OBErs (Alvarado, 2006b, p. 145). These 'astral travelers' have not only given detailed accounts about their OBEs, but also proposed several procedures to induce OBEs that might be approached more systematically by researchers.

2.1.1: Consciousness during OBEs

Often a question baffles the researchers – how much does out-of-body consciousness differ from normal consciousness? Those who have practiced OBEs confirm that out-of-body consciousness is very focused and directed. This single-mindedness usually stays with him during the experience and makes it easier to remember details later on. But this can also be an obstacle, because it's tempting to divert his full attention to some small distraction during the experience, rather than doing something that he had planned. As example, one experiencer had several times induced an OBE with the hope to visit his close friend, but always had been distracted and forgot his goal. One woman said though she was married for 13 years, in her OBE she thought of herself by her maiden name (Irwin, 1987, p. 56). A person may experience many frames of mind and states of consciousness during OBE. Usually, the consciousness is completely normal in all respects but at times the person may feel much stronger consciousness, and he may even feel more awake and aware than in normal life. In most of the incidents, perfect normal logical thoughts and use of logical deduction are reported. The emotions are also normal and sense of humor is not lost.

They often interact with other people – living, non-living (i.e., dead) and animals. When the experiencer meets someone on the astral plane, it is easy to tell if they are living or non-living. The living people usually seem busily preoccupied with various physical activities, and do not seem to notice the experiencer. So, the experiencer actually exchanges information with their subconscious minds. But later on when he goes to them to verify the experience, nobody remembered the conversations that occurred at subconscious level.

On the other hand, non-living people are not preoccupied. They usually notice the experiencer, and look at him when they are talking. They often wear out-of-place clothes, and they can be found suspended in midair or just about anywhere. Robert Peterson, an astral traveler, talked to his deceased father during his induced OBE. The interaction was cool and they were completely calm, rational and logical during the experience. Peterson (2013, p. 185) wrote,

> "...*I astrally projected last night and I talked to my dad who died less than two months ago. I had been flying.... My Dad was coming into view. I landed next to him. I couldn't see anything but him: There wasn't anything around for miles except blackness. He had a T-shirt on, and he looked very good. Here's what we said:*
>
> *Bob: Dad!*
>
> *Dad: Hi Bob. You guys a little preoccupied with my death, aren't you?*
>
> *Bob: Yeah, I guess so. What should I tell them?*

Dad: Tell 'em I love them. Tell Mom she shouldn't be so sad. It had to be this way.

Bob: What about the direction of my life?

Dad: Don't worry. Everything will turn out all right.

We exchanged one more line (which I don't remember). Then I remember (vaguely) flying for many miles downward and over, until I was next to my body. I woke up right away. I thought about it for a while but I was overcome by sleep. I have dreamed about him before, and this was not a dream. First, there is always scenery in a dream, and there wasn't any there. Second, in a dream I am watching myself do things against my conscious will. But there I was conscious. I didn't see myself because I was myself. And everything I did was my own conscious choice

The only thing I noticed about this projection was that I was strangely intellectual. I wasn't emotional, but had the feeling of a thinking mind. I didn't think to ask him any of a million questions I'd like to ask him. The lack of scenery makes me believe this incident took place on the astral plane, if there is such a place."

Crookall (1966, pp. 21-22) reported the case of Horace Wheatley, who felt himself "*floating in an atmosphere of peace and serenity*" while in a coma. A local government officer he knew well, greeted him and said, "*Welcome Wheatley; I shall have to see you later,*" and then faded from view. Only after recovering from his coma did Wheatley learn from his wife that this friend had died.

In many cases, the dead people do not seem to see the experiencer. In the below case of Peterson (2013, pp. 133-34) either the experiencer was seeing spirits from a different 'wavelength' or it was some sort of psychic afterimage.

"*I noticed [in my OBE] some sort of spirit form gliding from the direction of JH's room, into my room. The spirit figure I saw glided up next to me and came to rest to my left, near the bed. I turned my eyes to the left to look (I could not turn my head) but I could not make out the spirit figure too well.*

As I studied the ghostly figure, another spirit form glided in and joined the first. As I studied the two figures, their forms started fading in and out, so that parts of them were completely transparent, parts of them were visible but translucent, and parts of them were completely visible One of the spirits was a man, and the other was a woman, and they grasped each other while they reclined on the bed, less than a foot away to my left. They did not seem to notice me at all.

I wondered if the images I saw were really spirits, or if they were thought-forms, or just afterimages from a time when two such people occupied the same room years before. I was strangely calm and not alarmed at seeing the spirits. Since the spirits did not seem to care about me, I turned my attention away and concentrated again on trying to get away from my body.

I looked around once more, and as I looked, many other spirits started fading in and out of my vision. I concentrated on seeing them and as I looked, they became clearer in my vision, and soon it seemed as if the whole room was crowded with spirits of different kinds.

Most of the spirits were between the ages of 30 and 50, and they were talking to each other in this crowded room. It reminded me of a dance or a wedding reception... I moved my eyes back and forth, to scan the different spirits in the room. As I moved my eyes, the spirits seemed to move too, and it caused a strange effect. I was curious why, but it did not bother me.

I studied some of the spirits in the room, and I remember what some of them looked like: a man about 35 years old, wearing 50's style formal clothes, with some scratches and bruises on his face. He was talking to a woman, dressed also in a 50's style formal dress. None of these spirits seemed to notice me either, so I decided to ignore them..."

Sometimes others can observe the astral body during exteriorization. The Society for Psychical Research has a great number of such cases on record. One very interesting case came from Lucian Landau.

Landau (1963, pp. 126-28) reports that in 1955 his fiancé told him of her OBEs. One night he gave her his diary and asked her to move it to his room during her next OBE. Early morning, he saw her apparition came out of his room and returned to her room and soon vanished into her body sleeping on the bed. When he entered his room, he found her rubber toy dog which he had last seen on a chest of drawers beside her bed, lying beside his bed. When questioned about it, she stated that she had felt uncomfortable moving the diary as she had been taught as a child never to handle other people's letters and diaries.

Alex Tanous could do astral travel at will. In one experiment (Williams, 1989, pp. 35-36) Tanous was traveling astrally to a place few miles away to visit a particular office to see what was on the table and then report back. Tanous did not know that at this office a psychic, Christine Whiting, was waiting to see if she could see anyone coming to visit. With her clairvoyant sight, she was able to see Tanous come into the office and, as well, she described in detail his position and the shirt with rolled-up sleeves and the corduroy pants he was wearing.

Almost all the out-of-body experiencers claim that during an OBE everything is controlled by the person's thoughts. To travel, they say, all one has to do is to think of the person or place he wanted to visit, and he would be magically transported there. The experiencer also has the power to control his brain completely though it is uncertain which side of the brain interprets non-physical mystical experiences.

2.1.2: The astral body and cloths during OBE

In the disembodied state we have an astral body and we are clothed. This is despite the fact that soul is a pure energy state, and body and cloths are irrelevant. How is it possible that the apparition is clothed? Many critics have raised this highly challenging question. Muldoon and Carrington (1973, p. 283) stated,

> "*But one thing is clear to me – the clothing of the phantom is created. and is not a counterpart of the physical clothing. The absorbing question to my mind is this: How are they created. For whenever I was clothed in my projections, I invariably asked myself what the clothing was made of. where it came from, what it looked like.*"

Charles Tart suggested that a non-physical second body travels in a non-physical world that is capable of being manipulated or changed by "*the conscious and non-conscious thoughts and desires of the person whose second body is in that space*" (Tart, 1974, p. 369). Imprisoned in a gross physical body, the soul is restricted. That's why we still don't realize how mighty the power of the quantum soul is. About 93% people perceive their 'separated self' to be an invisible, non-material entity. A 48-year-old fireman who lapsed into a deep uremic (kidney failure) coma in 1977, experienced that,

> "*There was no feeling of being, it was more like a spirit... If you think about it, you can feel your cloths against your skin. But there was nothing there like that. There was no sensitive feeling as far as being.*" (Sabom, 1982, p. 39)

Another person, a 48-year-old during his cardiac arrest in 1976, experienced, "*I had a white robe on with a white belt which was interwoven and it had a tassel on both ends of it... I had a white hood but I didn't have it up*" (Sabom, 1982, p. 40). The question naturally arises – How and why is this happening?

Most of the researchers say that either our thoughts produce instant reality during an OBE, or our subconscious thoughts are more powerful than our conscious thoughts. Our beliefs, expectations, emotions, and fears also play a large part in what we experience. We certainly do not need an astral body or body parts. During the OBE when we want to pick something up, the hands will pass right through the object. We can also pass through solid walls. With mind-sensing, everything can be sensed around us and we can just float or fly wherever we want. So, eyes and legs are unnecessary. But we have astral bodies because we are so accustomed to operating with a physical body. In a physical world, a person's body is his self-image, and identity. We are so accustomed to look at our bodies in the mirror every day and to maintain this self-image that even during OBEs we carry this strong impression with us.

Since everything is controlled by a person's thought during OBE, an astral body is created. Probably, subconsciously, we create astral bodies for ourselves to use during an OBE as a convenience to others. How would we recognize a friend if he or she did not have an astral body with their familiar face?

For the same reason we are clothed during the disembodied state. Since most of us cannot think of going out naked, our thoughts create astral cloths in the same way as astral bodies. But few people who report being naked during an OBE usually 'feel naked' without their body. Similar for other styles such as combed hair. Devinsky et al. (1989, p. 1081) wrote about one patient who noted that his body, perceived from an external perspective, was dressed in the same clothes he was wearing, but curiously he always had combed hair even when he knew his hair was uncombed before the onset of the episode.

Rev. W. Stainton Moses gave an account in 'Phantasms of the Living' (case 13), where he had described his attempt to willfully appear to a friend as an apparitional figure few miles away. He did not inform him beforehand of the intended experiment. On seeing his friend a few days afterword, Rev. Stainton asked if anything had happened at his room on that night. His friend replied,

> "*Yes, a great deal happened. I was [about] to finish my pipe, when I saw you sitting in the chair. I looked intently at you, and then took up a newspaper to assure myself I was not dreaming, but on laying it down I saw you still there. While I gazed without speaking, you faded away.* ***Though I imagined you must be fast asleep in bed at that hour, yet you appeared dressed in your ordinary garments, such as you usually wear every day***." (Gurney et al., 1886, Vol. 1, pp. 103-04).

The apparition always appears in the way that the observer is used to seeing that person in real life. In Chapter 4, while discussing many case studies of ghosts and apparitions of discarnate entities the readers will find that the clothing the ghost appeared in, was what the deceased habitually wore, not necessarily those in which he had died. The material clothing does not pass on to the afterlife, but the outward appearance the discarnate entity takes is seen coincided with that of the percipient.

Many experiencers report that they were wearing white robes, unlike any clothes they own in physical life. Usually most of them believe that they are dead or they are temporarily spirits, and what else do spirits wear? Many people find themselves in astral clothes identical to the clothes they were wearing at the time of the OBE. Often these people do not realize at first that they are out of their bodies, as example, a person lies down for a quick nap, and the next moment he finds himself standing up and feeling light on their feet. And of course, they believe they are wearing the same clothes. More common, however, is the case where the subjects do not remember whether they were wearing clothes. They just do not seem to notice, because they hardly think about the cloths. The important point is, while we are out of the body our beliefs and thoughts do influence our experience. So, if we think that we should be clothed, we will be; if we think that we should have astral body or body parts we will have, and if we think that our astral bodies are malleable, they will be. Some people have reported their astral bodies were not in the shape of a human body. For example, Peterson (2013, p. 207) wrote,

> "... *I separated my head last, and then I felt just like a balloon. I was bouncing up and down but stuck to my body in a way I could not tell. I couldn't turn around. My consciousness was again very clear and concise.... If I had an astral body, then it was curled up into a ball-shape. And I was stuck to my body's right side; that is, by the right arm.... Another strange thing about this morning's projection is: I folded my arms around my chest to rest them, but they went right through my chest! They rested on the bed.*"

In the disembodied state we have freedom but there is a clause that restricts this freedom. It is not just the thought that fulfills our wishes, but our beliefs too. Some experiencers in their astral journeys were not always able to travel to a desired person or place. When trying to contact a friend, they often found themselves in unexpected, undesired, and unfamiliar surroundings. This problem stemmed mainly from their beliefs – the doubt and skepticism got in their ways. So, it takes more than just thoughts and desires to travel or to have astral body and cloths. He should have the faith on his capability. A thought like 'I am the master of my reality, and I control what happens here' may help to overcome all the barriers.

I will discuss more on apparitional clothing in Chapter 4.

2.1.3: Skeptic's views

"*We should not go for complete skepticism, but for degrees of probability.*"
Prof. Bertrand Russell

The skeptics often bring out a very logical question – what is the difference between lucid dreams (dreaming while knowing one is dreaming) and OBEs? They are right; at least some of the reported OBEs are hallucinations or daydreaming. Occasionally people who indulge in too much daydreaming confuse one experience for the other. But in real OBE cases after returning back to his earthly body, the person detects that he was fully aware during the experience, and not involved in a dream-fantasy.

Lucid dreams (a term coined by the Dutch psychiatrist Frederik van Eeden in 1913 – Windt, 2015, p. 105) are quite different from OBEs. The term 'OBE' belongs to parapsychology that implies that some invisible part of us leaves the body and is free to travel around in the physical world. The term 'lucid dreaming' belongs to psychology and this term doesn't even consider the issue of whether anything 'leaves the body' or not, but only deals with our level of awareness – we are aware that we are dreaming while we are within the dream. Gabbard and Twemlow (1984, chapter 6) had recorded several differences between OBEs and lucid dreams. Also, lucid dreams hardly have a positive lasting impact on the subject, and hence not easily remembered unless one is conditioned. OBEs are usually remembered vividly for years without prior conditioning. Many Lucid dreams contain sexual content. Author Patricia Garfield indicates that 'fully two-thirds' of her lucid dreams have sexual content and about half ended in orgasm (Peterson, 2013, p. 102). Lucid dream sex is 'convincingly' real. OBEs rarely have sexual content. When a person reports having "astral sex", the experience is more like a joyful mind-trip, a transfer of energy, or a euphoria, but it doesn't feel like physical sex.

In the disembodied state a person can differentiate between hallucination and reality. Greyson (2010, pp. 160-61) recorded the case of a 33-year-old man who had attempted suicide by overdose. In his drug-induced delirium state he started hallucinating small humanoid figures surrounding his body. As his condition deteriorated, he felt as if he had left his physical body and hovered above it. He watched his body looking around in puzzlement at the small humanoid figures. From his disembodied location he could not see those hallucinations – he was thinking and perceiving quite clearly – but he could see that his body was still hallucinating. By his account, his mind could function much more clearly and was not subject to drug-induced hallucinations once it was liberated from the brain.

How to explain the unconscious truck-driver's accurate description of his cardiac surgeon during his open-heart surgery 'flapping his arms as if trying to fly'? Should we dismiss all these phenomena as 'high-probability' guesses, or should we take them as evidence of veridical perception? What should we say about the 44-year-old man in the coronary care unit in 'deep coma and in the process of CPR', but who knew exactly where the nurse had kept his dentures? These examples, along with many similar others were confirmed by independent interviews with the doctors and nurses involved.

Skeptics sometimes argue that the OBEs provide no objective evidence that the person has in fact been separated from the physical body. Even if he later describes accurately events going on around him such information may derive from his persisting ability to hear during apparent unconsciousness. Hence, such experiences are probably imaginations. But there has been one notable attempt to determine whether the OBEs are subjective imagery or objective experience. In an experiment designed to test a subject's ability to perceive a distant object while he was having an OBE (Osis and McCormick, 1980, pp. 319-29), strain gauges situated near the target object were activated when the subject was successful in perceiving the target and perceived himself as being out of his body. The results suggested that some aspect of the subject's personality had been present at the target site, activating the strain gauges (Cook et al., 1998, p. 380). Morris et al. (1978) also conducted some experiments with another subject who was proficient at inducing OBEs in himself, and they used a variety of human, animal, and physical detectors to try to identify the times when the subject was having an OBE. Some of these experiments have shown positive results.

Many critics have argued that we cannot differentiate true out-of-body perception from extrasensory perception by the person inside the body. To address this problem Osis and McCormick (1980) designed a visual target that could be identified only if viewed from one particular visual perspective. A person skilled at inducing OBEs in himself successfully identified the target. This led Osis and McCormick to conclude that he had done so by viewing it while out of his physical body, rather than by clairvoyance while inside his physical body.

At last, those who still have doubt that OBEs are not real experiences, may please read the case of Olga Gearhardt (from the file of Melvin Morse), a 63-year-old woman who underwent a heart transplant. (Hogan, 2008, pp. 34-35). This case alone produces total evidence that the OBE cases are genuine.

When Olga Gearhardt was undergoing surgery, her entire family waited at the hospital, but her son-in-law stayed home more than 30 miles away. Though the operation was successful, at exactly 2:15 am, her new heart stopped beating. The medical team took three more hours to revive her. In the morning when the family called her son-in-law with the good news, he had his own news to tell. He already knew that the operation was successful. At exactly 2:15 am, while he was sleeping, he awoke to see his mother-in-law at the foot of his bed. She told him, "*I am fine; I'm going to be all right. There is nothing for any of you to worry about*". She asked him to tell her daughter (his wife). He wrote down the message, and the time of day exactly what she said and then fell asleep.

Later, when Olga regained consciousness on the hospital bed, her first words were "*did you get the message?*" She confirmed that she was able to leave her body and was able to travel to her son-in-law to communicate to him the message. When the family went in to see her, Olga began talking about the 'the strange dream' that took place during surgery. She said she had left her body and watched the doctors work on her for a few minutes. Then she went into the waiting room, where she saw her family. Frustrated by her inability to communicate with them, she decided to travel to her daughter's home, about 30 miles away, and connect with her son-in-law. She told them that she was sure she had stood at the foot of her son-in-law's bed and told him that everything was going to be all right.

There is no way to dismiss this story as a hallucination or as a phenomenon of a chemically imbalanced brain. Melvin Morse thoroughly researched Olga's testimony and every detail had objective verification including the scribbled note by the son-in-law.

2.1.4: Conclusion

Astral travel is real phenomenon. There is 'something' that leaves the physical body and are seen by others. This 'double' is composed of some 'finer' or more subtle material that is invisible to the untrained eye. OBEs have a profound impact on the experiencers. These are like platforms to develop farther psychic abilities. If the scientists can replicate OBEs in the laboratory condition, then we can understand many scientific laws governing mind and matter that psychic abilities are only hinting at today.

OBEs have some military application such as gathering secret intelligence by spying etc. If a person can induce an OBE at will then he can travel at great distance and obtain information that is not within the reach of the five senses. This is termed as 'remote viewing' which can be used to locate almost anything, from missing persons, hostages, secret hiding places of the criminals to the planets of our solar system as well as those of distant ones at the distant galaxies (Shrikhande, 2009, p. 59). Patrick Price, a retired police commissioner had been accustomed to use his remote viewing talents to track down crooks in Burbank, California. He could describe distant sites, given only their latitude and longitude (Thompson, 2003, p. 101). Major-General Edmund R. Thompson (US Army) commented (Spencer and Spencer, 1998, p. 129; Collingwood, 2011, p. 151), "*I never liked to debate with the skeptics because if you did not believe that remote viewing was real, you had not done your homework*". An expert in this field can even look at the past and into the future of any event.

1. In July 1973, an astral traveler Joe McMoneagle was shown a satellite photograph of a building at Soviet Union, and latitude and longitude were given to locate the building. With the information, Joe looked inside the building. There he viewed a large submarine under construction and described some of its technical details, such as driving mechanism, its hull and missile payload. He even looked at the future and saw the approximate date and manner of its launching. Later, a spy satellite took photograph that confirmed Joe's information (Shrikhande, 2009, pp. 62-3). On several other occasions Joe had provided fairly accurate information.
2. The Pentagon has used code names like 'Gondola Wish', 'Grill Flame' and 'Stargate' for the astral travelers who were used to spy on Soviet Union (Madsen, 2012, p. 197). The CIA asked one of them to look into a US embassy building in Moscow to check for 'bugs' (electronic monitoring device). The psychic spy found many such bugs planted in the building and predicted that it would have to be

pulled down. Strangely, it had to be broken down because the place could not be debugged, and it was of no use (Shrikhande, 2009, p. 63).

3. The 'Stargate' tried to locate Colonel Gaddafi of Libya during the 1986 bombing, and soldiers missing (or kidnapped) in battles (Krishnan, 2017, p. 42). The programme had above average success.
4. The Czech army also took assistance from astral travelers in 1919. "*It was a great advantage in the battle*", stated a spokesman for the army, "*the clairvoyant research party safeguarded the troops in action*" (Spencer and Spencer, 1998, p. 130).
5. Former President Jimmy Carter, recalling a 1978 remote-viewing operation, commented (Weintraub, 1998, pp. 208-09), "*She went into a trance. And while she was in the trance, she gave us some latitude and longitude figures. We focused our satellite cameras on that point, and the lost plane was there.*"

Harold E. Puthoff of Stanford Research Institute put it this way (Schnabel, 1997, p. 454), "*There were times when they wanted to push buttons and drop bombs on the basis of information given by the psychic spies*". Brenda et al. (1979, p. 17) recorded that in one remote viewing experiment even before a target site was chosen and the experiment commenced, one participant claimed to have received impressions of the targets. Her descriptions turned out to be extremely accurate even though the target locations had not been selected at the time these impressions were received. This shows the OBEr's mind or mental states are literally at the sites from which he seems to perceive.

There are clubs that do astral travel, such as the very active, proficient group in Hawaii named the Hawaii Remote Viewers Guild that does remarkable, consistently accurate remote viewing for entertainment.

NDEs offer more insights into the mechanisms involved in OBEs although their frequency was found to vary greatly between different studies. Nelson et al. (2007, pp. 794-95) found that 76% of subjects with NDEs also experienced an OBE, and 40% of these patients had their OBE only as part of the NDE episode.

2.2: Near-death Experiences (NDE)

"*There seems little doubt that NDEs occur in all cultures and have occurred at all times through recorded history ... the NDE happens to young and old, to people from all walks of life, to those whose life has a spiritual dimension and to those who profess no faith at all ... there are many examples of people who have a NDE at a time when they did not even know that such a phenomenon existed.*"

Peter Fenwick

> "*The near-death experience proves to be a challenge to the materialism of modern science, just as it challenges those who are spiritually inclined to interpret its meaning properly.*"
>
> Douglas Groothuis (1995, p. 179)

In various life-threatening situations, such as cardiac arrest ("*the mental state of cardiac arrest survivors is the closest model to that of a dying brain*" – Parnia et al., 2001, p. 150), people sometimes experience strong mystical and emotional feelings and "vivid sights of otherworldliness". These are grouped under the term of near-death experiences (NDEs). The word 'near' does not mean 'almost' dead, rather it should be read more as a temporary experience of the early stages of death. There are millions of stories on NDEs throughout human history in many places, cultures, and societies in every part of the world – what's strange is that all these accounts are strikingly similar (Zaleski, 1987, p. 5). The oldest surviving explicit report of an NDE comes from the famed Greek philosopher Plato, who describes an event in his tenth book of his legendary book entitled 'Republic' dated between 380 and 360 BC. Plato discusses the story of Er, a soldier who 'died' in battle but came back to life on his funeral pyre and described his journey into the afterlife.

> "*He once upon a time was slain in battle, and when the corpses were taken up on the tenth day already decayed, was found intact, and having been brought home, at the moment of his funeral, on the twelfth day as he lay upon the pyre, revived, and after coming to life related what, he said, he had seen in the world beyond.*" (Estrada and Newkirk, 2013, p. 143)

Er revealed that "*when his soul went forth from his body he journeyed with a great company*" which proceeded towards a meadow portrayed as "*a mysterious region where there were two openings side by side in the earth*" (Wright, 2000, p. 154) through which the souls of disembodied people traveled upwards and downwards in space in accordance with the judgment passed on their lives in that place. After an interval of 'seven days',

> "*they were required to rise up on the eighth and journey on, and they came in four days to a spot whence they discerned, extended from above throughout the heaven and the earth, a straight light like a pillar, most nearly resembling the rainbow, but brighter and purer.*" (Shorey, 1946, pp. 499, 501)

In that place, Er had watched how a large number of souls selected events for their next lives and drank from a river that erased their memories. Er was suddenly drawn back towards his body and awoke.

> "*Er himself ... was not allowed to drink of the water, yet how and in what way he returned to the body he said he did not know, but suddenly*

> *recovering his sight he saw himself at dawn lying on the funeral pyre*". (Shorey, 1946, p. 519)

Er's case does not seem to be a work of fiction since it contains sufficient details to warrant a reliable assessment. The vision commenced with an OBE – "*when his soul went forth from his body*", and ended with his return but he does not even know how he returned. These two components have the most striking parallel with modern NDEs. The sudden return is actually a trademark of NDE. Er had arrived in a strange world with a group of accompanying souls. This beautiful otherworldly landscape is often stated in modern NDE cases to feature beautiful colors, flowers, and music. Plato's original text portrayed this landscape as a "leimon", means a meadow (Parry, 1992, p. 231), on which the souls participated in a joyous festival.

On the fourth day of their travels they came to a magnificent new place where many goddesses were present. All the souls were organized into rows and they drew lots to choose their next life (reincarnation). Many animal souls choose human lives and many human souls choose 'easier' animal lives. During judgment every single deed in the lives of these beings was scrutinized as Er "*saw, by each opening of heaven and earth, the souls departing after judgment had been passed upon them*" (Shorey, 1946, p. 493). In sum; from Er's afterlife vision three core ideas are clear – an account of a mysterious place, an account of reincarnation, and finally the idea that souls receive judgment for their deeds, i.e., karmic justice.

Similar to modern NDE cases (Moody and Perry, 1988, pp. 12-13; Zaleski, 1987, p. 33), Er is denied access, despite his protestations, and is appointed as a 'messenger' to convey the wisdom of karmic fate of souls to other mortals.

> "*When he himself drew near they told him that he must be the messenger to mankind to tell them of that other world, and they charged him to give ear and to observe everything in the place*". (Collins, 2006, p. 183).

The message was clear – the character of our soul determines the next life we choose, and it is important how we train our souls during our mortal lives. Many modern NDErs receive the same wisdom.

Plutarch reported a similar incident in 'The Divine Vengeance'. A man by the name Aridaeus had fallen from a height and struck his neck. Though he had no wound, he 'died'. But after three days at his funeral, he revived and narrated his vision. While appeared dead Aridaeus was aware that "*his intelligence was driven from his body*" and that he "*had risen somewhat and was breathing with his whole being and seeing on all sides, his soul having opened wide as if it were a single eye*" (Marshall, 2019, p. 118). In this elevated condition, he felt the presence of many other souls around him.

> "*[He] recognized one soul that of a kinsman, though not distinctly, as he was but a child when the kinsman died; but it drew near and said.*

'Greetings, Thespesius' He was taken aback and said he was not Thespesius but Aridaeus. 'You were that before,' was the reply, 'but henceforth you are Thespesius. For you must further know you are not dead, but through a divine dispensation are present here in your intelligence, having left the rest of your soul, like an anchor, behind in your body." (Lacy and Einarson, 1984, p. 277).

This guiding soul then took care of him – "*swiftly taken by the guide over what appeared an immense distance, traversing it easily and unerringly, buoyed up by the beams of the light as by wings, until he came to a great chasm...extending all the way down ... called the place of Lethe [and another]... deep chasm in the ambient*" (Mead, 1907, p. 27). There was,

"*a large crater with streams pouring into it, one whiter than sea-foam or snow, another like the violet of the rainbow, and others of different tints, each having from afar a lustre of its own... [and a region with] ...those who were suffering punishment. [The] final spectacle of his vision [was that of] the souls returning to a second birth, as they were forcibly bent to fit all manner of living things and altered in shape by the framers of these. [When he was watching this scene] a woman interposed, and he was suddenly pulled away as by a cord and cast in a strong and violent gust of wind upon his body, opening his eyes again almost from his very grave.*" (Lacy and Einarson, 1984, pp. 271, 273, 277, 285, 287, 291, 293, 297, 299).

Like the case of Er, this case also includes all the three core ideas. Both of these extraordinary conscious experiences during a period of apparent coma emerge as convincing cases of NDE. Upon the detachment of his (Aridaeus) "intelligence" from his body "*nothing that he saw was familiar*" (Lacy and Einarson, 1984, p. 273). This is how the present day NDErs find it difficult to describe what they have seen. During those days the reports were rare, but today we have increasing frequency because of the improved survival rates resulting from modern techniques of resuscitation.

****

The enhancement of mental functioning at a time when the brain is physiologically impaired, as well as the paranormal and otherworldly experiences, cannot be easily explained by materialistic models. Sam Parnia, a physician from Southampton General Hospital in England and a famed NDE investigator commented in an interview with the Reuters news service,

"*The brain function these [near death] patients were found to have while unconscious is commonly believed to be incapable of sustaining lucid thought processes or allowing lasting memories to form. ... The brain itself is made up of cells, like all the body's organs, and is not really capable of producing the subjective phenomenon of thought that people have."* (Hogan, 2008, p. 5)

People experiencing NDEs regularly report clarity of perception and thought greater than that enjoyed during normal waking life, and even though "*according to conventional psycho-physiological theory, such activity should be diminishing or even not possible*" (Kelly et al., 2007, p. 386). Most of the NDErs have experienced all or some of the following (IFSR booklet, nd, p. 5; Zaleski, 1995, p. 391),

1. conscious awareness moves away from the physical body often to a spot above and looking down at the body (a 'spectator' perspective watching the scene of crisis) with medical personnel working to revive them,
2. a swift passage through a dark tunnel, outer space, a 'void', an emergence from the tunnel to brilliant light, brighter than any they had encountered before, yet not harsh on their eyes, seeing an "infinitely loving" being of light whose love is indescribable,
3. experiencing a panoramic life review of memories where each feeling is as vivid as it was in life, and feeling the impact their actions had upon others. In cases of sudden encounter with life-threatening danger, this life review often takes priority over other features, gaining insights into the purpose of their life, right and wrong choices and behaviors to adopt,
4. seeing deceased relatives and friends and sometimes communicating with them meaningfully and consciously, futuristic visions,
5. disappointment upon being revived out of their NDE, losing all fear of death after their NDE, experiencing a shift in values in which compassion, service, and a quest for meaning replace materialism, acquisitiveness, and skepticism.

NDEs follow "*universal laws of symbolic experience*" (McClenon, 1994, p. 172) which remain constant across cultural as well as social differences. Roberts and Owen (1988, p. 611) claim, "*The central features of the NDE have been recorded throughout history and across numerous cultures and religious groups*". NDE can also occur during depression, isolation, meditation (Owens et al., 1990, pp. 1175-77), and psychological critical life events (Facco and Agrillo, 2012). In rare occasions it may also occur in healthy individuals present during a close relative's death (Moody and Perry, 2010). NDE cases have been investigated widely over the past four decades, primarily with regard to their epidemiology, their psychophysiological correlates, and their effects on the lives of experiencers (Holden et al., 2009). Raymond Moody, a pioneer in the field of NDE research, had documented 150 narratives, and published under the title "Life after life" in 1975. According to Agrillo (2011, pp. 1-10) this book represented NDE as one of the most fascinating issues in cognitive neuroscience research both from scientific and philosophical points of view. The main reason these experiences generate interest among the general public is that they provide evidence that consciousness can function independent of the human body and therefore, be able to survive bodily death. Moody has talked to many NDE researchers around the world who he feels believe "*in their hearts that NDEs are a glimpse of life after life*" (Moody, 1975, p. 151). Moody continues,

> "*These medical and scientific researchers have yet to show 'scientific proof' that consciousness continues after we are physically dead, so they refrain from going public with their true feelings about what happens when we die*".

NDE cases are scattered throughout the literature for the past few centuries, but often negligently documented. Henry Atherton (1680, pp. 1-2) has recorded his 14-year-old sister's experience. Miss Anna Atherton was in trance for seven days, was thought to have died. She had no breath when a mirror was held to her mouth and no response was seen when live coals were put to her feet. But the girl recovered and related a vision of visiting heaven, which her relatives dismissed as "dream or fancy". The girl then insisted that she had seen several dead people. One of those she named was thought to be still alive; however, her family subsequently sent out inquiries and confirmed that the girl was correct. How she identified a deceased person not previously known to be dead unless she had 'really' seen the person while unconscious? In a similar case (Ring, 1980, p. 208), a man saw two of his brothers in his NDE, one of whom had been dead for years, while the other had died only two days ago – a fact unknown to the dying man. Only after he recovered from his near-death state did he learn of his brother's recent demise.

According to Greyson (2010, p. 161) 21% cases involved deceased person, For Kelly (2001, p. 233) the figure is 13%, for Ring (1980, p. 67) it is 8%, and for Fenwick and Fenwick (1995, p. 163) 39% cases included an encounter with a deceased person. On rare occasions, animals (deceased pets) are seen. The dead people often appear to welcome the person to the afterlife or send him back to this life. Kelly (2001, p. 232) gave two examples, one person who suffered cardiac complications during routine surgery said, "*I was in the brightest place I have ever seen.... I actually saw my friend Bill...coming towards me with his arms outstretched – he looked so healthy and smiling [not the way he looked before he died]* ". Another person, a utility lineman who was electrocuted, described his experience briefly as follows,

> "*I could see myself laying [sic] on the ground, very plainly. It was a feeling as though I was floating in a tunnel with a couple of white doves flying along. The further down the tunnel I went, it became lighter, and when I got closer to the end I could see a human figure, which was my*

> *[deceased] mother, motioning for me to go back – not to come any further. After she motioned me back, I came to, with the paramedics working over me.*"

Most people who meet a deceased person are at great comfort – "*seeing my dad made me truly believe that when a person dies a love[d] one will appear to ease the transition to the other side.... I knew I was dying and that he had come to get me*" (Kelly, 2001, p. 232). Rationally, communicating with a person who is dead is quite difficult to accept. Such was the case of a 23-year-old woman, who during her NDE perceived the very 'real' image of her deceased father – "*even then my mind was saying... but I can't be seeing Daddy and talking to him – he's dead... yet I could see him perfectly.*" (Sabom, 1982, p. 41). Myers (1968, pp. 55-56) related the case of a woman who viewed the hospital room and saw her distraught husband and the doctor shaking his head. Then she went to heaven and saw an angel and a familiar young man. She exclaimed, "*Why, Tom, I didn't know you were up here,*" to which Tom responded that he had just arrived. The angel then told the woman that she would be returning to Earth, and she found herself back in the hospital bed with the doctor looking over her. Later that night, her husband got a call informing him that their friend Tom had died in an auto accident.

Moody and Perry (1988, p. 136) recorded the NDE of a man who was on deathbed with heart problems at the same time that his sister was on deathbed in another part of the same hospital in a diabetic coma. The man reported that he left his body and watched the physicians work from his vantage point in the corner of the room. Suddenly he found himself conversing with his sister, who was up there with him. As she began to move away from him, he tried to go with her, but she told him, "*You can't go with me because it's not your time.*" Then she receded into the distance through a tunnel. When he awoke, he told the doctors that his sister had died, but they reassured him that she had not. At his insistence, they had a nurse check, and, in fact, she had just died.

Arthur E. Yensen had an NDE in 1932 after receiving severe injuries from an automobile accident. The vividness of what happened next remained fresh in his memory, not only after he revived, but throughout what later became a long and productive life. Yensen described,

> "*Gradually the earth scene faded away, and through it loomed a bright, new, beautiful world – beautiful beyond imagination! For half a minute I could see both worlds at once. Finally, when the earth was all gone, I stood in a glory that could only be heaven.*
>
> *In the background were two beautiful, round-topped mountains, similar to Fujiyama in Japan. The tops were snow-capped, and the slopes were adorned with foliage of indescribable beauty. The mountains appeared to be about fifteen miles away, yet I could see individual flowers growing on their slopes. I estimated my vision to be about one hundred*

times better than on earth. To the left was a shimmering lake containing a different kind of water – clear, golden, radiant, and alluring. It seemed to be alive. The whole landscape was carpeted with grass so vivid, clear, and green, that it defies description. To the right was a grove of large luxuriant trees, composed of the same clear material that seemed to make up everything". (Atwater, 1994, pp. 53-55).

The population of such a lovely world, as Yensen described, is young-looking and lively, yet possessing a weightless grace in their movements. Their bodies were somewhat translucent, so was the grass and trees; their clothing minimal. Atwater continued,

"*Everything over here is pure. The elements do not mix or break down as they do on earth. Everything is kept in place by an all-pervading Master Vibration, which prevents aging. That is why things do not get dirty, or wear out, and why everything looks so bright and new.*"

Even after almost 40 years of research into NDE phenomena, there is no final opinion among the scientific community with regard to its interpretation. Muriel E. Kelly, weakened by rheumatic fever and a serious heart murmur, became very ill and then had an NDE. (Atwater, 1999, p. 131; 2003, pp. 106-07). Later she came back to life and narrated,

"*I found myself standing on a cobblestone road with people around me dressed in bright robes – red, blue, pink. Everything was so bright and sunny. Birds were singing. Baby angels were smiling and flying around. I saw all different sizes of angels. The music was hauntingly beautiful.*"

Suddenly Muriel heard her name called. When she turned to see, she saw a holy figure beside her dressed in a white-and-red robe – "*He knelt down, and gave me a hug and I hugged him back. He told me we were going somewhere to talk.*" The holy man led her to an apartment building with many doors, and told her which door to knock on. A voice inside beckoned her to enter. It was her mother who had died when Muriel was nine, leaving behind five children. Their reunion was love filled.

"*I asked Mama where Daddy was, and Cecil, Willie, John, and Paul. Mother told me they weren't there 'cause it wasn't their time. I had no idea what she meant, so she took me to an area where we sat on a cloud and looked over the whole world. My mother located my dad and brothers riding in a car. We could see right through it. Dad was driving, and we heard my brothers and Dad crying, saying, 'I wish Muriel was still here. We miss her.'*"

Muriel began to cry for her earthly family and wished to be back with them. She got her wish and returned back to earthly life.

Cecil L. Hamilton drowned while swimming with his brother and stepped into the same light-filled world.

> "*I noticed everything – sky, buildings, glass – emitted its own light. And everything was much more colorful .... a river meandered around. On the other side was a city, and a road running through it to another city, and another city, and another and another. Right in front of me but across the river were three men. They projected themselves to me. They didn't walk or fly; they projected over. I didn't recognize them...*
>
> *I knew these three men were looking out for me, like a welcoming committee to escort me over the river to the first city. I had the feeling that if I went with them, there would be no coming back, so I hesitated. The first city was like first grade. People stayed there until they were ready to go to the next city – your eternal progression, from city to city. Behind me and to the left was a strong light source, very brilliant and filled with love. I knew it was a person. I called it God for lack of a better term. I could not see it; I felt what seemed like a male presence.*" (Atwater, 2003, pp. 45-47)

God and Hamilton engaged in a long conversation about the Universe and reasons for everything. Then God questioned if Hamilton wanted to return to the physical world. "*I do want to return,*" he said. God asked why. Hamilton narrated,

> "*I said I would help my mother whom my father had left with four children and one on the way. God kind of chuckled and asked for the real reason. I said I would leave the earth a little better than I found it. 'Then you may return with some of the knowledge of the things you have learned, but the rest will be veiled for a time. Live in such a way that you will not feel bad when you return here again.' I woke up face down in the mud of the river bottom and was 'lifted' to the top.*"

Habermas and Moreland (1992, p. 74) believe that NDEs are "*strong evidence for at least a minimalistic view of life after death,*" which they defined as "*life in the initial moments after death, not some detailed version of heavenly life or even necessarily eternal life*". A 26-year-old woman described the following experience full of mystical features that occurred during an emergency caesarean section,

> "*I heard my doctor say, 'I've lost her; she's gone!' Then four angels were carrying me through a great, huge auditorium. The two large doors of the auditorium opened, and we went out and up, through space. I saw a beautiful white city, with a wall around it and a set of gates facing me. I was so excited, because I wanted to go through those gates. There was a beautiful bright light over the city.*

I could not go through the gates into the city, but found myself back on the operating table. My doctor said, 'I'm so glad you are back; your husband will be so glad you are back.' I was crying as if my heart would break, telling him that I did not want to come back. I begged him to let me go again, it was so beautiful! It was the saddest time of my life, and yet it was the most beautiful!" (Greyson, 1985, p. 394)

The account of Pam Reynolds has been widely acclaimed by the researchers as the "*single best instance we now have in the literature on NDEs to confound the skeptics*" (Ring, 2000, p. 218), and as the one coming "*closest to providing solid, scientific evidence suggestive of the post-mortem survival of consciousness*" (Schmicker, 2002, p. 205). A weakness in the walls of two arteries in her brain had caused the arteries to swell, and rupture was considered imminent. Anesthesia was induced, and sooner her NDE began with the buzzing noise of the bone saw motor (Sabom, 1998, pp. 41-42),

"*As I listened to the sound, I felt it was pulling me out of the top of my head....I remember seeing several things in the operating room when I was looking down....I was metaphorically sitting on Spetzler's [Robert F. Spetzler who had performed the brain operation] shoulder. It was brighter and more focused and clearer than normal vision...There was so much in the operating room that I didn't recognize, and so many people....*

The saw thing that I hated the sound of looked like an electric toothbrush and it had a dent in it, a groove at the top where the saw appeared to go into the handle, but it didn't....And the saw had interchangeable blades, too, but these blades were in what looked like a socket wrench case....

I remember the heart-lung machine. I didn't like the respirator...I remember a lot of tools and instruments that I didn't readily recognize."

After the operation, Pam was placed on cardiopulmonary bypass to quickly cool her core body temperature. As her temperature fell to 60 degrees F, her heart stopped, her electroencephalogram (EEG) flattened into complete electro-cerebral silence, and her brainstem and cerebral hemispheres became unresponsive. The cardiopulmonary bypass machine turned off, and the blood drained from her head. In this critical condition her NDE progressed (Sabom, 1998, pp. 43-45),

"*There was a sensation like being pulled, but not against your will. I was going on my own accord because I wanted to go....It was like a tunnel but it wasn't a tunnel.*

At some point very early in the tunnel vortex I became aware of my grandmother calling me....The feeling was that she wanted me to come to her, so I continued with no fear down the shaft. It's a dark shaft that I

went through, and at the very end there was this very little tiny pinpoint of light that kept getting bigger and bigger and bigger.

The light was incredibly bright, like sitting in the middle of a light bulb....

I noticed that as I began to discern different figures in the light... and they were all covered with light, they were light, and had light permeating all around them... they began to form shapes I could recognize and understand....

They would not permit me to go further....I wanted to go into the light, but I also wanted to come back. I had children to be reared."

According to the "whole brain" definition (Uniform Determination of Death Act, drafted by the National Conference of Commissioners on Uniform State Laws, Kauai, Hawaii, 26 July to 1 August 1980) of death, life ends with the "*cessation of all functions of the entire brain.*" During Pam's surgery, her brain had been drained of blood and found "dead" by all clinical tests of brain function. According to Spetzler (CBS News, 1997), "*If you would examine that patient from a clinical perspective during that hour [of hypothermic cardiac arrest], that patient would by all definition be dead.*"

There are cases where the experiencer met an unknown person during NDE, but recognized him later from family photographs. These are strangest of all, and provide some of the most persuasive evidence for the ontological reality of deceased spirits and suggest the persistence of consciousness after death.

Rawlings (1978, pp. 17-22) described the case of a 48-year-old man who in an NDE, perceived a gorge full of beautiful colors, lush vegetation, and light. There he met both his stepmother and his biological mother who had died when he was only 15 months old. His father had remarried soon after his biological mother's death. He had never even seen a photo of her. A few weeks after this episode, his aunt, having heard about this vision, visited and brought a picture of his mother posing with a number of other people. The man had no difficulty picking his mother out of the group, to the astonishment of his father.

Kubler-Ross (1983, p. 208) reported the case of a girl who after almost dying during heart surgery, said she had met her brother who seemed familiar to her, even though she thought she never had a brother. Her father, very much moved by her testimony, told her that she did, in fact, had a brother who had died before her birth. Morse and Perry (1990, p. 53) described the case of a seven-year-old boy dying of leukemia who told his mother that he had traveled up a beam of light to heaven, visited a "crystal castle" and talked to God. A man there approached him and introduced himself as an old high school boyfriend of the boy's mother. The man said he had been crippled in a car accident but in the crystal castle he had regained his ability to walk. The boy's mother had never mentioned this old boyfriend to her son, but after hearing of this vision, she called some friends and confirmed that her former boyfriend had died the very day of her son's vision.

Van Lommel (2004, p. 122) recorded the extensive NDE of a Dutch man who, during a cardiac arrest, saw his deceased grandmother and an unknown man who looked at him very lovingly. More than a decade after his NDE, his mother, on her deathbed, confessed to him that he had been born from an extramarital relationship, and that her husband was not his biological father. His biological father was a Jewish man who had been deported and killed during World War II. She showed her son a photograph of his biological father, whom he immediately recognized as the man he had seen in his NDE a decade earlier.

These are the cases what the investigators call 'Peak in Darien' type. In this type, the person at a near death situation has reported seeing a recently deceased person of whose death the experiencer had no normal knowledge. Many investigators (Barrett, 1926, pp. 10-26; Callanan and Kelley, 1993, pp. 86-87, 93-94; Crookall, 1966, pp. 21-22; Gurney and Myers, 1888-89, pp. 459-60; Hyslop, 1908, pp. 88-89; Myers, 1903, pp. 339-42; Osis and Haraldsson, 1977a, p. 166; Ring, 1980, p. 208; Sidgwick, 1885, pp. 92-93) have recorded such accounts. The hypothesis of survival begins to seem worthier of consideration.

NDE reports are not related to gender, race, education, occupation, previous knowledge of these experiences, and method of resuscitation. Hundreds of thousands of reported cases, not only amongst religious people, but also from jungle dwellers to the canyons of Wall Street, from atheists to god-fearing – the universal message relayed from the other side is that life exists as an ongoing extension of itself. After presenting over 600 NDE accounts in his book 'Evidence of the Afterlife' Jeffery Long (2010, p. 50) concluded, "*The remarkable consistency of NDEs around the world is evidence that they are real events*".

We are mortal human beings when earth-bound, but as a soul we are immortal – a true extension of The Divine. As I will show later in this book, our earthly existence has a meaning, and this materialistic world is an illusion. We have a **GREATER PURPOSE.** Do these experiences mirror what quantum physics seeks to uncover and explain, that all is consciousness, and everything else is illusion? It is only the consciousness that matters, the physical body is the most insignificant; even our attitudes, thoughts, and feelings are more important.

2.2.1: NDE experiences are "realer than real"

"*The plain fact is that none of us understands these phenomena. As for the soul and life after death, they are still open questions, though I myself suspect that NDEs are part of the same continuum as mystical experiences.*"

Peter Roennfeldt

Many experiencers state that their experience was hyper-real – not dream-like, not hallucinatory – more real than the experience on Earth, as one experiencer commented, "*The memory of the near-death experience is more real than what I did yesterday*". Another person puts it this way – "*as real as you and I sitting here talking at this moment*". Greyson (2010, p. 160) wrote,

"*The vast majority of near-death experiencers report that during the time that their brains were demonstrably impaired, their thinking, by contrast, was clearer and faster than ever before, as if the mind had been freed from the distractions and limitations of the physical brain. Such enhanced mentation is in fact significantly more common during NDEs in which proximity to death was well documented in medical records than during NDEs lacking such documentation, and includes increased speed, logic, and clarity of thought; overall visual and auditory clarity; vividness of colors; and control of cognition.*"

Among eight hundred experiencers (Kelly et al., 2007, p. 386), 80% described their thinking during the NDE as "*clearer than usual*" (45%) or "*as clear as usual*" (35%); 74% described their thinking as "*faster than usual*" (37%) or "*at the usual speed*" (37%); 65% described their thinking as "*more logical than usual*" (29%) or "*as logical as usual*" (36%); and 55% described their control over their thoughts as in "*more control than usual*" (36%) or in "*as much control as usual*" (36%). In Pam Reynolds' case, "*[I was] the most aware that I think I have ever been in my life*" (Kelly et al., 2010, p. 517). Sometimes the "*senses are much more acute,*" such that details of the experience and of one's physical surroundings at the time "*are frequently recalled with great minuteness*" (Starbuck, 1906, p. 78). Long (2010, p. 56) reported that 94% of experiencers say that they were "*more conscious and alert than normal*" or "*just as conscious and alert as normal*" in their NDE. Other studies (Blackmore, 1993; Potts, 2002, pp. 233-58) confirm that most of the experiences are "*real*", or even "*realer than real.*"

"*In 45 years I dreamed a lot of things, but I never had a 'dream' like this.... When you dream, you know that it is a dream. When I remember my dreams, in the next five minutes I'm not sure any more about their content. This experience [NDE] instead, you'll remember it clearly, for years.*" (Palmieri et al., 2014, p. 9)

A deep sense of reality pervades the experience both while it is happening and later. Sabom (1982, pp. 32-33, 227) recorded these statements.

"*It's reality .... no fantasy. There was no so-called dream or nothing. These things really happened to me. It happened. I know. I went through it. Even though I was in a blackout stage I know myself that I went through it.*"

"*This was real. If you want to, I am perfectly willing for you to give me Sodium Pentothal [Truth serum] ... It's real as hell.*"

"*[My NDE was] realer than here, really. After that the world seemed like a mockery to real life – make-believe. Like people playing games. Like we are getting prepared for something but we don't know what.*"

One experiencer wrote (Blackmore, 1993, p. 137),

"*For many years, it was the most real thing that ever happened to me. Yes, far more real and vivid than any real-life incident. It was so real, detailed and so vivid and consistent ...; in fact, so totally un-dreamlike!*"

The overwhelming "realness" of an NDE is a second argument used to support the afterlife theory. Swiss geologist Albert Heim who had an NDE while falling on a ski trip refers to this aspect during his mountain fall.

"*All my thoughts and ideas were coherent and very clear, and in no way susceptible, as are dreams, to obliteration ... The relationship of events and their probable outcomes were viewed with objective clarity, no confusion entered at all.*" (Laureys and Tononi, 2009, p. 313)

Most people consider their NDE memories far superior (most powerful, intense, vivid, important, and founding experience of their life) to their real memories. In one review Van Lommel (2011, p. 20) highlighted this core issue,

"*Why is the experience of the self during NDE so real? How is it possible to experience enhanced consciousness with the possibility of veridical perception independently of the lifeless body?*"

NDE memories are characterized by a sense of "phenomenological certainty" of the experience, typical of the perception during daily life (Dell'Olio, 2010, pp. 113-28). Thonnard et al. (2013) have examined this aspect of NDEs in depth. They specifically investigated NDE memories with the Memory Characteristics Questionnaire (MCQ), built to evaluate peculiar characteristics of real and imagined event memories. They compared memories of real (such as, marriages and births – intense real-life events) and imagined past events (such as, dreams and thoughts – things that did not occur in physical reality) in three groups of people that survived from the coma, one of which was characterized as having had NDEs and a control group. The results were fascinating. The NDE memories were much richer than any imagined event or any real event of these survivors. Even if the patient had the experience a long time ago, its memory was as rich as though it was yesterday. These findings demonstrate that NDEs are not imagined events.

Palmieri et al. (2014, pp. 1-16) had examined the possibilities of using hypnosis to recollect the richness and thoroughness of the NDE recalls. Hypnosis, if used wisely, is an excellent aid to facilitate and to focus on the recall of both real and imagined memories (Erdelyi, 1994, pp. 379-90; Orne et al., 1996, pp. 354-69; Scoboria et al., 2002, pp. 26-32; Wagstaff et al., 2004, pp. 434-55). Hypnosis can be used successfully to evoke memories of NDEs that have happened before. In fact, some individuals are able to remember their NDEs only under hypnosis (Schroeter-Kunhardt, 1993, p. 221; Facco, 2012, pp. 284-97), or months to years later, when they come into contact with an appropriate association, for example another experiencer. The details of the NDE memories under hypnosis are well-organized sequence of events. Additional details also surface with the same intensity of feeling of re-experiencing the event and the original emotions. Memory features are strikingly similar. Also, the EEG pattern of NDE memory recall significantly differs from that observed for imagined memories. It means, NDE memories are episodic memories of events experienced in a peculiar state of consciousness.

Hence NDEs are real experiences. Eben Alexander, the author of a best-selling 'Proof of Heaven: A Neurosurgeon's Journey into the Afterlife' commented in an interview, "*A much richer consciousness exists when we are freed from the shackles of the physical human brain and mind.*" (Alexander, 2012). Penny Sartori did a comparison of NDE and hallucinations caused by sedatives and painkillers. She found that the hallucinations were much more confused and less likely to be remembered afterward. Also, these patients knew they were hallucinating, whereas, the NDErs (Sheehan, 2011, p. 22), "*remained adamant that their experience was real*". One NDEr had gone even this far to say (Sabom, 1982, p. 33),

> "*[The experience was] realer than here, really. After that the world seemed like a mockery to real life – make-believe. Like people playing games. Like we're getting prepared for something but we don't know what.*"

NDE memories can remain unchanged over a period of 20 years (Greyson, 2007, pp. 407-11). One experiencer said, "*My memory became exceedingly clear*" (James, 1902, p. 157). Our memories originating from real, everyday life have more perceptual information (e.g., color, sound, smell etc.), more contextual information, and more details than memories originated from thought or imagination; so are the NDEs with vivid and memorable visions. The large body of NDE data now points to genuine evidence for a non-physical reality.

2.2.2: NDE, timelessness, fine-tuning and biocentrism

The NDErs give us opinions that confirm our understanding of fine-tuning, biocentrism and illusion of space and time. Sense of time is greatly altered during NDE. This is a frequent feature of NDE but has not been described in detail in statistical and phenomenological terms. Albert Heim who had an NDE while falling on a ski trip reported that "*time became greatly expanded*" during his fall (Heim, 1892, pp. 327-37). Greyson (2003, pp. 269-76) found that 67% of NDE subjects reported an alteration of the sense of time. Sabom (1982, p. 32) concluded that all the people he had interviewed described their NDE events were being perceived all intuitive sense of the duration of the experience was lost, such as, "*You are like a state of suspended animation*", "*I cannot pinpoint time in a situation like that. It might have been a minute*", and "*There was no measurement of time. I don't know if it was a minute or five or ten hours*" and so forth.

In a timeless condition, the question how much time the NDE lasts is irrelevant. Heim's fall lasted less than 10 seconds during which he experienced a life-review and other elements, which he claims will take a very long time to describe. This is confirmed by the few survivors jumping from the Golden Gate Bridge who experienced NDEs – a fall of about four seconds (Marsh, 2010, p. 74; Woerlee, 2013, p. 306), as well as the syncope (temporary loss of consciousness caused by a fall in blood pressure) induced in healthy subjects under experimental conditions which lasted no longer than 22 seconds. During this short period 83% of the subjects had profound experiences including OBEs, entering other worlds, meeting other beings, life reviews and visual perceptions. So, the length of the experience is not corelated with the length of the experienced content as can be seen by the example of life reviews 'condensed' into short time periods of experience (Swaab, 2014, p. 310). What in narrative time is experienced as hours, can in experiential time take place in a few seconds and to date no researcher knows when that moment occurs. Ray Kinman, after an incident of accidental overdose had an NDE (Atwater, 2007, pp. 35-36), where he had experienced timelessness.

> *"Now this is very difficult to describe, time ceased to exist. Past and future were completely non-existent. I was traveling in an intense, burning 'now.' 'Now' was everything. I ceased to be a noun (person, place, or thing) and became a verb (an action)."*

Eternal souls live in timelessness. Statements from three experiencers in an astral body support the theory of fine-tuning and biocentrism.

> *"I was in the Void. I was in pre-creation, before the Big Bang. I had crossed over the beginning of time/the First Word/the First vibration. I was in the Eye of Creation. I felt as if I was touching the Face of God. It was no religious feeling. Simply I was at one with Absolute Life and*

> *Consciousness... When I say that I could see or perceive forever, I mean that I could experience all of creation generating itself. It was without beginning and without end. That's a mind-expanding thought, isn't it?* ***Scientists perceive the Big Bang as a single event which created the Universe. I saw that the Big Bang is only one of an infinite number of Big Bangs creating Universes endlessly and simultaneously.*** *The only images that even come close in human terms would be those created by supercomputers using fractal [a fractal is an object or quantity that displays self-similarity on all scales] geometry equations.* (Bailey and Yates, 1996, p. 44)

> "*God revealed to me that I had been created as a spiritual being at the beginning of the creation of the universe. ... It was also part of God's plan to create a physical world as a place of learning and growth.*" (Gibson, 2006, p. 336).

> "*The Light explained to me that there is no death. We are immortal beings. We have already been alive forever! I realized that we are part of a natural living system that recycles itself endlessly.*" (Arial, 2010, p. 193).

Therefore, the emergence of consciousness from inanimate matter and the interpretation of the physical fine-tuning of the Universe for life are interlinked. The quantum soul will continue to exist from Big Bang to Big Crunch. The body-linked waking consciousness only has a subjective reality and the physical world as we normally perceive is an illusion. The 'real self' is not the product of brain function, as one experiencer commented (Van Lommel, 2011, p. 27). "*I can live without my body, but apparently my body cannot live without me.*"

There is an eternal consciousness that existed even before Big Bang otherwise how the laws of physics took the forms which were just right for life? This eternal consciousness possesses the power and knowledge sufficient to create a Universe with life and a strong motive for doing so. Thus, a deep understanding of this eternal consciousness is required to understand various afterlife phenomena and our significance on Earth. We are not here by accident. We have a purpose and a mission to fulfill. As we learn more about the world, we will eventually understand that all of these fine-tuned laws, fundamental constants and boundary conditions will all be explained as part of a final and unique theory of everything.

2.2.3: The tunnel experience during NDE

The researchers have put several theories to account for the origin of tunnel experiences in near death studies. Most of the experiencers say that the tunnel is dark (rarely multicolored or spiral-shaped narrow space accompanied by visible or invisible beings or by music), and there is an exceptionally bright but nonblinding, beautiful, and alluring light source at the end – "*We want to reach the light. It is coming nearer*" (Blackmore and Troscianko, 1989, p. 15). People are often pulled towards the light source at an incredible speed. The tunnel experience is both exciting and mysterious. A 70 years old woman while undergoing surgery for a spinal tumor experienced this;

> "*Suddenly amidst all this pain (I was still in the dark tunnel) I saw a light very faint and in the distance. It got nearer to me, and everything was so quiet; it was warm, I was warm, and all the pain began to go. When I finally stood out of the dark [tunnel], and into this light, it was the most beautiful thing I have ever seen: soft, warm, translucent. I was finally there, and I felt as if someone had put his arms around me. I was safe, no more pain, nothing, just this lovely, caring sensation.*" (Blackmore and Troscianko, 1989, p. 16)

Experiencing a passage through some darkness or a tunnel is experienced by about 23 to 25% of subjects with NDEs (Lenggenhager et al., 2006, pp. 643-57; Sabom, 1982, p. 278). Woerlee (2005, p. 211) provides an example;

> "*After I had floated close to the ceiling for a short time, I was sucked into a tunnel ... It was black and dark around me, somewhat frightening, but this did not last long: at the end of the tunnel I saw a clear light towards which I traveled.*"

Sabom (1982, p. 278) found that 28 to 30%, and Van Lommel et al. (2001, p. 2041) that 23% of subjects with NDE reported seeing the intense light, but did not specify if this was associated with the experience of a tunnel.

> "*This is how I remember it...I was in a tunnel, traveling at enormous speed toward a light, which was incidental at this point. I had flown frequently on business, and participated in automobile racing..., and I was aware that the speed I was traveling was far in excess of anything I had ever experienced, and it was increasing all the time. The walls of the tunnel were a blur, but as I looked more carefully, I came to the realization that this tunnel through which I was traveling at such unbelievable speed was composed of planets; individual solid masses blurred together by speed and distance. Incredibly, I seemed to be hurtling through the universe!*
>
> *There was tremendous sound, too. It was as if all the great orchestras in the world were playing at once; no special melody, and very loud, powerful but somehow soothing. It was a rushing, moving sound, unlike anything I could remember, but familiar, just on the edge of my memory.*
>
> *I was suddenly frightened. I had no idea where I was bound at such speed, nor had anything in my life prepared me for this adventure.*

> *As soon as I realized I was afraid, a presence reached out to me; not physically, but telepathically. It was a calming, gentle presence and a voice, which said, 'Take it easy. Everything is O.K. Relax' and this thought transference immediately induced a soothing effect on me, far more powerful than anything within the experience of my stressful life"*. (Ring, 1991, p. 29)

Some people float gently down tunnels while others rush at a tremendous rate. Kevin Drab (1981, pp. 126-52) reported 67 cases describing movement, of which 12 said they were moving at a slow to moderate speed and 24 were moving very fast. A 23 years old woman had experienced this way,

> "*There was total blackness around me... I felt like I was moving very, very fast in time and space. I was traveling through a tunnel. It did not look like a tunnel, but when you are in a tunnel, all you see is blackness around you. If you move very fast you can feel the sides moving in on you whether there are sides there or not because of the darkness.*" (Sabom, 1982, p. 63).

A 60 years old woman 'watched' her cardiac resuscitation from an out-of-body location while surrounded by a region of darkness.

> "*[During the arrest] I had left my body and was to the side in sort of like a tube. It was real dark in there, but I could see what they were doing. I could hear them, I saw them doing all these stuff to me.... Whatever I was in was black, but I could see out and watch everything.*" (Sabom, 1982, p. 64)

A man felt he was moving through a dark corridor-like region while observing the resuscitation of his unconscious physical body. This mysterious region separated the perceptions of earthly events from the other-world features of his experience.

> "*I could see my body lying there... I saw the whole show... I was going up slowly, like floating in a dark or semi-dark corridor like. They were working the hell out of me. ... and I kept thinking: What is this? What's happening? And I kept going up and up and up.... And then I went further... I went to a different world.*" (Sabom, 1982, p. 64)

Drab (1981, pp. 126-52) studied 71 tunnel experiences obtained from 1,112 reports. He excluded descriptions of voids and black spaces and defined the tunnel as "*the perception of a realistic enclosed area of space much longer than its diameter*". He found, among other things, that the tunnel was more frequent in serious medical conditions than in non-serious conditions.

The tunnels are mostly dark or dimly lit (10% are brightly lit). None of the experiencers have reported touching the sides, although these varied widely and included scintillating darkness, luminous vapor with fine lines, and bricks with a cobblestone floor. One observer went down a tunnel made of leaves (Blackmore, 1982) and rare experiences included tunnels made of varying textures, bright lights, or bands of darker and lighter gray.

Almost half of Drab's cases reported a light at the end of the tunnel, and 73% of those described it as becoming larger in their field of vision and described themselves as moving towards it. Many described the light as extremely bright but it did not hurt their eyes. Almost all of Drab's experiencers described moving through their tunnels – most went through, some up, and some down, but only eight cases described coming back through the tunnel. It is not clear from Drab's description whether they came backwards through the tunnel or turned around and moved forwards in the opposite direction.

What kind of explanation are we looking for – spiritual and scientific? We want to know, why there is a tunnel and not something else? There could be gates, doorways, arches, chasms, or the great Ganga River of the Hindu faith. In fact, these other forms do occur later on in NDEs, but the tunnel appears regularly in predictable forms. Why it is dark as most people experienced? Why there is a light at the end? And, above all, why it seems so real? It is obvious that the tunnel is not an actual one but it is symbolic of blacking out of consciousness as it passes from one state to another. Celia Green (1968) proposed the tunnel as a symbol of a long journey and Kenneth Ring (1980) considered the tunnel a psychological phenomenon through which the mind shifts from its normal state of consciousness to a holographic or four-dimensional consciousness of pure frequencies.

The spirit world starts at the end of the tunnel where eventually people are wholly enveloped by this light and feel completely absorbed by it. This process is coupled with an indescribable feeling of bliss, a sense of unconditional love and acceptance. The tunnel and the light have become almost synonymous with NDEs.

2.2.4: The mystery of the Divine Light

The greatest discovery the vast majority of experiencers make is that one or more super-intelligence – the light (a godlike or angelic presence) – exist. Some seem to be using the phrase "seeing the light" in a symbolic sense, but others are clearly referring to what was for them a real and vivid sensory phenomenon. Regarding this NDE element, Moody (1975, pp. 49-50) wrote,

> "*What is perhaps the most incredible common element in the accounts I have studied, and is certainly the element which has the most profound effect upon the individual, is the encounter with a very bright light. Typically, at its first appearance this light is dim, but it rapidly gets brighter until it reaches an unearthly brilliance. Yet, even though this*

light [usually said to be white or "clear"] is of an indescribable brilliance, many make the specific point that it does not in any way hurt their eyes, or dazzle them, or keep them from seeing other things around them [perhaps because at this point they don't have physical "eyes" to be dazzled]".

"*Despite the light's unusual manifestation, however, not one person has expressed any doubt whatsoever that it was a being, a being of light. Not only that, it is a personal being. It has a very definite personality. The love and the warmth which emanate from this being to the dying person are utterly beyond words, and he feels completely surrounded by it and taken up in it, completely at ease and accepted in the presence of this being. He senses an irresistible magnetic attraction to this light. He is ineluctably drawn to it*".

A five-year-old child had the following experience during hernia operation.

"*I was in a place where everything was light around me – something like clouds and still not clouds the way you see them from an airplane. I was standing at the bend of a road of light leading to something at a far distance that it is not possible to describe straight out.*

In front of me, on the road, was a being of light, a presence rather than someone visible, a light in all the light. I immediately realized that this being could see right through me and reveal my deepest secrets. My very first impulse was to hide, but I realized immediately that this would not be possible and also not necessary. For between us I now felt a strong mutual wordless love, and I knew beyond any doubts that whatever he would see in me, he would understand and accept.

The being had no physical features except for the light. Nevertheless, he was quite definitely male. To put a name on him – God, Jesus, Smith would be utterly meaningless. Although he was far more powerful, wise, and loving than I ever expect to become, he was not superior to me. For on the deepest and most important level of them all – the level where we loved each other – we were equals. Thus 'him' – not 'Him'. And thus, no praise, no worship.

This hasn't made me think that I am superior to other human beings. On the contrary, the lesson is everybody is equal to everybody else when it comes to real love – irrespective of age, sex, education [etc.]". (Ring, 1991, pp. 37-8)

Tachibana (2003, pp. 27, 58, 60, 90) had recorded the accounts of three Japanese experiencers whose NDEs included the element of a bright light. Yasuda, a musician and a stage actor, encountered a strong, bright light in his NDE and commented, "*First of all, the nature of the light is quite different. It was much, much brighter than stage lights. Yet it is not blinding [it does not hurt my eyes]. Stage lights are blinding*". He felt extremely happy as he was walking in the light. Another experiencer met a colorful, unforgettably beautiful butterfly emitting bright light. Embraced in the bright light, she "*was in total sweet euphoria*".

The typical image of heaven for Japanese is a flower garden with a border or limit, such as a river, one as a pond, and one as a stone wall (Ohkado and Greyson, 2014, p. 195). In contrast the Westerners see the border or limit in various forms, such as a body of water, a gray mist, a door, a fence across a field, or simply a line (Moody, 1975, p. 65). Tachibana (2003, pp. 58, 60) recorded that a critic had an NDE where he moved through a seven-colored light column and reached a place like "*a lawn, or flower garden, fluffy and very soft as if made of cotton*". He described his feelings as this,

> "*I have never felt such a good feeling. I can't compare it with any other experiences. It was like going to heaven or the feeling of ecstasy. I was perfectly content. I didn't want anything. Like I was 100 percent content. Nobody will understand how I felt until they experience themselves*".

One important finding of NDE research is that about 89% of the experiencers who see the light also see deceased friends and relatives, and those who see deceased persons also mostly have experienced darkness and the tunnel.

> "*I had been gasping because of the pain, but somehow I just gave up and felt my last breath leave my mouth. At that instant, all the pain was gone, and I was flying at an enormous speed through darkness into a light. My flight stopped just with the darkness, and I gazed into the light, sensing the power that emanated from it.*
>
> *My Grandmother appeared within this wonderful, pure light. She was smiling, totally at peace and harmony with herself and her surroundings; an indescribable purity and unconditional love emanated from her and the light toward me. Grandma spoke no words. The love said everything. Her eyes were filled with deepest compassion, and I was swept with overwhelming longing to enter into the light with her.*" (Sorensen and Willmore, 1988, p. 37)

In all possibility the light being was a Deity or angel, as Pam Reynolds described in a BBC interview (Maksimonus, 2009; Zap, 2012, p. 54; Pam, 2003),

> "*I asked if god was the light. And the answer was 'no, god is not the light. The light is what happens when god breathes.' And I distinctly remember thinking, 'I am standing in the breath of god'*".

Probably God unveils His invisible qualities through several Deities and angels who command and control the afterlife realm full of love and bliss. People often encounter more than one Deity, and each Deity is so massive, so powerful, so encompassing that it is often described by them as more brilliant and mightier than a million suns, existing as a 'Presence' without need of name, identity, or definition. All that exists in the afterlife seems to exist within this 'all-ness', this oneness. It is as if there is only One Mind, yet many thinkers. A favorite phrase, experiencers come to use is – we are one with The One. And 'The One' teaches us that a moment taken to show another human being selfless and unconditional love without thought of reward and recognition can give incredible meaning to our lives. It is more fulfilling than becoming the President of a State, winning a Nobel Peace Prize, or becoming a billionaire. Likewise, moments that are simply spent on oneself, without a thought of service to another or without a thought of bringing something good into the world are as if they never existed. Our every action and every choice are incredibly powerful and significant.

A 31-year-old woman described the following experience that occurred during open-heart surgery,

> *"I found myself elevated. There was nothing underneath. I was in a dark place except there were patches of mist. I never saw myself below. . .. I wasn't frightened. I had no pain. And I think I was wondering, 'Why aren't I afraid?' But I wasn't afraid. It felt natural. I felt this feeling of love. It was like all of a sudden I could feel this whole feeling of love and joy. It was all around me. My eyes were automatically drawn to the side and I saw this circle of light off in the distance. I'll never forget it. And I could feel this love just coming from that light. It was all around me. It wasn't a beam. It was just the feeling of it coming from that light. It was so beautiful! I could never explain it in a million years.*
>
> *And I went towards that light with my arms extended. I just wanted to embrace it. And as I did this I started to move. I wasn't walking. But I could feel the vibrations, the air as I was going along, I could absolutely feel it. It didn't bother me and it was perfectly natural. And as I was getting closer to the light, I was having an argument with myself. And I was saying, 'Don't you think you should go back and take care of your children?' I remember I said, 'No!' I love my children. And I loved them up there. But it was a different kind of love. This is the hardest part for me to explain. It's a true love, a pure love, free of earthly worries. Absolute pure love!"* (Greyson, 1985, p. 392)

Experiencers always report direct communication with this being, as if it reads their mind and responds through the mind. While enveloped by this light, people experience total acceptance and unconditional love, and have access to a deep knowledge and wisdom. This Divine light answers most profound questions even before they are asked. As one man put it, "*you realize that you are suddenly in communication with absolute, total knowledge*" (Ring, 1984, p. 58). The Light being seems to know **EVERYTHING** about the person.

"I was immersed in a feeling of total love. It was crystal clear to me why I'd had cancer. Why I had come into this world in the first place. What role each of my family members played in my life, where we all were within the grand scheme of things, and in general what life is all about. The clarity and insight I had in that state are simply indescribable. Words seem to diminish the experience – I was in a place where I understood that there's so much more than we can fathom in our three-dimensional world. I realized that this was a great gift and that I was always surrounded by loving spiritual beings of light." (Van Lommel, 2010, p. 34)

"To me the Light doesn't need a word. So, if someone needs to call it Buddha or Jesus or God, I would say 'yes', but for me, it was love. I knew that I was forgiven for anything and everything. I was loved and I knew that would never, ever change. Bliss is a word that doesn't even come close to describing that moment." (Sharp, 1995, p. 163).

Often the skeptics say that the light is the creation of a dying brain. But what is the purpose of the dying brain for doing this? How an illusion can be so loving, so all-knowing, and so authoritative? If our brains are only a high-tech computer-like lump of tissue which produces our mind and personality, why does it bother to create such illusions at the time of death? If everything, including the mind and personality, are about to disintegrate, why would the brain produce a last wonderful super-intelligence? Even if NDE elements are reduced to only a series of brain reactions, this still does not explain how a self-conscious super-intelligence can be created by a dying brain.

"[The light was] so pure, so intense, so perfect. I knew it was a being I had to go to. I don't know how this happened. I didn't have to think, I knew everything. I had no mobility problems anymore. I had no body anymore. This dead weight had gone.... I passed through everything. At once I realized: there's no time or space here. We're always in the present here. This gave me a great sense of peace. I felt it as I experienced the Light. It's the pinnacle of everything there is. Of energy, of love especially, of warmth, of beauty." (Van Lommel, 2010, p. 34)

"There, before me, was the living presence of the Light. Within it I sensed an all-pervading intelligence, wisdom, compassion, love, and truth. There was neither form nor sex to this perfect Being... [He] contained everything, as white light contains all the colors of a rainbow when penetrating a prism. And deep within me came an instant and wondrous recognition: I, even I, was facing God.

I immediately lashed out at Him with all the questions I had ever wondered about; all the injustices I had seen in the physical world. I don't know if I did this deliberately, but I discovered that God knows all your thoughts immediately and responds telepathically. My mind was naked; in fact, I became pure mind. ...it was just my personal intelligence confronting that Universal Mind, which clothed itself in a glorious, living light that was more felt than seen since no eye could absorb its splendor." (Ring, 1991, pp. 15-16)

"*I had been traveling toward the tremendous light at the end of the tunnel; but just as I was about to enter it, everything went black. When I close my eyes in a dark room, I still have the sensation of sight. I also retain a sense of touch and feeling, of having a body. The black of which I speak was total, absent of any sensation. My consciousness simply WAS. I existed, but without any senses whatsoever. It was absolutely terrifying. This lasted but a moment, as had the entire journey. Then sensations began slowly to return, and I understood that these were positive only. There was no longer pain ... instead peace and joy and harmony and light. Oh, what a Light it was! As I became increasingly aware of it, it was gold and silver and green and full of love. As the sensations solidified, and this seemed timeless because there was no hurry in this place, I became aware of a being sitting beside me. He wore a white robe, and exuded peace. He was the one who had comforted me during the latter stages of my voyage, I knew instinctively. He was comforting me still. I knew he would be all the friends I never had, and all the guides and teachers I would ever need. I knew that he would be there if ever I needed him, but that there were others for him to look out for, so I needed to care for myself as much as I reasonably could.*

We sat side by side on a rock, overlooking the most beautiful landscape I had ever seen. The colors were outside my experience, vivid beyond my dreams, the composition exceptional. It was exquisitely pleasant and there was no pressure, for my friend knew me and loved me more than I could ever know or love myself." (Ring, 1991, pp. 29-30)

Here is another example in the account of a woman who was declared clinically dead in the middle of a surgery (IFSR booklet, nd, pp. 4, 5),

"*I remember moving away from my body and up to the corner of the room. ... Then I passed through a dark tunnel, but I could see light and I was rushing toward it. I reached the light. There are no words to describe its warmth and brilliance. I felt such peace and love. And suddenly I saw someone – pure light and pure love – and I've tried to describe this being to myself for years. It must have been God; it felt like God. I became keenly and instantly aware of a specific purpose for my life here, and then the light began to fade. I could feel myself moving away, and there I was back in the corner of the room, being drawn back into the body*"

Ray Kinman had a detailed encounter with the light during his NDE from an accidental overdose when he was a teenager (Atwater, 2007, pp. 35-36).

His NDE was not like any drug experience. It was truth, and he was shown the way things really are.

> "*I was given a huge message. The Being told me, 'This is Who You Really Are,' as the Universe opened up to me. I could not tell the difference between myself and the infinite galaxies. I became all powerful and all-knowing – yet I was still Ray. Then the Being introduced me to another Being of the most Incredible Beauty and Love that anyone could comprehend. It was a Greater Being of intense Light. It was God. The first Being guided me to this Light and let it enfold and swallow me up. I became one with Love times a million, billion, trillion forever and ever. We were made of the same stuff! Every Being that had ever existed in all of Creation was now part of this Greater Whole Being called God. I was one with all of them, and yet I was still Ray – all-powerful, little old me!*
>
> *'This is Who You Really Are,' thundered the Light. It looked like a galaxy except the points of light were not stars, they were Beings. Every Being there was singing this incredibly beautiful music and praising God. After some indefinite length of Now-ness, I was told that I must go back. I was given another message that was very important. I was told I may return anytime I wished to. Coming back to my body felt like I was stuffed into a vessel of pain and exhaustion.*"

Suzuki, a university professor from Japan had received an important message from the Light. In her NDE, Suzuki was surrounded by a very beautiful light that she had ever seen (Suzuki, 2005, pp. 14-17). The light was very bright but not dazzling. She felt that the light was life itself, with its own personality, and was connected and interacting with her at a deep level. She was wholly known, understood, accepted, forgiven, and completely loved – an experience of ultimate love. From that light, she received the message, "*When you go back to the earth, the most important things are to study and to love. Only these two are important*".

Iida (2006, pp. 71-94), a Japanese man during an episode of brain hemorrhage, had an NDE in which he met a very bright light. He was surprised by its astonishingly high frequency vibration, describing it as the ultimate light, and felt that if he had seen it with his physical eyes, he would not be able to open them. After a long dialogue with the light, he received the ultimate message, "*The only valuable thing in life is to study, to love, and to try to fulfill your mission*", which, interestingly overlaps the ultimate message Suzuki received in her NDE.

Tannis Prouten, a 20-year-old woman from Vancouver had an NDE after suffering from a severe anxiety attack where she saw small, round, glowing spheres around her that she came to realize were lost souls. But before she could react,

> "*Very rapidly I was enveloped within this most divine, living, golden-white light, my HOME. The joy, bliss, humility, awe were beyond human capability to bear. The LIGHT was an infinite, loving, accepting BEING without form. IT had personality. IT communicated with me telepathically. IT was pure TRUTH.*
>
> *I was the LIGHT and the LIGHT was me. I was still a unique, separate, point of consciousness with the same sense of humor and awareness that I had always had, but the paradox is that I was MORE. I had become homogeneous with the LIGHT. I was all love, wisdom, truth, peace, joy, for all eternity. Human words fail to express this experience. Not only was the message of my true nature conveyed to me telepathically, but I experienced the SPIRIT of the message – I felt IT with every speck of my being. There was absolutely no possibility of hiding, distorting information, or lying in communicating with the LIGHT. I fell madly in love with the SPIRIT OF TRUTH! There was no concept of space or time in the GREATER REALITY. All takes place or exists in the ETERNAL NOW. That is my last conscious memory of the experience.*" (Atwater, 2007, pp. 27-28).

More than a century ago, one experiencer commented, "*Indeed I cannot tell you whether I was in the body or out of the body but oh, the light came, – it was almost too much for me. I cannot express how I felt*" (Leuba, 1896, p. 372). Some people compare the brightness of the light to the sun or the beauty of a sunset – "*It looked like an orange – uh – [have] you seen the sunset in the afternoon?*" (Sabom, 1982, p. 65). The light seems to cover a larger area in the visual field when subjects experience a sense of motion into an image (Blanke and Dieguez, 2009, p. 312). For a young soldier, the light was, "... *a very bright, bright light. It wasn't the sun and yet it was like an overexposed picture of you shooting the camera into the sun*". A 50-year-old who recovered from an episode of profound shock, understood the light as, "*but the absence of darkness... this light was so total and complete that you didn't look at the light, you are 'in' the light. See what I'm saying?*" (Sabom, 1982, p. 65). Another person, when resuscitated from a cardiac arrest, narrated (Sabom, 1982, p. 66);

> "*... a bright light, I mean such a bright light, and it had the shape of – if you watch TV, there's an advertisement for Quasar television that has these little white lights that just brighten up and are not exactly in the form of a cross but are basically a cross except they have a little more flare at the center part. That is exactly what I saw in extreme intensity, brightness.*"

Often the light is interpreted as being the spirit of a religious figure. At times the light is felt as having more than one personality. A survivor of cardiac arrest observed (Sabom, 1982, p. 67),

"There was a big white light, but it wasn't like one man but maybe it was two in light. It wasn't a blinding, bright light at all. It was just a white light which looked like two people, but other than that, I actually didn't see who it was ... like two people that were coming toward me. Just outlines of light."

Another narration from Moody (1975, pp. 53-54),

"I began to feel a sort of drifting, a movement of my real being in and out of my body, and to hear beautiful music. I floated on down the hall... There, it almost seemed that clouds, a pink mist really, began to gather around me, and then I floated... up into this pure crystal-clear light, an illuminating white light. It was beautiful and so bright, so radiant, but it didn't hurt my eyes. It's not any kind of light you can describe on earth. I didn't actually see a person in this light, and yet it has a special identity, it definitely does. It is a light of perfect understanding and perfect love.... And all during this time, I felt as though I were surrounded by an overwhelming love and compassion."

This Divine Light is such an intelligence whose depth we human beings cannot fathom. This Deity exists as a "Presence" without need of name, identity, or definition – for a Hindu this is Lord Krishna, for a Christian this is Jesus Christ, for Buddhists it is Buddha, and so on. All that exists is seen to exist within this "allness", this oneness, because every living creature is an extension of The Divine.

2.2.5: The panoramic life review

"There is a destiny which makes us brothers; none goes his way alone. All that we send into the lives of others comes back into our own."

Edwin Markham

The panoramic life review is an important part of the NDE. A person's whole life comes up for instantaneous review without any significance to time and space. Psychologist and para-psychological researcher Charles Tart commented in an interview,

"It's extremely common in NDEs for persons to undergo a life review, where they feel as if they remember at least every important event in their life, and often they say every single event in their life. Sometimes it even expands out into not only remembering and reliving every single event in their life, but also into knowing psychically the reactions of other people to all their actions. For some it must be horrible, because it seems that you would really experience their pain." (Brown and Tart, 2009, p. 17)

After resuscitation the NDEr can talk for hours or even days about the content of their life review, even though the cardiac arrest lasted only few minutes. He is instantly taken to whatever he focuses his attention on. Everything appears to exist and be open to experience at once, and everything and everybody appears to be connected in an eternal present.

The review is the perception of "*unusually vivid, almost instantaneous visual images of either the person's whole life or a few selected highlights of it*" (Irwin, 1999, p. 204). After the review, the person takes some time see what worked, what didn't, and how he might improve upon the process the next time he tackles it. The review works the same way the postmortem concept in video game development. People experience not just their every action or word but also every thought from their various past lives. Van Lommel (2006, p. 140) wrote,

> "*Patients survey their whole life in one glance; time and space do not seem to exist during such an experience. Instantaneously they are where they concentrate upon (non-locality), and they can talk for hours about the content of the life review even though the resuscitation only took minutes.*"

They realize that their every single action affects both themselves and others because all of it is an energy field that influences oneself as well as others. All that has been done and thought seems to be significant and stored. They also get a sense whether love has been shared or withheld. A 35 years old man after suffering from a massive heart attack, had this review (Sabom, 1982, p. 74),

> "*... my life just flashed in front of my face. My whole life ... things that had happened to me in my lifetime, like when we got married, just flashed in front of my eyes, flashed and it was gone. When we ... had our first child flashed in front of my eyes.*"

The review is observed as a spectator and as an actor. It is something more than a speeded-up film. A Vietnam veteran observed while he was lying wounded on the battlefield (Sabom, 1982, p. 74),

> "*When I came down and hit the ground [after being blown up by explosion], I remember sitting up and I saw my right arm gone, and my right leg gone and my left leg was lying off to the left side. I fall back... and my whole life was just going in front of me like a very fast computer and I kept thinking about all the different things I had done or perhaps I hadn't done.*"

Swiss geologist Albert Heim had the following life review during a mountain fall (Blanke and Dieguez, 2009, p. 312),

> "*... I saw my whole past-life take places in many images, as though on a stage at some distance from me. I saw myself as the chief character in the performance. Everything was transfigured as though by a heavenly light and everything was beautiful without grief, without anxiety, and without pain*".

A 21-year-old woman described the following experience, dominated by cognitive features that occurred during a bicycle accident.

> *"I was riding my bike and failed to see a car coming towards me until I realized it would hit me, regardless of any maneuver I might make. That realization seemed to take forever as time slowed way down, and I consciously decided to let go of the handlebars, cover my head with my hands, and scream. During the next few seconds, or fractions thereof, while the car hit my thigh and the bike (at least), I was unaware of any bodily sensations, but rather 'saw' my life flash before me in a series of typical scenes. I felt very peaceful, and the thought, 'Well, if I die, that's all right; I've had a good life,' came very clearly into my mind. I felt apart from my body at this time".* (Greyson, 1985, p. 391)

Life review may happen anytime during NDE, or even before NDE starts prior to the full loss of consciousness. Various researchers have found life reviews in 13 to 30% of subjects with NDEs (Ring, 1980; Van Lommel et al., 2001, p. 2041; Greyson, 1983, pp. 327-34; Noyes and Slymen, 1979, pp. 313-21; Noyes and Kletti, 1977, pp. 375-84). Stevenson and Cook (1995, pp. 452-58) analyzed 122 subjects with NDEs and reported that the number of distinct life memories may range from a few images (one or two) to the impression of a rapid flow of countless images depicting their entire life – "all at once". It is usually experienced very vividly, associated with bright colors and can occur as moving in chronological order or in the opposite order, i.e., ending or starting with childhood (Blackmore, 1993). Life reviews seem to be more frequent for the drowning victims, as compared to other situations (Dlin, 1980, pp. 111-18; Noyes and Kletti, 1977, pp. 375-84). Suicide survivors (Rosen, 1975, pp. 289-94) and children with NDEs (Morse et al., 1986, pp. 1110-14; Serdahely, 1990, pp. 33-9) rarely report life reviews.

The life review incidents after full loss of consciousness show that the actual storage place of memories, i.e., the 'information storage unit' is not in the brain; rather in that part of us that survives the body. In waking life, we have sensory input from our physical senses essentially of a third dimensional perspective and within a three-dimensional recall mechanism. But in the afterlife the consciousness is flooded with abundant emotion and unbounded perceptions, and because of this, people report brighter colors, 360-degree vision and unearthly sounds, and greater emotions. These perceptions are consistent with what one would expect in a fourth or greater dimension.

The deep and intense life review is the final psychosis where the dying individual acts as his own judge, jury, accuser, prosecutor, defense attorney, and witness.

> "*There is no judgment in the next stage of life except by our own conscience. This voice of inner conscience is a part of God, as we ourselves are a part of the Creator, but the judgment which is meted out comes from our own being.... The veil is withdrawn, and we are able to see clearly where we erred and where we chose rightly and thus advanced perceptibly.*" (Montgomery, 1972, p. 123)

The individual alone renders the final verdict of guilty or not guilty. Sometimes the review experienced in the presence of a being of light, or a highly developed spiritual being. The purpose of life review is to teach us that there exists a cosmic law in which everything we do to another person will ultimately have an effect on us as well, and this applies to both love and affection, and violence and aggression. Nobody feels judged – we understand how we lived our lives and how this affected others.

If an NDE was experienced during a (failed) suicide attempt, the people generally refrain from making a second attempt because the experience taught them that they remain burdened with the problems they tried to escape. They realize that it is better to solve problems in this life because the other dimension offers little opportunity for solving their earthly problems. Sandra Rogers, after a failed suicide attempt on April 30, 1976, had an NDE. Later she wrote a book "Lessons From the Light: Insights From a Journey to the Other Side". The introductory chapter opens with the following statement describing her NDE and some of the insights she learned while in the light.

> "*I came into the presence of a brilliant, wonderfully warm and loving Light. While I was in the presence of this Light I was shown a review of my life and all the events that brought me to that point.*
>
> *I was fascinated as I watched my life unfold, that I was aware not only of my own emotions, but also the feelings of those around me as well as those whose lives we touched. I experienced their pain or pleasure and understood what motivated their actions toward others and me...*
>
> *As my life review continued, I encountered again all of the pain and hopelessness of my next several years; a series of bad relationships, pregnancies, miscarriages, broken marriages and suicide attempts. I saw myself as a young woman of twenty-five, married and divorced three times and hospitalized for drug overdoses six times. I felt how I hated my existence and could not understand how a loving God could allow these things to happen.*
>
> *I was aware as I relieved each of these terribly painful events in my life that the light, which was with me as I watched, felt all of my pain and sorrow and never judged me, but instead understood and loved me.*

> *The love I felt from the light was overwhelming and I never wanted to leave it. While I was in Its presence, I had unlimited knowledge about anything I wanted to know. I was given the choice of remaining with the light, provided I return later to the physical world and experience all that brought me to the point of shooting myself, or I could return now and pick up my life where it was. I was told that I would eventually have the family and love I so desperately yearned for. I was also told that I could only take back the knowledge I needed to sustain myself, although I would be given insights to help others and me along the way as I continued my life journey...*
>
> *During my NDE I followed my angel guide into the light. The angel was absorbed by the light and so was I. While in the light I learned that everything in existence was created from the essence of God, the light.*" (Rogers, 2009)

None goes to hell for committing suicide. An NDE after a failed suicide attempt is not predominantly unpleasant, rather what they experience provides a reason for continuing life – such self-destructive tendencies are serious mistakes because it destroys an opportunity for spiritual advancement – "*Do not seek death. Death will find you. But seek the road which makes death a fulfillment*" (a quote from Dag Hammarskjold – Thomas, 1982, p. 5). Life is a precious sacred gift which is meant to be lived meaningfully – "*No person has the right to take the life within himself, any more than that of another person, since all are a part of the Godhead.*" (Montgomery, 1972, p. 41). To end life prematurely is a refusal of that gift and a denial of all the opportunities for spiritual growth that could have come throughout one's natural lifetime.

Spiritual regressionists believe that people choose their own destiny in life before they are born. This destiny is changed by committing suicide. It means nobody is predestined to commit suicide. The life reviews reveal a perfect universal plan being worked out by higher spiritual guides in the spirit world (Chapter 9). When a person cuts short his destined time for life because he has problems coping with life's demands, his problems may not necessarily go away. Rather the problems may also be complicated by the added burden of their knowing the full horrible consequences of their action on others. Therefore, those who are thinking of killing themselves can learn a great deal from NDEs. There is a reason for everything that happens on Earth.

In our waking reality our memories are not recalled with 100% accuracy because we fill-in-the-gaps or add emotions and excuses unconsciously (Freud, 1950, p. 89). But, in the life review people can have more than 100% recall of every earthly event that happened to them even if the events were forgotten or happened before they were old enough to remember. They will describe how their actions on Earth affected other people (even though we were not aware of it while alive, or the people that wronged us first). We get to feel the happiness we instilled in others by showing compassion and kindness. We get to see people's actions and reactions to us and the ripple effect it caused even when we were not physically present to see them. The rule is simple and straightforward – you cause pain and suffering to someone in this life, and you have to feel and experience it yourself during your life review. Van Lommel (2010, p. 36) recorded one experience full of important details.

> *"Throughout [the life review], I not only saw everything from my own point of view, but I also knew the thoughts of everybody who'd been involved in these events, as if their thoughts were lodged inside me. It meant that I saw not only what I had done or thought but even how this had affected others, as if I was seeing with all-knowing eyes. And so even your thoughts are apparently not wiped out. And throughout, the review stressed the importance of love. I can't say how long this life review and insight into life lasted; it may have been quite long because it covered every single subject, but at the same time it felt like a split second because I saw everything at once. It seemed as if time and distance didn't exist. I was everywhere at once, and sometimes my attention was focused on something and then I was there too.*
>
> *To start with, I was shown images of my two previous lives. The first time I died was during a campaign in England during the Roman era. ... I also experienced my death [second life] in World War I. ... Why I also saw excerpts from these two lives, I don't know.... What I remember much more vividly are images from my latest or, if you like, current life. First I witnessed my own birth.... I also saw my school years pass before my eyes, and the teachers I used to torment. The war years were quite prominent. I saw some people I'd known in the camp and whom I had, on occasion, robbed of the little food they had in a bid to survive.*
>
> *But some of my good deeds also flashed past.... I saw a lot of situations in which, as a serviceman, I'd been rather ruthless. But my NDE also brought back some memories of incidents in which, in defiance of orders, I'd let mercy take precedence over law. Among them were quite a few incidents I had long since erased from my memory. For instance, there were things in my life that I'd come to accept as bad but that were now suddenly deemed good. The same applied to things that I'd always considered to be good and that were now branded wrong....* ***What I mean to say by this is that up there they judge by different standards than down here.****"*

In a typical life review, the events constitute a "unifying vision" which gives the person insight into his life's purpose. We realize how we have played a role in all that has happened to us. Our actions, thoughts, and lives are our responsibility alone. When we show true forgiveness, we release themselves from the binds of hurt and bitterness. Forgiveness isn't about accepting wrongful behavior; it is about choosing to let go of the hurt and resentment that keeps us from living in peace.

Many people fear that they will be judged when they die, but no. The individual person judges himself and his own actions. And then he decides if he will forgive himself for the pain he caused others or if he will beat himself up for it. The purpose of getting to feel the pain we caused others in life is not punishment. It's designed to help us understand and grow. The Golden Rule (treat others how you would like to be treated) is a Universal Law and a constant reminder that whatever we do (or don't do) for others, we do (or don't do) for ourselves ... and either way, we will get to experience that. Fortunately, this also goes for the loving words and deeds, which hopefully outweigh the other kind.

Sometimes the life review takes a different form, such as for few Indian cases they were "*taken to other realms by messengers or someone*" and then were "*passed on to the man with a book*" containing a list of deeds or mistakes (Pasricha, 1995, p. 86). However, the core meaning of a life review remains the same. It always gives the person guidance to make him aware of his life's purpose.

In sum; the life review teaches us that we are going to reap what we sow, whether that is happiness and joy, or terror and misery. It's our choice – we have a free will. So, before we take any action we should ask ourselves if we are willing to be on the receiving end of the consequences, because someday we will be. It also comforts those who had ever been on the receiving end of pain, abuse, and trauma. The person who inflicted this upon others will eventually feel it himself. It means, it's the person who inflicts the pain who owns it. From here the karmic debt starts. The victim should not carry around the trauma because it's not his. Let them bear that burden, not the other.

2.2.6: Future visions during the NDE

During an NDE, many people have reported seeing the future (flashforwards). In the future review, both future images from personal life events as well as more general images from the future occur. George Gallup's nationwide survey of Americans on the afterlife found that "*during near-death encounters or other related experiences, they learned of events that were in the process of happening at some distance or would happen in the future*" (Gallup and Proctor, 1982, p. 54). One experiencer (Van Lommel, 2010, p. 38) wrote,

> "*And in a flash I saw the rest of my life. I could see a large part of my future life: taking care of my children; my wife's illness; everything that would happen to me, both in and out of the workplace. I could see it all. I foresaw my wife's death and my mother's passing. One day I wrote down all the things I saw back then; over the years I've been able to tick them all off. For instance, I saw my wife on her deathbed, wrapped in a*

white shawl, just like the one she was given by a friend of hers shortly before she died..."

Many people compare future visions with the concept of 'forbidden knowledge' of the Universe. They ask "Isn't knowledge of future events prohibited by the Universe?" The humble answer is, if we are supposed to know something, such as a major event of our future, our spiritual guide will confirm that we receive that data. If, however, we are not supposed to be aware of certain future events, then no person, place, or thing will give us that information unless and until we are ready to receive it (Goldberg, 2004, p. 138). Melvin Morse shares the case of a 66-year-old-man who recalls,

> "*My wife and I had been told that she couldn't have any more children. But then, in June 1959, I was involved in a serious pit accident at a coal mine. I was taken to the hospital and found to be dead on arrival. But somehow, I was revived and remained in a coma for a week.*
>
> *While unconscious, I had a vision of walking along the sun's rays and seeing a hand with a long white sleeve reaching down. I was almost touching the hand when I felt myself being pulled back, and I heard a voice say: 'Don't worry. You are going to be all right and your son will be all right.'*
>
> *A few months later we learned my wife was pregnant and our son was born almost a year to the day after my accident*". (Morse, 1992, p. 115)

Bertha, a Canadian woman saw her future children during an NDE in 1913. This is a very interesting case. She was the mother of 13 children. Life was too difficult to her and she decided not to bring any more children into the world. Soon afterwards Bertha became seriously ill, and a nurse Sister Edwards came to the home to care for her. In those days, in remote rural communities, going to hospitals was usually out of the question. In this serious condition, suddenly Bertha first had an OBE and then an NDE.

> "*Thinking Bertha had died, Sister Edwards later said she wanted to call the others into the house, but was prompted to do nothing. She had a peaceful feeling that everything would be all right if she just waited a few minutes.*
>
> *[In her NDE] Bertha felt relieved. She was greeted by a woman who escorted her into a large room where she was greeted by many of her departed friends. One was a young man she had befriended and encouraged to develop his artistic talents. He was sitting in front of an easel, painting. Though he was very happy to see Bertha, he quickly returned to his work as though his time was very precious.*
>
> *Bertha was then taken into another room where there were many children. On the far side of the room she saw two little girls, whom she*

did not know. They were so beautiful she could not look away from them.

'Do you want them?' the guide asked.

'Yes. Oh, yes,' she responded quickly. 'Can I return to earth life and have them'?

'Yes', said the escort. This is the purpose of this visit, to let you see them. Now we must return'. Bertha returned to her body, much to the relief of Sister Edwards. After recovering from the illness, Bertha told Jonathan [her husband] she wanted more children. A year later, after moving to Oakley, Idaho, Bertha gave birth to a new little girl whom she named Alberta. Two years later she delivered another little girl, LaVirle. For the remainder of her life, Bertha insisted these were the two little girls she had seen in the large room" (Nelson, 1988, pp. 38-39).

Jenny Somers wrote in her book of her NDE which accurately predicted her mother's death in an accident two years later, but that her sister would survive the accident (Somers, 2009, p. 27). A woman had a powerful NDE in 1972 while recovering from surgery. While she was having a life review what she described as an "enormous television screen", she saw in vivid color various scenes from her life in a very rapid sequence of realistic images. Suddenly the screen vanished and a second screen followed. This screen was dark and the images were in black and white, foggy and difficult to discern. However, she remembered being shown, among other events, the deaths of two members of her family (who were not ill at the time of her NDE) and told that she would play a special role in caring for these persons during their terminal illnesses. Later it was confirmed that these futuristic events did indeed come to pass (Ring, 1988, p. 5). Some of the future visions are prophetic visions, i.e., the visions have a planetary focus and seem to represent something of the Earth's future. This type of futuristic visions is rare.

"*Among the many volcanic eruptions that are going to occur, I saw the one that just occurred in Hawaii. As I saw the pictures on the television, it was really quite uncanny, as I had already seen it taking place during the vision I had seen at the time of my near-death experience.*" (Grey, 1985, p. 125)

"*I was shown Mt. St. Helen's eruption.... I was also shown other volcanoes.... I was shown Mt. St. Helen's ...and on May 18, Mt. St. Helen's really erupted its heaviest. I turned to my husband and said, 'Mt. St. Helen's just blew its top', and the people there just laughed at me. Later that night we were watching TV and the very scenes that I had seen in my mind were shown on the TV and no one continued to laugh at me then*". (Ring, 1984, p. 200)

An NDEr becomes aware of the futuristic events by two different ways. First, a flashforward life review; second, a guide or a being of light, or a deceased relative or some person in the otherworld foretells a future event or events that are yet to occur on Earth. Lundahl (2001, p. 234) commented that the prophetic visions have five distinctive features, such as, geophysical changes, meteorological changes, supply and economic breakdowns, nuclear war, and a new era of human history characterized by universal love and world peace.

How to explain these "future memory phenomenon"? The information these people gain were accurate more times than it was inaccurate. Some people believe that such revelations are absolute, while others believe that these futuristic events can be altered if people were willing to change certain attitudes and behaviors. Whatever is the fact, the future visions baffle the researchers. Raymond Moody and Paul Perry (1988, p. 25) wrote that even "*as science struggles to get a handle on near-death experiences, it cannot even begin to grasp flashforwards during NDEs*".

The future vision events are confirmed with people under deep hypnosis for spiritual regression. One person saw his future wife, an attractive aerobics instructor, for the next life. He saw himself meeting his future wife in a gym, "*I studied her body and facial features carefully because I didn't want to mess up our meeting.... The scent of her body bathed in sweat was embedded in my mind ... her gestures ...her smile ...and most of all her eyes. The moment I saw her in this life it was like two magnets pulling together*" (Newton, 2016b, p. 274). This premonition prepared both parties for future relationships.

Some researchers had attempted to explain these future memory cases and offered a variety of interpretations. However, there is not a single explanation which is adequate. The spirit world is a 'timeless' zone. If NDE occurs in a timeless dimension, the future may remain in many possibilities. As example, our karmic issues are changing our future events in every moment. So, when a person sees a future vision, it is correct at that particular moment. I will show later that earthly life is similar to a huge stage play where there is no fixed script. Future is not predetermined as Newton (2016b, p. 371) commented,

> "*If someone saw themselves being killed in a certain place and time and it didn't happen, this potential causality could mean it was only the most dire of alternative possibilities*".

However, these alternate possibilities may not be unlimited in number. And we cannot just choose the best aspects of all the possibilities. We can only choose one possibility and accept the good with the bad. Only the person himself can make this choice. Goldberg (2004, p. 183) wrote,

> "*there is no predestination. The soul always has free will. What will be somewhat predestined is the basic framework of the frequency.*

The specifics can be changed by varying the choices along the way, but the basic framework can't be altered."

We all are bound by the irrefutable law of Karma, and since we all have free will our future is changing continuously as per our choices and actions. Neither our fate is chiseled in stone nor are we puppets on a string. The NDEr, as a passing visitor to spirit world, simply study alternate timelines of future events. Changes in life are conditional on our free will toward a certain action, and the future vision that he sees is a single possibility that could change when the time actually arrives.

2.2.7: The perception of a border and the return journey

The adventure at the spirit world comes to halt when the experiencer becomes aware of a border – a point of no return. Sometimes the experiencer sees a thick fog, a wall, a valley, a river, a bridge, or a gate. Instantly he becomes aware that once he crosses this border, he will not be able to return to his body and continue his earthly existence (only the dead do not return but cross over the border). At this point the person can have some communication with a departed soul of relative or friend, or with a holy man or a being of light. The experiencer hears that he is not welcome because his time has not yet come, and hence he must return to his body because he has a purpose in life and a mission to fulfill. This purpose or mission may be to care for a newborn baby, a child, or a relative. On some occasions, the person cannot remember clearly why he was sent back. The decision to return sometimes belongs to him; otherwise it is forcefully imposed by the higher being.

"*Then I reached a border. Even at the age of ten I needed no further explanation. I simply understood that I'd never be able to return if I crossed this border. But some of my ancestors were on the other side, and they caught my attention because they were communicating through a kind of telepathy. I was born profoundly deaf. All my relatives can hear, and they always communicate with me through sign language. Now I had direct communication with about twenty ancestors via some kind of telepathy. An overwhelming experience....*" (Van Lommel, 2010, p. 39)

"*Without a word the figure encouraged me to decide whether I wanted to remain in this state or whether I wanted to return to earthly life. I could either enter the gate or return to the lifeless body, which I immediately sensed below me. I had the impression that entry through this gate meant definitive physical death. Aware that this was my chance to go back knowing that this state of being is a reality that feels more real than what we call reality and thinking of my young wife and our three small children, I opted to return....*" (Van Lommel, 2010, p. 39)

While serving in Vietnam as a military policeman Steve was badly injured by a hand-grenade explosion. In the hospital his heart stopped and then,

> "*he found himself being carried away by two beings, one on either side of him, toward the gates of Hell. The walls were built from what looked like large black blocks, outlined in red light; the overall impression was of a place that absorbed light rather than giving it off. From somewhere, Steve heard a booming voice say, 'This one has not yet fulfilled my purpose,' and he found himself back in his body*". (Sharp, 1995, pp. 167-68).

This border experience is followed by a forceful return to the sick, damaged, and aching body. Most people are disappointed at this moment.

> "*When I came to in my body it was dreadful, so dreadful.... The experience had been so beautiful that I didn't want to come back. I had wanted to stay there...and yet I came back. From that moment it was a real struggle to live my life inside my body, with all the limitations I experienced at the time.... But later I realized that this experience was in fact a blessing, for now I know that the mind and body are separate and that there's life after death.*"

> "*Before I get a chance to turn around and dive into that heavenly light, I notice a slender hand on my back, from my right shoulder down to my waist. This large hand pushes me very firmly yet lovingly back into my body. For a moment I feel like I'm doing a couple of somersaults in the air. Then I realize that I've landed back in my body. Back to the pain and to the doctor's deafening screams and slaps. I'm furious, incredibly furious!*" (Van Lommel, 2010, pp. 40-41)

In Arthur Yensen case, he did not want to leave but an entity told him,

> "*You have more important work to do on earth, and you must go back and do it! There will come a time of great confusion and the people will need your stabilizing influence. When your work on earth is done, then you can come back here and stay.*" (Spencer, 2011, p. 171)

In the majority of the NDE cases the 'return' is influenced or directed by other spiritual beings, or dead relatives. Few excerpts from Sabom's (1982, pp. 282-84) cases are these,

> "*God said in loud, thundering voice... 'Go back, work not done yet'.*"

> "*All spirits, with their hands up, waving, said, 'Go back, ... Your children and a lot of people are going to need you.'*"

> "*Spirits 'push me back' and 'tell me it's not time yet.'*"

> "*Father said, 'Go back and stay with your sister. Everything is going to work out.'*"

"Father said, 'Go back to your mother for a while.'"

"Grandmother said, 'We'll see you later but not this time.'"

"A spiritual being said, 'You have one little black spot you have to clean up and then I will come get you. Go back'."

"A voice said, 'You cannot go yet. You have unfinished businesses'."

"God said, 'It's all right dear, you will make it. I'm not ready for you yet.'"

Lundahl (1992, pp. 49-50) recorded the account of a nurse who described angels holding hands to form a stairway to heaven. Once she reached the top of this stairway, she met another angel who suggested to her that she ask the Lord to let her go back to raise her child. In some cases, people want to return back voluntarily though they are given choices to stay at the spirit world.

"Asked God for more time with children in 'clear loud voice.'"

"Brother presented a choice of either 'staying' or 'returning' to body."

"I told God in my prayers I wanted to go but was needed here."

"Asked Lord, 'Please don't take me now. Let me stay and raise my kids.'"

"Spirits said, 'We are here to show you the way.... If you don't wish to go, we've got to get on. We'll be back for you.'"

The NDE-people return, often against their will, through a still-open tunnel back into their physical bodies. In Tibet those who have returned from the dead are called "delok". The great Buddhist teacher Sogyal Rinpoche wrote that these people 'die' as a result of an illness, and then travel to "bardo" (the soul world). They visit the hell realms, where they witness the judgement of the dead and the sufferings of hell. They sometimes go to paradise and Buddha realms. Often, they are accompanied by a deity who protects them and explains what is happening. After a week the delok is sent back to the body with a message from the Lord of Death for the living, urging them to spiritual practice and a beneficial way of life (Rinpoche, 1993, p. 330). These are very similar to classic NDE reports.

2.2.8: Distressing near death experiences

Though the great majority of NDEs are pleasant, even glorious with profound feelings of peace, joy and cosmic unity, some experiences are deeply disturbing. These NDEs are of four types,

In first type of cases, the person feels extreme fear or panic because what is happening is out of his control – *"I expected the Lord to be there, but He wasn't...I called on God and He wasn't there. That's what scared me.*" (Rommer, 2000, p. 53). This is an intense unpleasant event. One man in such a horrible condition called for help to his sister who had recently passed away. He got timely help and came back into his body lying on the hospital bed. One man while falling down to an intolerably hot bottomless pit screamed for assistance "*God, I am not ready, please help me*". Later he described his NDE, "*I remember when I screamed an arm shot out of the sky and grabbed my hand and at the last second, I was kept from falling of the end of the funnel.*" (Bush and Greyson, 1992, p. 100). In some cases, the features usually reported as pleasurable or interesting are perceived as threatening because of loss of control or the bizarreness of the situation.

In second category, the person has an acute awareness of nonexistence or of being completely alone forever in an absolute void. He may receive a totally convincing message that the real world including himself never really existed. A woman in childbirth had an NDE. She found herself into a deep, empty space middle of a group of circular entities. These entities informed her she never existed, that she had been allowed to imagine her life but it was a cruel joke; she was not real. She argued with facts about her life and descriptions of Earth. They said, "*No, none of that had ever been real; this is all there was.*" She was left alone in deep, empty space with a sense of despair (Bush, 2012, pp. 1-5). She awakens thinking, predestination. Several years later she learns that the entities were Chinese Yin-Yang symbols. Another woman had interacted with similar type of creatures,

> "*There were beings all around me and they acknowledged my presence. The beings were quite amused at me. They totally accepted me into their midst and didn't seem to mind one bit that I was cranky and demanding to know where I was and who did they think they were anyhow, snatching me away like that! Put me back, damn it, put me back! Slowly my ruffled feathers became smoothed and I felt peaceful and calm. So, I began going along with this weird experience and became accepting of them too. We began to have a question and answer time. I would ask the questions and instead of receiving a wordy reply they would 'show' me the answer. We moved from place to place with no effort at all and I learned a great deal...Finally the beings made it clear to me that I could return...*" (Bush and Greyson, 1992, p. 101).

These entities are neither fearsome nor tormenting, but only mocking in a machine-like manner. The message they give is that we are only allowed to imagine our existence which is actually a cruel joke of some mischievous power (Bush and Greyson, 1992, p. 102). Throughout the experience, these entities keep laughing and mocking, but don't do any serious harm.

In third type of cases, the person arrives in an ugly or sinister landscape, intensely cold or unbearably hot, where they hear loud, annoying noises and sounds that resemble the wailing of 'souls' in torment. They also see wrathful demonic creatures, frightening animals, faceless or hooded beings, and human and nonhuman entities in extreme distress (Grey, 1985, p. 58). In most of these, the experiencer is present as an observer or guided traveler; except in experiences of shamanic initiation, torment may be witnessed or interpreted but is not actually felt (Turner, 1993, p. 102; Zaleski, 1987, p. 44). In rarest cases people in this condition feel personally tormented. As example, a man experienced being pinched maliciously and then torn apart by human-like beings.

These experiences of encountering blatant "hellish" images often begin with a sense of falling down to a dark pit (Bush and Greyson, 1992, p. 99). One woman in her NDE engaged in a life-and-death struggle with a demonic being. The evil force was so powerful that she, for the first time in her life, called out to God for help, and a superior being helped her out of the situation. In these cases, often the individual identifies loss of ego control as the terrifying aspect of the experience. Another woman reported an NDE involving,

> "*horrific beings with gray gelatinous appendages grasping and clawing at me. The sounds of their guttural moaning and the indescribable stench still remain 41 years later. There was no benign Being of Light, no life video, nothing beautiful or pleasant.*" (Bush and Greyson, 2014, p. 373)

The last and rarest of all, the person feels negatively judged by a higher power during his life review. One important difference is that other three types of experiences don't have a life review.

The conventional assumption is that "good" people get pleasant NDEs and "bad" people have distressing ones. But there is no evidence to support this. NDEs do not function as clear-cut reward or punishment, or that character is a determinant. Saints who have lived a pious life reported extremely disturbing NDEs (Cressy, 1994, pp. 63-75), while criminals, murderers, rapists and suicide attempters have encountered bliss (Flynn, 1986, pp. 41-44). Sabom found from his large hospital study,

> "*In each case in which unpleasant emotions (e.g., sadness, loneliness, fright) were encountered ...they were perceived to be but a momentary impression in an otherwise pleasant NDE, the overall content being later described as enjoyable. It is conceivable that this overall assessment might have been different (i.e., unenjoyable) if the experience had abruptly ended at the point at which the unpleasant emotion was perceived.*" (Sabom, 1982, p. 20)

The opposite is also reported where the NDE started as a blissful experience but changed to a frightening one upon an unexpected encounter with a devilish creature. Irwin and Bramwell (1988, pp. 38-43) had reported one such case of a 50-year-old woman.

Scott, a six-year-old boy, encountered both the devil and God following a near-fatal car accident (Bonenfant, 2001, pp. 87-100). Eight hours later when Scott regained consciousness in the intensive care unit, he told his parents about what he had experienced following the accident. He recalled witnessing the entire accident from the vantage point of a nearby tree some 30 feet away. Apparently, Scott was able to hear and see everything that was going on around him at the scene of the accident. When the tunnel experience started, which was looking "*like a tornado lay flat on the ground*", Scott found himself face to face with the devil. The devil spoke to Scott in a deep, raspy voice saying, "*You're bad*," and made an attempt to grab him. He was completely terrified.

Scott described the devil as being composed of rotting, putrid flesh, and covered with sores and slime. The devil appeared to be both mentally and physically ill. Its head was deformed and sickly looking. Scott desperately tried to keep his faith in God. He believes that God rescued him but he cannot remember exactly how it occurred. He next found himself being whisked through the tunnel toward a distant point of light. When asked about the characteristics of the tunnel, Scott could remember only that it seemed to contain the faces and voices of all those who had ever known and loved him.

Distressing NDEs have been reported under a wide range of circumstances, from cardiac arrest to spontaneous events. There is no distinguishing data mark those who have a distressing NDE, and such an experience should not be perceived as the imminence of hell.

2.2.9: OBE and NDE in the blind individuals

"*Death is no more than passing from one room into another. But there's a difference for me, you know. Because in that other room I shall be able to see*".

Helen Keller

It is reasonable to ask questions like these – do the blind individuals have OBEs and NDEs? If they do, are they the same as or different from those of sighted persons? Do they have visual perceptions during these experiences?

Research had been conducted on this issue, and it is found that blind persons, including that blind from birth, do report classic NDEs very similar to sighted persons. They also provide visually-based knowledge that could not have been obtained by normal means, can be independently confirmed. Kenneth Ring and Sharon Cooper studied NDE/OBE cases of 31 blind people, almost half of them were born-blind, yet all of them were able to 'see' accurately of the doctors operating on them, the colors the visitors were wearing. They also had visions of angelic beings and deceased relatives (Champlain, 2013, p. 80). Here I will discuss two cases from Ring and Cooper (1997, pp. 108-13).

Vicki Umipeg, a 43-year-old woman received extensive and life-threatening injuries in a car accident, and had an NDE. She was born-blind, suffering complete atrophy (withering) of the eyeball and optic nerve. In her own words,

> "*I've never seen anything, no light, no shadows, no nothing. A lot of people ask me if I see black. No, I don't see black. I don't see anything at all. And in my dreams I don't see any visual impressions. It's just taste, touch, sound, and smell. But no visual impressions of anything.*"

After the accident, first she caught a brief glimpse of the car wreck from above. Then she had a passing image of herself lying on the metal table.

> "*I knew it was me. ... I was pretty thin then. I was quite tall and thin at that point. And I recognized at first that it was a body, but I didn't even know that it was mine initially. Then I perceived that I was up on the ceiling, and I thought, 'Well, that's kind of weird. What am I doing up here?' I thought, 'Well, this must be me. Am I dead?'. I just briefly saw this body, and ... I knew that it was mine because I wasn't in mine. Then I was just away from it. It was that quick.*"

She suddenly realized that she was being pulled up headfirst into a tunnel. The enclosure itself was dark, yet she was aware that she was moving toward light. As she reached the openings of the tunnel, the music that she had heard earlier transformed into hymns. Next, she found herself lying on grass surrounded by trees and flowers – a place of tremendous light that could be felt as well as seen. The light conveyed love, and the people she saw were bright and reflected the light of this love – "*Everybody there was made of light. And I was made of light. There was love everywhere. It was like love came from the grass, love came from the birds, love came from the trees.*"

There five of her friends and relatives welcomed her including two of her blind schoolmates, Debby and Diane, who had died years before, at ages 11 and 6, respectively. In life, they had both been profoundly retarded as well as blind, but here they appeared bright and beautiful, healthy and vitally alive, and no longer children, but, as she phrased it, "*in their prime*". There were also two of her childhood caretakers, Mr. and Mrs. Zilk a married couple, and her own grandmother – all had previously died. In these encounters, no actual words were exchanged, but only feelings of love and welcome. In the midst of this reunion, suddenly she overcame with a sense of total knowledge.

> "*I had a feeling like I knew everything ... and like everything made sense. I just knew that this was where ... this place was where I would find the answers to all the questions about life, and about the planets, and about God, and about everything ...It's like the place was the knowing.*"

She was flooded with information of a religious nature as well as scientific and mathematical knowledge. She came to understand languages she did not know. She was overwhelmed and astonished. Then she noticed that a figure is standing next to her whose radiance was far greater than the illumination of any of the persons she had so far encountered. He greeted her tenderly, and telepathically, communicated to her; "*Isn't it wonderful? Everything is beautiful here, and it fits together. And you'll find that. But you can't stay here now. It's not your time to be here yet and you have to go back.*"

She reacted with extreme disappointment, but the being reassured her that she would come back, but for now, she had to "*go back and learn and teach more about loving and forgiving*". Still resistant, however, she then learned that she also needed to go back to have her children. With that, she who was then childless but craved for a child, was almost eager to return and finally consented. She has since then given birth to three children. But, before she could leave, the being said in these exact words, "*But first, watch this*". It was her life-review – "*everything from my birth*" in a complete panoramic review of her life, and as she watched, the being gently commented to help her understand the significance of her actions and their repercussions. Once the life-review had been completed, she heard the words, "*You have to leave now*". Soon she was back in her body, and "*it was excruciatingly painful and very heavy and I remember feeling very sick.*"

How to make sense of Vicki's case? A born-blind as a result of an atrophied eyeball and optic nerve and who has an undeveloped visual cerebral cortex can still see people and surroundings raise significant questions.

The second case involves an eight years old boy, Brad Burrows. Blind from birth, Brad contracted a severe case of pneumonia and eventually had severe breathing difficulties. In this condition, he had an OBE. He felt himself lifting up from the bed and floating through the room toward the ceiling, and saw his apparently lifeless body on the bed. He also saw his blind roommate get up from his bed and leave the room to get help (later confirmed by his roommate), then found himself rapidly going upward through the ceilings of the building until he was above the roof. At this point, he could see clearly the snow everywhere except for the streets, which had been plowed, though they were still slushy. He was able to give a very detailed description of the way the snow looked.

After this, he had the tunnel experience. When he emerged from it, he found himself in an immense field illuminated by a tremendous, all-encompassing light. At first, he was puzzled by the sensation of sight. He started walking on a path surrounded by tall grass and tall trees with immense leaves. No shadows were visible. While in this field, he became aware of beautiful music that he had never heard on Earth. Walking toward the sound, he came to and climbed a hill, eventually encountering a glittering stone structure so brilliant that he thought it might be burning hot. But it wasn't, and he entered it. The music continued here as well. In this structure, he encountered a man who emanated an overwhelming love. The man, without a word, gently nudged him backward, initiating a reversal of his experience. Soon he found himself in bed gasping for air.

These two cases show an obvious structural similarity and conform to the classic form of the NDE. Both of them, though blind from birth, had perfect visual perceptions very clear and detailed, particularly when they were in the otherworldly portions of their journeys. However, not all the NDEs described by the blinds are as rich as these two, but in general, all report the same kind of visual impressions as sighted persons do in describing NDEs. Whether one is blind from birth, loses one's sight in later life, or suffers from severe visual impairment, the type of NDE reported appears to be much the same. The experiencers say that their visions are "*perfectly natural*" or "*the way it's supposed to be*".

Researchers have cited many such cases to make a powerful argument for near death phenomena. Psychiatrist Stanislav Grof commented,

> "*There are ...reported cases where individuals who were blind because of a medically confirmed organic damage to their optical system could at the time of clinical death see the environment. ... Occurrences of this kind, unlike most of the other aspects of near-death phenomena, can be subjected to objective verification*". (Grof, 1994, p. 31)

Experts say that a born-blind person cannot immediately begin to see normally if his vision were somehow restored. Thus Irwin (1987, p. 54), in a discussion of OBEs in the blind, concluded,

> "*Because people who surgically regain their sight take some time to learn visual identification of objects, the initial OBEs in the congenitally blind should exhibit the same property if the experience depends upon the visual pathways of the nervous system*".

Therefore, they reported what they had actually seen independent of their physical nervous system. Many such testimonies indicate that subjects were seeing in an omnidirectional fashion, not limited either by location or by the limited visual field of physical eyeballs. We can see it in this testimony by a pregnant woman who lost consciousness upon being checked into a hospital for pneumonia.

> "*The [hospital] room was much more interesting than my body. And what a neat perspective. I could see everything. And I do mean everything! I could see the top of the light on the ceiling, and the underside of the stretcher. I could see the tiles on the ceiling and the tiles on the floor, simultaneously. Three hundred sixty degree spherical vision. And not just spherical. Detailed! I could see every single hair and the follicle out*

of which it grew on the nurse standing beside the stretcher. At the time I knew exactly how many hair there were to look at. But I shifted focus. She was wearing glittery white nylons. Every single shimmer and sheen stood out in glowing detail, and once again I knew exactly how many sparkles there were." (Ring and Cooper, 1997, p. 139)

This visual experience is literally in three dimensional, rather than two dimensional. A person while in a deep meditative state had a very profound and startling experience,

"*Although my eyes were closed, I could suddenly see everything – the whole room and myself in it – and I couldn't tell where I was seeing from! I wasn't seeing from my eyes or from any single point of view. I seemed to be seeing from everywhere. There seemed to be eyes in every cell of my body and in every particle surrounding me. I could simultaneously see from straight on, from above, from below, from behind, and so on.... There seemed to be no observer separate from what was seen. There was simply awareness*". (Ring and Cooper, 1997, p. 139).

Physical eyes can see only from a particular vantage point in space. In an out-of-body state the soul is freed from the restrictions of the physical body and it is able to perceive according to its own natural powers. The quantum soul has the 'awareness' of everything. A seer's power of omni-vision may be explained in the same way.

2.2.10: NDE with the children

Very young children, as soon as they are able to speak, have reported NDEs structured similar to the adult ones that they had as infants, or even in the process of being born. These accounts are different from the family teachings of death. In the OBEs, they see themselves as adults and not as baby spirits. Sometimes they see their living playmates in their NDEs. They rarely experience a life review and they do encounter favorite pets that have died more frequently than do adults.

Atwater, who herself had three NDEs in 1977, posits that *"the child you get back after a near-death episode is a remodeled, rewired, reconfigured, refined version of the original"* (Atwater, 1999, p. 121). Frightening childhood NDEs are rare but happen and these experiences begin or end with a positive note. Children's narration of NDEs is particularly valuable and enlightening because they report accurately what they experience without undue apprehension over the rational interpretation of their experiences.

In one case (Steiger and Steiger, 1995, pp. 42-46), a nine-year-old, Eddie Cuomo, came out of coma after 36 hours, and told his parents that he had been to heaven where he saw his deceased Grandpa Cuomo, Auntie Rosa, and Uncle Lorenzo. His father was embarrassed and tried to dismiss it as hallucination. Then Eddie added that he also saw his 19-year-old sister Teresa, who told him he had to go back. His father then became agitated, because two nights ago he had spoken with Teresa who was attending college in Vermont. Later that morning, Eddie's parents telephoned the college, and learned that Teresa had been killed in an automobile accident just after midnight, and that college officials had tried unsuccessfully to reach the Cuomos at their home to inform them of the tragedy.

Sam Parnia (Hogan, 2008, p. 29) described a child two-and-a-half-years old whose heart had stopped beating. He was unconscious and clinically dead, but was revived. Afterward, the child's parents contacted Parnia to tell him that the boy had drawn a picture of himself portraying what it was like during the trauma, but in the picture, he was outside of his unconscious body looking down at himself. In the drawing, there was a balloon-like area. When the boy was asked what that was, he said, "*when you die, you see a bright light and you are connected to a cord*". Six months later, he was still drawing the same scene with the same details.

Melvin Morse (Hogan, 2008, p. 141) presents the report of a 29 months old child, Todd who during 1972 bit into an electric cord from a vacuum cleaner. Medical records document that he was in ventricular asystole with no spontaneous respirations for about 25 minutes. After his resuscitation, he slowly recovered cortical and neurologic functions over the next four to six months. At the age of 33 months, he was playing in the living room when his mother asked him about the accident. He stated; "*I went into a room with a very nice man and sat with him. [The room] had a big bright light in the ceiling. The man asked if I wanted to stay or come back with you*". He then looked up at his mother, smiled and stated; "*I wanted to be back with you and come home*".

Atwater (2000) reported the case of a four-year-old who drowned in a backyard swimming pool. After resuscitation, he revealed that he met his little brother "over there" who told the story about Mommy having him pulled out of her tummy when she was 13. This statement upset everyone, since the four-year-old was the only child (there was no 'little brother'), and because Mommy's tearful admission afterward set the record straight about her secret abortion.

One five-year-old boy had following experience after he contracted meningitis and fell into a coma.

> *"I died, and drifted in a safe and black void where I felt no fear and no pain. I felt at home in this place.... I saw a little girl of about ten years old. I sensed that she recognized me. We hugged and then she told me, 'I'm your sister. I died a month after I was born. I was named after your grandmother. Our parents called me Rietje for short'.*
>
> *She kissed me, and I felt her warmth and love. 'You must go now', she said.... In a flash I was back in my body. I opened my eyes and saw*

the happy and relieved looks on my parents' faces. When I told them about my experience, they initially dismissed it as a dream.... I made a drawing of my angel sister who had welcomed me and repeated everything she'd told me. My parents were so shocked that they panicked. They got up and left the room. After a while they returned. They confirmed that they had indeed lost a daughter called Rietje. She had died of poisoning about a year before I was born. They had decided not to tell me and my brother until we were old enough to understand the meaning of life and death."

Some people can have NDE at an early childhood stage but no memory of it later on. If they have a second one later in life, sometimes they suddenly realize that they had one when they were little even though the content of a second NDE is seldom identical to the first. The cardiac arrest patients who had an NDE earlier in life are significantly more likely to have a second one than the other patients.

Children NDEs are important for several reasons. Critics often say that NDEs are culturally conditioned. Hence if pre-adult experiences resemble those placed on record by more mature witnesses, the cultural expectancy model can be rejected. With this kind of rationale in mind, Nancy Bush published a study of 17 childhood NDEs and found childhood and adult NDEs are comparable. However, she warned,

"*In the accounts presented here, it is not possible to determine how much of the affective interpretation is an adult overlay, though the specificity of memory detail in some cases..., suggests that this is not a major issue*" (Bush, 1983, p. 192).

Children are also able to describe quite clearly the experience in later stages of their lives. As example, Twemlow and Gabbard (1984, pp.157-58) reported a case where a seven-year-old girl had an NDE, and when she was twenty-nine, "*although it was approximately 22 years later, she remembered it with vivid clarity*". Morse had the same conclusion, "*The mind does not alter the childhood NDE over time, nor does the experience change or embellish the story after years of retelling the event*" (Morse and Perry, 1990, p. 152). Bush (1983, p. 199) agreed,

"*There is no indication here that children's experiences are simpler, less detailed, or different in structure from those occurring in adults as described by Raymond Moody, Ring, Sabom, and George Gallup. What may be most remarkable about them is that, when compared with the content of adult experiences, they are so unremarkable*".

Hence, there is little, if any, difference between adults' retrospective accounts of childhood NDEs and contemporary accounts of pediatric NDEs. Morse's assertion that "*the mind does not alter the NDE over time*", is correct.

Children generally are not motivated by personal, cultural, or religious agendas. A child under the age of two has no concept of death, and from two to five years, the child has a limited understanding that death is when the body stops moving. Hence, they are unlikely to report data to help any religious agendas. Also, the vast majority of children have never heard or even had the occasion to hear about near-death experiences. Hence, their accounts cannot be biased by others' reports.

2.2.11: NDE is a life changing experience

"*The man who dies before he dies does not die when he dies*".

Austrian Augustinian monk Abraham a Sancta Clara

"*Is there any scientific explanation for comprehensive and permanent life changes after a two-minute cardiac arrest?*"

Pim Van Lommel

"*My belief is that if everyone had an NDE there would never be another war, no one would starve or be the victim of violence and greed would become a thing of the past.*"

Christine Stewart (had an NDE at the age of 11)

Those who have visited the other world have a much lower fear of death than others. Whether they had vivid and wonderful memories of a flower-filled heaven or a brief and passing experience of light – almost all have permanent life changes. The deeper their experience, the deeper is the positive transformation of their attitudes towards others. This finding is in sharp contrast to people who have come close to death but no NDE. They have higher death anxiety than normal. Also, those people who are intensely religious have the same death anxiety as those who did not have NDE (Morse, 1992, p. 66). It means we cannot control our anxiety about death by religious faith alone. This is the reason the long-term effects of NDEs can be measured with a fairly high degree of objectivity and they stand in stark contrast to the general population.

"*I'm no longer afraid of death because I'll never forget what happened to me there. Now I'm certain that life goes on. Over the years I've undergone a number of changes. I feel a strong connection with nature. The garden now plays an important role in my life. I've become much more emotional. I've acquired a great sense of justice. I've become more patient and peaceful. I can see things in perspective now. My aggression is a thing of the past. I feel a strong inner urge to never lie again. I'd rather keep silent than tell a little white lie. I do struggle with deadlines: things must get done within a certain time. But I can handle it reasonably well. Before I never knew anything about spirituality; I wasn't interested.*

But now I've become aware of prophetic powers with which I can help others. I have a sixth sense. Over the years I've learned to live with it. It has simply become a part of my life. I really rely on my instincts these days. ... I enjoy life immensely. Now I'm aware of things that I never noticed before in my experience. I believe that people have stopped living from the heart.... I'm so glad and grateful that I can discuss it with my wife." (Van Lommel, 2010, p. 47)

The positive changes develop with the passage of time after NDE. A person with a strict religious upbringing copes with the experience differently than the less religious people and atheists. Those who were raised with material values find it harder to accept the new insight that money and power are no longer essential to happiness. NDE is a life-insight experience, and this newfound insight concerns to what matters in everyday life, i.e., acceptance of unconditional love for oneself, others, and nature. This understanding also relates to connectedness – a deep feeling that everything and everybody is connected, that individual personality is a drop of water dissolving into the ocean of Divine Unity. That's why an NDE is also an experience of unity. An NDEr, by putting his experience into words, can teach us a great deal about the "cosmic law". People become more forgiving, more tolerant, and less critical of others. They are more likely to donate to charities or to dedicate themselves to a social cause. They are also more willing and able to share emotions with others.

The NDE reveals that the quality of our lives is not determined by how we die, but by how we live. It also increases openness toward the idea of reincarnation. Ring (1984, p. 160) commented,

"*Of course, there is no reason why an NDEr's openness toward reincarnation must stem directly from his NDE. In fact, I am quite convinced that in many cases it is more likely to be a response to an NDEr's reading and other life experiences following an NDE.*"

Ring's study also indicates that in addition to the acceptance of reincarnation hypothesis, the NDErs openly have a more general acceptance of Eastern religions. One woman commented,

"*[I] hadn't given it [reincarnation] much thought before that [her NDE]. I was brought up in a fairly conventional religion – Catholicism. I was not a particularly practicing Catholic at the time, but more or less hadn't explored much Eastern philosophy. After the experience, I did. I read a great deal of different philosophies, not just Eastern, but all of them, and found that it [reincarnation] was plausible.*" (Wells, 1993, p. 28)

A review of interview data revealed that 13 of the 14 NDErs either believed in reincarnation or were at least open to the idea. Seven of them did not believe in reincarnation before their experience, but did believe in it afterwards

(Wells, 1993, pp. 18, 22). Many people who had believed in reincarnation 'a bit' became more convinced afterword (Sutherland, 1989, p. 100). Other researchers found a similar shift in religious beliefs among individuals having not only NDE but OBE also. Wells (1993, pp. 27, 28, 30) recorded many such statements,

> "*So, what happened to me is, before either of these experiences [two NDE] happened I didn't believe in reincarnation at all.... After these experiences what one of the things that happened to me was, I started getting memories of my own past lives. A lot of times just spontaneously something would trigger it and I'd get this memory, and I see visions, and then I started getting them of other people's lives.*"
>
> "*This didn't come about from the experience but afterwards, since then. [I've received] messages, my brother-in-law [deceased] had a message ... that his soul would be reincarnated into my sister's son*".
>
> "*I had ongoing experiences after the near-death experience. In that after process I experienced souls. On one occasion it's like I followed a soul, went through a process with a soul, in how they were reborn, how it came about that they were reborn.*"
>
> "*I didn't even know what reincarnation was before I had an NDE. It was afterwards that I was led to find out what it was. Some of the things I'm telling you [about reincarnation] came out in other conversations and some in the reading that I've done, and some just thoughts I've had. And it made total sense to me*".
>
> "*It is a matter of personal knowledge from what the Being with whom I spoke during my NDE told me about my older son, that he had had 14 incarnations in female physical bodies previous to the life he has just had.*"
>
> "*My whole life went before me of things I have done and haven't done, but not just of this one lifetime, but of all the lifetimes. I know for a fact there is reincarnation. This is an absolute. I was shown all those lives and how I had overcome some of the things I had done in other lives. There was still something to be corrected.*"
>
> "*I had a lot of questions, and I wanted to know what they [light beings she encountered in her NDE] were doing? Why are you just kind of milling around here? And someone stepped forward ... it wasn't just one ... I got information from a number of them ... that they were all waiting for reincarnation.*"

When we come to discuss reincarnation and the law of Karma (Chapter 7 and 8), complex issues surrounding the idea of soul will emerge, and will be explored more deeply at that time.

Though NDE literature mostly concentrates on the positive nature of these changes, there are cases when many people struggle to accept and integrate their newfound insight, especially when faced with negative reactions from family and friends. One person said (Van Lommel, 2010, p. 62),

> "*It had such a profound effect on the rest of my life: the timelessness that I experienced; the knowledge that my consciousness will survive outside my body. It was enough to destabilize my life.*"

Atwater (1994, p. 19) believes that the changes resulting from the NDE are exactly what the person needed. Those who had rigid personality usually became soft and began to enjoy the simple things in life. An underachiever learnt to be a more productive person, thirsting for knowledge and a chance to give back. She calls the NDE as,

> "*one of nature's more accelerated growth events, a powerful and complex dynamic that not only can foster psychological changes in both adults and children, but can cause physiological mutation the equal of species evolution*". (Atwater, 1994, p. 18)

Atwater (Sheehan, 2011, p. 15) recognizes four types of experiences that correspond to the amount of change a person needs. First, those who do not need a 'shake up' in their lives feel the initial experience of just peacefulness and light. Second, those who need some inner cleansing may have an unpleasant type. Third, those who have repressed guilt and those who need to learn to fight for themselves would have some hellish experience, as example, an abused woman found the strength to change her situation for the better following her hellish NDE. And the last one, i.e., the pleasant experiences give those who want reassurance that they are loved, the self-validation they need. A person can have multiple types of experiences simultaneously. The enlightenment of the experience comes from being bathed in the light. Atwater's research concentrates on the spiritual awakening in NDErs. She says (1994, p. 212), "*We as a species are always changing and NDE is a breakthrough in higher consciousness and the next stage of human evolution*".

An NDE can put a severe strain on marital relationships. A woman was blissfully married to a fundamentalist preacher for many years. They had a busy lifestyle with three children. But after an NDE it became increasingly difficult for her to attend her husband's church services. As she put it (Atwater, 1988, p. 118),

> "*He's wrong. I know now deep in my heart he's wrong. What he's preaching, that's not the way it is. I feel like he's telling everyone a lie and I don't know what to do about it. I love my husband and I love our children. I don't want to upset him or anyone else. I don't want a divorce or anything like that. But I can't listen any more. I try to pretend I'm too busy to come.*"

Nobody feels the change more acutely than a spouse. The divorce rate is between 75 to 78%, and most of these divorces happen within seven to 10 years of the episode because the NDEr is no longer the partner he or she originally married. The most common complaints from spouses are "I don't know this person anymore," or "This unconditional love nonsense is just an excuse to insult me by flirting with others." A common attitude of the experiencer is, "Since I no longer fit in, I'll move on." While others think that the experiencer is out-of-touch with reality, the experiencer thinks others are not interested in making changes. This created emotional distance between the partners.

A man after having an NDE said, "*I love my wife and children more than I ever thought I could. I love everyone. My experience taught me real love, unconditional love!*" (Atwater, 1988, p. 69). His family recognized how wonderfully he had changed, but he seemed somehow unreachable to them. A gap developed between them, and soon he became annoyed by facing challenges from others. He failed to understand why people had trouble getting along with him since he was so filled with joy and love for all of them. He was generous and openly affectionate, yet people tended to turn away or back off when he was around. At last he left the town and drifted for a while until he could figure out what was wrong.

Child experiencers often face troubles in the society. For instance (Atwater, 2003, p. 97), a young boy drowned at the age of five but revived 15 minutes later, and immediately began to see 'through' people and act in 'odd' ways. As he matured, what interested his age-mates bored him. This resulted in behavior problems. At 18, he joined the Army, hoping he would die. He met an accident and had another near-death scenario during resuscitation. The second NDE 'explained' the earlier one and gave him the courage he needed to turn his life around. The paranormal element in his experiences is thought-provoking.

Some people feel that they have a personal bond with God. One person said after an NDE, "*I now have a much, much stronger bond with God. I see and feel him as the greatest force in my life. He entered my life unbidden, but I welcomed him*". However, sometimes this belief causes trouble. An NDE may lead some people to believe that they are one of God's chosen. This 'sense of salvation' can make them feel relatively invulnerable and extremely important and may result in a strong urge to spread word of the NDE as a deeply religious experience. Such proselytizing is often seen as intrusive and stirs a great deal of resistance.

In addition to major psychological transformations, they also report important physical changes. They become more sensitive to light, especially sunlight, and to sound (tastes in music often change). The experience can trigger a heightened sensitivity to all sensory impression and a cross-connection between them. A person affected in this way talks of seeing smells and hearing or smelling colors (for example, 'smelling red'). They may have greater sensitivity to loud noises, a desire for silence, and a newfound preference for soothing music. Some show insatiable curiosity, lower blood pressure and bright skin and eyes. One experiencer wrote,

> "*After my NDE I felt like a child learning how to walk. The world around me overwhelmed me. I couldn't find my place in the world. For months I couldn't bear light and noise, TV and radio, not even music, which I used to love. Sometimes I think I've got a new problem because I've become hypersensitive to too much noise.*"

Some people experience an allergy to conventional medicines and become interested in alternative medicine. Metabolic rates and energy levels change, and people recover faster and look younger. Van Lommel (2010, p. 60) observed, some people discover the ability of self-healing, or to direct healing power at others which enables them to help people with physical or psychological problems.

The 'electromagnetic field' that surrounds the average person alters after an NDE. As a result, more than one-fourth of all adults who survived near-death as children said that they could not wear watches because they simply stopped running (Atwater, 1994, p. 132). A man had purchased three watches over the course of five years, none of which worked when he wore them. He was perplexed when they would begin to run, without repair, for his sons. Another bought a very expensive watch that would run while in his dresser drawer, but not when he wore it. Those changes are more profound who have experiences of the light (Atwater, 1994, p. 159). According to Van Lommel (2010, pp. 59-60) the electrical phenomena is very common. The electromagnetic field can interfere with electrical equipment – lights go out, the computer crashes, the car starter fails, or the supermarket checkout scanner refuses service. One person said, "*another strange thing was that after my NDE every piece of equipment I touched, such as lamps, dishwasher, kettle, the light in the cooker hood, it broke. I gave off energy everywhere.*"

Distressing NDE is harder to absorb because it is often accompanied by strong feelings of guilt. The hell experience may prompt revulsion, and in many cases, self-rejection. It is almost impossible to talk about a frightening NDE to others. As a result, there is total silence that generally precludes any chance of integration and actually increases the fear of death.

2.3: Skeptic's view

> "*I began my eight-year study as a cynic. But by the time it ended, I was convinced that near-death experiences are a genuine phenomenon.*"
>
> Penny Sartori

The skeptics have presented several theories as possible explanations of NDE, such as conscious and subconscious fabrication, oxygen deprivation, autoscopic (autoscopy means self-visualization) hallucination, dreams, prior expectation, drug-induced illusion, endorphin release, temporal lobe seizure and relieving birth memory. All these physical explanations for the accounts given by experiencers can be demonstrated to be implausible.

An individual who had a glimpse of the afterlife often describe it as a 'peak' event, which had done more to shape the depth and direction of life goals and attitude than any other prior single experience. The impact is evident in many different and unique ways. Death anxiety is dramatically reduced and they live their lives more fully day to day. Many people develop psychic abilities. When a person becomes permanently changed by an NDE during a cardiac arrest of only some minutes' duration, it is a scientific challenge to discuss new hypotheses other than traditional one. If the tunnel, the OBE, and many other experiences are "just imagination", then we need a useful theory that can explain why everyone's imaginations are of very similar types rather than different.

Also this 'just imagination' explanation cannot explain the paranormal aspects of NDEs, such as; telepathic communication with a living person (example, George Rodonaia), communication with unknown deceased persons (example, Colton Burpo), deceased loved ones give paranormal information (example, Eddie Cuomo), NDEr appears as an apparition to others (examples, Mary Gosse, Olga Gearhardt, Laurin Bellg's cancer patient), psychic abilities (example, Cherylee Black) and miraculous healings (example, Anita Moorjani). These paranormal events cannot be explained by science, and are in that sense facts that prove that NDEs include other dimensions. They cannot be explained or reached by a materialistic view. Another proof for the spiritual nature of NDE is that the born-blind people can see clearly during the experience.

NDEs are also not drug-induced hallucinations. During the experience, people report being hyper-alert – "*I saw clearer than I've ever seen*". They remember in great detail things that happened around them and in adjacent rooms, meaningful conversations with deceased relatives and seeing scenes very clearly. The reports are of sensations and consciousness that are more lucid than normal, an effect opposite to that of a brain clouded by drugs. With major hallucinogenic drugs tunnel experiences are common, but so are lattices, spirals, cobwebs, and other simple forms. In all NDE cases, the tunnel has a special place which is as real as anything in normal perception. Sabom (1982, p. 234) commented,

> "*In sum, the hallucinations and delusions reported by persons during extreme illness or after the administration of medicinal narcotics differ significantly from the NDE in both content and structure. Moreover, we*

have clear documentation of many cases in which the NDE occurred in the absence of any medicinal hallucinatory agent, thus making the drug-induction hypothesis completely untenable in such situations."

B-endorphin is a substance produced within the human brain that possesses many characteristics of morphine sulfate. This explains why some people report having little or no pain following overwhelming trauma. Some skeptics propose this property of B-endorphin as the cause of the profound painlessness during an NDE. Experimentally, when an injection of B-endorphin is administered to 14 volunteer patients with intractable pain associated with disseminated cancer, all of them reported complete relief of pain which lasted from 22 to 73 hours (Oyama et al., 1980, pp. 122-24). Similarly, a person having an NDE also reports complete relief of pain. However, there is a difference – the painlessness occurs only during the NDE itself and as soon as the experience ends, i.e., the astral body returns to physical body, the physical pain abruptly returns, as in the following account.

"*I was hurting real bad... But all of a sudden the pain completely stopped and I could feel my being rising out of my body... I looked dead.... Then I started floating back down to my body. As soon as I got down to my body, the pain came back. Tremendous pain.*" (Sabom, 1982, pp. 235-36)

If painlessness state during NDE was caused by massive release of B-endorphin, the relief would be expected to persist much longer than the NDE experience. When patients are injected with B-endorphin, drowsiness and sleep are reported to be major psychodynamic effects of the chemical. But during NDE, the individual is hyper-alert with an exceptional clarity of vision and thought and the panoramic life review is presented to him in the most organized sequence.

NDE phenomenon is not same as autoscopic hallucination. Autoscopy denotes seeing one's own self or one's double in normal mental condition. This is a rare psychiatric disorder seen primarily in patients with depression, epilepsy and schizophrenia. Usually the patients will suddenly and without warning perceive a visual image of their own face or upper trunk projected a few feet in front of their own bodies. The image is usually colorless and transparent and will often imitate all movements and facial expressions of the original as if the person is seeing his own reflection in the mirror (Sabom, 1982, p. 225). This phenomenon has been known to all races from time immemorial. Unlike NDE, autoscopic hallucination consists of a physical body (original) perceiving the projected image (double) but without any direct interaction between the original and the double. Autoscopic hallucinations are perceived as unreal and commonly evoke negative emotions. In contrast, the NDE experiences are 'realer than real' and have a profound positive impact on the person's life. Hence, this is not a possible explanation for NDE.

NDE is not same as Temporal Lobe Seizure (TLS). During TLS, the perception of the environment is distorted and the patient feels fear, sadness and loneliness. But in NDE, the environment is not distorted, and calm, peace and joy pervade (unless it is distressing NDE). During seizure the senses of taste and smell are present, but absent in the NDE. Forced thinking is present during the seizure, but not in NDE. Hence, seizure can mimic some elements of NDE but does not cause the actual experience. Other possible explanations are a lack of oxygen in the brain, or too much carbon dioxide. However, these theories would not explain why some patients are able to give full and clear reports of things that went on around them during their NDE. In a laboratory set up, two physicians placed human volunteers in an air chamber and gradually lowered the concentration of oxygen. As the level was lowered, the person's mental and physical abilities became progressively impaired until convulsions occurred and respiration ceased. No experiences resembling an NDE were reported (Henderson and Haggard, 1927). When oxygen supply to the brain decreases, a progressive muddling and confusion of cognitive abilities are observed. In contrast, the NDErs report hyper-alertness. Hence, brain hypoxia cannot account for the typical manifestations of an NDE. Similarly, hypercarbia (elevated levels of carbon dioxide in the brain) also does not explain an NDE.

Another theory is that the NDE is a reliving of one's birth and that the tunnel is really the birth canal. It is something like the re-enactment of the birth experience. A baby being born leaves his mother's womb to travel down a tunnel towards a light, and what waits for it in the light is usually a great deal of love and warmth. What happens at the point of death is only a stored memory of what happened when life began. This theory is simple, beautiful and easy to understand and therefore, many skeptics cling to this idea when all other explanations fail. But there are a lot of points that don't match. How an infant would perceive the world in a form that could later be recalled by an adult with totally different perceptual capabilities is difficult to understand. The birth canal is nothing like a tunnel with a light at the end, and in any case the fetus is pushed along it with the top of its head usually emerging first, not its eyes. Hence, for a critical thinker it takes a vast leap of the imagination to make the two comparable.

Secondly, if we agree that the tunnel experience is reliving birth memories, then the kind of birth should make a difference. In particular, people born by cesarean section have never been along the birth canal and so, presumably, should not be able to relive it. Hence, when a survey was carried out, the researchers found that those who had been born by cesarean section did not report more or fewer tunnel experiences than the others. Moreover, an infant being born does not exactly float at high speed down a tunnel, but is buffeted along with difficulty by its mother's contractions. This theory also does not explain the meeting with dead friends and relatives. If the "Being of Light" is supposed to be the midwife or the doctor who rules the delivery room, then many babies are born without a midwife or doctor present, or perhaps with many people present. It is a medically proven fact that an infant's nervous system is not sufficiently developed to allow it to assimilate and store memories of the birth process. When skeptics argued that the tunnel is not actually reliving one's birth but is a kind of symbolic representation of birth in general, then the counter-argument is that the theory is equivalent to the previous kind of theory and suffers from the same weakness.

Can a physical brain mechanism ever be shown with certainty to cause a dark tunnel experience, or the overwhelming presence of the light? Radiologist Andrew Newberg has extensively studied brain function during spiritual experiences using nuclear imaging techniques, and concluded,

> "*The fact that spiritual experiences can be associated with distinct neural activity does not necessarily mean that such experiences are mere neurological illusions. It's no safer to say that spiritual urges and sensations are caused by brain activity than it is to say that the neurological changes through which we experience the pleasure of eating an apple cause the apple to exist.... There is no way to determine whether the neurological changes associated with spiritual experiences mean that the brain is causing those experiences...or is instead perceiving a spiritual reality.*" (Woznicki, 2007, p. 328)

Neuropsychiatrist Peter Fenwick and his wife Elizabeth Fenwick argue that modern medical practices have devalued end-of-life experiences, and call for a more holistic approach to death and dying.

> "*Messages about the outside world come from the sense organs and are relayed to the brain. The brain uses this information to create a model of the world...[F]or a sensory experience to come into consciousness it has to make its way to the appropriate analysis system in the [brain] cortex....Each brain area contributes part of the picture of our experienced world....To bring a complete model of the world in to consciousness the brain has to be working as a whole in an integrated way. If one area is damaged then its particular function will be absent or distorted, and so too will that part of the 'world model'.*" (Fenwick and Fenwick, 1997, pp. 199-207)

Dreams and an NDE are not same. Many subjects who were asked to compare reality of the NDE versus the fantasy of the dream made the following emphasis.

> "*I've had lot of dreams and it wasn't like any dream that I had had. It was real. It was so real. And that peace, the peace made the difference from a dream, and I dream a lot.*" (Sabom, 1982, p. 227)

Dreams appear to be very real at the time of their occurrence, but the NDE is perceived as stark reality both during the experience and later in reflection. The contents of dreams vary extremely from person to person and from night to night, but there is a consistency of events in NDE cases.

Susan Blackmore popularized the dying brain theory, according to which the NDErs have the same pattern of experience, and going through remarkably similar stages of incidents on the way, makes a powerful case against the reality of NDE. It means, the "sameness" evidence is actually a function of the dying brain. All human brains, regardless of where in the world they come from, die in the same way. This is the reason the essential core elements of all NDEs are strikingly similar. The dying person is not traveling toward a beautiful afterlife, but because the neurotransmitters in the brain are shutting down, in the dying process these are creating the same lovely illusions for all who are at death's door.

However, an intuitive mind has some questions. First, how all the dying brains throughout the world do this, if it is just a highly sophisticated lump of tissue? Second, how all the brains of all human beings are connected so that they see same lovely illusions? Third, if death is the ultimate ego annihilation, why the brain bothers to show same hallucinations? Fourth, if an NDE is nothing more than a series of brain reactions, why do a great many people report being told, "*Your mission has not been completed,*" or, "*The time for your death is not yet,*" during their NDE? Last, if death is the final end, how the brain shows future events during NDE which later proves to be correct? For logical people, it is easier to believe that NDEs are a real afterlife experience than answering these questions. Since all NDEs are similar around the world and throughout our history, these are real journeys to a common place. The dying brain theory though seems to have strength, is actually a logical fallacy. During NDE the EEG activity is often flat and hence the brain can't produce any activity probably not even if it's dying.

There is no end of skepticism on the face of concrete proof that OBEs and NDEs are real experiences. If the NDE research done so far on the question of survival is not compelling, then mere speculation about alternative explanations of these data is even less compelling. As David Lester, a disbeliever in survival hypothesis, disapproved his fellow skeptics, "*Although the research conducted by those who argue that NDEs are evidence for life after death is often methodologically poor, the critics of this position have published no research*". (Lester, 2003, p. 255). Simply pointing out that investigators are at fault, patients are at delusion, and presenting bizarre theories such as birth canal memory etc., will not help. Anyone can accuse a serious investigator in any field of fraud but such an accusation without supporting evidence is not even the weakest of arguments. This is not actual skepticism, but rather skepticism's evil twin, 'denialism'. The serious researchers can ignore such arguments and move on. As Henry Sidgwick said about 140 years ago in his President's address at the first meeting of the Society for Psychical Research, "*We have done all we can when the critic has nothing left to allege except that the investigator is in [on] the trick. But when he has nothing else left to allege, he will allege that.*" (Sidgwick, 1882, p. 12). Harold Widdison reminded us,

> "*Judging each other is not a weakness of any field but a sign of growing maturity. We should question each other's research. Then, if we find weaknesses, we can correct them and do more research. So brick by brick correctly placed, we create a theoretical model that fits and helps to understand near-death phenomena*". (Widdison, 2002, p. 285).

Today there is a 'mountain' of scientific evidence suggesting consciousness can survive bodily death. OBE and NDE research are in good shape and the truth will take its own course in the coming years. Jeffrey Long manages the largest database of NDEs available today. He had used "scientific" methodology and gathered as many "reliable" accounts as possible. According to the "scientific evidence" provided by the more than 1,300 reports studied, Long (2010, p. 48) concluded, "*By studying thousands of accounts of NDErs, I found the evidence… it is reasonable to accept the existence of an afterlife*".

A major goal for future research is to address the question of why some people experience NDEs whereas others, in apparently similar physiological or psychological conditions, do not. One related question is why some people experience particular features of NDEs, such as an apparition of a deceased person, whereas others do not. Another important issue is the relationship between NDEs and related phenomena, such as mystical experiences, deathbed visions, ghostly encounters, mediumship and reincarnation.

Many physicians are unresponsive to their patient's NDEs. One physician went so far as to say that if someone tells him of an NDE he just changes the subject. Some patients receive a judgmental reaction from their physician or nurse causing them less likely to share their stories – who wants to be devalued? Medical staff show this negligent attitude because not many of them had some training on NDE in medical school. In traditional medical text books NDE cases are rarely mentioned. As Sabom (1982, pp. 185-86) noted, one text book had a small comment on NDE in the psychiatry chapter. Aside from this brief account no farther comment was made regarding the causes or implications of these strange experiences. Hence, naturally, the medical reader is left with the impression that such occurrences have clear psychiatric implications because the material was included in the 'Psychiatric Complications' section of the chapter devoted to 'Complications to other organs and systems in cardiac resuscitation'. Furthermore, it was sandwiched between paragraphs dealing with 'severe personality decomposition', 'acute brain syndrome', and 'other psychiatric reactions' to the stress of medical care in hospital intensive care facilities. The text book does not even show the NDE as an abnormal psychiatric reaction. As a result of all these the numbers of NDEs are underreported, especially in a hospital setting. For example,

> "**Dr. Sabom:** *Did you mention this [NDE] to anyone there?*
> **Patient:** *Yes. To several doctors and nurses who were there, but they just sort of scoffed at me. You know how they do... and I said, 'I don't believe what just happened to me.' Of course, they wanted to know what and I told them and they looked at me and sort of scoffed and that was it. ... They just said it was the pain that caused it and that I couldn't have seen all this."*
>
> *"People will think I'm crazy. I wouldn't dare tell my wife. She would have me a candidate for the second floor [psychiatric ward]. But you've expressed an interest in it and you seem sincere. I'm not telling you everything, Doctor. Just enough so that you won't get too uptight with me. Maybe later, when I know you better and know how serious you really are about this thing. It's a pretty kinky experience".* (Sabom, 1982, pp. 186-88)

OBEs and NDEs are eyewitness testimonies. If we can draw an analogy between an eyewitness to a crime and an NDEr's visualization of a medical procedure, we will find that the person gets a brief glimpse of an unexpected and unfamiliar scene under stressful circumstances in both the situations. Crime researchers have confirmed that eyewitness testimony is most reliably obtained when the witness is allowed to give a free, unstructured account of events. Witness confidence in the account also has a positive correlation with its accuracy. Similarly, each individual should be allowed to describe the experience in a free, unstructured format. The person has very high confidence on the accuracy of his experience, as we often hear remarks like these – 'it was realer than real', 'clearer than normal vision', 'this is no figment of my imagination' etc.

Raymond Moody brings this point to our attention in his book, The Light Beyond, as he relates an account he witnessed at a lecture on NDE by Michael Sabom. An angry cardiologist in the crowd stood up and announced, "*I've worked as a cardiologist for 25 years now, and I've never come across such absurd stories in my practice. I think this is complete nonsense; I don't believe a word of it*". Before anyone could react, a man sitting behind the doctor replied, "*I'm one of your patients. A couple of years ago I survived a cardiac arrest and had an NDE, and you would be the last person I'd ever tell*". (Finnegan, 2014, pp. 225-26). This is a very common problem. Some people maintain silence because they prefer to come to terms with their NDE in silence. Some find it extremely difficult or painful, if not impossible, to live their lives according to their newfound insights (Hoffman, 1995, pp. 29-48). There are cases when people took more than 50 years after the event to talk about their NDE and its consequences for the fear of rejection; they preferred to keep their NDE a lifelong secret. However, that trend is changing.

2.4: Conclusion

"If conscious life can continue while the brain is temporarily out of commission, it is natural to ask what will happen when the body actually dies."

Richard L. Thompson

"... what happened to them at death's door will happen to every human who crosses that threshold of death, and that people deserve to know the truth".

Regina M. Hoffman

The OBEs and NDEs combine prove that what we have been taught for several thousand years – that there is life after death – is true. NDE researcher P.M.H. Atwater had analyzed thousands of cases for 23 years. She concluded that the cases have following very meaningful pattern (Atwater, 2000).

1. Most cases happen during exact moments of unusual stress in the person's life when spiritual guidance or direction would be most helpful. An NDE contains a message that fulfills almost exactly the subconscious needs of the person at that moment in time. The life review and any session that covers lectures or advice reflects whatever was omitted, ignored, or not yet learned in life by the experiencer involved.
2. In a child's NDE, parents, relatives and caregivers are often affected the most as if the child had the experience for them. Often the experience is a quiet but powerful directive in the life path the child takes once grown.
3. The discarnates at the other side always try to help the experiencer.
4. After an NDE, the person desires to grow psychologically and spiritually. The growth indicates that whatever qualities are missing in the person's overall maturing process are now being filled up.

Most of the aspects of consciousness during NDE are similar to quantum-like phenomena. Does quantum physics have something critical to do at fundamental level with how consciousness and memories relate with the brain and the body during normal activities or during NDE or actual death? Quantum physics confirms that particles can propagate like waves, as example, light behaves like particles (photons) in some experiments, and in other experiments it behaves like waves, and both experiments are true. Since there is a lack of objectivity, it seems the consciousness of the researcher and his design of the experiment define the result. During life our consciousness has an aspect of particles, but when we die our consciousness will no longer have an aspect of particles, but only an eternal aspect of waves. This new concept can explain all the reported elements of an NDE.

In science, confirming the reality of a concept comes from many independent studies with different methodologies. This cross-checking among scientific studies has always been the foundation for validating scientific discoveries. From this view, the OBE and NDE research is scientific. All the evidence show that NDE is a model for the final stage of dying, and anyone who has reached the death's door should perceive some aspects of a reality like the NDE. No matter how the skeptics explain the NDEs, the major question remains unanswered unless we adhere to the afterlife hypothesis. Melvin Morse wrote,

> "*I have re-examined a generation of scientific research into higher brain function and have found that the soul hypothesis explains many 'unexplained' events. It explains out-of-body experiences, the sensation of leaving the body and accurately describing details outside of the body's field of view. Events such as floating out of the physical body and giving accurate details of one's own cardiac arrest – things a person couldn't see even if their eyes were open – are virtually impossible to explain if we do not believe in a consciousness separate from our bodies that could be called a soul.*" (Morse and Perry, 1990, pp. 169-70).

Wettach (2000, p. 89) pointed out the possibility that NDE is the reason that religions developed. Suppose in a primitive, prehistoric society an apparently dead person comes back to life and describes travelling to a strange and beautiful place. The elders cannot explain this. Hence to assure their dominant position in the tribe, they invent the concept of God and an afterlife and tell others that only they can interpret God for the rest of the tribe. Thus, the children of the tribe are taught religious concepts to store in the primitive centers of their minds. In later generation if someone has an NDE, his experience will prove to the tribe that the elders were right and God exists.

NDE is a legitimate field of scientific study. But a few people are willing to bend facts to fit certain testimonies of 'religious' books. If facts are dramatized and twisted to conform a set of religious beliefs, then future research will certainly hamper. NDEs occur within the context of a person's entire life and that their full meaning can only be understood in that context. Hence, we need to spend more time taking a critical look at not just the experience but its aftereffects and implications as well.

Chapter 3

Deathbed phenomena

"It is very beautiful over there."

Thomas Edison on his deathbed (Sandberg, 1977, p. 65)

Those who have years of working experience with the dying and the bereaved often notice commonly shared experiences that remain beyond our ability to fully understand. These strange experiences, commonly known as pre-death experiences describe a wide range of phenomena – deathbed visions (or visitations, phenomena, communication), apparitional experiences, nearing death awareness, end-of-life dreams and visions etc. The reports have many similarities to NDE cases and have been well documented throughout history and across cultures and folklores although scientific study of them is relatively recent.

For a terminally ill patient the veil between life and death is lowered. There are numerous reports of terminal lucidity (TL – sudden return of mental clarity shortly before death). The dying person often reports having glimpses of places not of this world, seeing deceased relatives, friends, angel-like figures and religious figures, and having conversations with them or be overcome with a feeling of joy and happiness. If we accept deathbed visions at face value, they provide glimpses of what awaits us when we ourselves make the transition. The impact of pre-death experiences on dying individuals and their loved ones can be profoundly meaningful. Recent reports from nurses and doctors suggest that paranormal experiences consist of a much wider range of phenomena such as,

1. seemingly veridical spatial clairvoyance and accurate future predictions related by the dying, spontaneous telepathy,

2. feelings of love or light spreads out to fill the room that assists to calm grieving loved ones, dying person speaks of 'transiting' to new reality,
3. synchronistic auditory or physical phenomena such as knocking sounds, hearing music, strange noises, voices/dialogue, crying or moaning from unknown source, hearing voices coming from a place where there is nobody, unexplained object movements, such as moving of doors, falling and breaking of objects without outside force, odd behavior of electrical devices, such as lights turning on and off, and stopping of clocks,
4. emanations of mists, shapes, lights or a radiance from dying persons, or replica of the dying person's body seen by others; winds felt, plants affected, changes in pet behavior (howling or behaving as if someone has arrived when no one is visible) etc., change in room temperature during the final moments of dying and at death (either icy cold or unusually hot),
5. coincidences are experienced by someone emotionally close to the dying person but physically distant who is somehow aware of their moment of death, or says the person "visited" them at that time to say goodbye, again providing comfort.

Palliative care nurses' experiences of paranormal phenomena are neither rare nor surprising. More people now die in hospitals than before, but unfortunately the nurses have neither the time nor the training to deal adequately with the spiritual aspects of the dying process. Since deathbed incidents are not a part of medical studies, this special awareness is often ignored, missed or overlooked. Hence, the estimated number of unreported cases may be high. In this chapter we will look into several case studies to find their paranormal connections and their relevance in afterlife research. Increased awareness of unusual end-of-life experiences could help physicians, caregivers, and bereaved family members be prepared for encountering such experiences, and help those individuals cope with them.

3.1: Strange mist and light observed at deathbed

Staff working in hospices frequently report of a strange mist that is seen over a deathbed which they describe in various ways. It may look like smoke or as subtle as steam. This strange mist usually drifts upward and disappears soon. Sometimes it seems to have a human shape.

"*As he died something which is very hard to describe because it was so unexpected and because I had seen nothing like it left up through his body and out of his head. It resembled distinct delicate waves/lines of smoke (smoke is not the right word but I have not got a comparison) and then disappeared. I was the only one to see it. It left me with such a sense of peace and comfort.*" (Moreira-Almeida and Santos, 2012, p. 183)

Moody and Perry (2010, pp. 101-02) quoted a Georgia physician who twice saw a mist coming up from deceased patients. He explained that as the patients died they lit up with a bright glow, their eyes shining with a silvery light. The mist formed over the chest and hovered there. After close observation he saw that the mist had depth and complex structure and seemed to have layers with energetic motion in it. During the second occurrence, he felt an unseen presence standing beside him and seemingly waiting for the patient to die. A few days after the second experience, he had a spontaneous out-of-body experience. These multiple experiences had profoundly affected his worldview – "*I can say with assurance that there is more to the world than there seems*".

When the former Beatles guitarist George Harrison died on November 29, 2001, after a battle with lung cancer, his wife Olivia Harrison and many others witnessed at his deathbed that,

"*There was a profound experience that happened when he left his body. It was visible. Let's just say, you wouldn't need to light the room, if you were trying to film it. He just…lit the room.*" (Taylor, 2014, p. 244)

Neuropsychiatrist Peter Fenwick found in a survey of palliative caregivers that one in every three reported accounts of "*a radiant light that envelops the dying person, and may spread throughout the room and involve the caregiver*". This description sounds remarkably similar to the "profound experience" recounted by Olivia Harrison. In a similar study more than half of all caregivers reported observations of this 'dying light'. Fenwick (Kean, 2017, p. 140) described the incident of a woman who witnessed the spiritual image of her husband.

"*Suddenly there was the most brilliant light shining from my husband's chest, and as the light lifted upward, there was the most beautiful music and singing voices. My own chest seemed filled with infinite joy, and my heart felt as if it was lifting to join this light and music. Suddenly, there was a hand on my shoulder, and a nurse said, 'Sorry, love. He's just gone. I lost sight of the light and the music and felt so bereft at being left behind.*"

Another woman reported what she saw when her mother passed away.

"*It was then that I saw her face appeared to be glowing with a gold light. The light began to leave through the top of her head and go towards the ceiling. Looking back to my mother's face I saw that she was no longer breathing*". (Moreira-Almeida and Santos, 2012, p. 182)

A hospice psychologist in North Carolina described that the deathbed visions are unearthly. Although she is not religious, hospice work has awakened her to a spiritual dimension of life.

> *"In my opinion, everyone who works with the dying long enough must have some awareness of these experiences. I believe the spiritual experiences of dying people somehow leak out and pervade the area around them. If you step into that area with the right temperament, you will receive, I feel, a sense of the sacred in the presence of the dying.*
>
> *I have experienced the room taking on a different configuration a number of times. The only way that I can describe it is that moving energy pulses through the room. I often feel something I can't name.*
>
> *The bedside of the dying offers a view into eternity. Like looking through a window into elsewhere, from time to time I see light and twice have had clear views of what appear to be structures. On both occasions I saw patients leave their bodies in a cloud form. I saw them rise out of their bodies and head toward these structures.*
>
> *I would describe these clouds as a sort of mist that forms around the head or chest. There seems to be some kind of electricity to it, like an electrical disturbance. I don't know if I see it with my physical eyes, but it's there all the same. There is no doubt in my mind that you can sometimes see people depart for the other side.*" (Moody and Perry, 2010, pp. 102-03).

One pioneering researcher of deathbed phenomena was late Robert Crookall. Following two cases are from his file. In the first case the observer saw a replica of a dying person's body.

> "*I approached the ward as the child drew its final breath. Then I saw mist above the little body. It took the shape of the body which lay on the bed. This was attached by a very fine silver cord. The replica was about three feet from the body on the bed. It rose gradually to above five feet above the body, then gradually lifted itself into an upright position. It then floated away.*" (Crookall, 1967, p. 40)

Crookall also cites the case of R. B. Hout, a physician who encountered both anomalous mist and light in the room during the death of his aunt.

> *"My attention was called...to something immediately above the physical body, suspended in the atmosphere about two feet above the bed. At first I could distinguish nothing more than a vague outline of a hazy, fog-like substance. There seemed to be only a mist held suspended, motionless. But, as I looked, very gradually there grew into my sight a denser, more solid, condensation of this inexplicable vapor. Then I was astonished to see definite outlines presenting themselves, and soon I saw this fog-like substance was assuming a human form... The eyes were closed as though in tranquil sleep, and a luminosity seemed to radiate from the spirit body."* (Taylor, 2014, p. 247)

A report from Ed Bodin in the January 25, 1945 issue of 'Psychic Observer', stated that a young soldier saw a strange mist in the battlefield.

> "*I have watched it emanate from a badly wounded soldier and then disappear as that soldier breathed his last. One hillbilly comrade from Kentucky called it 'soul mist,' revealing that many natives in his part of the country considered it quite a normal thing, although they seldom talked about it.*"

This soldier asked not to be identified since his orthodox Christian family prohibits such discussion. In the battlefield another soldier lay badly wounded about 10 feet from him. He continued, "*I looked at him with pity, forgetting my own pain. Then in the deepening twilight I saw strange smoke begin to curl above him as though coming from his stomach as he lay on his back moaning*".

A hospice nurse reported seeing mist rising from many patients as they die, including her father, with whom she saw the mist rise from his chest "*as if off a still river*" (Moody and Perry, 2010, p. 26) and then hovering for a few seconds before dissipating. One man saw that the room became "uncomfortably bright," so bright that he couldn't shut it out even when he closed his eyes. A hospice nurse reported seeing a "*luminous presence floating near the bed, shaped somewhat like a person*". The head nurse saw the light in the room and light coming from the dying person's eyes but did not observe the presence (Moody and Perry, 2010, p. 83). In another situation the whole family saw an unusual light in the room which was like looking at light in a swimming pool at night.

How to interpret this mist or light that some people see at the point of death? This cannot be a hallucination because the mist or light appears at the same time in the dying process and often witnessed by many people. It's possible that the mist or cloud seen leaving the body at deathbed is actually the soul, or the spirit body, etheric body, astral body whatever name be assigned to it. Ernesto Bozzano believed that these represented the initial stages of death, involving the separation of an etheric body; more precisely, the "*initial phase of deathbed 'bilocation' phenomena*" (Bozzano, 1934, p. 120). Whether it is non-matter, or matter (have particles and weight), or a form of energy – at present it is beyond the grasp of modern science. But calling it a hallucination makes no sense at all. Those who have witnessed this 'dying light' will not be swayed by skeptical arguments.

3.2: Terminal lucidity (TL)

> "*The history of science is full of examples in which important observations and theories were dismissed as 'impossible' or 'misinterpreted' only because of obsolete prejudice.*"
>
> Michael Nahm

The unexpected return of mental clarity and long-lost memory often occur in the last few seconds, minutes, hours, or days before death in patients suffering from severe psychiatric and neurologic disorders. This is commonly known as 'terminal lucidity' (TL) which involves deathbed patients with both mental and physical illnesses, patients suffering from brain abscesses, tumors, strokes, meningitis, dementia or Alzheimer's disease, schizophrenia, and affective disorders. TL can manifest in two ways. First, the mental clarity can improve steadily in contrast to the gradual decline of physical vitality. Second, the mental clarity can reappear abruptly and unexpectedly shortly before death. Rush (1812, p. 257) wrote that "*most of mad people discover a greater or less degree of reason in the last days or hours of their lives*". In France, prominent physician Alexandre Brierre de Boismont (2003, p. 243) observed,

> "*In certain diseases, the senses acquire an extraordinary delicacy on the approach of death, when the sick person astonishes those about him by the elevation of his thoughts, and the sudden lucidity of a mind which has been obscured during many long years*".

There are enough published cases during the last 250 years, but this mysterious phenomenon has so far not received much attention among psychiatrists and physicians. Many scholars of classical times, such as, Hippocrates, Plutarch, Cicero, Galen, and Avicenna noted that symptoms of mental disorders decrease as death approaches (Nahm, 2009, p. 90). The earliest systematic survey was carried out by an author, Julius in 1844. He documented statistics on 139 patients of a British asylum who died there from 1796 to 1841. In 13% of the cases, the mental state was considerably improved at the time the patients died. Biggest symptom reduction at the end of life was displayed by patients diagnosed with mania (16%) and melancholia (17%). Julius also mentioned that in a few cases the patients died of a sudden death such as stroke. In only 2% of the patients the terminal mental condition was considerably changed for the worse, in 63% it remained unchanged, and in 22% it changed in quality, e.g., from mania to melancholia.

How to explain the cases where full mental clarity had appeared quite abruptly and unexpectedly shortly before death? It is unclear how severely demented patients can sometimes recognize their family members and remember their lives again shortly before death. The strange case of Anna Katharina Ehmer is one of the most intriguing cases of terminal lucidity that we can find.

Anna Katharina Ehmer was a severely disabled woman. In addition, she had suffered from repeated and severe attacks of meningitis which had destroyed much of the brain tissue required for intelligent reasoning (Nahm and Greyson, 2013, p. 78). An eye-witness, Friedrich Happich characterized her personality as follows,

"*Kathe [Anna Katharina Ehmer] was among the patients with the most severe mental disabilities who have ever lived in our institution. She had never learned to speak a single word. She stared for hours on a particular spot, then she fidgeted for hours without a break. She gorged her food, fouled herself day and night, uttered an animal-like sound, and slept. In all the time she lived with us, we have never seen that she had taken notice of her environment even for a second. We had to amputate one of her legs, she wasted away.*" (Ringger, 1958, p. 219)

Chief Physician Dr. Wittneben (1934, p. 153) characterized her in similar terms. She suffered from tuberculosis, and the reason for the amputation of her leg was osseous tuberculosis. Despite the amputation, the disease progressed and finally led to her death. Happich had witnessed Kathe's deathbed scene as this,

"*One day I was called by one of our physicians, who is respected both as a scientist and a psychiatrist. He said: 'Come immediately to Kathe, she is dying!' When we entered the room together, we did not believe our eyes and ears. Kathe, who had never spoken a single word, being entirely mentally disabled from birth on, sang dying songs to herself. Specifically, she sang over and over again 'Where does the soul find its home, its peace? Peace, peace, heavenly peace!' For half an hour she sang. Her face, up to then so stultified, was transfigured and spiritualized. Then, she quietly passed away. Like myself and the nurse who had cared for her, the physician had tears in his eyes. He stated repeatedly: 'I cannot explain this in medical terms. If demanded, I can prove by autopsy that ... from an anatomical perspective, thinking could not have been possible*'." (Ringger, 1958, p. 220).

"*This appeared like a miracle to us. Even bigger, however, was the miracle that Kathe, up to now entirely mute, could suddenly recite the text of the song clearly and intelligibly. Dr. W. [Wittneben] stated over and over again: 'From a medical perspective, I am confronted with a mystery'. Kathe has suffered so many severe infections of meningitis, that due to the anatomical changes in the cortical brain tissue, it is not comprehensible how the dying woman could suddenly sing so clearly and intelligibly.*" (Stritter, 1930, pp. 176ff).

How did this woman regain her long-lost mental faculties and sing dying songs in a very intelligible manner before death? Can our modern medical knowledge give a logical explanation to this? Dr. Wittneben was dumbfounded as he wrote,

"*I hurried to her room to observe what would contradict all medical experience. But it is true: Kathe sang, very intelligibly: 'Where does the*

> *soul find its home, its peace?' A smile caressed her stultified face, the soul flung off restraints*". (Roesermueller, 1957, p. 24)
>
> "*Who has witnessed something like this will not dare to kill "life not worthy of living." He will realize that we can ultimately not solve the mind-body problem as earthbound humans, but he will also realize that we bear a special responsibility for the souls of the mentally ill who are bound to their frail bodies*". (Wittneben, 1934, p. 154)

Both Friedrich Happich and Dr. Wittneben were well-known and highly respected personalities of their time and held high positions in the educational sectors. It is unlikely that they simply invented this case to support their personal agendas. Moreover, at least another five authors have recorded this case and all the original records are still available. Since the case had been reported so often that it cannot be considered a mere fiction.

In Britain, Andrew Marshal published a number of cases in persons with mental illness including a report (Marshal, 1815, p. 150) of a mad and very violent ex-lieutenant of the Royal Navy, who also suffered from severe memory loss to the extent he did not even remember his own first name. On the day before his death, he suddenly became rational and asked for a clergyman. With him, the patient conversed attentively and expressed his hope that God would have mercy on his soul.

Martensen-Larsen (1926, p. 128) reported the case of a farmer's wife who was seemingly imbecile for eight years. During TL, she remembered the past events as a 'bad dream' and said that she was possessed by an alien that would quit the scene at the approach of its host's death.

> "*Usually, the woman just stared in front of her; and – if at all – uttered only detestable swear words. When visited by the doctor or the priest, she displayed an odd virtuosity in successfully spitting on their shoes. One day, she began to converse rationally with her caretaker and apologized from deep within her heart for her bad behaviour. Broken and remorseful, she affirmed she was not able to behave in any other way since she had been forced to act like this. It was her utmost concern whether she would be forgiven for these and other sins. When the priest arrived, he handed her the requested Lord's Supper. The next morning, she died in peace.*"

In 1861, German naturalist and entomologist Josef Anton Maximilian Perty reported the case of a young man whose intellectual capacities did not exceed those "*of a dog or a monkey*". Yet, four days before he died, he entered a fully lucid state of mind and surprised all around him with his clear thoughts and speech (Perty, 1861, p. 60). In a recent study, seven out of ten caregivers in a nursing home reported that they had observed patients with dementia and confusion becoming lucid a few days before death during the past five years

(Brayne et al., 2008, pp. 195-206). Another recent survey of nursing home staff reported that "*interviewees from all units reported first-hand accounts of previously confused residents suddenly becoming lucid enough in the last days of life to recognize and say farewell to relatives and carers*" (Fenwick et al., 2010, pp. 173-79). Psychiatrists in the USA and Europe had noted that patients with chronic schizophrenia sometimes showed unexpected decrease of their psychosis shortly before death.

Nahm and Greyson (2009, p. 943) recorded the case of a 92 years old woman who had been diagnosed with Alzheimer's disease for nine years and did not recognize close family members, including her son. But just 24 hours before death, she recognized them again. Moreover, she knew how old she was and where she was, which she had not known for many years.

Several members of a palliative care team have observed that patients who had been in a deep coma suddenly became alert enough to coherently say goodbye to loved ones at their bedside before they died (Nahm, 2009, p. 94). Nahm et al. (2011, p. 2) reported the case of a five-year-old boy who had been in a coma for three weeks dying from a malignant brain tumor. Various family members almost constantly surrounded him. Finally, on the advice of their minister, the family told the comatose child that they would miss him but he had their permission to die. Hearing these words, the boy regained consciousness unexpectedly and thanked the family for letting him go, and told them he would be dying soon. He died next day.

Surya (1921, p. 14) recorded an incident of his friend who had a brother living in an asylum for many years because of serious mental derangement. One day he received a telegram from the director of the asylum saying that his brother wanted to speak to him. When he visited his brother, he was astonished to find him in a perfectly normal mental state. On leaving again, the director of the asylum decently informed him that his brother's mental clarity is an almost certain sign of his approaching death. Indeed, the patient died within a short time. Subsequently, an autopsy of the brain was performed, to which Surya's friend was allowed to attend. It revealed that the brain was entirely formed into pus which must have been present for a long time.

Nahm and Greyson (2013, p. 84) described one case concerning George, a young man with severe mental deficits for 14 years. He arrived as a boy of six years in the mental asylum and spoke only in ruptured curses. He did not learn even the easiest activities. Confronted with the slightest obstacles, he bit himself and hit his head painfully against walls and tables. Though he could not even remember the names of his caretakers, he could memorize songs without understanding their meaning. One day he fell sick and brought into the hospital, as he had been many times before. Ringger (1958, p. 218) wrote,

> "*On his way to the hospital, he sang 'though I wandered through the dark valley, I do not fear any harm'. When laid down in a hospital bed,*

he sang all verses of the Christian dying song 'O world, I have to leave you, I pass over my streets to the eternal fatherland'. On the next morning, his first words were 'George goes to heaven today'. After a carer asked him to sing another song, he sang a song about a mill. As he reached the phrase '... and the millwheel didn't turn anymore', he shook hands with everybody present, said 'Good night!' – and died."

How George was able to relate these songs to his current situation by understanding their meaning? How did he develop an appropriate conception of death with all confidence and correct anticipation? How did he converse until the end and then expire with a farewell?

Nahm et al. (2011, p. 2) referred a case originally published in 1822. A 17 years old boy was suffering from constant pain, extreme sadness and loss of memory. He fantasized, blinked continuously, and looked for hours at particular objects. In the hospital he was not able to sit or get out of bed for 18 days. On the morning of the 19th day, he suddenly left his bed and appeared very bright, claiming he was free of all pain and feelings of sickness. The hospital decided to discharge him the next day. But 15 minutes after the attending physician left him, he fell unconscious and died within a few minutes.

Haig (2007, pp. 108-09) reported the case of a young man dying of lung cancer that had spread to his brain. On his deathbed, a brain scan showed little brain tissue left, the metastasized tumors simply did not push aside normal brain tissue but actually destroyed and replaced it. Few days before his death, he lost all ability to speak or move. According to a nurse and his wife, however, an hour before he died, he woke up and said good-bye to his family, speaking with them for about five minutes with full awareness and reason. Then he lost consciousness and died soon.

In one case (Nahm et al., 2011, p. 3), after a failed surgery a 42-year-old man became bedridden, blind in one eye, incontinent, and increasingly confused in his speech and bizarre in his behavior. Soon he appeared to be unable to make sense of his surroundings, and when his family touched him, he would slap as if at an insect. As he came closer to death, he stopped sleeping, talking deliriously through the night. After several weeks of that, suddenly at one night he appeared calm and started speaking coherently, and then slept peacefully. The following morning, he remained coherent and conversed with his wife, discussing his imminent death with her for the first time. However, he stopped speaking later that day, and lay immobile on his bed, not eating or drinking for two more weeks, after which he expired.

In another instance (Nahm et al., 2011, p. 3), a man after suffering his first stroke was almost entirely paralyzed for 11 years without any ability to read or speak. After three years he had learned to recognize certain persons and speech again, but his mental faculties did not develop any further. Seven days before his death he suffered the second stroke. After this stroke, he regained almost full consciousness. He was able to speak in full sentences and understood lengthy passages of speech. Although he was an atheist for all his life, he now asked to see a minister and died in peace.

There are many cases where a dying person talked coherently with loved ones before passing away a short time later. This has been known to occur even when the patient's speech center has been destroyed and some have gained mobility where they previously had none. Schubert (1967, pp. 145, 354) reported three TL cases. The first case was of a deaf-mute man who was educated in a special school for deaf-mute persons, but still never managed to speak understandably because of an "organic defect" (not specified by Schubert). But, surprisingly "in the elation of the last hours", he could speak comprehensively for the first time in his life. The second case involved a previously nonresponsive patient. This old and sick man had lied "debilitated and entirely speechless" in his bed for 28 years. On the last day of his life, his awareness and ability to speak suddenly returned after he had a joyful dream in which the end of his suffering was announced. The third case involves a dying woman who was suffering from nightmares for 20 years. Four weeks before death she recovered, and as death approached others saw in her an extraordinary positive change.

> "*Those who knew her before her madness hardly recognized her in her last state of transformation – so ennobled, enhanced, and elevated were all powers and sensations of her mental nature, so ennobled her articulation. She spoke with distinctness and inner brightness about things, which man learns only rarely to understand superficially in his ordinary state of being. Her story aroused furor. Literate and illiterate, educated and uneducated crowded at this dignified sickbed. All had to confess that even if she would have been taught by the most learned and enlightened men during the time of her illness, her mind could not have been more educated, her knowledge could not have been more substantial and higher than now, as she seemed to awaken from a long and deep confinement of all powers.*" (Schubert, 1967, p. 146)

Famous biologist and philosopher Hans Driesch (1951, p. 40) described the death of his mother suffering from peritonitis. She was unconscious and everyone thought that she would die in her sleep,

> "*[but] something very strange happened. After having uttered only unintelligible words in the past hours, she suddenly awoke and became brightly aware, but at the same time she was very unwilling to find herself in life again! It had been so wonderful to be united with my father, her parents, and friends – all of whom were dead. In this respect one might be reminded of certain reports of Bozzano [Ernesto Bozzano was an Italian parapsychologist who had done extensive research on deathbed*

visions]. The period of being awake did not last for long. Soon, my dear mother fell asleep once more, never to wake up again."

At present there is no satisfactory explanation of TL cases in medical terms. Most often, a medical explanation is not even attempted because it doesn't fit any current fundamental theory of medicine which is viewed in strictly materialistic fashion. Skeptics say that lucidity is due to the sudden boost of the brain one last time before shutting down permanently. But what is the biological need for people to suddenly regain lucidity within hours of dying? A biological system at the face of termination is in decline and it doesn't make sense for one part of that system to have a sudden positive change that creates lucidity, but then goes away forever shortly after.

After careful future studies and collection of further well-documented case reports, these cases hold the potential to contribute to an enhanced understanding of the nature of human consciousness and, perhaps to the development of new forms of therapies.

3.2.1: A paranormal explanation of TL cases

"*People associate death as losing our life force, when actually the opposite is true. We forfeit our body in death, but our eternal life energy unites with the force of a divine oversoul.*"

Michael Duff Newton

TL incidents prove that we are far from understating the mind and its relationship to the brain. As put by the philosopher of mind David Chalmers, despite the extraordinary advances of neuroscience, explaining conscious experience "*poses the most baffling problems in the science of the mind. There is nothing that we know more intimately than conscious experience, but there is nothing that is harder to explain.*" (Chalmers, 1995, p. 200). Human consciousness cannot be fully explained by quantitative mechanistic science, and a paranormal explanation is more logical. If we believe in the existence of an eternal soul, these TL cases become much easier to understand.

The soul is much more than a byproduct of brain chemistry. Hence, it remains basically intact when the brain is affected by disturbance of the mind and/or physical malfunction. As death approaches, the soul prepares to return to its eternal abode, and the transcendental faculties of the soul start releasing. During and after death, the soul is freed from material constraints, regaining its full potential. The only purpose of a soul to reincarnate on Earth is for its spiritual growth. Hence even if the body and mind cease to function effectively, the barriers enable the hidden development of higher aspects of the soul on deeper levels. So, when a person with severe physical or mental difficulties recovers before death, he can display an extraordinary change in his thinking and speech because the veil that separates life and death is lifted and he is more in touch with the next world than with ours.

Therefore, TL cases are always connected with death – no cases have been reported where the patient recovered after this phenomenon, became healthy again and lived farther.

The common belief that people with severe mental illness or mental disability are inferior or even unworthy of living is a big mistake. This belief was particularly promoted by the German Nazis in their heydays (Nahm, 2009, p. 95). A 'hidden inner life and purpose' exist under the mental surface of even the most disabled imbeciles. Before leaving the body, sometimes the soul displays parts of this hidden inner life. This is terminal lucidity which cannot be explained in brain physiological terms. The existence of the non-material component in the Universe is more logical and more scientific than the materialistic science itself.

3.3: End-of-life dreams and visions

"It was striking – (the) dramatic increase in frequency of dreams and visions and particularly in seeing the deceased (as death neared)."

Christopher Kerr

"I have come to realize that for some experiences there is no explanation, just a deep knowing that I have encountered the Divine."

Janis Amatuzio, a practitioner in forensic medicine for 25 years

End-of-life dreams and visions (ELDVs) are intrinsic to the dying process. About 50 to 60% of conscious dying patients experience ELDVs (Mazzarino-Willett, 2010, pp. 127-33). Perhaps this number is even higher, as research has shown that patients, families and clinicians knowingly under-report end-of-life experiences for fear of judgment, ridicule, and embarrassment (Barbato et al., 1999, pp. 30-37). The majority of published literature on ELDVs is based on surveys or interviews with families of the deceased or with clinicians who work with the dying. Out of 668 telepathy cases, 399 were death-related, "*in the sense that the percipient's experience either coincided with or very shortly followed the agent's death*" (Gurney et al., 1886, vol. 2, p. 26). Also, 79 out of 149 veridical dreams "*represented or suggested death*" (Gurney et al., 1886, vol. 1, p. 303). On the basis of statistical considerations, it can be said that the coincidence of such experiences with death could not be the result of chance.

Also, there are many cases where one or more people had experiences that apparently coincided with deaths occurring far away. Sylvia Hart Wright had recorded four such cases. One person saw the bedroom becoming "*dark as if death itself was at the doorstep*". Another "*saw a black cloud obscure the light shining in the kitchen*". One person felt the 'presence' and 'closeness' of a discarnate entity. The fourth person unexpectedly "*broke into sobbing*" without any reason (Wright, 2002, pp. 21-23). In some cases, the deceased loved one asserts that he/she is fine and asks the dreamer not to grieve.

These end-of-life experiences are regarded as "*profoundly subjective and meaningful events, which usually occurred in clear consciousness*" (Fenwick, et al., 2010, p. 177). From various cases, it seems that one primary way the departed soul can reach a living person more easily when the person is in dream state (Newton, 2016b, p. 22) as indicative in the case of Jerry (Botkin, 2014, pp. 187-88).

Jerry was living in the Midwest and his ex-wife was living on the East Coast with their three children. One night, Jerry saw a clear image of his ex-wife in a vivid dream. She looked beautiful, peaceful and happy and she wanted to tell him about something of great concern to her. She told him that he should start playing a more important role in rearing their children and even offered very specific suggestions about each child. Jerry awoke right after his experience baffled by its remarkable clarity. He remembered each detail and for him it was like a real conversation with his ex-wife. Next morning his ex-wife's sister rang him and informed him tearfully that his ex-wife had been killed in a car accident during the night. Immediately the meaning of his experience became clear. Since then, his ex-wife has appeared to him five times in spontaneous after death communications, each time offering further advice about their children. In all instances, the advice turned out to be very helpful. While narrating his story to a psychiatrist, Jerry commented, "*Every time, she did all the talking.... She hasn't changed much. She was always hyperverbal and bossy.... I didn't believe in this stuff before it happened, but now I have no doubt whatsoever.*"

The unconscious mind is more open for telepathic reception from the other world during deep sleep. One reason is, our oversize ego stops functioning once we enter the sleep cycle. Ego is a defence mechanism which acts as a barrier to spiritual receptions. Many people have received forewarning from the discarnate entities about some future event in their dreams. ELDVs rarely occur in wakeful state and typically manifest with clear consciousness. A common element reported by bereaved family members and clinical staff is the personal or spiritual solace provided by the dreams/visions for deathbed patients. Most clinicians confirm that ELDVs are not hallucinations, because hallucinatory experiences frequently elicit anxiety or perplexity, but ELDVs evoke peacefulness, comfort, and a sense of wonder, and help patients accept death more peacefully and agreeably.

Christopher Kerr (chief medical officer at Hospice Buffalo) led a research team from the Palliative Care Institute in Cheektowaga, New York in a long-term study on dreams and visions in the dying. The team wanted to do a thorough study. They conducted more than 450 interviews with 59 dying patients (range of days before death for interviews was zero to 87) at Hospice Buffalo's in-patient facility between January 2011 and July 2012. All participants were terminally ill and had no cognitive impairment. In this study, 52 (88.1%) reported experiencing at least one dream or vision. Almost half of the dreams/visions (45.3%) occurred while asleep, 15.7% occurred while awake, and 39.1% occurred while both asleep and awake. Nearly all ELDV events (99%) were reported by patients to seem or "feel real". Most daily reports included a single ELDV event (81.4%) with two (13.2%), three (4.1%), and four events (1.4%) on other days (Kerr et al., 2014, p. 298). The contents of their dreams varied, as example,

1. **Deceased friends/relatives:** A 51 years old man saw in his dream his deceased parents, grandparents, and old friends who were "*telling me I will be okay*". Many of those people he had not seen for years, and "*I know we are going somewhere but don't know where*" (died after 14 days). Another patient (age 88) dreamt of driving somewhere unknown and was comforted by hearing his mother say, "*It's all right. You're a good boy. I love you*" (died after 28 days). A 96 years old woman had dreams of her mother in a beautiful garden saying, "*Everything will be okay*". She told her family she wanted to sleep as her mother will return (died after 71 days). A 71 years old woman recalled comforting dreams of her deceased mother and a deceased sister who "*practically raised*" her, saying, "*Remember what I taught you*" (died after 38 days). Another patient (age 88) dreamt that he walked to his childhood home and his deceased father walked him back to the inpatient unit and said, "*We're going to stay here*" (died after 56 days).
2. **Other:** An 87 years old patient reported, "*I just knew I was dead in my dream*" but was mad because "*I really wasn't*" (died after two days).
3. **Past meaningful experiences**: A 54 years old woman dreamt of a childhood friend who caused her great pain. The friend, now deceased, appeared as an old man and said, "*Sorry, you're a good person. If you need help, just call my name*" (died after nine days). One army man of 88 years had dreams/visions of war, stating, "*There is nothing but death. Dead soldiers all around me*" (died after eight days). Just six days before his death he dreamt of an unknown soldier who told him, "*They are going to come get you next week*".
4. **Religious figures**: An 81 years old woman reported seeing "*five little angels*" in her room and immediately told a priest she was ready to die and wanted to write a letter to God (died after seven days). A 79 years old woman dreamed about talking to Father Sean, a local Catholic priest who had been murdered during 1960s and reported, "*He [the priest] told me the end of the week. I'm going to die in seven days*" (died after seven days). A 64 years old woman reported a dream in which God held her hand. She stated, "*I am ready to die. I just want to go peacefully*" (died after 13 days).

5. **Departure**: About 38.9% of all dreams included a theme of going or preparing to go somewhere. A 52 years old woman dreamt of her deceased father and brothers, hugging her and "*welcoming her to the dead*". They seemed to be preparing to go somewhere but "*they haven't said where*" (died after 37 days). A 91 years old woman stated she was "begging" to God to take her so that she could see her mother. She reported comforting dreams/visions of going to heaven to see her mother, who sent her back saying, "*It's not your time yet*" (died next day).

This study demonstrated a clear pattern of association of ELDVs of the deceased with greater levels of comfort with approaching death. It also suggests that a person's fear of death often diminishes as a direct result of ELDVs, and what arises is a new insight into mortality. About 60.3% of all the dreams are rated as comforting or extremely comforting. The investigators had made a strange observation while conducting the study. The pre-death dreams were frequently so intense that the dream carried into wakefulness and the dying often experienced them as waking reality. Regardless of whether the experience occurred during waking (19%) or sleep states (46%) or both (35%), they conveyed a sense of realism. Lawrence and Repede (2013, pp. 632-39) had observed that patients who experienced ELDVs had peaceful and calm deaths. As the death approaches, the dreams become more vivid, intense, memorable, and rich with personal meaning that frequently carry great emotional significance for the patient. Another significant observation is that, although very little spoken dialogue within the dreams/visions takes place (between the dying person and deceased relatives), the message is still conveyed without distortion.

Sometimes the discarnate soul of a person who had died recently leaves a message to his close relatives. At New York, an elderly man died of cancer. He died alone because he wanted it that way. Just two hours after his death, his nephew dreamed of his uncle.

> "*I was asleep and 'dreaming'. My uncle took me through a man-sized tunnel that opened out onto a beautiful landscape. A green meadow by a hill, a tree, a lake – All illuminated by a silvery sun. 'I'm here now', he said. And he looked extremely happy.*" (Van Lommel, 2010, p. 42)

The caregivers themselves sometimes receive visit during dreamtime from deceased relatives or even the dying person. Carla Wills-Brandon (2007) described one such caregiver's experience. She had just returned home fully exhausted from caring for her dying mother at the nursing home. She went to bed but,

> "*During the middle of the night, I awoke from a very deep sleep. I had dreamt my mother had come to visit me. In this dream, she was with my*

father who had passed 5 years ago. Both of them looked happy and healthy. My mother blew me a kiss. Then she and my father turned around and walked off, over a hill. When I awoke, tears filled my eyes, but I also felt a sense of peace. My parents look so joyful. I looked at the clock and noted it was 3 a.m., then lay back down and went to sleep. The next morning my brother called to tell me my mother had left us. When I asked him about the time of her death, he replied she had passed at 3 a.m."

These archetypal dreams are different from normal dreams. Everyday dreams have no special meaning, and full of opposition and conflicts, but these archetypal dreams show us universal stages of life without any ambiguity. The themes include; creation, great passage or journey, crossing over water or bridge, reformation of person in a new body, weighing or judging of the soul, return to another realm of existence, and occasionally the cycle of reincarnation and Karma. These dreams are very clear and meaningful, as if a particular dream is specially designed for a particular patient, something like custom-built, and the recipient has no difficulty to come to a final conclusion. Though the contents of the dreams vary from one patient to another, the common metaphor for all dreams is that "life is an eternal journey."

3.4: Deathbed visions

The wish of a dying person to see and to be in the presence of a loved one once again who has died is among the most touching and deep-seated of human desires. This wish is sometimes fulfilled in the form of visions or apparitions of the deceased. These "deathbed visions" are often reported within few hours of a death. In their study Brayne et al. (2006, p. 20) reported, their small sample of nursing home staff stated that these visions "*were neither rare nor surprising*". Typically, the dying person sees a deceased loved one who urges the dying person to follow. Hence deathbed visions are also known as "take-away" visions. Sometimes, the deceased person in the vision has died recently, but the death was not known to the viewer. In some rare cases, when the dying person sees the vision, it is simultaneously seen by relatives and/or medical personnel present there. These discarnate entities are like God's counselors – they bring reassurance to those who are about to crossover. It is their express purpose to collect the dying person and taking him on a smooth journey through physical death.

Michael Barbato (2009, p. 18) a palliative-care physician with deep spiritual interests, claims that the term 'deathbed' is somewhat misleading for, although "*many deathbed visions occur when death is imminent, a significant number happen days, weeks or even months beforehand*". In their important work on deathbed visions, Osis and Haraldsson (1997, p. 64) found that in the majority of cases (62%), visions heralded death within a day of it occurring and 27% died within the hour. Other researchers found that 50% of the deathbed visions occurred within 24 hours of clinical death and 38% experienced visions more than a week prior to death (Jackson, 2012, p. 62). Though most visions are pleasant and welcomed by the dying person, Haraldsson and Osis reported in their 1977 transcultural study that 29% of their subjects, mostly from their Indian sample, responded negatively to the apparitions. Negative emotions were directly related to the nature of the apparition. In the Indian sample, the negativity was most commonly in response to seeing the apparition of 'Yamadoot', the Indian messenger of death, the agents of 'Yamaraja', the lord of the dead (Osis and Haraldsson, 1997, p. 71). The terminal patients appeared to be rational and clear-minded at the time that their deathbed vision occurred as indicated in this case summary.

> "*A sixty-five-year-old American (male) cancer patient seemed to be clear and rational in his thinking, but 'saw the other world'. He looked into the distance, these things would appear to him, seemed real to him. He would look up at the wall, eyes and face would brighten up as if he saw a person – he'd speak of the light and brightness. He saw people who seemed real to him, said 'Hello', and 'there's my mother'. He gestured, stretched out his hands after it was over, closed his eyes and seemed very peaceful. Before the hallucination he was very ill, nauseous; after it he was serene and peaceful.*" (Osis and Haraldsson, 1977a, p. 64).

In the beginning of last century, Myers (1903, two volumes) and Hyslop (1908) recognized some possible paranormal elements in few selected cases of visions of dying patients. Sir William Barrett, a professor of physics of the Royal College of Science (Dublin), was interested in such cases and presented a number of them in a small book entitled 'Death-bed visions' – the first book that tried to understand this paranormal phenomenon in a scientific manner. Barrett was particularly impressed by those visions that seemed to mirror some form of contact between patients who were fully rational and aware of their physical surroundings and their deceased relatives, who, presumably, had passed on to the other world. Often in these cases, the ostensible purpose of the deceased was to take the patient away to a postmortem plane of existence. Barrett gave more importance to those cases in which the apparitions ran contrary to the patient's expectations, for example, apparitions of the persons the patient thought were still living, but who in fact were dead. Here is a typical experience of a patient,

> "*On the night of January 12, 1924, Lady Barrett rushed home from the hospital to tell her husband about a remarkable deathbed vision seen by one of her patients, Dora, who delivered a child safely but died after the delivery. As Dora lay dying, she suddenly looked across the room and broke into a radiant smile. When Lady Barrett asked what she saw, Dora replied, 'Lovely brightness – wonderful beings'. Dora was fully and intensely absorbed in the vision. Then she announced to Barrett that she*

saw her father who was indicating to her how glad he was that she was coming to join him. When the nurses brought Dora her newborn baby for her to see, Dora wondered aloud whether she should stay for the child's sake. But then announced that she couldn't turn her back on the beautiful world she was seeing in the vision. She wanted to go there." (Hogan, 2008, pp. 73-74)

This is an extremely real and attractive vision. The beauty of the 'afterlife' is such that even the mother is willingly giving up her own baby and her life as well, to embrace it. Such complete and total belief in the reality of deathbed vision by the dying is rare. However, the surprise does not end here; what makes the case so strong is what happened next. Dora turned to Lady Barrett with a puzzled expression and said, "*He had Vida with him*" (Hogan, 2008, p. 74). Vida was Dora's sister who had died three weeks before. Her family was afraid that the news of Vida's death would upset Dora's fragile health. Hence, they withheld the news from her. This was the reason of Dora's surprise at seeing her sister with her deceased father.

Another typical experience recorded by M. J. Savage in his book 'Life Beyond Death' (1899) is like this (Hogan, 2008, p. 75) – two young girls, Jennie and Bessie, ages eight and nine were close friends, and both suffered from the usually fatal disease diphtheria at the same time. Jennie died, but Bessie's family did not tell her because she was very ill and they did not want to upset her. Bessie realized that she would die, and on the day of her death, she began to tell brothers and sisters which of her belongings she wanted them to have. She included some items she wanted to give to Jennie, showing she did not realize that Jennie had died. Later in the day a short while before her death,

"*... she began seeing deceased grandparents and others gathered around her bed. And then she turned to her father, with face and voice both expressing the greatest surprise, and exclaimed, 'Why, Papa, why didn't you tell me that Jennie had gone? Why didn't you tell me of it?'*"

Hyslop (1908, pp. 88-89) had also mentioned this incident in his book. The dying child still had no way of knowing her friend had died unless she genuinely saw her in her deathbed visions. Greyson (2010, p. 161) argued;

"*Some experiencers on their deathbeds see, and often express surprise at seeing, a recently deceased person of whose death neither they nor anyone around them had any knowledge, thereby excluding the possibility that the vision was a hallucination related to the experiencer's expectations.*"

Famous spiritual teacher and psychic Sylvia Browne had witnessed one such incident when her friend, Shelly, was on deathbed. Browne and Harrison (2000, p. 55) recorded,

"*Her name was Shelly, and I met her while visiting terminally ill patients in a northern California hospital with my son Christopher. Shelly was clearly in her final hours, in and out of consciousness, and her heartbroken family was gathered around her bed when, with what little strength she had left, she raised her arms as if to be embraced, smiled, and said, 'Ruth, you're here!'*

The family exchanged sad glances with each other, shaking their heads. I quietly asked the gentleman next to me what was going on.

'Ruth is her sister,' he explained. 'She tried to get here, but she's stuck in Colorado.' I turned to Chris and whispered, 'That's what they think.'

Less than an hour after Shelly passed away the family got a call from Colorado telling them that Ruth had died unexpectedly earlier that afternoon. So, Shelly knew what the rest of the family didn't, that Ruth wasn't stuck in Colorado after all, she was safely on The Other Side, waiting to welcome her sister Home."

Elsewhere Sylvia Browne narrated the strange experience of Ted. He was lying alone on his deathbed stricken with tuberculosis, regretting the misguided life he had led. No one was there to comfort or mourn him, but suddenly,

"*... a lovely, kind looking woman slipped silently into the room and stood beside him. She seemed familiar, but he couldn't place her, and he was trying to dismiss her as a delirious vision when she reached out, took his hand, and gently urged him to follow her.*

Amazed that he had the strength, he stood and started with her toward the door of the small, barren room. The wall ahead of him drew back like a huge, brilliantly colored curtain as they approached it, and he saw that she was leading him into an unspeakably beautiful meadow beyond the curtain. He glanced back over his shoulder and was shocked to see his cold, wasted body still lying on the bed.

They were almost to the meadow when he turned to the woman and asked, 'Who are you?' She smiled at him with infinite love and reassuringly squeezed his hand as she replied, 'I died giving birth to you'." (Browne and Harrison, 2000, p. 75)

These visions where patients get a surprise are of three types – first, the deceased person seen had died some time before the vision, although that death was unknown to the experiencer as far as could be ascertained; second, the deceased person seen had died at the time of (or immediately before) the vision, thus not allowing any possibility for the experiencer to have learned of the death. The third type consists of cases in which the deceased person seen was someone whom the experiencer had never known. Such cases are scattered throughout the medical records and literature. Though they are often inadequately documented, there are enough of them to warrant giving them serious attention.

A dying woman suddenly showed joyful surprise and spoke of seeing three of her brothers who had long been dead. She then apparently recognized a fourth brother, who, as everyone knew, was still living in India. One of those bystanders was so shocked by the fourth brother being seen that she "*rushed half-senseless from the room*". Sometime thereafter letters arrived announcing the death of the brother in India, which had occurred prior to his dying sister recognizing him (Cobbe, 1877, p. 378). Communications during those days were quite slow, and it often took weeks, months, or even years to know that a loved one had died.

Psychologist Edmund Gurney and the scholar F. W. H. Myers reported the case of two brothers – three and four years old – who died of scarlet fever on successive days (Gurney and Myers, 1888-89, p. 459). Harry, the younger brother, died on November 2, and David, the older brother, died 14 miles away on November 3. David's family took care to keep him from knowing about Harry's death, and they felt sure that he did not know. Nevertheless, about an hour before he died, David sat up in bed and, pointing, said distinctly, "*There is little Harry calling to me*".

In a similar incident (Gurney and Myers, 1888-89, pp. 459-60) John Alkin Ogle, just one hour before his death saw his brother who had died 16 years earlier, calling him by name. Ogle then called out in surprise, "George Hanley!" – the name of a casual acquaintance in a village 40 miles away – before expiring. His mother, who was visiting from Hanley's village, then told that Hanley had died 10 days earlier, a fact that no one else in the room had known.

Kalmus (1949, p. 30) wrote of her sister Eleanor's last moments, in which she began calling out the names of deceased loved ones whom she was seeing. Just before she died, she also saw a cousin named Ruth and asked, "*What's she doing here?*" Ruth had died unexpectedly the week before, and Eleanor had not been told because of her condition.

Psychiatrist Ian Stevenson, famous for his work on reincarnation, described the deathbed vision of an old woman from USA (Stevenson, 1959, p. 22). When she was terminally ill and no hope to recover, her grandchildren gathered around her bed. Suddenly she seemed much more alert, and the expression on her face changed to one of great pleasure and excitement. She raised herself slightly and said, "*Oh, Will, are you there?*", and fell back dead. No one named Will was present, and the only Will her family could recall was a granduncle who lived in England. Not long after, her family received word from England that her brother Will had died about two days before her death.

Elsewhere Stevenson (1995, pp. 359-61) investigated a case where a young girl of about 14 years saw her dead grandmother at the deathbed of her grandfather on January 4, 1965. Her maternal grandfather was suffering from leukemia and in such an enfeebled condition that family members decided to admit him to a hospital. On the fateful day she stayed home with her grandfather while all others were out at work, or school. She wrote in a letter to Stevenson,

> "*Granddaddy called to me to give him a drink of water. I failed in my attempts to lift him enough to wet his lips. The disease had reduced his once tall, strong stature to [that of] a frail, weak, invalid. I called mom at work to ask for help, but she told me it would have to wait until dad returned from work at noon.*
>
> *Shortly thereafter I heard granddaddy calling out to his wife, Hazel. Grandmom had died nine years prior [October 13, 1956], so I thought he must be losing his mind. I ran down the hall to make another attempt to help him. I was amazed to find him sitting up, smiling with his arms reaching out. The room was filled with a warm, bright light. He spoke to grandmom, who was standing at the foot of his bed. Neither of them acknowledged my presence. She was there but a brief moment, and when granddaddy laid back down, his soul escaped with her. He died with a smile on his face.*" (Stevenson, 1995, p. 360)

The young girl was sure that the figure she saw (and her grandfather seemed to see) was really that of her grandmother. Her grandfather's calling out the name "Hazel" in a very loving sweet voice was part of the evidence, but apart from that she had known her grandmother well as she had been five years old when her grandmother had died. When Stevenson asked her for more details the girl said,

> "*I just recall that it ... a very bright white light and that her face is there and I see her hands. I can see an image of arms but I don't see clothing. She is either in all white or the white light is so bright I can't see the clothing... I can tell that the arms are outreaching but the light is so bright ...*
>
> *I didn't see her feet. But she was above the floor. And if a conversation was held between them it was not to my ears. You could see very beautiful, peaceful expressions on their faces. That is the most vivid part of it for me. That they both were just so at peace at seeing each other.*" (Stevenson, 1995, p. 361)

Osis and Haraldsson (1977a, p. 164) wrote of a man who died in a hospital in Connecticut the day after his sister's death in Ohio. Before expiring, he mentioned seeing his sister Mary in his hospital room, although he did not know that she was dead. Another case documented by the same authors (1977a, pp. 80-81) is that witnessed by a nurse at the deathbed of an intelligent 76-year-old female patient who had suffered a heart attack. She was fully conscious cheerful and happy – no sedation, no hallucinogenic history. Also, she was confident that she would recover and return to her daughter who badly needed her at home. But suddenly she stretched out her arms and smilingly called out to the nurse,

> "*Can't you see Charlie [her dead husband] there with outstretched arms? I'm wondering why I haven't 'gone home' before.... What a beautiful place with all the flowers and music. Don't you hear it? Oh, girls, don't you see Charlie?*".

During this episode, the woman had a feeling of peace and serenity came over her. She remained oriented to her surroundings, and was able to talk with the nurse and the family at her bedside during the vision.

Gallup and Proctor (1982, p. 14) reported the case of a woman who announced to bedside witnesses, "*There's Bill,*" immediately before dying. Bill was her brother, of whose death a week earlier was unknown to her.

Mehra Shrikhande, a paranormal researcher from India, recorded the strange experiences of her friend Aruna Jethwani (Shrikhande, 2009, p. 84). Aruna witnessed twice a strange beam of light passing across the room when someone dies. The second time she saw the light her mother died within few hours. The dying woman (her mother) made an interesting request on her deathbed. When Aruna was sitting near her, she repeatedly asked her to call her brother. Because of her repeated requests, she telephoned her brother and on seeing him, the dying woman heaved a sigh of relief. When Aruna asked her why she had been so desperate to speak to her brother, she replied, "*The souls had come to take me away, but I did not want to go before I spoke to him*". Aruna was surprised, "*Which souls?*" The dying mother replied, "*Those who come to take you away when you die.*"

Since the hospice nurses care for the dying patient and provide the emotional and spiritual support, grief counseling etc., they have more chances to witness their experiences. This is a reliable source for data collection. Nurse Joy Snell (1959) reported her many visions of spirits leaving the body at the moment of death and apparitions around dying persons. She also claims to have experienced music, smells, and lights from other dimensions. The researchers need to study more systematically such gifted people who are particularly open to repeated experiences.

Two hospice nurses, Callanan and Kelley (1993, pp. 93-94) wrote of a 93-year-old Chinese cancer patient who had repeated visions of her deceased husband calling her to join him. One day, she was puzzled to see her sister with her husband, and both were calling her to join them. She told the hospice nurse that her sister was still alive in China, and that she had not seen her for many years. When the hospice nurse later reported this conversation to the woman's daughter, the daughter stated that the patient's sister had in fact died two days earlier of the same kind of cancer, but that the family had decided not to tell the patient to avoid upsetting or frightening her. When her daughter then told the patient about her sister's illness and death, she relaxed, the puzzle solved, and she died at peace shortly thereafter.

In another case, the above two hospice nurses reported (Callanan and Kelley, 1993, pp. 86-87) the case of two childhood friends, Steve and Ralph who died around the same time hundreds of miles apart. After college their friendship ended as they hardly corresponded. At age 27, an automobile accident left Steve paralyzed from the neck down. In the nursing home he eventually succumbed to pneumonia. Weeks later a letter arrived from Ralph's widow in Ohio, saying that Ralph had died recently of cancer. Ralph had not known of Steve's paralysis or death, but in the last few weeks before he died, Ralph began to have visions. Just before he died and just after Steve had died, Ralph said excitedly, "*Oh, look! Here comes Steve! He's come to take me swimming*".

An intensive care nurse Sartori (2008, p. 300) reported the vision of one of her hospitalized patients whose condition was so severe that his family was called to the hospital at 3:00 a.m. to say goodbye to him. At one point, he smiled and appeared to converse with someone no one else could see. He subsequently told his family that his deceased mother and grandmother, and his sister had visited him. His sister had died the previous week, but the family had made a point of not telling him for fear of setting back his recovery. He died a few days later.

A young dying patient reported (Callanan and Kelley, 1993, pp. 94-95) that the previous day she had been drifting in and out of sleep, remembering back to a happy time in her childhood when she and her brother were taken in by a beloved aunt. She woke up with a start when she felt a warm, caring hand on her shoulder, and looking around behind her saw her aunt, who lived in another state, smiling and touching her. She felt her aunt with her off and on all day, and late that night her uncle called to say her aunt had died at the same time that she was first aware of her presence.

Sidgwick (1885, pp. 92-93) had presented a very interesting case. An English Lady had engaged Julia X, a trained public singer and the daughter of a local tradesman, to spend a week to sing with some visiting children. Julia X was very happy. Shortly thereafter Julia married and moved away.

Six or seven years later, the English Lady was on deathbed but appeared "*perfectly composed and in thorough possession of her senses.*" Suddenly she changed the topic and said, "*Do you hear those voices singing?*" No one else present heard them, and she concluded, "*[The voices are] the angels welcoming me to Heaven; but it is strange, there is one voice amongst them I am sure I know, and cannot remember whose voice it is.*" Suddenly she stopped and, pointing up, added, "*Why there she is in the corner of the room; it is Julia X.*" No one else present saw the vision, and the next day, February 13, 1874, the Lady died. On the next day February 14, Julia X's death was announced on the newspaper. Her father later reported (Barrett, 1926,

p. 104), "*On the day she died she began singing in the morning, and sang and sang until she died*". According to her husband, her voice "*had never been so exquisitely beautiful as when she sang just before her death*".

The next case is very strange and heart-touching (Crowther, 2005, pp. 268-70). It had components of both NDE and deathbed vision with future memories. During 1923, Mr. Walter P. Monson was stricken with intense pain from a strangulated hernia and had not much hope to survive. At night his dead daughter appeared to him and foretold the future death-event of his son (dead daughter's brother) that eventually occurred in his lifetime. The daughter came to take away the soul of her brother when he was on his deathbed. The narration is lengthy but worth reading.

> "*At midnight I was fully awake.... Suddenly, a coldness attacked my feet and hands. It moved up... and I felt it reach my heart. There was a slight murmur. I gasped for breath and lapsed into unconsciousness, so far as things mortal.*
>
> *As I turned my head in the direction I intended to go, I saw my little daughter, Elna, who had died twenty-one years before. She was more mature than when she passed away, and was most beautiful to my eyes, so full of life, intelligence, and sweetness. As she came towards me, she raised her right hand and said, 'Go back, Papa, I want Richard first. Then Grandma must come, and then Mama is coming, before you'.*
>
> *The next thing I knew was my body gasping for breath. I felt my heart action start and was conscious of the coldness leaving my body. All numbness left me and the natural warmth returned. I felt the nurse shaking me and heard her say, 'Mr. Monson, you must not let yourself slip like that again'.*
>
> *For five weeks I remained in the hospital, gaining a little strength each day.... Mrs. Monson visited me every day with my son Richard. She was told by the doctor, C. F. Wilcox, that there was no hope for my recovery, and of course, her visits were attended with deep emotion.*
>
> *Many times little Richard, for he was barely six years old, took my hand and pressed it affectionately against his cheek. 'Daddy', he would say anxiously, 'you're not going to die, are you?' I could not control my emotions, try as I would, but I managed to say, 'No, Dick, it is not my turn'.*
>
> *Four weeks after I returned home, my boy, Richard passed away. During the last hours of his life he sat up in bed, opened his big blue eyes and looked toward the door with intense interest. 'Come in, Elna', he said, 'there's only papa and mama here'.*
>
> *I asked him whom he could see and he answered, 'Elna is there. It's funny you can't see her. And there are a whole lot of people with her who want me to come'.*
>
> *He called his mother to the bed and put his arms around her neck. 'Can I go with Elna?' he asked.*

'Yes, my dear', she answered, 'you have suffered enough'.

'Then I'll go. And I'll be happy if you will promise not to cry once for me', he pleaded.

Mrs. Monson gave him the promise he wished and left the room.

'Daddy', he said to me, 'come here. I guess mama has gone out to cry'.

He paused a moment, then turned and looked in the direction of the door and listened intently at something he evidently heard.

'Dear old daddy', he went on at length, 'so you promised at the hospital I could go. Now I know why you cried when I said, 'you are not going to die, are you, daddy?'

Three hours later his eyes closed in eternal sleep.

How he knew that I wept because I had been told by Elna that he was to go first and that my coming back was equivalent to a promise that he might precede me to the great beyond, can only be explained through knowledge given to him from Elna herself, for he knew nothing of the circumstance of what I saw and heard while my spirit was separated from my body at the hospital.

Three weeks after his passing, I visited my mother, Ellen Monson, at Preston, Idaho. Mother had been a sufferer for many years, but her constitution was strong and the doctor had told her that she had every chance of living for ten or fifteen years. She lamented the fact that she was spared, while my boy was taken. She said she had desired to die for twenty-two years. Without realizing what I said, I made her this promise, 'Mother, you haven't twenty-two days to suffer'.

Nineteen days from that time, mother left us. And six years from the time of mother's death, Mrs. Monson passed away".

Johnson (1899, p. 290) reported a case in which Mrs. Hicks, on her deathbed in England, had a vision of her absent son Eddie in Australia. A few days before her death, on October 3, 1887 she looked earnestly at the door to the room and said to her nurse, husband, and daughters, "*There is someone outside, let him in.*" Her daughter assured her there was no one there and opened the door wider. After a pause, Mrs. Hicks said, "*Poor Eddie; oh, he is looking very ill; he has had a fall.*" Her family assured her that the last news they had heard from him was that he was quite well, but she continued from time to time to say, "Poor Eddie!" After she died, her husband received a letter from Australia announcing their son's death. He had fallen from his horse and died at about the same moment of his mother's vision.

Rosen (2006, pp. 9, 10) described the case of a Native American woman in her 30s who was struck by a hit-and-run driver on a highway. She had been left lying on the roadside curb for hours. A stranger stopped his car to help her. When he asked her if there was anything he could do for her, she said, "*If you ever get near the Indian reservation, please tell my mother that I was*

OK. Not only OK, but very happy because I am already with my dad." She died a few minutes after giving her mother's name and address. The stranger was so moved that he drove far out of his way to the Indian reservation, where the mother of the victim told him that her husband had died of a coronary 700 miles away, just one hour before the car accident had occurred.

In another example (Kubler-Ross, 1983, p. 210; Habermas and Moreland, 2004, p. 163), a mother and two young sons had an automobile accident. The mother had died at the scene and one son died in the hospital shortly. The second son, who was also dying in the hospital, had a vision. He told the nurse, "*Everything is all right now. Mommy and Peter are already waiting for me.*" Although in considerable pain, the child was peacefully quiet. Then smiling, he slipped back into a coma and died. The second son had no way to know that his mother and brother had already died.

Brian Weiss (2004, pp. 10, 11) confirmed that many dying patients have long-deceased people to take them to the realm of souls. One dying man described his grandmother waiting patiently in a chair in his hospital room for his time to come. A woman was visited by her child who had died in infancy. Among these dying patients there is calmness and a serenity about dying, and their fear of death decreases. Following is the experience of a man, who witnessed these changes when his wife died on May 23, 1902 (Jackson, 2012, p. 64).

> "*Two figures in white knelt by my wife's side, apparently leaning towards her; other figures hovered about the bed, more or less distinct. Above my wife and connected with a chord proceeding from her forehead, over the left eye, there floated in a horizontal position a nude, white figure, apparently 'her astral body'. At times the suspended figure would lie perfectly quiet, at other times it would shrink in size until it was no larger than perhaps eighteen inches, but always the figure was perfect and distinct ... with her last breath and last gasp, as the soul left the body, the chord was severed suddenly and the astral figure vanished. The clouds and the spirit forms disappeared instantly and strange to say all oppression that weighed upon me was gone.*"

This case of a 91-year-old woman includes both deathbed vision and terminal lucidity. As a result of two strokes she was entirely paralyzed and speechless. A daughter looked after her. One day the daughter saw her mother smiling brightly, although her facial expression had been frozen since her second stroke. The mother turned her head and sat up in bed with no apparent effort. She then raised her arms and exclaimed in a clear, joyous tone the name of her dead husband. Her arms dropped again, and she sank back and died (Noyes, 1952, p. 65). She had experienced a deathbed vision of her deceased husband, but unquestionably regained her ability to use her body and speech during that experience.

All these cases reveal that deathbed visions are relatively common and are an intrinsic part of the dying process. But knowledge and management of these events are inadequate. The reasons, as Barbato et al. (1999, p. 35) proposed are "*maybe a lack of awareness of such phenomena by palliative care workers or a reluctance by them to talk of such events*". Barrett (1926, p. 10) concluded that the type of deathbed vision in which experiencers "*appear to see and recognize some of their relatives of whose decease they were unaware, affords perhaps one of the strongest arguments in favour of survival*". Betty (2006, p. 37) concluded,

> "*Whether dying persons are telling us of the glimpse of the next world or conversing with people we can't see, we should consider ourselves immensely blessed when it happens.*
>
> *If we don't make the mistake of assuming they are 'confused' we are likely to feel some of the excitement they convey, for we are witnessing the momentary merging of two worlds that at all other times remain tightly compartmentalized and mutually inaccessible.*
>
> *That merging is what I mean by the spirituality of death.*"

In most of these cases, the appearance of the vision suggests strong motivation on the part of the deceased individual to communicate a message to the dying person. It is timely that research into these phenomena is treated as a legitimate subject for medical and health research.

****

English parapsychologist Sir William Barrett pointed out that deathbed visions often do not conform to cultural stereotypes, e.g., dying children were surprised to see "angels" without wings (Osis and Haraldsson, 1977b, p. 238). Children are truth-tellers because of their heavenly innocence, hence when they experience such visions, they describe them matter-of-factly. As example, a seven years old girl sat up in bed just before her death from Leukemia and said, "*The angels, they are so beautiful, can't you hear them singing Mommy?*" A boy dying of Leukemia said that God spoke to him and that he asked God to live another year so he could explain his death to his three years old brother. Strangely, the boy lived one more year against all medical predictions. (Komp, 1992). A healthy four years old girl saw in a vivid dream a beautiful golden heaven and that was, "*really, really, real*" with gold angels, diamond and jewels. There she met a holy man who told her mother not to worry because the holy man would take care of her. She then went out to play and was murdered only hours later (Kubler-Ross, 1983). Pre-death visions of the children are devoid of any emotional or religious exaggeration.

James L. Hallenbeck, director of palliative care services with the Veterans Administration Palo Alto Health Care System, estimated that deathbed visions of deceased loved ones occur for at least 25% of deaths (Moore, 2006).

However, the number of people who experience such visions should be significantly higher, because only 10% of dying are conscious shortly before their deaths (Hogan, 2008, p. 66). It means around 50 to 60% dying patients experience deathbed visions. Survival researcher Dianne Arcangel (2005, p. 120) boldly stated, "*I have never sat with a dying patient who was not in the accompaniment of an apparition as their time grew near.* ***No one ever dies alone***".

Deathbed visions have remarkably similar characteristics. Hands passionately reaching upward to some unseen force are witnessed in many deathbed encounters. The otherworldly visitor mostly stands toward a corner of the room. According to Hogan (2008, pp. 66-7), the investigators found the following consistencies,

1. Some dying people reported seeing angels and other religious figures, but most reported seeing familiar deceased people. During the vision, the dying person is actually aware of their real surroundings and conditions, not absorbed in a fantasy.
2. Often the close friends and relatives in the visions tell them that they have come to take them away. The dying person is reassured by the experience, expresses great happiness with the vision, and very willing to go with the deceased greeters.
3. Often the dying person's mood and health change when they have such visions. Sometimes, during these visions, a once depressed or pain-riddled person is elated and relieved of pain.
4. The experience and reactions afterwards are same for all the experiencers, whether they believe in afterlife or not.

Yet, some of the deathbed visions are frightening similar to negative NDEs. It is not clear why one person has a positive experience and another, a distressing one. The nurses say that as some approached death, they were "restless, fighting, fussing, and arguing" with someone unseen. One patient spoke of seeing dark beings moving from the wall to the floor coming to get him. He was said to have been so frightened that he tried to get away by crawling out of the room. One man thought he could avoid death by never lying down. He died on his knees by his bed.

During 1959, inspired by Barrett's work, Karlis Osis (Psychology professor, University of Freiburg) systematically studied deathbed experiences using modern survey methods and statistical evaluations. It was the first of its kind (hence called "pilot survey"). The study confirmed that the terminal patients see apparitions of identified persons – 90% were of relatives of the patient, and out of these, 90% were close relatives, such as, mother, father, spouse, sibling, and offspring. The report was published in the book, 'Deathbed Observations by Physicians and Nurses' during 1961. When the extensive interaction analysis of the data observed from pilot survey was done, it led to the discovery of many patterns that supported the postmortem survival hypothesis.

Later two new cross-cultural surveys were carried out to replicate the pilot survey in both the USA (1961-1964 by Chester F. Carlson) and India (1972-1973 by J. Prasad and P. Dayal). Total 714 terminally ill patients were interviewed – 471 patients confirmed seeing apparitions of human figures, 112 vision cases were primarily of heavenly abodes, landscapes, gardens, buildings. In 174 cases, the patients did not report (or reluctant to report) anything unusual, but their moods became elevated to serenity, peace, elation or religious emotions.

A full description of this lengthy survey process and complete statistics is outside the scope of this book and I will not try to review them here. Few excerpts of the survey result are outlined below.

3.4.1: Characteristics of the apparitions seen by terminal patients

The distinctive feature that terminal patients saw apparitions but others around him did not see anything is by far the most interesting part of this investigation. Percentage may not add up to 100 due to rounding off.

1. Duration of apparition: 48% (one second to five minutes), 17% (six to 15 minutes), 18% (16 to 59 minutes), 13% (one hour to one day), 4% (longer than one day)
2. Interval between apparition and death: 12% (zero to 10 minutes), 15% (11 to 59 minutes), 20% (one to six hours), 15% (seven to 24 hours), 38% (longer)
3. Identity of apparition: 18% (living), 47% (dead), religious figure (30%), combination of above (5%)
4. Sex of apparition: 57% (male), 43% (female)
5. Purpose of apparition: 14% (Taken for visitor), 6% (to comfort patient), 47% (to take patient away with consent), 18% (to take patient away without consent), 1% (to send patient back), 6% (threatening), 9% (reliving memories). The take-away purpose (with or without consent) is dominant in all three surveys – 76% (pilot), 69% (USA), 79% (India)
6. Emotional reactions: 30% (no effect or relaxation), 20% (serenity), 21% (elation), 29% (negative), 27% (positive, nonreligious), 14% (positive, religious). Percentage does not add up to 100 because one patient can show more than one emotional reaction.

The identity of the apparitions experienced within this group varied greatly. American patients for the most part saw deceased persons while Indian patients predominantly saw religious figures. Female figures were extremely rare for the Indian patients. It means, while the frequency of survival-related apparitions is same in both samples, the characteristics of these apparitions are strongly molded by cultural forces.

These apparitions are self-conscious and aware of the patient's dying condition. If the main purpose is to make the patient's final journey comfortable, then certainly those deceased will come with whom the terminally ill patient is most comfortable with. The identity of the entities varies, as example,

1. Identity of the apparition (secular): 23% (mother), 9% (father), 18% (spouse), 13% (sibling), 13% (offspring), 4% (other relatives, previous generation), 4% (other relatives, same generation), 1% (other relatives, next generation), 7% (unidentified relatives), 9% (friends, acquaintances), 0% (unidentified persons).
2. Identity of the apparition (religious): 28% (God or Jesus), 12% (Hindu deities: Shiva, Rama, Krishna), 8% (female deities: Mary, Kali, Durga), 17% (God of death and messengers), 8% (saints and gurus), 24% (Angels, Devi, etc.), 3% (demons and devils), 0% (unidentified religious figures).

The percentage figures do not sum up to 100 because in many cases the patient saw several apparitions together. The religious figures were usually identified according to the patient's faith, e.g., no Hindu reported seeing Jesus; no Christian a Hindu deity. Some patients who did not believe life after death also saw apparitions. So, belief in an afterlife has no significant influence on the frequency of the kind of apparition seen, though it did seem to influence the patient's communication with it.

Majority of the patients who saw apparitions with a "take-away" purpose eagerly consented "to go" with them, although some did not consent. In extreme cases, patients reacted with fright and screamed for help. Terminal patients usually suffer from pain and other kinds of discomfort; consequently, their moods are rather depressed. The elation and serenity that the apparitions aroused in most of the patients (about 70%) contrasted sharply against the gloom of dying. During encountering the apparition, 43% the patients (total number 457) were in a normal state of consciousness. In 29% cases, awareness was mildly impaired, and only 17% were in a severely impaired state that little or no communication was possible. For the rest, clarity fluctuate and could not be accurately determined.

Today there is a growing recognition that these experiences hold much intrinsic value, and these phenomena are psychologically and existentially significant. There is also a growing body of literature that describes the prevalence and therapeutic value of these experiences as they signify patients' attempt to find meaning, to process or reconcile traumatic events and therefore come to terms with their death.

3.5: Shared deathbed visions

Sometimes people in the same room with a dying person see the same vision or experience some kind of event at the moment of the patient's passing. This is called shared deathbed visions. These visions rule out hallucinations since multiple witnesses would not have identical hallucinations.

The Society of Physical Research had documented many cases. In one well-documented case, a dying woman Harriet Pearson and her three relatives who were caring for her had seen the same apparition. When a young boy was dying, two witnesses independently saw his recently deceased mother at his bedside (Hogan, 2008, p. 76). Linn et al. (2016, pp. 84-85) narrated the experience of a woman who had shared her husband's life review. Her husband was dying of cancer. She was beside him the whole time in the hospital and was holding onto him when he died. The review was vivid, and it contained images and events that she had previously been unaware of.

> *"When he died, he went right through my body. It felt like an electric sensation, like when you get your finger in the electrical socket, only much more gentle.*
>
> *Anyway, when that happened our whole life sprang up around us and just kind of swallowed up the hospital room and everything in it in an instant. There was light all around: a bright, white light...*
>
> *Everything we ever did was there in that light. Plus, I saw things about Johnny... I saw him doing things before we were married. You might think that some of it might be embarrassing or personal, and it was. But there was no need for privacy, as strange as that might seem. These were things that Johnny did before we were married. Still, I saw him with girls when he was very young. Later I searched for them in his high school yearbook and was able to find them, just based on what I saw during the life review during his death.*
>
> *In the middle of this life review, I saw myself there holding onto his dead body, which didn't make me feel bad because he was also completely alive, right beside me, viewing our life together.*
>
> *By the way, the life review was like a 'wraparound'. I don't know how else to describe it. It was a wraparound scene of everything Johnny and I experienced together or apart. There is no way I could even put it into words other than to say that all of this was in a flash, right there at the bedside where my husband died.*
>
> *Then, right in the middle of this review, the child that we lost to a miscarriage when I was still a teenager stepped forth and embraced us. She was not a figure of a person exactly as you would see a human*

being, but more the outline or sweet, loving presence of a little girl. The upshot of her being there any issues we ever had regarding her loss were made whole and resolved.

One of the funny things about this wraparound view of our life was that we had gone to Atlanta in the seventh grade, to the state capital, where there was a diorama. So at one point we were watching this wraparound and watching ourselves in another wraparound – a diorama – where we stood side-by-side as kids. I burst out laughing and Johnny laughed too, right there beside me.

Another thing that was strange about this wraparound was that in certain parts of it were panels or dividers that kept us from seeing all of it I don't have the words to this, but the screens or panels kept particular parts of both of our lives invisible. I don't know what was behind them ...".

A woman in her seventies described her experience of nursing to her dying mother. As her mother died, the light in the room suddenly became much brighter and more intense, and she felt a rocking motion through her whole body. She then found herself seeing the room from a different angle, from above and to the left side of the bed instead of from the right side. Moody (2012, pp. 234-36) wrote,

"*This rocking forward motion was very comfortable...*

I don't know whether I was out of my body or not because all the other things that were going on held my attention. I was just glued to scenes from my mother's life that were flashing throughout the room or around the bed. I cannot even tell whether the room was there any more or if it was, there was a whole section of it I hadn't noticed before. I would compare it to the surprise you would have if you had lived in the same house for many years, but one day you opened up at it and found a big secret compartment you didn't know about. This thing seemed so strange and yet perfectly natural at the same time.

The scenes that were flashing around in midair contained things that had happened to my mother, some of which I remembered and others that I didn't. I could see her looking at the scenes too, and she sure recognized all of them, as I could tell by her expression as she watched. This all happened at once so there is no way of telling if that matches the situation.

The scenes of my mother's life reminded me of old-fashioned flashbulbs going off. When they did, I saw scenes of her life like in one of the 3-D movies of the 1950s.

By the time the flashes of her life were going on, she was out of her body. I saw my father, who passed seven years before, standing there where the head of the bed would have been. By this point the bed was kind of irrelevant and my father was coaching my mother out of the body. I looked right into his face and a recognition of love passed between us, but he went right back to focusing on my mother. He looked like a young man, although he was 79 when he died. There was a glow about or all through him – very vibrant. He was full of life.

One of his favorite expressions was 'Look alive!' and he sure did look alive when he was coaching my mother out of her body. A part of her that was transparent just stood right up, going through her body, and she and my father glided off into the light and disappeared.

The room sort of rocked again, or my body did, but this time backward in the opposite direction and then everything went back to normal.

I felt great tenderness from my mother and father. This entire event overflowed with love and kindness. Since that day I wonder: ***Is the world we live in just a figment of our imagination?***"

Carla Wills-Brandon (2007) describes her husband's experience of a shared deathbed vision before the death of his father whom they called 'Da'. Her husband told her the story the morning after he sat up all night with his father in the hospital.

"*Tonight while snoozing in the chair in his room, I had a wonderful dream about Da. In this dream he said to me he was going soon, but that he would always watch over us. Upon awakening, I looked over at Da as he slept, and noticed he was very much at ease. Suddenly, I saw something rise from his body. It was absolutely beautiful. A whirl of pastel color, vibrant in not only appearance but also movement, was leaving his chest area. It was so comforting.*"

The following week Da gently passed away in her husband's arms.

Countless hospice workers have seen a wisp of "something" leaves the body at the moment of death. Visions of vapors, mists, and shapes around the dying person are very common – more common than we think. Crookall (1967, pp. 37-44) had mentioned many such cases. The famous medium Eileen Garrett wrote that while attending the death of a friend, "*I perceived two small clouds emitted from his body – one from the right side of the torso, at the level of the spleen, the other from the top of his head.*" (Garrett, 1943, p. 151). Generally, these visions are seen by a single individual, but they can be collectively perceived. Dorothy Monk (1922, p. 182) and other family members saw a strange color around her dying mother.

"*I and three sisters all at once noticed a pale blue mauve haze all over her as she lay. We watched it and very gradually it deepened in colour until it became a deep purple, so thick that it almost blotted out her features from view, and spread all in the fold of the bed clothes like a purple fog. Once or twice she feebly moved her arms and the colour travelled with them.*"

Hospice workers sometimes describe a radiant white light which envelops the dying person and may spread through the room involving the caregivers as well. This light is full of love (Fenwick, 2004). Other synchronistic events e.g. clocks stopping, bell ringing, changes in pet behavior are also reported Some caregivers report of a sense of being "pulled" shortly after death. Sometimes the room temperature changes quickly at the time of death (Sondermann and Janzen, 2011, p. 6). The following experience (Van Lommel, 2010) includes components of both shared deathbed vision and NDE. It's a very strange experience.

> "*I was in a relationship with Anne when she suddenly died in a serious traffic accident. Her son, who'd just turned seven, sustained severe head trauma... it took him about five days to make the transition. He was the eldest grandson... Some sixty relatives had gathered around his hospital bed, and since I'd only been his mother's boyfriend, I was standing somewhere at the back by the window. The moment he died, when his EEG flatlined, I 'saw' that his mother came to collect him. You must bear in mind that she'd died five days earlier. There was this incredibly beautiful reunion. And at one point they reached out for me and included me in their embrace. This was an indescribable, ecstatic reunion. Part of me left my body and accompanied them to the light. ... I was fully conscious and with Anne and her son as they went to the light, just as I was fully conscious and in the room where all the relatives were incredibly sad. And I joined them, we were heading toward the light, but at a certain point it was clear that I had to return, so I fell back. I simply fell back into my body.*
>
> *It was such an overwhelming experience, I glowed with happiness, but then I suddenly realized that I had a big smile on my face amid all these people who'd just lost a child dear to them. I quickly covered my face with my hands because I didn't want to be disrespectful toward all these mourning and crying people in the room. And I never said a word about the experience. Talking about it seemed completely inappropriate at the time, and besides I didn't have the words to describe what had happened to me. I used to think that I knew what was what. But my worldview underwent a radical transformation.*"

Many people have experienced physical phenomena that coincided with death with someone important to them at a distant place. The most commonly reported phenomena are clock stopping/starting and objects falling without any outside interference. It appears that before leaving the physical world, the discarnate entity wants to announce his death to his loved ones by this way. Rhine (1968, pp. 245-46) recorded this case, where Frank, a young man was accidently shot and killed.

> "*When the rest of us had chicken pox, my brother Frank was sent down to my grandmother's... about forty miles [away] where we lived. Two*

days after Frank left, Mom and our neighbor were having their morning coffee and talking... All of a sudden, this cut-glass dish that Frank had given Mother popped and broke right in two. It was just sitting on the sideboard. Mother screamed and said, 'My God! Frank has been killed'. Everyone tried to quite Mother, but she said she just knew."

A dying person was given water with a spoon from a glass. The glass was placed on a table. The moment he died, three persons present in the room heard tinkling sounds. One person narrated, "*It came from the glass in which there was only a little water, and before our eyes, the glass split in two parts, a rim about a half inch from the top breaking from the rest of the glass*" (Whitmer, 1924, p. 575). We should study these strange coincidences in more details.

Physical phenomena may continue after death with or without manifestations of apparitions (Piccinini and Rinaldi, 1990, pp. 110-11). Different physical phenomena had been reported at distant places coinciding the death of a person. Those who experience these phenomena are always meaningful to the dead person. As example (Flammarion, 1922, pp. 307, 139-40), on the death of an old woman on February 9, 1913, a clock stopped near her at quarter to two. Around the same time, her son living in USA saw his mother's apparition by his bed. In another case, at three different locations people have reported such phenomena. Someone was dying in Spain, sounds like clock were heard at Buenos Aires, a silhouette was seen on a wall in a city in the interior of Argentina, and dogs were heard howling in Spain.

Sometimes strange music and/or sound of singing ("*sweet music without distinguishable words*" – Rogo, 1972, p. 108) is heard around the dying person which could not be attributed to any earthly source. A child, by the name Lilly, died on Tuesday evening. Several family members heard a music that started on previous Saturday and continued till her death. The music was heard in all parts of the house, but strangely the dying child did not hear it. Her father described the music as (Gurney et al., 1886, vol. 2, p. 222) "*the soft, wild notes of an Aeolian harp, which rose and fall distinctively, until the room was full of sound*".

Statistical analysis shows that when many people are present at the time an apparition is perceived, in two-thirds of such cases two or more persons perceive it (Stevenson, 1982, p. 349). It means, the apparition has an objective reality. Collective apparitions appear as though the phantasm were actually physically present and reflecting light into the eyes of the witnesses.

The new generation researchers should study these cases systematically and scientifically so that our knowledge of these strange phenomena increases. We should not limit our research to mere documentation of the occurrences. Rather we should in some way find out the mode in which some unknown energy is operating to produce the main result. We should also explore the interrelationship of features, their clustering, or their relationship to other variables.

3.6: Skeptic's views

"The man who denies spiritualism today is not entitled to be called a skeptic, he is simply ignorant."

Thomas Jay Hudson, author of 'The Law of Psychic Phenomena'

Skeptics have a ready, stand by argument – deathbed visions are medical or psychological hallucinations. But leading researchers on this subject, such as, Ernesto Bozzano, William F. Barrett, Douglas Scott Rogo, Moody, Osis and Haraldsson, Ring, Robert Crookall and many others have studied thousands of such reports, and after examining the patients carefully they have confirmed survival hypothesis. Patients who received drugs, e.g. Morphine and Demerol do not have greater frequency of visions than other patients. Also, brain disturbances caused by disease, injury or uremic poisoning decreased the vision phenomenon or did not affect it at all. Osis and Haraldsson (Hogan, 2008, p. 71) had a thorough search of past medical record of the dying patients to find any hallucinations. No support was found for this thesis.

Various psychological factors, such as stress, expectations of dying or recovering, a desire to see someone they loved did not affect how often people had deathbed visions. There is no evidence to suggest that psychological factors encouraging hallucinations also encouraged afterlife visions. Patients didn't automatically see in their visions people they specifically wanted to see. People who didn't expect to die also saw deathbed visions.

Some skeptics bring the issue of cultural factors, i.e., established beliefs, values, traditions, ethics etc., induce in the dying patient some bizarre hallucinations. Agreed that the culture of an individual often decides the way he behaves but deathbed visions were not just wishful projections of the patient Ernesto Bozzano believed that the discarnate agency explanation had stood the test of time, "*far from showing weakness or defeat... it appears like a lighthouse pointing to the port for sailors who are lost in the ocean of life*". (Bozzano, 1910, p. 308). Hogan (2008, p. 87) put forward his argument,

1. The dying person often saw something that was "*unexpected, untaught and a complete surprise to them*".
2. Deathbed visions often do not conform to religious beliefs about the afterlife. As example, among Christian American patients, there were many reports of visions of heaven. But visions of hell and devils were almost totally absent. Christian ideas of 'judgment', 'salvation' and 'redemption' were not mirrored in their visions. In India, basic Hindu afterlife beliefs like reincarnation and dissolution in Brahma were occasionally mentioned in their visions.

3. Eleven core phenomena (from the research of Karlis Osis and Erlendur Haraldsson) suggestive of an afterlife were found to be common to both Indian and American deathbed visions. Similarities outweighed the differences by a large margin. It indicates a universal human experience rather than a culturally-produced experience.

Hence, deathbed phenomena can only be explained as genuine visions of deceased loved ones helping the dying person through the transition process.

3.7: Conclusion

End-of-life dreams are real. The departed souls use dream to reach the dying because during sleep state the unconscious mind is more open for reception. The souls carefully select the dream sequences so that the dreams they project to the dying people are very simple. Sometimes the dying gets much useful guidance from apparently unknown persons in their dreams. These unknown people might be our guides, teaching souls or soulmates who come as messengers to assist us (Newton, 2016b, p. 24). As example, one mother was walking alone (in her dream) in the fields around the house. Sylvia, her recently died daughter wanted to say a last goodbye to her mother before leaving for the spirit world. Hence, she entered her mother's dream from the other end of the field by matching her energy pattern to her mother's thoughts. Sylvia projected an image of herself as she was the last time, she saw her. Then she came slowly across the field to let her get used to her presence. She waved and smiled and then came to her (Newton, 2016b, p. 27). Sometimes existing dreams are altered by a skillful discarnate entity – "*spirits place themselves as actors between the lines of an unfolding play so the dreamer is not aware of script tampering with the sequences*". Sylvia was doing this with her mother. A discarnate entity can also organize a dream to contact a living person.

> "*[the entity] must create and fully implant a new dream from scratch and weave the tapestry of these images into a meaningful presentation to suit their purpose. Creating or altering scenes in the mind of a dreamer is intended to convey a message. I see as this an act of service and love. If the dream implantation is not performed skillfully to make the dream meaningful, the sleeper moves on and wakes up in the morning remembering only disjointed fragments or nothing at all about the dream.*" (Newton, 2016b, p. 28)

Therefore, dream is a very effective method for information transfer from spirit world to our Earth. When a dying person informs us that the dead people had contacted him through dreams, we should not discredit them because these dreams light a lamp in the darkness of despair and give them solace. Rather we should try to find a meaning of their dreams. If the discarnate entities have difficulty reaching the mind of a troubled adult, they might resort to using children as conduits for their messages. Children are more receptive to spirits because they do not doubt or resist the supernatural. But these are rare incidences.

Many deathbed vision cases are explainable only within the framework of the survival theory. Ernesto Bozzano had done one of the most important historical studies on deathbed visions (Bozzano, 1923). Morselli (1908, p. xvi.) referred to Bozzano as "*unquestionably the most learned and authoritative of the connoisseurs of psychic studies in Italy*". French jurist and physician Joseph Maxwell considered Bozzano's studies to be "*among the most important that have been devoted to the examination of metapsychical phenomena. They are distinguished by a wide erudition, by fair critiques, by a deep knowledge of the subject*" (Maxwell, 1920, p. v). Bozzano published many books and articles, revising them in later years, and updating them with new cases.

After carefully studying numerous case examples of each, Bozzano had classified deathbed visions into six categories of phenomena – cases in which the apparitions of the deceased appear solely to the dying person and relate to persons he knew were dead (24 cases); cases in which the apparitions of the deceased are still perceived only by the dying person, but refer to persons whom he did not know were dead (six cases); cases in which other people gathered about the dying person perceive the same phantoms that he does (eight cases); cases of apparitions at the deathbed coinciding with predictions or similar confirmations obtained by means of mediums (seven cases); cases in which the intimates of the dying person are the only ones to see the phantoms of the dead (nine cases), and examples of apparitions of the dead, appearing a short time after a death and observed in the same house where the corpse lies (one case).

For many years medical culture has attempted to find ways to explain deathbed phenomena. After the first systematic study by Barrett in 1926, and then the 1961 study by Karlis Osis, further studies confirm that DBP are experienced in very similar ways around the world. Additional evidence of postmortem survival comes from the "mediums," people who claim to communicate with deceased spirits on behalf of bereaved clients (chapter 6).

Deathbed visions are clear and rational, contain reasonable, uplifting messages, and are always calm though some visions are scary similar to negative NDEs. From various case reports, we can find few reasons behind these scary visions.

1. Karmic issues: A disturbed spirit, or ghost may make contact with the dying person because of some unresolved karmic issues they had on Earth on any of the past lives.

2. Misunderstanding: Occasionally, a friendly spirit has been trying to reach the person on deathbed. But due to severe death anxiety the person has misinterpreted the intent of this spirit who only wished to bring comfort and love.
3. Miscommunication: Discarnate spirits have no trouble with telepathy between themselves, but this does not mean all souls are adept communicators with living persons.

In a classic trilogy of books Camille Flammarion grouped a variety of phenomena according to the time at which they took place – whether before, during and after death. In these three books, he described what appeared to be similar features among the three groups of cases. In Flammarion's (1922, p. 83) view, phenomena happening around death will gradually bring us to a knowledge of what exists after death.

In the beginning of present century, systematic investigations have increased because of the recent western culture shift and interest in the paranormal. A 2006 study in a hospice in Camden, England found that deathbed visions and shared deathbed visions occur relatively frequently. All staff felt that these visions are intrinsic part of the dying process, and about 89% caregivers have witnessed patients experiencing a vision (Sondermann and Janzen, 2011, p. 12). Though the medical training teaches them to ignore this phenomenon we all know that the court of law treats a dying person's last words as the truth. Hence, we still require well-planned and rigorous study protocols in order for study outcomes to be accepted by mainstream medical science.

CHAPTER 4

Ghosts, apparitions and after-death contacts

"If you are lonely, dim all the lights and put on a horror movie. You won't feel like you are lonely anymore."

Anonymous

"Accounts of haunting phenomena, no matter how terrifying they may be, provide evidence that existence continues for the spirit on more than one dimension, and that human beings are multidimensional entities that consist of mind, body, and soul."

Brad Steiger

Ghosts and apparitions (a form of a person not physically present) is consistent with the argument that we all survive physical death. The idea of "ghosts" had haunted the human mind from time immemorial and existed in practically all stages of culture. For instance, the Roman author Pliny the Younger (AD 61 – 115) had given an account of an encounter that the philosopher Athenodorus Cananites had with the ghost of an untidy old man in chains in a haunted house in Athens, Greece. According to a Latin translation of this account, Athenodorus waited at the haunted home with a pen and a paper to write down his experiences. The first part of the night passed silently, but then suddenly he heard a clanking of iron and rattling of chains. Athenodorus neither lifted up his eyes nor laid down his pen, but in order to keep calm tried to pass off the sounds to himself as something else, but,

"The noise increased and advanced nearer, till it seemed at the door, and at last in the chamber. He looked up, saw, and recognized the ghost

exactly as it had been described to him: it stood before him, beckoning with the finger, like a person who calls another. Athenodorus in reply made a sign with his hand that it should wait a little, and threw his eyes again upon his papers; the ghost then rattled its chains over the head of the philosopher, who looked up upon this, and seeing it beckon as before, immediately rose, and, light in hand, followed it. The ghost slowly stalked along, as if encumbered with its chains, and, turning into the area of the house, suddenly vanished." (Eliot, 1909, p. 328)

Apparitional beliefs and experiences are persistent and widespread phenomena. As I will show throughout this chapter, if there was an honest investigation, the outcome would prove that the majority of stories are genuine and such cases are not within the realm of physics rather than psychical research. In this scientific age of discovery, we know the presence of ghosts and apparitions by way of case studies and in controlled laboratory settings. All the evidence suggests survival hypothesis.

Much contrary to popular belief, however, many of the ghostly encounters are not frightening. We can also detect the presence of ghosts and apparitions through channeling and mediumship.

According to a Gallup survey conducted in June of 2005, about 32% believe in the existence of ghosts and spirits of dead people (Lyons, 2005). A poll of 808 Americans by CBS News in October of 2005 indicated that 22% have seen or felt the presence of a ghost (Alfano, 2005). Amongst British, a survey conducted in February 1998 showed that 40% believed in ghosts, while 37% had seen or felt one (MORI, 1998). W. D. Rees, a British physician, found that of a sample of widows in Wales, 47% had experiences – often repeatedly over a number of years – that convinced them that their dead spouses had been in contact with them (Rees, 1971, pp. 37-41). An earlier British experiment by Marris (1958) had found a figure of 50%. Dunn and Smith (1977, pp. 121-22) repeated this study in Canada, and found that 50% widows and widowers had contact experiences. Most percipients confirm that they were helped by their contact experiences (Rees, 1971, p. 40). A study conducted by Douglas Davies shows that about 35% of the people contacted for his survey of 1,603 people in four regions of the UK "*had gained some such sense of the presence of the dead*" (Davies, 1997, p. 154; Davies and Shaw, 1995, p. 96). Davies also notes that sensing the presence of a parent is the most common type of experience (15.4%); next is grandparents (10.3%), then spouses (5.0%), siblings (2.2%), children (1.1%), other kin (3.6%) and 1.7% feels the presence of friends (Bennett and Bennett, 2000, p. 140). Bereavement researchers agree that these sort of experiences are commonplace.

Generally, the apparitions do not appear at random, but only to those who dwell on their memories – "*Memory itself attracts ghosts*" (Dernbach, 2005, p. 101). Apparitions can be visual (69%), auditory (28%), tactile (13%), olfactory (4%) or only with a vivid sense of presence (10%). The percentage figure does not round up because of combined modality.

> "*This happened three years ago. I sat in a chair in my room and was reading. Then I looked up and saw my deceased grandmother standing in front of me, as fully alive. I told my mother about this the following day. She said, 'That is nice, it was her birthday'. I had not remembered it.*" (Haraldsson, 2012, p. 6)

> "*I had recently started working in a factory when one day I see a man walking at the further end of the machine at which I was working. He walks up to a wall near which the machine was placed and back. I went to see who the man was but found no one. When I told my co-workers about this experience and described the man to them, they were sure that this had been a ghost which some others had also seen. It was the former director of the company who had committed suicide.*" (Haraldsson, 2009, pp. 95-96)

> "*I brought my wife to the hospital in February 1960. She had been sick for several weeks. I visited her that same evening again and she was dressed in a blue nightgown. I had expected to see her again the following day but she died in the night. The next day my daughter-in-law comes to select a gown for her burial. A day later I come home late and take out the psalm book to select the psalms to be sung at her funeral. Then the astounding thing happened. My wife suddenly stands in front of me, bathed in white light of an oval form. I see her very distinctly and vividly as she holds both hands around the collar of her nightgown, not that one I saw her in when I saw her the last time, but a pink fancy gown she used only rarely. She held the collar together with both her hands under her cheek. I became startled and then she disappears. I had not known what gown my daughter-in-law had selected for her but discovered later that it was exactly this dress.*" (Haraldsson, 2009, p. 96)

In most of the visual cases (about 89%), the apparition was seen through open eyes. In about 7% cases, the observer saw the deceased person as if by the mind's eye, i.e., as a vivid image in the mind. Auditory cases were the second most common. Voices alone without other modalities are rare, but here are two such cases, both reported by fishermen who were being warned of impending danger.

> "*This happened when I was a teenager. I was alone fishing on a small boat. Suddenly I heard a voice that says I should leave the fishing line and row ashore. I heard this quite clearly. It was said to me in a commanding tone. I do as ordered, I do not know why, but I found it so odd. Just as I am about to arrive at the harbour, suddenly there sweeps over a violent storm. I barely managed to dock. I did not recognize the*

> *voice, but later I connected it with my brother who had recently drowned.*" (Haraldsson, 2009, p. 97)

> "*I was on a fishing boat. We were out in the bay in the storm and rain and had just laid our nets and should be wakened at six the following morning. I slept in the narrow cabin with the others and one man was on duty in the deckhouse. About five in the morning I and some others wake up as someone calls 'rise'. I went up to the cabin door and called to the man in the deckhouse and asked if he had been calling. No, he said, it was not time for that. I went back to my bunk, and was not yet asleep when again there was a shout, 'rise, are you not going to get out of bed?' It was as if someone was calling loudly from the cabin door some two meters away. Everyone woke up and jumped out of bed. That surprised me; generally the crew was not that quick. I told the machinist to run aft and start the donkey engine to haul in the nets. As the machinist went down to the engine room he saw the dynamo catching fire. He barely managed to disconnect from the electricity so that it came to a halt. I am convinced if he had gone later, we would have caught fire and there would have been a fatal explosion in the engine room. I did not recognize the voice. It called in a typical seaman fashion. I had reasons to suspect that it was my deceased grandfather*". (Haraldsson, 2009, pp. 97-98)

Auditory cases (about 30%), where noises from various human activities that had been typical for a particular deceased person, are fairly common. A widow reported that just before an operation she was nervous. Suddenly she heard clearly the flute her husband had always played at home. It was as if he was standing at her bedside. This incident left her free from fear. Another illustrative example is this specific one.

> "*Shortly after our father died I came to his house with my brother. We knew that there was nobody in the house and then we heard the old man at his desk. He was walking around, opened the door and closed it again. Both of us stopped and listened when we entered and then I remarked, 'I guess there is no doubt who is up there'. 'No there is no doubt about it,' my brother replied. Both of us went upstairs, no one was there. We had heard this so clearly. He was 85 years when he died, walked slowly you know, had the typical old man's way of walking.*" (Cook and Delanoy, 1994, p. 3)

About 13 % cases are tactile, i.e., it involves a touch sensation. Three quarters of these tactile cases involve two or more modalities. This case combines vision, hearing, and touch.

> "*The night after my husband died I could not sleep, was at home in my bed and very lonely. Suddenly I sensed him standing by my bed. He seemed to be covered in something like mist. I saw him and felt his hand as he*

> *stroked my head and he recited part of a well-known poem that was about how good it was to rest and then wake up one day surrounded by eternal joy. I felt quite differently after this*". (Cattoi et al., 2015, p. 120)

The olfactory cases were the fewest, only 4%. Some olfactory cases have very interesting features.

> "*I was alone in the house. My husband was out working. Suddenly I see that a man enters through the front door and goes to the kitchen. This happened suddenly and was over. I then felt a strong smell of liquor. I never use alcohol. Well, then my husband comes home, and he says, 'Who has been here?' Nobody, I tell him. 'Oh, there is such a strong smell of liquor'. 'Yes', I say, 'but nobody has been here'.... The next day my husband comes home for supper and says, 'No wonder there was a liquor smell here yesterday.... Erlingur from whom we bought the house was missing yesterday.... He had been quite drunk and it was feared that he had fallen into the harbour and drowned'. Two weeks later his body was found floating in the harbour. When this incident occurred, we had no idea about what had happened.*" (Haraldsson, 2009, pp. 99-100)

In a study of 68 widows and widowers in Boston, four respondents have seen their husbands sitting in their favorite armchairs or going into another room. Many felt the presence in connection with experiences they had shared, such as getting breakfast or watching TV. The researchers concluded, "*The greater part of our sample seemed to maintain some sense of their husband's presence during the first two months of their bereavement*" (Glick et al., 1974, pp. 136-37). Many people thought that they were "going crazy" and kept quiet to avoid ridicule.

The next account is fairly typical (Bennett and Bennett, 2000, p. 150). One night a woman was sleeping in a room while her mother was on her deathbed in the next room. Suddenly she saw her father 'who had been dead for many years' entered the room and wake her up. Later the woman narrated, "*He came in. I heard him cough, and he came in, and he shook her and said, 'Your mother wants you'.*" When asked what happened next, she replied, "*Oh, she died. She died very soon after that*".

The experience of 'sensing the presence' of dead husband ranges from the classic ineffable 'feeling' that he is there, to clear sensory experiences which "*often lasted many years but were most common during the first 10 years of widowhood*" (Rees, 1971, p. 37). The most common experiences reported are hearing or sensing the voice of the dead husband giving advice or making comments on changes around the house. Other reports include smelling an odor particularly associated with their husband, or may see or hear him. The sense of touch is also involved often especially in bed at night.

> "*I really saw my husband now, about six or seven weeks after. I'd gone to sleep. I'd had a sleeping tablet. I couldn't sleep, and I woke up to hear somebody say, 'Lucy, Lucy, Lucy', and I woke up, and it was like I am now, and just inside the bedroom door was John, HONESTLY! And he gave me the loveliest smile, and he'd got his lovely silver-grey suit on, and that was it. Never dreamt about him since or anything. But it was real. It was really real*". (Bennett, 1999, p. 108)

Stevenson (1995, pp. 353-54) investigated a case which is worth mentioning here. N. E. (50 years old woman from Charlottesville, Virginia), had an apparitional experience following her mother's death in 1971. One among eight siblings, she was strongly attached to her mother. When her mother was terminally ill, about one month before her death, N. E. asked her mother to try, after her death, to give her a signal of her survival of death, and her mother agreed. When she died, N. E. was severely grief-stricken. The funeral took place two days after the death. She returned home from the funeral in a desolate state and went to bed with her husband.

She could not sleep but kept thinking about her mother. All of a sudden, she became aware of a very strong yellow-green bright light, which she thought it might be coming from a neighbor's automobile. When the light entered in her room, she was at first frightened and pulled the bed covers over her head. Then she received the word "Mother," and uncovered her head. After that, she saw her mother, but not in full length; only the upper part of the body and the face were visible.

The apparition was laughing at N. E. but no sound heard. At first, N. E. was so awestruck that she could not talk. The apparition moved across the room. N. E. asked the apparition whether she (her mother) was in heaven. The figure smiled silently and bowed affirmatively. N. E. then asked, "*Is Daddy with you?*" The figure again smiled and bowed with affirmation. By this time, the apparition had moved near the window, and then disappeared. N. E.'s husband was awakened by the sound of her voice and asked her whom she was speaking, but she did not reply. For N. E., this experience was satisfying evidence that her mother had survived death and rejoined her husband in a heavenly realm.

A high proportion of parents of children who die expect to sense an apparition of the deceased child within a few months of the child's death. Stevenson (1995, p. 362) narrated the strange inner feeling of a physician,

> "*As a pediatrician B. I. had often treated children who had died. He had sometimes prayed for their sufferings to end. Sometimes, after a child had died, he had a kind of inner 'flash of seeing' the child running around and playing after being released by death. B. I. attributed these images to 'my own hopes that they were at last free to do so [run and play] and my own somewhat vivid imagination'*".

Many experiences are collective encounters, i.e., more than one person had the same experience at exactly same time.

> "*I was around twenty. My father and I sat in the kitchen around noon. Then I see clearly a woman coming towards us. I was not going to mention it but notice that my father also sees this. I asked him what he was looking at and he replied, 'Surely the same as you'. Then he said he knew this woman. She had died a while back. Three or four hours later there was a phone call for my father who was a clergyman. The husband of the deceased woman we saw had died. We had seen the woman around the time her husband had died.*" (Haraldsson, 2009, p. 109).

> "*Mrs. P. is lying in bed waiting to feed her baby. A lamp is burning. Suddenly she sees a tall man, dressed in naval officer's uniform, come to the end of the bed. She rouses her husband, who also sees the figure. It speaks reproachfully to her husband. He then leaps out of bed.* ***The figure moves away, transiently blocking the light from the lamp, and vanishes into the wall.*** *Mr. P. tells her the apparition was that of his father, who had been dead fourteen years. Later she learned that her husband was prevented by this vision from taking financial advice which would have proved ruinous.*" (Gauld, 1982, pp. 234-35).

Here the uniformed figure blocks light like a solid object, but apparently exits through the solid wall. Though seems illogical there are many reports like this.

In some cases, the apparition is perceived by one amongst several other persons present in the same location. The experiencer does not recognize the apparition, but when he describes his experience to others present, one or some of them recognize the figure (Stevenson, 1982, p. 344). It seems that the discarnate had intended to come to the person(s) who knew him, but could only be perceived by another – a more sensitive person.

Erik died in a tuberculosis sanatorium at the age of sixteen. When his death was known, some people had seen Erik more than once although it was never more than one person at the same time. One incident is particularly interesting.

> "*This happened in the winter. The sheep were out in the valley. I round them up and want to drive them into the barn. Whatever I do they do not go in and run to the side. Then I see where Erik is standing in the door. With his arm he points west to the farm where his mother was living. Erik then disappeared and I was able to get the sheep into the barn. Later in the winter his mother died of tuberculosis.*"

Erik's family members believe that by pointing to the farm where his mother was living, the apparition was expressing concern about his mother's health or indicating that she might soon die, which she did, although not immediately. Other people also saw Erik.

> "*I was skating on ice in the open when I felt I saw my friend Erik. I thought this was some nonsense and skated on. A little later I see him again and close to me, and think again this cannot be and I must be hallucinating and try to shake it off. I felt a strange feeling going through my body and I look behind and see his face. Then I felt sure he must have died. I went home and told them. They said of course that I was talking nonsense. The next morning there came a telegram announcing his death.*" (Haraldsson, 2009, p. 110)

Famous spiritual regressionist, Newton had regressed one of his clients to her pre-birth (means, the period as a soul between two incarnated lives) memories and found to his surprise that the woman under deep hypnosis remembers her existence as a ghost for a good amount of time after a former life (Newton, 2016b, pp. 54-55). This case is different from others because it explains the phenomenon from the perspective of the ghost rather than from those who experience them. In previous life, the woman was a teacher. She died young in a schoolhouse fire while saving the children. After death she stayed around town for few months as a ghost. During this time, she was checking on the kids and other people who were grieving at her untimely death. When Newton asked her, what prompted her to finally leave she replied that eventually she got bored. This case indicates that discarnate spirits may take some time to adjust before leaving Earth's astral plane.

Newton (2016b, pp. 58-59, 64) narrated the case of another woman who also had recalled her pre-birth memory as a ghost. In previous birth her name was Elizabeth. After death she resisted moving away from Earth's astral plane because she wanted to wait at the farm for Stanley, her husband, who went to Africa. Her suffering and non-acceptance of the situation was so severe that she ultimately became a ghost. She hovered around crying over her abandonment and knocking things down to frighten others. She thought that if she could scare away any potential buyers the estate might remain in the family. In this condition she remained as a ghost for 26 years but her husband did not come back. Ultimately, she returned to the spirit world. This Elizabeth-Stanley case also includes a karmic lesson which I will discuss in a later chapter. In another case, the husband of a newly married woman became a ghost because he was so overcome with despair and concern for his wife he wouldn't leave. He remained tormented for 30 years before being rescued by a higher entity from the spirit world.

The spiritual guides never compel or coerce the discarnate to move into the spirit world if the discarnate does not want to leave. The higher beings are instantly aware of our death, yet the wishes of the deceased are always respected. I will discuss more on this in chapter 9.

Newton (2016b, p. 56) recorded an incident that had happened during 1994. A young mother was driving at night on a road at the Sierra Nevada Mountains with her three-year-old son. Suddenly, her car tumbled down a steep embankment. She died on the spot but her son miraculously saved. The accident had happened in such a secluded place that no one had seen the accident or noticed the wreck 50 feet down the hill. Five days had passed and her son clung to life. On fifth day, a passing motorist saw a ghostly apparition of a nude young woman lying on the highway directly above the wreckage. This was the ghost of the mother who found a dramatic way to be noticed. Luckily, her son was found just in time to save his life. This accident attracted national attention.

A man was coming home early morning around four o'clock. In the middle of summer there was full light, and while walking over a bare hill he suddenly found a woman following him. This woman was,

> "... *kind of stooping, with a shawl over her head... as she passes me I say 'Good morning' or something like that. She didn't say anything. Then I notice that she has changed her course and follows me a bit behind. I got slightly uneasy about this, and found it odd. When I stopped, she stopped also. When I came close to home she disappears.*
>
> *I go up to my room. My brother Agnar wakes up and says half asleep, 'What is this old woman doing here? Why is this old woman with you?' And I tell him not to speak such nonsense but to continue sleeping, although I knew what he meant. I did not see the woman at that time but my brother appeared to see her when he woke up.... Agnar gets up again and says, 'Why has this woman come back?' And I tell him not to act like that, that there is no woman in here, that he is confused and should go to sleep.*
>
> *At lunch the following day I say to my brother, 'What nonsense was this last night? You thought you saw a woman in our bedroom.' 'Yes', he said, 'I felt as though an old woman came with you into the room'. Then our father became attentive and said to me 'Did you see something last night?' I told him that I had seen this woman. 'That is strange,' he said, 'around three o'clock this morning old Vigga died.' What I had seen fit her description perfectly.*" (Pearson, 2015, pp. 99-100)

Karlis Osis (1986, pp. 175-93) had investigated the apparitional sighting of a young businessman named Leslie, who had died in a plane crash. After this mishap, a distant relative of Leslie had sent out a mental appeal to his discarnate spirit, asking him and his infant son (who had died from drowning one year ago) to appear before his deeply grieving mother as a sign of comfort and survival. After two nights, between 1:00 and 3:00 a.m., Leslie's mother suddenly awoke to find someone standing at the foot of her bed. Looking up, she was startled to see Leslie standing there with his infant son.

"*There he was, Leslie, with the baby, and he was holding the baby's hand ... they were at the foot of the bed. They looked at each other. I was wide awake then. They were content; they were happy that they found each other, that they were together now. And they were letting me know that it is so; I got that feeling.*" (Osis, 1986, p. 181).

Leslie's mother apparently became so lost in her experience of seeing them that the external world around her seemed to fade away. It was quite brief, estimated at about 15 seconds total. By her account,

"*They were solid. There was like grayness around, like a gray cloud around them. I would say there was a mist in the whole room, nothing you could touch, just the grayness all around. But they were solid, both of them. The room was dark; electric light was coming from outside through the venetian blinds .... but I didn't need light to see them. There is a lot of traffic around my area. No matter what time you got trucks and buses. Not one sound then, all was excluded at that moment, everything, as though the world had stood still. And there was nobody but us three in the world.*" (Osis, 1986, p. 181).

The ghosts of Leslie and his son did not speak, but his mother felt that they were able to convey a nonverbal message.

"*They looked at me and they communicated. [(Osis): What did they communicate?] I really don't know. I got a peaceful feeling, everything around was completely serene. I felt them as if they were breathing into me, breathing my life into me. He was giving my life back to me. And it's the most lasting feeling: I will never, never forget this. Never, never forget this. It never happened before and never happened since. They were just there, I believe, to give me peace of mind. It really helped. I have not gotten over it [the grief] yet, but it made me able to live through very hard times without killing myself, because I was very despondent. I tried to keep them longer and they just went...They got smaller [into the distance] and faded out*".

The non-verbal communication moved her profoundly. If Leslie's spirit had appeared to comfort his grieving mother (in response to his relative's plea), then the spirit was exhibiting some degree of purposeful action and self-awareness (i.e., a form of intelligence). This in turn suggests a form of survival on his part.

The Cheltenham Ghost case (also known as Morton Ghost case) was one of the earliest cases investigated by the Society for Psychical Research, concerning reports of a persistent apparition in a house in Cheltenham, a town in the west of England, occupied by the Despard family. Between 1882 and 1886, several people have seen the figure of a tall woman dressed in black, habitually holding a handkerchief to her face and heard her footsteps as she passed. The principal witness was Rosina Despard, then a 19-year-old girl, resident in the house. Rosina, under the pseudonym R. C. Morton, wrote,

> "*The figure was that of a tall lady, dressed in black of a soft woolen material, judging from the slight sound in moving. The face was hidden in a handkerchief held in the right hand. ...on further occasions, when I was able to observe her more closely, I saw the upper part of the left side of the forehead, and a little of the hair above. Her left hand was nearly hidden by her sleeve and a fold of her dress. As she held it down a portion of a widow's cuff was visible on both wrists, so that the whole impression was that of a lady in widow's weeds. There was no cap on the head but a general effect of blackness suggests a bonnet, with long veil or a hood.*" (Morton, 1892, pp. 313-34)

Inquiries by the Despard family suggested that the apparition was the second wife of a previous occupant of the house. This well-documented case may represent a conscious survivor of death, or it had been an empty shell, i.e., appearance without consciousness like zombie images we see on movie screen.

The Proceedings of the Society for Psychical Research (Society for Psychical Research, 2012, Vol. 11, pp. 547-49) contains one of the most curious and well-authenticated cases in which a haunting spirit along with two other ghosts established communication with a living person and was laid to rest after its wishes were carried out. The incident (Grosso, 2004, pp. 58-61; Green and Carrington, 2012, pp. 57-59; Kingsford, 1920, pp. 219-27) occurred in 1893 to Mrs. Clara Claughton in a house reputed to have been haunted by the spirit of Mrs. Elizabeth Blackburn, its former owner.

Clara Claughton, a psychically talented woman, once visited a haunted house in October 8, 1893. Curious, she settled in her room with heightened attentiveness. At night while in bed with one of her children, she heard footsteps in the hallway outside that stopped at the door. She lit a candle and then opened the door, but found no one there. She went to sleep but soon awakened by a loud sigh. This time she saw a woman wearing a white shawl at the foot of the bed. "Follow me", said the phantom. Clara followed her into the drawing room, where the phantom turned back, and said in a distinct voice "tomorrow" and disappeared.

On the following morning Clara came to know from her friend that the ghost was Mrs. Blackburn who died in the house on December 22, 1878 at 5 a.m. Next evening, after Clara's daughter fell asleep, Mrs. Blackburn appeared again with the ghost of a dignified man who introduced himself as George Howard and announced "*I am buried in Meresby Churchyard*". Clara never heard of him or of Meresby Churchyard. After making her take solemn oaths of secrecy, these two polite and rational ghosts invited Clara to verify certain facts for herself at Meresby such as her (Mrs. Blackburn) date of marriage which took place at India. George Howard also gave the dates of his marriage and death, and asked Clara to verify them by the registers in Meresby, and if found correct to go to Churchyard at Meresby at 1:15 a.m. and wait at the grave of Richard Hart. Howard's ghost also told Clara that a man named Joseph Wright would help her to carry out her mission. And that she would lodge with a woman whose drowned child was buried in the churchyard. Towards the end of this conversation, Clara saw a third ghost behind Mrs. Blackburn's right. Then all three disappeared. Clara checked all the dates and found them to be accurate.

Clara was so curious that she took the noon train to Meresby (an obscure village four to five hours from London) on October 14, 1893, and found exactly what the ghost had said. Around 01:20 a.m. Clara reached to the grave of Richard Hart. The ghost of Howard appeared again and asked Clara to pick a white rose from his grave and give it to his daughter. Clara also delivered a message to Howard's daughter which was unrevealed to public. After accomplishing these, the ghosts of Meresby fell silent. The desires of the dead had been carried out in full.

This case is well researched and well documented. Grosso (2004, p. 58) reported that about this case famous psychical researcher Frederic Myers wrote, "*The evidence for the external facts of the narrative is absolutely conclusive*", and Andrew Lang, mythologist and psychical researcher wrote that the case was "*such as we seldom meet in modern science*".

****

Ghosts can appear on photography. Alex Imich, a famous and renowned parapsychology professor and investigator had an experience when studying a psychic medium who had the power to converse with the dead. The medium stated that she would attempt to make contact with his deceased wife. While she was meditating and going into her trance Imich's assistant took a picture of the medium's face. When the picture was developed, instead of seeing the face of the medium, Imich saw the face of Wela, his dead wife (Imich, 2007, p. 32). Furthermore, he says, "*To confirm my impression, I made copies of the photo and sent them to five nieces and nephews of my wife. Two of them called and excitedly declared: This is Wela, the name of my wife*".

Can we dismiss all these cases as 'just hallucinations' by following the prevailing academic attitude? One of the reasons that apparitions have remained a mystery despite their relatively common occurrence is the difficulty in systematically studying the apparitional experience. Another reason for the persistent mystery is the conventional psychological perspective, which assumes that apparitions are nothing but hallucinations and are therefore unworthy of serious study. Hence the facts are often ignored.

> "*Behavioral scientists and other investigators have rarely permitted mystical, other-worldly, extrasensory occurrences to become part of their personal interpretation of the world*". (Kalish and Reynolds, 1973, p. 210)

However, even if we cannot fully understand the basis for these paranormal phenomena, the weight of evidence suggests we cannot continue to ignore them.

> "*Science may keep saying: 'such things are simply impossible'; yet, so long as the stories multiply in different lands, and so few are positively explained away, it is bad method to ignore them.*" (James, 1978, p. 49).

> "*When a loved one dies, grievers may experience feelings of hopelessness and despair. However, post-death encounters suggest the existence of an afterlife, and establish a bond with the deceased. [They] can have a positive and therapeutic effect on the griever, and can be an important part of healing*". (Nowatzki and Kalischuk, 2009, p. 103)

Though we often use the term apparition as a synonym for ghost, apparitions are a bit different from ghosts. This term came from the Latin word "apparere", means, "to show oneself" (Peterson, 2006, p. 253). More precisely, it is "*an experience, usually visual but sometimes in other sense-modalities, in which there appears to be present a person or animal (deceased or living) ... who/which is in fact out of the sensory range of the [witness]*" (Thalbourne, 2003). Hence, this term is a bit broader than the more popular term ghost (from the German word "geist", means mind or spirit – Smith, 2010, p. 85). The parapsychologists are interested to investigate the apparition related incidents for four main reasons.

1. To determine whether or not such phenomena may have a rational explanation in terms of the known principles and laws of physics.
2. Seeing an apparition involves the use of ESP (extrasensory perception). Why some people can see or "sense" apparitions, while others cannot?
3. Some physical phenomena associated with apparitions (such as odd sounds and occasional object movements) may involve the use of psychokinesis (PK), or "*the mind's ability to affect or move an object at a distance by intention alone*" (Henry, 2005, p. 126). Are the apparitions seen somehow formed through a PK-related process?
4. Apparitions are certainly relevant to the issue of possible life after death.

Apparitional experiences were commonly reported and accounts of them frequently published in the late nineteenth century. However, nowadays they are rarely reported. Stevenson (1995, p. 352) had surveyed many such reports that are fairly recent, and it shows that these experiences still occur with notable frequency and are acknowledged, at least in surveys. The reason that such published reports are comparatively less today is that the experiencer fears to be identified as having 'hallucinations' and therefore, by implication, they are mentally ill. These experiences are worthy of study in their own right, like other aspects of human experience.

The popular belief that apparitions are mostly seen in darkness or twilight is not correct. The manifestations can take place anytime – in broad daylight, full electric light, twilight, darkness, and under variable conditions. Haraldsson (2012, Ch. 8 and 15) examined both the time of day and the state of mind of the observers at the time when the apparitions appeared. The percentage of apparitions which appeared in the evening was almost same as the percentage of those which appeared during the day (30% vs. 29%, respectively). And there was actually a higher percentage of experiences during the day (29%) than there was at night (21%).

Apparitions tend to occur when the mind is not actively engaged and in a restful state. Some researchers believe that a telepathic impression may have reached the experiencer before the apparitional experience takes place. A sizable number of the encounters occur just prior to falling asleep or upon awakening. From various cases, it seems that grief is the major cause of apparitional experiences.

There are various types of apparitional phenomena categorized and documented by psychical researchers and parapsychologists since the late nineteenth century, such as deathbed visions, crisis apparitions, postmortem apparitions, haunting apparitions, and apparitions of the bystander-type. Deathbed visions are already discussed, and now I will discuss other types.

4.1: Crisis apparitions

Crisis apparitions constitute by far the largest category of visions with paranormal transmission of knowledge (Thompson, 2003, p. 140). In this category, the apparition appears in a visible but immaterial form to a witness at a time when the person whose apparition is seen is experiencing a state of crisis, i.e., an unexpected tragedy, whether it is an accident, an illness, or a threat of death. An illustrative example of a crisis apparition is this particular case where a man was in hospital in serious condition. His wife left him at the end of the visiting hour to notify relatives and caring for their small son. Rhine (1981, pp. 150-51) continued,

> "*Completely exhausted, she fell asleep around 10:30 p.m. About 2 a.m., she found herself sitting upright in bed. She was looking at her husband standing in the doorway of the room. But he could not possibly be there. As she said in reporting the occurrence, 'I felt like a complete fool, but I*

> *couldn't get back to sleep so I called the hospital. Sheepishly, I told the floor nurse what had happened so she graciously said to wait while she checked up on him'.*
>
> *Minutes, then half an hour went by, when all she could hear was the sound of running feet, wheeling carts, etc. But finally, the nurse came to the phone out of breath, but happy. It seemed that when she went to the sick room the patient was in a crisis. He was choking. The delay had been while the nurse got two doctors and another nurse. It took all four to keep the patient alive. The nurse said if the wife had not called, by the time the intern made the next check it would have been too late*".

These are often once-in-a-lifetime events and the apparition seems to appear as a gesture of farewell, a wish on his part to say goodbye. The apparitions must have some factual basis because these apparently coincided with events that were taking place somewhere else. Hence many researchers have seen in these cases a possibility for empirical research into the question of continued existence after bodily death.

> "*In April 1888, Miss Hervey was in Tasmania, while her cousin was working in Dublin as a nurse. The two women had been close friends, but had not seen one another since Miss Hervey moved to Tasmania in 1887. The cousin's apparition was seen coming upstairs, dressed in grey, between 6 and 7 p.m. on April 21. The experience was so vivid that Miss Hervey ran to Lady H., in whose home she was staying .... At the time, Miss Hervey was unaware of the fact that her cousin had been stricken by a sudden and quickly fatal attack of typhus fever, lasting only five days. Death came on April 22, 1888, at 4:30 p.m., about 32 hours after the apparition occurred. News of the event did not arrive until June.*" (Braude, 1991, p. 175).

Crisis apparitions usually occur in less than 12 hours of death but may occur within 24 to 48 hours (Shrikhande, 2009, p. 99). Alvarado (2006b, p. 143) observed that apparitions seen more than 12 hours after death shows significantly higher frequencies of instances of being seen repeatedly, and they have an emotional bond to the location where they were seen. The apparition tries to communicate with the participant by means of look, touch, or even speech. When the apparition is seen by more than one person, it is called collective apparition. British psychical researcher G. N. M. Tyrrell (1953, p. 72) pointed out that in collective apparitional cases, the people observe the same apparitional figure "*each appropriately according to his position and distance from the figure*". Let me illustrate this with this case.

> "*A woman and her fifteen-year-old daughter had recently moved to California from their previous home in Washington D.C., where they had left the woman's father very ill. One day not long after moving, they*

> *entered the dining room, and to the woman's great surprise, there stood her father. 'Why Dad, when did you get here?' she exclaimed.*
>
> *At that point, her daughter turned around to look, and she, too, saw the figure of her grandfather, his hand upraised in a gesture of greeting or perhaps blessing, but he slowly faded away, and they both suddenly realized that he was not really in California in their house. Shortly afterward, they received the news that he had died*". (Feather and Schmicker, 2005, p. 254)

There are three interesting aspects of this experience. First, the apparition was collectively perceived, it was witnessed by more than one person. Hence, we cannot dismiss it as hallucination, wish-fulfillment or the product of the unconscious mind. Second, the apparition was apparently so real looking to both of them that they actually mistook it for their real father/grandfather. This observation goes against the traditional view that apparitions are often only misty, translucent outlines. Third, the apparition of the man acknowledged the presence of his daughter and granddaughter, meaning that the apparition has intelligent awareness.

> "*My mother lived in California and I lived in Wichita, Kansas. At 9:40 a.m. on February 17, I was sitting in my bedroom ... in front of the mirror. Suddenly the room was illuminated with the strangest light, one I can't fully describe. I then felt a rustle of wind across my shoulders, and a faint sound like the brushing of birds' wings. Then I looked in the mirror.*
>
> *My mother was standing behind my chair ... She just stood and smiled at me for a full thirty seconds. I finally said, 'Mom!' and rushed for her, but she disappeared, light and all. I was so upset by this that I shook for an hour. When my husband came home for lunch, I told him about it and got myself ready for a phone call that mother was dead ... Sure enough, about one p.m. that same day, the call came that my mother was gone ...*". (Feather and Schmicker, 2005, pp. 261-62).

Few cases show selective percipience – some people have experiences while others don't. On some occasions, two persons can perceive different things. One case involved two persons (one man and one woman) in the same house. They heard a voice while a family member was dying at a distant place. In the corridor of their house, both of them thought that the other had uttered a call. Though both heard at the same time, they heard differently. One of them heard her name called, while the other heard the word "uncle" – both three times (Gurney et al., 1886, vol. 1, pp. 227-29). These auditory cases have some pattern. The sound generally ceases when the percipients recognize they were death-related. But if there is no recognition it continued to be heard at least once more.

In another case, a man saw a female figure but could not recognize her features. However, his wife felt a presence and saw a "*misty shadow passing through the chamber*". That evening her mother-in-law fell ill and died (Gurney et al., 1886, vol. 2, pp. 236-37). Few more cases are as below,

> "*One day while I was shaving, Earl stood before me in his army uniform and looked me over for a few minutes and then disappeared... Several weeks later I found out that he had been killed in action at the time he appeared to me.*" (Rhine, 1968, p. 84)

> "*My wife and I had living with us a little girl about two and a half years old whom we fostered. One night I wake up and feel as though a woman were standing beside the bed. She says to me, 'my name is Margret'. Then she vanishes out the door. I look at the clock and see that it is exactly three thirty. The day after or the same day I learn that the girl's grandmother had died at that same minute, from a heart attack at Hvammstangi (a town in another part of the country). Her name was Margret. I knew nothing about her health, am not even sure I remembered her name. I had never seen her when she was living.*" (Haraldsson, 2009, p. 107)

> "*One winter's day I went out to the stable.... When I had been shoveling for a while, I suddenly felt Karl Kristjansson standing in front of me in one of the stalls in the stable and he says something rather peculiar, 'You were lucky, you did fine,' and that was all; then he disappeared. That evening his death was announced on the radio. While pondering about the incident and trying to figure it out, I learnt that he had suffered a heart attack and been brought to the Reykjavik City Hospital where he died. I had been admitted to that hospital a year earlier after suffering a similar attack. I luckily recuperated and could go home, whereas he died. In that context I understood his words, 'You were lucky, you had good luck.'*" (Haraldsson, 2009, p. 108).

There are many recorded cases that the wives and mothers of soldiers dying in World Wars I and II had seen apparitions. It seems, if a man dying on the battlefield had an intense desire to see his mother or wife before death, he could appear to them as crisis apparitions. Stevenson (1982, p. 351) had noted that,

> "*No fewer than 78% of apparitions of the dead were perceived by a [witness] to whom the [deceased person] had had strong emotional ties, such as a husband, wife, or fiancé; and among apparitions of the living the percentage of such appearances rose even higher, to 92%.*"

The members of the Society for Psychical Research had made detailed investigation on crisis apparition phenomenon during the nineteenth century.

Edmund Gurney was the first author to argue that telepathy could provide information about distant individuals who were passing through a crisis or were close to death. The participation could be either apparitional or visual such as through dreams, or intuitions, auditory and tactical impressions, or physical and emotional reactions. But in every case death is the major topic of the distant agent's situation (Alvarado, 2006b, p. 132). There are incidents when mothers have seen crisis apparitions of friends telling them their child is in danger. The mother checks on the child and finds him in some type of serious trouble.

> "*Early one morning a United States serviceman stationed in Germany showed up quite unexpectedly at his family home in a Detroit suburb. His mother, who was in the middle of preparing breakfast, was both startled and overjoyed and set another plate for her son.*
>
> *"Sorry, Mom," he said, declining the meal with a gentle smile, 'I can't stay for breakfast. I just wanted to say goodbye'. The young soldier waved farewell and walked out the door. His heartbroken mother ran after him, shouting for him to return and stay longer, but he had completely disappeared. A few hours later, an officer appeared at their door to inform the family that their beloved son had been killed in a training accident 6,000 miles away in Germany. He had died half an hour before his mysterious visit.*" (Steiger, 2003, p. 171)

From various cases, it seems that the discarnate entity wants to convince the person grieving that the individual they love is still alive. By one last contact, the departed allows the grief-stricken person to come to terms with their loss by acquiring an awareness that absence is only a change of reality and not final. The discarnate hopes that this will help the bereaved to move on and complete their own life constructively. Famous ghost researcher Brad Steiger wrote,

> "*[It seems] that at the moment of physical death, the soul – the essential self in all persons – is emancipated from the confines of the body and is able to soar free of time and space. In some instances, the soul is able to make one last, fleeting moment of contact with a loved one. These projections at the moment of death indicate that something nonphysical exists within the human body and is capable of surviving physical death.*" (Steiger, 2003, pp. 155-56)

Newton (2016b, p. 41), in a session of spiritual regression had the following conversation with his client who in a previous life, had died by car crash.

> "*Dr. N: Tell me what you did for your wife after the crash?*
> *S: I stayed around for three days with Betty to lessen her heaviness. I positioned myself over her head so our energy fields crossed in such a way that I could soothe her by matching our vibrations.*"

In another case (Steiger, 2003, p. 171), two friends started a business on partnership and opened a clothing store at Boston, but one of them betrayed and left the town with all the money. In spite of the partner's disloyalty the business prospered. About 12 years later, the owner of the clothing store was stunned when his former partner walked in the door. By waving aside all amenities he immediately got to the point of his visit. He said that he had come back to say sorry for his betrayal. The old friends embraced, and the disloyal partner was forgiven. The long-lost friend's face brightened at once. "Thank you," he said, then quickly left the store. It was several days before the businessman learned that his ex-partner had died three hours before he walked into the store to ask forgiveness.

> "*I sat one evening reading, when on looking up from my book, I distinctly saw a schoolfriend of mine, to whom I was very much attached, standing near the door. I was about to exclaim at the strangeness of her visit when, to my horror, there were no signs of anyone in the room but my mother. I related what I had seen to her, knowing she could not have seen, as she was sitting with her back towards the door, nor did she hear anything unusual, and was greatly amused at my scare, suggesting I had read too much or been dreaming.*
>
> *A day or so after this strange event, I had news to say my friend was no more. The strange part was that I did not even know she was ill, much less in danger so could not have felt anxious at the time on her account, but may have been thinking of her; that I cannot testify. Her illness was short, and death very unexpected. Her mother told me she spoke of me not long before she died. ... She died the same evening and about the same time that I saw her vision.*" (Hogan, 2008, p. 76)

There is a case of prolific horror/sci-fi director Reginald Le Borg, who helmed such films as *Voodoo Island, The Mummy's Ghost, The Black Sleep*, and *Diary of a Madman*. While living in Los Angeles in 1938, Le Borg was awakened by a vivid dream one night at 2:15 a.m. In the dream his father had shouted, "*Stay here! Don't say no!*" Le Borg's father had strongly opposed his decision to travel to the USA and pursue a career in Hollywood. Later in the morning a telegram arrived informing him that his dad had expired. The precise time of death corresponded to the moment he had awakened, and that his last utterances as he lay dying were, "*Stay here! Don't say no!*" (Steiger, 2003, p. 159). Such powerful cases support the view that the departed soul persists after death.

In one case (Shrikhande, 2009, p. 100), a housewife by the name Jayshree Mande whose husband was working in Saudi Arabia, woke up around 3 a.m. on June 14, 1985 to find her mother-in-law sitting on her bed. She was surprised, "*Mother, how come you are here at this hour?*". She replied, "*I have come to meet you and the children. When will my son come?*". The wife said that her husband will be coming during Diwali (a Hindu festival). "*It will be too late, I will not be able to meet him. I am worried about you and children staying alone in this lonely place*". Then the apparition got up to leave. "*Have a cup of tea*", she said, but after five minutes when she came out from the kitchen with the tea, the apparition had vanished. The front door was bolted from inside.

Later that day, the phone rang – it was her brother-in-law who informed her that his mother had passed away that night. She rushed to her mother-in-law's house and found her dead in the same white sari with a pink floral design and green blouse that she had seen her wearing a few hours earlier. The brother-in-law told her that she had slipped into a coma earlier that night and had regained consciousness around 3 a.m. He asked his mother if she wanted something to drink. She said, "*No, thanks. I just went to Jayshree's (daughter-in-law) house and had some tea*". Then she died.

Steiger (2003, p. 244) recorded the case of Patricia Mann that appeared on Fate Magazine, February 1967 issue. Around 2:00 a.m. on July 17, 1957, Patricia opened her eyes and glimpsed a shadowy form of her mother who lived 10 miles away. The apparition said to her, "*Come, I need your help*."

Puzzled, she picked up the phone and dialed her mother, but got a busy signal. She called the telephone company and came to know that the line was out of order. Patricia sensed danger, and drove to her mother's house. When she arrived, she found all the lights on, and she could hear the television set blaring at full blast. She pounded on the door and called her mother's name but received no response. Finally, she found an unlocked window and crawled through. Her mother was lying in a pool of blood, clutching the telephone receiver in her hand. Patricia called an ambulance. After her mother's forehead had been stitched up in the hospital's emergency room, she told Patricia what had happened. In short, about 2:00 a.m. her mother had a fall and sustained a deep cut. She tried to phone Patricia but blacked out. She only remembers calling her daughter's name before sensory loss.

Mrs. Jean Bettany remembers having a strange vivid sensory-like vision at the age of ten. While walking on a country lane,

> "*... in a moment, I saw a bedroom known as the White Room in my home, and upon the floor lay my mother, to all appearance dead. The vision must have remained some minutes, during which time my real surroundings appeared to pale and die out; but as the vision faded, actual surroundings came back, at first dimly, then clearly.*
>
> *I could not doubt that what I had seen was real, so, instead of going home, I went at once to the house of our medical man and found him at home. He at once set out with me for my home, on the way putting questions I could not answer, as my mother was to all appearance well when I left home.*

I led the doctor straight to the White Room, where we found my mother actually lying as in my vision. This was true even to minute details. She had been seized suddenly by an attack of the heart, and would soon have breathed her last but for the doctor's timely advent..." (Gurney et al., 1886, Vol. 1, p. 194).

Many investigators have recorded this incident. The kind of vivid and detailed imagery seen by Mrs. Bettany is very similar to the kind that people often describe when they see the detailed apparitional figure of a person. Perhaps this offers a hint that ESP is involved in both types of experiences.

Crisis apparitions materialize when people least expect them. They suddenly pop up, completely unannounced by prior feelings of distress or anxiety about the person whom they represent. The visions usually manifest while the percipients are engaged in their normal duties or while they are preparing for sleep. As example (Shrikhande, 2009, pp. 100-01), a South African student saw a crisis apparition of her sister. One night while reading a novel by the bedside lamp, she saw her bedroom door open and her sister walking in. Her sister was injured and blood was dripping from her head. She screamed and rushed out of the room and out of the house. Later she gathered her senses and returned to the room, but her sister was not there. Next day, she received a telephone call informing her about her sister's death in a car accident the previous night.

One night, a priest, Arthur Bellamy, saw an unknown lady sitting on his wife's side of the bed while she was sound asleep. He stared at her for several minutes, especially noting her elegant hair style. Then she vanished. When Mrs. Bellamy awakened, Arthur described the mysterious visitor. He was astonished to learn that the description fit that of a schoolgirl friend of his wife. The two friends had once made a pact that whichever of them died first would appear to the other after death. Arthur asked if she remembered her friend having any distinguishing physical characteristics, so that they might be certain it had been the same individual. "*Her hair*," his wife replied without hesitation. "*We girls used to tease her at school for devoting so much time to the arrangement of her hair.*" Later, Arthur saw a photograph of his wife's friend and identified her as the ghost that had appeared at his wife's bedside. (Steiger, 2003, p. 155). Later Arthur identified the 'lady' from a photograph which proved that vision was authentic.

In the next case a suicide victim keeps his promise.

"Jacob was a patient in a sanatorium where I worked. He was sometimes depressed, and I tried to brighten his stay with a bit of humour. One day I had talked to Jacob that he should visit us because he came from the same county as my husband and they would enjoy talking about the people from there. He says yes to that, is glad, and I say to him: 'You promise to come tomorrow.' 'Yes, yes, I promise,' he says. During the night, I wake

> *up, and all strength is like taken away from me. I am unable to move. Suddenly I see the bedroom door opened, and on the threshold stands Jacob, with his face all covered with blood. I look at this for a good while unable to speak or move. Then he disappears and I felt as if he closed the door behind him. I became my normal self, call my husband and tell him about the incident: 'I can swear that something has happened at the sanatorium.' I telephone in the morning and ask about if everything is not alright with Jacob. 'No,' said the nurse, 'he committed suicide this night.'"'* (Haraldsson, 2009, p. 104)

The postmortem report of Jacob declared the cause of death as suicide by drowning, and there were "two large wounds on his head and the cranium (upper portion of skull) much broken." This fits the percipient's description that she saw Jacob "with his face all covered with blood." The river is rather shallow, but it flows over sharp rocks of lava that must have caused the severe head injuries.

From various similar cases, it seems a violent and sudden, unexpected death makes the appearance of an apparition more likely than a natural death. Do apparitions of those who suffer such a death have an invasive character? Since violent deaths are almost invariably sudden, some researchers have speculated that suddenness or unexpectedness may be more crucial than the actual mode of death.

In rare cases, a person sees something that seems to be a superimposed image of the dying individual and its surroundings as if the whole image is projected from a slide. Mrs. Taunton of Brook Vale (Birmingham) had this experience on November 14, 1867 while sitting in Town Hall concert with her husband.

> "*... I saw with perfect distinctness, between myself and the orchestra, my uncle Mr. W, lying in bed with an appealing look on his face, like one dying. I had not heard anything of him for several months, and had no reason to think he was ill. The appearance was not transparent or filmy, but perfectly solid looking; and yet I could somehow see the orchestra, not through, but behind it... The vision gradually disappeared...*" (Gurney et al., 1886, vol. 2, p. 37)

After enquiry, it was found that her uncle had died around the time of her vision. In rarest cases, the discarnate entity announces his death information. Flammarion (1900, p. 140) collected one such case where a woman saw, "*a figure standing upright, surrounded by a circle of light... I recognized my husband's brother-in-law... who said: 'Warn Adolphe' [her husband] – 'tell him I am dead'*".

Crisis, usually of death-threatening magnitude and violent deaths are most likely to be sudden. I think, this feature of suddenness increases motivation on the part of the person in distress (or, already dead) to communicate with someone they think likely to be interested. Those who are dying slowly have enough time in which to communicate normally with those from whom they wish to take leave before dying. Minot J. Savage, a Unitarian clergyman, describes an incident in which a young boy who had befriended a judge of some prominence living in the neighborhood, received a paranormal visit from his friend.

> "*After the boy was put to bed one night, his parents heard him crying. They rushed to him and asked him what was wrong. 'Judge says he's dead! He has been here and told me that he is dead!' the boy sobbed. The next morning the parents found out that the judge had died at about that time the night before*". (Hogan, 2008, p. 80).

Some cases involve visual and perception. Flammarion (1900, p. 84) recorded one such case where a person awakened at night and then,

> "*I looked up and saw at the foot of my bed... a shining disk... Without seeing any figure, without hearing any noise, there came into my mind the persuasion that I had before me one of my cousins... who was very ill.*"

The case of Vice Admiral Sir George Tryon is well-documented. On June 22, 1893, Lady Tryon was entertaining her guests in London's fashionable Eaton Square. The mansion was crowded with the cream of the capital's society. Suddenly, in full public view (some 300 guests), Sir George walked down the decorated curved staircase towards the guests in full dress uniform. As Lady Tryon screamed, the apparition reached the foot of the stairs, calmly and silently crossed the room, opened a door and vanished. The guests were surprised because at that time admiral was supposed to be far away at sea with the Mediterranean fleet. Later they realized that they had seen a ghost when they came to know that Sir George died when his flagship 'Victoria' had collided with a battleship 'Camperdown'. His ship sank causing the death of 22 officers and 336 seamen. (Boar and Blundell, 1991, p. 91; Young, 2015, p. 40). The admiral's sudden appearance at the party was obviously his way of saying goodbye to his wife and guests.

It seems, when a person is in a physically dangerous situation (either dying, already dead or likely to die) his ability to communicate with others 'paranormally' increases.

> "*I was out in the country and going to visit my grandfather. I was having a pleasant trip, stayed at Blanda for two nights, or rather was going to. I was not in any hurry. All of a sudden I sensed my grandfather right there with me. I instantly knew that he had passed away, went to the post office and called. It was confirmed that he had died the day before.*" (Haraldsson, 2009, p. 101)

There are cases when some information unknown to the percipient is apparently passed on to the recipient in an inexplicable manner by the apparition. Often the crisis apparition expresses a specific purpose to the percipient.

> "*This happened shortly after my father died. I was in bed sleeping but woke up and felt there was something at my side. I saw my father there, I looked at him, reached out and felt him. He was just as he had been, wearing a blue shirt over his underwear.... He got out of the bed and walked to the room he had lived in and was across from mine. As he walked, he pointed to the wall without saying a word. On that wall there was a large clock that he had earlier asked me to deliver to his grandson in Reykjavik.*" (Haraldsson, 2009, p. 109)

All these accounts prove that the soul, when detached from the physical body, can exist independently and display intelligence and memory. A person undergoing a tragic experience can somehow project his external self to another person if his wish to do so is strong enough. In previous chapter, I wrote that at the time of severe life-threat, the soul comes out of the physical body even before death. When the soul is free, the soul may wish to visit his near and dear ones before starting an eternal journey.

4.2: Postmortem apparitions

This type of apparitions is visible after a person's death, anywhere from several days to several years after. Survival researcher Dianne Arcangel (2005, pp. 70-72) documented a case where a woman and her pet dog saw an apparition.

One day in June 1995, Mrs. Beverly, an elderly woman was out with her son's dog. Her son, Tommy was murdered about four months ago. When the woman with the dog was passing by the parking lot where Tommy had kept his Scout Jeep, suddenly the dog began barking and pulling on the leash. The woman looked up and saw a young man standing in a blue outfit about 30 feet away. At first, she could not see him clearly because she was not wearing her glasses. When she finally put them on, she recognized the apparition as her son standing there on the sidewalk and smiling at her, wearing a blue outfit he had bought but never got to wear before he died. The woman was shocked, immediately called out to him, and began running with his dog towards him. But then, the apparition seemed to slowly turn around and glide away, his feet being about an inch off the pavement. Despite how fast they ran, the woman and the dog could not catch up to him, even after pursuing the apparition for three blocks. Then, the woman's sight of her son was abruptly obstructed by some passing schoolgirls, and when she looked up again, the apparition had vanished into thin air.

In this case, if it was a hallucinatory image produced by the primary visual areas of the elderly woman's malfunctioning brain why the dog was alarmed and reacted hastily?

An Argentinian woman, Maria Elena lost her eight-year-old nephew, Pablo, in an accident on June 22, 1999. Maria's mother was devastated. Though she was a strong critic of afterlife, about a year after Pablo's death she saw his apparition.

> "*Mother came to me in a state of shock. 'I saw Pablo! I saw Pablo!' After I calmed her down, she said that around four a.m. she was sitting on the bed getting ready to get up and go to the toilet when she saw him standing at her bedroom door. He was smiling at her, and there was a luminosity around him, even in the jeans, and blue and green sweater he was wearing. He looked healthy and very real. She couldn't talk to him, or even try, because she was scared to death, so she pulled the covers over her head and started to pray. She stayed like that for hours and didn't even go to the toilet. When she looked again, he wasn't there anymore.*" (Arcangel, 2005, p. 54).

Sometimes a postmortem apparition tries to convey information unknown to the witness, as example the famous "Chaffin Will" case. James Chaffin was a farmer living in North Carolina in the early 1900's. On November 16, 1905, he wrote a will leaving his entire estate to his third son, Marshall, which was attested by two witnesses. In 1919, he appeared to have changed his mind about his will and wrote a second will leaving all of his property equally amongst his four sons. This will was not witnessed but the handwriting could be verified to be his. He hid this copy of the will in the family diary, and wrote a note referring to the will and sewed it into the inside pocket of an overcoat belonging to him, apparently telling no one of either the second will or the note. On September 7, 1921, James Chaffin died suddenly due to a fall and all of his property went to his third son, as per the instructions of the original will. In June 1925, James Chaffin's second son, James Pinkney, began to have vivid dreams of his father visiting him at his bedside. In one dream his father appeared to him dressed in his overcoat, pulled it back and said, "You will find my will in my overcoat pocket." The son then went to his oldest brother's house, where he found his father's old overcoat. After undoing the stitching, he found the note, and went to his mother's house with three witnesses, where he found the second will in the family bible.

The case then went to court, but the situation was amicably settled out of court prior to the judgment after twelve witnesses, including the wife and son of Marshall (Marshall had died within a year of his father) agreed that the handwriting of the will matched the handwriting of James Chaffin. The Court accepted it as legitimately superseding the earlier one.

One particular feature of the Chaffin will case provokes further questions about the power and the preoccupations of the dead. It took four years for the senior Chaffin to change his mind. We are not sure about the experience of time in the afterlife, but probably senior Chaffin was suffering from indecision about his property even after his death. Perhaps the death of Marshall motivated him to communicate with James Pinkney. Probably Marshall, now himself in the next world, personally encouraged and helped him to communicate to avoid family conflict and stress over his father's property. It is difficult to understand, how much do the discarnates value the thoughts and emotions of the living.

Italian poet Dante Alighieri was a moral philosopher best known for the epic poem 'The Divine Comedy'. Stevenson (1982, p. 348) wrote that after Poet Dante's death his son saw his father beckoning to him and then guided to a place where the poet had hidden the final cantos (a principal form of division in a long poem) of the 'The Divine Comedy'. Dante's son had no idea when his father had written those last cantos, much less any knowledge of where he had hidden them. The son had a strong desire to acquire and publish as much of his father's work as possible. Yet another such case was the Conley case where his daughter became aware paranormally of money that her father had hidden in his cloths, which had been discarded after his death (Myers, 1892, pp. 200-05). In all these cases the motivations of the discarnates are very strong. In 'Phantasms of the Living' Gibson (1944, p. 104) concluded,

> "*... at the conscious level motivation of the percipient is usually weak... [and] motivation of the [discarnate] agent is strong in most of the cases.... A large number of these incidents are teleological in character, the general purpose being to inform the percipient that the presumed agent dying or dead.*"

Some apparitions tend to be seen in the geographical location where they once lived or worked. One case comes from Dianne Arcangel (2005, pp. 18-20). Her family had a dry-cleaning business where amongst the workers there was the ghost of a man named Dyer who had worked there diligently at his spotting board from morning till night for about 30 years until his sudden death from a heart attack. Not long after, a female co-worker walked in and saw Dyer working behind his spotting board. She smiled and waved at him, and he waved back. The woman turned to put her things down, and when she looked back Dyer was gone. Twenty years later, several workers and tenants of the apartment that was later built above the business by Arcangel's husband also reported seeing the spectral figure of Dyer. People had noticed that one particular area of the apartment, located directly over the area of Dyer's spotting board, was constantly cold, even in the summer months. Neither the later workers nor the tenants had ever known about Dyer prior to their experiences.

Postmortem apparitions are also called residue apparitions since 'something' remains at the locality after the death of the material body. They have certain characteristics, such as, they repeatedly appear in the same place (usually the place of death or a great disaster) over time to different witnesses. The duration of the sighting is over three seconds and the witness can make out enough visual details to provide a good description which can later be verified as factual about the deceased. Often multiple people, either together or independently, describe the exact same details of the phenomenon they have witnessed without prior knowledge of the location or its history. If the apparition is unknown to the witness at the time of the sighting, it is later identified by other means (historical research, photograph etc.) that it is a factual person. Sometimes, the apparition either directly tells them or shows them something important (a family secret, a lost will, how they died, who killed them, etc.) that is later independently verified to be true.

The "Lon and Gordy" case (Roll and Persinger, 2001, p. 160) is a very interesting one. A little girl (three-and-a-half years) named Heidi Wyrick moved to a new home with her parents in Ellerslie in 1988 and became friendly with a man in her neighborhood named "Con". Her new friend invited her to play on a swing. When Heidi asked her mother for permission to do so, she enquired about Con and Heidi described him as "having blood all over." Concerned that Con may be a kidnapper or a child molester, the parents had the neighborhood searched for the man, but were unable to find him. Shortly after, Heidi began speaking of regularly meeting with another man in the neighborhood named "Mr. Gordy" to play on the swing. As her parents could not find Con or Mr. Gordy in the neighborhood, they thought that those two men were the girl's imaginary playmates. Eventually they discovered that an elderly person named James Gordy and a man named Lon [Con] Batchelor had actually lived in the neighborhood many years back. Lon had lost his hand in a machinery accident. The descriptions that Heidi gave of the two men were later found to closely match photographs of them. Heidi was also able to correctly pick them out of a random collection of old photos.

American parapsychologist William Roll who had investigated this case in the late 1980s, could find no normal way in which Heidi could have learned about them prior to her family's discovery of their identities. The Lon and Gordy case contains a parapsychological component. Heidi was able to somehow psychically perceive the apparitions of people who had once lived in her local surroundings.

Psychic researcher H. M. Denning investigated the case of a young married couple who heard knockings and footsteps in their home. The wife saw an apparition of a woman whose description seemed to fit her husband's recently deceased mother. Denning visited her home with a psychically gifted medium who allegedly contacted the deceased mother. The mother indicated that she was very unhappy about being 'earthbound'. The bereaved son had thought of his mother so often and with so much grief, that 'the energy' had held her to him, and she had tried very hard to demonstrate that she was still 'living'. Two weeks later no further manifestation was reported (Denning, 1996, pp. 65-66). We do not know how the deceased agent produced the phenomena. If the apparition was not hallucinatory and in some sense objective, then we know what motivated her.

Postmortem apparitions frequently haunt their former habitats. They are seen in graveyards, cemeteries, old mansions, castles and houses where a number of suicides or murders had taken place, on the lonely stretches of roads where many accidents have occurred, and in certain doomed locations where a tragedy, like a fire or other mishap had taken a large number of lives (Shrikhande, 2009, p. 76). The ghost adopts a "habitual" activity and continues to perform these actions long after death. Perhaps the entities do not realize they are dead, or perhaps they are so comfortable that they simply refuse to leave and pass all the way to the other side.

Ghostly incidents can reoccur regularly at a certain hour, in certain month, yearly, in every few decades or on a special anniversary. Often the ghost is completely unaware of anything going on around him. They are oblivious to the passage of time or transitions of ownership or observations. For them, only that moment exists. There is nothing else, no one else. However, they can sometimes interact with familiar objects such as keys, furniture, toys and objects in their living space such as doors and windows.

From various cases, it appears that sometimes the extended self or the soul, when separated from the body, might get stuck in a time loop. This is something like a no man's land. The soul neither belongs to the physical world nor the soul world where they should be. In my opinion ghosts are less developed souls. That's why they have trouble freeing themselves from Earth. At present, we don't know what the real reason is, and hence, a lot of research needs to be done. But before terming any incident as ghostly, or calling a place as haunted, all rational logical explanations must first be carefully scrutinized. In this scientific age, superstitions are greatly reduced, but strange, inexplicable incidents still happen.

4.3: Bystander-type apparitions

Apparitions of this type are relatively rare. These apparitions have been witnessed in close proximity to people who once knew them in life rather than being seen in the place where they once lived or worked. Louisa Rhine had coined the term bystander-type case to label this type of cases, noting that, "*...these cases are suggestive of the haunting cases, the main difference, however, being that in these the link is a person rather than a geographical location*" (Rhine, 1957, p. 39). For instance,

> "*I was cleaning a large room in a business where I had recently started to work and was alone as far as I knew. Suddenly the door is opened and I hear 'God bless you'. I turn around and see a large woman walking into the room. I was sort of hypnotized and could not move because of fright. She stopped at a machine that was out of order and disappeared. She was in a long dress with a shawl over her shoulders and had grey hair. As she disappears the director enters and walks the same way as the woman. I heard it much later that she had been the mother of the director.*" (Haraldsson, 2012, pp. 155-56).

Stevenson (1995, p. 362) had once interviewed a medical doctor who had witnessed such apparition while keeping vigil at the bedside of his mother-in-law. The old woman was in a coma and very close to death. Her children and her physician agreed to keep her comfortable at home and to avoid any life-extending procedures. According to the doctor,

> "*I was standing by her bed and no one else was in the room. She had an agonal inspiration, and at that moment I had a very clear picture of G. C. [her late husband] standing across from me with his arms outstretched, and he said, 'Flora, I've been waiting for you.'*
>
> *I did not really have to look to see that my mother-in-law had died, but the physician in me pushed me to verify that.*"

The doctor noticed that his late father-in-law was "... *quite opaque, as he would have seen him in life*". He was only able to see the figure from the waist up, but believed that the surrounding furniture had blocked his vision of the rest. Prior to his encounter, the doctor believed that he had only seen his father-in-law once or twice while his father-in-law was still alive, but he was familiar with his father-in-law's appearance from family photos. Though he did not expect to see his father-in-law at the time of his mother-in-law's passing, "*I was surprised but comforted by what I saw*". This is a bystander-type apparition because the doctor was able to see the apparition of a man in close proximity to the man's dying wife, and thus the doctor was acting as a third person "bystander" witness (hence the term). Although this case was similar to a deathbed vision, but it cannot be classified as one in the strictest sense because the mother-in-law was comatose and did not herself perceive the apparition of her deceased husband. This case has two very interesting aspects – the apparition was solid like a living human being, and the apparition has some degree of intelligence because it can speak and has emotion.

Gurney and Myers (1988-89, pp. 422-26) reported a similar type case. A widow died in a house on the same day a new tenant moved in. The new tenant, a woman, knew neither the widow nor her late husband who died three years ago. She saw the apparition of the long-dead husband. The appearance of the husband makes sense – probably he came to help his wife through the transition of death.

Boar and Blundell (1991, p. 185) reported a bystander case of one Mary Goffe who lived in 1691 at Rochester. As she lay dying at her parent's home, on June 3, 1691, she pleaded to be taken to see her children (about 14 kilometers away) for the last time. Her parents refused because the journey would be too much for her. Mary slipped into a coma and died, whispering that she was at peace because she had seen her children. Her mother thought that the dying woman was dreaming. After few days, the nurse who was caring for the children at Rochester, met Mary's mother and revealed that at 2 a.m. on the day she died, Mary had spent 15 minutes beside the beds of her little ones, gazing silently down at them before vanishing.

On rare cases, a bystander perceives the apparition while the primary percipient to whom the apparitional figure intends to appear does not see it (Rhine, 1957, p. 39). A classic case (Kirti-Iyengar case from India) is that of Ms. Suman Kirti and her teacher Dr. (Mrs.) Bhanu Iyengar, lecturer in the Department of Pathology of the Maulana Azad Medical College (Delhi). This case (Haraldsson, 1987, pp. 64-67), occurred in March or April 1968, can be categorized both in crisis and by-stander type. The essential details of the case are as below.

Dr. Iyengar, Kirti's teacher and mentor, was hospitalized in a nursing home in New Delhi because of complications arising after childbirth. In the afternoon, Kirti went to the nursing home to spend at the bedside of her friend Dr. Iyengar. Iyengar's mother, Mrs. T. Iyengar, was also there. Dr. Iyengar was very sick, had high fever, though not in danger of death. After initial greetings, both women sat silent at her bedside. Iyengar suddenly turned somewhat excitedly to Kirti and asked her to go home immediately to her grandparents. Kirti had for a long time been living with her grandparents since her parents were at that time living far away, Africa. Kirti answered that she had come to spend the whole afternoon with her and she refused to go. There were some arguments between them, and Iyengar kept insisting that Kirti should go home or at least telephone her home.

At around 4.30 p.m. Kirti finally agreed to make a call to her home. Her uncle, who happened to be visiting there, came to the phone and told her that Kirti's grandfather had passed away at four o'clock unexpectedly.

Iyengar then described to the two women the following incident – while lying in bed silent and drowsy, she suddenly saw Kirti's grandfather standing at the further end of her bed. She had only seen Kirti's grandfather two or three times before when she had happened to pick up Kirti on her way to or from work, and on one occasion when he, with Kirti, made a brief visit to Iyengar. He appeared excited, stood at the foot of her bed and said to her "*Would you not send my child home?*". By that Iyengar understood Kirti, who lived with her grandparents.

By seeing the old man, Iyengar was surprised, and her first reaction was that she was hallucinating because of high fever. She therefore rolled to the other side of her bed and expected the hallucination to disappear. However, the old man appeared again in front of her and indicated with his eager countenance that she should send Kirti home. In this way, the deceased grandfather appeared two or three times. Iyengar decided to ask Kirti to go home urgently. When she rushed home, her grandfather had died almost at the same time Iyengar saw him.

Famous paranormal researcher Erlendur Haraldsson had investigated this case. The apparition was very real and life-size. As she rolled over to dispel her hallucination, the apparition changed his position two / three times to remain within visible sight of her. It was so real that at first Iyengar thought he was really there, but when she noticed that Kirti and her mother did not see him, she thought she was imagining his presence. He was wearing his usual clothes and spectacles. Iyengar saw him only a few seconds each time. For that reason, she thought he was not real. This was the first and only time that Iyengar had hallucinatory experience or any psychical experience. All three persons present testified that the death of Kirti's grandfather coincided with Iyengar's sudden urging Kirti to go home.

Also, the fact that the grandfather appeared repeatedly (two or three times) till Iyengar reacted to his wishes, confirms that the apparition was self-conscious and had a strong desire and affection to 'see' his granddaughter at home. He wanted her to go home immediately, we may guess, to help and console his wife. Kirti did not see him, probably because he did not want to confuse her. He used Iyengar to bring his message to Kirti, perhaps because Iyengar was in a mental state that was better receptive to his appearance. The percipient, Iyengar, acted as an intermediary, even rather unwillingly between the deceased and Kirti. Hence, this case falls into the rare category of both bystander and crisis cases.

Two sisters, Emmeline and Susanna, were around the deathbed of their sister Charlotte Bingley on June 8, 1843 and saw the faces of two deceased brothers. Gurney et al. (1886, vol. 2, p. 629) noted Emmeline's statement,

> "*... I saw a golden light above Charlotte's bed, and within the light were enfolded two cherub's faces gazing intently upon her... I put my hand across the bed to Susanna, and I only said the word: 'Susanna, look up!' She did so, and at once her countenance changed, 'Oh Emmeline', she said, 'they are William and John'. Then both of us watched on till all faded away like a washed-out picture; and in a few hours Charlotte died of sudden inflammation.*"

There was an interesting case concerning American poet Horace Traubel (1858-1919) and Walt Whitman (1819-1892). Traubel was a student and admirer of the work of Walt Whitman. When Traubel was on deathbed, he saw and heard Whitman among other people. Moore Cosgrave, who had been with Traubel for last three nights of his death, shared one of his visions (he has similar experiences in the past). Cosgrave looked at the same place Traubel was staring at, and in his words,

> "*Slowly the point at which we were both looking grew gradually brighter, a light haze appeared, spread until it assumed bodily form, and took the likeness of Walt Whiteman, standing upright beside the bed, a rough tweed jacket on, an old felt hat upon his head and his right hand in his pocket... he was gazing down at Traubel, a kindly reassuring smile upon his face, he nodded twice as though reassuringly, the features quite distinct for at least full minute, then gradually faded from sight.*" (Prince, 1921, p. 119)

Cosgrave confirmed that Traubel also saw Whitman.

> "*At the same moment, Walt passed apparently through the bed towards me, and appeared to touch my hand, as though in farewell, I distinctly felt it, as though I had touched a low electric charge, he then smiled at Horace, and passed from sight.*" (Prince, 1921, p. 121)

A nurse was attending a young dying girl. Her doctor was also present in the room. When the patient showed 'adverse' symptoms, they did not call her mother because she was exhausted and resting in the next room. The nurse wrote,

> "*As I looked there passed around from the head of the bed the figure of a woman in white whose face was turned away from me, and who paused for a moment by the girl's side before passing by the doctor and myself, still with averted face, and going out of the door back of me which led into the room in which the mother was sleeping.*
>
> *Immediately after the figure passed the doctor, he started and said sharply, 'Who hit me on the shoulder just then?'*" (Hyslop, 1915, p. 393)

The young girl was still conscious. She died next day in her mother's arms.

4.4: Haunting and poltergeist cases

'Haunting' is a traditional term. Psychical researchers generally apply the term 'haunting' to spontaneous cases featuring recurrent manifestations of a paranormal nature that seem to be linked with particular places rather than specific people. Various witnesses experience these happenings there over a lengthy period sometimes exceeding five hundred years.

The royal Hampton Court Palace was home to many British monarchs for over 500 years, and it is now a popular historical attraction. The palace is also frequently referred to as 'one of the most haunted places in England' with both staff and visitors reporting unusual phenomena in many areas of the building, and allegedly contains the ghost of Catherine Howard, the fifth wife of Henry VIII. Fifteen months after her marriage to the King in 1540, Catherine Howard was found guilty of adultery and sentenced to death. Legend suggests that upon hearing the news, Catherine Howard ran to the King to plead for her life, but was dragged back by the guards. After her death at the block, her phantom was said to haunt the gallery that, today, had become associated with various unusual experiences, including sightings of a woman in a white gown and reports of inexplicable screams. Some visitors have experienced poltergeist phenomena.

Some haunting cases are purely auditory, i.e., they manifest as sounds reflective of human activities, as example, the alleged haunting phenomena witnessed aboard the Queen Mary cruise ship. W. G. Roll (1991, pp. 55-61) had thoroughly investigated this case. According to the ship's crew, sounds of loud metal impacts, voices, and rushing water are sometimes heard coming from the lower forward compartments near the ship's bow. But when the compartments are checked, no one is found in the area, nor is there any sign of damage or a leak. To see if these sounds might represent an objective event rather than being purely subjective, Roll attempted to record them by leaving a voice-activated tape recorder overnight in the bow. When retrieved in the morning and played back, it was discovered that,

> "*... the tape recorder picked up a strange sequence of noises. You could hear heavy blows of metal, sounds of rushing water and voices, one of which, low pitched and gravelly, was almost intelligible.*" (Roll, 1991, p. 58).

The recorded sounds were found to be strikingly similar to a description given by the ship's chief engineer, who heard the sounds on several occasions when he was in the bow area with no one else around. The nature of the sounds seemed consistent with a tragic event occurring early in the Queen Mary's sailing history, when it had been a military transport during World War II. During an evasion maneuver on October 2, 1942, the bow of Queen Mary had accidentally collided with the British battle cruiser Curaçoa, tearing the smaller cruiser in half and resulting in the deaths of 338 British sailors

Common public is most aware of this type of ghostly phenomena because there is no shortage of third-rated movies made on this theme. Though apparitions are often experienced at allegedly haunted sites, they do not take the form of the classic ghosts of folklore, such as, ferocious demonic creatures, humanoid figures etc. Instead, they appear as shadowy forms, floating lights, and hazy mist-like clouds. However, most haunting events have some theatrical quality. In fictional films, haunted sites look spooky but with real paranormal events the settings are often quite ordinary as in this case,

> "*I once lived in a three room apartment on the ground floor. All the doors were locked so I was sure that nobody could have come in and I*

was all alone. It was evening and I was making my bed when all of a sudden I had the feeling that somebody was in the room with me. Looking up I saw a young man standing in the room, looking at me as if he wanted to say, 'This is my house. What are you doing in here?' He was dressed in a brown suit, a red necktie and black shoes. Before I had a chance to come to my senses he was gone. Now I had the habit of visiting my landlady every evening so I told her my experience. No sooner did I finish than she turned almost green in her face. She told me that not so long ago the same man once lived in my apartment and took great pride in fixing it up. But he died in those same rooms leaving a young wife and baby." (Rhine, 1957, p. 36).

Auditory phenomena are more common than visual, such as footsteps, voices (meaningful or blabbering), knockings, sounds of doors opening and closing, music, and sounds of furniture being moved etc. Often, they are experienced by other senses, such as sensing an unseen presence (at times accompanied by feelings of apprehension or fear), and hearing various kinds of sounds that may either be suggestive of physical disruptions (crashes and banging noises) or be suggestive of a presence (voices, footsteps, doors opening and shutting). Then there are phenomena that may have some degree of physical objectivity, such as floating lights (orbs), temperature variations (cold spots, which can be measured with a thermometer – a drop of about 9 to 10 degrees Fahrenheit – Turner, 1970, p. 352), electrical disturbances, and the occasional instance of apparent object movement (Williams et al., 2007, p. 1). There are often disturbances of bedclothes. Pet animals sometimes show signs of distress.

Can we dismiss these cases as hallucinatory while there is not a single advanced idea to explain them? For example, a witness in a London-based case was in her bedroom when she suddenly heard heavy noises downstairs, including bangs and crashes. Expecting to be greeted with a scene of 'total destruction' when she went downstairs in the morning, she was surprised to find nothing out of place. The sounds might be hallucinatory, but some of the phenomena in this case were physical. When she entered a room, she found that a box containing some beads had disappeared. She left the room, but found the box back in position when returned five minutes later. Her father witnessed an incident in the same house in which five bedroom doors, one after another, banged shut (MacKenzie, 1982, pp. 198-99). How to explain this phenomenon?

MacKenzie (1982, pp. 200-04) discussed another case where there were apparitions, noises, cool breezes, cold sensations and displacement of objects. A witness reported that the side of a bed had been pressed down as if some unseen person sat on it. These physical occurrences prove that the phenomena of hauntings are for the most part objective. Early researchers, such as Mrs. S. Sidgwick (1885, p. 142) while discussing cases that had come to her attention, took the view that "*the evidence connecting [haunting apparitions] with some crime or tragedy is extremely slight*". However, in 1929, Bozzano (Collins, 1948, pp. 68-77) studied 532 sufficiently well documented haunting cases, and out of these, he classed 374 cases as "*hauntings properly so-called*", and in the majority, there was a connection with a death in the haunted location. Denning (1996, p. 128) suggests that some rare cases, which she calls 'pseudo-hauntings', do not entail the active intervention of spirit entities, but rather an "*energy form created by traumatic events [that] seems to be charged with a powerful energy that continues to exist...for a considerable length of time*".

MacKenzie (1982, pp.102-13) had described an unusual and complicated case in which apparitions of discarnates had communicated coherently with a percipient, providing information that was subsequently verified, and giving detailed instructions that the percipient carried out. This case can be seen to be lending credence to the spiritualist standpoint of afterlife survival. Moreover, this case also suggests that the deceased may have some capacity to direct and/or foretell the course of future events in the lives of the living.

Like haunted houses, road ghost sightings cases, though rare but happen and occasionally reported in newspapers and investigated by paranormal researchers. As example, a certain 15 miles stretch of Scotland's A75 motorway is dangerously haunted for more than six decades. In 1955, Jim Carlyle, a 75-year-old man was driving a taxi on the highway with his future wife. Suddenly both of them saw that "*there was a woman, dressed in white, a long cape, and she just floated right across the road in front of me. I braked, but I went right through her – it was a ghost.*" (Annandale Observer, October 29, 2010 edition)

Another incident allegedly occurred at 10.45 p.m. one misty night in October 1957. A lorry driver called Hugh Watson Reid reached a bend in the road, at the junction with the A75, and saw a middle-aged couple, wearing old-fashioned clothes, walk arm-in-arm in front of his lorry. After bringing his lorry and trailer to a halt and switching on the hazard warning lights, Reid jumped out. He intended to remonstrate with the couple, but found that the couple had vanished without a trace. There hadn't been time for them to jump clear of the vehicle, and there was no sign of them beneath it. What's more, an impenetrable hedge bordered the road at that spot. However, Reid learned months later, "*that he had not been the only witness to [this] sudden and potentially dangerous manifestation... Other night drivers have experienced an identical incident at the same spot.*". This means, the ghostly phenomena are recurring events. Some night drivers also saw near this area "*a ghostly car which ... travels the same road at night with dipped headlights, and then suddenly disappears.*" (McCue, 2011, p. 26). These two incidents were reported in the newspaper. Later in 1960, a woman called Margaret Ching, while driving with her fiancé reported her experience that came in the newspaper – "*she saw an old woman in Victorian clothes standing in the middle of the road*". The couple thought that they had driven straight through her, and they described feeling a terrible chill.

British Parapsychologist Peter Underwood (1980, pp. 14-17) recounts an experience of two brothers, Derek and Norman Ferguson that occurred one night in April 1962 when they were driving through that "15 miles stretch of Scotland's A75 motorway". A large hen flew towards their car, but disappeared just before striking the windscreen. Shortly after, an old woman rushed towards the car, waving her arms. But she also vanished exactly at the moment she would have been expected to collide with the vehicle. After this, a succession of other unexpected figures appeared from nowhere, such as big vehicles, wild-looking dogs, goats, etc. Derek, who was 22, swerved and braked repeatedly, trying to miss the apparitions. He noticed that none of them actually hit the car, and he initially thought that it must all be his imagination. But when he glanced at his 14-year-old brother, he realized that Norman was also seeing them. They were aware of a drop in the temperature in the car, and Derek felt as if a force were trying to take control of the steering wheel.

The brothers felt suffocation, but when Derek opened a window, it was bitterly cold outside. They heard screaming, high-pitched laughter and crackling noises. Derek eventually stopped the car, but then they felt it bouncing up and down and rocking from side to side. Derek came out of his car and found that everything was quiet. But when he got back in and slammed the door, the shaking and high-pitched laughter resumed. A strong wind seemed to blow up, and invisible fists started striking the vehicle. Driving on, they experienced more apparitions and frightening noises. After some time, they observed a small red gleam ahead which appeared to be the tail light of a large furniture van. Derek then realized that he was approaching it far too quickly, although he found himself unable to take any evasive action, his foot would not move from the accelerator pedal. But when they were about to crash into the van, it disappeared. As they drove on, Derek noticed that the car had slowed to a crawl, and that the noises and high wind had died away. The experience continued for about 30 minutes.

During March 1995, a couple called Garson and Monica Miller were driving when the figure of a man dressed in a cloak jumped out in front of them. They were apparently convinced that their vehicle had made contact with the figure, and they immediately notified the police but nothing was found (Annandale Observer, October 29, 2010 edition). During July 1997, a woman called Donna Maxwell with two children was driving home when a man jumped out in front of her car. She slammed on her brakes and closed her eyes for a second, but heard nothing. The man had vanished before she opened her eyes. All three of them had witnessed the incident. Police were unable to trace the man but many other people had seen the same man standing in a particular place near the road just looking at the cars (Annandale Observer, August 01, 1997 edition). Shortly before midnight on November 8, 1992, 54-year-old Ian Sharpe was driving when a young woman ran in front of his car with her face turned towards him. His vehicle seemed to hit her, and she disappeared beneath it. Two weeks later, in the same general area, another driver, 19-year-old Christopher Dawkins had the same experience.

By reading all these reports Derek McCall, a member of a local paranormal investigation group (with the fanciful name 'Mostly Ghostly'), drove through the same highway, and had an experience on December 12, 2010, between 8.20 and 8.25 p.m. McCall was driving along at 60 m.p.h., listening to the radio, when he became aware of the figure of an elderly woman suddenly appearing at the side of the road. She wandered into the road in front of him. McCall hit the brakes, but just at the moment of the collision, the woman vanished. When he checked his rear-view mirror, he found nothing. In the previous night, McCall and his fellow investigators had been in the area of the sightings, and had been discussing them. Probably the ghostly encounter somehow staged for his benefit.

From all these reports, it seems that different types of apparitional figures appear at respective localities. Except the Ferguson brothers' case, all other cases are very similar. These cases are not hallucinations because not everyone can have same type of hallucination in that exact stretch of highway, and driver and passengers cannot have same hallucinations together. The traditional assumption that the apparitions are the earthbound spirits of the dead is more reasonable. However, there is a question because there are reports of apparitions of inanimate objects such as cars etc.

There is a common theme in all these reports – vehicles running into apparitional figures. In my view, the discarnate entities want to pass a message to us with their symbolic dramatic acts. These are the warnings about dangerous driving. Probably the ghosts were victims of careless driving when they were human beings on Earth. May be, those annoyed ghosts remind us about the environmental damage caused by motorized transport and road building. Otherwise, these mischievous spirits are randomly picking on road users just to give them a fright.

4.4.1: Poltergeist disturbances and related phenomena

Poltergeist (German for 'noisy ghost' – 'poltern' means noisy and 'geist' means ghost – Klinge et al., 2011, p. 196) cases are much similar to haunting cases. The only difference is that it is physical, such as the breakage of glass and crockery, rapping and knocking sounds, and the movement of objects without any apparent reason. But unlike haunting cases, it is relatively short-lived. W. G. Roll (1977, pp. 383, 399) discusses 116 cases; in respect of 98, where the duration was recorded, the average was 5.1 months. Poltergeist cases are reported all over the world and from time immemorial. The earliest was in 355 AD, when people from a small German village were hauled from their beds by unseen hands and subjected to an onslaught of stones and strange noises. One of the most gruesome incidents on record was in 1878 at Amherst,

Nova Scotia where a 19-year-old Esther Cox was under severe attack. People were pelted with plaster and planks of wood, mystery fires flared up in the cellar of her home, and the entity left a message on the wall, "*Esther Cox, you are mine to kill.*" (Boar and Blundell, 1991, p. 48). Roll (1977, p. 386) recorded one case at 1960 Sauchie (Scotland) that involved loud knocking emanating from the bed-head, A 50-pound linen chest standing near the bed began rocking spasmodically and unevenly rising from the floor. Then it shifted sideways "*with a jerky kind of motion through a distance of about 18 inches and back again*".

Researchers regard these cases as instances of 'recurrent spontaneous psychokinesis' (RSPK), and the effects are often attributed to a living agent, a 'poltergeist focus' (if a person can be identified which is not always the case), and it is sometimes assumed that the manifestations reflect some form of psychological tension within that person, or changes associated with puberty. However, Stevenson (1972, p. 234) cautions against dismissing the possibility that some poltergeist cases entail discarnate agency because sometimes the self-conscious apparitions are seen in the place. As example, during the beginning of April 1663, unexplained knockings, musical drumming sounds and sounds of panting and scratching were observed in a house. Rooms became inexplicably hot and filled with offensive smells. Objects moved or flew through the air, doors opened and shut spontaneously, and strange lights were seen moving through the house. Apparitions were also seen. English philosopher Joseph Glanvil wrote, "*the house was several nights beset with seven or eight in the shape of Men, who, as soon as a gun was discharged, would shuffle away together into an Arbour and disappeared*" (Glanvil, 1682, pp. 107-08). After a thorough examination of this case, Glanvil concluded that the noise was made by some demon or spirit.

These apparitions don't always represent human figures, but can take form of animal figures, body limbs, demonic figures and formless (indistinct, shadowy or mist-like) shapes (Roll, 1977, p. 397). There are cases where shadowy beings such as the face of a woman are seen clearly reflected in the mirror (Steiger, 2003, p. 63). Sometimes footsteps, snorting and whistling are heard. So, if an 'agent' is posited, we need to find out whether that person or entity is incarnate or discarnate, and whether the agent is conscious of his or her involvement in the phenomena.

Often the agent shows intelligent behavior. Once when a witness was about to leave the Slawensik castle (Poland) where such incredible phenomena were taking place, his hat was hidden from him. After the household had looked for several minutes in vain, the missing hat was seen floating teasingly in front of its owner. As the frustrated and frightened person reached for his headpiece, it jerked out of his grasp. With him running in pursuit, the hat led its owner on a merry chase before it finally dropped at his feet. In the same place, one family member was exhausted from months of sleep deprivation.

He firmly announced to the ghost one night that he did not want to have a single object thrown at him while he attempted to rest on his bed. It seemed for a while that the entity was going to cooperate with him. But the person had just drifted off into a deep sleep when he was rudely awakened by a large quantity of water being dumped on his face (Steiger, 2003, p. 65). On another day,

> "*[the family] saw a jug of beer rise slowly from a table and begin to pour its beverage into a tumbler. Then, before their unbelieving eyes, the glass was lifted and began to empty, just as if someone were drinking from it. As the glass was put back on the table, the men went to the spot where the invisible being had just drunk the entire tumbler of beer. There was not a drop of beer to be found on the floor. The men were terrified that the invisible thing could actually swallow liquid*". (Steiger, 2003, p. 66)

Prof. Gudmundur Hannesson (1924, p. 253) mentioned one case where the poltergeist agent had snatched a chair from under a person about to sit on it. It is less likely that the unconscious mind of a living agent would discriminate objects in this way. In many cases objects are seen flying through the air, then suddenly float through a gentle rest. Sometimes the objects show abrupt variations in the speed of flight. The objects can turn at a sharp angle to continue flight in a new direction (Stevenson, 1972, p. 247). By supporting Stevenson's opinion, Gauld and Cornell (1979, pp. 351-52) and Roll (2006, p. 7) commented,

> "*If there are indeed both living agent cases and discarnate agent cases we should surely expect, not the absence of intelligence and purpose in the former, but different kinds of purposes and different degrees of intelligence in the two sorts of cases*".

> "*The totally blind and purposeless poltergeist is perhaps a rarity even among obvious living agent cases. ... There is ...a good deal of evidence that living agents can produce not just mere whirlwind-like explosions of energy around them, but, for example, communicative rappings through which pseudo-personalities manifest themselves*".

A logical mind will try to find better reasons, such as a discarnate entity is actually carrying the objects transported or by some means controlling their flight. The unconscious mind of a living agent cannot cause intelligent pranks, such as pulling chair from under a person or throwing a large quantity of water on a sleeping person or drink beer or cause apports (objects appear in, or disappear out of enclosed spaces and objects have materialized in mid-air). Also, the purposes exhibited by the phenomena appear quite alien to the known aims and purposes of any living person in the household (Gauld and Cornell, 1979, p. 354). The same authors have discussed one remarkable case – the Sandfeldt phenomenon.

Sandfeldt is a village in Germany that was the scene of a violent poltergeist outbreak on January 26, 1722. A farm in the village had many empty rooms which had become a scene of peculiar arrangements. Once a servant of the owner was investigating the phenomena. He was in the kitchen with the children when they heard noises from the empty living room. When he looked around, to his astonishment he found that,

> "*objects in the room were gradually being arranged into a little scenario. Each time he looked, more objects had been added. ... A cloth was spread on the floor, and on it were laid numerous dishes and various kinds of foodstuffs. The figures of two picnickers were made out of clothes ingeniously put together*". (Gauld and Cornell, 1979, p. 110)

The children also saw ghostly animals and an apparition of a child or angel causing some of the incidents. When arrangements of objects into patterns are made inside empty rooms it is obvious that only discarnate agents are involved.

In one case, the discarnate entity, identifying himself as Bill Hobbs, said that he came from a graveyard. His voice was taped "*I am 72 years old and I have come here to see my family. But they are not here now.*" His activity stopped with these last words. An American family found a quilt in a box when they moved into their new home. When they decided to use it, the disturbances started. At midnight, the daughter heard a voice say, "*Give me back my Christmas present.*" (Boar and Blundell, 1991, pp. 42, 48). Hence, at least some poltergeist effects are caused by discarnate entities, and to explain these phenomena we need a paranormal connection requiring the notion of postmortem survival.

The Grottendieck stone-thrower is a famous poltergeist case of Sumatra (Indonesia) occurred in September 1903. Local poltergeist activities are commonplace and often reported in the newspapers. Dutch engineer W. G. Grottendieck witnessed a strange phenomenon of falling stones which were appearing near the inside of the roof, not puncturing the material. There was no trickery or natural explanation for the fall of stones. He tried to catch the stones at the appearing-point, but though they moved extraordinary slow, they evaded him (Grottendieck, 1906, pp. 262-63). Grottendieck fired five sharp cartridges from his Mauser rifle, "*but the stones, far from stopping, fell even more abundantly after my shots than before*" (Podmore, 2011, p. 165). The stones were warmer than usual. The warmth of the object is a trademark of poltergeist cases. In such cases, when objects are flung about rooms by unseen hands, often at angles, speeds and in trajectories that defy the known laws of physics, they are found to be quite warm to the touch. Additionally, the stones seemed to be falling slower than they should, another interesting trademark of such cases. The sound they made in falling down on the floor was also abnormal, yet another hallmark of the poltergeist phenomena.

In another case, "*the objects fell slowly, or even floated down, as if under the influence of some anti-gravitational force*" (Michell and Rickard, 2007, p. 2). In December 1965, an eleven-year-old Brazilian girl Maria José Ferreira was the target of similar indignities and injuries. Large number of stones dropped from the ceiling. Michell and Rickard (2007, p. 176) wrote, "*a particularly large stone [the largest weighing 3.7 kg] was observed to descend from the ceiling of a room, breaking into two pieces close to the floor. When one of the witnesses brought the pieces together, they 'snapped together' as though they were magnets*".

One investigator visited a home with poltergeist disturbances in 1968. The family told him that objects disappeared and were then seen falling to the ground outside the house. He put bottles containing perfume and tablets on the kitchen table, asked the occupants to go outside, closed all the windows and doors and also went outside. However, "*after a short time the perfume bottle appeared in the air outside the house, the bottle of tablets appeared in the air at the height of the roof and fell to the ground in a zigzag manner*" (Bender, 1969, p. 96). In another incident (Boar and Blundell, 1991, p. 49), coins were found coming from the stairwell and bouncing off the floor and walls of the room.

From a three-dimensional reality this is a logic-defying occurrence. However, such incidents become less mysterious in a four spatial dimensional worldview. When we see an object disappears in front of our eyes, the entity is simply picking up the object from our three dimensional surrounding and carrying it within its higher spatial dimension and brings it back again to our known three dimensional surrounding. Hence, an object can appear in, or disappear out of enclosed spaces.

4.5: Characteristics of ghosts and apparitions

The first characteristic deals with the physical appearance. The apparitions can be solid looking life-size with physical or non-physical features, such as, some appear to cast shadows and reflected on mirrors while some appear as unrecognizable mists. In the Morton Ghost case, the ghost of the dead widow "*... was so solid and life-like that it was often mistaken for a real person*" (Morton, 1892, p. 315). Apparitions can appear or disappear in enclosed rooms, or pass through solid materials, such as doors and walls and sometimes move about by gliding instead of walking. (Stevenson, 1982, p. 353; Tyrrell, 1961, pp. 56-58). Attempts to touch an apparition have either resulted in the figure apparently eluding the hand to where it is unable to be touched, or the hands simply passing through the figure. When Rosina attempted to touch the spectral widow, she found, "*It was not that there was nothing there to touch, but that she always seemed to be beyond me, and if followed into a corner, simply disappeared*" (Morton, 1892, p. 315). In the crisis case earlier, we have seen that the woman and her daughter initially took the apparition to be the woman's real father, and in the bystander case, the doctor described the image of his late father-in-law as being opaque and life-like. Many apparitions have exhibited physical power, can communicate, have intelligence and self-awareness. Since apparitions belong to a higher spatial dimension that we human beings cannot intrude, they have at least one more degree of freedom than us which we can neither experience nor access directly.

From various cases it seems that the farther one gets from a person's time of death, the less frequently that person's apparition appears. Edmund Gurney and Frederic Myers had conducted a survey of early apparition cases, and after studying 211 cases they concluded, "*... the recognized apparitions decrease rapidly in the few days after death, then more slowly, and after about a year's time they become so sporadic that we can no longer include them in a steadily descending line*" (Gurney and Myers, 1888-89, p. 427). Rosina (Morton, 1892, pp. 314, 318, 321) noted that from 1882 to 1884 she saw the spectral widow "*... about half a dozen times*" with several other members of her family. It was reportedly seen frequently throughout the year of 1885, but by 1887, "*... we have few records; the appearances were less frequent*". From 1887 to 1889, the spectral widow was rarely seen, and then, "*From 1889 to the present, so far as I know, the figure has not been seen at all*".

When an apparition is seen (or sensed by hearing, touch etc.) certain kinds of subjective effects, such as feeling sensations of cold or wind are observed. Tyrrell observed that the experience of cold breezes and similar cooling sensations was fairly frequent across witness accounts, such as, "*... felt myself grow perfectly cold*", "*A cold, shivering feeling came over me*", the apparition "*laid a cold hand on his cheek*", and "*As if a cool wind was blowing about me*". Witnesses suggest that the cold sensation had emanated from the apparition itself, "*As the figure passed, we distinctly felt a cold air,*" or "*Her kiss was like a waft of cold air upon my cheek*" (Tyrrell, 1961, p. 73). Rosina stated that similar cold sensations were sometimes felt in proximity to the spectral widow of the Morton ghost case (Morton, 1892, p. 325). The cold feelings would even sometimes occur in the room while it was being warmed by an active fireplace.

Dean Radin and William Roll had attempted to find out the physical composition of the ghosts. During their investigation in a popular Kentucky music hall, a psychic had sensed a rather strong ghost in the basement of the hall. All three of them rushed to the basement and the psychic was able to corner the ghost in one area of the room. The investigators placed a Geiger counter (an instrument used for detecting and measuring ionizing radiation) both 'inside' and 'outside' the supposed ghost. The Geiger counter sounded an alarm, detecting the presence of radiation. On two other occasions, when taken out of the ghost as a control comparison, the Geiger counter remained silent. But sadly, before they could repeat the test, a photographer snapped a photo of the room which according to the psychic the ghost did not like and disappeared into the wall (Radin and Roll, 1994, pp. 337-46). This experiment offers the hint that some ghosts may be radioactive.

Some ghosts maintain their own schedule and the unpredictability is one major factor that makes an objective investigation difficult. So, the observer should be at the right place at the right time to see it. However, for an investigative purpose, the ghosts can be categorized as below,

1. One-off ghosts: These ghosts appear one time only with a very strong manifestation. Sometimes they can be triggered by an investigation, i.e., when an investigation takes place, the ghost manifests, perhaps to just get some attention or maybe it is just curious. It then moves on, never to be seen again unless it is provoked again. These cases are most difficult to document because, perhaps by intent, they never reappear.
2. Intermittent ghosts: They have no obvious schedule. The ghost may be seen several times in one day and then not show up again for several weeks or even for several years or decades.
3. Reactive ghosts: These ghosts manifest with disturbing phenomena when a living person modifies the local environment until the change is undone, as example, if a sword is removed from the wall of a museum or if their portrait is moved to a new location. They can also appear as a result of remodeling or other building modifications. Probably those ghosts were creatures of habit when they were alive.
4. Circulative/wandering ghost: Some ghosts haunt more than one site. Probably these ghosts follow a residual energy path. Some researchers feel that these ghosts may have encountered major problems in several places and as a result, they visit them all. In rare cases, the ghost may attach itself to a significant person who has a direct connection to the spirit, and it follows that person to different locations by paranormal induction. On occasions they attach themselves to a well-loved pet.
5. Cyclic ghosts: They present themselves on a regular schedule. We can see them every day at the same time, or on a particular day every week or perhaps once a month or on a particular date.
6. Anniversary ghosts: They will appear on a specific date which is almost always is the anniversary of an event that was important to them when they were alive. Unlike cyclic ghosts, anniversary ghosts usually appear on a particular date, regardless the day of the week. Sometimes time of the day is also a factor.

Except cyclic ghosts and anniversary ghosts, other types are easy to explain because we can clearly see what motivates them to manifest.

The cyclic and anniversary types have something in common, i.e., the regularity or punctuality which often they show for hundreds of years. Their repetitive acts are so predictable that sometimes it seems that their ghostly forms only represent an earthly shell without consciousness. Newton (2016b, p. 55) had explained that the discarnate entities don't have a linear clock in their heads so staying behind for months, years, or even centuries doesn't have the same relevance as with incarnates. A ghost who has haunted a castle of historical importance where a great number of murders and much injustice took place for five hundred years and finally returns to the spirit world may feel in spirit time this amounted to forty days, or even forty hours. These two types of ghosts don't lurk around Earth to disturb living beings and prefer to live in seclusion. Their repetitive behavior has following two motivating factors.

Their actions are the result of something unfinished, traumatic and overwhelming which they are unwilling to forgive and forget (Newton, 2016b, p. 65). This behavior is not unusual, and we have seen this behavior amongst living beings also. As example, some hurtful words, or behaviors from our loved and trusted ones often leave permanent scars on our minds or remain in our minds for a very long time. These mental scars bother us repeatedly and make us unhappy, but not many of us want to take help from a professional psychiatrist. Similarly, these discarnate entities are so unhappy because of the injustice caused to them that they don't even want to take assistance from their spiritual guides. It is their free will and hence, their guides cannot take charge and pull them up deeper into the spirit world despite their resistance.

As example, a restless ghost of a 22 years old American marine had haunted a house at Portland for two years to convince his mother the truth about his violent and mysterious death. Lieutenant James Sutton belonged to an honest, upright and respectable family. James went for his training as an officer in the Marine Corps. He used to write cheerful and affectionate letters to his beloved parents regularly. On October 11, 1907 his mother Rosa Sutton suddenly had a strong feeling that something was terribly wrong. Next evening, she had sharp attack of pain and feeling of shock without any apparent reason. She felt that James would come back home unexpectedly. On October 13, James' father received a telegram from the Naval Academy that his son had committed suicide by firing a fatal shot into his brain.

Mrs. Sutton refused to believe that her son had committed suicide. "*At that instant*", she wrote later, "*Jimmie stood right before me and said, 'Mamma, I never killed myself... my hands are as free from blood as when I was five years old*'" (Constable, 1988, p. 66). No one else in the room saw or heard anything. She said her son was trying to tell her something vitally important – James had been hit on the head with the butt of a gun, and three other men jumped on him, beat him ruthlessly, kicked him, broke his wristwatch and then tried to rub his face on the ground – "*Oh, if you could see my forehead and put your hand on my forehead, you would know what they did to me. But*

I did not know I was shot until my soul went to eternity." Wrapped in his overcoat, the ghost began to vanish, "*Oh, Mamma, don't lose your mind because you have got to clear my name*".

On October 16, James appeared again and gave further details about his death, describing how his attackers had tried to bandage his head to hide what they had done – "*My face was all beaten up and discoloured, my forehead broken and there was a lump under my left jaw*". As a final proof, next time Mrs. Sutton saw her son with a face hideously disfigured. Still wrapped in a big coat he seemed to be looking for something – "*It's my shoulder knot I can't find.*"

Slowly other family members started feeling the presence of the ghost. Dan, James' younger brother saw him and Louise, his sister was keenly aware of his presence. James also appeared in the dream of another sister, Daisy, where she saw the photo of James' fellow officers, a man called Utley. Soon James informed Mrs. Sutton that his body had been hidden in a basement and a lieutenant called Utley had been responsible for his murder.

First confirmation of Mrs. Sutton's extraordinary experiences came about three weeks after Louise returned from James' funeral at Annapolis bringing her brother's belongings with her. Among them was a shattered wristwatch.

The ghost continued haunting at Portland house. Ultimately the Suttons asked for their son's body to be exhumed, and soon an independent enquiry revealed some staggering facts. The remains had shown that he had been severely disfigured. The injuries were exactly as the ghost had revealed to his mother. The shoulder knot of the uniform was missing. After the autopsy it was confirmed that the shot had been fired from at least five feet from his head, and that the wound showed conclusively that it was a physical impossibility for James to have fired the shot. Soon an anonymous eye-witness testimony confirmed that James was murdered.

Once Mrs. Sutton removed the stigma of suicide from her son's name, the departed soul of James was satisfied. Once justice had been done, Mrs. Sutton still caught a glimpse of him from time to time but the image grew fainter and then disappeared forever. This intriguing tale of the death of a young Marine Corps officer, a military cover-up, and a mother's crusade that brought it to the nation's attention had fascinated reporters, members of Congress, high-ranking military officials, lawyers, doctors, clergymen, and even spiritualists. A book was written on this murder mystery by Robin Cutler (2007), named 'A Soul on Trial: A Marine Corps Mystery at the Turn of the Twentieth Century'. The ghost had been sighted by dozens of credible witnesses over two years.

Like lonely persons these repetitive ghosts create a world for themselves where they design their own reality with memories of the physical life, they had experienced. Some may stay in nice places, as example, gardens, children park etc, while others may design terrible spaces for themselves like a prison, an isolated room, old castles, etc., so that they can't experience much light or make contact with anyone. It is self-imposed punishment. The psychiatrists have observed that in our society those who like to live in loneliness show repetitive behavior. Since the ghost was once a living human being, they show the same tendency.

Some ghosts show their repetitive behavior because they want to return as quickly as possible in a new body (reincarnation) without going through the normal process of returning back to the spirit world, receiving counseling from masters and guides, studying their lessons and taking some part in the selection of a new body. They perceive that a sudden change in their 'planned karmic direction' is not only unexpected but also unjust (Newton, 2016b, p. 56). In their physical life they had bravely faced many difficulties like frontline warriors in a battlefield. An untimely death seems to them as some kind of 'injustice' of spiritual guides, and hence they want to maintain the continuity with their physical life. By showing repetitive behavior they want to show that nothing had happened to them. Since for the discarnate entities time does not pass same as living beings, they are unaware of the fact that they are repeating their behavior for several hundreds of years. In spirit time this amounted to, may be, few days, or even few hours. Hence, they seem to be caught in a time-loop replaying the same scene over and over. Newton (2016b, pp. 68-69) commented,

> "*Souls of silence know they are immortal but they feel impotent. Consider what they do in solitude without help. They relive their acts over and over again, playing back all the karmic implications of what they have done to others and what has been done to them in their last life. They may have harmed others or been harmed by them. Quite often I hear they feel victimized by events over which they had little control. They are sad and mad at the same time. They have no interaction with their soul groups. These souls suffer from self-recrimination [the act of accusing or blaming oneself] and restricted insight. I must admit these conditions fall within some of the definitions of purgatory.*
>
> *In their space, the souls of solitude have given up their imaginary Self for a large dose of self-flagellation. Solitude and quiet self-analysis is an important and normal aspect of soul life within the spirit world.*"

Since a soul cannot be destroyed or made non-functional, ultimately all the earth-bound spirits will be released one way or another through different forms of encouragement, but "*no one can do anything for them until they themselves make the effort*" (Montgomery, 1972, p. 62). The guides take it as a challenge to let the spirit to give up their self-imposed places of confinement and move to spirit world. But several hundreds of years may pass in this process. Do we see haunted places with pre-historic ghosts?

We are fearful about the ghosts – it's natural, but many ghost-researchers conclude that there should be no reason for us to fear ghosts more than the living people. Death necessarily does not make a living person more powerful when he becomes ghost. Since ghosts were once living people, there are as many different personalities among them as there are among people, as example, forceful, passive, introvert, extrovert and so on. But for the sake of simplicity, I will discuss two general types – Benign ghosts and Malevolent ghosts.

Benign ghosts mean no harm and in fact, they may even provide help and comfort in some way. Most of the ghosts are of this type – perfectly harmless. They can act in a variety of ways, but mostly they tend to be benevolent. Generally, they were nice people while they were alive, and logically they would also be nice after death, as example the famous and well-documented case of Mary Roff and Lurancy Vennum (Stevens, 1887; Myers, 1903, vol. 1, pp. 360-68; Auerbach, 1993, pp. 257-58). This case had attracted a great deal of publicity, and many paranormal researchers had investigated this case.

On July 5, 1865, a young woman, Mary Roff in Watseka, Illinois (about 70 miles south of Chicago) died after a period of suffering from psychological disturbances which apparently included some extrasensory experiences. On the day of Mary Roff's death, Lurancy Vennum was a fifteen-month-old baby living on her parents' farm in Iowa, seven miles south of Watseka. After thirteen years, Lurancy began showing abnormal mania and odd aggressive behavior. Under hypnosis conducted by physician E. Winchester Stevens, Lurancy said that she was under some form of influence by evil entities. It was suggested that she ask for a good spirit to help her control the evil entities. Mary Roff, the same woman who died about thirteen years ago, came to help her.

Roff was requested to possess Lurancy in order to help her from the attacks of the evil entities. On February 01, 1878, the 'control' of Lurancy, or the 'spiritual possession' as some researchers have called it, began. Soon Lurancy became mild, passive and polite, began to behave like Roff, and ultimately 'became' Mary Roff. For fifteen weeks Lurancy Vennum lived as Mary Roff among her family and friends, and everything she did convinced people that she was the real Mary Roff, whom she had never known. During this period her handwriting had changed. From within Lurancy's physical body, Mary Roff not only recalled events that occurred before Lurancy's birth, but even went to live with Roff family. On May 21, 1878, Mary Roff told her family that Lurancy was coming back, that the healing was over and that she would have to leave. Soon Roff tearfully bade everyone goodbye and left. Lurancy reappeared in her own body in perfect mental condition and returned to her own house. In the words of her mother, Lurancy was,

> "*perfectly and entirely well and natural ...Lurancy has been smarter, more intelligent, more industrious, more womanly, and more polite than before... Several of the relatives of Lurancy, including ourselves,*

now believe she was cured by spirit power, and that Mary Roff controlled the girl."

In January 1882, Lurancy had a happy married life and became mother of eleven children. Though Lurancy was alright, Mary Roff kept a vigil watch over her, even coming through her from time to time by pushing her into a trance state.

Stevens wrote a book called 'The Watseka Wonder' about the case. This case attracted wide attention at the time and contemporary newspapers in and around Chicago devoted a lot of space to it.

This is the kind of love, sympathy and 'humanity' that a ghost had shown to her neighbor. But still the benign ghosts can be little bit chaotic because they are not always aware of their surroundings. Though they will not intentionally do harm, but occasionally accidents can occur because they do not realize what might be going on around them. Sometimes these ghosts are "playful" to children not realizing what they are doing is creating a dangerous situation. We must realize that here we are dealing with things that are not scientifically explained very well. We are one kind of being, and spirits are another. We are subject to the laws of physics but they are not. And we don't know how immaterial and material substances interact. Hence, when a child talks about an imaginary playmate we must investigate the matter.

Malevolent ghosts are of much concern and we must take utmost care about these ghosts because they can do severe physical and mental harm. Ghosts can be good or bad, just as good and bad people exist in our world. If in life a person was hateful or cruel, he often maintains this mean personality after death. One good point is that malevolent ghosts are quite rare, just as in life there are more good people than bad people. Some malevolent ghosts may not be ghosts at all, they are demons (next chapter) who never had experienced physical life on Earth.

Many apparitions are reported to be wearing clothes or carrying objects, which creates a problem in explaining whether or not objects can survive bodily "death", however, as apparitions are regularly reported as appearing to have a solid body that can cast a shadow, then it could be equally as easy for the apparition to appear to be wearing clothes too. In OBE and NDE cases, while the person's physical body is on operation table and complicated surgery is in progress, he finds himself fully clad rather than naked during his experience. Researchers have varied opinion on this issue. Steiger (2003, p. 246) views, "*I believe that since near-death experiences involve the essential stuff of human personality, the projected mind may – if it wishes to do so – "create" its clothing by exercising the same kind of mental machinery that is utilized in dreams*". To support his point, Steiger (2003, p. 246) narrated the experience of a person, namely Wiltse, during his OBE.

"When he first projects his true self from the skull, he perceives himself as 'something like a jellyfish as regards color and form'. Then, because his mind had been conditioned on the temporal plane to think in terms of physical body concepts, the "jellyfish" expands into the full stature of a naked human male. When Wiltse confronts his sober-faced friends at the door, he suddenly finds himself clothed. Even though he is certain that they cannot see him in his spiritual body, a lifetime on the Earth plane living in a conservative culture had conditioned him not to go about in the nude. It may well be this same psycho-spiritual mechanism that explains why we never perceive naked ghosts."

The logic is that one's subtle body has a certain degree of malleability, so that it can alter its age, size, and other features (such as whether or not it has a beard or long hair). This malleability can also extend to the simulation of clothing. If after death we go forth into the world unclad, one would expect at least some reports of naked apparitions. Yes, it happens – there are cases when the ghost is seen at first fully naked but "quickly became clothed" (Irwin, 1985, p. 229). Since a ghost was once a living human being living in a traditional culture on the Earth for a lifetime, it obeys the same conservative culture. Granted some spirits may be confused or unable to accept their deaths, once they learn to manipulate energy sources and to use energy around them to become visible then it is just a matter of how they choose to show themselves to.

4.6: Apparitions of the living people

So far, in all the discussed cases we have noticed that every case coincided or nearly coincided with a death. However, on occasions we can see the apparitions of the people who are still alive physically and in a perfect physical and mental health. These incidents are very similar to out-of-body experiences only from another perspective view. Louisa Rhine had documented the following case,

"A little old lady came around every Thursday morning selling eggs from door to door and she always stopped at my house. This Thursday I had to go to town and as I was coming up the little road leading to my house I saw the egg lady standing on the porch. I noted that she was wearing a new pink dress and a sort of little bonnet to match. Just as I spied her she turned to step off the porch and I called to her to wait and then she just disappeared.

She never came out of my gate, she didn't go anywhere, she just wasn't there. I was not more than 50 feet away when I first saw her and there were no bushes or plants to obstruct my vision. Later in the afternoon a knock sounded on my door and when I responded there stood the little

egg lady dressed in pink and with her basket on her arm. I told her I was sorry I was not at home when she called about an hour earlier. She looked very surprised but smiled as she answered, 'But this is the first time I have been here today. An hour ago I was just leaving the ranch. I was thinking about you and wondering if you wanted some eggs.'" (Rhine, 1957, p. 22)

The apparition of the old lady was not self-aware. She was not even aware that she was projecting herself to the observer. Her words to be noted – "*I was thinking about you and wondering if you wanted some eggs*". Only by thinking, she unintentionally created the apparition. Various case studies had shown that many apparitions of the dead people are not self-aware. Are they also projecting themselves from the spirit world by only 'thinking' about the living people they left behind? In the following case (Hart, 1959, pp. 159-60) of Walter E. McBride, a farmer who lived near Indian Springs, Indiana, the apparition exhibited behavior suggesting that he had some degree of awareness of his surroundings.

On 23 December 1935, McBride had been concerned during the entire day about his father that he might be ill. At about 8 p.m. that evening, while wide awake, he felt himself to be floating in the room, in a whitish light which cast no shadows. In this condition, he moved upward to a certain height, and when he looked downward, he saw his physical body lying on the bed. He floated further upward through the building; the ceiling and floor failed to stop him. Almost at once, he somehow realized that he was moving through the air towards the north, going to his old home several miles away where his father lived.

Passing through the walls of his father's house he stood at the foot of the bed where his father was resting. His father's eyes were fixed upon him. The father was surprised but he did not seem to hear when McBride spoke to him. When McBride understood that his father was well, he found himself traveling back to his bedroom and again saw his own body still lying on the bed where he had left it. After reentering his physical self, he was instantly alert, with no feeling of drowsiness. Throughout this excursion, McBride was aware of a presence, which he was unable to identify, but which he subsequently came to regard as a guiding angel. This is a clear case of out-of-body experience.

Then McBride got up, made a light, and wrote down the time and the account of what he had experienced. Two days later, on Christmas Day, 1935, he visited his father, who verified his experience confirming that he had seen McBride exactly at the same time just as he had stood at the foot of the bed. Two more witnesses of this incident signed this statement, "*I can vouch that the above-described meeting and discussion did take place.*"

It seems in the cases of unintentional projections the apparition is not self-aware, while in cases of deliberate projections the apparition shows intelligence and awareness. Kelly et al. (2007, p. 396) described one famous case from 1863 that involves a Mrs. Wilmot, whose husband was onboard a ship on a storm-tossed Atlantic crossing,

> *"[She] had an experience, while she was awake during the middle of the night, in which she seemed to go to her husband's stateroom on the ship, where she saw him asleep in the lower berth and another man in the upper berth looking at her. She hesitated, kissed her husband, and left. The next morning Mr. Wilmot's roommate asked him, apparently somewhat indignantly, about the woman who had come into their room during the night."*

Some investigators describe these cases "reciprocal apparitions" where one person deliberately tries to "project" his personality or is having a spontaneous OBE or is having a dream in which he or she seems to go to a distant location, while a person at that location, unaware of the first person's experience sees an apparition of that person. So, apparitions of the living can be the active, purposeful vehicles of conscious, living selves which can function separately from its body, even while the body is alive. Thus, if apparitions of the dead are found to be identical in character with the apparitions of the living, would it not then follow that apparitions of the dead can also be active, purposeful vehicles of conscious surviving selves?

4.7: Psychomanteum: laboratory induced apparitions

For investigators, the most important question is whether the apparitions are subjective fantasies or whether they reflect some form of objective reality. The best way to experiment with an apparition would be to bring it into the laboratory, where its physical and psychological aspects could be studied under controlled conditions. To do that, parapsychologists have made use of a custom-built chamber called a psychomanteum (also known as 'apparition booth') where an apparition can be experienced under controlled setting.

The idea of a psychomanteum is derived from Greek mythology, in which people would often journey to special locations (such as the oracle at Delphi) to hold audience with the gods through visions and to see images of their deceased ancestors in the reflective pools of oil or water. Homer and Herodotus had written about this. Homer even provided a graphic account of a ceremony for calling up the dead. Very little was known about the Greek psychomanteums until 1958 when Greek archaeologist Sotirios Dakaris and his team uncovered a series of small underground rooms connected by a passageway that led to the main chamber believed to be the place where seekers could consult spirits of the deceased.

World's foremost expert on NDE, Raymond Moody had a deep interest in Greek history. When he read the Greek magical papyri, i.e., scrolls of magical recipes found in Egypt, but written in Greek, he followed the instruction of the magical papyri in a facility designed for just this purpose and then had created a modern psychomanteum in the style of the ancient Greeks in the early 1990s as a technique for bereavement and grief counseling.

The psychomanteum (Greek for "theater of the mind" – Houran and Lange, 2001, p. 166) is a darkened room with black curtains all around it. Inside the room there is a comfortable chair and a mirror on one of the walls. The mirror is angled so that the person sitting on the chair cannot see his own reflection. A candle is normally placed behind the chair to create subdued light. Moody's technique generally proceeded as follows.

The person would first be asked to select a deceased friend or relative with whom he wished to have a visionary reunion. Prior to the actual session, Moody would extensively discuss with him about the deceased person, their relationship with him, and his motivations for wanting to have a reunion. The person shared photographs and objects that had once belonged to the deceased person, and discussed their significance to help them remember and reconnect with that person.

> "*We discussed in detail the person who had died and the relationship that had existed between the two of them. We explored such areas as the type of person the deceased had been, his or her appearance, habits – virtually every aspect of personality....*" (Moody and Perry, 1993, p. 85)

After the preparatory session, towards dusk the person was shown into the psychomanteum, and was instructed to relax in a comfortable chair while gazing passively into a large mirror hanging on the wall (angled upward to reflect the darkness) a few feet across from the chair. The person begins to stare at the mirror. After a few minutes to a half-hour in the psychomanteum, people typically report that the mirror gradually transforms into a window, swirling clouds appear in this window, and then intensely vivid visions are seen through it. Often visions from the "other side" of the window extend into the psychomanteum itself. The person can stay inside as long as he wants, but should not wear a watch so that he would not be tempted to glance at the time. An attendant sat outside the chamber during this whole time, prepared to render any needed assistance.

> "*A number of persons participating have experienced full-sized, appropriately moving, three-dimensional, aptly colored apparitions of departed persons. All subjects were psychologically normal adults who were in a waking state of awareness during the process. Some of the subjects reported complex communication with the apparition and most described having a convincing sense of the presence of the departed person during the interlude. All subjects so far have voiced their unequivocal personal convictions that the visitations were real.*" (Moody, 1992, p. 85)

In all, Moody led 300 subjects into the psychomanteum that he wrote about in his book, 'Reunions'. About half of the people reported seeing apparitions of the dead in the mirror. Other researchers using the psychomanteum had varying degrees of success. Dianne Arcangel (1997) had a strong degree of success, with 58 of her 68 participants (85%) having a reunion experience. Participants see several visual images in the mirror including black robed figures, animal faces, flowers, a starry night, a landscape, and unknown faces. Some people also saw light that is "*brightest ever seen, but is not of the eye*". Angels and spirit guides and religious leaders appeared in some sessions. (Hastings, 2012, p. 15). These three-dimensional visions are often described as "hyper-real," that is, as more intensely real than the reality experienced under ordinary consciousness.

Arthur Hastings had 27 people participate in a psychomanteum study. During these episodes participants' sense of time is altered or distorted. Many of them are surprised when their time was up ("*I had no sense of it,*" commented one). One participant sought to contact her grandmother who had died 13 years ago. She could not contact her but had the following experience.

> "*Feeling deep grief at the beginning; black robed figures coming toward me; black spinning ball with trailing energy moving clockwise in mirror; unidentified faces in the mirror; energy streaming out of mirror into space in front of me. A foot (light skin then changed to dark skin). Hand and faint formulations of a human [?] shape*" (Hastings et al., 2002, p. 217).

Some participants mention telepathy either one sided, with the deceased person giving a message, or a mutual dialogue. Most of the communication was brief. One participant had received a very meaningful advice from his departed friend.

> "*I experienced a flash of light not in the mirror but above me to the right. I experienced some mental "knowings" and my friend chided me for resorting to such trappings in order to contact her. She "said" (internally) that she did not want her energy used for my amusement. If I really wanted to connect with her, I could be more connected with the part of her that lives on in her sister who is alive.*" (Hastings et al., 2002, p. 218)

Other advices from the departed seemed trivial to an outsider, e.g., "*Don't try to make things happen...they are happening to you*", and "*Look for love inside yourself [not from me]*", could have been significant to the recipient because of timing, circumstances, and salient concerns.

Hastings (2012, pp. 13, 14) reported that some sessions are like clear understandings, i.e., they are messages in themselves with or without an explicit sense of the deceased. As example, one person wrote that he was "*trying to understand more about the origins of my family's anger and rageful attitudes towards children*". Another person who had issues with his father wrote,

> "*I was immediately in a space of talking to my father, in my mind.... I went over the things he said to me when I was a child. He would call me 'no good', would say I never could do anything right.... I cried and pleaded with him for explanations for his behavior toward me, rejecting behavior*".

After about 20 minutes of pleading, "*the mirror and I sort of became one*", and he began to experience the situation with his father from a deeper, more all-around perspective.

> "*I began to see how he viewed our experience as a family.... I entered into his view and expectations of us.... He expected that we would provide us [i.e., the family] with the love and acceptance he was looking for. He saw himself burdened with duties and responsibilities that he had not wanted and blamed my mother and myself for this scenario.... I was expecting him to show his love for me. He was expecting I would love him. Like he could not show me love until he got it first.*"

This was a transformational experience for him because he could see his father's expectations from his viewpoint as if "*I became him.*" Seeing this from his perspective has answered a lot of questions at once and his view of their life relationship completely changed – "*... [the session] has eased off my blame toward him and helped me accept myself".... My abuse was not because there [was] inherently something wrong with me as I was told, but had more to do with my father's own view of himself.*" Not many people reported an experience of merging like the above.

Moody (2012, p. 220) wrote, "*The Oracles of the Dead and psychomanteums aren't the kind of thing that some doctors even care to understand*". Curiously, Moody talks about how his father, a well-respected physician had him committed to a mental hospital for psychiatric issues when he had talked to him about his work with the psychomanteum.

When Moody first built his psychomanteum he assumed that only 10% would experience seeing an apparition in the mirror, a vision of the departed person they had been prepared to see. He also assumed that even the small number of experiencers will be doubtful about what they see. However, in his utter surprise he found that he had grossly underestimated himself.

> "*The picture that has emerged from this project is dramatically different from what I had initially imagined... 12 of the 25 persons who have been guided through the entire procedure, and four other persons who were subjected to briefer versions of the preparation, have experienced apparitions.... all were articulate and intelligent.*" (Moody, 1992, p. 110)

The apparitions were not only visualized but also spoke intelligibly including meaningful exchange of information not known to participant before, as Moody wrote, "*These ranged from a few words of reassurance and love to lengthy, involved, interactive communication.*" The experiences were not frightening but quite natural while they were going on. The participants had little feeling that they could control the experience or ever tried to control it. Always the relationship between the discarnate and the person is the centerpiece of the whole encounter. In brief (Moody, 1992, pp. 110-12),

1. A female journalist came hoping to see her son on the mirror who had committed suicide some months ago. When he appeared, he told her that he was fine and that he loved her.
2. A man saw his deceased mother who expressed surprise and curiosity as to how her son had come to where she was.
3. A person met his adolescent nephew who had committed suicide a decade earlier. The teenager instructed his uncle to tell mother (his sister) that he was fine, that everything was all right. The person felt completely sure that he had actually been in the presence of his nephew.
4. In some cases, there were nonverbal communications. One man reported that the apparition of his mother indicated to him nonverbally that she felt the woman to whom he had recently become engaged was good for him and that she approved of her. This man had been very close to his mother, and this reflected a concern that had been on his mind. Another man, a psychologist, saw two of his cousins who acknowledged his presence during the encounter.
5. Not everyone met the person he or she had expected to see. An old man spent a long day with Moody preparing to see his father, but his departed business partner showed up instead. A woman tried to see her husband but her father came to her. Moody sought a meeting with his maternal grandmother, but his father's mother appeared to him.

All those who had seen apparitions asserted that they had completely real experiences. When Moody asked a smiling man what his judgment was, whether he felt his experience was a projection of his own mind, he said with emphasis, "*Oh, no! I saw my mother!*". A woman assured with complete confidence and equanimity that she had indeed been with her deceased father. A journalist insisted that he had in fact seen and visited his father. One woman said mirror gazing session had "opened (her) up" in some way difficult to describe. Many others described a compelling sense of the presence of their lost loved ones during these encounters.

Often the apparitions do not confine themselves to the mirror, or even to the psychomanteum. One man was shocked when his three departed relatives actually emerged from the mirror and surrounded him. Wondering at first if it was a deceptive trick, he reached up as if to touch them but his hand went right through the apparitions. A woman felt the presence of her grandfather so realistic that she felt him comfort her in an embrace.

Sometimes the apparitions occurred after the person had left the psychomanteum. A woman came in hopes of seeing her husband but saw nothing inside the psychomanteum. But shortly after she returned home, she experienced two separate apparitions of her father, during which she had lengthy conversations with him. The female journalist whose son appeared to her while she was in the psychomanteum spent that night in a motel. After she had already locked the door and was preparing to go to sleep, she found her son again standing in her motel room. She at first took the apparition as an intruder who had forced his way into her room. It is unknown why this delayed effect sometimes takes place.

Moody wanted a vision of his deceased maternal grandmother in his psychomanteum. The hour passed, and nothing happened. Later on, when he was sitting alone in a room a strange woman walked in. After about a minute of bewilderment, he realized that she was his deceased paternal (not maternal) grandmother. The reason Moody had not recognized her at first was that she appeared much younger than she was when she died, in fact even younger than she had been when he was born. Moody (1992, p. 113) commented,

> "*It is very difficult to put this experience into language; I am at a loss to explain some of it in words. When I recognized her as my grandmother and confronted her with this fact, she immediately acknowledged it and began to use the nickname she alone had used for me when I was a child. She talked with me about events only my grandmother and I knew. She imparted to me certain very personal information about my early life that has been quite important and revealing.... I look forward to meeting her again when I make my transition.*"

The apparition reminded Moody of several events that he had forgotten. Her voice was clear, the only difference being that there was a crisp, electric quality to it that appeared clearer and louder than her voice before she died. Most of their conversation was through spoken word, but from time to time he was immediately aware of what she was thinking, and obviously it was true for the apparition also.

The apparition did not appear 'ghostly' or transparent during the reunion. She looked completely solid with no difference from any other person except that she was surrounded by what appeared to be a light or an indentation in space, as if she were somehow set off or 'offbeat' from the rest of her physical surroundings.

Moody did not touch his grandmother. When he indicated that he wanted to hug her she put up her hands and motioned him back. Moody declared that the experience was completely coherent with his ordinary waking reality – "*If I were to discount this experience as hallucinatory, I would be almost obliged to discount the rest of my life as hallucinatory too*" (Varga, 2009, p. 13). He took the experience as proof of the reality of life after death.

From the above first-hand experiences, it is very clear that none of the above participants were victims of hallucinations. Actually, it is impossible for a human brain to produce strong hallucination which Daniel Dennett defines as "*an apparently concrete and persisting three-dimensional object in the real world*". This would be something like "*a ghost that talked back, that permitted you to touch it, that resisted with a sense of solidity ...*" (Dennett, 1991, p. 7). Only a small part of the brain's information processing power could be devoted to generating a hallucination. Much of the brain's visual processing system cannot produce hallucination and large sections of the brain is 'wired' for unrelated functions, such as control of the bodily limbs etc. (Thompson, 2003, p. 130). Thus, hallucination does not appear to be an adequate explanation. Rather by their very occurrence, these fascinating encounters bear witness to the existence and wonder of the immortal soul – the quantum consciousness.

4.8: A scientific analysis

The English Society for Psychical Research instituted the first systematic inquiry into apparitions in 1882. Members of that society included William James, Sir Oliver Lodge, Physicists Wilhelm Weber and W. F. Barrett, French astronomer Camille Flammarion, English naturalist Alfred Russel Wallace (the co-inventor of Darwin's theory of evolution), and a host of Nobel laureates, such as J. J. Thomson, Sir William Crookes, Charles Richet and Lord Rayleigh (Kaku, 1994, pp. 50, 53). They wanted to examine these phenomena scientifically. Later, in 1889, a far more detailed international study was commenced where 32 thousand cases of sightings of apparitions were received. Further studies were conducted by the American Society for Psychical Research and by Camille Flammarion, who compiled thousands of cases. The Society thus collected narrative descriptions of messages from the dead and allied data, cases that are still among the most useful descriptions available today.

Gurney and Myers (1888-89, pp. 403-85) examined 27 of these cases in details and concluded that apparitions of the dead are real. Hudson (1901) attributed these encounters to the brain's ability to reach maximum power at the very hour of death and project itself into another's mind. Myers (1903) came to a similar conclusion that the ghosts are manifestations of persistent personal energies and that the soul is a definable component of the organism that can survive the body at death.

However, the nature of the apparitions remained a mystery to the society members. Equally mysterious were the deaths of the leading three members, as Siegel (1980, p. 916) wrote, Myers suffered from a fatal disease that encouraged his thoughts of death and spiritualism, Gurney died from a mysterious overdose of chloroform and Podmore was found mysteriously drowned in a few inches of water.

British spiritualist William Harrison, while discussing apparitions of dying, and those perceived after death, commented, "*There is no break of continuity in the phenomena of apparitions in consequence of the death of the body*" (Harrison, 1879, p. vii). Myers (1903, vol. 1, p. 8) had the same view as he wrote, "*We gradually discovered that the accounts of apparitions at the moment of death ... lead without perceptible break to apparitions occurring after the death of the person seen*". After few years, Delanne (1909, p. 12) affirmed the existence of a "*perfect resemblance between the extra-sensory manifestations of the soul during life, and after death. A phantom of the dead is identical to a phantom of the living.*" In other words, such apparitional experiences indicate survival of bodily death.

Some of the leaders in the scientific research of life after death are extremely intelligent and astute medical doctors who began their investigation as skeptics. Glen Hamilton was a highly respected physician and member of the Canadian Parliament. In his laboratory under strictly controlled conditions he had a battery of fourteen electronically controlled flash cameras which photographed apparitions simultaneously from all angles. He summarized the results in this sentence, "*Time after time, I saw dead persons materialize*" (Hamilton, 1942). Observers present at his experiments included four other medical doctors, two lawyers, an electrical and a civil engineer.

Today, investigators want to explain the ghostly phenomenon and appearances of apparitions in strict scientific terms. Brian A. Schill, an investigator from American Society for Paranormal Research and Investigation, pointed out that every living being has a bioelectric cycle that functions at 60 Hz that enables our hearts, brains, and central nervous system to function and to communicate within the organism itself. This medical fact, if examined, within the context of the first law of thermodynamics (energy can neither be created nor destroyed, only transformed), we can recognize that two-thirds of our life experience exists within our intangible mind and spirit (life force, soul, etc.), while the third part is made up of our physical body. Now, if two-thirds of our total existence is in the form of intangible energy, we need to know what happens to this energy when we die. Schill (Steiger, 2003, p. xi) commented,

> "*When a person dies the bioelectric energy is released from the body into the local environment where it may perform one of two actions. The unconscious energy may dissipate into the local environment and there will essentially be no manifestation thereafter or it may, through covalent bonding, remain in the local environment and attach itself to a certain place or object that the person was attached to in life, or any place that*

has an electron deficit (this is the theory behind 'repeat' hauntings). The energy may, upon rapid release from the physical body (such as in accidental death, tragic situations, or a rapid natural release, etc.) coagulate within the local environment over a short period of time, maybe only a couple of minutes or so, and amass to such a degree that the greater portion that was originally in the body has now become self-aware outside of the body."

When self-awareness occurs, there is generally a degree of confusion because of the new form that the person is in. The new form is one of pure energy state rather than a physically manifested body.

Various cases documented over last few centuries had shown that the ghostly hauntings are strikingly similar, and these are consistent with other non-physical phenomena, such as OBEs, NDEs, astral projections, poltergeists, manifestations of religious figures, spirit possession, mediumship, glowing orbs, and animal spirits. Each of these non-physical phenomena comprises an interesting side of human experience that may one day help us define the farthermost reaches of the soul.

It's a common misconception that ghosts don't know they are dead or how to escape their pathetic situation. They are trapped because they are confused. They are not lost in some confined astral plane and they do know they have made a transition out of life on Earth. Their confusion lies in the obsessive attachment they have to places, people and events that they can't let go. These actions of self-displacement are voluntary. Spiritual guides honor poor decision-making also.

The apparitional occurrences challenge the materialistic views of mind currently prevailing in cognitive sciences, pointing towards a spiritual dimension co-existing with the human mind.

4.9: Skeptic's views

While disproving this specific area of supernatural, the skeptics put forward following arguments,

1. No evidence of ghosts exists. There is no theory in any life science that makes a prediction that ghosts exist. Ghosts have no properties that can be described.
2. There has never been a reproducible ghost event. This makes it unlikely that the perceived phenomenon was a real one.
3. The logic that most people use to arrive at a conclusion of "ghost" is faulty. It's usually that something inexplicable happened, what else could it be? A ghost is an unknown. How a set of unknown properties be considered consistent with your experience? When searching for

the explanation for a strange experience, a process of elimination of causes can never logically leave "a ghost" as a reasonable explanation.

4. Anomalous magnetic fields are possibly inducing haunt experiences.

Literally hundreds of thousands of well-documented cases of apparitions and poltergeist phenomena exist. It is questionable to believe a single person's claim to have seen a ghost but when more than one thousand people (including several members of the royal family) declare they have all seen Anne Boleyn's ghost in seven different locations it is unreasonable to disbelieve them. The existence of ghosts is an evidently proven reality. There are paranormal research societies that have been around since the 19th century that publish all sorts of journals and literature and case studies. The researchers are often highly qualified people who had done notable research on other subjects. It would be unjustifiable to call all these records as fabricated or biased. Today there are actually plenty of respected institutes and university research groups pursuing these paranormal entities.

Life sciences involve mainly the scientific study of living organisms, such as microorganisms, plants, animals, and human beings. Hence, afterlife research is not within the scope of life sciences, and a new science is required to explore the objective side of human consciousness. Ghosts are fully consistent within our understandings of quantum physics.

Ghosts have certain common properties, such as some ghosts are radioactive, block light from electric bulbs, exchange intelligent information and can be captured on photography. If ghosts are hallucinations how brain activity would corroborate such things? Also, meaningful voices can be recorded which is called Electronic Voice Phenomena (EVP). The discarnates can manipulate the sound waves that have previously been recorded on a device. So, the sound of a fan or raindrops can be changed into the sound of spoken words (Champlain, 2013, p. 76). Most of these voices sound like whispers but sometimes a loud, clear word or message can be heard. Once EVP experiments were conducted in soundproof studios, and in a duration of 27 minutes some 200 voices were received. No one could break the mystery.

Based on the laws of physics and atomic structures, no known particle is small enough to pass through walls and at the same time big enough to block light. It means, either ghosts are made up of a material that cannot exist in three-dimensional reality, or ghosts are not 'things' that are observed directly through the optic nerve, but rather in the mind where sight is decoded by the brain, i.e., some outside force projecting it to the mind. They can float midair, means, gravity does not apply to them. They can interact with each other and have a very tiny bit of power also to move something small (like a penny or slam a door). Ghosts by default do not collide with anything, but can willingly choose to interact with other masses and therefore collide with them – these self-contradictory properties of a ghost raise many serious questions that present-day scientists cannot fully understand. One possible explanation is that astral beings can dematerialize or materialize their forms at will. So, when a ghost is in materialized state it can block lights, and when it is in dematerialized state, it can pass through walls. Famous Hindu Yogi Paramhansa Yogananda wrote that his guru Sri Yukteswar appeared to him in physical form after his death. On asking him if he was truly in a physical body, Sri Yukteswar answered,

> "*Yes, my child, I am the same. This is a flesh and blood body. Though I see it as ethereal, to your sight it is physical. From cosmic atoms I created an entirely new body, exactly like that cosmic-dream physical body which you laid beneath the dream-sands at Puri [a pilgrimage city of India] in your dream-world. I am in truth resurrected – not on earth but on an astral planet. Its inhabitants are better able than earthly humanity to meet my lofty standards. There you and your exalted loved ones shall someday come to be with me.*
>
> ***... my new body is a perfect copy of the old one. I materialize or dematerialize this form any time at will,*** *much more frequently than I did while on earth. By quick dematerialization, I now travel instantly from planet to planet or, indeed, from astral to causal or to physical cosmos.*" (Yogananda, 1981, pp. 400, 414-15)

Anomalous magnetic fields are not the entire explanation for all reported hauntings, as there are some experimental studies and field investigations which have not found magnetic fields around haunt areas. Moreover, it is unclear how these fields can produce apparitions showing self-consciousness and intelligent behaviour. And as Cornell (2002, p. 388) had wisely pointed out, apparitions and their related phenomena "*...were widely reported long before the development and use of manmade electromagnetic utilities*" nullifies the claims of the doubters.

There are "reproducible ghost events", such as cyclic ghosts and anniversary ghosts who appear at regular schedule. If there is only one ghostly event it can be dismissed a hallucination, but when the cyclic and anniversary ghosts are seen at regular intervals and witnessed by many people it cannot be disregarded as hallucination or thinking error. It seems the skeptics are blind to the evidence that's right in front of them.

We cannot say that ghosts are unknown because we cannot see them normally as we see people walking on the street. Montgomery (1972, p. 37) had a fine logic on this issue;

> "*Simply accept for the time being that your family and friends will not be able to see and converse with you, even though you are able to see and talk with them.* ***This proves that you are more alive than they are, because your faculties are so much greater now that you have left the body.*** *But for the time being they will view you as nothing but thin air and think of you as beneath the ground. Such a pity...*".

There's as much scientific evidence to support their existence as there is for the existence of black holes. People claim to have photographed, observed, and studied black holes, but they haven't been tested under laboratory conditions. That doesn't mean that they don't exist. By the same token we can't dismiss the existence of the supernatural either.

According to some skeptics, the image of the apparition is in the mind of the experiencer, i.e., the experiencer is actually projecting the image of a dead person which he perceives again as a ghost. But this hypothesis does not explain the significant coincidences of apparitional experiences with crisis in the life of a person. There are also cases when an experiencer sees an apparition with physical changes of which the experiencer had no formal knowledge. In one case, the experiencer saw his brother drowned when his foot got entangled in a ship's towline (Sidgwick, 1891, pp. 32-35). In another case, the experiencer saw the apparition with a beard of which he was completely ignorant (Gurney and Myers, 1888-89, pp. 412-15; Sidgwick, 1894, p. 379). Stevenson (1982, p. 343) studied a similar case at Nigeria during 1978. As per his report, one person was shocked to see the apparition of his younger brother in his (the experiencer's) room wearing an unusual towel wrapped around his middle. He later came to know that in another city his brother has gone for an emergency surgical operation at about the time of the apparitional experience and had worn such a towel-like garment during the operation. This proves that the ghosts and apparitions are objective reality, not hallucinations or projections of mind. If this type of cases is caused by telepathy between a discarnate entity and a living person, then obviously all the details come from the side of the discarnate entity which again prove that the discarnate is actually 'living' on the other side of death. The entities are not only in conscious states, but have a strong desire to communicate to living persons they think likely to be interested, or when some purpose arises such as the Chaffin Will Case and Lieutenant James Sutton case.

Here it is worth mentioning how a hardcore skeptic changed his views after death. Steiger (2003, p. 223) narrated the case of Deon Frey, an exceptionally powerful medium. Her father was a strong disbeliever of afterlife. But on the night her father died, she received a visitation from him.

> "*I was 15. Eternal life was proved to me that night. The spirit of my father, who had never been a churchgoer or a believer in the afterlife, appeared at my bedside and said, 'If I live after death, then everyone.lives.*'"

It should be remembered that, two hundred years ago, skeptics had rejected the scientific idea that things like bacteria and viruses existed, largely because it seemed absurd to imagine that creatures could exist that are too small to be seen with the naked eye. Once the microscope was perfected, of course, all that changed, leading to the advent of modern medicine. Could "ghosts" then be the next revolution in science that awaits only the development of the technology needed to detect them?

4.10: Conclusion

Presently, greatest degree of evidential support from parapsychological findings pertaining to ghosts and apparitions is available. The more we examine the cases scientifically, the more our strength increases for the evidence that points towards survival. Ghost investigation is 'science' in proper sense of the term which has the potential to make a huge difference in a society still tormented by superstition and fear.

If the psychomanteum reunion experiences are produced in the brain then obviously the material for these experiences are taken from the participant's subconscious mind which by hypothesis is part of his brain's mental system. But how the brain can use this material to create a meaningful conversation that unfolded interactively and appeared to involve two conscious persons? How the transmission of meaningful information takes place (Moody and his grandmother)? The logical conclusion is that they are genuine contacts with the deceased. When a person dies, the relationship does not necessarily end. It continues, but in a different form when they were alive. Therefore, psychomanteum experiments are purely scientific.

However still there remains a lot that is unknown about their scientific nature, and their possible implications for survival. Keeping that in mind we should pay attention to the words of experimental parapsychologist, Michaeleen Maher,

> "*...it is evident that research on ghosts (poltergeists, hauntings. and apparitions) has as yet exposed little of the vast, uncharted domain of death and possible immortality. Far from resolving the mystery, we have hardly begun to penetrate its outer shell. It would be unwise to "give up the ghost" at this unsatisfying stage of our knowledge. An honest inquiry into death and its aftermath is both bold and necessary for the true progress of humankind*". (Maher, 1992, p. 138)

As a good start we should do more research on psychomanteum which is still at its infancy. Parapsychologists, psychical researchers and dedicated paranormal enthusiasts can be quite helpful in this regard and can potentially contribute to the efforts. They may also continue to open new doors to better answers, and thus shed more light on the nature of ghosts and apparitions.

Chapter 5

Demon possession

In last chapter I have discussed about the discarnate entities who were once human beings in a physical body. In this chapter, I will discuss other type of entities who had never lived as humans on Earth but strongly desire to occupy a human body. These nonhuman entities want to feel the emotions and sensual expressions that are unique to the human experience. Some of them use their psychic abilities to assume a humanlike appearance when they manifest in our material, three-dimensional world. Traditionally they are called demons but a more appropriate term is "spirit parasites". Steiger (2003, pp. 174-75) indicated,

> "*There are shadow beings and spirit parasites that inhabit unseen areas at the edge of our material world who take delight in assuming control over humans, or even in entering and taking possession of a physical body... there are entities in the spiritual dimension that will masquerade as something or someone they are not. They do this for the sole purpose of deceiving us and wreaking havoc in our lives.*"

By the word 'demon' I don't mean anything like devils with tails and pitchforks as depicted in comic books. It is unknown how they appear to each other in their world. These extraterrestrial entities are pure evil or 'evil' itself who are coming from other dimensions of reality. Occasionally they speak of hell. According to famous psychologist Wilson Van Dusen,

> "*They invade every nook and cranny of privacy, work on every weakness and credibility, claim awesome powers, lie, make promises, and then undermine the patients' will. They never have a personal identity, though they accept most names or identities given to them.*" (Steiger, 2003, pp. 114-15).

By seizing the controlling mechanism of a host body and by undermining the victim's will, they direct the enslaved human to perform harmful acts against himself and others. When an unwilling person is taken over by a demon for devious purposes or for no reason at all, we call it demon possession. Possession is the symptom, not the problem, and therapeutic processes (exorcism or adorcism) aim to lessen such problems. The external phenomena of possession may resemble symptoms of psychic disturbance or disease. Hence there is a possibility that a person who shows psychological disturbance will be dismissed as a mere psychotic, and not considered to be under the demonic influence.

The quantum souls and spirit parasites are entirely different. A spirit can show intelligent and kind behavior while a demon is always low in intelligence, utterly cruel and insensible to us. Most of the times they are not identifiable. Hence when an exorcism is performed, the experts first try to find out the name of the demon (though some demons are nameless) and then use that name to cast out the evil entity. Demons have a tendency to return until they are convinced it would be more comfortable for them to abandon the victim permanently. This part is also taken care of.

In reported cases of ghostly encounters, the entity tends to behave like they would if they were alive because ghosts are just people without a 'living' physical body. In other words, ghosts are people too. Just as there are nice people, there are not-so-nice people. Hence just as there are nice ghosts, there are not-so-nice ghosts. Though a ghost can be obnoxious and insulting, in general the ghosts don't misbehave. The hauntings are not, in and of themselves, evil. We fear ghosts and apparitions because we still don't understand the phenomena scientifically, and that which we are afraid of is generally labeled as 'Evil'. But demons are inherently evil entities "*whose sole reason for existence is to persecute, attack, and possess living people*" (Auerbach, 1993, p. 249). Hence ghost possession and demon possession cases are of different nature. Possession takes two forms – one form of possession causes a change in bodily functioning and the other form alters consciousness, awareness, the personality or will of the individual (Bourguignon, 1976, p. 3). In general, ghost possessions take the first form while demon possessions take the second form. Ghost possession can be beneficial to the victim as we have seen in Mary Roff and Lurancy Vennum case. When a demon possesses a person, the power it exercises in its victim is beyond the capacity of any human being. The possessed body becomes a blind instrument. Here I discuss four cases.

5.1: The Tennessee Demon

Farmer John Bell and his family began experiencing disturbances in 1817 in their remote farmhouse home Clarksville, Tennessee. First, mysterious rappings were heard on the doors and windows. John looked outside but saw nothing. Then in one fateful night the mysterious being succeeded in entering the house. Frightening sounds filled the rooms – the rush of wings, a rat-like gnawing and the muffled pad of animal paws. As days passed the noises grew louder and stronger as if whatever was causing them was growing in power.

In the upstairs room, John's thirteen-year-old daughter Elizabeth, known as Betsy, woke up one night screaming. An invisible force was pinching and slapping her. Other children also reported similar attacks that steadily grew in ferocity. At first, the terrified family tried to keep their horror a secret because they did not want to become the subject for common gossip.

Soon another strange noise that sounded like the sucking noise of a baby being nursed, and lips smacking together filled the entire home. Several demonologists have noted the peculiar sounds of psychic "nursing" that often signal the beginning of a particularly violent episode of disturbances. The phenomenon is a result of the manifestation of an entity in the form of an obscene infant, born from some dimension of reality that borders our own. English poet and cleric Sacheverell Sitwell (1988, p. 108) wrote that such a being might be "*an embryonic phantasm*" that comes into existence on "*the borderlands, upon one frontier or the other, of human life.... It is in all things unholy, unhallowed, and not human.*"

Finally, the Bell family could not take it any longer and invited a neighborhood preacher, James Johnson, to exorcise the demon. Despite his hymns and prayers, the attempt failed, and the angered demon slapped Betsy, knocking the screaming girl to floor. A number of neighbors took Betsy out of the house and into their homes, but the demon simply followed her to the other abodes. By now the haunting had achieved wide notoriety. The demon grew stronger and the gargle turned to a husky, rasping whisper. Most of the words were frightful gibberish and each message carried the same thing. It hated John Bell and swore it would hound him to the grave. Soon the demon became powerful enough to venture outside the farmhouse and away from Betsy, its center of energy. Betsy began to suffer from seizures and fainting spells, similar to those that spirit mediums undergo while in or entering a trance. Neighbors reported seeing lights like candles or lamps moving through the fields, and farmers began to suffer attacks of stones thrown by the demon. This evil entity was outspoken in its dislike of John Bell, "*I'll keep after him until the end of his days! Old Jack Bell's days are numbered.*"

Soon another four nasty entities, each speaking in a distinctive voice of its own, made every night a maddening, wild party during their stay with the demon. The visitors who stayed the night had the covers jerked from their beds, and some were slapped soundly on the face. When a visitor questioned the demon concerning its identity, it once answered, "*I am a spirit who was once very happy, but who has been disturbed and made unhappy. I will remain in this house and worry old Jack Bell until I kill him*" (Steiger, 1966, p. 28).

This demon was having the voice and attributes of a woman. It was invisible to the eye, yet it would hold conversation and even shake hands with certain individuals.

John's mind and body finally broke under the terrible assault and he suffered frequent seizures. Even during John's illness, the cruel entity would not leave him in peace; rather, it continued to torment him by slapping his face and throwing his legs into the air. A doctor had prescribed medicine for John, and during one attack his son went to get it. Instead of doctor's medicine, he found the bottle filled with a murky liquid. The family called the doctor, but while they waited, the demon rampaged triumphantly through the house. Its whisper was a hoarse grunt, "*I have got him this time! I gave him a big dose while he was sleeping and old jack is done for now.*"

John Bell died December 20, 1820 after lapsing into a deep stupor. The doctor tested the medicine on a cat – and it died. The demon sang vulgar songs all during John Bell's funeral and annoyed the assembled mourners with the sounds of its crude celebration throughout the man's last rites. After the funeral, the demon told the family that it would return in seven years. Right on time, the demon again visited the family, but both the sons and Betsy were happily married. Disappointed, the demon said it would return in 107 years. But the threat was never carried out and 1935 passed safely for John's heir Charles Bailey Bell.

5.2: Demon-infested house in Amityville

This house was a scene of a multiple murder when Ronald DeFeo, a 23-year-old son of a wealthy car dealer had drugged his parents, brothers and sisters at supper and at 0315 a.m. slaughtered six family members by shooting each of them in their back with a rifle on November 13, 1974. The dead bodies were found face down in their beds. Ronald claimed in the court that 'voices' had ordered him to commit the crime. He was sentenced to six consecutive life sentences (Boar and Blundell, 1991, p. 32). From the date of this gruesome multiple murder incident this beautiful three-storied colonial-style residence seemed to have an evil life of its own.

On December 18, 1975, George and Kathleen Lutz purchased the house and moved in with three children. A local priest, Father Ralph Pecoraro came to bless the house. He went from room to room and said prayers in each room using holy water, but he was a bit uncomfortable in the upstairs back bedroom. The bedroom was abnormally very cold. While sprinkling holy water he heard a rather deep voice behind him saying 'Get out'. It seemed so directed toward him that he was really quite startled. At one point, he felt a slap on his face, but nobody was there. Later he claimed that blisters appeared on his hands after the blessing. He commented that he went to the doctor, but the physician couldn't explain the wounds.

For the first two nights in their new home, the family was awakened by strange noises at 0315 a.m. But the real horror began on third night. Before going to bed George had checked that all the doors and windows were locked from inside. The strange noises aroused him at 0315 a.m., and he went downstairs to investigate. He could not believe what he saw. The heavy, solid-wood front door had been wrenched open and was hanging by one hinge. With horror he realized that the door has been forced open from inside the house. The thick steel doorknob spindle was twisted and the surrounding metal plate had been forced outwards.

Two weeks after the front-door incident George woke in the night to find that his wife Kathy had levitated and moved towards the wall away from him. George pulled her down by her hair and switched on the light. He was looking not at his attractive young wife, but at a hideous vision. She had turned into an old crone, a really ugly old woman. Kathy caught a glimpse of her reflection in a mirror and screamed, "*That's not me. It can't be me.*" It took six hours for her face to change back to normal.

A few nights later, the couple was in the sitting room when Kathy looked up and saw two glowing red eyes at the darkened window. They hurried outside and found strange tracks on the snow. The keyholes from the old-style doors on the second and third floors started emitting some strange substance. The drips got longer and longer. The mysterious drippings were black, almost like epoxy, and the longer they were in the house, the longer the drips came out of certain keyholes. Also, a large number of flies did form against the sewing room window that didn't go away. Even the dog was scared to enter that room. The hauntings seemed to escalate day by day, and after 28 days of living in the house, Lutz family fled the dream house. The house was pure evil. The Amityville Horror case has reached legendary status in the annals of paranormal history.

5.3: A demon-possessed man in a Chinese monastery

Possession and exorcism cases are common in Communist China where belief in supernatural is a taboo. During the 1920s at a monastery near Shanghai, a young farmer with "*a wild, roving look in his fevered eyes*" was brought for exorcism. The abbot approached holding "*an elongated ivory tablet, the symbol of wisdom and authority*" and commanded the evil entities (for there were two) to come out of the man in the name of Shang Ti (the supreme Taoist Godhead), the demons coursed him, "*out of the energumen's distorted mouth in a strange, shrill voice, which sounded mechanical, inhuman – as if pronounced by a parrot*" (Goullart, 1961, pp. 86-87). Then with extreme horror the people saw that the man's body began to swell visibly. It continued until he became a grotesque balloon of a human shape. The abbot concentrated and commanded more fiercely, and then "*streams of malodorous excreta and effluvia flowed on to the ground in incredible profusion*" with a terrible stench (Smith, 2012, p. 178). After about one hour the man finally resumed normal size. However, the demons were not finished. Goullart (1961, p. 89) continued,

> "*Another scene of horror evolved itself before our dazed eyes. The man on the bed became rigid and his muscles seemed to contract, turning him into a figure of stone. Slowly, very slowly, the iron bedstead, as if impelled by an enormous weight, caved in, its middle touching the ground. The attendants seized the inert man by his feet and arms. The weight was such that none of them could lift him up and they asked for assistance from the onlookers. Seven men could hardly lift him for he was heavy as a cast-iron statue.*"

Eventually the man regained his normal weight and the final struggle began. When the abbott started yelling at the demons, the onlookers saw the man's body tremble, his fingers claw his body until it was covered with blood, his eyes roll up under his skull, and then the final twisting outburst as the demons came out of him with a wild scream, "*Damn you! Damn you! We are going but you shall pay for it with your life*" (Goullart, 1961, p. 89). The exorcism was completed successfully, and the man resumed his normal personality and asked where he was. He had absolutely no memory of anything that had happened. The abbot was completely exhausted and had to be helped away.

5.4: Demonic molestation of a teenager

In the night of May 10, 1953, a teenage girl, Clarita Villanueva, was found walking lonely on the streets of Manila, sobbing for someone to protect her from a monster. Her strange behavior had attracted a small crowd of local observers and soon police arrived and took her in custody. When police medical officer Mariano B. Lara gave the teenager a cursory examination, he diagnosed her as having suffered an epileptic episode and advised that she be closely watched so she could not injure herself. The police officer put her in a prison cell and reassured her as she crouched in terror behind the bunk in her cell – "*No monster can get you in there. He couldn't get through the bars.*"

Suddenly Clarita screamed, "*He is drifting right through the bars!*" Then, before the officer's startled eyes, prominent teeth marks began to appear on her upper arms and shoulders. She cried in extreme pain, and more bleeding wounds and marks appeared on her arm as if an invisible beast had wrapped its entire mouth around her slim arm and had sunk its teeth deep into her flesh. The frightened officer helped Clarita into the hall, and together they fled the cell to seek out his senior who in turn quickly informed higher authorities, and within a short time, the chief of police and the city's mayor had gathered around Clarita, attempting to decide what could be done to help the girl.

Mayor Lacson questioned Clarita while medical officer Lara examined her. The wounds were not self-inflicted. She cannot bite herself on the back of her neck. But what was attacking her? The sobbing girl described that it resembled a man with a long, flowing black cloak. It was very ugly and came at her with its fangs bared and ready to sink into her flesh. Lara traced a forefinger over the indentations in the girl's skin. They certainly appeared to be the prints of teeth.

Clarita spent the rest of the night on a bench inside the police station, closely attended by an officer. The next morning, the girl was brought to court to face the charges of vagrancy that had been levied against her. There, before the skeptical eyes of the entire court, Clarita endured another attack by the demon. Reporters rushed to stand beside her for a closer look as she collapsed from severe pain of the unseen jaws that had attached themselves to her flesh. "*This girl is definitely not having an epileptic fit,*" Lara told the reporters. "*These teeth prints are real, and they are most certainly not self-inflicted.*" There was no need to attest to the reality of the teeth marks to the reporters. They were serving as startled witnesses to the cruel indentations that were appearing on the girl's arms, shoulders, palms, and neck. Lara told a police officer, "*Perhaps a clergyman will be of more value in this case than a doctor.*" With more attacks, soon the unfortunate girl had become a veritable mass of deeply embedded teeth prints and swollen and bruised flesh.

When mayor took one of Clarita's hands into his own deep teeth marks appeared on opposite sides of her index finger, as if a hungry beast was trying to chew the finger off. An ambulance was called to take her to a hospital. Inside the ambulance, Clarita shouted that there were two creatures attacking her, each of them with large, bag-like eyes and awful teeth. Lara and Mayor Lacson watched in horror that teeth marks appeared on both sides of the girl's throat and on her hands. The demonic attacks ceased when Clarita entered the hospital. Six weeks later she had recovered her health almost completely, and never again suffered from the terrible invisible jaws that had torn at her flesh. Her body would forever bear the scars of those vicious attacks by her invisible assailant. Lara commented, "*What happened to Clarita Villanueva is a complete mystery, something that simply defies rational explanation. I don't mind saying that I was scared out of my wits*". This case had received worldwide publicity (Weise, 2017, p. 151). Till date no one knows what the reason of this demonic attack was and from where the demons came.

One similar case from 1925-26, discussed by Michell and Rickard (2007, p. 66), was of an illiterate 13-year-old Romanian peasant girl named Eleonore Zugun. Deep cuts resembling bites from teeth, and punctures and scratches from needles suddenly appeared on her skin. Objects were moved, materialised and dematerialised. Locked doors seemed no hindrance to their transportation.

She was brought to London for a series of experiments at the National Laboratory of Psychical Research by Countess Zoe Wassilko-Serecki who described this as follows,

> "*Then there appeared suddenly on her hands and forearms marks, which one could recognize only as bites. There were sharp teeth-marks, completely and unmistakably recognizable as such, exactly as though she [Eleonore] had been bitten by somebody. There would be from six to nine teeth above and below, the size of the oval varying, just as though this hypothetical mouth had been more or less widely open*". (Wassilko-Serecki, 1926, p. 595).

The bite marks did not correspond to Eleonore's own teeth; whoever was responsible for the bites, it was not Eleonore inflicting them. Large amount of 'saliva' appeared around the bites, which was found to be linked with a variety of infections when tested in the laboratory. To Eleonore, the scratches and bites were simply the work of 'dracu' – Romanian for 'the devil' only she could see, but the word "Dracu" spontaneously appeared (Evening Standard newspaper, October 1, 1926). The press coverage came to the attention of the German papers leading to a visit from a German psychical researcher Fritz Grunewald of Berlin. During experiments, investigators covered Eleonore's skin with a heavy layer of rouge in the areas where the bites and scratches tended to appear, but these marks appeared on the rouge as well as on the underlying skin.

****

Ghost possessions are much easier to deal with than demon possession. In 1924 Carl Wickland, a psychiatrist from Los Angeles, published a book 'Thirty Years Among the Dead' a unique record of exact conversations he had with departed souls using his wife, a trained spiritualist medium. He carefully divided his book into chapters based on what kind of spirit spoke through his wife, such as, both before and after their deaths, tormented women, alcoholics, criminals etc. The departed souls of alcoholics sometimes continue after death to 'drink' by possessing living people. Once Wickland talked to a discarnate who was parasitically using the body of a woman named 'Mrs. V' to drink. Wickland used electric shock to dislodge the spirit, then transferred the spirit to his wife's (a trance medium) body on April 04, 1923. Once inside his wife's body, Wickland tried to persuade the spirit to leave (Wickland, 1924, p. 188). Eventually he succeeds in making the spirit understand who he is, that he has died, that he is ruining a woman's life, and that he can get help for himself. As the session ends, the spirit, guided by his deceased mother, departed (Betty, 2005, p. 15). Wickland closed the account with these words,

> "*After the foregoing experience a friend reported a marked change for the better in Mrs. V., saying that no further desire for intoxicants was*

manifested. Mrs. V. herself acknowledged this change and expressed her gratitude for the relief obtained." (Wickland, 1924, p. 196).

Hence, ghost possession cases are different from demon possession cases. Possessing ghosts are obliging, but when they are treated rudely or violently, they can make a spectacle of themselves. Also, there are ghost possession cases where the possessing entity has a karmic link (The law of Karma – Chapter 8) from a past life with the person being possessed. Many expert paranormal investigators take this matter into account while resolving a possession case.

5.5: Warning signs of demonic possession and exorcism techniques

The signs of demon possession vary depending on the cultural and/or religious belief system (Auerbach, 1993, p. 229). The most common feature is extreme shift of the victim's personality and change of identity. At the extreme end, the person has such a drastic change in personality that people who know him or her can say confidently that he or she never behaved 'like that before'. Such shifts in personality and behavior patterns may appear and disappear for short periods of time or even for days at a time. Further to the extreme, the person showing new personality characteristics may claim to be someone other than the original personality. According to Bletzer (1986, p. 481),

1. The demon substitutes his own mind for the length of the seizure. The new personality unfolds quickly which is incoherent and incalculable. Facial features change and are sometimes grotesque. The demon triggers strong irresistible impulses to perform acts contrary to the victim's personality. The victim may prefer nakedness, otherwise his dress sense and appearance deteriorate. Also, there is a tendency of self-mutilation. He may start foaming at the mouth and speaks language unknown to himself. He may reveal very personal knowledge about members in the room which he could not have known otherwise.
2. The victim makes inhuman noises with drastic change of tones. Sometimes sounding guttural and masculine, and then it is high pitched – "*A woman may start speaking in a husky voice like a man, or a mild-mannered person may begin speaking in a snide, insulting tone of voice*" (MacNutt, 1995, p. 78). Once a possessed woman began to tremble, then a dreadful growl filled the room. But in spite of the rising chorus of animal howls that were ostensibly coming from the woman, neither her tongue nor her lips moved. (Steiger, 2003, p. 117). Body performs mannerisms and body gestures that

are impossible to do in normal consciousness. He may pronounce revulsion to holy objects, places and people.

3. Automatic writings may appear on the wall. Words such as 'evil' and 'hell', along with other various marks, appear on the victim's body. Sounds and voices arise from nowhere. Marked decrease of room temperature where the person is kept is observed.

In this pathetic condition, the victim may show superhuman strength, e.g., a person who used to work in a psychiatric hospital was tossed once by a very petite woman he outweighed by well over one hundred pounds. Some patients who show extreme psychopathology, such as a psychosis or form of schizophrenia are also reported to have momentary burst of great strength. Other common features are levitation and clairvoyance. The victim may rise off the ground defying gravitation without any particular reason, and can also disclose something that happened at a distance and at another time which he could not possibly know.

MacNutt (1995, pp. 77-78) summarizes the signs under three headings – bodily contortions, changes in the voice, and changes in facial expression.

> "*Perhaps the most common external indication of demonization comes when the person's facial expression changes. It is as if you are no longer looking at the same person you started talking to. The old saying 'The eyes are the windows of the soul' becomes especially meaningful. It is as if the evil spirit is peering out at you. The eyes become filled with hate, mockery, pride or whatever the nature of that particular spirit is. Now that the evil spirit has surfaced, you are no longer directly in touch with the person you have been praying for*".

The demon becomes too violent and abusive towards the victim during an exorcism, and tortures the victim with new ferocity in the hope that the priest will discontinue the exorcism. The victim could be a bloody mass of pulp before the exorcism is over. It is also risky to attain an exorcism, because there are cases where after being driven out, the demon will try immediately to enter into another person. MacNutt (1995, pp. 170-71) reported of many cases.

> "*She probably will remember nothing she said or did during that time. She may have been shouting curses at you, or thrashing around and screaming, but afterward, mercifully, she will have no memory of it at all. In the end she will probably feel refreshed and ready for a celebration, while you and your team will feel exhausted and ready to sleep on the spot!*"

Exorcism is a strange, terrifying, overtly bizarre experience and a risky task. But it is an effective cure, and on certain occasions this is the only effective cure. Peck (1983, p. 189) wrote,

> "*Difficult and dangerous though they were, the exorcisms I witnessed were successful. I cannot imagine how otherwise the two patients could have been healed. They are both alive and very well today. I have every reason to believe that had they not had their exorcisms they would each be dead by now.*"

The exorcism should be the last option. No responsible exorcist claims that all mental illnesses are caused by the presence of evil spirits. MacNutt (1995, p. 67), for example, reports that his wife, Judith, when counseling clients as a licensed psychotherapist, "*ended up praying with [only] about a third of them to be freed from the influence of evil spirits*". Father LeBar, an exorcism specialist, commented,

> "*We look at every medical, psychiatric, and psychological evaluation and profile to make sure that there are no unanswered problems in those areas. And before a person is allowed to even be considered for an exorcism, we have to have the assurance that every available treatment has been given to the person ... and had not produced any results.*" (Nightline, 1991)

But who are these spirit parasites? Newton (2016b, pp. 69, 70, 72) noted from his various clients that between their lives on Earth they travel as discarnate entities to other worlds both in and out of our dimension. During their inter-dimensional journeys, they see other non-physical entities. One client, under deep hypnosis remembers, "*... sometimes I see strange beings I don't know.... Odd, strange shapes, wispy or dense ... not human-looking*". Some of them are good, friendly, helpful, peaceful and quite advanced (such as the light beings which I will discuss in Chapter 8: The law of Karma), while some of them are ugly, distant, aggravating and even contentious with bad temperament. The good entities don't get entangled with people's lives in any major way because Earth's inhabitants are afraid of them. Another reason is that they don't want to step on our karmic path and jeopardize our spiritual growth. In contrast, there are bad ones,

> "*who travel inter-dimensionally who we consider to be maladapts. They do not seem to have any sensitivity to Earth. They are not knowledgeable about human beings.... Sometimes we might run into a dark, heavy entity who is disoriented by the Earth sphere. This place is dense but they come from places even more dense. Anyway, they want to cling to us because they don't know what they are doing. We call them the 'heavies' because of their lack of mobility.*"

These parasitic entities are coming from cruel and ruthless worlds where kindness, sympathy and love might be unheard of. When benevolent spirits come across these rogues, "*we put a stop to it and try and push them away*" (Newton, 2016b, p. 73). After studying many cases of demon possession,

I came to the conclusion that neither the demons are 'fallen angels' (as some holy scriptures say) nor they have any unresolved karmic issues with human beings. The game is purely evil and one-sided.

5.6: Ouija board

The Ouija board (also called 'Mysterious Talking Oracle') is a piece of compressed wood, with the letters of the alphabet, some numbers, punctuation marks and 'yes' and 'no' printed on it. People using it place their fingers lightly on a pointer, which then rapidly and without the conscious knowledge of the members present, moves to spell out a series of messages. It is sold at many toy stores and occult supply and book stores. Ouija is a combination of two words, 'oui' and 'ja' which mean 'yes' in French and German respectively.

The board itself is not dangerous but the form of communication that can be attempted often is. Since the Ouija board is very similar to automatic writing, a doorway to the spirit world may open unknowingly and accidently while using it. This innocent looking Ouija board is even more dangerous when the user is under the influence of alcohol or mind-altering drugs. The game has achieved popularity in times of crisis. During World War I, England experienced a surge in attempts to contact dead soldiers by attending séances featuring Ouija boards. Psychic investigator Prof. Archie Roy likens using a Ouija board to the practice of picking up total strangers in a bar and inviting them home (Roy, 1996, p. 176). An evil entity could be described as a cat trying to get into a house. Leave a door open just a crack for just a second and that cat is in the house before we realize it. Steiger (2003, p. 112) wrote,

> "*Young people, with their unfettered imaginations and undisciplined lives, are also very susceptible to possession, especially if they are excited, even titillated, by the lure of exploring the unknown through devices such as the Ouija board. Venturing into the dark areas of the occult or attempting communication with spirits become especially dangerous when attempted by those who have not taken the time to study the arcane. Explorations into the world of shadows require discipline and experience with the precautions that must be exercised before venturing into realms that can be very dangerous. If ... under the influence of drugs or alcohol ... the result may be temporary or extensive possession by a spirit entity who enthusiastically takes advantage of the psychic doorway that has been unknowingly opened by the unprepared.*"

Edgar Cayce had once seen a woman who liked playing with a Ouija board. Once unknowingly, the board opened the door to spirit world and many departed souls came through at once. As a result, she started hearing unknown voices consisting of strange, confusing pattern of words, such as idle gossip, dirty stories, dire predictions, teasing kinds of comments about the lady personally etc. Eventually her husband put her in a mental hospital where she was treated to help rid her of the voices. The voices continued disturbing her for a long time, then suddenly stopped.

Many of us have seen the horror movie 'The Exorcist', the story of the horrific demonic possession. The movie was based on a true case of a 14-year-old boy Roland Doe.

The events began in mid-1949, when Aunt Harriet bought Roland a Ouija board and taught him to use it. After her death, Roland attempted to contact her by using the board but an evil parasite deceitfully took refuge in his soul. Soon a series of strange events were set off, such as, family members heard strange footsteps throughout the house and religious icons and artifacts being thrown about, blankets started flying and hovering across the room, beds shaking uncontrollably on their own, and pictures of Christ shaking powerfully against the wall. Soon Roland was getting scratched and lacerated by unseen claws. His mother took him to several hospitals but the phenomena continued. Deep scratches appeared on his abdomen that spelled out the word "Hell" carved into his flesh.

Roland gathered incredible strength and started speaking in foreign tongues. Often he levitated into the air and spoke in tongues. His mother thought that the change of location would cure him of his 'illness', but the paranormal phenomenon continued to plague the Doe family without any real suspect to blame. Father Raymond Bishop performed the exorcism and with the ritual being repeated over thirty times before it was successful. When the ritual was complete, witnesses reported a strong smell of sulfur permeating the air.

The room where the exorcism was performed never felt the same after Roland left. It remained sealed for many years and nobody dared wander inside. In 1978, before the room was destroyed, workers found a copy of Father Bishop's diary that later on, was the basis for William Peter Blatty's novel "The Exorcist" and William Friedkin's film of the same name. This is a well-documented case.

Here I will discuss few more recent cases in short.

1. Van Gelder (1987, p. 151) writes of a young man on "*all fours snarling like an animal*" soon after playing with a Ouija board. A crucifix fell to the floor, and nails in the wall melted.
2. In November 2014, 35 students at a school in Santa Cruz de la Sierra, Bolivia, were taken to hospital after playing with a Ouija board. They were suffering from mental agitation and confusion, profuse sweating, rapid pulses, and trance states.
3. Between October 2006 and June 2007, at a girls-only Catholic boarding school in Mexico reported a variety of symptoms including

headaches and difficulty walking. Some students could only walk with the help of their friends. Symptoms would suddenly go away, and just as suddenly recur. In total 512 students were affected out of 4,000 students. After investigation, a psychiatrist diagnosed it as a case of mass psychogenic illness (mass hysteria) and traced it back to a student who had used a Ouija board to try to influence the outcome of a school basketball game. The accused girl, Maria, was expelled for using the board. But before leaving, she cursed the school, and soon after the symptoms appeared. The first few victims were Maria's fellow Ouija board players, but soon spread across the school.

4. In May 2015, four students in Columbia were hospitalized when they began "screaming and babbling" after playing the game. In the same year, schools in several countries across the Caribbean reported a wave of symptoms after playing the game including trance states, confusion, and fainting. Outbreaks in small groups of students were reported in Jamaica, St. Lucia, Antigua and Barbuda, and Barbados.
5. Early June 2015, the game resulted in several students reportedly being "possessed by the Devil" at a Primary School in the Dominican Republic.

Use of a Ouija board is very common in South and Central America, where there have been many reports of mass fainting and spirit possession, especially in Mexico. In the USA, there was "*a 750 percent increase in the number of Exorcisms performed between the early 1960s and the mid-1970s*" (Martin, 1992, p. xviii). Strangely there are people who willfully want to be possessed by demons. As example, one possessed person of Prof. Malachi Martin's record wrote after few months of his successful exorcism, "*Solemnly and of my own free will, I wish to acknowledge that knowingly and freely I entered into possession by an evil spirit*" (Martin, 1992, p. 403). In England, "*incidents of demonic interference... since 1960 have become 'virtually an explosion'*" (Malia, 2001, p. 66). There are many chapels in the Philippines for worshipping demons where people want to be possessed by demons for power and supernatural knowledge etc. At the front in place of the altar, there is a large Ouija board. With this device, some worshippers make themselves sacrificial victim of evil forces. There are reports confirming that possession and exorcism cases are on the rise in Philippines.

5.7: Skeptic's views

The critics don't accept an occultic explanation for the demon possession occurrences. According to them all can be explained as a psychotic or epileptic experience. But a close study of the possession cases shows that there are some differences between individuals who are under demonic control and those who suffer from organic brain disorders.

Demons show strong aversion towards religious artifacts and religious counseling particularly during an exorcism, while many deeply mentally disturbed are often devoutly religious. Psychologists have observed that in mental hospitals many patients desire religious instruction (Koteskey, 1979, p. 182).

Demons speak through the victim in a rational manner and carry on a real dialogue. The speech and logical process of those suffering from organic brain disorders are often incoherent. They produce 'word salads' and irrationalities that are often utterly nonsensical (Sall, 1976, p. 288). Hence in those cases where people hear meaningful and well-balanced voices, we can strongly suspect of paranormal influences.

Demons can convey messages through the victims revealing very secret knowledge which they have not acquired by normal means of learning. By no way a mentally ill person can show such abilities. Also, clairvoyance and xenoglossy are very common in possession cases. They are certainly not signs of mental illness. A mental patient will never be able to speak in a voice or a language he has previously not learned.

In possession cases there are occurrences of levitations, trances, telepathy and strength out of proportion to age. Reputed individuals have witnessed and videotaped occasional cases of levitation by apparently possessed persons (Martin, 1992, p. 363). What about the horrific phenomena reported by Goullart, the weighed-down rock-like body that bends iron bedsteads or the horribly inflated body resembling a balloon? Can the critics rule out such events as being optical illusions or fraudulent displays? How to explain the terrible stench, coldness, and voices that arise from no known sources? How the automatic writings appear on the wall or on the victim's body? How the body performs gestures that are impossible to do in normal consciousness?

Possession cases are different from MPD (Multiple personality disorder). MPD is a common psychiatric disorder in which a secondary personality, called an 'alter', splits off and dissociates itself from the primary one. The altar has a life of its own, and when it surfaces it completely displaces the core personality. The altar personality is usually strikingly different from the primary. The core personality is always unaware of the existence of the alter, at least until close to the very end of prolonged, successful treatment. But in cases of demon oppression the patients are either aware from the beginning or are readily made aware of the demonic part of them which has a distinct and alien personality (Peck, 1983, pp. 192-93). Secondly, trying to cast out an alter is a very difficult task since these alters are mostly fragments of the person's personality (MacNutt, 1995, p. 231). But casting out an oppressing entity is possible when the necessary expertise is available. Hence demonic possession cannot be reduced to MPD.

Lastly, if possession is purely a medical issue why exorcism cannot be done by antidepressant drugs? At last, in no mental illness cases the caretakers say that the patient had lost human qualities. MacNutt (1995, p. 23) attained a case where psychiatry failed but prayer worked for a schizophrenia patient.

> "*I once prayed for a young woman who had been confined in a mental hospital for twelve years, suffering from schizophrenia. After two hours of prayer for healing and deliverance, the glazed look in her eyes left and she was able to converse in a normal way. Several weeks later the doctors recognized a dramatic change in her behavior and released her from the hospital. I could cite many more prayer for healing and deliverance examples from a steady stream of supplicants ...unable to find help from psychotherapy or from those who are ministers of religion who had not learned to deal with the demonic*".

How the prayer for healing and deliverance worked so dramatically, completely, and permanently in this case where conventional psychiatry failed? Prof. M. Kemal Irmak, a doctorate in Biochemistry, suggested,

> "*Demonic possession can manifest with a range of bizarre behaviors which could be interpreted as a number of different psychotic disorders... it is time for medical professions to consider the possibility of demonic possession in the etiology of schizophrenia, especially in the cases with hallucinations and delusions... it would be useful for medical professions to work together with faith healers to define better treatment pathways for schizophrenia*". (Irmak, 2014, pp. 775-76).

The effectiveness of spiritual treatments for schizophrenia in this case indicates that spiritual causes, such as demonic possession, are in fact the cause of these experiences. The fact is, the exorcist has correctly diagnosed the ailment and the psychiatrist has not. John M. Stanley, a trained social scientist had visited many Hindu temples in India where exorcism is done regularly by Hindu Priests. After interviewing many people in a variety of conditions, he wrote,

> "*...my conversations with spirit victims and friends and relatives of victims, as well as with people who had been cured, confirmed the claims without exception. Nearly all who come regularly are, after a certain period of time, fully restored to feeling their former selves. Some few do come to sessions regularly for years without complete recovery, but even in these 'incurable' cases the relatives and friends of the victim report that the sessions help the individual a great deal – especially that they feel much better immediately after an 'arati' [a tray of oil-lamps and flowers] session*". (Stanley, 1988, p. 40)

Furthermore, if possession cases were unique to one culture, religion or geographical region, we can ask a very logical question, why the evils harass only one kind of people? But they do not discriminate; they work their mischief all over the world. The demons feel just as threatened by a Taoist priest holding an ivory tablet as a Catholic Priest holding a crucifix or an Indian 'baba' (holy man) waving 'arati'. Most important, such cures are usually total. This makes us take them more seriously.

Today psychiatrists do not rely solely on drugs to treat mental illness, but use 'shock therapy' (ECT, electroconvulsive therapy) because drugs have limitations. However, no one in the psychiatric community can say for certain why ECT works, but the therapy works, as Harold Sackheim, says, "*Not only is the probability of getting well higher than with any other treatment, but the likelihood of getting residual symptoms is less*" (Horgan, 1999, p. 133). Back in the 1920s, Carl Wickland used electric shock to patients to rid them of possessing spirits. No doubt ECT is more developed today than in the 1920s but the treatment is essentially the same. Does shock therapy create a hostile environment in the brain for oppressing spirits? This is a possibility we cannot ignore.

Secondly, how to explain these phenomena – a man blowing up like a balloon, exudes a pool of excreta from his pores as he deflates, becomes as rigid and heavy as a cast-iron statue, caves in an iron bedstead while remaining motionless, resists being lifted by seven men, and writhes like a mortally wounded snake at the moment of expulsion. Betty (2005, p. 20) put forth a clear logical argument,

> "*The question before us is this: Is it easier to believe human beings can do such things on their own with their bodies and minds, or that these things are unnatural and/or extra-human and can be done only by something alien to them using their bodies? If you observed first-hand someone in your own family inflate before your eyes and then speak a language you know he has never learned, in a voice that is not his, would it be easier and more plausible to assume he was showing a hitherto unknown side of his personality for the first time or that he was possessed by an alien spirit?*"

Demonic influence and mental disorders are conceptually distinct phenomena, but a good amount of overlap exists among symptoms. However, it is not very difficult in a given instance to make a firm conclusion regarding which phenomenon is present.

5.8: Conclusion

There is no shortage of documented cases that give the most credible evidence for the existence and power of demons. We can no longer relegate these experiences simply to the field of psychology because good empirical evidence exists to confirm the supernatural. Psychologists themselves are beginning to question the phenomena and are looking for new frames of reference.

> "*Within recent years, however, there has been increasing interest in the demonic. Even some secular writers have acknowledged that evil forces do exist, forces that are not explained by scientific knowledge.*" (Bufford, 1988, p. 8)

In 1987, a doctoral thesis was presented at the California School of Professional Psychology (Berkeley) where the author Craig T. Isaacs did some fascinating research on demon possession. His research question was, "Is possession a phenomena independent of the current commonly accepted psychodiagnostic categories?" The study concluded that possession is different from other established categories of mental illness.

> "*Therefore, certain psychological researchers began to turn their attention to possession as a distinct phenomenon .... demonic possession should be accepted on its own merits, and that psychiatry and psychology must begin to take seriously the active presence of evil in the lives of patients.*" (Isaacs, 1987, p. 266)

In 1976, Prof. Malachi Martin published a book 'Hostage to the Devil: The Possession and Exorcism of Five Americans'. This book is the most convincing and authoritative book available on the subject. In 1983, Harvard-educated psychiatrist M. Scott Peck wrote a book 'The Road Less Traveled' that startled the psychiatric community by describing his participation in two exorcisms. Peck had personally confronted a profoundly evil spirit on both occasions. The two patients he observed "*were gravely ill from a psychiatric standpoint before their exorcisms*" (Peck, 1983, p. 202). But after exorcism the patients completely recovered, as one patient commented, "*Before, the voices were in control of me; now I'm in control of the voices*" (Peck, 1983, p. 198). According to Peck, genuine demonic cases with complete possession are rare.

From various research papers published in scientific journals, it seems many psychiatrists are quietly wondering if there is something to possession. Besides Peck, another professional, Colin Wilson (2000, p. 261) mentions two others who occasionally treat their patients as if they were possessed. One of them, Ralph Allison, a specialist on MPD, occasionally ran into personalities that did not act at all like split-off alters. Of one of these Allison wrote, "*Despite all my efforts, I was unable to find a more plausible explanation for his existence than the spirit theory*".

MacNutt (1995, pp. 73, 88, 93), a leading authority on evil spirits estimates that most people under the influence of evil spirits are only 'oppressed' by demons, but not completely possessed. For them exorcism is neither necessary nor desirable. True demons from hell for which usually requires a full-scale exorcism represent a relatively small percentage, around only 10%. Many mentally ill people – both within and outside of mental asylums – are oppressed by evil spirits. These spirits range from the truly satanic to the "*dead who are not at rest*". Huston Smith agrees with MacNutt, "*Our madhouses may contain souls that are ravaged by principalities and powers on the psychic plane; in a word, possessed*" (Smith, 1976, p. 43). These 'earthbound spirits' are not so much evil as confused. However, in their blind selfishness these spirits can do serious harm, though sometimes unintentional. In relation to us, therefore, they are evil.

Hence, instead of approaching possession cases with the disease-oriented models of medicine, research should turn to a culturally-minded model. In this regard we can safely rely on the data being gathered by the anthropologists. Peck (1983, p. 200) though commented that America and Europe have not studied scientifically the possession and exorcism phenomena, acknowledges that Western anthropologists have long studied possession phenomena in the countries like India.

CHAPTER 6

Psychical unfoldment through mediumship and channeling

"Positive observation proves the existence of a psychic world as real to us as the world known to us by our physical senses".

Camille Flammarion

"I am well aware that many will say that no-one can possibly speak with spirits and angels so long as he is living in the body; many say it is all fancy, others that I recount such things to win credence, while others will make other kinds of objection. But I am deterred by none of these: for I have seen, I have heard, I have felt."

Emanuel Swedenborg

A medium is a gifted person who communicates with beings from the afterlife. The ability to communicate with spirits is as old as time itself, such as, the oracle at Delphi in Greece. The Delphic oracle spoke with the words of God Apollo (Auerbach, 1993, p. 141). The organized effort to speak to discarnate spirits using a code started when two young sisters made contact with the discarnate, they playfully called "Mr. Splitfoot".

On March 31, 1848, two young sisters Kate and Margaretta Fox began receiving rational response from some mysterious rapping noises in their home in Hydesville (New York). The Fox sisters discovered that the rapping would respond to their hand clapping. So, they worked out a code to communicate with Mr. Splitfoot, the discarnate entity. Mr. Splitfoot rapped out his name as Charles B. Rosna, and told them he had been murdered in that house some years ago. The discarnate entity responded to all their questions immediately and definitely. Though it started out as a kind of game neighbors came to witness the rapping, and the news of the Fox sister's mediumship spread, and shortly many psychics, such as slate mediums (the spirits wrote their messages with chalk on slates), tipped tables mediums, trance mediums and physical mediums, appeared (Melton, 1978, p. 94). It became quite clear that some kind of intelligence was manifesting, and then,

> "*a Committee of Investigation was formed, a definite code of signals agreed on, and it was then established that the communicator was one Charles B. Rosna, a peddler who had been murdered by a previous occupant of the cottage and buried in the cellar; This information was subsequently verified.*" (Leonard, 2005, p. 62)

The Fox incident commenced a new era of mediumship, and brought the psychic mediums into a principal focus of psychical researchers. From 1880 onwards numerous books were written which were channeled works by mediums from all walks of life. By definition, mediumistic phenomena involve a person (or persons) serving an intermediary between the physical world and the spirit world. The intermediary, or medium, is either at the center of the communications, or is the actual channel through which contact comes.

Today mediumship phenomena are divided into two distinctive areas – Physical Medium and Mental Medium. Physical mediums are those whose séances or contact sessions bring about not only verbal messages from the dead, but also more commonly, physical disturbances. An efficient physical medium can produce a wider range of phenomena, such as, anomalous sounds, materialization of objects and spirits, "ectoplasm", levitation, anomalous exposure of film, etc. Today, we don't find many physical mediums outside the spiritualistic camps.

Mental mediums are those who speak directly with one or more discarnate entities. We call them channelers (or channels) because the medium is channeling information from the dead. They limit themselves to receiving information from apparently anomalous, 'personality-like' sources. A channel usually alters his/her consciousness somewhat and 'allows' an intelligent and self-aware source to manifest and communicate. The source can 'download' information and/or be questioned to provide answers. Channelers usually speak, but can write on a paper or use keyboard.

Hence, mediumship is the older academic term while channeling the newer. While mediums purportedly obtain this information from deceased persons, channeling has put a newer twist on things because some of the discarnate intelligences that now speak through the channels are not only spirits of dead humans, but also extraterrestrials, "daemon" (not to be confused with "demon," a negative, possessing entity. Daemon is a guardian angel), dolphins, long dead Atlanteans and entities from other dimensions, or from off-planet, such as from the future (Auerbach, 1993, pp. 2, 140). Kelly (2010, p. 248) observed that mediumship "*is the only phenomenon directly relevant to the survival problem that can be produced and observed under conditions of experimental control*". Whether mediumship or channeling, if the evidence contained in this chapter is seen collectively, the case for survival after death is absolutely stunning and irrefutable.

6.1: Physical mediumship

"*The point is, if you want real conviction of life after death, physical mediumship is the answer.*"

Leslie Flint

"*The evidence of man's immortality rests on spirit manifestations. Without them we could have no certain knowledge of the future life. I make this broad statement, including the manifestations of ancient times and of all races, but more especially is it true of the modern phenomena.*"

Hudson Tuttle

Physical mediumship is 'state-of-the-art' mediumship. World's leading authority on this subject, Jon Klimo provides a fairly standard definition of physical mediumship as the purported ability of certain mediums to "*channel unknown energies that affect the physical environment in ways that can be directly experienced by persons other than the channel*" (Klimo, 1987, p. 200). All experts at this level usually have surpassed the abilities of straight mental mediumship (Dreller, 1997, p. 41). Manifestations of these "unknown energies" that defy all known physical laws take many forms including, levitation and manipulation of physical objects (knocks and raps, table levitations, levitation of the medium's body, temporary loss of weight, voices of discarnate spirits heard etc.), the production of anomalous environmental changes (breezes and unusual drops in room temperature), the generation of so-called "spirit-lights", the "teleportation" of physical objects into and out of the séance room, and the materialization of ectoplasmic forms (limbs, heads or, occasionally whole bodies), amongst many others. While some mediums gain impressions from the spirits in a fully conscious state, others enter a trance, which is often accompanied by manifestations.

The mediums claim that while they are in a trance, they fall under the control of a particular special guide who speaks through them and works all manners of mysterious phenomena on their behalf. The spirit guide also serves as an intermediary between themselves and the discarnate spirits. While many mediums may admit that the subjective mind is not entirely eliminated when they are in a trance, they insist that their subconscious mind is taken over and controlled by a mysterious power of great compassion and wisdom. Irene F. Hughes, a Chicago-based medium, explained how her spirit guide brings messages from a discarnate entity. As she engages herself in the spirit world, her body becomes as "*icy cold as death itself*," yet a delightful warmth engulfs her inner self.

> "*I am quiet, completely relaxed and deep in meditation... I may be alone at home or among friends in a prayer circle. A tingling sensation, similar to a chill, begins on my right ankle, then on my left. Slowly the tingling spreads to cover my entire body. It is as though a soft silken skin has been pulled over me, glove-tight – even over my face, changing its features – yet comfortable and protective. At this point I am on the way to that golden flow of consciousness that we earthlings term the spirit plane. I am in semi-trance. Were I in full trance, I could not recall a single detail.*" (Steiger, 2003, p. 223)

Renowned psychical researcher Harry Price had witnessed the materialization of a child spirit (Steiger, 2003, pp. 234-36). On December 8, 1937, Price had just concluded a radio broadcast regarding psychic phenomena when a listener contacted him and informed that she regularly participated in a family séance held every Wednesday evening, at which the family materialized the spirit of a child. She invited Price to attend on the condition that he would never reveal the location of the séance circle or the identity of the members, and never touch the spirit without permission. Price immediately agreed to those terms and the family permitted him to attend one of the séances and to conduct any examination that he wished.

Accordingly, Price made arrangements to attend a séance on December 15. The spirit child, Rosalie, was the daughter of one of the sitters, whom Price referred to as "Mrs. Z." in his notes. The girl had died of diphtheria in 1921 at the age of six. One night in 1925, Mrs. Z. had sensed the etheric presence of her daughter and heard the child's voice calling to her. Before dawn, Rosalie had materialized and had become sufficiently solid for her mother to clasp her hand. When members of her family and certain close friends learned of Rosalie's remarkable return, they agreed to meet for one night each week for the purpose of establishing a systematic schedule that would encourage the spirit to visit her mother on a regular basis. The séances had proved to be most successful, and by the time they invited Price to join them, the circle had been meeting weekly for 12 years.

Price thoroughly examined the room before sitting. He removed all ornaments, the clock, and any small items of furniture so that the room might be as bare as possible. He locked the door and slipped the key into his own pocket. The door and windows were sealed with adhesive tape. The fireplace was covered with sheets of paper. Every drawer was emptied, every cushion examined, and every inch of the floorboards was sounded. Then he sprinkled liberal coatings of powdered starch around all the movable objects that remained in the room, and in front of the door and fireplace. When Price had completed these extensive preparations, he indicated that the séance could begin. Price's notes reveal that it was just a few minutes after 10:00 p.m. when Mrs. Z told others that she sensed the presence of Rosalie. The mother began to weep softly and cautioned others not to speak. The room was by no means dark. A small lamp gave enough light for Price to clearly distinguish the mysterious shape of a small girl materializing beside him.

When the materialization completed Price asked "*May I touch Rosalie?*" With permission, he touched the spirit child, and found her flesh to be much cooler than that of a living human. His fingers moved up to test the soft, silken quality of Rosalie's hair. Then, with the mother's permission, Price lifted the spirit girl to his knee, just as he might any living child. To his astonishment, he was able to hear a heart beating when he placed his ear to Rosalie's chest. The rate of her pulse was 90 beats a minute. Price turned her face toward the lamp and noted that Rosalie's classical features would have "*graced any nursery in the land.*" With Mrs. Z.'s indulgence, Price asked the girl about conditions in the spirit world. Interestingly, Rosalie responded to none of these questions, but when the investigator asked her if she loved her mother, the spirit child responded rapidly in the affirmative. Mrs. Z. could no longer contain herself, and she went to Price's chair and took the spirit child from his lap. Price later told that he also was deeply affected by the emotional scene. Rosalie was with the circle for about five minutes, and then she slowly began to fade back into her ethereal state. Within a few moments, the spirit child had completely disappeared.

Price called for the lights to be switched back on and conducted an immediate inspection of his seals and coatings of powder. He found all of the tape intact, and discovered no tracks of any kind in the powdered starch that he had dusted about the room. When Price made public certain details of the remarkable return of Rosalie, many other investigators were greatly intrigued by his account and wished to learn more about the incredible materialization of a spirit child. Price remained true to his word and never disclosed the names of the individuals in the circle that summoned Rosalie back from the grave each Wednesday night.

This case does offer the testimony that the strength of a mother's love can summon the spirit of a deceased child to revisit Earth in a physical form for a limited period of time.

Probably, the most influential innovator in early physical mediumship was the Scottish-born Daniel Dunglas Home (1833-1886). In his early life Daniel had many spiritual visions and premonitions. He conducted his first séance at the age of eighteen and swiftly gained a reputation as a powerful medium. By 1856, he was conducting séances in Britain. In 1868, he performed his most famous paranormal feat – the levitation of his body horizontally out through a third-story window at Ashley House in London. Many highly reputed and honest people have witnessed this (Doyle, 2006, p. 99; Lamont, 2005, pp. 185-87). In 1874, his mediumship received further support with the publication of Sir William Crookes' report which confirmed after laboratory experimentation that he was able to manipulate physical objects paranormally. Using specially designed laboratory equipment Daniel's ability to change the weight of physical objects and to play tunes on an accordion suspended out of reach in a cage was tested (Lamont, 2005, pp. 204-07; Alvarado, 2006a, p. 142; Melechi, 2008, pp. 198-200). Doyle (2006, p. 106) noted that his séances often featured the alleged materialization of glowing hands that would playfully touch the sitters, though he never produced full-body materializations.

On the evening of July 7, 1874, a lady by the name Comtesse Caterina sat in a seance with him and five others. The seance took place in a room of the hotel in Florence. Many unusual phenomena were reported and a particularly impressive spirit communication took place that astonished Comtesse. She initially disbelieved, and then thought to herself, "*If you are really the spirit you claim to be, I ask you to take that rose from Henrietta, and bring it to me.*" She testified that,

> "*The thought had hardly taken shape in my mind, when a hand, visible to everyone present, the large nervous hand of a man, grasped the rose, and disengaging it, brought it to me, and placed it in my fingers. This was not done in darkness or in a dim light. The room was well lit, the hands of every person present rested on the table, and there hovered in the air before us a hand as perfect in form as human hand can be.*" (Home, 1879, p. 480).

Although accusations of fraud were made, none could prove it.

Most physical mediumship is carried out under red light and the medium sits in a black wooden cabinet. This combination of lights concentrates the energies better and makes the manifestation a bit easier for the spirit world. It takes many years of sitting in development circles for the medium to develop physical mediumship, and also great dedication.

A gifted physical medium can produce ectoplasm (ghost slime – from the Greek, meaning 'exteriorized substance') is by now practically synonymous with physical mediumship and is well documented in the early literature of psychical research. Ectoplasm is a cloud-like substance that leaves the body of the medium in thick strands and at times from different exits such as the nose, mouth etc. This substance then joins together to form either a spirit voice box in the air near to the medium from where the spirit communicator will speak (direct voice) or it may take the form of a spirit communicator who wishes to make contact with someone in the room (spirit manifestation). Another form is 'Transfiguration' – the medium sits and takes on the physical attributes of the spirit communicator. This may mean their face changes because an ectoplasmic mask has been placed over the face that forms the face of the communicator. The voice of the medium also alters. The onlooker can with their own sense verify a full-blown manifestation of a spirit person formed from the ectoplasm which has been formed from within the medium.

The term 'ectoplasm' was coined by Prof. Charles Richet in 1894, who wrote,

> "*It is a whitish substance that creeps as if alive, with damp, cold, protoplasmic extensions that are transformed under the eyes of the experimenters into a hand, fingers, a head, or even into an entire figure.*" (Tabori, 1972, p. 144)

Sometimes, ectoplasm is first visible as fluid and then form bodies gradually. Otherwise the bodies seem to appear and disappear abruptly (Thompson, 2003, p. 192). French physician and psychical researcher Gustave Geley wrote,

> "*The substance exudes specially from the natural orifices and the extremities, from the top of the head, from the nipples, and the ends of the fingers... the most easily observed from the mouth.... The substance has variable aspects; sometimes, and most characteristically, it appears as a plastic paste, a true protoplasmic mass; sometimes as a number of fine threads; sometimes as strings of different thickness in narrow and rigid lines; sometimes as a wide band; sometimes as a fine tissue of ill-defined and irregular shape.... In fine, the substance is essentially amorphous, or rather, polymorphous.*" (Geley, 1920, p. 54)

Gustave Geley explains that ectoplasm is very variable, sometimes very little and at other times covering the medium completely, like a cloak. It most frequently appeared white, but occasionally black or gray.

> "*Sometimes it is slowly evolved, rises and falls, and moves over the medium's shoulders, her breast, or her lap with a crawling, reptilian movement; sometimes its motion is abrupt and rapid, it appears and disappears like a flash. It is extremely sensitive, and its sensitiveness is closely connected with that of the hyper anesthetised medium, and touch reacts painfully on the latter.... The substance is sensitive to light rays; a light, especially if sudden and unexpected, produces a painful start in the medium. However, in some case the substance can stand even full light. The magnesium flashlight [flash camera] causes a violent start in the medium.... It shrinks from all contact and is always ready to avoid them and to be reabsorbed.*" (Geley, 1920, pp. 55-56)

> "*Observation shows this ectoplasm as an amorphous substance which may be either solid or vaporous. Then, usually very soon, the formless substance becomes organic, it condenses, and forms appear, which, when the process is complete, have all the anatomical and physiological characters of biologic life. The ectoplasm has become a living being or a fractional part of a living being, but is always closely connected to the body of the medium, of which it is a kind of prolongation, and into which it is absorbed at the end of the experiment.*" (Geley, 2006, p. 176)

The production of ectoplasm by physical mediums is not fraudulent. No doubt, many charlatans took advantage of the darkness of the séance room and the desire of believers to communicate with the dead. Many were unmasked and physical mediumship was ever after suspect. In spite of this, there are still instances that seem genuine. Prof. Richet, who won the Nobel Prize in 1913, commented,

> "*There is ample proof that experimental materialization (ectoplasmic) should take definite rank as a scientific fact. Assuredly we do not understand it. It is very absurd, if a truth can be absurd... Spiritualists have blamed me for using this word 'absurd'; and they have not been able to understand that to admit the reality of these phenomena was for me an actual pain... It is prodigiously strange, prodigiously unusual, and it would seem so unlikely as to be incredible; but we must give in to the facts...* ***Yes, it is absurd; but no matter – it is true.***" (Richet, 1923, pp. 618-19)

Prof. Richet after attending experiments with medium Eusapia Palladino began taking an active interest in psychical research. After almost thirty years of studying the mediums he accepted the reality of mediumship and other psychic phenomena. He explained how the ectoplasms are formed. Initially the ectoplasms are invisible to others, but capable of moving objects and giving raps on a table. Soon they become visible though hazy and unclear. Still later slowly they change their forms and consistence, and evolve under our eyes to a human form. Soon the substance becomes an actual being with the "*astral presentment of a garment, a hat, an eye-glass, or a walking-stick*" (Richet, 1923, p. 618). Here a question arises – does the materialization of these earthly things discredit the hypothesis that a deceased human is materializing? Richet (1923, p. 476) explained,

> "*It seems to me much wiser to verify without pretending to understand, and to admit that any explanation we can give can hardly escape being ridiculous. Instead of claiming that unknown powers pertaining to deceased humanity are capable of producing these phenomena, it is better to admit that we are dealing with facts as yet inexplicable, and await further elucidation. But there is no reason to deny a fact because it is inexplicable. Can anyone have the unpardonable presumption to claim to give an adequate explanation of all-natural phenomena? In metapsychics we come up against the inexplicable at every turn.*"

The phantom may appear suddenly without passing through the phase of luminous cloud, but this phenomenon is probably of the same order as the slower development (Richet, 1923, p. 618). In an interview Richet said, "*I find myself unable to adopt [the spirit hypothesis] ... nevertheless I oppose it half-heartedly, for I am quite unable to bring forward any wholly satisfactory counter-theory*". Though publicly he leaned toward a physiological explanation, but privately at least in his later years he apparently accepted the spirit hypothesis as the best explanation.

6.1.1: Skeptics' views on physical mediumship and ectoplasm formation

Skeptic scientists insisted that ectoplasm was nothing more than cheesecloth or some other substance cleverly packed in the body which is regurgitated (vomited) at an opportune moment. No doubt some people are able to use the stomach as a hiding place and later bring it back up. In fact, some mediums had been caught red-handed while playing this trick. But we cannot dismiss all the cases as fraudulent.

There are only few mediums in the world strong enough or developed enough physically to produce ectoplasm which would result in full body materialization. But they are often overshadowed by the crooks and con artists who are only looking to see how much money they could cheat of their unwitting clients. Many tricks that were carried out seem just as silly to us now but they were still amazingly effective under the heightened conditions of the séance. As example, one used a long evening glove (that reached beyond the elbow) stuffed with wool to reach over and touch her sitters, another had a black glove painted with luminous paint, yet another concealed a 'spirit baby' beneath her skirts (a stuffed shape attached to a stick and worked by her foot) who came up and peered over the table whenever called.

These crooks often portrayed the entire movement in a bad light, and many people believed in them enough to part with their money in order to hear from those in their families who had died. Some of these sittings are almost comical, but they are not amusing when one considers how many bereaved people are deceived. They were so desperate to believe these messages that on the medium's instructions they sometimes parted with their jewels, gave away their houses and remade their wills.

Ectoplasms are not cheesecloths. It is difficult to believe that some of the most eminent men of science who observed it, examined it, tested it, and proclaimed it real, could have been fooled over and over again, especially under laboratory conditions. Thus, many paranormal researchers concluded that the most productive way to get in touch with spirit world is physical mediumship. A typical séance, which was presided over by a physical medium, could boast all sorts of strange and logic-defying activities even under strictly controlled conditions.

Albert Von Schrenck Notzing (German physician, psychiatrist and notable psychical researcher, who devoted his time to the study of paranormal events connected with mediumship, hypnotism and telepathy) pointed out to the skeptics, more than half of the 180 observations of ectoplasm by him did not involve ectoplasm flowing from the mouth. It sometimes came from the nose, from the ears, from the female genital tract, and quite often just from the pores of the skin. Since the ectoplasm formed spontaneously, deception can be ruled out.

Charles Richet had conducted experiments in which ectoplasmic hands made molds in paraffin. He had used chemically marked paraffin so that he could detect phony molds that might be substituted by sleight of hand. He pointed out that the molds he obtained were narrow at the wrist and thus they could not have been made by simply inserting a hand into the paraffin and pulling it out (Thompson, 2003, pp. 192-93). It means, the materializing hand had disappeared (de-materialized) mysteriously by melting away into vapor leaving the molds intact. Another Nobel Laureate, Sir William Crookes had a similar observation,

> "*I [Sir William Crookes] have retained one of these hands in my own, firmly resolved not to let it escape. There was no struggle or effort made to get loose, but it gradually seemed to resolve itself into vapour, and faded in that manner from my grasp*" (Braude, 1991, pp. 107-08).

De-materialization is possible if there is a dimensional shift, i.e., the mysterious hand had moved from a three-dimensional space to four-dimensional space. No other explanation seems to fit here. The laws and systems governing the higher spaces do not in any way conflict with the well-known laws governing action in ordinary three-dimensional space. But the interactions passing between physical space and higher spaces do require a modification of these familiar laws.

In the case of medium called Eva C. (real name Marthe Beraud), Von Schrenck Notzing often observed ectoplasm oozing from the pores near her shoulder. He was so cautious that he had her completely strip before many of the sittings and then subject herself to a gynecological exam. She was then given special attire, consisting of knitted tights and an apron tunic closed down the back. Before each sitting, the tunic was sewed up at the back, the wrists, and the junction of the tights with the dress. According to Notzing, there was absolutely no opportunity for her to smuggle any kind of foreign substance or object into the room. On several occasions, Eva C. volunteered to sit in the nude and did so to satisfy various skeptical scientists who observed the phenomenon with Notzing. Eva C.'s ectoplasmic manifestations are graphically described by the following narration.

> "*On 2nd December 1910 a particularly interesting phenomenon occurred. As the by now exhausted medium asked me to give her more strength; she moved towards me, her hands outstretched, and I made a movement to take her hands. At that moment, and in full view of all the sitters, a fully modeled arm and hand seized the medium's left arm around the elbow and thrust her roughly backwards. Eva, frightened, cried out and started to tremble; she had an attack of nerves that I had to calm. Some minutes later the arm and hand reappeared on the medium's knees; this time they were flat and motionless. This phenomenon is all the more*

remarkable in that it suggests a will operating independently of the medium, myself and others." (Barrington, 2011, p. 5)

Gustave Geley, along with some prominent scientists, had investigated Eva. C. and wrote,

"*These were formed under our eyes, the curtains being half-drawn. Sometimes they proceeded from a cord of solid substance issuing from the medium, sometimes they were progressively developed in a fog of vaporous substance condensed in front of her, or at her side.*" (Ramesh, 2014, p. 95)

Richet, Notzing and Geley were all hardcore scientists. All of them and many other researchers have all resisted the spiritualistic hypothesis, the idea that the phenomena were being produced by spirits. However, publicly or privately all of them had accepted the idea that spirits were producing the phenomena, despite the fact that as hardcore scientists there was no room for spirits in their belief system. Many other researchers simply wrote it off as something that was beyond science at the time.

Since Eva C. was strictly an amateur and apparently was not paid for her sittings, she had no financial gain from her mediumship. Secondly, if she had been the only person producing ectoplasm and related phenomena, then there might be justification for being skeptical, but the fact is that the phenomena were observed by many distinguished men and women and their reports were consistent with those of Notzing, Geley, and Richet.

The sequence of materializations is not same for all mediums because there is a vast difference in psychic powers in various mediums which the discarnate entity uses for materialization. In case of the séance of Eusapia Palladino, an Italian physical medium, Richet (1923, p. 478) wrote,

"*At first, touches and raps produced both easily and frequently; this is the first stage, in which nothing is visible, for the material energy disengaged from her body is formless. In the second stage the hand is formed, but still cannot be seen, though it can execute well-defined mechanical actions, can take hold of a bell or book, and can touch one's head with fingers that are felt to be warm and jointed. Finally, in the third stage, which was rarely reached in my experiments with Eusapia, the hand becomes visible and can be photographed.*

In a still rarer, fourth stage, not only a hand but a whole body is formed and detached. Vassallo, Porro, Morselli, and Bottazzi have been able to witness these complete materializations. [And], luminous phenomena are relatively frequent."

The Society for Psychical Research had sent Hon. Everard Feilding, Hereward Carrington, and William Wortley Baggally – three skeptical experts in trickery to Naples in 1908 to put Eusapia to the test. After rigorous test, Feilding commented,

"*My own frame of mind, when starting on this investigation, was that, in view of the concurrent opinion of practically all the eminent men of science who have investigated Eusapia's phenomena, it was inconceivable that they could, in turn, have been deceived by the few petty tricks that have, from time to time, been detected, and that it was therefore probable that the phenomena were real.*" (Feilding, 1963, p. 171)

Many highly qualified scientists had accepted her as genuine. Eusapia was not detected in fraud in any one of the 470 phenomena that took place at the eleven séances. Baggally (Schmicker, 2002, p. 113) concluded,

"*Taking into consideration the manner of the control, that no mechanism was found on the medium's person, that no accomplice was present, and also that the three S.P.R. investigators were men who had been accustomed for years to the investigation of so-called physical phenomena of every variety, and who had detected fraud after fraud, I find it impossible to believe that Eusapia could have been able to practice trickery constantly during the many hours that the séances lasted and remain undetected*".

About the mysterious hands that appeared in a séance, Carrington remarked,

"*That human hands – having all the peculiarities of hands, even to the presence of finger nails, should become visible and tangible during a séance – these hands not being Eusapia's nor any of the sitters' – this is so utterly at variance with common sense that one finds it next to impossible to believe it. And yet these hands are real, and by no possible means could they have been Eusapia's.*" (Feilding, 1963, p. 166).

One of most curious phenomena of Eusapia investigation is the formation of cold strong breeze that emanated from a scar on her forehead in good light. Baggally held a small paper flag to her forehead, nose and mouth. The flag blew right out several times, and then out so forcibly that it turned completely over (Barrington, 1992, p. 333). The three investigators thoroughly searched Eusapia's clothes and body but found no concealed apparatus.

Another famous physical medium Mina 'Margery' Crandon could produce a wide range of effects in a darkened séance room – everything from levitations to glowing ectoplasm, from ringing bells to the linking of wooden rings (Auerbach, 1993, p. 144). Walter Franklin Prince, one of the chief investigators of Margery's mediumship, provides a survey of some of her feats.

"*At hundreds of sittings, it is claimed, 'ectoplasmic' limbs – extruded from her body and afterwards reabsorbed – have performed various acts, such as touching persons seated nearby in the darkness, shoving, lifting and throwing objects, overturning a small table, ringing the bell in a box activated by contact cover, producing phosphorescent lights, etc.*" (Prince, 1926, p. 431)

Famous magician and escape artist Harry Houdini (real name Ehrich Weiss) and William McDougall declared her performance as fraudulent. Houdini even took the elaborate steps to duplicate her feats. However, Houdini was unable to find ultimate fault with her and merely duplicated her effects in an attempt to defame her (Auerbach, 1993, p. 145). Over the course of his public debunking, Houdini employed increasingly tight controls on the medium including, at one point, completely sealing the medium within a specially constructed wooden box, with only her head and hands visible (Polidoro, 2001, pp. 143-45). But in spite of his best efforts Houdini could not prove that she was faking it all.

Spiritual writer Harry Edwards (1978, pp. 96-97) reported the materialization and dematerialization process in Welsh spiritualist medium Jack Webber's séances.

"*... at first a vague, shadowy form is seen, darker than the prevailing light. This form then becomes denser, and the hands and head are held to the red light for closer examination. The red light is about nine feet from the floor, yet the materialized people are able to rise to it from the floor and expose their heads in close proximity to the bulb... When a form has built up in the red light, its disappearance is of interest. Standing full length in the centre of the circle, it is seen to diminish downwards as if passing through the floor. The period of time necessary for the disappearance is about two seconds. After the disappearance of a form, throat action is heard from the medium – gulp like sounds, rather similar to those made when ectoplasm is returning to the medium's body.*"

The accounts from the séances of Helen Duncan (other name Hellish Nell), feature many of the same characteristic descriptions of ectoplasmic materializations and dematerializations as earlier accounts of other mediums.

"*Witnesses used terms such as disappeared, vanished, melted, sinking towards the floor... Mrs. Lock stated her mother disappeared down to the floor when seeing her on the 17th and 18th of January and her friend Pinkie who did so displaying a clear face with a red complexion with hair. He drifted down to the ground. Mrs. Jennings was so struck by the way the figures disappeared... [she] took a special interest and stood to observe the method.... the head portion went first, then the shoulders down. The last thing she could see was a lot of white on the floor. She explained they all disappeared in the same way. Mr. Lock also described this same method for a figure purporting to be his sister Sally... He described how the white form disappeared towards the ground.*" (Hartley, 2007, p. 205)

In 1941, Helen Duncan was able to fully materialize the spirit of a sailor who wore his naval cap mentioning the name of his ship – HMS Barham. The discarnate then announced that he had recently died while the enemy had sunk his ship in the Mediterranean (Ludden, 2011, p. 273). This information had not at the time been made public by the government who had kept it a secret that HMS Barham had sunk when a German U-Boat U331 had torpedoed the ship from a range of only 750 yards on Nov. 25, 1941 (Suckling, 2006, p. 78; Howell, 2008, p. 44). Apparently, government had only informed some individuals on a confidential basis that they had lost loved ones but kept secret from the public at large that 861 British seamen had died (only 395 were rescued), in order to protect public moral and mislead the enemy (Winsham, 2016, pp. 120-21). When the secret was revealed, the authorities were aware of her psychic power. As a result, they got her arrested and convicted her under an old witchcraft act (the British Witchcraft Act of 1735) in March 1944 (Deer, 2009, p. 153). With arrest warrant, the police came to one of Duncan's séances in plain clothes. In the darkened room when a luminous figure appeared, one policeman ran for the light, and the other one to the stage and grabbed for the gauge he expected to find, but all collapsed into a bit of dust (Arnold, 2008, p. 43). Duncan was the last person to be imprisoned (nine months in prison after a seven-day-trial) under this Act, and after that the Act was abolished. The event was a public scandal and media event because of this unfair treatment.

How is it possible that a medium with no prior knowledge of a dead person can fully materialize him in full uniform and give accurate information about Britain's top military secret during WW II? If physical mediumship is an outright fraud, why the British military authorities were paranoid that Duncan might reveal further details of classified information? Finally, it is difficult to believe that as much 'cheesecloth,' as seen in many of the photographs, could be stored in an orifice of the body, especially the ears and pores, and so dramatically extruded, then to have human forms shaped from it or within it, and then, in some cases, to have those human forms emerging from the ectoplasm and carry on meaningful conversations with those present, sometimes about personal matters known only to the sitter.

For those skeptics who are still in doubt, I will give the final proof of life after death. Harry Houdini, the genius of all time, had spent most of his time exposing fraudulent mediums. In fact, he really did spiritualism a great service by weeding out the imposters. As a final challenge, he had left a widely publicized message that if there were anything to the claim for survival he would get through to his wife, Bess, with a coded message. This is known as 'Houdini Code' which he had with his wife, Bess Houdini, and told her that only a true medium would be able to give her his message. After Houdini's death an American medium, Arthur Ford (1897-1971) broke the Houdini Code on January 5, 1929, and proved that the great skeptic magician himself had survived bodily death. Ford gave Bess Houdini the message "ROSABELLE, BELIEVE!" which was done in the long, complicated code which the two Houdinis had agreed to use many years before (Buckland, 2005, pp. xvi, xvii). Bess Houdini confirmed that the code was such a secret that no one except Houdini and herself knew the cipher or the key and its application. She even signed a statement validating Ford had communicated Houdini's secret message (Guiley, 2010, p. 52; Montgomery, 1972, p. 23). This made Ford world famous.

With this final proof, the great Houdini gave us evidence from other side that all physical mediums are not fake as the old saying goes that it only takes one white blackbird to prove that not all blackbirds are black.

Those who have studied mediumship and séance carefully decisive proofs are repeated daily. The authority of the witnesses and the accumulation of repeated proofs are such that the authenticity of these supernatural phenomena is founded on granite – on thousands of exact observations and rigorous experiments. Physical mediumship is a certainty – even though among these observations there are few cases of trickery, errors, and illusions – still the thing is certain. I don't say that there are no 'gaps', but the whole represents such a large and homogeneous evidence that no criticism however acute, will be able to disintegrate and disperse the facts. Physical mediumship has more truth in it than we can imagine.

6.1.2: Conclusion

Basically, both telekinesis (psychokinesis, or PK – the ability to move objects through mind power) and ectoplasm are synonymous with physical mediumship. However, sadly these are grossly under-researched and hence poorly understood. But can any scientist worthy of the name affirm that materialistic science has classified, analyzed, and penetrated all the energies of immeasurable nature? Can any learned professor of physics make the strange and pretentious claim that we know all the dynamic manifestations in the world?

Since there is no such thing as final proven knowledge in science, we cannot discredit all the researchers as insane or duped by an illusion. Their competence and honesty cannot be called into question as they had spent decades on researching these phenomena and witnessed thousands of observations and experiments. Instead, if we agree that there are intelligent and self-conscious energies that can act on matter, it would not destroy even the smallest fragment of science. This is not an unscientific hypothesis. What is unscientific is not to accept such forces exist but to affirm that they do not exist. In fact, our little steps towards our understanding of the quantum physics are leading us that way. Richet (1923, p. 601) commented,

> "*Then why be indignant, when on the basis of thousands of observations and experiments, we affirm one of those unknown energies?... Everything that is not in formal contradiction with known facts is possible. Well, materializations and telekinesis do not contradict one single established scientific fact. That a hand having all the attributes of a living hand should be formed from a whitish cloud in no way nullifies the laws of circulation, nutrition, and structure of a normal hand. It is new fact but not a contradictory one.*"

The 'unknown energies', in other words the faculty of cognition that differs radically from the usual sensory faculties that Richet had pointed out indicate the power of quantum soul. Richet talked about unknown energy in his 1923 book, 'Thirty Years of Psychical Research' when the scientists had not even a slightest idea about the behavior of matter and its interactions with energy on the scale of atoms and subatomic particles. His contemporaries might have ridiculed him for his bold ideas, but today with the advent of quantum physics when we are slowly replacing the classical physics of Newton, Maxwell, and Einstein with the quantum physics of Planck, Bohr, and Heisenberg we know he was not wrong. The quantum soul that survives death is made of energy that is not only intelligent but also self-conscious. We don't have to reject some or the entire quantum soul hypothesis, rather this hypothesis helps us to reject some of the classical Newtonian physics which are absurd.

6.2: Mental mediumship (Channeling)

"*They want to talk to you as much as you want to talk to them!*"

John Holland, a famous mental medium

Channeling flourished when physical mediumship suffered a lull in interest. Roughly from 1848 onwards till 1945 was the prime time for the physical mediums. The main reason for the fall was that the harsh ways in which physical mediums had been tested in the experimental conditions put people off developing mediumship. Also, numerous exposures of fraudulent mediums had given the profession a bad reputation which put people off entering into it (Hunter, 2012, pp. 38-39). As a result, people became more prone to mental mediumship which was a bit easier to develop. So, the channelers are following the legacy of the physical mediums.

Channeling is like a cell phone. The device does not create the sound but receives it from a source external to its own identity. The only control it has over the sound it channels through itself is the care with which it has allowed itself to be connected. A good cell phone has good reception and a bad one has bad reception. However, no matter how good or bad the device is, it must obey the mechanical rules which are quite simple but unavoidable. The channelers generally enter a trance state (though some can do it in conscious state) and allow these other intelligences to speak through them. Some expert channelers can channel a person who is still alive while he is 'dreaming' in his sleep. In rare cases channelers claim to have channeled the consciousness of trees, plants and even such things as crystals. Channelings are of three types – conscious channeling, relay channeling and trance channeling.

Conscious channeling involves a light trance state. The person is completely conscious of everything as it happens through him. His consciousness simply moves into the background and lets others into the foreground. Here the channeler knows what he spoke or did, and the channeler's voice and mannerisms will usually appear unchanged although the material being given can be quite profound and involve demonstrations of obvious psychic ability. In relay channeling the channeler hears or sees messages telepathically from paranormal sources and then relays them to the interested person or group.

Here one question arises – why it is no longer necessary for some people to be in a deep trance in order to allow channeling to occur? Once one discarnate entity has answered this question, that the veils between the Earth plane and other dimensions are slowly thinning down. Many people who are present on the Earth plane at this time have a vibrational rate that is already high enough to allow an entity to join with them without inducing a deep trance state. For this reason, today more and more people are finding that they can consciously channel if they devote some time to practice and to learn how to relax the mind and body and allow the entity to speak through them.

Trance channeling involves completely giving over the channeler's body and consciousness to other non-physical independent conscious beings. The channeler is not aware of what is being said through him and when it is happening. He generally remembers nothing after coming out of the trance state. So, trance channeling could be categorized as a type of 'willful possession' – "*a trance state interpreted by the culture as a condition during which the practitioner's own personality is temporarily displaced by the personality of another entity.*" (Winkelman, 1986, p. 194). However, the trance channelers prefer the term 'blending' to describe their trance state as this term brings harmony and mutual cooperation between the channeler and the entity rather than domination of the channeler by the entity. Since the trance channeler fully steps aside and allows the entity to take full and direct control over all speaking and physical movement, the voice used by the entity to speak through the channel is usually distinctly different from the channeler's 'normal' voice. The facial movements and other physical mannerisms also become distinctly different. The interactive conversation becomes more meaningful because there is zero distortion of information. In this respect, the conscious or semi-conscious channelers do not get extremely 'clean' transmissions.

Since each entity has its own distinctive personality, trance channeling can be quite dramatic than other forms of channeling – the channeler's delivery format of information, personality, facial movements and other physical mannerisms change from one sitting to another.

For those with extremely faint of heart or who holds a great deal of religiously based fear may feel very uncomfortable in trance channeling. However, some interactions are really funny. As example, when a teenage girl who lived in 17th century France (and did not reincarnate after that) was channeled by a trance channeler she was completely unaware of modern inventions. So, the sitters spent a good deal of fun time discussing the differences between her "time" and ours. When someone played the radio or the stereo cassette deck, she was totally amazed, and asked "But where are you keeping the musicians?" She loved the running water in the kitchen and when she saw the gas burner on the stove she stepped back and asked "Are you witches?" When a Sioux Indian girl was trance channeled, she could not confirm what "time" she was from. When someone told her that the sitters have white skin she said "I have heard that some of our warriors have told stories about men with white skin". This girl did not realize that she was physically dead. She thought that she was dreaming in her sleep and due to some reason was unable to wake up. So, trance channeling can be extremely horrifying or utterly funny.

The trance channeling incidents owe a great debt to the controversial Helena Petrovna Blavatsky (1831–1891) popularly known as Madame Blavatsky, who was the first to popularize 'channeling' wisdom from ancient teachers and masters, as well as the mystique of past-lives and lost worlds. Perhaps the most famous and most documented trance channeler was Edgar Cayce. He was referred to as "The Sleeping Prophet", because he only channeled when he was in a deep trance state. He would lie down on a couch, fold his hands over his stomach and enter the trance state, which made it seem like he was asleep. In this condition he lost all muscle tone and had to be lying down, and his secretary would be present there to take dictation and then transcribe the notes from the channeling session. The Association for Research and Enlightenment in Virginia has 14,306 of his recorded readings on astonishing 10,000 different topics in their archive, most of which dealt with health and the treatment of illness. His messages (known as 'readings') brought us other modern metaphysical (Meta, meaning over and beyond – and physics. Thus, the combination means over and beyond physics) terms like meditation, holistic, akashic record, aura, and soulmate that has until his time never been heard of before.

The most prominent trance channeler of Iceland was Hafsteinn Bjornsson (1914 - 1977) about whom several books and research papers had been written (in Icelandic) with interesting accounts of individual cases, including drop-in communicators (discussed later) and one impressive case of xenoglossy.

Hafsteinn's abilities as a channeler had attracted much attention in Iceland that there was always a long waiting list for his sittings. He used to bring messages from the discarnate entities, often giving their full names so that they were easily identified, and at each séance 20 to 30 entities or more might thus be described or identified. The sitters were often deeply impressed by the characteristic features, manner of speech, and behavior expressed by the direct communicators.

Hafsteinn could see discarnate entities around people while in a waking state. Sometimes in public meetings, usually in a cinema or assembly hall, held in semi-darkness, he would describe 80 to over 100 deceased persons giving accurate details of their names, relations to each other, appearance, and sometimes short messages from them. Hafsteinn would invite the audience to ask questions, which he would apparently relay to the deceased entities and which might bring out further details about the deceased persons (Haraldsson, 2008, p. 68). During Hafsteinn's séance once there was a case of xenoglossy (the ability to speak a foreign language not normally learned). Professor Sven Fredriksen of Denmark attended a séance with Hafsteinn in 1966 and conversed for a short time in the Eskimo (Inuit) language with a discarnate entity supposed to be an Eskimo witchdoctor whom Fredriksen had known in his childhood and youth in Greenland, where he learned the local language (Stevenson, 1974a, p. 8). Since Hafsteinn had received only minimal schooling and knew no foreign language, this case cannot be dismissed as fraud. Xenoglossy is common in reincarnation cases (next chapter).

Two most celebrated and tested trance channelers were Leonora Piper (1859-1950) and Gladys Osborne Leonard (1882-1968). Often when thinking about a medium, we envision a gypsy-like person hovering over a crystal ball. That was not their image – both were quiet women of common sense, integrity, and expertise, and lived their lives by a set of principles. They had excellent psychic powers. Many persons, including hard scientists and skeptics who came for sittings with them during their long period of activity became convinced they had communicated with their deceased relatives and friends.

Leonora (famously known as Mrs. Piper) used to have mystical experiences as a young girl. At the age of eight while playing in the garden she felt a mild blow on her head, and on the right ear she heard "a prolonged sibilant sound" followed by the clear words, "*Aunt Sara, not dead but with you still.*" (Fontana, 2005, p. 123). She was terrified and when she told her mother, her mother noted the time of day. A few days later they learned that at that exact time, her mother's sister Sara had unexpectedly died. Few weeks later she called her mother and complained that she couldn't sleep because of the "*bright light in the room and all the faces in it*" as well as because "*my bed [a big old-fashioned four-poster] won't stop rocking*" (Richardson, 2006, p. 260). In the late June 1884, she discovered her psychic and channeling abilities when she visited J. R. Cocke, a blind healer and clairvoyant, seeking treatment for a tumor. She was part of a circle meeting, and when her turn came, she saw in front of her "*a flood of light in which many strange faces appeared*". Both Cocke and Leonora went into trance. She then rose from her chair and unaided walked to a table, and wrote down a remarkable message to a Judge Frost of Cambridge (another of Cocke's clients), from a son he had lost some thirty years ago (James, 1986, p. 398). Shortly a number of discarnates made themselves known and exchange of meaningful information took place. As word of Frost's experience spread, Leonora herself began receiving requests for sittings. She tried doing this at home with relatives and friends with some success.

Soon Professor William James of Harvard University, a founder of the American Society for Psychical Research was so impressed by her séances that he devoted the next eighteen months to carefully controlling everything she did, making all arrangements. Prof. James (1986, pp. 82, 88) wrote,

> "*This lady can at will pass into a trance condition, in which she is 'controlled' by a power purporting to be the spirit of a French doctor, who serves as an intermediary between the sitter and the deceased friends. This is the ordinary type of trance-mediumship at the present day.....I am persuaded of the medium's honesty and of the genuineness of her trance, and although at first disposed to think that the 'hits' she made were either lucky coincidences or the result of knowledge on her part of who the sitter was and of his or her family affairs, I now believe her to be in possession of a power as yet unexplained.*"

> "*I repeat again what I said before, that, taking everything that I know of Mrs. Piper into account, the result is to make me feel as absolutely certain as I am of any personal fact in the world that she knows things in her trances which she cannot possibly have heard in her waking state, and that the definite philosophy of her trances is yet to be found*".

The investigations and experiments of Prof. James with Leonora that continued until shortly before his death convinced him that the veridical phantasms, haunted houses, trances with supernormal faculty are natural phenomena which must, just like other natural events, to be followed up with scientific curiosity.

Prominent author Henry Holt had several sittings with Leonora. He related that after being seated a minute or two, her eyeballs rolled upward, her face became slightly convulsed, and then she began talking in a rough voice not her own. He recalled the voice affecting him as if it were coming from a statue,

> "*pouring forth at one moment some brusquerie [bluntness of manner] in the rough deep tones of Phinuit; at the next, in the same voice softened to gentleness, petting a child; then, perhaps, a return to the gruff tones in some biting sarcasm to some interloping control; then perhaps issuing*

from the same mouth, a child's voice singing the little boat song – all going on amid the weeping relatives who join in the song." (Holt, 1919, p. 482)

One observer described it as "*perhaps the most shocking sight I ever witnessed*" (Hodgson, 1892, p. 97). On March 6, 1889, Alice James and Robertson James (Prof. James' wife and brother) sat with Leonora. Alice asked about Aunt Kate who was seriously ill and living more than two hundred miles away at New York. Leonora in a trance state replied, "She is poorly". Alice was disappointed, and towards the end of the séance she asked again, "*Can you tell me nothing more about Aunt Kate?*" Suddenly Leonora threw back her head and said in a shocked way, "*Why Aunt Kate's here. All around me I hear voices saying, 'Aunt Kate has come'.*" Then followed the announcement that she had died very early that morning shortly after two o'clock (Martin and Zacharias, 2003, p. 295). Leonora also confirmed that a letter or telegram saying she was gone would be received later that day. Alice and Robertson knew that Aunt Kate had been seriously ill, but neither was aware that she had died. Later Robertson wrote that after leaving the séance "*on reaching home an hour later I found a telegram as follows – 'Aunt Kate passed away a few minutes after midnight – E. R. Walsh'.*" (Holt, 1914, p. 411).

Between 1885 and 1915, Leonora Piper became one of the most investigated channeler of all time. Barrett Wendell described her recovery from the trance states as "*perhaps the most shocking sight I ever witnessed.*" It involved convulsion-like movements that alarmed many people. Minot Judson Savage, one of Prof. James' friends maintained a written record of his first sitting with Leonora early in 1886. After three years of his 31-year-old son's untimely death, once Savage "*tried to see if I could get anything that appeared to be a message from my boy*". Leonora informed him that his son was present.

In deep trance Leonora wrote down the message from his son "*Papa [and this with a great deal of earnestness], I want you go at once to my room. Look in my drawer and you will find a lot of loose papers. Among them are some which I would like you to take and destroy at once.*" Immediately Savage ran to the apartment his son had been sharing, searched the drawer, gathering up all the loose papers, inspected them, and "*at once saw the meaning and importance of what he had asked me to do*", as he later wrote, "*there were things there which he had jotted down and trusted to the privacy of his drawer which he would not have made public for the world.*" (Peden, 2010, p. 84; Pye and Dalley, 2013, p. 121). Savage ended the story, commenting that he would not violate his son's privacy by disclosing the contents of the papers.

Various other distinguished authors, such as, David Fontana, Chris Carter, Greg Taylor, Michael Tymn, Michael Prescott and Robert McLuhan had investigated her and confirmed that no tricks would explain the many documented occasions when she had produced names – sometimes both family and surname and nicknames, and gave accurate details about people and incidents, with no prompting and at the first attempt. The genuineness of the trance state was tested on several occasions by subjecting Leonora to physical discomfort. Richard Hodgson wrote that he could not detect '*the smallest signs of discomfort*' after she had taken several inhalations of strong ammonia (special care was taken to see that the ammonia was actually inhaled) (Hodgson, 1892, p. 4). Leonora suffered somewhat after the trance was over. It caused her nose to bleed and brought on chronic sensitivity. Similarly, she appeared to be quite unaware of a spoonful of salt which he placed in her mouth.

Sir Oliver Lodge wrote in his own account of Leonora's mediumship that,

> "*the trance is, to the best of my belief, a genuine one. In it, Mrs. Piper is (sometimes, at least) insensible to pain, as tested by suddenly pushing a needle into her hand, which causes not the slightest flinching; and her pulse is affected beyond what I can imagine to be the control of volition*". (Myers, et al., 1890, p. 447)

Frank Podmore made it clear that "*by an almost universal consensus of opinion her trance is a genuine one*". Charles Richet investigated her mediumship and declared her trance to be genuine. Psychologist(s) Stanley Hall and Amy Tanner used an esthesiometer to measure tactile sensitivity of her hands, finding no response. They also pressed camphor to her nostrils, then placed a one-third teaspoonful of camphor in her mouth, neither having any effect. But after becoming conscious her lips had painful blisters. They concluded, "*certainly her respiratory functions, taste, smell, general tactile sensibility and motor innervation are asleep*" (Tanner and Hall, 1994, p. 268). So, how did she fool scientists and physicians that her trance was genuine, showing no reaction to pain sensitivity tests including surprise needle jabs, flames held to her skin, and long inhalations of ammonia?

In later years, a number of 'advanced spirits' took over control of 'the machine' (their name for Mrs. Leonora Piper), and most communications were in writing. The long period of the Mrs. Piper investigation even resulted in a number of the original researchers 'returning' as spirits communicating from 'the other side'. As example, Frederic Myers' (died on January 17, 1901) departed soul communicated through her while she was undergoing rigorous investigation by George Dorr in Boston. Myers was a distinguished classical scholar and in the conversation with Dorr, the departed soul gave many accurate references to one question. When Sir Oliver Lodge learned of this, he posed the same question through another medium known as Mrs. Willett in London. In response the departed soul gave another long series of references in front of many classical scholars which were equally accurate. When Lodge asked why 'Myers' had not given the same responses, the reply was that had he done so, critics would have dismissed the evidence as mere telepathy between the mediums (Keen, 2003, p. 293). This had convinced nearly all researchers that she had access to information that was not available by 'normal' means.

British medium Mrs. Gladys Osborne Leonard began trance channeling early in the twentieth century. Her controlling discarnate was Feda, who claimed to be her great-great-grandmother, allegedly the Hindu wife of one of her ancestors who lived around 1800 and died in childbirth at the age of fourteen. Leonard recalled hearing a story about an Indian ancestress from her mother but did not remember any details. Unlike Mrs. Leonora Piper who was controlled by several discarnates, Mrs. Leonard was controlled by Feda from beginning to end except that other discarnates occasionally sent messages through her. There was no similarity between Leonard's voice and that of Feda, who spoke like a young girl with different accent and substandard English (frequent lapses of grammar) and on some occasions sent messages through automatic writing (Xiong, 2010, p. 267). It means, Feda used her own voice and used Leonard's speech mechanism.

As a young child Leonard had many visions which she called "Happy Valleys". In her autobiography, 'My Life in Two Worlds', she wrote,

> "*In whatever direction I happened to be looking, the physical view of the wall, door, ceiling, or whatever it was, would disappear, and in its place would gradually come valleys, gentle slopes, lovely trees and banks covered with flowers, of every shape and hue. The scene seemed to extend for many miles, and I was conscious that I could see much farther than was possible with the ordinary physical scenery around me.*" (Leonard, 1931, p. 11)

She could see spirits "*like clearly cut shadows, which showed up perfectly against the light background*" (Leonard, 1931, p. 31). When she was entering her teens, the family came upon a period of great financial trouble. She trained herself to be a professional singer, but an attack of diphtheria affected her voice. At about this time at a Spiritualist Church, a medium told her "*your guides are preparing you for an important spiritual work*" (Leonard, 1931, p. 290). One day she went away from home to stay with friends for a night, but during the early morning hours, she was suddenly awakened with a strange feeling that something unusual was happening. She looked up and saw in front of her but about five feet above a large, circular patch of light about four feet in diameter. In this light she saw her mother's face quite distinctly. Her face looked several years younger, her eyes were clear and shining and a smile of utter happiness was on her lips. She gazed down on her for a moment, seeming to convey to her an intense feeling of relief and a sense of safety and comfort. Then the vision faded. The next morning, she learned that her mother had died at 2 a.m. (Leonard, 1931, p. 23; Smith, 1964, p. 18). This incident made a great impression on her mind, and she finally decided that she must continue to find out much more about these psychic faculties.

Feda told Leonard that she had been watching over her since she was born, waiting for her to develop her psychic powers so that she could put her into a trance as she (Feda) had work to do through her because of a big and terrible happening (apparently World War I) that would soon take place. Feda further confirmed that she was fulfilling work required of her to make spiritual progress of her own soul. Initially, Leonard was reluctant because the idea of being controlled while in the trance state did not appeal to her,

> "*I was not pleased with this, as I wanted to develop normal clairvoyance, but Feda said, 'No, you must be controlled, because otherwise your own mind would interfere with everything we wish to give, through you'. So I began to think seriously about it, although I did not want to be entranced.*" (Glenconner, 1921, p. 141)

Feda then told Leonard to become a professional medium and promised her that she would look after her. After WW I, Feda asked her to give up her public sittings and begin private sittings for those who had lost loved ones in battle. Thus began her long life of dedicated service as a trance channeler.

Leonard was one of the most thoroughly investigated and carefully documented channeler of the twentieth century. Hundreds of pages of the Society for Psychical Research's Proceedings were devoted to the Leonard's trance channeling. For more than fifty years she gave undeniable evidence of afterlife survival to countless number of people. World's most noted psychic researchers of the time had conducted investigations, such as, Rev. Charles Drayton Thomas, Rev. Vale Owen, James Hewat McKenzie, Mrs. W. H. Salter, and Whately Carington, to name a few. Charles had over 500 sittings with her, all fully recorded. Lady Troubridge had weekly sittings with her for eight years, and carefully preserved every word that was spoken. Rev. W. S. Irving sat two or three times a year for more than 22 years. Mrs. Lydia W. Allison made frequent trips to England from USA from 1921 to 1927 in order to sit with Leonard and other mediums. Mrs. W. H. Salter, a prominent member of the Society for Psychical Research, gave countless hours to sittings with Leonard. Miss Nea Walker, Sir Oliver Lodge's psychical secretary, made regular visits for nineteen years as a 'proxy sitter' on behalf of other people. During these sittings, Leonard was subjected to very close scrutiny. However, amazingly enough she never seemed to be bothered by this because she knew that she had nothing to hide in her work. Talking to a spirit was just as natural as talking on the telephone.

The most significant amongst all was a series of sittings she had with Sir Oliver Lodge, the renowned physicist. In 1915, Oliver and his wife anonymously visited Leonard. With the information given by Feda, they were convinced that they were communicating with their son Raymond who had recently been killed in the war on September 14, 1915. Oliver was a skeptic, and hence he put Leonard through a severe series of tests. But the evidence kept coming forth, and it became impossible to deny the obvious – Raymond lived on the other side of life. Leonard gave Oliver such information about which he knew nothing about, but later confirmed from his son's diary. Oliver's book, 'Raymond or Life After Death', is an examination of his search for survival evidence. The publication of Raymond gave great push to Leonard's career.

Alec Lodge, one of Raymond's older brothers, was still skeptical. He sat with Leonard on December 21, 1915, and as a test of his own, asked Raymond about his favorite music. Alec noted that he then heard Feda questioning Raymond, asking him "sotto voce" (whispering) "*An orange lady?*" Still confused, Feda then told Alec "*He says something about an orange lady.*" Alec felt that this was very evidential as "My Orange Girl" was the last song Raymond bought when "alive". Raymond also mentioned "Irish Eyes," another of his favorites (Lodge, 1916, p. 212). Alec's siblings Lionel and Norah also heard such whispering of Feda to Raymond in another sitting. Once Rev. Charles Thomas heard such whispering too, of which he could catch fragments, such as "*Yes, Mr. John [Rev. John Thomas – his deceased father], Feda will tell him…Yes, all right…Feda says she is having trouble understanding Mr. John.*" (Thomas, 1922, p. 23). It was not that Feda was referring to herself in the third person but while relaying messages from other spirits they were interacting amongst themselves. Curtis (2011, p. 115) reported that many mediums talk about the need to exercise 'crowd control' when many discarnates appear and talk all at once.

Leonard received information from Feda in a variety of ways such as book test, newspaper test, proxy sitting and cross correspondence. In book tests, Feda would direct the sitter to a certain book in a certain place (e.g., on the third shelf from the top, the ninth book from the left) in his or her home where on a given page the sitter would find a special message. Significant results from these tests were reported by many investigators. Newspaper tests were futuristic, something like, in tomorrow's Times, on third page, column five, about eight inches from the top, you will find a name which will recall intimate associations of your youth between the ages of sixteen and eighteen. There were several book and newspaper tests between late Rev. John Thomas and his son Rev. Charles Drayton Thomas on different sides of the veil of death with the help of Feda and Leonard. Soon it was abruptly clear that the senior Thomas was experimenting on his side as much as junior Thomas was on the material side. Leonard had never visited Thomas' house and knew nothing of the library of books in it. Over a period of two years the father and son carried out 348 tests. After book test, the discarnate father told the son to start newspaper test. The discarnate Thomas started providing information to be found in newspapers and magazines not yet printed. The game went on between a dead and a living person. Many newspaper tests were carried out. In each case, junior Thomas would immediately write down the information and file it in a sealed envelope with the Society for Psychical Research at a time before the type was set at the newspaper office. Further, Thomas would check papers from at least 10 other days, being sure that the same names did not appear in those editions, thereby ruling out coincidence.

In proxy sitting, the person present with her would be acting as a proxy on behalf of the actual sitter. The sitter was known neither to the medium nor to the person acting as a proxy. Leonard was very successful in these cases also, and gave information right away with high degree of accuracy (Braude, 2003, p. 78; Broad, 1962, p. 265). Cross correspondence is a way of information transfer in which part of a message would come through her mediumship and part through another medium with no ordinary contact between them. The information produced by one medium does not make sense, but when put together a complete and meaningful message can be obtained (Moreira-Almeida and Santos, 2012, p. 202). These cases are relatively rare.

At the end of World War I in 1918, the Society for Psychical Research had investigated Leonard rigorously. Out of seventy-three sittings, all of those involved agreed that "*good evidence of surviving personality had been obtained and the complete trustworthiness of the medium could not be questioned.*" (Buckland, 2005, p. 226). Leonard became a professional medium of such quality that she was called "The Queen of English Mediums," "The British Mrs. Piper," (a reference to Mrs. Leonora Piper) and "Greatest Trance Medium." Sir Arthur Conan Doyle said that she was "*the greatest trance medium with whom the author is acquainted.*" (Doyle, 2008, p. 249). What is most interesting about Leonard's channeling is the way in which she and Feda worked together. She achieved such a great success because there are two mediums – one in body and one in spirit – both working together, as one channel for communication. This beautiful team effort had not only strengthened death but also beautified it.

Another two gifted channelers were Arthur Ford and Eileen Garrett. Arthur's guide was a discarnate, named Fletcher who stayed with him throughout his carrier. Eileen Garrett was interested about paranormal from her childhood days when both of her parents committed suicide. Eileen was not aware of her psychic power, but once she fell asleep at a public meeting in London and the spirits of deceased relatives of the men and women seated around her began to speak through her. One person sitting nearly was familiar with the phenomenon of mediumship, and he explained to Eileen what had happened to her. He went on to say that he had communicated with an Asian spirit named Uvani that had manifested through her while she was entranced, and the entity had informed him that henceforth he would serve as Eileen Garrett's guide and spirit control. Hereward Carrington, one of the leading researchers during that period, conducted a series of tests with Eileen Garrett and declared her to be a "medium's medium". Throughout her life Eileen was a supporter of the scientific enquiry of mediumship and channeling. In her autobiography 'Adventures in the supernatural' she wrote (Briggs, 2010,

p. 134), "*I have a gift, a capacity – a delusion, if you will – which is called 'psychic'. I don't care what it may be called...I have been called many things, from a charlatan to a miracle woman. I am at least, neither of these.*"

There are countless other brave pioneers in this paranormal field who blazed a path for the rest of us at a time when the world was even more judgmental than it is now. The trance mediums were not always given the credit they deserve for their work and the spiritual gift they bring to the world. But we should pay attention to the messages they bring from supernatural sources because it can help us to change the world and bring new hope to humanity.

6.2.1: Futuristic newspaper tests – a possible explanation

A while ago we have talked about futuristic newspaper tests between father and son (John Thomas and Charles Drayton Thomas) on different sides of death with the help of Feda and Leonard. The question that struck immediately is, how the late father was able to obtain information from newspapers not yet typeset that he had passed on to his son? Did the medium receive the information clairvoyantly before the page had been set up? Is precognition an alternative explanation to survival hypothesis?

When Thomas asked his father how he was able to obtain futuristic newspaper information, the father replied that he didn't quite understand it himself but referred to it as some kind of "etheric foreshadowing", similar to seeing the shadow of a man around the corner before actually seeing the man at the door. It means, whatever is about to materialize on Earth (i.e., a future event), has its spiritual counterpart in the spirit world. It is the 'intention' that is sensed in the spirit world before it is put into action by the person who has intended. As example, when a criminal wants to kill someone, the potential victim may feel a sense of impending danger. Sometimes we call this as sixth sense. Animals have this sense more than human beings. The late father explains from the spirit world,

> "*Now the things I see are frequently but the spiritual counterparts of things which are about to take form; some of my tests from the Times might be called shadows of a substance.... When you see a shadow it is but an outline, and you do not look for detail, and that explains the difficulty of these tests; we cannot always sufficiently observe detail.*" (Thomas, 1922, p. 206)

Senior Thomas further explained that while moving from 'sensing' to seeing, he could not always see the word clearly, as in one case he gave the word 'rain' for what proved to be 'raisin'. Although the words may not be in type, someone's thoughts are in them and someone has formulated the wordings. The discarnate father had 'sensed' the words, not actually read them. This is not the case of simple telepathy. This discarnate clairvoyance is much beyond human comprehension.

Mrs. Piper also suggested the exercise of discarnate clairvoyance. In early March 1892, a personality claiming to be the recently deceased George Pelham manifested at sittings with Mrs. Piper. George regularly disclosed the names of many of his personal friends and intimate details of his associations with them throughout his life. During one sitting, this discarnate entity claimed to have watched his father compose a letter to his brother Frank (George's uncle) on a particular day. Although his father did not actually write such a letter, he had intended to do so on the day in question (Hodgson, 1898, p. 315). The father's thought had created a spiritual counterpart, i.e., a shadow of the 'letter' that the father intended to write. His son, the discarnate spirit had 'sensed' the futuristic letter even though it was never written.

6.3: The Seth material channeled by Jane Roberts

"*The Seth books present an alternate map of reality with a new diagram of the psyche ...useful to all explorers of consciousness.*"

Deepak Chopra

Dorothy Jane Roberts (1929–1984) was an American author, poet, self-proclaimed psychic, and spirit medium. While in a trance state Jane channeled a spirit teacher who called himself 'Seth'. Seth was an "'*energy personality essence' no longer focused within the physical system; that he speaks through my subconscious but is independent of it.*" (Roberts, 2000, p. xxii). The popular phrase "you create your own reality" is said to have been first coined by Seth speaking through Jane, who is the author of what is known today as the "Seth Material". Jane dictated the words to her husband, Robert Butts, from late 1963 until her death in 1984. During these 21 years Jane held more than 1500 regular or private 'ESP class' trance sessions in which she spoke on behalf of Seth. With this, Jane established her as one of the preeminent figures in the field of paranormal studies.

Seth indicated he had completed his earthly reincarnations and was speaking from an adjacent plane of existence. The Seth personality described himself as a 'teacher', and said, "*this material has been given by himself and others in other times and places, but that it is given again, in new ways, for each succeeding generation through the centuries.*" (Lewis, 2004, p. 584). In the material, Seth had given many references of consciousness, reincarnation, karmic cycle, spirit world, illusion of time and space etc. in a very objective way. I briefly mention below some of the wisdom which are relevant to our topics, and put my comments in square brackets.

1. Consciousness creates matter. Physical reality arises from consciousness, not the other way around. Our beliefs (both individual

and collective) form reality, and the intensity of a belief is extremely important. "*Your beliefs meet you in the face when you look in the mirror. They form your image. You cannot escape your beliefs*". [Quantum physics – The 'physical' world that we have taken for granted to be solid and separate from us is a trick of the senses. The strange behavior of quantum particles confirms that the apparent 'materiality' of the world is no more and no less 'real' than a dream-image. Seth's wisdom is fully consistent with the discoveries of quantum physics. Only for this reason, the Seth Material holds particular interest for those engaged in the study of quantum physics.]

2. God exists as a self-replicating and inexhaustible mental energy whom Seth referred to as "All That Is" and described as a "primary energy gestalt". The mental energy of God is the composite substance of all things, including all beings, all Universes, and all events and phenomena. God contains all of creation within it. God is a gestalt of all existence (a gestalt, as a whole, is greater than the sum of its parts), as in Pantheism and Panentheism (Pantheism means that all is God; panentheism, that all is in God.). God's consciousness extends into all things as they are created and is therefore omnipresent. All things in existence including physical matter have life and consciousness. God experiences existence in all its forms and consequences through its creations. God is therefore dynamic and ever-changing and shares in the failures, triumphs, perfections and imperfections of its creations. Every creature, though part of God, has free will and self-determination. Seth personality was not aware if there is any reality outside of God. [This explains why the Universe is fine-tuned for life. The life of each and every living being has a purpose.]

3. There was a creation, but it differs markedly from the Christian and Muslim versions. Initially the Universe existed in a state of potentiality within God's dreams. The power of God's consciousness was so great that the individuals in its dreams had self-awareness, and they appealed to be made real. The creation occurred when God made its dreams real. [Here Seth confirmed that souls existed even before Big Bang.]

4. Consciousness is an attribute of the soul, a tool that can be turned in many directions. I (the physical being) am not my consciousness. It is something that belongs to me and to my soul. I am learning to use it. [This perfectly explains quantum consciousness.]

5. All probable worlds, and all probable variations on the most minute aspect in any reality exist now. Seth referred this as a "spacious present". [The multiverse theory fits well with quantum physics that

all possibilities can coexist. Also, both past and future coexist with the present.]

6. No event is predestined. Any given event can be changed not only before and during but after its occurrence. An individual's future actions are not dependent upon a concrete finished past, for such a past never existed [If time and space are illusions of mind, then past, present and future – all are changeable. The parapsychologist Helmut Schmidt has performed PK experiments which seem to show that actions in the present can influence the past (Schmidt, 1976). This is called retrocausation. Past is neither written on stone nor it is immune to further influence.]
7. No one is at the mercy of the unexplainable, or at the mercy of events (psychological or physical) over which we have no control. [The free will of the soul is always honored.]
8. The human race is a stage through which various forms of consciousness travel. [We are multi-dimensional beings; more than our physical bodies.]
9. After death we travel in other dimensions where we will find ourselves in another form, an image that will appear physical to us to a large degree as long as we do not try to manipulate within the physical system in it. [The spirit realm is beyond our three-dimensional understanding where we can manipulate by thought process.]
10. Death will not bring us an eternal resting place. After death we have to face up to ourselves for those that we did not use during our previous existence. In answer to someone arguing against reincarnation, Seth replied that all of us will reincarnate whether or not we believe that we will. Our personal beliefs and choices will not change the nature of reincarnation one iota. The purpose of reincarnation is to purify the soul. Purification does require change, and the soul needs the trials of a new physical life. Often past-life memories come to the surface but are not recognized as such, since they appear in fantasy form, or are projected into art creations. But below the fantasy form and projections there is authentic material. The past-life memories enrich the present live. [Reincarnation is not a hypothesis but a hard fact. It's a natural law.]
11. If we examine our own life now carefully, the challenges that we have set for ourselves will become apparent. This is not easy to do, but it is within the grasp of each individual. If we release ourselves from the hatred then we automatically release ourselves from any such relationships in the future or any experiences that are based upon hatred. The entire structure of our existence will begin to change with these realizations, and an acceleration of spiritual and psychic growth will develop. [This is how we can work out our Karma.]

12. Everyone lives all of our reincarnations at once though we may find this difficult to understand. Time, as we think of it, does not exist. [When we think in terms of reincarnation it seems that one 'tracing' exists before the other, but the entire 'chart' exists at once, with all the individual life tracings.]
13. Illness and suffering are not thrust upon us by any supernatural power. They are byproducts of the learning process. All our mishaps have a purpose for the growth of the soul. [The miseries and rewards that our life gives us have meaning. The earthly life is a continuous learning process for the development of the soul. In that sense the Earth is a training ground for the soul.]
14. A human is actually his entity (your soul). He is its materialization in space and time as he understands it. There is no division between your entity and what you are. [We are all spiritual beings in a human body.]
15. There is never any justification for violence, for hatred, for murder. Those who indulge in violence for whatever reason are themselves changed, and the purity of their purpose adulterated. [Only love is real.]

In short, Seth's teachings are full of wisdom and the effect upon New Age thinkers has been profound. Many things that were explained by Seth are now proven to be true. Hence Seth and Roberts have attracted critics from outside the paranormal community as well. As example, the late physician Michael Talbot wrote, "*To my great surprise – and slight annoyance – I found that Seth eloquently and lucidly articulated a view of reality that I had arrived at only after great effort and an extensive study of both paranormal phenomena and quantum physics.*" (Ludden, 2012, p. 443). Seth wants us to doubt as he had confirmed that his messages are for doubters.

> "*The information was not to be given to 'born believers', but to intelligent people, and to a 'medium' who questioned it, not only for [herself] but for all those given to the same kind of questioning.*" (Roberts, 1972, p. 321)

The Seth wisdom withstood the test of time and affected the lives of people in every corner of the globe. By now the material had been translated over a dozen languages and sold over eight million copies.

6.4: Skeptic's views

Psychologist Gary Schwartz has extensively studied the spirit mediums where he tried to rigorously exclude the possibility that the mediums used normal sources of information to learn about deceased persons. He reports that mediums are in many cases able to report large amounts of accurate, detailed information about the departed, even though they do not have voice or visual contact with the sitters or know their identities. Also, that objective methods of tabulating data eliminate the possibility that these positive results could be due to selective memory on the part of the sitters (remembering hits while forgetting misses), vague information (that could apply to anyone), and lucky guesses (Schwartz, 2002). These results can be explained only by communication with the dead or by some form of paranormal information transfer not involving the dead.

Famous psychologist Arthur Hastings had done extensive research on trance mediums, and concluded that fraud, schizophrenia and mental disturbances are explanatory in some cases, while the large majority of cases are genuine (Hastings, 1991, pp. 159-60). The strongest evidence for channeling comes primarily from outside, separate disincarnate entities that include, the distinctness of their personalities from that of the channeler once cases of schizophrenia and multiple personality are excluded, the expression of skills and knowledge that the channeler does not possess, and examples of coded information coming through several channelers (Hastings, 1991, Chapter 15). Information received from one particular channeler in one sitting makes no sense individually, but when put together the meaning is evident. As example, medium Arthur Ford deciphered the Houdini's coded message to his wife after ten sittings with Houdini's spirit.

Can 'Super-psi hypothesis' explain away the channeling phenomena? As per this hypothesis, the trance channeler is telepathically getting the information from the deceased person before he died using retrocognition (knowledge of a past event which could not have been learned or inferred by normal means), or the channeler is telepathically tapping into the mind of some living person who has intimate knowledge of the dead person being channeled. Simply speaking, this hypothesis is an extension of the original telepathy concept which presumes psychic functioning among living persons.

However, there are reasons to discard this hypothesis. First of all, if the channeler is plucking out both the name and the incident most closely related to the individual of the sitter's head, how can we explain proxy sitting cases when a person who is present with the channeler would be acting as a proxy on behalf of the actual sitter about whom the channeler has no knowledge? Mrs. Piper provided detailed information that was not known many times to the sitter, who had to search to verify what she had told them (Cox, 2009, p. 114). Secondly, 'retrocognition hypothesis' can be ruled out because in many trance channeling cases, the discarnate persons have highly specific knowledge of living agents and the physical world acquired after their death. Finally, when most mainstream scientists wholly dispute regular ESP and telepathy between a single individual to another, to assign the super-psi answer is even harder to accept. In other words, if the skeptics deny regular telepathy, then how could we ever accept a 'super' version of it? What Super-psi hypothesis can explain the origin of Seth wisdom?

How to explain the voice, handwriting and the art produced by the mediums? The celebrated Irish medium Geraldine Cummins produced about fifty different personalities and styles in her career, many matching deceased persons known to their survivors. Writing in a light trance, she wrote at astonishing speed with no idea of what her hand was to produce.

There are indications that discarnate entities keep a vigil eye on what is going on in this physical world. Rev. David Kennedy documented with considerable details, a large number of ostensible communications from his deceased wife Ann during a six-month period after her death which came through a dozen different mediums. Once Ann said that she was with her husband 10 minutes prior and knew that he was reading about a particular person (Rev. Drayton Thomas) at the time. In another time, Ann concerned the whereabouts of clean clerical collars, which Kennedy was looking for at that particular moment. Ann not only knew where the collars were located in the house but she knew that Kennedy was going to be giving a memorial service for a specific person later that evening. One day a channeler phoned Kennedy and said that Ann had just been watching her husband doing laundry and that he had put too much soap in the wash, resulting in an overflow of foams. She also knew the specific items of clothing that were in the wash. On another occasion, Ann claimed to have watched Kennedy cook fish earlier in the day. She knew the kind of fish, and added that the pot which Kennedy had placed in the cupboard, wasn't properly cleaned. Once Ann revealed that her husband had withdrawn £45 from his bank account earlier in the day and that the lights on Kennedy's car needed to be replaced. Ann also disclosed the location of a very specific pair of earrings Kennedy had never seen before (Kennedy, 1973, pp. 69-70, 105-06, 115, 125-26, 147-48). In all these Ann/David Kennedy communications, telepathy would arguably be insufficient to explain them since neither Kennedy nor any other living person was aware of the facts at the time. The undeniable fact is that Ann was watching her husband from an afterlife realm and warned him whenever required.

In one sitting of Mrs. Piper, the sitters asked G.P. (a discarnate entity) to provide a description of the activities of his friend Mrs. Howard at the time of the sitting. G.P. correctly described Mrs. Howard's activities from the previous day (Hodgson, 1898, pp. 305-07). How the discarnate entity provided reports of what other people were doing at specific locations while the sitting was underway? A hypothesis cannot do any explanatory work unless independent evidence supports it. The telepathy and Super-psi hypothesis for mediumship cases are not supported by a single independent evidence, and to borrow words from Almeder (1992, p. 52) "*before one can appeal legitimately to super-psi as an alternative way of explaining anything, one should have some empirical evidence that in fact super-psi exists.*" When all arguments are refuted, if skeptics cannot accept the answer of "the dead," then what else is there?

Some skeptics believe that every action and information is recorded at a quantum level and the channeler is simply accessing this information. However, the question still remains, from where the information is coming and how the channeler is receiving it. Can we explain the Ann and David Kennedy communications from what skeptics believe? Some channelers even exhibit apparent knowledge of future events when in trance, such as the afterlife communication between late Rev. John Thomas and his son Rev. Charles Drayton Thomas. The newspaper tests between father and son from different sides of the death effectively eliminated telepathy, recordings at quantum level, super-psi with the living as the source of the information, because the front page of the newspaper was typeset in the evening before publication, hours after the reading occurred. This future memory phenomenon is certainly an interesting topic.

6.5: Further Evidence from 'drop-in' mediumistic communications

Among all the data collected from physical and mental mediumship cases there is a significant group that "*consists of those in which a communicator appears whose existence neither medium nor sitters know anything about at the time of the manifestation*". (Stevenson, 1965, p. 47). Such cases are called "drop-in mediumistic communications" – a term coined by Ian Stevenson. Here the communicating personality, unknown to all, appears spontaneously and provides specific details that are later found to be accurate. Stevenson continues,

> "*if subsequent checking verifies the existence of a person and details corresponding with the communicator and his message ...[then] the explanation of the communication as resulting from telepathy between the medium and the sitters breaks down*".

Stevenson (1970, p. 53) mentioned that he had collected about 60 published reports of drop-in cases and was preparing a thesis on them. Unfortunately, by the time of his death he had not done this. These cases provide strong evidence for survival hypothesis because they can't be explained by telepathy or clairvoyance. "*The verified information contained in the communication was not obtainable through any single source*" (Kelly, 2010, p. 255). One aspect of these communications is 'motivation' – the discarnate usually has a purpose to communicate, such as to give an important information, console a relative in mourning, take care of an unfinished business etc.

Stevenson (1965, p. 48) quoted the case of Abraham Florentine that was first published by the highly regarded medium Stainton Moses in 1875. In one sitting on September 01, 1874, a discarnate identified himself as Abraham Florentine, and said that he had fought in 1812 war, and he had entered spirit-life at Brooklyn, USA on fifth August, at the age of 83 years, one month, and 17 days after a painful illness (Podmore, 1897, p. 128). Inquiries in the United States led to the identification of Abraham Florentine and an interview with his widow. She verified all the details, except she said that her husband had died at the age of 83 and 27 days (not one month and 17 days, as reported in the communication). Much later, in 1921, British anthropologist and psychical researcher Eric John Dingwall was curious about the case and made further inquiries and found obituaries of Abraham Florentine in the Brooklyn Daily Eagle and New York Daily Tribune, both of which stated that Abraham Florentine, a veteran of the war of 1812, had died on fifth August after a painful illness at the age of 83 years, one month, and 17 days. Stevenson undertook new inquiries more than 40 years later and checked the records of veterans of the United States Armed Services, as well as records of the Greenwood Cemetery in Brooklyn. The age of Abraham Florentine given by the communicator and the obituaries was right. The widow was wrong.

During September 1950, one such incident took place in Camerino University (Italy). Guiseppe Stoppolini, professor of anatomy wanted to do a paranormal experiment and so introduced medium Maria Bocca to his students. Maria went into a trance, and in a typical séance type interaction she was answering questions and relating messages from the dead friends and relatives of students in the room. Suddenly her voice changed and became unfamiliar, and she begged the audience to have mercy and listen. The discarnate said (Boar and Blundell, 1991, p. 64),

> "*I was born Rosa Manichelli. When I died, I was Rosa Spadoni, but my husband has died since then, too. We are both in the cemetery at Castel-Raimondo a few miles from Camerino. I am asking only that you help others, because the same thing can happen to them. Two days after the death certificate was signed, I was taken to the cemetery in a deep coma and buried alive*".

The students sat in a shocked silence while Maria toppled to the floor in a faint and the ghost of Rosa Manichelli was gone. Stoppolini did some research and quickly found that a woman named Rosa Spadoni, who had been born Rosa Manichelli, had died in September 4, 1939 at the Civic Hospital in Camerino at the age of 38 years, and two days later had been buried at Castrel-Raimondo. The cause of death was given as puerperal infection and subsequent heart involvement.

On September 13, 1950, the students accompanied by the professor and many other curious people gathered around the grave of Rosa Spadoni for the exhumation. When the lid was removed, they were shocked. The skeleton inside was leaning to the left instead of flat on its back. The left arm was bent up and fingers jammed into the mouth and throat cavity. The knees were bent as if to open the lid and there were parallel scratches inside of the coffin lid where Rosa had tried to claw her way out. She had been buried alive to awaken in her coffin sealed from the outside world. Maria had spoken the truth, and this incident had offered genuine proof of the survival phenomenon.

The discovery of this burial of a living person confirmed every detail of the communication from Rosa Manichelli made at the séance and it profoundly shocked all the witnesses of the digging up.

Another 'drop-in' was experienced by Frau Schutz, a non-professional trance channeler who gave regular sittings to a small private circle in Zurich. On Feb. 02, 1962, the discarnate spirit of a little boy appeared unexpectedly and said, "*You have never known me*" and gave his name as Hans-Peter Pasona. He said he had dark hair and brown eyes, died of something to do with the appendicitis and "*an unusual illness with a lot of fever*" in a children's hospital "*a long time*" ago. He lived in the seventh district in Zurich, and had two living brothers. His father had something to do with tea. When the channeler asked, "*What do you want child?*", the answer was "*give my love to my mother*" (Smith, 2000, p. 179). After enquiry, only one family of the name of Passanah was found in the telephone directory of Zurich. They had three sons and lived in the seventh district. The father was in the business of importing merchandise from India including tea. The whole family liked Indian tea. The youngest son had dark hair and brown eyes and died in 1932 when about twenty months old. Although the boy was named Robert, not Hans-Peter, nearly all the other details were accurate (Stevenson, 1970, p. 60). John Passanah, his elder brother was four years old when Robert died in a kinderspital (children hospital) not because of appendicitis but Pneumonia (Xiong, 2010, p. 221). The cause of death could not really be necessarily wrong as the discarnate had said that he had 'much fever' when he died and it could not exclude the possibility that the doctors failed to find anything wrong with his appendicitis. It seems, Robert (Hans-Peter) appeared to reassure his grieving mother of his survival at a time when the removal of his tombstone in the cemetery had renewed her sorrow.

Drop-in communication cases are not rare, but often the researchers fail to notice them because the episode ends very fast. Those discarnates arrive uninvited and then after passing some meaningful information, they just quickly 'drop out' without further reappearance most of the time. So drop-in cases occur only spontaneously; we must wait for them to appear if and when they will. But when they do appear, they are extremely important because the motivation behind the cases comes entirely from the deceased persons.

Sometimes these uninvited cases are forceful and abusive. The aforementioned Icelandic medium Hafsteinn Bjornsson held his séance regularly in his home at Reykjavik. In the autumn of 1937, an uninvited discarnate manifested through him when he was in trance. When asked to identify himself he said, "*My name is Jon Jonsson or Madur Mannsson [common Icelander names]. What the hell does it matter to you what my name is?*" When someone asked him what he wanted, his reply was, "*I am looking for my leg. I want to have my leg.*" When asked where his leg would be, the uninvited guest replied, "*It is in the sea.*" The discarnate kept appearing at sittings and demands for snuff, coffee, and alcohol very rudely. Throughout this period, he repeated the same request concerning his missing leg and always refusing to reveal his identity.

When a new member, Ludvik Gudmundsson, joined the group in January 1939, the discarnate finally said that Ludvik knew about his leg which was in his house. Annoyed by his rude behavior, the sitters finally gave the discarnate an ultimatum. They demanded to know his identity and said that otherwise they would do nothing for him. After this, the discarnate did not appear for many sittings, but one day he finally returned abruptly. The sitters had the impression that he literally forced himself into the medium by jostling aside another communicator. Then he began his story (Larusdottir, 1946, pp. 203-04), "*Well, it is best for me to tell you who I am. My name is Runolfur Runolfsson and...*".

In short, the annoying discarnate, Runolfur Runolfsson was a 52 years old man who had alcohol addiction. Once on a late-night journey to his home he was drunk. Weather was bad, and he was wet and tired. He sat down on a rock, opened his bottle and drank more brandy, and then fell asleep. At night the storm carried him out to sea. He died on October 16, 1879, and later his dismembered body was washed ashore. Dogs and ravens came tore him to pieces. The remnants (of his body) were found and buried in graveyard on January 8, 1880. But then the thigh bone was missing. It was carried out again to sea, but was later washed up again ashore (Braude, 2003, p. 46). There it was passed around and now it is in Ludvik's house. When Ludvik asked where he could find proof of the accuracy of his testimony, the discarnate replied, "*In the church book of Utskalar Church*". When the church books were examined all the information were found to be correct.

The discarnate made twenty claims about himself including dates, places, family history etc. Eighteen of them were verified by written records and testimony through interview. The remaining two claims could not be verified (Sudduth, 2016, p. 96). However, the mystery of the leg remained for some more time.

When Ludvik had purchased his house at Sandgerdi, he had heard a rumor that the house was haunted because the previous owner had kept two skulls in the house. A young boy living there had thrown one of these skulls into a corner with a disdainful remark about trash lying around. The next night the inhabitants of the house felt the presence of "two men" who seemed to go around looking (or trying to do so) at everyone who was sleeping. "They" stopped particularly at the bedside of the boy who had thrown the skull which made the boy utterly terrified. Ludvik collected the skulls and placed them in a glass box. An inhabitant of the area suggested that perhaps the house contained other bones that might be found if one searched for them.

However, Ludvik thought no more about this suggestion at the time, but when the discarnate, Runolfur Runolfsson, affirmed that his leg was at Ludvik's house in Sandgerdi he recalled the incident of the skulls. So he asked many elderly men of the village if they knew anything about a leg bone in the area. Some of them recalled vaguely that a thigh bone (femur) had been "going around," but they did not know what had happened to it. Ultimately, the thigh bone was found in 1940 when a wall was torn apart. Ludvik kept it for a year and then had a religious burial ceremony performed for it (Hugenot, 2016, p. 106). The thigh bone was extremely long. It matches Runolfur's claim that he had been very tall.

Runolfur came and expressed gratitude at a séance held immediately after the burial ceremony for the femur. He declared that he had been present at the ceremony and reception, and described them in detail, even mentioning the names of the different cakes served at the clergyman's home. He expressed thanks particularly to Ludvik and his wife for arranging the burial ceremony. Though the question remains why this discarnate still needs his thigh bone after more than sixty years of his death, the incident confirms that his consciousness was still continuing in the afterlife realm after sixty years of his physical death.

British medium Margo Williams had most of the drop-in cases. Margo said she was not aware of her psychical powers until a day in April 1976, when she heard a voice say "My name is Jane", and felt an impulse to write. She described herself later as writing 'furiously'. Jane communicated a lengthy account of parts of her life and of how she died. Soon many uninvited discarnates joined her. By January 1978, she had written scripts from more than sixty such communicators, which soon crossed one hundred. She usually wrote these scripts at the places of the supposed hauntings. Most of the discarnates were either the victims or perpetrators of serious crimes when alive. Sometimes they remembered two or more past lives in a series of reincarnations (Stevenson and Beloff, 1980, p. 430). Many discarnates wished to unburden themselves of guilt felt for a crime or lesser sin that they had committed when alive. They did not always state this motive explicitly, but it was nevertheless often apparent. As example, Mary Todd Lincoln (wife of President Abraham Lincoln) repents of her bad temper and frequently included a self-approach from other side of death, "*I should have been sweeter*". When she was alive her notorious outbursts of temper and violence saddened her husband and terrified many people. Staff at President Lincoln's office referred to her as 'A Perfect Devil', 'The Hell-cat' and 'Her Satanic Majesty' (Burlingame, 2008, p. 201). The discarnate of a highway robber often used the phrase "Life is for living", or a slight variant of it. Death makes a person humble.

Famous parapsychologist John Beloff (Stevenson and Beloff, 1980, p. 430) took a strongly positive view of Margo's drop-in cases and argued that the evidence definitely favored a paranormal interpretation despite the occasional lapses or inconsistencies that could be attributed to what he liked to call the "Margo component" of the scripts.

Super-psi hypothesis cannot explain these dramatic communications. Extrasensory perception between the medium and living persons who knew the communicator when the latter was alive, or to clairvoyant reading of printed information about the communicator can also be ruled out as a possible cause. Hence drop-in communications must be "*authentic and ostensibly paranormal*" (Stevenson and Beloff, 1980, p. 428). All other explanations lack independent evidential support.

6.6: The Scole experiment

"*Talking to someone who is deceased is a natural thing. It's the same as you and me talking right now. There is no difference except the fact we are aware they are no longer in this world*".

Robin Foy

"*The spirit world is our true home. I don't think that our earthly life is the real world at all. I think we come here to gain experience but when we shake off our physical bodies we return home because we are always spirit and so the spirit world is where we belong.*"

Sandra Foy

Towards the end of last century when the practice of physical mediumship almost had died out, two middle-aged couples had dedicated themselves to its revival. They sat in a small farmhouse (the home of physical mediums John and Sandra Foy) in the English countryside village of Scole, England, and the phenomena they had witnessed have led us towards a new form of physical mediumship. In the history of paranormal science, this is known as 'The Scole Experiment' which was a series of séances conducted by a group of sitters over a five-year period (1993 to 1998) in which a variety of visual, audible and physical phenomena were witnessed under controlled conditions. (Karl, 2007, p. 140). Grant and Jane Solomon had compiled the results of this research from original recordings made by the sitters and published in their book 'The Scole Experiment: Scientific Evidence for Life After Death' in 1999.

With the first few weeks when many discarnates materialized through the mediums (Robin Foy, Sandra Foy, Alan Bennett and Diana Bennett), the Scole group invited guests to witness the activities and sometimes as many as twenty-five people would watch in awe the utter paranormal activities. Then the Scole group contacted the oldest and most respected of psychic research bodies in the UK to properly authenticate and record the incidents – The Society for Psychical Research. The Society sent three noted investigators, David Fontana, Arthur Ellison and Montague Keen to examine the claims. Keen (2001, p. 168) wrote,

"*Our objective was to obtain evidence of a permanent nature which could be experienced or examined independently outside the séance room and which was not wholly reliant on subjective assessment, experience, memory or feeling; evidence which had been produced under circumstances which precluded human interference and which would satisfy external critics.*"

The mediums performed demonstrations in full view of audience consisting of these three noted researchers, intellectuals, paranormal investigators and scientists from other fields including those from the NASA (Higgins and Bergman, 2011, p. 67). Other notables were from the Institute of Noetic Sciences (San Francisco) and Stanford University, James Webster (a professional stage-magician and former member of the trade's prestigious Magic Circle, who has more than fifty years' experience in psychic research), and a host of other highly credible witnesses with many years of experience in dealing with the paranormal. They were interested to examine mediums and mediumship without any financial or publicity motives. After witnessing the paranormal trait, some fifteen scientists from the NASA group formed their own psychic group to continue to communicate with the afterlife entities (Solomon and Solomon, 1999, pp. 73, 189). In all, over the five years, there were a total of around 500 sessions – average duration of each session was two hours, so totaling over 1,000 hours of group activity. Supernatural phenomena occurred at every sitting; not a single one went blank and concrete evidence stood at every test.

1. In the beginning the messages came in the form of voices, and heard by all in the room.
2. Physical touch and levitation of objects took place, followed by actual materialization of the discarnates (shadowy figures described as angelic forms). Objects appeared from no known source and by no known means – "*The experimenters reported many instances during which they saw shadowy floating figurines – angelic beings ... appearing in front of them, visible in the dim light provided by apparently animated entities and accompanied by gentle brushes against hands or face, as of gossamer, brushes for which no mechanism was apparent.*" (Keen, 2001, p. 170). More than fifty small objects were materialized, including a silver necklace, a Churchill coin, a small rose quartz crystal ball, a 1940 British penny, a 1928 one-franc piece, a silver charm of the "Grim Reaper," two original copies of The Daily Mail (April 01, 1944) and The Daily Express (May 28, 1945).
3. Spirit forces operated cameras independently. On unopened rolls of film inside a locked box images were imprinted, such as actual photos of people (occasionally half-formed human faces), animal and places, sometimes from the past (the past images were actual memories of one of the spirits who lived in that time), and various obscure verses

and drawings that took some effort to identify. "*On the film were quotations in French and Greek, together with a stanza of an oddly precognitive poem describing the* ***survival of the human soul even when worlds eventually collapsed into what are now called black holes.***" (Keen, 2001, p. 171). Pyramids can be seen in one photo. Also, there were pictures of other dimensions and the beings that inhabit them. These films had been exposed in total darkness initially via cameras held by one or another member of the Group (Keen, 2001, p. 168). After much investigation Keen and his fellow investigators were entirely satisfied that the images on the film had been produced by paranormal means. Video cameras were able to record disincarnate images.

4. Manifested psychic lights had whirled around the room performing various maneuvers, including throwing out beams and passing through solid objects. When the lights touched people, there was a definite sensation, and when they entered someone's body a healing was observed. Keen (2001, p. 169) wrote, "*[participants] confirmed that they had felt touches, usually in places that were physically inaccessible to any member of the Group... The light phenomena were the most immediately impressive because of what we considered to be the impossibility of a natural origin or mechanism*". Once a visiting scientist, Graton Guinness, in an effort to check if the lights were attached to any wires cupped his hand around one. It buzzed around angrily inside his hand for a while until he released it. It indicated that the lights were intelligent and self-aware. All of these phenomena were accompanied by sudden and dramatic drops in temperature.

5. Single light points moved around at great speed and performed 'dances' which appeared inconsistent with physical manipulation. Keen (2001, p. 169) wrote,

   "[The light can] alight on our heads, frequently responding to spoken or silent requests, appear to enter bodies, "dive-bomb" the table top with a sharp "ping" and emerge from below it, ... and illuminate crystals, bowls and the interior of the glass dome... On one occasion a light settled on a crystal... spread its effulgence throughout the crystal, which was then levitated before our gaze and gently placed in the base of a translucent kitchen bowl... The glowing crystal remained clearly visible, and no hand or instrument could have effected this without visible detection. The entire experiment was repeated for my benefit, the crystal having mysteriously rematerialized for the purpose, and was then repeated once more.... The light itself was more than once enclosed in the hands of skeptical sitters, and the lights were sometimes sufficiently strong and durable,

occasionally lasting from 15 to 20 minutes, to enable us to observe other phenomena."

Though the source of the self-aware lights was mystery, Keen planned an experiment aimed to eliminate the possibility of fraud. He along with other investigators brought factory sealed rolls of 35 mm Polaroid film to the sessions, and placed the rolls inside a specially constructed wooded security box, padlocked it and then one investigator held the box firmly during the entire session. Spirits would then work on the film directly, no camera being necessary. Immediately after a sitting was completed the film was developed in a special instant processor supplied by Polaroid. This way any results could immediately be viewed. And the results were truly staggering. Later the spirit team working on other side, informed that the lights were actually animated spirits or discarnate entities that were not yet fully formed.

On November 23, 1998, Robin Foy had stopped all future Scole sessions. The explanation for this termination was as remarkable as the evidence they collected. Foy explained that the opening of an 'inter-dimensional doorway' that had been created by the spirit team to assist in the experiments was causing serious space-time problems and that experimenters from the future had been attracted to this doorway. He explained that since the interference was contrary to the strict laws of space and time, it must not be allowed to continue.

One important point throughout the experiment was that the Scole group had received unconditional love from the same spirit friends working on other side. Though initially they referred to themselves by a pseudonym, soon many of them gave their real identity in the process of communication. In fact, after two years of regular séances the Scole group's chief claimed that they had established contact with a "team" of spirit communicators comprising, or in contact with, a number of former scientists (Keen, 2001, pp. 167-68). The spirit team consists of 'thousands of minds' that exist in another dimension of reality normally invisible to the senses. Foy (2008, p. 425) reported that the mediums had used a germanium crystal that had optimized the reception of spirit communication on a one-to-one basis with remote and distant dimensions.

The Society for Psychical Research had prepared reports of 300 pages for validating the phenomena. Many of those who had witnessed the supernatural activities consider them as irrefutable evidence of the existence of an afterlife. Some Skeptics argued that such effects could be produced by stage magicians using long hollow strands of fiberglass with laser lights projected through them. But James Webster who had attended three sessions with the Scole group sent a letter to the English newspaper 'Psychic World' declaring,

"*I discovered no signs of trickery, and in my opinion such conjuring tricks were not possible, for the type of phenomena witnessed, under the conditions applied….*" (Schmicker, 2002, pp. 248-49)

The Scole group also invited many magicians to replicate the phenomena under the same controlled conditions, but no one came forward to take the challenge (Higgins and Bergman, 2011, p. 68). The sitters were encouraged to search the cellar before and after each sitting. To enable observers to monitor any movement, all members of the group wore luminous velcro wristbands (Keen, 2001, p. 168). Montague Keen speaking on behalf of three investigators, commented, "*None of our critics has been able to point to a single example of fraud or deception*" (Buckland, 2005, p. 363). In spite of this some critics still tried to dismiss the whole experiment as fraud, but all of them had failed to explain the 'tricks' employed by the mediums. Finally, Higgins and Bergman (2011, p. 68) had a very appropriate remark for the skeptics on Scole issue,

> "*If you are unable to make up your mind about these experiments, remember that though it is good to be a skeptic and question things, it is also to have an open mind about phenomena that cannot be explained by mainstream science.*"

The amazing wealth of paranormal material that the experiment had produced shows that life after death is not a matter of faith, it's about evidence – the spirit world is the most important reality. To date no one has found any evidence to show that the findings were anything but genuine.

6.7: Mediumistic art through channeling

The 'mediumistic art' (also known as spirit painting and art from afterlife) is a strange phenomenon in which a discarnate entity would drive the artwork making process through a channeler. This is not a form of abnormal expression of human creativity. These cases are genuine, i.e., some channelers without having conventional artistic skills and with no art competence or know-how are able to create (at some point in their lives and under specific conditions) some artworks that they would never have been able to perform in normal conditions. We still don't know by which psychic mechanism this artistry is activated. This paranormal ability has some specific features, such as,

1. Many channelers start to create suddenly and spontaneously as if they were moved and driven by an inner urge or possessed by a mysterious force. It occurs in a trance or semi-trance state, automatically, unconsciously and with amazing speed. The motivation is irresistible, involuntary and independent of the will and consciousness of the channeler.
2. He is not aware of what he is doing and finds out the painting only when the work has been completed. There is no preliminary sketches, outlines, or advance planning. He does not even know how to explain what he represented. He may disavow the artwork as soon as he is back into himself.

3. He can work in the dark or with closed eyes and under various impossible conditions for any ordinary artist, such as, backward painting, huge brushes and coarse, or the colors are distributed with the fingers. Even in these adverse conditions he can produce artworks by using the exact style of the most famous departed painters, such as Van Gogh, Modigliani, Michelangelo, and Renoir. No changes or corrections are made because the work produced is already perfect and finished.
4. He can also paint with both hands and feet, or work on more than one canvas simultaneously using different artistic styles of famous dead painters. When the artwork is in progress, he may undergo an appreciable change in vital signs, such as blood pressure or heartbeat, presenting in some cases sweating and weight loss. Almost all of them report that they have felt inspired by otherworldly entities or guiding spirits.
5. Many channelers have paranormal experiences or manifest paranormal abilities. Some of them even manage to draw the portrait of unknown deceased persons whom he had never seen.

From the above points it is clear that the channelers are actually conveying messages from discarnate spirits. No other hypothesis other than the survival hypothesis is the only explanation of the above evidence that had been gathered in controlled laboratory conditions.

6.8: Conclusion

"*It is entirely possible that behind the perception of our senses, worlds are hidden of which we are unaware.*"

Albert Einstein

"*Life [on his side] is far more wonderful than I can ever tell you, beyond anything I ever hoped for; it exceeds all my expectations*".

The spirit of Sir William Barrett through Feda and Leonard

Relying on a broad range of observational data we can confidently say that physical mediums and the channelers are actually talking to dead. Mediumship is a fact, and the descriptions of the afterlife communicated by mediums often confirm the descriptions of afterlife conditions given by individuals who had NDEs.

The discarnate entities possess the ability to communicate with living persons intelligently by directly sending information, or influencing the mind of the medium. They can also acquire practical knowledge of happenings in our world and in some cases bring about physical effects in our world starting from raps and knocks on tables and walls to more large-scale physical effects like levitating tables, materializations of objects, teleportation, and disembodied voices. Sometimes they even exhibit apparent knowledge of future events.

However, the whole mediumship phenomena need farther research despite more than one hundred years of high-quality study. How exactly the discarnate entities are able to interact with living people? How they convey meaningful messages to mediums? How they acquire knowledge about events taking place in our physical world, and influence physical matters in our world? For obvious reasons we have exactly the same questions about ghosts and apparitions. Several prominent parapsychologists, such as Frederic Myers, Antony Flew, H. H. Price, C. D. Broad, Terence Penelhum, and more recently Alan Gauld and Stephen Braude have tried to answer these questions scientifically but no significant progress. It means, the discarnate entities possess independent powers or capabilities that are beyond our understanding, and they rely on some strange and unusual modes of reasoning and action in their communications with the living beings.

Chapter 7

Reincarnation

"Human beings do, in fact, enjoy a life cycle that comprises much more than just bodily life."

Eric Weiss

"If survival occurs, then reincarnation may be one form it could take, for all, for many, or only for some human beings. Survival could occur without reincarnation. On the other hand, reincarnation by definition cannot occur without some preceding survival of a physical death. Thus evidence for reincarnation is ipso facto evidence for survival while the reverse is certainly not true."

Ian Stevenson (1960, p. 52)

Reincarnation (repeated incarnation), literally "to be made flesh again" as a doctrine holds the notion that the soul of any living being (or in some variations, only human beings) can survive death with its integrity partly or wholly retained, to be reborn in a new body. Cooper (2007, pp. 15, 21) wrote,

"It is a universal process, and prevails not only in the human kingdom but throughout the whole of nature. Whenever we find a living form, the consciousness of that form is also evolving, using temporarily for that purpose the physical form in order that it may gain physical experience."

"In each incarnation we have a different physical body, a different name, and may have different souls acting as parents, but these changes do not in the slightest imperil our individuality."

The idea of reincarnation and cases of past-life experiences appear early in the history of philosophy, according to which every living being is an eternally existing spirit. Upon physical death this soul survives and subsequently passes from one body to another in accordance with the laws of Karma (next chapter). Mills and Lynn (2000, p. 285) define past-life experiences as "*reported experiences or impressions of oneself as a particular person (other than one's current life identity) in a previous time or life*". Stevenson (1977a, p. 305-footnote) proposed the following explanation of the reincarnation phenomenon,

> "*Reincarnation, briefly defined, includes the idea that men [and women] consist of physical bodies and minds. At a person's death, his [and her] physical body perishes, but his [and her] mind may persist and later become associated with another physical body in the process called reincarnation. Some persons find the word "mind" in this definition unclear or otherwise unattractive. They may certainly substitute another word such as "soul" or 'individuality'. I intend only to indicate a component of human beings not comprised in our present understanding of their physical bodies, which component may persist after physical death.*"

Therefore, reincarnation is a category of transpersonal experience that involves reliving or remembering vivid episodes from other historical periods and various parts of the world. Reincarnation is the essential life-cycle of a quantum soul.

> "*[The possibility of reincarnation] presents to us the idea of a long succession of lives on earth for the individual, each of them as if it were a day in the school of experience, teaching him new lessons through which he develops the capacities latent in human nature, grows in wisdom, and eventually reaches spiritual maturity.*" (Ducasse, 1961, p. 210)

Belief in reincarnation is an ancient phenomenon; its presence ranges from mythology to folklores, and religious books to literature and poetry. Eastern religions do not have a corner on reincarnation thinking. Most of the preliterate or primitive religions as far back as the Stone Age also considered the idea of pre-existence of the soul and rebirth. Great philosophers, such as Hume, Goethe, Lessing, and Schopenhauer have either endorsed the idea of reincarnation or expressed sympathetic interest in it. Many others have interested themselves in reincarnation as a mechanism of survival, that is, as explanatory of the further fate of the deceased personality. Scholar and past-life researcher Hans TenDam wrote,

> "*The general assumption that reincarnation is a typically Indian idea is as persistent as it is wrong. Ideas about reincarnation are found in diverse cultures all over the world.... Anthropologically, belief in reincarnation is better conceived as an original category which has arisen independently in separate cultures.*" (TenDam, 1987, p. 29)

Studies have shown that the belief in the continuity in life originates in children altogether spontaneously (Goswami, 2013, p. 8). In Greek culture, this theory has sometimes been attributed to Pythagoras and Plato (Frederick, 1983, p. 79). Pythagoras is said to have distinctly remembered a number of his previous incarnations, and at one time pointed out a shield in a Grecian temple as having been carried by him in a previous incarnation at the siege of Troy. Some see reincarnation as a part of their religion, and for others this doctrine is an answer to many common moral and existential dilemmas, such as "Why are we here?" and "Why do bad things sometimes happen to good people?" However, the historical and geographical universality of these experiences suggest that they represent a very important cultural phenomenon. They also have critical implications for understanding the nature of consciousness, psyche, and human beings and for the theory and practice of psychiatry, psychology, and psychotherapy.

Though mainstream science does not accept yet that reincarnation is a proven phenomenon or that it happens, many people throughout the recorded history of humankind allegedly "remember" their past lives and used that knowledge to help them with their current lives, and "*experiential sequences of this kind constitute the empirical basis for the widespread belief in reincarnation.*" (Grof, 2000, p. 235). Past-life recalls occur in two forms – spontaneous and hypnotic.

Spontaneous recalls are relatively rare and uncommon phenomena (Mills and Lynn, 2000, p. 286). Some of them are almost mechanical, for example, when someone with healing talent discovers a past life as a great healer. Most spontaneous past-life memory cases develop within cultures that hold beliefs about reincarnation. Most subjects reside in small towns or villages and are born into relatively uneducated and impoverished families (Stevenson, 1987, p. 96). Hypnotically-elicited recalls, on the other hand, occur relatively often whenever it is suggested (implicitly or explicitly) that the hypnotically-regressed person does so. Past-life memories are retrieved either in a therapeutic environment during past-life regression therapy or in related controlled studies. Today, both these types are under rigorous scientific investigation. Recalls may happen regardless of the participant's belief in past lives.

Amongst all the spontaneous past-life recalls, children memories are most authentic and pure because of two main reasons. First, a toddler is far too young to acquire much information about remote unknown persons and places through the usual media of communication of adults, such as newspapers, radio, TV, cinema, and carry such knowledge in the shape of buried and disguised memories. Thus, we cannot ignore a child who from early infancy talks sincerely of an 'earlier life', while retaining his normal consciousness without apparent personality shifts, and uses the present tense with respect to 'this life' and the past tense with respect to the 'other life'. Secondly, occurrences of delusions and true psychotic conditions are rare in children. Reincarnation fantasies in small children who otherwise seem normal, intelligent, and cooperative cannot be ascribed to a split of personality. These children, apart from their impressive and detailed 'memories' of 'another life', do not exhibit any evidence for psi capacities. If the capacities exist, why they restrict themselves only to past-life memories and not to any other areas of life?

Stevenson's investigatory studies have become a benchmark in this challenging research field. Stevenson had a lifelong interest in parapsychology, and was familiar with the concept of reincarnation since childhood. He had analyzed forty-four 'apparent memories of former incarnation cases' as a group in a paper published in 1960. The reports came from a number of sources, such as books, magazines, and newspapers. He told Tom Shroder years later, "*these forty-four cases, when you put them together, it just seemed inescapable to me that there must be something there .... I couldn't see how they could all be faked or they could all be a deception.*" (Shroder, 1999, p. 103). Stevenson's this 1960 paper caught the attention of Chester Carlson, the inventor of the photostat machine. He financed Stevenson's researches because he believed that he got the inspiration for his invention paranormally. Stevenson traveled an average of 55,000 miles every year (many of his field trips were not only expensive, but logistically complicated, difficult and even dangerous also) for about 45 years to bring back reports of young children who speak of remembering previous lives, providing detailed and accurate information about people who died before they were born — people they say they once were.

Stevenson had authored about 200 papers and nine books. For him reincarnation is "*not a matter of belief, but an empirical issue, based on very specific experiences and observations*" (Grof, 2000, p. 235). The Journal of the American Medical Association reviewed one of his books in 1975 and stated, "*in regard to reincarnation he has painstakingly and unemotionally collected a detailed series of cases...in which the evidence is difficult to explain on any other grounds.*" (King, 1975, p. 978). Though his efforts did not produce mainstream acceptance of his work, it did garner some respect in mainstream circles. His interests also spread to apparitions, poltergeists, mediumship, NDE and deathbed observations.

Stevenson took an analytical approach to the cases. On a commentary on Stevenson's early work (Stevenson, 1977b, pp. 152-70) psychiatrist Harold Lief later described him as "*a methodical, careful, even cautious, investigator, whose personality is on the obsessive side.*" (Lief, 1977, p. 171). Stevenson never assumed he knew the cause of the cases but instead simply worked to determine precisely what the facts of each case were. He cautions that such evidence is suggestive of reincarnation, but that more research must be conducted – "*reincarnation is the best – even though not the only – explanation for the stronger cases we have investigated.*" (Stevenson, 1987, p. 254).

He made no grand claims about the work, as indicated by the title of his first book on the phenomenon, 'Twenty Cases Suggestive of Reincarnation' despite the massive evidence that was accumulated as a result of his painstaking research for about five decades. Stevenson (1977, pp. 307-08 - footnote 4) preferred to use the term 'previous personality' because,

> "*the term can be used whether or not an actual deceased person has been found whose life corresponded to the child's statements; nor does its use imply any commitment to a particular explanation of how the child obtained any correct knowledge he [or she] showed about the person identified*".

He always referred to his case studies as "suggestive of reincarnation," and "of the reincarnation type," and maintained that the data he uncovered were consistent with the reincarnation hypothesis. However, most of the arguments that Stevenson had advanced in favor of reincarnation are so strong as to entitle them to be classed as "proofs" that warrant serious consideration, that upon recognizing it one would be irrational not to believe in reincarnation. Stevenson had a brilliant mind; he had prepared his cases to present to his scientific peers. He knew his work would be carefully scrutinized, so he was careful to cover all bases with his methodologies and explore all possible alternative explanations for what he was finding.

Stevenson has left us a mighty legacy. Even his staunchest critics have a very high opinion for his scientific methodology, scientific honesty, and also for his towering personality. Stevenson's research is notable in the high standards he set for himself, as Grof (2000, p. 236) commented,

> "*Some of the cases [Stevenson] eliminated because the family benefited financially, in terms of social prestige, or public attention, others because Stevenson found a connecting person who could have been the psychic link. Additional reasons were inconsistent testimony, false memories (cryptomnesia), witnesses of questionable character, or indication of fraud. Only the strongest cases were included in his final reports*".

Stevenson (1977, p. 324) commented, "*friendly critics of my investigations have pointed out that reincarnation is itself an irrefutable hypothesis. We can never show that it does not occur; nor are we ever likely to obtain conclusive evidence that it does occur*".

His book 'Reincarnation and Biology' is a classic study of parapsychology, heralding a paradigm shift from physics to biology. He had conducted meticulous studies of over three thousands of such cases and reported them in his books 'Twenty Cases Suggestive of Reincarnation' (1966, revised 1974), 'Unlearned Languages: New Studies in Xenoglossy' (1984), and 'The Children Who Remember Previous Lives' (1987), reporting only several hundred of them, because many have not met the highest standard. American Philosopher Robert Almeder commented,

> "*the data in the richer reincarnation cases overwhelmingly suggests [sic] as the first plausible hypothesis that the subjects in these cases are indeed reincarnated persons… for Stevenson, the behaviors in question have no better, or as plausible, an explanation as the belief in reincarnation*". (Almeder, 1996, pp. 498, 513)

Elsewhere Almeder (2001, p. 497) argued that it is not necessary for the reincarnation hypothesis to demonstrate how or why the phenomena of reincarnation produced the data in order to provide acceptable explanation for it in the rich cases.

> "*So, there is a prima facie plausibility to the reincarnation hypothesis as an explanation of the data in the richer cases because the content of the richer cases is precisely what we would expect or predict if we thought there was any evidence at all that would confirm the hypothesis of reincarnation.*"

Stevenson (Oct. 31, 1918 – Feb. 8, 2007) retired in 2002 but continued writing that included a final paper summarizing his career (Stevenson, 2006, pp. 13-21). He left his work to successors led by Bruce Greyson. Child psychiatrist Jim Tucker has carried on Stevenson's work with children focusing on North American cases. Tucker said that toward the end of his life, Stevenson had accepted that his long-stated goal of getting science "to seriously consider reincarnation as a possibility" was not going to be realized in this lifetime.

7.1: Spontaneous past-life memories in children

> "*Either he [Ian Stevenson] is making a colossal mistake. Or he will be known as 'the Galileo of the 20th century'.*"
>
> Harold Lief (1977, p. 171)

In several instances, small children seem to be remembering and describing their previous life in another body, another place, and with other people. Chari (1978, p. 316) described,

> "*the children…claim awareness of a psychic identity binding two 'successive personal lives'. Even the habit-patterns, skills and dislikes, phobias, scars, or marks of inquiry on the skin appear sometimes to be a 'carry-over' from the 'earlier life'*".

Children's memories about previous lives have better scientific credibility and contain more promising evidence in support of reincarnation (Stevenson, 1974b, pp. 3, 4). These past-life memories lie closer to the surface of consciousness than that of the adults, and therefore are easier to retrieve. Moreover, since children have fewer experiences than adults, any memories of previous lives would have less danger of becoming contaminated with memories of the present life. The past-life memories emerge usually spontaneously shortly after these children begin to talk. Between ages five and eight, memories fade from consciousness although some subjects claim to be able to remember the previous life even into adulthood.

Stevenson (Shroder, 1999) investigated a case where Suzanne, a middle-class girl from Beirut remembered the life of a woman who had died undergoing heart surgery in Richmond, Vancouver. When she was 16 months old, she pulled the phone off the hook and said, "Hello, Leila?" into it over and over. Soon Suzanne claimed that she was Leila's mother. By the time she was two, Suzanne had mentioned the names of total 13 people including this woman's other children, her husband, parents and brothers. At three, she had recited portions of a funeral oration for the woman's brother and begged her parents to take her to her 'real' home in a Lebanese town. After inquiry, ultimately the parents found the family of Suzanne's past life. And there they learned that shortly before undergoing her heart surgery, the woman in question had tried desperately to call her daughter Leila. This family confirmed much of what Suzanne had been saying – names, places, the funeral oration. Suzanne identified members of the dead woman's family from photographs. Though she was a child, she treated the dead woman's grown children as a mother would. She asked if their uncles, when they returned to Lebanon, had distributed 'her' jewels to Leila and her sisters — which had been a deathbed request known only to the family. The dead woman's relatives gave it, but grudgingly as they had been rocked by Suzanne's claims. That reluctance made their testimony all the more valuable, in Stevenson's view.

On a UK television program on mysteries, there was a report of a young Druse boy who was adamant on meeting someone of whom his parents had never heard. He was eventually tracked down in another village the boy had never visited. The boy knew his way around, embraced his apparently unknown friend as 'his' son in a former incarnation, identified clothing that had belonged to 'him' before his death in action in Lebanon two weeks before the child's birth, and even correctly stated that 'he' had left a cigarette in a pack in a shirt. (Keen, 2001, p. 180).

Stevenson (1997a, pp. 5-9) identified several types of behaviors that occur in childhood and may persist into adulthood for which reincarnation provides a better interpretation of the observed facts than other alternative theories, including,

1. strong fears or phobias that can neither be traced back to earlier trauma nor shared by other family members, strong interests in certain activities or areas of knowledge, unexpected appetites and unusual

desires that do not conform with family upbringing, and proficiency in skills not taught through instruction or learned through imitation,

2. troubled child-parent relationships, special family attachments, and other departures from expected family relationships,
3. revengeful, prejudicial, and warlike attitudes toward certain individuals, social groups, or nations that cannot be traced to ordinary socialization processes,
4. gender identity confusions that cannot be satisfactorily explained by faulty parenting or biological factors,
5. the location of unusual birthmarks, birth deformities, and internal diseases in which genetic factors, family medical history, or chance factors can be ruled out,
6. observed personality, behavioral, and physiological differences between members of monozygotic twin pairs and conjoined (Siamese) twins,
7. maternal craving or aversion for particular foods during pregnancy.

Many children demand to be called by the name of the previous person, and some seem to expect that they should be recognized as from the previous life (Stevenson, 1983a, p. 94). Many of them do not at first distinguish past from present, and they may use the present tense in reference to the previous life (Stevenson, 1997a, p. 5). Most often, the child uses the same kind of hand gestures as the deceased person when talking. Recognitions of persons or places are frequently the initiating stimuli to the memories. He is usually better at recognizing persons in photographs taken during the periods when the previous persons knew him than he is in recognizing. Also, he likes and dislikes special idiomatic phrases, and recollects nicknames and names for objects of his past life. Stevenson (1974b, p. 5) commented;

> "*The identification by these children with the previous personality seems to me one of the most important features of these cases. Such personation [personification], with components of strongly emotional behavior, transcends the simple recital by the child of information about another person who lived before. In my opinion, these behavioral features of the cases both add considerably to their authenticity and greatly increase our opportunities for studying human personality.*"

In several instances, two or more researchers have investigated the same case independent of each other, and agreed upon major facts and interpretations. In many cases, the children claim to remember the lives of grandparents, deceased siblings, or other relatives. In the majority of cases, only a single previous life is recalled. But there are few reported cases where the child claimed to remember more than one previous life. As example,

Swarnlata Mishra (Stevenson, 1974b, pp. 67-91) claimed memories, and performed dances and songs she said were related to a life intermediate between her present life and the previous life to which the majority of her memories referred. In a few cases, subjects have recalled lives of persons who themselves claimed to remember previous lives.

Strange characteristics are observed in cases involving twins. Researchers have special interest in twin cases because any observable differences between the twins would seem to be attributable to non-genetic factors. Stevenson (1987, p. 187) noted that of 36 cases of twins in his files, 26 have been solved (means, past-life claims found authentic and the deceased person is identified) for both twins. Among these 26 cases, the previous persons had been related in 19 cases and been friends or acquaintances in the remaining seven. In none of the 26 doubly-solved twin cases were the previous persons strangers. Stevenson (1975, pp. 337-56) describes in detail a case involving one set of twins, Ramoo and Rajoo Sharma (born in August 1964 in the village of Sham Nagara in U.P.), who remembered lives as twins (Bhimsen and Bhism of the village Uncha Larpur, about 16 kilometres from Sham Nagara) who were murdered at the same time and thrown together into a well. In another case, the Pollock twins gave evidence of being the reincarnations of their sisters who had died together in a hit-and-run accident (Stevenson, 1997a, Chapter 23). Fielding-Hall (1902, pp. 339-41) describes the case (known as the Okshitgon twins) of twin boys who recognized themselves as husband and wife from a previous life in which they had died together. Cook (1986) reports two published cases where only one of the twins recalled a previous life. Rankawat (1959, pp. 76-80) mentions a case in which one twin claimed to remember a previous life in which his brother was his cook.

In extreme rare cases, the subject remembers animal lives (Stevenson, 1987, p. 210). One child believed she had been a monkey in one or two previous lives anterior to the two human ones she remembered (Stevenson, 1983a). Elsewhere Stevenson (1987, p. 302) briefly describes third such case, in which a Burmese girl claimed an intermediate life as an ox. Fielding-Hall (1902, pp. 298-300) records an amazing case of a woman who saved the life of a fawn, believing it to be the reincarnation of her son, and then was sued in court by the hunters who had been pursuing it. The court ruled that either party had made its case, and retained custody.

One question is often asked, if there is a possibility of reincarnating in more than one body at the same time. Some tribal societies, such as Igbo and other West African tribes, and American Indian societies in Alaska and British Columbia believe in multiple identifications. Some Tibetans, Burmese, the Eskimos also have such beliefs. Few cases of multiple identifications of the same previous person are found but they are all of the very weak, undeveloped variety and lack sufficient data. No children have claimed the lives of more than one deceased personality living in the same period.

The pattern of relationships between the two families bears some relation to social rules and practices. Hindus, generally speaking, marry outside their families but within their castes, and their cases show a relatively large proportion of cases with the two families unknown to each other before the cases develop. The Tlingits (indigenous peoples of the Pacific Northwest Coast of North America), on the other hand, trace descent within family groups, and place emphasis on being reborn in the same family. A large proportion of their cases are same-family cases.

One important observation is that no child had claimed the memories of living ones. Mostly they are in the ordinary waking state when speaking of memories, except a few cases the memories are related to sleep, and even more occasionally to illness. They require no apparent stimulus to speak about past memories. These children are often found to be more intelligent and more mature than their siblings or peers. They may learn to speak earlier and to use adult language more readily, and they may be too interested in religion or sex or their desire for cigarettes or alcohol.

Stevenson's cases were not only from 'primitive, 'exotic' cultures with prior belief in reincarnation, but also from Western countries, including UK and USA. Past-life memories are cross-cultural phenomena which is not necessarily reliant on the belief in reincarnation common to a specific cultural environment. These cases with similar main features had also occurred "*in areas of the world whose peoples find the idea of reincarnation uncongenial or even heretical*" (Stevenson, 1977a, p. 308). Often, the children's past-life recalls are surrounded by mystery and disbelief even causing resentment and scolding by the parents because such claims represented a concept that is not taught at schools and "*often conflicted seriously with the beliefs of their parents and other members of their families*" (Stevenson, 1983b, p. 744). In such cases, parents are resistant to acknowledge the children's statements and dismiss them.

It seems that the circumstances of early death (most cases violently through accidents, murder, or acts of war) involve shock due to sudden interruption that can possibly break through the memory loss during the time-gap between two lives, and the most vivid memories involve events leading up to it. Another strong motivation for reincarnation is "unfinished business", such as young children to care for, thought of revenge etc. Stevenson (1980, pp. 355-60; 1987, pp. 211-13) has noted several patterns related to the previous person and his or her circumstances at death when death was natural and when death was violent.

There is also a behavioral aspect as many suffer from phobias, which they associate with the mode of death they described. These children do not know anything about events that had occurred after the former person's death. This is an important point in deciding whether they are unconsciously reconstructing the details of this life by telepathically reading the minds of those who knew the deceased or possess these details as genuine memories.

7.1.1: Behavioral memories, unusual phobias and untaught skills

Most often, these children identify with previous persons through their behaviors as much as through their statements and recognitions. They may exhibit a wide range of behaviors, habits, aptitudes, unlearned skills, philias (strong interests), and phobias related to the previous life, some of them quite specific to the persons they are talking about. As example, during the British period a Burmese boy named Maung Htun Kyaing preached Buddhism from very early age of four with profound understanding of the subject and better than any religious teacher could have done. He was born in a very poor and illiterate mat-weavers family. He visited a Buddhist monastery in the local village, where he lived in his previous life as an abbot (a head of a monastery) named U. Pandesia (Govinda, 1988, pp. 190-97). He recognized the present abbot and correctly mentioned his name and showed the room where he meditated, and identified the things that he used. At the monastery, the child read the scriptures written in ancient Pali language and explained its meaning. People were so impressed by the sermons that they came by thousands to listen and see him. Stevenson (1977a, pp. 310-11) wrote,

> "*We have known that a person may carry out instructions to perform a certain action while at the same time having complete amnesia for the fact that he has been given such instructions. The hypnotist can first give the subject a suggestion of something he will do after he is brought out of hypnosis, and then tell the subject that he will forget that the hypnotist has told him to perform the action. The subject will then not remember later the real cause of his posthypnotic behavior. Many of our actions in everyday life provide even similar examples. We know how to walk, but few of us remember the days of infancy when we learned to walk. I am not therefore saying anything new if I remind readers that we can have behavioral memories in the absence of any imagined memories about the origin of the behavior.... Furthermore, the related behavior often persists some or many years after the subject has completely forgotten whatever imaged memories of the previous life he had. These facts make it possible to envisage that some persons may have had previous lives of which they have no imaged memories, but from which nevertheless they may have derived important ingredients of their characters.*"

Here lies the practical significance of reincarnation. The common belief of most of the psychiatrists and psychologists is that infancy and childhood are more important periods in the formation of personality than any later periods. Stevenson's argument challenged this age-old idea – "*although personality is indeed being formed in childhood, its development actually begins much earlier in other terrestrial lives anterior to the child's personal life.*" (Stevenson, 1977a, p. 306). Researchers group this tendency together as behavioral memories. Even if a child doesn't speak directly about a previous life, the memories can manifest prominently almost any aspect of a child's personality. In these cases, some gentle probing may elicit a past-life story.

Those who had a change of sex through reincarnation may dress in the style of the opposite sex, and exhibit similar personality traits. Those who claim to belong to foreign countries in their previous lives may exhibit behaviors consistent with the habits of the countries they say they were from. Stevenson (1983a, pp. 216-17), and Stevenson and Keil (2005, pp. 178-80) list several behaviors characteristic of a group of 24 Burmese subjects (16 males and 8 females – all the female children claimed to have lived last life as male) who said they were Japanese soldiers killed in Burma.

1. Nostalgia for Japan / wish to return to Japan. A child lay on the ground writhing and crying to return to Japan. A child boasted of being Japanese – "*I am Japanese. What do you think of me?*" When the Japanese War Graves Commission came to her area she proudly remarked, "*They are our nationals*".
2. Interest in war games. Thirteen of the twenty-four children engaged in play at being a soldier. Fourteenth, a female child showed an unusual interest in guns.
3. Preference for Japanese clothing. One of them habitually dressed as much like a Japanese soldier as he could – "*rousers, belt with large buckle, and boots; all this was quite different from the sandals and longyi tied at the waist worn by Burmese men and women.*"
4. Annoyance with British / Americans, complaints about heat in Burma, desire for Japanese food (raw or partially cooked fish, raw eggs, strong tea) and rejection of Burmese food.
5. Speaking a strange language (assumed to be Japanese) other than Burmese, persistence of 'foreign' accent in adulthood.
6. Reluctance or refusal to show respect to Buddhist monks / refusal to go to Buddhist temples / worshiping while standing up / sitting on floor with buttocks resting on heels (common Japanese style).
7. Insensitivity to pain (three children rubbed salt in wounds to show how little affected by pain they were).
8. Greater industriousness than Burmese children. One child came home from school and found his parents seated in front of their house and chatting, he rebuked them for idleness, saying "*Why do you not go and do some work? At home we have to earn our bread by working. In my country, everyone goes to work when a siren sounds and remains at it until it sounds again*".
9. Japanese-like extreme cruelty, such as pulling limbs off live frogs. One child said he needed a pair of pliers to pull out the fingernails of playmates who annoyed him. This is the exact style of the Kempetai (the Japanese military police).

10. Either expressing the hope that the airplane would take subject back to Japan or showing fear and running for cover.

Stevenson and Keil (2005, p. 174) concluded, "*the subject's [Japanese-like] behavior differed markedly, often startlingly so, from that of his or her siblings or other Burmese children.*" These behavior features are unusual in Burma, but typical of Japanese people, especially Japanese soldiers during their occupation of Myanmar (Burma). Some children had quite clear, distinct, and vivid imaged memory for the details of those Japanese soldiers who they claimed to have died at Burma. During World War II, the Japanese soldiers had shown extreme cruelty to the rather peaceful Burmese Buddhists as indicated by the following statements.

> "*...these militarists surpassed all others the Burmese had ever known. The brutality, arrogance and racial pretensions of these men remained among the deepest Burmese memories of the war years.*" (Ba Maw, 1968, p. 180).

> "*The period of Japanese military rule lasted only three years, but to the Burmese people it was more irksome than sixty years of British rule ...The Japanese imposed a reign of terror.*" (Htin Aung, 1967, p. 301).

As the British defeated the Japanese in the early 1945, the Japanese army retreated in some disorder and many soldiers remained behind. The British army captured some of them, and the Burmese villagers took revenge by capturing and killing many of them. The unusual behavioral patterns strongly suggest that some of the dead Japanese soldiers had returned back as Burmese children. There are many coincidences, such as,

1. Most of these reincarnated children were born particularly in the triangular area of upper Burma where the major battles and most of the Japanese army casualties of 1945 took place.
2. The Japanese Army suffered some casualties when it first invaded Burma in early 1942. After three years, the army again suffered much casualties in the early 1945. After reincarnation, the oldest Burmese child of the group was born in late 1943 or 1944. One child was born in 1945, and all other children were born later. The youngest was born in 1980.
3. In a few cases the child himself or herself stated where the soldier had died. These places were usually close to the subjects' birthplaces – sometimes as close as only ten meters. A girl remembered the life of a Japanese soldier who was killed near her parents' home. It was found after investigation that a Japanese soldier had really died in the same place, same manner and same time.

The strong manifestation of Japanese-like traits and the amazing coincidences cannot readily be explained by genetics and environmental influences, alone or together. It can only be explained by reincarnation – the personality of the dead Japanese soldiers reappeared as Burmese children.

Another odd behavior pattern is a variety of unusual types of play in young children that corresponds to their past-life memories. These plays are unusual in the child's family, but appropriate for the person whose life the child had lived. Sometimes the play is so strange that it gives the parents their first indication that the child might be remembering a previous life. As example, a two-year-old girl pointed at the collapsing twin towers on the screen and said very clearly, 'I die'. Sometimes, a child reenacts the mode of death of the previous personality in a playful nature. Here, I pick up few notable cases from Stevenson's (2000, pp. 561-67) file.

Shopkeeper: The two-and-a-half years old son of a university professor in India made a model that appeared to be his shop, with wires running around them. He made 'biscuits' from mud and served these with 'tea' (actually water). During his play he also showed surprising knowledge of soda water production. While engaged in this kind of play, he gradually revealed a previous life in which he was a rich businessman who had owned shops, manufactured biscuits and produced soda water in his factory. The child played little with other children and became so totally absorbed managing his shop and factory that he fell markedly behind at school.

Pickled tea seller: A young girl of Burma, whose father was a cotton farmer, set up a stall in her play, where she had sold pickled tea (a stimulant very popular in Burma) and dried tea leaves. She was so absorbed in her world that she would not play at other games and would not change the commodity she sold. She remembered the life of a woman of similar profession as previous personality.

Cross-dresser: Nearly all the children who claim to remember a previous life as a person of the opposite sex engage in cross-dressing when they are young children.

Commanding officer in British army: In 1918, a three-year-old child from India played the role of a soldier from British army. He gave much accurate military commands in professional manner to his imaginary regiment in English holding a stick as his rifle, though he was taught by no one. He also had numerous western behavioral traits. When asked, he revealed that he had been a soldier named Arthur who had been killed in the "German War" (World War I).

Bandit: A young boy from Turkey took pleasure in throwing stones at soldiers and policemen. Later he remembered the life of a bandit who had committed suicide rather than be captured and probably executed by the police.

Operator of a flour mill: The two-year-old son of a small farmer in India, while playing with sand erected what amazingly looked like a flour mill. Then he said to his grandmother, "Bring some grain for grinding". The family suspected that the child was remembering a past-life. On being encouraged to say more, he remembered the life of a prosperous owner of a flour mill and gave numerous details.

Nightclub owner: The child of an unskilled laborer from Turkey regularly played at managing a nightclub. He arranged boxes to represent a bar and placed bottles on them. He assigned roles in the club to neighborhood girls and gave one a stick that represented the microphone held by a singer, and put out two chairs for the wives of the club's owner. He remembered the previous life of a man with two wives who owned a nightclub in Istanbul.

Role-playing of a guardian: A very young boy of Syria had collected five eggplants and two potatoes. He then gave male names to the eggplants and female names to the potatoes. If anyone touched these vegetables he became angry, and he wanted to keep them forever. He remembered his past-life as one of his deceased relatives who had five sons and two daughters. His collection of eggplants and potatoes had the same names.

Play reenacting the mode of death in the previous life: A young boy from Burma would sometimes in his play enact a scene of a man trying to escape from a sinking ship. He would shout, "*The boat is sinking. Help! Help*!" He remembered the life of a man who had drowned when a ferry on which he was a passenger capsized and sank.

Children like these types of unusual play because they have done this several times before. Stevenson (2000, p. 567) calls it "*the unconscious expression of a habit*" which is forceful enough to cross the barrier of death, to manifest, not only in inwardly experienced images, but in the physical activity that we call play. Many children who engage in unusual play talk spontaneously about previous lives. If they do, parents should listen to them carefully. They should not be laughed at or be accused of 'wild imagination'. If they do not, parents may legitimately ask them why they engage in such unusual play. If open-ended questions are asked, the past-life memory may keep flowing.

****

Phobias are irrational fears. Many of us have observed that strong, irrational fear sometimes occur in children. Towards the end of 19th century, a pioneering American psychologist and educator G. S. Hall while studying various root causes of fears observed that the fears of infancy and childhood were often focused on dangers that, although prevalent during earlier centuries, no longer presented any important threat – thunderstorms, snakes, drowning, nighttime darkness etc. Hall (1897, pp. 246-47) commented,

> "*their relative intensity fits past conditions far better than it does present ones. Night is now the safest time, serpents are no longer among our most fatal foes. ... The weather fears and the incessant talk about weather ...fits [sic] a condition of life in trees, caves or tents, or at least of far greater exposure ...than present houses, carriages, and even dress afford. ... The first experiences with water, the moderate noise of the wind, or distant thunder, etc., might excite faint fear, but why does it sometimes make children on the instant frantic with panic?*"

Did the phobias, that the children exhibit, somehow inherited from ancestors? Hall (1897, p. 244) concluded that the inheritance theory (genetic memory) may explain some of the fear phenomena, but not all. There are some remote origins for these unexplained fears of childhood. In this respect, Hall gave casual hints towards the Platonic idea of metempsychosis – what today we know as reincarnation.

About 36% of the children who claim to remember a previous life manifest phobia concordant with the lives they say they remember (Stevenson, 1990, pp. 243, 246; 1994, p. 191). Such phobias relate to the mode of death of the previous individual. They usually manifest between the ages of two and five, and sometimes the child showed the phobia in early infancy before it had begun to speak about a previous life (Stevenson, 1990, p. 243; Cook et al., 1983b). The phobias did not derive from imitating another person or from any postnatal traumatic experience.

> "*The phobias nearly always accord with the claimed mode of death in the previous life. A child who claims to remember a life that ended in drowning may have a phobia of being immersed in water, one who claims to remember a life that ended in stabbing may have a fear of bladed weapons, and so on.*
>
> *Most of the phobias occurred in relation to violent deaths of all kinds. They occurred much less frequently in the cases of children who remembered natural deaths.*" (Stevenson, 1990, p. 247)

As example, among 47 cases in which the subject remembered a life that ended in drowning, hydrophobia occurred in 30. Among 30 cases in which the deceased person had died of snakebite, phobias of snakes were reported in 13. Few short examples from Stevenson's (1990, pp. 247-49) collection,

1. One child who remembered dying (severe gastroenteritis, perhaps with peritonitis) from eating too much contaminated yogurt showed a strong aversion for yogurt.

2. One child who remembered the life of a young woman who died after a prolonged illness due to congenital heart disease had a severe phobia of drugs, injections, and blood.
3. One child from Lebanon who remembered the life of a man who was fatally injured by a truck had a phobia not only of trucks, but of all motor vehicles.
4. A child from Turkey remembered the life of a man who had been murdered by a man called 'Hasan'. The child had a phobia of all persons called 'Hasan'.
5. A young boy from Turkey remembered a past life that ended when a van in which he was riding crashed against the support of a narrow bridge. He showed a phobia of automobiles and also a marked phobia of the bridge where the accident had occurred. The bridge was not far from his birthplace.
6. A child from Turkey remembered the life of a man who had drowned in a river. The river flowed near the child's village. It was noticed that the child avoided going near the part of the river where the drowning had occurred.
7. A child from India remembered the previous life of a child who had been murdered near a temple by a barber and a washerman. He had a generalized fear of all barbers and washermen. He also showed strong fear when taken to the area of the temple where the murder had occurred.
8. One baby from Sri Lanka struggled so much against being bathed that it took three adults to hold her down for this. Also, before she could speak, she had manifested (at the age of six months) a strong phobia of buses and cried when transported in one. The life she later described was that of a young girl (of another village) who had been walking on a narrow road that crossed flooded paddy fields. A bus had come along, and this girl, stepping back to avoid it, had fallen into the flood water and drowned.
9. A boy from Turkey showed a marked fear of airplanes before he could even speak. When he saw or heard one, he would run to his mother and cover or hide under a bed. Later, he described the previous life of a man who had been killed in an airplane crash.
10. A boy from Sri Lanka showed a phobia of policemen when he was just beginning to speak at the age of one and a half years. When he was about four years old, he gave details of a previous life that corresponded closely to events in Sri Lanka in April 1971 when the police and army suppressed a serious insurgency during which they killed hundreds of the insurgents. His parents believed that their child was describing the life of one of the insurgents killed in the uprising.

11. A child from Sri Lanka was found responding obediently whenever her mother happened to mention the word 'lorry'. The child showed a notable watchfulness in the presence of policemen. In addition, he showed a craving for tobacco and alcohol that was quite unusual for a child of his age. This child remembered the life of a distiller of illicit alcohol whose premises the police had frequently raided. He was a heavy smoker and an even heavier drinker of alcohol. He died one day when, being drunk, he stepped into the path of a speeding lorry.
12. A four-year-old child from Burma (an unsolved case) was observed to cringe with fear whenever airplanes flew over. When her father asked, she replied that she was afraid the airplanes would shoot her. She was a Japanese soldier (presumably in World War II) in her previous life who had been shot and killed in an airplane attack. In addition to the phobia of airplanes she liked to play at being a soldier, and she was markedly masculine in her behavior. Her refusal to wear girls' clothes eventually led to her being expelled from her school.

We should study these memories carefully because they offer us the finest evidence for the continuation of a personal consciousness after death. In most of the cases these phobias tend to recede as the memories of past-life diminish. However, in some cases the phobia persists after the subject has lost the imaged memories of the previous life. These phobias are past-life wounds to the soul which are traumatic enough to cross the barrier of death and to reappear to the new life even if the sources no more exist. In case the wounds are not healed by their own, one should contact clinical psychiatrists who have expertise in past-life regression therapy to resolve the brought forward issues so they are not carried into adulthood – or into future lives.

****

Some past-life memories in children manifest as talents or unlearned abilities – we often call it "God given gift". Stevenson (1974b, pp. 67-98) had investigated one such case from India. Swarnlata Mishra, a girl at the age of five or six years had performed unusual songs and dances first in front of her mother and then in front of others which she had no opportunity to learn so far as her parents knew. She remembered two of her previous lives – in one life she was a married woman, and in another life she was a boy, named 'Kamlesh' from Sylhet (presently at Bangladesh). Stevenson (1974b, pp. 69, 82, 88) wrote,

> "*The songs and dances of Swarnlata apparently belong to the life in Sylhet. The language of the songs was identified as Bengali by Professor Pal, who transcribed some of them for further study. Sylhet is in a Bengali-speaking area whereas in Madhya Pradesh Swarnlata had lived entirely*

among Hindi-speaking people .... Swarnlata always performed the songs and dances together, never one without the other. It was as if she had learned them together and could not (or did not care to) separate them from each other. Professor P. Pal shared this impression because on a visit he made to Swarnlata and her family in 1965 he observed 'she had difficulty in recollecting the words of the songs without performing the dances'. Professor Pal, who is a native of Bengal, identified the songs as Bengali and upon returning to his home in West Bengal he learned that two of them derived from poems by Rabindranath Tagore. The third song, also definitely Bengali, was by some minor poet whom Professor Pal could not identify... My own conclusion is that Swarnlata's songs and dances belong to the paranormal components of the case and are among its strongest features."

The text of her two songs (a spring song and a harvest song), when compared to the original words of Tagore's two poems, showed some minor deviations. Prof. Pal observed that her dances associated with the spring song were of the "Santiniketan style" which he had himself observed during his visit to the Visva Bharati. It means she did not learn the songs by hearing them alone but actually practicing both the songs and dances together.

Swarnlata said that she had learned the songs and dances from a friend, Madhu, during the previous life as Kamlesh. Her performances were of paranormal origin as she had no chance to learn during present life-time. Songs and dances are skills and skills can only be acquired by practice. Talents had been carried forward from past life to present life.

Haraldsson (2000, pp. 16-24) investigated a Sri Lankan case of Purnima Ekanayake who remembered the past life of a man whose family was making incense and had no other job. When the girl was asked if she knew how incense is made, she gave a detailed reply. There are two methods to make it, and Purnima had extraordinary practical knowledge of both the methods. Since her parents had hardly any idea how the incense is made, the knowledge must have been carried forward from her previous birth.

Highly skilled or gifted children, even prodigies, might be experiencing the carryover of spectacular talents from past lives, and are able to utilize and enhance them in their current lives. As example,

1. Mozart played whole pieces of music at four and wrote his first composition at five, Mendelssohn wrote his first piece at age 11, and Camille Saint-Saens could play any of Mozart's piano concertos from memory at age 10.
2. Jay Greenberg at around age two started drawing instruments. His mother, who had no musical background, reported, "*he managed to draw a cello and ask for a cello, and wrote the word cello. And I was surprised, because neither of us has anything to do with string*

instruments. And I didn't expect him to know what it [a cello] was." (Ward, 2008, p. 14).

3. Dhanat Plewtianyingthawee from Thailand had his first art exhibition at the age of three and a half. He started violin lessons at the same age, and at the age of four he performed a violin solo at Thailand Cultural Center, playing in a way that mature violists would envy.
4. Thomas Greene Bethune, though born blind and a slave boy, played on the piano 'par excellence'. He gave many concerts at different places to several audiences. His parents had never seen such a musical instrument called 'piano' and much less heard about it. This blind boy neither knew anything about music lessons nor had anyone taught him. Whatever he performed were his own original compositions.
5. Richard Hoffman, only three years old, played a piano solo before an audience after only eight months of lessons, Jackie Evancho from Pittsburgh, United States, sings opera like a seasoned star at the age of 11.
6. Jay Greenberg was born in a family which did not have any musical background. However, from age two he started showing talent in music. Some say he is the greatest musician to come in last 200 years.

People are amazed by these phenomena – How these little children are able to sing like stars? The answer to this question is much simpler than most people think – they are stars because they had learned it in the past. These young talents are simply the result of the reincarnation of passed away singers and musicians who had toiled to expertise their crafts. Natural talents and abilities can stem from past lives.

Sometimes a brain damage unlocks the genius within. In medical terms, we call it "Acquired Savant Syndrome" (a person acquires prodigious capabilities or skills following dementia, a head injury or severe blow to the head, or other disturbance). Treffert (2010, pp. 65,75,195) narrated the strange case of Orlando L. Serrell.

Orlando was an ordinary boy until at age 10 he was struck by a baseball on the left side of his head. He fell to the ground but didn't report it to his parents or receive medical attention, although he suffered from a headache for a long time. However, he found that he then was able to perform calendrical calculations of incredible complexity. That means if Orlando was asked what day of the week January 4, 1966 (Author's birthday) would fall on, he will be able to tell you, "Tuesday", instantly, without a pause to calculate and with perfect accuracy. The change happened immediately after the accident.

At six years of age, an autistic child named Matt Savage suddenly began playing 'London Bridge Is Falling Down' perfectly on the piano without trial and error to learn it, "*from nothing to playing perfectly*", his mother said. Before that day when he spontaneously started playing the piano, he did not like to be exposed to any noise (Hogan, 2008, p. 48). Such cases, where most ordinary people had their talents unlocked after an illness or injury affected the brain, are found from all the nations and at all times, such as Anthony Cicoria (mysterious capability to compose songs), Tommy McHugh (unusual painting skill), Sabine (unusual ability to solve mathematical problems), and Alonzo Clemons (can look at any animal for just a few moments, and then, using only his hands, create a very detailed, three-dimensional replica out of clay or wax. And while he sculpts, he will only access the images in his mind for reference). Since skills can develop only after rigorous practice, many reincarnation researchers believe this syndrome is a strong argument for reincarnation. The idea is, we suppress our past-life experiences to make room for new learning. Somehow this suppression has been damaged and the previous learning is suddenly "remembered".

A child who is usually adept in any field should be encouraged to pursue that interest because the child could be rekindling the use of instinctive abilities from a literal "life-time ago". The reawakening of latent talents in the current life could be one of the most exciting, practical uses of past-life recall.

7.1.2: Birthmarks and birth defects

One strong evidence in support of the reincarnation hypothesis is the incidence of striking birthmarks that reflects injuries and other events from the remembered life. Cultural influences are out of question for the formation of birthmarks because birthmarks are formed in the embryo before the child is born. These birthmarks and the birth defects are almost always of rare types, i.e., they differ noticeably from the kind of birthmark and defects that almost everyone has.

Phobias and birthmarks appear to be strongly related to violent death cases. About 35% of children who remembers past-lives have birthmarks and/or birth defects that they (or adult informants) attribute to wounds on a person whose life is remembered (Stevenson, 1993, p. 403). In some cases, the child has two or more birthmarks each corresponding to a wound on the deceased person whose life he remembers. As example, Stevenson (1993, pp. 407-412) noted,

1. A Thai child had a major abnormality of the skin on the back of his head and a deformed toe nail of the right great toe. He recalled the life of his uncle, who had been struck on the head with a heavy knife and killed almost instantly. The uncle also had chronic infection of the same toe from which he had suffered for some years before he died.
2. A Thai child had a small round birthmark on the back of his head and a larger, irregularly shaped birthmark on his forehead. He recalled the life of a man who was shot with a rifle in the head from behind.

These two birthmarks corresponded to the bullet wound of exit on the man whose life the child remembered. These observations accord with the fact that bullet wounds of exit are nearly always larger than wounds of entry.

3. A Thai woman had three separate scar-like birthmarks near the midline of her back. As a child she remembered the life of a woman who was killed when struck three times in the back with an axe.
4. A Burmese woman had two perfectly round birthmarks in her left chest which slightly overlapped, and one was about half the size of the other. As a child she remembered the life of a woman who was accidentally shot and killed with a shotgun. The shotgun cartridge had contained shot of two different sizes.
5. A Burmese child said that she remembered the life of her deceased aunt who had died during surgery for congenital heart disease. This child had a long, vertical linear birthmark close to the midline of her lower chest and upper abdomen. This birthmark corresponded to the surgical incision for the repair of the aunt's heart.
6. Two Burmese children remembered the lives of persons who had died after being bitten by venomous snakes, and the birthmarks of each corresponded to therapeutic incisions made at the sites of the snakebites on the persons whose lives they remembered.
7. One Burmese child remembered the life of a child who had been bitten on the foot by a snake. The child's uncle had applied a burning cheroot to the site of the bite (a traditional remedy for snakebite in Burma), but the child died. After reincarnation, the child's birthmark was round and located at the site on the foot where the bitten child's uncle had applied the cheroot.
8. A Turkish boy had diminished and malformed ear and underdeveloped face at the right side. He remembered the life of a man who had been shot (with a shotgun) at point-blank range. The shot had penetrated the right side of the skull.
9. A child from India had birth defect of fingers almost absent on one hand. He remembered the life of another child who had put his right hand into the blades of a fodder-chopping machine and lost his fingers.
10. A Burmese girl had a birth defect of absence of the lower right leg. She remembered the life of a girl who was run over by a train which had severed her right leg first, before running over the trunk.

In Haraldsson's (2000, p. 17) case of Purnima Ekanayake, she had "*a large cluster of hypopigmented birthmarks to the left of the midline of her chest, and over her lower ribs*". She remembered the past life of a man, Jinadasa Perera, who died at traffic accident two years and four months prior her birth. The postmortem report revealed that wounds had been inflicted on him in the same area as her birthmarks.

Stevenson (1974b, pp. 91-106) had investigated the case of Ravi Shankar, who was born with a long, stippled mark across his neck. When he was between the ages of two and three, he began to speak about a previous life during which he said he had died after having his throat cut. He related his birthmark to the murder he said he had suffered.

Perhaps the most striking birth defect so far published is that of Wijeratne. Wijeratne was born with an undersized right arm and webbed fingers which he credited to his having killed his wife with his arm in his previous life. This case is from Stevenson's file which I will discuss in details in next chapter. Except in the most extreme cases (e.g., that of Wijeratne), birth defects generally heal and internal diseases disappear over time. Birthmarks may also shift position and fade.

In countries with a traditional belief in reincarnation, such as India, Burma, Sri Lanka, and Thailand, birthmarks and birth defects are often regarded as an indication that a previous personality has been reborn. Stevenson (Keil and Tucker, 2000, pp. 1071-72) described the strange case of Bruce Peck. His grandfather had repeatedly expressed the desire to Bruce Peck's parents, along with another person to return with only one hand or arm in his next life. After his grandfather died, Bruce Peck was born with his right hand and part of the forearm missing.

These birthmarks and birth defects are not medical malfunctions but the soul is reconstructing the baby in mother's womb in a very specific way and for some unknown reasons. In 1997, Stevenson published a weighty two-volume document called 'Reincarnation and Biology: a contribution to the etiology of birthmarks and birth defects'. In this monumental work, Stevenson documented 225 cases of birthmarks and birth defects on children that corresponded to fatal wounds, injuries, or illnesses of the person the children remembered being in their former life. Stevenson (1997a, pp. 2-3) asserts that these cases are especially important for the following three reasons.

First, these birthmarks and birth defects provide an objective type of evidence – "*for many of the cases, we have a medical document, usually a post-mortem report, that gives us a written confirmation of the correspondence between the birthmark (or birth defect) and the wound on the deceased person whose life the child, when it can speak, will usually claim to remember*". Second, they provide evidence that a deceased personality – having survived death – may influence the form of a later-born baby; and finally, these cases provide a better explanation than any other now available [e.g., genetic factors, chance, postnatal environment] about why some persons have birth defects when most do not and for why some persons have birth defects have theirs in a particular location instead of elsewhere.

Stevenson (1986, pp. 205-08) wrote that about 68% of the reincarnation cases, a birthmark or birth defect appears in exact places. Some of them have more than one birthmark or birth defect and few of them have both a birthmark and a birth defect. Phobias also occur and many of the phobias are rooted into the previous personality's mode of death. Stevenson (1997a, p. 11) concluded,

> "*The [irrefutable] correspondence between wounds and birthmarks and the child's correct statements about the life of the deceased person usually leave no doubt that the correct previous personality has been identified.*"

The belief of reincarnation is widespread amongst the Igbo tribe of Nigeria; nearly everyone is thought to be reincarnation of another person. Stevenson (1986, p. 213) commented, "*Many Igbo subjects may have abundant imaged memories of previous lives, but they may learn early in life the undesirability of talking about these in front of disapproving adults.*"

They also have a bizarre belief that some children who die in infancy do so deliberately to torment their parents. The 'spirit-child' or 'repeater-child', known as the 'ogbanje' in the Igbo language and the 'abiku' in the Yoruba language of Western Nigeria, is imprisoned in an endless cycle of birth, death, and rebirth. Indeed, the Igbo word 'ogbanje' means "*to make several trips to and from a place*" (Williamson, 1972, p. 404). The tribal people believe that the child who is unduly linked to the spirit world cannot complete a normal life cycle because these children are unable or unwilling to break ties with the spirit world, thus compromising their earthly existence (Harler, 2013, pp. iv, 6). So an 'ogbanje/abiku' child has 'decided' beforehand when he would die.

Such babies are not only a burden and a sorrow to their parents, but they are also an 'insult' to the tribal community itself because they break the cycle of fertility and render it useless. Hence, they must be stopped. The most extreme of the ways a suspected 'ogbanje/abiku' may be stopped is by mutilating the child's body, perhaps by amputating a portion of a finger.

The belief is that the 'ogbanje' works in a group. Every member in the group had taken an oath in the discarnate realm that he or she would die as a child and return back to other members in the spirit world. The 'ogbanje' dislikes ugliness and deformities. Hence, in mutilating a living or dead suspected 'ogbanje', other members of the group would expel anyone whose body was disfigured. When an ogbanje child has died and his body has been mutilated, the parents closely observe the next child born into the family. If a child is born with a birth defect corresponding to a particular mutilation of a deceased ogbanje such as absence of tip of the left little finger they identify the newborn child as the ogbanje reborn. They consider that he or she has now returned to stay because the parents have broken a cycle of ogbanje deaths in infancy.

Whether or not this act has the desired effect of preventing premature deaths, some Igbo children are really born with a missing finger end or other deformity that seems to correspond to a mark made on a deceased sibling (Stevenson and Edelstein, 1982, pp. 178-79). As example, Wenger and Chesi (1980, p. 91) described the case of a Yoruba woman whose first ten children died young. Enraged by the death of the tenth of these children, she threw the dead body on the ground and broke its lower jaw. Her eleventh baby was born with the lower jaw missing (or greatly reduced in size), and she survived into adulthood. Stevenson (1986, pp. 207-08) had investigated many 'ogbanje' cases and his findings would astonish anyone.

1. One person had been born after the death of two older siblings. He bore two birthmarks that corresponded in location with different marks made on both of the deceased siblings after they had died.
2. One girl was born with severe birth defects of the hands and feet. Though she displayed some past-life memory, her father did not want her to speak because he believed that the girl was the reincarnation of his deceased daughter. After the death of his daughter in infancy, he had been enraged at the child for dying so young, had mutilated her hands and feet. Then he had performed a ritual to prevent her for reincarnating. Later he by mistake neutralized the ritual unintentionally. Soon after, the present girl child was born to his other wife.
3. After the death of the third baby, the father mutilated the hands and feet of the corpse. Later a niece of the father of these infants was born with severe congenital deformities of the hands and feet. She was thought to be the reincarnation of the mutilated baby.
4. A baby was born with deformities at his left little finger and both little toes. These deformities correspond to customary mutilations of 'ogbanje' children in Igbo community. His family believed that the child had been an 'ogbanje' in his immediate previous life
5. A boy was said to be the reincarnation of an older sister who had died at the age of eighteen months. When the sister had been born, she was believed to be the reincarnation of her parental grandfather. When she died in infancy, she was judged to be an 'ogbanje'. Her parents then chopped her body in two places with a hatchet and warned her discarnate soul that, if she again reincarnates in the family, she should remain or would be cut again. The boy had two birthmarks at the exact sites where the older sister had been cut. He had lived up to adulthood.

The physical imprints are not the result of DNA, because the molecular codes are new and come with the present body. The soul mind does affect the biological body by influencing the DNA. This is the power of the quantum soul. Newton (2016b, p. 137) commented, "*Indeed, there are countless other elements involving thought sequencing which we bring into our host body from hundreds of former lives*". Since the former bodies we had in previous lives are almost never genetically related to our current family, what critics think as genetic memory is actually the soul memory emanating from the unconscious mind. The memories are forceful enough to cross the barrier of death and to manifest in the new body. This mind-over-matter power of the quantum soul is something that new age scientists call as 'quantum mysticism'.

Birthmark and birth defect cases show that human body is constructed by the soul (the quantum consciousness) while the baby is inside the mother's womb. Quantum physics showed us that consciousness creates matter and the quantum double slit experiment is one way we can see how consciousness affects the physical material world. Also, the core teaching of the Seth material is that the physical reality arises from consciousness, not the other way around. Therefore, within our understanding of Quantum physics, birthmark and birth defects perfectly explain the reincarnation hypothesis. It is quite possible that everything in the normal body is also constructed individually in a unique way by its soul.

The whole matter has quite practical significance. If birthmarks and birth defects can be carried forward from one life to another, then it is also possible that many of our health problems (both physical and mental) have origins in past lives, that neuroses have a basis in previous life experiences. It is quite possible that many present-life diseases are due to past-life accidents, sickness or ailments.

These behavioral, emotional and physical residues from many earlier lives have critical karmic issues. Newton (2016b, p. 272) explains,

> "*The time we spend in the spirit world between lives should eliminate all residual effects of our past life experiences. In most cases it does but, as I have said, some people do carry physical and emotional body imprints from one life to the next. This is especially true if that imprint bears upon a particular karmic lesson in the life to come*".

7.2: Spontaneous (non-therapeutic) past-life memories in adults

> "*The knowledge of rebirth is the turning point in the history of mankind.*"
> Friedrich Nietzsche

Spontaneous vivid recollection of past-life memories occurs most frequently during unprompted episodes of non-ordinary states of consciousness such as spiritual emergencies. Various degrees of remembering can also happen in more or less ordinary states of consciousness in the circumstances of everyday life during normal waking state, in dreams, fantasies, psychotherapy, reiki, drug-induced states, various trance states, meditation and during psychiatric treatment. Most often, these are "one-timer view". A young Thai woman of 20, Pratomwan Inthanu, was meditating when she recalled events from two previous lives as well as the intermission between her most recent past life and her present one (Stevenson, 1983a, pp. 157-60, 168-69). The past-life memories often appear unsolicited in sessions with therapists who do not aim for them and do not even believe in them, catching them completely off-guard. Professional psychologists and psychiatrists are aware of such memory collections but treat them indiscriminately as indications of serious psychopathology.

Adult past-life memories are more often triggered by memory cues resembling unusually strong deja vu experiences when a person is able to provide descriptions of environments and circumstances related to the observed events without any prior knowledge of them (Mills and Lynn, 2000, p. 289; Neppe, 2010, pp. 61-97; Brown, 2003, pp. 394-413). Often we have strange feelings towards others which we do not find any reason why they last so long in some persons and quickly vanish in others. We are attracted or repelled by certain nations, people, names, food, or other common objects. In all probability, such fondness and fears are related to apparent memories originating from past-lives. Stevenson (1960, pp. 56-58, 60) mentioned three such cases.

> "*An American couple cruising around the world stopped at Bombay [India]. Walking around the city, they both found themselves extraordinarily familiar with parts of it so that they had no need of a guide and could tell each other in advance of coming to a place, say around a corner, what they would see. They tested this knowledge by going to a particular quarter they thought they remembered and looking for a house and a banyan tree they remembered standing in the garden of the house. When they reached the place where they expected to find the house and tree, they did not find them. They then noticed a policeman who happened to be there and asked him if the house and tree had formerly stood there. He recalled having heard from his father that they had been there as this couple described them. He added an additional item of information. The house had belonged to a family named Bhan. This couple had, for some reason unknown to them, liked the name Bhan and given this name as first name to their son.*"

It is practically out of question that something like this is a mere coincidence. It rather suggests a situation that characterizes past-life experiences.

Previously, I had talked about 'mediumistic art' phenomena in which an individual appears to be possessed by an entity that guides the artwork creation process. Following reincarnation case supports this view.

> "*A Dutch portrait painter named Henriette Roos married a man called Weisz whom she subsequently divorced. Although it is the custom in*

Holland for women to resume their maiden names after a divorce, Mrs. Weisz for an unaccountable reason liked her married name and did not want to give it up. When her mother reproached her with not resuming her maiden name, she replied, 'I don't know, it is a strange feeling, I can't explain, that name somehow suits me. I feel one with it, it is more me than my own name, Roos. Each time I call myself that way I have the feeling I'm talking about someone else'. So she decided to call herself Mrs. Weisz-Roos.

Some time after her divorce, she was in Paris working hard to support herself by her painting. One evening she went to bed extremely fatigued hoping to benefit from a good sleep. She then heard a voice say, or was impressed by the thought: 'Don't be so lazy, get up and work'. After further importuning which she at first resisted, she did get up and went to her easel. She was impressed to paint in the dark and did so with feverish haste and hardly knowing what she was doing. After a time she felt better, naturally sleepy and returned to bed and to sleep. Upon awakening the next morning, she discovered that she had painted a beautiful little portrait of a young woman.

Puzzled by this experience, she described it to a friend who persuaded her to consult a sensitive who practiced psychometry. Mrs. Weisz-Roos took her portrait to the sensitive and without saying anything to her, placed it on a table from which the sensitive picked it up. The sensitive went into a trance and after a time said, 'I see very large golden letters. A name is spelled to me ...G-O-Y-A now he speaks to me. He says: He was a great Spanish painter. He had to fly from his country from his enemies and it was you who received him in your home in a big southern city in France until the end of his life. He still is so thankful for this that he wants to guide you but he is not satisfied, you resist too much, you are too much tied up in your academic education, you never relax and let him guide you, you make it very difficult for him, he therefore made you paint in the dark so you couldn't see what you were doing ....'

At the time of his communication, Mrs. Weisz-Roos had never read anything about Goya. However, that same evening, she went to a home where her host owned a copy of a life of Goya. She borrowed this and was astonished to find in it an account of Leocadia Weisz, in whose home Goya had lived during his exile from Spain at the end of his life."

Yet, another strange incidence is like this.

"*When I was at Heidelberg, Germany ... in company with some friends, I paid my first visit to the ruined Heidelberg Castle. As I approached it, I was impressed with the existence of a peculiar room in an inaccessible portion of the building. A paper and pencil were provided me, and I drew a diagram of the room even to its peculiar floor. My diagram and description were perfect, when we afterwards visited the room.... Still another impression came to me with regard to a book, which I was made to feel was in the old library of Heidelberg University. I not only knew what the book was, but even felt that a certain name of an old German professor would be found written in it.... A search was made for the volume but it was not found. Still the impression clung to me, and another effort was made to find the book; this time we were rewarded for our pains. Sure enough, there on the margin of one of the leaves was the very name I had been given in such a strange manner.*"

Sometimes memories appear in fantasy daydreaming (Parish, 2004, p. 23). Pnina Cohen, a 15-year-old girl had developed a pet fantasy after reading Daniken's "Chariots of the Gods". In her daydreams, she would hike in Peru flying over the plain of Nazca in a helicopter, looking at the gigantic land drawings and making discoveries that would change the face of the world. Soon after her marriage, her daydreams started appearing as vivid visions at night just like a movie on a television. Every night she saw something new – "*long skulls with a hole in the left side of the forehead, bizarre drawings on rock walls, temples and rocky beaches*". She began to draw sketches of what she had seen and shown to her husband. He was surprised and took her to the temple of Nazca, where "*She easily identified the central square shaped like seven trapezes, as well as the gigantic drawings of monkeys and rats, the rocky beaches and the flat deserts. She felt that she knew each place*". After six months, they went to the local Shaman, where after a special ceremony, the Shaman went into a trance and unearthed the roots of Pnina's strange recollections and informed her confidently that, "... *she had lived there hundreds of years ago. She had been the doctor who had treated patients and had exorcised the evil spirits that possessed them by piercing their skulls on the left side of their foreheads*" (Parish, 2004, pp. 66-67). Pnina's daydreams were not mere fantasies; they had intrinsic meanings for two earthly existences separated by a tiny fence of death.

In 1922, five scientists went to Gobi Desert (Mongolia) in search of ancient fossils. Among them were Kirk Grainer and Yvette Andrews, Kirk's girlfriend. After an exhausting journey in burning heat, these five explorers reached their destination – Gobi Desert, the godforsaken part of the world. For 20 days, the team travelled among the huge colorful cliffs that were 75 million years old. But, except Kirk and Yvette, other members did not succeed to find fossils. Kirk and Yvette found more and more fossils each day. They discovered a huge treasure trove of fossils and remains of rare animals as if they simply "knew" which cliff to look behind and where to check the ground.

Soon other people gave up leaving the task of primary location to them. Night after night, Kirk and Yvette would sleep in the same tent. From the very first night they began to have dreams that seemed to be not only meaningful but also matching with each other's dreams. On one night Yvette had a very strange dream. Parish (2004, p. 194) described, she dreamed that she was in a large cave, sitting next to a campfire. There were other women and children and all were wearing skins and furs. Yvette identified herself despite the fact that she looked very different mainly because of her skin clothes and facial expressions.

Yvette realized that her dreams revealed a past-life probably several thousand years ago. Gradually, many facts from her previous life came under limelight. She held an important position in that small tribe. She prepared paints from various mixtures that were used for cave painting. She also made other mixtures used for spreading on the men's bodies before they went hunting.

She remembered the life-style and food-habit of her tribe. One morning she began describing her dreams to Kirk. Surprisingly, Kirk became pale upon hearing her story. Strangely...very strangely...Kirk "*continued from the place she had left off. He told her about the cave, about the women waiting for the men and even about the cave paintings that she had not bothered to mention to him.*" (Parish, 2004, p. 195). The joint dreams of Kirk and Yvette revealed a different period of life, an ancient one, during which they were both partners and lived in the same cave.

It was not the hand of chance that brought them back to the place of a past existence. In this Universe no information is lost. Life is an ongoing and continuous process. The karmic link that connects the present with the past is never broken.

Stanislav Grof, a psychiatrist with more than sixty years of experience researching non-ordinary states of consciousness, had recorded the case of one of his participants in a month-long seminar at Esalen (Grof, 1988, pp. 92-95). This is Karl's case history.

Karl was a talented artist. During the seminar, suddenly he started experiencing fragments of dramatic scenes full of powerful emotions and physical feelings not connected with present life that seemed to be happening in another land and time. In his visions, he saw tunnels, underground storage spaces, military barracks, thick walls, soldiers in various defensive positions and ramparts in a fortress situated on a rock facing a sea shore. He felt puzzled because the soldiers looked like Spanish but the scenery looked more like Scotland or Ireland.

As the vision continued, the dramatic scenes started representing fierce combat and bloody slaughter. Karl experienced himself as a priest and at one point saw himself with a bible and a cross. He saw a seal ring on his hand and could clearly recognize the initials that it bore.

Being a talented artist, he produced a series of sketches and paintings of this strange process. Some of these depicted different parts of the fortress, others were scenes of slaughter, and a few were his own experiences including being attacked by someone with a sword. The enemy threw him over the ramparts to die on the beach. Among these pictures was a drawing of the seal ring with the initials.

As Karl was recovering bits and pieces of this story, he found more and more meaningful connections with his present life. He noted that many emotional and psychosomatic feelings, as well as problems in interpersonal relationships that he had at that time in his everyday life, were clearly related to his inner process, involving the mysterious sequence of events in the past.

A turning point came when he suddenly felt a strong desire to spend his holiday in Western coast of Ireland. After his return, he showed the photographs that he had shot on his vacation. He realized that he had taken eleven consecutive pictures of the same scenery that did not seem particularly interesting. He took the map and reconstructed where he stood at the time and in which direction he was shooting. He realized that the place that attracted his attention was the ruin of an old fortress called Dunanoir, or Forte de Oro (Golden Fortress).

Karl suspected a mysterious connection between his experiences and his vision. He studied the history of Dunanoir thoroughly and discovered to his enormous surprise that at the time of Walter Raleigh, the Spaniards took over the fortress, and then the British besieged it. Walter Raleigh negotiated with the Spaniards and promised them free exit out from the fortress if they would open the gate and surrender to the British. The Spaniards agreed on these conditions but the British did not hold their promise. Once inside the fortress, they slaughtered mercilessly all the Spaniards and threw them over the ramparts to die on the ocean beach.

Karl was thrilled and continued his library research until he discovered a special document about the battle of Dunanoir. There he found that a priest accompanied the Spanish soldiers and was killed together with them. The initials of the name of the priest were identical with those that Karl saw in his vision of the seal ring and depicted in one of his drawings.

Spontaneous evoked past-life memories have important implications for psychology and psychotherapy because of their therapeutic potential, such as,

1. They feel extremely real and often facilitate access to accurate information about historical periods, cultures, and even historical events that the individual could not have acquired through the ordinary channels. Accuracy of these memories can be objectively verified sometimes with amazing details. Their emergence is also completely independent of the subject's previous philosophical and religious belief system.
2. The root cause of various emotional, psychosomatic (involving both mind and body), and interpersonal problems can be better understood because there are karmic links among various incarnations. These memories are more powerful than memories from the present lifetime, and often associated with amazing meaningful synchronicities.

The criteria for adult's past-life verification are similar to that of children, except that the memories of a child are more recent, hence easy to verify. For an adult, evidence is harder to come by as they are much older. However, they are still verifiable with independent historical research. In addition, the karmic pattern started to emerge when their past-life memories are compared with the present life situation. For children such comparison is not possible since the child is yet to experience his present life.

7.3: Hypnotic past-life regression

"*If I didn't believe in reincarnation on the evidence I'd received I'd be mentally defective... none of my colleagues have found me psychotic.*"

Arthur Guirdham (forty years of research experience in regressive hypnosis)

Many people can recall past-lives through hypnosis and such memories can be checked against existing historical records and public documents for their accuracy. Often, while the person describes many details of his various past-lives, the professional psychologists and psychiatrists can also see how the divine law of Karma takes its inevitable and unaltered course through birth and reincarnation.

Logically, any previous life recollection could be brought to the surface by a method that would relax the person sufficiently so that the past-life memories could make themselves known. Hypnotism is one such method (dreams and deep meditations are other common methods) of uncovering such memories in the same way that it can allow subjects to remember forgotten incidents from childhood in therapy. The hypnotic state is a variation of the usual state of consciousness. Waking state is characterized by rapidly changing thought-content, every five to six seconds, and hypnotic state characterized, at deep levels, by steady, connected thought-content.

First, let us understand what hypnotism is, how it works, and what the limitations are. Experts differ on the nature and workings of hypnosis. Some believe hypnosis is a special, alternate state of consciousness, while others believe hypnosis is little more than an ordinary, highly motivated waking state of consciousness. Hypnotic trance refers to a quite normal state of consciousness in which an individual narrows the focus of his awareness and concentrates attention upon a particular idea or belief to the exclusion of others, thereby activating subconscious mechanisms that dutifully materialize those suggestions in physical experience. This is "*a situation in which the subject is asked to set aside critical judgment without abandoning it completely, and to indulge in fantasy and make-believe*" (Perry et al., 1988, p. 129). In this state of focused concentration with the elimination of all distractions in which attention is directed away from exterior, physical stimuli and directed inward toward images, ideas, feelings, and sensations, often the subject recollects lost memories from one or more previous existence on Earth. Here hypnosis is used as a research method and not as a form of therapy.

Not only man, even lower animals can be hypnotized (Nee, 1972, p. 20). It is a misconception that hypnosis is a potentially harmful, coercive, or manipulative procedure (Council et al., 1997, p. 258). Another erroneous belief is that hypnosis can produce powers not ordinarily available in an individual (Gravitz, 2002, p. 8). This is a natural state that we all enter spontaneously. There is no acceptable, scientific evidence that hypnosis and the experience of trance is in itself harmful (Rossi, 1987, p. 492). Many third-rated movies and novels have contributed to these misconceptions. The person in deep tears over a lost love is experiencing hypnosis, as is the person who has unintentionally clicked off into a daydream state during a boring talk. Psychiatrist Milton H. Erickson, in a paper titled 'Possible detrimental effects from experimental hypnosis' (1932) concluded, "*The author's own experience, based upon several thousand trances on approximately 300 individual subjects, some of whom were hypnotized at least 500 times each over a period of four to six years, reveals no evidence of such harmful effects*" (Rossi, 1987, p. 497). Actually, the subjects demonstrate a full capacity and ability for self-protection, ready and complete understanding with critical judgment, avoidance, evasion, or complete rejection of commands. Also, repeated hypnosis does not make a person 'addicted' to hypnosis or there is no 'weakening' as a result of hypnosis. Hence, clinical use of hypnosis is harmless. Most of the reports of complications arising in the use of hypnosis have involved hypnotic situations in which hypnosis is practiced by amateurs and stage hypnotists (Kost, 1965, pp. 220-22). Sometimes the subject mischievously fakes it so cleverly that even an expert hypnotist may not be able to detect the deception.

In a clinical hypnosis trial, the power lies less with the hypnotist and the experimental setting, and more with the individual subject who receives and accepts the suggestions that the hypnotist offers. Hence, all hypnosis is self-hypnosis. If the subject does not believe the hypnotist's suggestion, no matter how cleverly packaged it will have no effect on him, but if the subject does, then he will even see a flying elephant in the middle of a crowded room if requested to do so.

In the hypnotic situation the memories or habits belonging to an earlier period of life are readily activated. This feature makes possible hypermnesia (unusual power or enhancement of memory) and age-regression. Cunningham (2009, p. 133) wrote,

> "*If the past events of childhood form memories that we cannot consciously recall but to which we react are stored in the subconscious mind, then there is no reason why memories of past events even further back in time [if a mechanism by which those memories are encoded and stored can be proposed] are not repressed in the same manner. If repressed childhood*

memories can be recovered through hypnosis, perhaps recall of past lives can be obtained through hypnosis as well. Current experimental investigations of the reincarnation hypothesis using hypnotic regression have given no proof, scientifically speaking, but there is enough evocative evidence [e.g., xenoglossy, children who remember previous lives, hypnotic past-life therapy outcomes] to lead us to conclude that the reincarnation hypothesis is worthy of further serious consideration."

Based on this age-regression principle the subject is put in a trance state in an experimental setting. The hypnotic induction is then followed by a three 'five-minute-suggestions' administered by the experiment that informs the participant that he is regressing in time to age fifteen, age five, and age one, and then to a time "*beyond the point of their birth*". When the hypnotic regression suggestion, "*You go back to an age preceding your birth; you are somebody else, somewhere else*", as "*secondary personalities*" and "*multiple personalities*" (Kampman, 1976, p. 218), or "*You are regressing in time, beyond your birth and into a new dimension… You are now in a different life, living in another life that you have lived before in another time. You are now reliving that other life that you lived once before in a different time*" (Spanos et al., 1991, p. 310), or "*I am going to count backwards from ten to zero. Now as odd as this might seem, when the count is finished you will see scenes from a time before you were [give present name]*" (Roberts, 1993, pp. 185-86), is given, what is often observed is the "*secondary identity enactments*" (Spanos et al., 1991, pp. 309-10) producing appropriate behavioral and psychological changes. Past-life regressions occur even in skeptical individuals who do not believe in hypnosis, regression, or past-lives.

Hypnotic regression techniques have been used ever since Colonel Albert de Rochas published a detailed account of his mesmeric experiments in 'Les Vies Successives' in 1911 (Cunningham, 2009, p. 7). However, hypnosis does not always lead to truth and people can lie unconsciously in hypnosis just as they can lie in the waking state. Also, distortion of memories (commonly known as additional recall) can occur when remembering is attempted during hypnosis (Pettinati, 1988, p. 277). The courts of law do not accept statements under hypnotic trance as evidence. Hence, such past-life memories should not be taken on faith. We must take every effort to check the information against existing records and documents.

Even in the deepest hypnosis the subject is conscious, and under appropriate circumstances he can retrospectively (and concurrently) describe his hypnotic experiences accurately (Shor, 1979, p. 108). The behavioral and psychological manifestation of a person who recalls past-lives under hypnosis differs from those who report spontaneous recall. The person may show major changes of mood, speech, and behavior. With a convincing sense of vividness and certainty they may claim to be in other locations and other periods in history. They may exhibit foreign accents and xenoglossy (responsively speaking an unlearned language). They claim to have different names and identities, and may claim to belong to the opposite sex. Often they display funds of information that are surprisingly appropriate to the personalities they claim to be (Venn, 1986, p. 409). However, the individual can report a past-life experience without its associated emotions. When an experience is perceived from the point of view of outside-the-image (i.e., passive observation), the image and the emotional aspect of the experience becomes separated from its visual aspects (Bandler, 1985, chap. 3). All experience requires a 'point of view' or 'perspective'.

Hypnotic past-life recalls have various common features (Knight, 1995, p. 92).

1. The past-life experiences often mirror issues in the person's present life that have roots in the past lives, i.e., prominent manifestation of the law of Karma. Regressions develop according to meanings, not historical time.
2. They are usually visual and have a life of their own. The imagery has an uncanny feeling of familiarity, and the person identifies with one character. Most past lives are ordinary. Past-life regressions become easier with repetition.
3. Regressions are often followed by a genuine improvement in mental state. It may affect medical conditions also.

Often a simple therapeutic age regression for reliving an early event can lead to a past-life regression. As example, Brian Weiss (1988), documented the account of his treatment in 1980 of a highly hypnotizable young unmarried woman, named Catherine, who suffered from a number of psychological problems including phobias, panic attacks, depression, and recurrent nightmares. Weiss made a nondirective suggestion to her during one hypnotic session – "*Go back to the time from which your symptoms arise*". He expected that the woman would go back to her early childhood as expected, but surprisingly recalled a past life 4,000 years ago in which she had lived. There was a big flood that devastated her village and she died by drowning with her baby in her arms. She identified that mishap as the origin of her present difficulties.

After this session, her symptoms gradually went into remission and within months completely vanished. In the hypnotized state, Catherine gave detailed accounts of many past lives spanned a wide range of times and places from ancient Egypt to England in the days of sailing ships. Weiss said his clinical evaluation of her showed she was not making things up and was not delusional at all.

As we have seen in Stevenson's cases, Catherine's past lives all involved humble circumstances, including poverty, prostitution and even servitude.

Thus, they were by no means complimentary to her ego. The most important feature of Catherine case is that she would repeatedly describe intermediate states between incarnations that strangely resemble the states reported in NDEs. At the end of one past-life account she said,

> "*I have left my body. I see a wonderful light. ... There are people coming to help me. Wonderful people .... The soul ... finds peace here. You leave all bodily pains behind you. Your soul is peaceful and serene .... The light is so brilliant! Everything comes from the light! Energy comes from this light. ...*" (Weiss, 1988, pp. 82-83).

Catherine spoke of personalities called 'Masters' who lived in the intermediate realm and provided wise advice to incarnating souls. Her testimony paints an overall picture of repeated rebirth as a learning process, a school of hardship in which souls gradually progress to higher spiritual destinations.

During 1952, a businessman and amateur hypnotist, Morey Bernstein, regressed a young married woman named Virginia Burns Tighe (born 1923, and had never visited Ireland). Tighe recalled several previous lives under hypnosis – one of which was an Irish girl named Bridey (Bridget) Kathleen Murphy, born on December 20, 1798 in Cork, Ireland and died in 1864 at the age of 66 in Belfast, Ireland. Between November 29, 1952 and August 29, 1953, Morey Bernstein regressed her for total six times, and in 1956, he wrote a book 'The Search for Bridey Murphy' on this case that caused a public sensation because of the many concrete and obscure (an uninteresting) details about peasant life in 18th century Ireland that would be verified, but that could not have become known to Tighe by normal means.

In spite of extensive investigation, it could not be established that Bridey Murphy ever existed, and no documents of her birth, marriage, and death could be found. Still the case cannot be dismissed because aside from some church records, vital statistics in Ireland do not go back beyond 1864, and Bridey Murphy was assumed born in 1798, and other details reported by Virginia are found mostly accurate. Ducasse (1961, pp. 9, 11) and Jayatilleke (2000, pp. 151, 152) presented many examples,

1. Bridey mentions the names of two Belfast grocers from whom she bought foodstuffs – Farrs and John Carrigan. After considerable search by the Belfast chief librarian John Bebbington and his staff, these two grocers were found listed in a Belfast city directory for 1865-66. They were the only individuals of those names engaged in the 'foodstuffs' business there at the time.
2. Bridey's husband, Sean (John) Brian Joseph McCarthy, really existed and worked as a bookkeeper listed in the 1858-59 and again 1861-62 Belfast directory.

3. The existence of 'The Meadows' where her house was allegedly located was verified on an 1801 map of Cork on which a number of houses were built in an area identified as 'Mardike Meadows' just to the West of the city. This is the only 'Meadows' on the map spread through 82 acres of land, and not more than eight buildings are shown. The area perfectly fits Bridey's description in location, population and name.

There were many attempts to disprove the accounts of Tighe's past-life regressions. Some of the statements that Bridey made were refuted by experts based on known facts, but these were later shown to be correct after extensive research. Goldberg (1982, pp. 48-50) recorded,

1. Bridey mentioned a rope company and a tobacco house operating at Belfast. It was verified to be true.
2. As a child Bridey received a spanking for scratching all of the paint off her metal bed. Skeptics said that iron beds were not introduced into Ireland until at least 1850. The Encyclopedia Britannica stated that iron beds appeared in Ireland in the eighteenth century.
3. Bridey said that her husband taught law at the Queen's university in Belfast during 1847. Experts said that Queen's college was not founded until 1849 and Queen's University was established until 1908. However, subsequent research revealed that on December 19, 1845 Queen Victoria declared that "*there shall and may be erected... one college for students in arts, law and physics... which shall be called Queen's college*" (Gunaratna et al., 2011, p. 264). On August 15, 1850, Queen Victoria founded Queen's University in Ireland and stated, "*the said Queen's colleges shall be, and .... are hereby constituted colleges of our said university.*" (Registrar's office, 1851, p. 59).
4. Bridey mentioned that little sacks of rice were tied to the leg as a sign of purity. There was an objection from the Life magazine's expert on folklore, Richard Hayward, that rice had never been part of Irish folklore traditions. But investigation confirmed that rice was imported into Ireland around 1750. Since rice is white it would naturally suggest purity. This custom is quite possibly accurate.
5. Bridey talked about reading a book 'The Sorrows of Deirdre'. Skeptics pointed out that according to English catalogue of books published since 1800, the first appearance of this book was in 1905. But it was later discovered that an inexpensive paperback was published in 1808 by Bolton entitled, 'The Song of Deirdre' and 'The Death of the Sons of Usnach'.
6. Bridey mentioned the tuppence as one of the coins used in her days. Very few researchers know that this particular coin was in use in Ireland only from 1797 to 1850.

Time and time again the 'experts' have claimed that Bridey was wrong about one point or another but with farther investigation later found to be accurate. It seems that Bridey gossiped and exaggerated her actual position in life (as example, her husband was not a barrister, but a clerk / bookkeeper who kept books for several of the business houses in Belfast and perhaps also for Queen's College) because she had exhibited much awe and jealousy to the higher class of people.

Under hypnosis Tighe told Morey Bernstein many Irish stories, sang Irish songs, and spoke Irish colloquialisms. Bridey said that she had danced to an Irish tune called, 'The Morning Jig'. When a post-hypnotic suggestion was given that she would perform that dance, she performed exactly at the same manner (Bernstein, 1956, p. 162). Gravitz (2002, p. 5) recorded that Morey Bernstein at one point asked her to regress even before Ireland, whereupon she related that she had led a prior life in America, where she had resided with her parents, Vera and John, in New Amsterdam, as New York City was named between 1626-1664.

One final note on this case concerning the last years of her life at Belfast strongly suggests that the case was genuine. Tighe spoke with a weary, half whine and a throaty Irish accent that defies all explanation except reincarnation. Since the accent of the Belfast slums has never been used by American actors, Tighe could hardly have been exposed to it in this life. Also, to have mastered such an accent, Tighe would have had to be a skilled actress. As a 'typical American housewife' during the 1940s, she possessed none of these qualities. These last recordings of her voice under hypnosis illustrating this accent are more convincing of her life as Bridey Murphy than many of the controversial facts she stated that have subsequently been verified.

The 1952 case of Bridey Murphy became a landmark event in the history of hypnotic past-life regression, and the 1956 publication 'The Search for Bridey Murphy' written by Morey Bernstein became an internationally bestselling book written for lay readers. The book, which was even made into a movie, was a significant factor associated with a resurgence of public and professional interest as the book showed that reincarnation is a demonstrable fact.

Past-life psychotherapist Linda Tarazi describes the case of one client who never visited Spain, and neither speaks nor reads Spanish. This client (non-Catholic) revealed a volume of information over a three-year period and in some 36 formal hypnotic sessions about a past-life as a 16th century Spanish Catholic woman named Antonia Ruiz de Prado (Nov. 1555 – Mar. 1588). Tarazi (1990, p. 309) wrote,

> "*hundreds of hours of research over three years in two dozen libraries and universities, travel to Spain, North Africa, and the Caribbean, and correspondence with historians and archivists verified well over 100 facts, but uncovered no errors*".

The 'Antonia' personality provided with astonishing accuracy numerous out-of-the-way, detailed, and highly specialized facts unknown to even the learned professors "*who teach courses in Spanish history or the history of 16th-century Europe*". These facts could only be verified with great difficulty in fairly obscure sources, such as old Spanish books, inquisition records, and municipal records in the town of Cuena, Spain for which no expert could suggest an easier source. The information 'correctly' contradicted the authorities, e.g., the description of a building that housed the Tribunal of the Inquisition in 1583, the existence of a college in Cuenca in the mid-16th century, the number of Inquisitors at Cuenca from 1584 to 1588 among many others.

While some of the information in 'Spain' personality could be found with difficulty in history books and encyclopedia and in specialized history books at big libraries, many of the detailed facts could only be found in very old obscure Spanish books or never published at all and found only in local Spanish town or church archives. The 'Antonia' personality also gave accurate dates and descriptions of various events that were never published in English but only in Spanish. Tarazi (1990, pp. 327-29) concludes,

> "*After going over all this information, I am convinced that she knew no Spaniards.... In short, no one could have contributed any of the facts that she reported as Antonia.... When one considers the number and obscurity of the sources and the difficulty in extracting the pertinent information from them, it seems improbable that she would have read all of them. Add to that the facts that could only be obtained from the archives, both municipal and diocesan, in the town of Cuenca, and we approach the realm of impossibility for one who had never been to Spain and reads no Spanish*".

In spite of all the accurate details there seems to be no historical record documenting that Antonia herself had ever lived. Similar to Bridey Murphy, Antonia had lived a most ordinary life without any meaningful events. Therefore, even if Bridey and Antonia had really lived, their records were very unlikely to be found. As example, Antonia was baptized at a small, local church that she could not name. If recorded, those records probably would have disappeared long ago. Probably the church does not exist anymore or renamed. Her marriage by an unofficial priest at her husband's home and her death by drowning off an unnamed Caribbean island are also unlikely to have been recorded. Does history record the ordinary lives of every insignificant people who lived centuries ago? If a person supposedly remembered had an obscure station in life, it is very unlikely that we shall find any record to prove his existence. However, the great amount of obscure yet accurate factual information in other locations and other periods of history that these two personalities had revealed even baffles the historians. What is the source of their accurate practical knowledge with different names and identities, unless we agree that reincarnation is the only possible explanation?

Psychotherapist Peter Ramster (1994) described the case of Gwen MacDonald, a highly hypnotizable Australian woman who had no previous past-life memories, never traveled outside of Australia, and did not believe in reincarnation. However, during a series of hypnotic past-life regressions, she began to recall memories of being a young woman named Rose Duncan who was born in 1765 in Somerset, England and died in 1782 of pneumonia. Under hypnotic trance in Sydney, she revealed great many details about her past-life as Rose Duncan that could be checked easily.

After investigation, her revelations proved to be historically accurate, including names of people she had known, descriptions of clothing she wore, places and locales where she had lived and worked, such as her house and the name of the estate it was attached to and the surrounding towns and villages, and the routine of daily life in 18th century England.

During the time of Rose Duncan, there was a nearby abbey in Glastonbury about seven miles from her house. She described the place and its surrounding countryside in remarkable details where she spent many hours in peaceful solitude and tranquility. She narrated under hypnotic trance about the arches in the building, feathers, and plumes etched out of stone that adorned the sides of the arches and doors.

The revealed details fascinated Ramster. After researching as much as he could at libraries in Sydney and over the telephone in search of evidence, he decided to go to England to verify as much of G.M.'s (Gwen MacDonald) story as he could, accompanied by G.M., a film crew that would film and document what was uncovered in his investigation, and Basil Cottle of Bristol University who served as an independent witness. Ramster (1994, pp. 75-76) wrote,

> "*Some of the villages she [G.M.] mentioned no longer existed, and we had to search older maps to find them. One place called Blawerton, was today spelled Blotton. However, when we referred to the old maps we found that in 1790 the name of the village was Blawerton. Stone Chapel, another village she had told us of, doesn't exist today, but did in the year 1782. All the other villages she spoke of were there: East and West Penard, Bradley, Langport, Somerton, Taunton, and Croscombe.*"

At Somerset, G.M. correctly identified unmarked photographs of paintings of people of her past-life hanging on the walls in the house of the owners of a nearby large estate. An old manuscript printed in 1794 confirmed the accuracy of her identification. The existence of buildings was verified from old municipal records at Somerset. Other details of G.M. story were confirmed in local historical libraries, museums, and community records. Ramster (1994, p. 77) wrote,

> *"In the library of Taunton in Somerset, I [Ramster] researched the word 'tallet', which G.M. had used, but for which we could find no entry in current dictionaries. In a book of obsolete west country words, we found it. 'Tallet' was a word used in the west country of England, during the time of G.M.'s previous life, to refer to a room under a roof, such as a loft. It isn't used now and was never used anywhere but the west country of England. This information confirmed also that she has used the word correctly under hypnosis."*

G.M. gave so much extremely accurate details that even a historian would not know though she had never been outside of Australia in her present life. As time went on, G.M. began to become conscious in her waking state of many of the memories uncovered in hypnosis. Ramster (1994, p. 82) wrote.

> *"Before we had come to England, G.M. had no doubts about her past life when under hypnosis, but when she was awake, she was unsure. In England, much of the life became conscious to her and was no longer vague. She was able to talk of events and places that she could remember, at least in part. She knew where she was. The whole area was completely familiar to her. Although she was in a country 12,000 miles from her home, G.M. appeared to be on familiar ground."*

Then Ramster attempted to locate the abbey, G.M. correctly provided details about the surrounding countryside that were not on any map, such as small streams, valleys, the shape of hills, ruins of buildings, location of graveyards etc. Once G.M. helped Ramster to identify the location of the beloved abbey he brought her there and recounts what occurred.

> *"We finally took G.M. to the place in Glastonbury that she had pointed to on the map. G.M. stood on the pavement and waited for the blindfold to be removed. We did this to prevent her from getting road sign clues whenever we took her to a new location where we might test her ability to find something. As her vision cleared, she saw herself standing outside the much loved abbey she remembered. When G.M. entered the abbey she was visibly moved, and a little shaken. She walked and she talked, she showed us the feathers on the doorway that she had previously talked of, also the buildings.... Consequent to this conversation, I checked G.M.'s recall of the old abbey and its surroundings from a 1790 description of the area, written in an old manuscript printed about 1794 and this verified G.M.'s description well. It was described as being surrounded by marshy ground and the other things G.M. had talked of... The abbey was the same as she remembered it... Even the things that were missing, such as certain paving stones in some places, the pyramids, and the evidence of the Druids, through checking, were found to have been there."* (Ramster, 1994, pp. 80-81)

A local historian confirmed that such minute details of the abbey could never be found in any book. Therefore, unless G.M. had visited the place in her past-life, there is no other way she would have known about it. She also talked about an inn that she would pass on her way to and from the abbey that she called 'The Pilgrim's Inn' located near a hill she called 'Wearyall Hill' that she described as being humpbacked in shape. Though the name of the inn is changed, a quick check of the past records confirmed she had named it correctly for the 18th century. The inn stood exactly as she had described it. It was built of sandy colored stone, had two points on the roof, a bow type window on one side, and an opening in the middle through which the coaches used to pass.

At last, Ramster searched for the old house that Rose Duncan lived with an old 18th century survey map. They reached the place where a little village used to be, and the spot where five houses used to stand, one of which sold cider during her previous life. A very old man nearby had confirmed G.M.'s recollection. The five houses were torn down, but a fork in the stream and waterfall, and prominent landmarks along their path were correctly identified. The house of Rose Duncan was no more, but in the same place G.M. correctly identified a very odd-shaped stone hidden beneath the dirt resting in the same place from her previous lifetime. Under hypnosis in Sydney, she had drawn the peculiar markings on the stone, and after checking Ramster (1994, p. 87) found,

> "*There was enough to show that G.M.'s drawings of the markings certainly matched the markings on the old, blue-grey stone she had led us to. The most noticeable markings were the three vertical lines on the top left hand corner of the stone that G.M. had referred to as the stone mason's mark of three fingers. This was a most remarkable find. I would venture the odds against achieving that by chance are enormous. G.M. had found the very stone that she had drawn in Sydney, a feat far beyond any element of chance as it was in a place, in a country, she had never been to.*"

What is the best explanation for G.M/Rose Duncan case if not reincarnation? The well-known psychological fact is that a person may subconsciously hear, see or otherwise become aware of details which escape conscious awareness, and subconsciously store up these impressions. However, it is impossible that a person to all appearances sane and normal may gather a wealth of information on certain topics such as sixteenth century Ireland by a subconscious process while the conscious awareness learns almost nothing on these same subjects.

Skeptics often define hypnosis as a fantasy-generator and then define past-life experiences fantasy because they are elicited or evoked during hypnosis. However, one does not have to believe in reincarnation in order to recall a past-life during hypnotic regression session. Recalls can occur even in skeptical individuals who do not expect to experience a past-life during hypnosis. Secondly, past-life experiences do not occur only under hypnotic regression. It may happen in conventional psychotherapy sessions with therapists who neither work with past-life therapy nor believe in reincarnation and in patients whose philosophic beliefs and religious upbringing do not support such experiences. Also, how to explain the spontaneous recalls?

The evidence supporting the reincarnation hypothesis has been accumulating over the last fifty/sixty years. As Carl Sagan, a renowned skeptic, wrote (Sagan, 1996, p. 302), "*at the time of writing there are three claims in the [paranormal] field, which in my opinion, deserve serious study*". The third claim is "*that young children sometimes report details of a previous life, which upon checking turn out to be accurate and which they could not have known about in any other way than reincarnation.*"

Today past-life regression therapy represents a growing field of interest in clinical psychology in which there is a specialized peer-reviewed journal, Journal of Regression Therapy, that provides a forum for the communication of theoretical and empirical research into past-life therapy. Many professional hypnotists have regressed between them several hundreds of thousands of subjects throughout the world. If hypnotic regression is fanciful then how to explain the effectiveness of past-life therapy in resolving some psychiatric disturbances in the clinical setting that have received a good deal of experimental and clinical research interest during the past several decades?

7.4: Psychically channeled past-life readings by Edgar Cayce

"*You have inherited most from yourself, not from family! The family is only a river through which it [the entity, soul] flows!*"

Edgar Cayce

Edgar Cayce (March 18, 1877 to January 3, 1945) was an uneducated, poor, orthodox Christian who spent most of his life at Virginia Beach. His psychic abilities began to appear as early as his childhood. He was able to see and talk to his late grandfather's spirit, and often played with "imaginary friends" whom he said were spirits on the other side. He regarded them all as incorporeal because he could see through them if he looked hard enough.

Later in life, Cayce would find that he had the uncanny ability to put himself into a sleep-like state by lying down on a couch, closing his eyes, and folding his hands over his stomach. In this meditative trance state, he was able to place his mind in contact with all time and space – the universal consciousness, also known as the super-conscious mind. His specialty was in diagnosing medical conditions of people he had never met. Goldberg (1982, p. 55) noted, when in trance he would not only correctly diagnose the patient's medical problem but would recommend the correct treatment in approximately 99% of the cases he handled despite the fact that he had no conscious knowledge of medicine. If he would receive a letter from someone he did not know (and never had seen), and just from the patient's name, would recite diagnosis and prescription.

Cayce was a devoted churchgoer and Sunday school teacher, and had read the Bible from cover to cover every year for much of his life. Though initially he did not believe in reincarnation (orthodox Christianity does not support the doctrine of reincarnation), at the very late-stage in his life he changed his opinion when during one of his trance states he provided some "life readings" that traced the past-life of individuals with its consequences of a karmic past and aided them greatly in understanding their present problems. At the time of his death, he had given about 2,500 "life readings" that traced man's experience in past lives and the soul's return to Earth in a different body so that it can continue as an instrument of its own development. Some "life readings" were about individuals he did not know and never met, being given only their names and location just prior to the session. Sometimes Cayce would trace a portion of the origins of present health problems to a past-life difficulty.

From his perspective, the purpose of reincarnation is to enable a soul to understand the consequences of previous choices and to know that each individual is ultimately responsible for shaping and creating his or her life in the present. In other words, the past merely provided a framework of potentials and probabilities. With free will, we can turn the challenges life presents to us into stepping-stones toward growth, or we can see them as obstacles and stumbling blocks. Either way, we reap what we have sown. We constantly meet the consequences of previous deeds and attitudes. Each soul's wealth of experiences from the past acts as subconscious memory in the present. It is better to make an erroneous choice than to be idle and to do nothing because soul development is only possible through movement, growth, and activity.

Cayce is the most documented psychic of the 20th century. Since he would get his information while lying down in a self-induced hypnotic trance, he was popularly called "sleeping prophet". Some of his "life readings" took the subjects back to not only such exotic known lands as ancient India, China, Persia, and Egypt, but to such legendary places as 'Lost' City of Atlantis and sunken Lemuria in the Pacific. Cayce claimed that he once lived at Atlantis in a previous incarnation. He described that the lost race was a sophisticated technological civilization whose power source was crystals. The abuse of this power led to three nuclear disasters, the last in 10,000 BC. (Natsis and Potter, 1995, p. 29). Cayce revealed that a great number of souls who lived at Atlantis had been incarnating to America for a long time now. Their purpose is to create a new era of enlightened human consciousness. In all, Cayce referred to Atlantis no fewer than seven hundred times over a span of twenty years.

Cayce also revealed information about the history of humanity ranging from the creation to a time in the future when humans will evolve into beings with supernatural powers. But he also believed that those horrible future events he prophesized about could possibly be averted if humanity changed its behavior. In fact, that is the purpose for giving prophesies – to warn people to change, so that prophesies won't happen.

7.5: Xenoglossy: speaking an unlearned language

Xenoglossy (also written xenoglossia) is a rare and unusual paranormal phenomenon in which a person is able to spontaneously speak (and/or write) a foreign language without first having learned it, or even been exposed to it during the present lifetime. This term is derived from two Greek words, Xenos (means foreign or foreigner), and glossai (means tongues or languages). An event in which an individual who knows only English, has never been exposed to any other language, and who suddenly starts to speak in fluent Swahili with appropriate vocabulary, pronunciation, and grammar would be an example of xenoglossy. Charles Richet coined the term xenoglossy in 1905.

There are two types of xenoglossy – recitative and responsive. Recitative xenoglossy refers to the repetition, as if by rote, of phrases and sometimes longer passages in a foreign language. In responsive xenoglossy, subjects can converse intelligibly in the unlearned language. They can reply to statements or questions spoken in the language with appropriate responses in the same language (Stevenson and Pasricha, 1980, p. 332). The person may converse with native speakers sometimes in obscure dialects that have not been in use for centuries. There are also cases when the person under trance have communicated in languages no longer in use or known only to a handful of experts.

1. Harold Jaworski, under hypnosis, wrote down twenty-two words and phrases that he 'heard' himself speaking in a past Viking life. Working independently, linguists identified and translated ten of these words as Old Norse and several of the others as Russian, Serbian or Slavic. All words were associated with the sea (Whitton and Fisher, 1987, p. 210).
2. In 1931, a young English girl from Blackpool, known in the files of the Society for Psychical Research as Rosemary, began to speak in an ancient Egyptian dialect under the influence of the personality of Telika-Ventiu (lived some time in 1400 BC). In front of Egyptologist Howard Hume, she wrote down 66 accurate phrases in the lost language of hieroglyphs and spoke in a tongue unheard outside academic circles for thousands of years (Lazarus, 1993, p. 85). Today, only a few specialists in the world could even recognize or comprehend this lost language.
3. An eleven-year-old English-speaking boy under hypnosis was taped for eleven minutes as he spoke in an ancient Chinese dialect. When

the tape was taken to a professor at the Department of Oriental Studies at the University of California it turned out to be a recitation from a forbidden religion of Ancient China. (Fisher, 1986, p. 202).

4. American medium George Valentine under trance conducted séances in Russian, German, Spanish and Welsh. The Brazilian medium Mirabelli spoke and wrote long technical documents in more than thirty languages in the presence of scientists and crowds up to 5,000. (Lazarus, 1993, p. 121).
5. In 1977, doctors discovered that a convicted rapist named Billy Mulligan had two additional personalities, both of whom communicated in a different language. Mulligan was born and raised in the USA and spoke no foreign languages. But when taken over by Abdul, Mulligan could read and write in perfect Arabic. As Rugen he spoke perfect Serbo-Croat with a thick Slavic accent. (Lazarus, 1993, p. 83).
6. Biologist Lyall Watson described the case of a ten-year-old child, an Igarot Indian, living in the remote Cagayon Valley in the Philippines, had no contact with any language or culture other than his own. Yet under trance conditions, the child communicated freely in Zulu, a language he could not have even heard. Watson only recognized it because he had spent his early life in Africa. (Lazarus, 1993, p. 84).
7. Pearl Curgen, a medium from Saint Louis who was barely literate, began to write in astonishingly accurate Middle English. Under the guidance of a spirit entity she produced sixty novels, plays and poems, including a 60,000-word epic poem. (Lazarus, 1993, p. 119).
8. Jamie, a two-year-old boy from Ohio was very slow to start talking. He made sounds and his parents soon noticed that Jamie had his own vocabulary because if he wants drink, he would say 'iki', for daddy and mommy he would say 'baba' and 'seziz'. A family friend solved the mystery; Jamie was speaking Turkish though no one in the family had ever been to Turkey. At the age of four Jamie reverted to English. (Smedley, 2010, pp. 177-78).
9. A similar case was triggered by a car accident in 2007. Prior to the accident Czech speedway racer Matej Kus could barely fumble along in broken English. Yet after being knocked unconscious in the accident, paramedics and others at the crash site were amazed that Matej could suddenly speak clear and perfect English with a British accent and stopped speaking Czech, his mother tongue. But the ability didn't last long. Matej retained no memory of his temporary English fluency after recovery and started speaking Czech. (Vintini, 2013; Weaver, 2008, pp. 115-16).
10. Australian psychologist Peter Ramster, author of 'The Search for Lives Past', found that he could maintain fluid conversations in

> ancient French with his student Cynthia Henderson when Cynthia was under hypnosis. When she was out of the trance state, she possessed only a basic knowledge of the language. (Ramster, 1990, p. 227).

A mother of three children observed that her third child, Carol, was different in all her reactions from the other two. Carol did not speak English and formulated a complete language of her own. She was taken to several psychiatrists for treatment of her speech aversion. Her mother said,

> "*This attitude continued until she was four years of age. Several months before her birthday I said, 'Carol, let's go for a walk. Go upstairs and get your hat.' She looked at me blithely for awhile and trilled, 'Mais oui, Maman, ou est mon chapeaur'. ... I followed a strong hunch and took Carol to a private kindergarten run by a delightful French woman. Carol joined in the singing of French songs and after a month of joy in an atmosphere peculiarly her own, began to speak English volubly.*
>
> *She is now twelve years of age and continues to reach back to another life and time, with constant references to the beauty of France and her love for Paris. She said to me the other day, 'you must really go to Paris with me, Monie. It is beautiful. Of course, England is lovely too, but I always liked France much more than England.'*" (Curtiss, 1949, pp. 54-55)

There are thousands of recorded xenoglossy cases involving modern and ancient languages from all over the world. Stevenson (1974a, pp. 14-18) had investigated several spontaneous child xenoglossy cases, including those of Swarnlata Mishra, Bishen Chand Kapoor, Uttara Huddar, and Kumkum Verma Psychic investigators used scientific method to illustrate xenoglossy and claim that there are only two possible explanations – either spirit contact or past-life memory – both of which are evidence for the afterlife. Every alternative explanation has failed.

Sometimes this phenomenon happens spontaneously but more often it occurs while the person is under hypnosis or in an altered state of consciousness. Stevenson and his associates (1974b, 1976, 1984; Stevenson and Pasricha, 1980) have investigated several cases of recitative and responsive xenoglossy. One case involved a woman named Dolores Jay. She could not speak German, never studied German in school, whose ancestry did not include any Germans. However during a hypnotic past-life regression, she displayed a personality that called itself "Gretchen" who spoke only German. Over a period of three years (1971-72-73) more than 19 tape recordings of sessions with Gretchen where "*she could give sensible answers in German to questions put to her in that language*" (Stevenson, 1976, p. 70). On this case, Stevenson (1976, pp. 75-76) concludes,

> "*How then did DJ [Dolores Jay] acquire the ability to speak German that she showed during the periods of Gretchen's manifestation? In*

> *reporting the Jensen case [described next], I argued that the ability to speak a language is a skill that skills cannot be acquired without practice, cannot be transmitted either normally or paranormally, and that if it can be shown that a person has not normally learned a foreign language that he can speak responsively, then we have evidence of the existence and influence on him of another personality which at some time has learned that language. In short, authentic cases of responsive xenoglossy provide for me important evidence of the survival of human personality after death. A surviving personality capable of continuing to speak a foreign language and expressing it through an entranced person may do so through processes that we call reincarnation or possession*".

The Jensen Jacoby case involves a Swedish male personality manifested by a 37-year-old American housewife from Pennsylvania. The age regression technique purportedly moved the woman back beyond her youth to an earlier life as Jensen Jacoby, a Swedish peasant born in the 17th century. As Jensen, she was able to communicate in Swedish though she had never been exposed to Swedish language. Jensen appeared in eight hypnotic sessions, all during 1955-56. Stevenson (1974a) had studied this case in depth. He went at great lengths to rule out, as an explanation for Jensen's Swedish speech, all possibility of fraud or of forgotten experiences with Swedish or other Scandinavian languages. Finally, he commented that she could only have known Swedish if she remembered it from a previous existence. Stevenson's theory is supported by the woman's ability to name daily artifacts of the place and time in which Jensen Jacoby was said to have lived.

The case of Swarnlata Mishra (already described) is an example of xenoglossy. Swarnlata, at the age of four from India could perform of dances and sing songs in Bengali that she claimed have learned from one of her previous incarnations. In that life she was a man by the name Kamlesh who had learnt such songs and dances from her friend Madhu.

On xenoglossy phenomena, Stevenson (1984, p. 166) presented two hypotheses – the reincarnation hypothesis and the possession hypothesis – "*a personality surviving death [can] express in another physical body – whether through reincarnation or temporary possession – a language that he had learned in a previous life*". Stevenson's (1976, p. 76) hypothesis of reincarnation is,

> "*With the concept of reincarnation, we can think of a deceased personality which had once learned to speak the language in question as surviving death as an enduring personality which later becomes associated with a new physical body. Under the special circumstances provided by hypnosis, and perhaps at other times, the previous personality could come to the surface – albeit perhaps only partially, but yet with sufficient control to speak its native language.... If we interpret the case as one of*

reincarnation, this does not bind us to believing that DJ [Dolores Jay] is a 'one-to-one' reincarnation of a previously living Gretchen. It is conceivable that DJ lived a previous life in Germany when she could speak German and that the Gretchen personality provided an appropriate dramatic vehicle for the partial expression of memories of that previous life. The Gretchen personality might then resemble an historical novel comprised partly of fact, partly of fiction."

Stevenson's (1976, p. 76) hypothesis of possession is this,

"*In considering the hypothesis of possession, we can imagine a deceased personality capable of speaking its native language persisting in a discarnate state until a suitably entranced living person gives it an opportunity to manifest temporarily through that person's body. In the present case this would imply that DJ became a medium when hypnotized by C.J. [her husband, the Rev. Carroll Jay] and that at such times Gretchen became a communicator capable of controlling DJ with sufficient power to speak her native language.... Nor does the interpretation of possession oblige us to believe that the manifest personality of Gretchen corresponds exactly, or even closely, with a real person who once lived a terrestrial life and is now discarnate. On this hypothesis also, the phenomenal Gretchen personality could be a mixture blended from parts of DJ's own personality and elements of a real discarnate Gretchen lying behind and influencing the manifest communicator.*"

In the above case, no matter whether it fits into the reincarnation hypothesis or the possession hypothesis, one point is very clear – the afterlife exists.

Stevenson and Pasricha (1980, pp. 331-48) investigated the case of a 32-year-old Indian woman named Uttara Huddar born in Nagpur (India) in 1941. She had no memory of a past-life as a child, never been to Bengal and had not learned its language. However, she began to display memories and knowledge of foods, customs, and places in Bengal allegedly derived from a previous life lived 150 years ago when a personality that called herself 'Sharada Chattopadhaya' spontaneously emerged in 1974 and continued to do so at intermittent intervals until 1979. Stevenson and Pasricha (1980, pp. 332, 335, 337, 338) described,

"*Sharada could not speak Marathi (Uttara's native language) but spoke fluent Bengali. Although Uttara was (and is) married, Sharada dressed and behaved like a somewhat shy, married, Bengali woman. She did not recognize Utarra's parents or friends. She gave many details about her life and mentioned the names of places in Bengali with which she was familiar. From the information she gave ... it seems probable that a person corresponding to Sharada's statements lived during the years*

> *between 1810 and 1830...When Sharada first appeared, she was completely unfamiliar with tools, instruments, and appliances developed after the industrial revolution. For example, she knew nothing about electric appliances, gas stoves, fountain pens, or modern vehicles such as automobiles and trains. ... Her Bengali [was free of all English loan words and] had more Sanskrit words than modern Bengali has, as did Bengali in the eighteen and early nineteenth centuries. ...The Sharada personality and Uttara in her normal state appeared, at least at first, to know nothing about each other. Uttara seemed to be completely amnesic for what happened during a Sharada phase, and Sharada regarded Uttara's family as strangers. ...The Sharada phases have lasted from one day to about six weeks. .... [Sharada] gave the correct relationship she would have had to five of the male relatives of Brajanath Chattopadhaya [Sharada's purported father] whose names appear around his on the genealogy.*"

According to Stevenson and Pasricha (1980, pp. 344-45) this case is unusual because of three factors. First, the late age (Uttara was 32 years old) at which the past-life memories emerged is unusual since in most reincarnation cases that Stevenson has investigated, children are between the ages of two to four when they first speak of past lives and few memories occur spontaneously after the ages of eight to ten. Second, the complete displacement of memories of the primary personality (Uttara) by the past-life identity (Sharada) is unusual because most children who remember previous lives retain their primary identity and generalized reality orientation while simultaneously being aware of their past memories without their primary identity being suppressed or dominated or taken over by them, except in few exceptional cases. The last point is the relatively long duration during which the 'Sharada' personality remained in control – "*the average duration, because of two long phases lasting 41 and 43 days, was a little over eight and half days*" (Stevenson and Pasricha, 1980, p. 335) – is unusual for those few exceptional cases of children reported being "taken over" by their memories of past lives for only hours or a few days at the most.

Sharada could also write Bengali script. V. V. Akolkar (1992, pp. 223, 230) had extensively researched this case and included two samples of her writing in his paper. Skeptics say that Uttara learned Bengali by cryptomnesia or is perpetuating some hoax on the investigators. Such an explanation is not acceptable because "*if Uttara had learned Bengali – accidentally or fraudulently – she would have acquired modern Bengali, not that spoken 150 years ago*" (Stevenson and Pasricha, 1980, p. 342). Sharada's Bengali was free of English words and much more 'Sanskritized' than is modern Bengali. Few skeptics argue that Uttara genetically "inherited" Sharada's memories and facility with Bengali language. However, "*this hypothesis requires us to believe that memories of events and linguistic abilities can both be inherited. ... [and] further requires us to discard Sharada's own statement that she had no children.*" (Stevenson and Pasricha, 1980, p. 343).

Sharada cannot be a multiple personality of Uttara. Generally, the secondary personality demonstrates behaviors and memories related to different periods in the same life as the primary personality, but to have the secondary personality display behaviors and cognitions related to a period of 150 years ago and express memories of events that occurred before the primary personality's birth is logically not possible. Stevenson and Pasricha (1980, pp. 345-46) concluded,

> "*We are therefore entitled to conjecture, at least provisionally, that Sharada was a previous incarnation of the person now identified as Uttara. If that is so, then the Sharada memories are a part of Uttara, but one that remained hidden until they began to emerge periodically when she was in her thirties*".

In the search for an all-inclusive explanation for xenoglossy, many researchers have come to agree with Stevenson's understanding that points towards previous lives. According to this theory, following a trauma or in a hypnotic state, the personality from a previous incarnation comes through and the person exhibits knowledge that he could not possibly have known in this life. Some skeptics such as Sarah Thomason argues that Stevenson's evidence is simply too thin to make such a claim but cannot give any better explanation. Initially Stevenson was also highly skeptical with regard to cases of regressive hypnosis. However, as time passed he became one of the most prolific authors on the subject. Later, as his research progressed, he turned his attention to the cases involving young children because they were more easily able to recall information from past-lives without the need for hypnotizing or a traumatic event to reveal their hidden distant past. Goldberg (1982, p. 56) commented,

> "*When children are regressed and speak or write foreign languages fluently, which they have not been exposed to in this life, I consider this proof of reincarnation. One could rationalize a word or a phrase being mastered in a foreign language by a child, but not an entire language. There is no way that a person's subconscious mind could have been exposed to an entire foreign language without conscious awareness of this. When adults or children start writing in hieroglyphics or other dead languages, I start thinking about past lives.*"

In the reliable historical sources there is a wealth of examples involving xenoglossy. Religious scriptures and pseudoscience have tried to explain this in various ways but there is not a single adequate explanation except reincarnation theory. While the xenoglossy phenomenon is intriguing, perhaps even more fascinating is the prospect of imagining where such ability could originate. Here the cause is more mysterious than the phenomenon itself.

7.6: Intermission memories between two reincarnated lives

In addition to one or more reincarnated past-life recalls, some people can recall events that occurred between the deaths of the previous persons and their own births (the intermission period) and give accounts of how they came to be born (the intermission memories). People in these cases make more verified statements about the past-life they remember than do other people who cannot. They also recall more number of past-lives. Studies had shown that these people have an unusually strong memory, and demonstrate more ability to recall a variety of memories from the past-life either accurate in most details or totally accurate. Cases of this type are reported from all over the world, but mostly come from Burma (Myanmar) and then Japan. Masayuki and Akira (2014, p. 481) noted that those children who speak intermission memories are eloquent, speak very clearly, and speaking with concentration. One parent reported that her stammering child became fluent only when he talked about life-between-life memories. Accounts of intermission experiences vary, and no two accounts are identical. There are, however, recurring themes, events, and chronologies.

During intermission period, the discarnate may remain in a terrestrial environment, or in a heavenly environment. In a small number of cases the discarnate remains in both the environments (with movement between them). An English girl, Nicola Wheater, told her parents, "*I went to sleep and died and I saw God in Heaven before I was born*" (Harrison and Harrison, 1991, p. 13). When both terrestrial and heavenly environments were described, the subjects said they spent most of their time in heaven but sometimes visited the earth. An Indian girl, Pratima Saxena, said that she "went up" after she died but whenever her (previous) son was in trouble, she "came down" to attend to him (Stevenson, 1997b, vol. 1, p. 594). A Thai girl, Ratana Wongsombat, said that she went first to heaven but came down to look for something she had left in a meditation hut (Stevenson, 1983a, p. 36). One unnamed Dutch girl told her mother, "*I was with the angels in the sky and I looked down upon the earth. . .. I flew to the earth, walked into a house and looked around*" (Rawat and Rivas, 2007, p. 197). Virginia Tighe (Bridey Murphy) recalled under hypnosis that following her death as Bridey in 1864, she had lived a long time "in the spirit world" before her rebirth in 1923 as Virginia Tighe in the American state of Iowa (Bernstein, 1956, p. 119). In this intermission period, Virginia said that while in a state of "purgatory" after her death and prior to her present reincarnation, she had seen and conversed with several persons whom she had known while living in Ireland. She also talked to her younger brother who had died "when just a baby", but who nevertheless was said to have been able to converse with her in English.

Kazuya, a Japanese boy, said that after killing himself he spent some time in a "reflection room" before deciding to be reborn to his former mother. Kazuya made a prebirth compact with three other spirits to be reborn around the same time. When they met after reincarnating, the children recognized each other (Ohkado, 2016, pp. 529-30). Masayuki and Akira (2014, pp. 477-78) referred the case of a Japanese boy born in 1806 called Katsugoro. This is one of the earliest cases with intermission memories from Japan (Hirata Atsutane wrote original report in Japanese in 1823). When he gave detailed memories of his past-life, he was taken to his house in a nearby village where he claimed to have lived, and was eventually accepted by his previous parents as their son Tozo reborn. He talked about his life-between-life memories, saying that after his death, he was guided to a beautiful field by a man with long white hair, and after spending some time there, he was led by that man to his present house and reborn.

Sharma and Tucker (2004) had conducted a scientific investigation based on the reports from 35 Burmese subjects, and indicated that the intermission memories consist of three stages – the transitional stage, the stable stage in a particular location or in another realm, and the return stage involving choosing parents, conception, and of being reborn. This model may extend to include a fourth stage, life in the womb, and a fifth stage, memories of birth and its immediate aftermath (Matlock, James G. and Giesler-Petersen, 2016, p. 6). All the stages, collectively leaves the impression of a continuous experience from death to birth. Everyone may not remember all the stages, but this described format suited the majority of the cases, and set up a stepping-stone for further analysis.

There are many published cases with intermissions of less than nine months, and a few cases with intermissions of one or a few days or even a few hours. Stevenson (1987, p. 171) found from his investigations that the intermission length varies from a few hours to 20 years or more. Elsewhere Stevenson (1973, p. 31) mentions a solved Sri Lankan case with an intermission of 82 years, which may be the record-holder. Amongst the Igbo tribe, who are strong believer of reincarnation, the intermission period varies from six months to 540 months (Stevenson, 1986, p. 206). In even rarer cases the intermission is a negative one; that is, the subject was born before the previous person died. The case of the Buddhist monk Chaokhun Rajusthajarn illustrates this phenomenon. Chaokhun Rajusthajam was born about a day before the death of the previous person and claimed to recall the events surrounding the transition from one body to another. Some researchers suggest a significantly shorter intermission in cases where previous person had a violent death than in cases where the death had been normal. The presence of intermission memories perfectly strengthens the cases of reincarnation by showing the continuation of journey of the astral body from one life to another.

The transitional stage: This stage most often includes the memories of the previous personality's funeral. One person remembered seeing the burned house in which the previous personality and her mother died. Often some of the events recalled during this stage are uncomfortable or unpleasant.

The person may see the preparation of his dead body for funeral. When he tries to contact grieving relatives, he finds that he is unable to communicate with the living. One person said he did not realize he was dead. Many people reported being repelled by the weeping of their relatives (Sharma and Tucker, 2004, p. 107). Departed souls who choose to comfort someone who is grieving, or have other reasons to stay near the place of their death for a while, experience no sense of time loss (Newton, 2016b, p. 1). Thai monk Chaokhun Rajsuthajarn reported attending the funeral of the previous personality and trying to interact with the guests, only to realize that he was invisible to them. Purnima Ekanayake, a child from Sri Lanka reported that she had observed 'his' (in her past-life she was a man, Jinadasa Perera – a 35 year old man who died on the spot in a road accident) dead body, funeral process and gave complete details how people mourned and cried (Haraldsson, 2000, p. 18). Jasbir (Stevenson, 1974b, p. 47) reported that after death he (as Sobha Ram in past-life who died in a chariot accident) met a Sadhu (a Hindu Holy Man or saint) who advised him to "take cover" in the body of Jasbir.

The tunnel experience or the sense of entering a dark region of the NDErs is not present in intermission memory cases. Some people with intermission memories say that they were offered a food, usually a fruit, by the "man in white", but managed to dispose of it when he was not looking. They credit their ability to recall previous lives to having done this. The "fruit of forgetfulness" has been reported from several cultures, but sometimes with transformations. In the Vietnamese case of Le Quong Hu'o'ng (1972, pp. 535-39), it is a soup and the subject disposes of it by slipping it to his dog. The dog had been killed at the same time as he. However, Ampan Petcherat (Stevenson, 1983a, p. 68) and Santosh Sukla (Stevenson, 1997b, vol. 1, p. 556) said that they ate the offered fruit; nevertheless, they recalled their previous lives and the intermission before their present lives anyway.

This stage often ends when an elder (dead) relative or an old man dressed in white directs the discarnate to a place where he then stays for the bulk of the intermission experience. This is the next stage.

The stable stage in a particular location: Most people remember this stage more clearly than other two. Here the discarnate is more stable, and lives in a particular location with peace of mind. Sometimes they are given a schedule or duties to which they must attend. Most of them stay in a tree, others live in pagoda, abandoned places, and some hang around near the place of death. Stevenson (1983a) reported the case of Bongkuch Promsin from Thailand who lived in a tree for seven years after death and then followed his present father home on a bus. Time has no meaning for a discarnate entity. One woman reported not being able to leave the site where she had buried her jewellery in life – such is the attraction for materialistic life. They often say that they observed events that actually occurred at this time.

Veer Singh (Stevenson, 1975, pp. 328-29) said that during an 11-year intermission he had lived in a peepal tree after his death. He mentioned lawsuits involving the previous person's family, and a camel bought by the family. He also stated the names of the children born after the previous person's death and recognized two of them. Furthermore, he said that he had become annoyed with some women who were swinging from a branch of his peepal tree, and caused the plank on which they were sitting to break. All these incidents had actually occurred as he had described. In another case that Stevenson (1972, p. 237-footnote) had investigated, the subject claimed that as a discarnate spirit he had lived near the house of his family and sometimes took the food they prepared. His statements accorded with observations by the family that often some food they had prepared had in fact mysteriously disappeared during this period.

During this stage, they often see or interact with other discarnate personalities. These interactions are generally pleasurable but can be abusive. Perhaps there are variations in social practices in discarnate existence, just as there are in physical life. One person reported being abused by other spirits who threw objects at him, and having to walk long distances (Sharma and Tucker, 2004, p. 108). The discarnate entity is often assigned some task such as that of guarding temples or treasures (Stevenson, 1983a, pp. 209-10). Sometimes the discarnate goes to a strange location, as example, Purnima Ekanayake floated in the air in semi-darkness for a few days with many other discarnate personalities floating around. Then she saw some 'light', went there and then reincarnated in a new body (Haraldsson, 2000, p. 18). Purnima had reincarnated after two years and four months. The specific imagery of the place of "semi-darkness", where discarnate personalities float, most probably was a symbolic culture-specific theme.

Masayuki and Akira (2014, p. 482) investigated a total of 21 children with life-between-life memories. Thirteen of the 21 children described the place as "cloud or sky", and three of them as "light." The remaining five described the place variously as "a wide space where you can see the Earth", "a place like a star", "a place where there are a number of levels", "up there", and "a place in the shape of a long ellipse". All of them said they were not alone in the life-between-life states. Fourteen claimed there was a god or god-like entity who was like a counselor, making suggestions about their future parents or giving permission to be born to the parents they chose. Twelve claimed that they were with their current family members (mostly brothers or sisters) and/or friends. One child said that there were many "light balls" present, but that it was difficult to say who they were, although he believed some of them were somebody close to him in current life. Thirteen children described how they felt in the life-between-life state. Eight of them said they felt "peaceful" or "calm", and two said "joyful" or "excited". The remaining three said "difficult to describe", "not different from what I feel now", and "lonely".

Fifteen said they were able to see "earthly affairs" from that place, but their memories were limited, relating only to their parents and households.

The recurring thematic elements of intermission memories, particularly the interaction with other discarnate personalities, taking guidance from a mystical being or presence (elder person, a man in white cloths, Sadhu) and occasional suggestions of being in another realm, bring to mind accounts of NDEs. However, if we compare NDEs with that of intermission period experiences, the 'life' of an earth-bound discarnate is not that beautiful, but pleasant. One woman reported that she was far more beautiful as a discarnate and had pretty dresses of gold. A poor woman reported that all her needs were taken care of as a discarnate and that her experience was "quite pleasant". One person said, "*I was quite happy*", and the other stating a more ambiguous, "*It appeared to be a very pleasant life*". More common were statements of discomfort, particularly when the discarnate is around weeping relatives, as example, "*the relatives started weeping. ... I could not bear it*"; "*We felt very hot if any of our relatives wept for us. ... We would have to flee*"; and "*Weeping scares away discarnates*" (Sharma and Tucker, 2004, pp. 108-09). Some people reported that they could change form during intermission period as they wished, and not having to eat. These two points suggest a lack of bodily sensation or limitations. Many people described the clothes they were wearing, usually the clothes of the deceased.

Next is the final stage when the discarnate decides to come back to experience another earthly life in a new human body.

The return stage: In this stage, the discarnate chooses his parents for the next life. More than half of the 35 Burmese subjects reported characteristics of this stage. Some discarnate personalities follow their future parents to home as apparitions, usually on their own initiative, as the parents passed by while performing everyday tasks, such as bathing in the pond or returning home from work etc. Stevenson and Keil (2005, p. 177) reported that some Burmese children who were Japanese soldiers in the past-life also remembered their intermission period. One child remembered being killed as a soldier near a monastery, which was about two kilometers from the child's birthplace. His father went to the area of the monastery to gather firewood; and the child as a discarnate personality followed his father home. Another child also claimed to have followed his father home, after committing suicide (the wounded Japanese soldier had shot himself) in the zoo at Rangoon. Further investigation confirmed that the child's father had really visited the zoo in Rangoon before his wife became pregnant with the child.

Often the elder, or the old man in white direct them to their future parents. Some of them commented on how they gained entrance to the mother's body. This was most often by transforming into a grain of rice or speck of dust in the water and being ingested by the mother. A few went to considerable lengths, having to try repeatedly when either the guardian spirits have rebuffed them or the water was thrown out as dirty (Sharma and Tucker, 2004, p. 108). An Indian boy named Sunder Lal recalled having been a man who had died of plague. The dead body was thrown into a river where Sunder Lal's mother-to-be happened to be bathing; he saw her and accompanied her home (Sahay, 1927, p. 17). One person said that he had waited by the village well for the mother of the previous life to come when his mother came instead. Sometimes they say they remember 'sending' announcing dreams to their future parents and on rare occasions, they claim to remember having visited their parents as apparitions before they were born. Occasionally the announcing dreams are so vivid that the person wakes up expecting to see the discarnate beside the bed (Stevenson, 1982, p. 354-footnote). Such cases occur particularly often in Turkey, Burma and among the Tlingit and other tribes of north-west North America.

In the investigation of Masayuki and Akira (2014, p. 482) 12 out of 21 Japanese children said that they remembered when they came to their mother's womb. Three of them said 'somebody' (a god, a shining ball, or an angel-like entity) helped them to come to their mother. Stevenson (1997b, vol. 2, p. 1812) recorded the case of a Burmese girl named Ma Par who recalled being a British officer aboard a reconnaissance plane that ran out of fuel and crashed in Burma during World War II. She thought of England and found herself there, but the King of Death forced her to return to Burma. Later she went to England a second time, but again was pulled back to Burma and told she would have to be reborn there, although the choice of family was left up to her.

The reason not all reincarnated souls remember life-between-life memories is that all people are not equally mindful. Memory is a function of what we could call "mindfulness". The more mindful, alert, or logical we are in a given moment of life, the more likely we are to have recall of that moment later in our existence. It is possible that people who are generally more mindful live their intermission periods in a more memorable way, while people who are less mindful might pass their intermission periods in a more dream-like state of mind so that their intermission memories just fade away.

There are cases when a child can remember his intermission memories without remembering a past-life. For these children, the term "life-between-life memories" or "intermission memories" may be regarded as inappropriate because it implies the existence of past-life memories. However, anyway I will use the term. The existence of children with life-between-life memories and no past-life memories is not unexpected if the survival of consciousness and reincarnation are real. Masayuki and Akira (2014, p. 477) have recorded several such incidents, as example, a six-year-old boy recalls his experience before he was born, saying, "*I was flying in the sky, looking for my mother. Looking down, I could see my mother and chose her. I thought she was the best person. She looked lonely, and I thought, 'If I come to her, she will not feel lonely anymore.*'" A nine-year old girl describes the place where she was before she came to her mother, "*There were many children, or souls, and a God, an entity with authority*". When she was asked if the authority was like a schoolteacher, she replied, "*No, no, no! He is much more generous…he was looking after us, like a counselor.*" Many children in Japan claim to remember such life-between-life experiences.

Often these discarnate spirits select their parents. Masayuki and Akira (2014, p. 484) reported that out of 21 cases, 17 children said that they chose their parents. Nine of them said that they chose only their mothers. Eight of them said that they chose their fathers as well as their mothers. Of the eight, four said that they chose their fathers and mothers simultaneously, and the remaining four said they chose their mothers first. Often their statements matched their parents' memories before they were born. A female child of five or six years said to her mother, "*When you were young, I frequently came to you.*" This statement matches her mother's experiences before she got married. She often felt that a small child (or a child-like entity) was looking at her and bustling around her.

Another child, who started talking about her life-between-life memories at the age of five, said to her mother, "*I saw you in a gorgeous white dress. You were holding a dog.*" The mother had indeed held a dog while wearing her wedding dress (a photograph of this event had confirmed this; she emphasized that the child had never seen it before the statement). After the wedding ceremony, she had entered a room where the dog was awaiting her return. She clearly remembered this experience because holding a dog in a wedding dress is not something you are supposed to do. A six years old child drew a picture of a four-storey building surrounded by mountains and said, "*This is where you lived. I saw you there.*" Her mother was astounded because, as a child, she lived in a four-storey building from which she could see the surrounding mountains.

Leininger et al. (2009, pp. 153-54) investigated the case of James Leininger, an extremely strong American case of the reincarnation. James who was a World War II fighter pilot, made statements similar to those made by these Japanese children. When his father, Bruce, picked up four-year-old James and told him how happy he was to have him as a son, James said, "*That's why I picked you: I knew you would be a good daddy.*" Perplexed, Bruce said, "*What did you say?*" James replied, "*When I found you and Mommy, I knew you would be good to me*". Bruce then asked, "*Where did you find us?*" James replied, "*Hawaii. It was not when we all went to Hawaii. It was just Mommy and you. I found you at the big pink hotel.*" Bruce and his wife had indeed stayed at a pink hotel in Hawaii 11 months before their son James was born.

When they are asked why they decided to be born, the reasons were – to meet or help their mothers, to help other people, to become happier than they were in their previous lives, and to enjoy life. One child said he did not remember why he was born because he forgot the reason when he was born in order to find what it is in the current life (Masayuki and Akira, 2014, p. 482). Though apparently life-between-life memories of children without past-life memories have little evidential value, there is no notable difference between those who remember of intermission period with past-life memories and those without such memories.

Therefore, intermission memories are part of the overall reincarnation phenomena. Intermission experiences and NDEs have many extraordinary parallels. A near-death experiencer returns to the same body (the brain's hold on consciousness is reduced or impaired temporarily), whereas the recounters of intermission memories have died but were reborn in new bodies (the brain's hold on consciousness is severed permanently, and hence the consciousness adopts a new body). This is the reason the first stages of the NDE are extremely similar to the first stages of the intermission experience. Hence, intermission experiences pick up where NDEs leave off. While NDE phenomena are well-researched, the intermission memory studies did not receive much attention as they are usually unverifiable. However, a careful examination of these stronger memory cases is required to understand how much control we do have over the reincarnation process, and how the law of Karma regulates the details of our rebirth in the world of mortals.

From some rarest cases, it seems that during intermission period the memories of two discarnate entities about their past lives may join together and then remembered in confusing manner when they reincarnate. As example, one of Stevenson's subjects, Imad Elawar recalled many details concerning the life of a certain Ibrahim Bouhamzy, but he also recalled a truck accident in which Ibrahim's cousin and good friend Said had been involved. A claimant to Said's memories was also found. Imad seems to have been somewhat confused over which of his memories related to Ibrahim and which to Said. The case is complicated but genuine because the facts are verified. Ibrahim knows everything what Imad remembered. The second subject, besides recalling the truck accident, spoke of many events in the life of Ibrahim's cousin which played no part in Ibrahim's memories. Apart from the events surrounding the truck accident, the memories of Imad and the other subject were completely different. We seem to be confronted with nothing more exotic than the independent memories of two subjects whose previous persons had been intimately acquainted.

Various researchers such as, W. G. Roll, Stevenson, M. Grosso, D. S. Rogo and G. R. Schmeidler had tried to interpret this case but it seems that a final conclusion could not be reached. Is it possible that the individual memories of Ibrahim and Said have joined postmortem and then reappeared in both Imad and the second subject, resulting in 'merged' (as Imad came from two bodies) and 'divided' (Said split apart and went to two bodies) rebirth? In my opinion, this is a classic case of split incarnation i.e., a single soul living parallel lives.

In this respect the case resembles Stevenson's (1980, pp. 194-235) cases of Ismail Altinkilic (past-life name, Abit Suzulmus) and Cevriye Bayri (past-life name, Sehide Suzulmus), who independently recalled lives of persons who had been married. In previous life the married couple was murdered on the same night (January 31, 1957), and in present life they are united again. But how they united? Even if two people are reincarnated, how in the world could they find each other in the next life?

7.7: Pre-birth communications and reincarnation

Pre-birth communications in the form of announcing dreams (before / during pregnancy and after birth) usually occur to pregnant women but may occur to fathers as well as to other relatives or close acquaintances of the mother (Mills, 1988, pp. 23-59). Following these highly significant dreams, extraordinary experiences, such as visions, apparitions, poltergeist activities and messages passed through mediums might occur. Tucker (2005, p. 9) wrote that 22% of 1100 cases in a computerized database at the University of Virginia had announcing dreams. Expectant fathers sometimes dream of their unborn children before their wives do. Dreams of men and women have no apparent difference in content. Some expectant parents had exactly the same dream content.

When they occur in reincarnation cases, these experiences help parents to know the past-life identities of their unborn children, prepare for the unexpected and can lead to life-changing decisions as indicative in the case of Alexandrine Samona (Johnson, 1936, p. 281; Curtiss, 1949, p. 58). On March 15, 1910 Alexandrine died of meningitis at the age of five. After three days she visited her mother in her dream and said, "*Mamma, do not cry any more. I have not left you for good…I shall return as small as that (showing a little embryo)*". The dream was repeated after three days. A few days later while the parents attended a séance, Alexandrine assured them that she would be reborn through her mother 'before Christmas' and her father's sister, Jeanne, who died at the age of 15 would incarnate with her. Alexandrine cautioned her mother that if she did not stop grieving she would give them greatly depleted bodies. Jeanne stated that Alexandrine would be reborn '*at least a little more beautiful*'. On November 23, the mother gave birth to twin girls who differed perceptibly in height, complexion and figure. The smaller was a faithful copy of Alexandrine at the time she was first born. There was such a striking resemblance, likes and dislikes, as the child started growing up that they named her Alexandrine II. This perfect identification between the two – living and the dead – cannot be a chance coincidence.

Announcing dreams are more vivid and realistic than other dreams, and there are so many symbolic elements that they are easily and intuitively understood, and do not require interpretation as ordinary dreams often do. Mascaro (2016a, pp. 192, 201-02; 2016b, p. 7) confirmed that announcing dreams are not exclusively visual and lucid but may have sensory or auditory dimensions also.

Francis Story and Ian Stevenson had independently studied a Burmese reincarnation case where a woman shortly before her pregnancy had a strange dream. An elderly sage dressed in white came to her house and told her that he was 'entrusting' to her a recently deceased man. Then the sage told her the name of the man and went out of the house and returned with this man, left him there, and vanished. Next day, a widow came to tell the woman that she had dreamed of an elderly sage dressed in white informing her that he was sending her late husband (same name) to be the woman's child (Story, 1975, pp. 197-98; Stevenson, 1983a, p. 245). Sometimes a discarnate entity requests permission to be reborn in the family. Stevenson (1987, p. 100) heard one such petitionary announcing dream. The husband of a Burmese woman was away from home on a long journey. In her dream a deceased friend asked to be reborn as her child but she did not allow. When her husband returned home, he told her he had dreamed of the same old friend, making the same request, and he (in his dream) had welcomed him in their family. Their next child had the past-life memories of his parents' friend, which suggests that his father's acceptance had prevailed over his mother's rejection.

In 1942, Burma was under Japanese occupation. Though Burmese people had strong hatred for the Japanese, due to some unknown reasons a Burmese woman, Daw Aye Tin, became friendly with a regularly bare-chested Japanese army man who had been working in a military camp as a cook near her house. They regularly discussed the relative merits of Burmese and Japanese food and various cooking techniques. When the war ended life returned to a semblance of normality. Later, during 1953 when Daw Aye Tin was pregnant with her fourth child, on three occasions (in an interval of five to ten days) dreamed of this Japanese cook wearing shorts and no shirt with whom she had long lost contact. The dream contents were exactly same – the cook said that he would come stay with her. On December 26, 1953 Daw gave birth to a daughter and called her Ma Tin Aung Myo. The baby was perfect with one small exception – a thumb-sized birthmark on her groin.

At the age of four, Ma Tin Aung Myo recalled for the first time the past-life memories of a Japanese man who had five children, and that he had been an army cook. She remembered that she (as the Japanese soldier) was near a pile of firewood next to an acacia tree wearing short pants with a big belt and no shirt. An Allied aircraft spotted him and dived at him spraying machine gun bullets. He ran for cover and as he did so, he was hit by a bullet in the groin, which killed him instantly. She described the plane as having two tails.

This was later identified as a Lockheed P-38 Lightning, an aircraft used by the Allies in the Burma campaign. Stevenson (1977b, pp. 202-06) had recorded this case after interviewing Ma Tin Aung Myo three times between 1972 and 1975 about her reincarnation memories. Announcing dreams, birth marks, past-life recall and firsthand verification by Stevenson – the simplest explanation is best one that this case strongly supports the reincarnation hypothesis.

Many women get the first indication that they are pregnant (or will be shortly) through announcing dreams. They may also come to know about the unborn child's sex and many physical and behavioral details. There is no shortage of examples when announcing dreams gave specific information about the child's identity, past-life history, and advice on how to care for the child's special needs after birth (Bowman, 2001, p. 213). Hinze (2016, pp. 27-28) talked to a woman who with her first pregnancy dreamed three times that her baby was a boy with blond hair, born two months premature, yet perfectly all right. Indeed, her baby was born at 33 weeks, a blond and healthy boy. Before the same woman knew she was pregnant a second time, she dreamed that she had twin girls, as was later confirmed by the doctors. Another woman dreamed that she was sitting on the floor playing with a two years old boy. The baby told her that he was going to build her a castle with blocks and giggled. When the boy was born, he turned to have exactly the physical features as in the dream and he had the same giggle as she had heard in the dream (Hallett, 2002, pp. 45-46). Bowman's (2001, pp. 200-01) opinion is, these strange visions later prove to be so accurate, matching the appearance of the child after birth, that parents are convinced that they had been given a pre-birth glimpse of their children.

Stevenson (2003, p. 152) studied the case of Samuel Helander whose mother became pregnant shortly after her stepbrother died unexpectedly. She did not want a child and considered an abortion. Then she received an announcing dream where her stepbrother told her, 'Keep that child!' She did, and after he was born, Samuel displayed a variety of behaviors suggestive of the reincarnation of the stepbrother. He started speaking of past-life memories at the age of eighteen months and continued to do so for several years.

Similar to announcing dreams, there are also departure dreams, in which a deceased person tells his family where he will be reborn or has been reborn. Pasricha et al. (2005, p. 378) investigated one such case from Turkey. A young man called Salih Girisken had an accidental death in 1974 when a factory building collapsed during a heavy storm. His mother dreamed that he had been reborn in a certain house in a village some 20 km away. She and later two brothers of Salih went there, but they were not allowed to see the boy, and only confirmed his identity years later when the boy began to speak about the previous life at the age of one and a half to two years. The two families were not related and had no contact before the case developed. It means,

Salih's mother had received accurate information in her dream. The baby had birth marks and birth defects at the exact locations where Salih had received injuries.

In a Burmese case, a newly deceased man appeared in the dream of a relative and said, "*I am going to live with Ma Htwe. Please look after my children*". Ma Htwe was then a young single woman. Later, she married and gave birth to a child who recalled the life of the man in the dream (Stevenson, 1997a, vol. 2, p. 1405). Departure dreams are much rarer than announcing dreams, and usually come after the birth of the child. In some cases, the reincarnated child complains to his previous family about his present circumstances. One mother dreamed her deceased son told her "*Help! I have got myself in a poor family. Come rescue me*". Another person dreamed of being told that the new father was an alcoholic, and in a third instance, the previous person alleged that his new mother was feeding him at her convenience, rather than when he needed food, leaving him hungry.

Stevenson (2001, p. 175) had observed that reincarnation-related announcing dreams were frequent among the Burmese, the Turkish Alevi, and indigenous peoples of northwestern North America, but reported rarely from the Sinhalese of Sri Lanka, from the Druze of Lebanon, and the Igbo of Nigeria, though all of whom have abundant reincarnation cases. Tlingit and Sri Lankan announcing dreams are symbolic. In Burma, the dreams are polite and petitionary. Rather than announcing their intention to come to the family, Burmese figures request permission to be reborn there (Stevenson, 1987, p. 99). Several researchers, such as Bauer et al. (2005), Carman and Carman (2013), Hallett (2002), and Hinze (2016) had recorded a great number of pre-birth communications in recent years, but follow-up investigations or analysis are lacking. However, Mascaro (2016b, p. 7) believes that serious research with announcing dreams is only beginning.

Reincarnation messages can also be delivered by waking visions, apparitional experiences, words heard from unknown sources and information through mediums. Many cases are recorded, e.g., the case of Maung Yin Maung from Stevenson's file. Announcements may also be associated with haunting or poltergeist effects (Mills, 1988, pp. 23-59). Other announcements come in the form of mediumistic communications. The cases of Alexandrine Samona (Shirley, 1936), Paulo Lorenz (Stevenson, 1974b, pp. 203-15), Hair Kam Kanya (Stevenson, 1983a), and Jacira (Andrade, 1980) provide examples of announcements in mediumistic communications.

When apparitions appear with a birth announcement, they typically match the deceased person whose life the child later recalls. Stevenson (1997a, vol. 2, p. 2091) recorded nine such cases with apparitions of deceased persons sighted between death and rebirth.

In the 1902-06 Italian case of Blanche Battista (Dillon, 2001, pp. 35-36; Gustus, 2011, pp. 123-24), the Battista family had a little daughter born in

Rome whom they called Blanche. They employed a French-speaking Swiss 'Nanny' called Marie to look after the child. Marie taught Battista to sing in French a lullaby song (for babies to sleep relax). Blanche was very fond of this song and it was sung to her repeatedly. Unfortunately Blanche died during 1902, and Marie returned to Switzerland. Mr. Battista wrote, "*The cradle song which would have recalled to us only too painful memories of our deceased child, ceased absolutely to be heard in the house ... all recollection of it completely escaped our minds.*" Three years after the death of Blanche her mother, Signora Battista, became pregnant, and in the fourth month of pregnancy she had a strange vision. She was wide awake when Blanche appeared to her 'with childlike joyousness' and said in her old familiar voice, "*Mother, I am coming back.*" The vision then melted away. Though the family was skeptical, when the new baby was born in February, 1906, they gave her the name Blanche. The new Blanche resembled the old in every possible way. When the second Blanche was six years old, an extraordinary thing happened. In her father's own words,

> "*While I was with my wife in my study which adjoins our bedroom. We heard, both of us, like a distant echo, the famous cradle song, and the voice came from the bedroom where we had put our little daughter Blanche fast asleep. ... We found the child sitting up on the bed and singing with an excellent French accent the cradle song which neither of us had certainly ever taught her. My wife asked her what it was she was singing, and the child, with the utmost promptitude answered that she was singing a French song. 'Who, pray, taught you this pretty song?' I asked her. 'Nobody, I know it out of my own head,' answered the child.*"

Sometimes words are heard from unknown sources. Bowman (2001, pp. 195-97) described a two-year-old girl named Lauren who spoke with her deceased brother Roger on her toy telephone. Roger died in a road accident. After a year of regular conversations with Roger, Lauren informed to her mother, "*Roger said he's coming back very soon*". When her mother tried to explain that Roger was dead, Lauren insisted, "*But I've been talking to him and he told me he's coming back!*" A few days later when shopping, Lauren wanted to buy clothes for an infant boy. In the following year her mother became pregnant. She gave birth to Donald, who when he was able to speak made dozens of accurate statements about the accident, other events in Roger's life, and changes in the house after his death.

Pre-birth communications are real. Beliefs and commitments held in life are carried over into death and continue to help shape the behaviors of discarnate spirits. The actions of the discarnate entities appearing in dreams and visions show that they can act on their own volition to a certain extent and they have at least some personal control over where reincarnation takes place.

7.8: Do we have control over reincarnation process?

Reincarnation is not random, not accidental, but follows a pattern controlled by our Karma. We are students on a journey toward ultimate perfection. Since we have free will, we have some control over the reincarnation process as the cases suggest. A discarnate entity chooses the new human host, but there are some limitations. And the discarnate always has the choice of not reincarnating.

If one believed firmly that one could not change sex between lives, one might not be inclined to try. Sex change cases are rarely found in cultures in which it is believed to be impossible to change sex between lives. If one believed that one ought to be reborn in one's family that is where one might choose to go. In Nigeria male and female subjects have claimed to recall previous lives as the opposite sex equally often. In other cases outside Nigeria, Stevenson (1987, p. 174) noted that where sex change cases are found, female subjects have more often claimed previous lives as males than vice versa by a three-to-one margin.

However, there is a point. Since through birth and rebirth karmic debts are fulfilled, and good and bad Karma are balanced, hence it is not always possible that every terrestrial existence through birth and rebirth there would not be any change of sex. It appears that unless extremely required by the law of Karma, the sex change does not take place. The soul grows through reincarnation when new lessons are learnt through past mistakes. Certain lessons cannot be learnt unless change of sex occurs (Montgomery, 1972, p. 47). Therefore, it is not surprising to discover that some of us were members of the opposite sex in our past-lives.

Past-life incidents do not need to follow the genetic principles of inheritance. Hence, people are often unlikely to have a past-life as one of their biologically related ancestors. Instead, it is very common of one to have a past-life in some faraway locality that is completely removed from any place that one's biological ancestors came from. For this reason, it is also very common for one to be a member of a different race in a past-life. Since there is no guarantee that we will return back in the same family and in the same country, becoming too attached to current family identity or national identity, or living too selfishly for own sake or one's own family sake only are detrimental to us, to our next life, and to our future wellbeing.

If law of Karma necessitates then we may be reborn as animal also, though very rare. All past-life experiences are basically 'Karmic' experiences, and hence they are typically accompanied with a strong positive or negative emotional charge with subjective quality of authenticity and reality.

If one believed that the period before one's next life (intermission time) ought to be of a certain length, one might strive to make it as close to this length as possible. The Tlingit and other Northwest Coast tribes believe they have control over the process, and some of their cases suggest that they do in fact have such control. Control is also suggested in those cases in which subjects claim to recall having chosen their parents in the interval between lives. The wishes of the discarnate are certainly honored, but within the premises of that person's karmic cycles. Curtiss (1949, p. 34) explained in this way,

> "*As a rule the more advanced one is, the longer he remains out of incarnation, unless there is some special reason such as helping humanity in some special way, such as spiritual teaching, etc., that brings him back earlier. Some advanced Masters have had to wait for centuries for the proper planetary and racial cycles and karmic conditions to arrive which would permit them to accomplish their mission.*"

Some sacred texts of Tibetan Buddhism suggest that many highly developed human beings are able to gain far-reaching knowledge about reincarnation process including the possibility of exerting influence on the time of one's death, predicting or even directing the time and place of one's next incarnation, and maintaining consciousness through the intermediate states (bardos) between death and next incarnation. Many Hindu monks in India can also do the same. Tibetan Buddhist monks can receive various clues through dreams, meditation, and other channels to locate and identify the child who is the reincarnation of the Dalai Lama (known as *tulku*). The child is then exposed to a test during which the child has to identify correctly from several sets of similar objects those that belonged to the deceased. This is how a new Dalai Lama is selected once the old Dalai Lama is dead.

Stevenson (1974b, pp. 259-69) recorded the case of Corliss Chotkin, Jr. who had expressed his intention to be reborn into Corliss' family and said he would be recognized by birthmarks representing scars he had. Corliss was born with marks in the places indicated. In the case of William George, Jr. the previous person (William George, Sr.) had expressed a similar intention, also apparently fulfilled (Stevenson, 1974b, pp. 232-33). The senior George had reportedly told his favorite son Reginald and daughter-in-law Susan, "*If there is anything to this rebirth business, I will come back and be your son*" (Ebon, 1969, p. 78). He added that they would know him as he would have same birthmarks – one on his left shoulder and the other on his left forearm. He gave his son a gold watch to keep for him. Shortly after his death, his daughter-in-law became pregnant and during her labour dreamed about William George, Sr. When the baby was born, he turned out to have the two exact birthmarks. When he grew into a toddler, he recognized the gold watch among his parents' possessions. Both of these are Tlingit Indian cases.

However, this idea of the control over the process leads us to ask a serious question. Suppose, if I do not believe in reincarnation, should I then not reincarnate? This question may be anticipated as the first skeptical response to this description of the reincarnation hypothesis, but it does not follow logically from what has been said. Reincarnation is a natural process, and we all incarnate. We may not have full control over the process as such, but merely over some aspects of its operation. There may be other constraints on the process. One of these may be the impossibility of reincarnating in the bodies of other species, and another may be the requirement that we reincarnate in only one body at a time.

7.9: Skeptic's views

"*If you don't believe in karma or reincarnation, don't worry. Probably you will in your next life*".

Bruce Goldberg

"*It is not more surprising to be born twice than once.*"

Voltaire (Francois Marie Arouet)

Past-life recall incidents have received a mixture of interpretations from the skeptics and have been associated with a variety of phenomena such as, conscious and subconscious frauds, altered states of consciousness, fantasy constructions, repressed memories, genetic memories, psychological projections and many others. Stevenson himself recognized one glaring flaw in his cases i.e., the absence of any evidence of a process by which a personality could survive death and transfer to another body as he says that he finds himself "*thinking increasingly of some intermediate 'nonphysical body' which acts as the carrier ... between one life and another..*" (Stevenson, 1974c, p. 406). In response to Stevenson's statement, Goswami (2006, p. 144) wrote, "*I agree. The subtle body in the form of the quantum monad [an indivisible and hence ultimately simple entity] is the carrier of the attributes of one life to another*". The doctrine of reincarnation merits our extreme respect because the greatest minds throughout the ages have followed this.

There are always chances of fraud. The parents of some of these children have been alleged to make money out of them by training them to enact the drama of reincarnation. However, there are many genuine cases as well where plenty evidence are available to rule out fraud. Another probability is that the child may have received information about the deceased person's life through extrasensory perception. Relatives still mourning the deceased might unconsciously be sending thoughts which are picked telepathically by the child. The observation that these children do not show any unusual paranormal ability in other situations is a counter-argument against the telepathic hypothesis.

Skeptics dismiss xenoglossy cases as telepathy, cryptomnesia or genetic memory. However, no skeptic had even presented a documented case of a person being able to speak a foreign language they learned by telepathy.

Practice is required to master a language. The other explanation, i.e., genetic memory is equally hard to accept. The claim that somehow an ancient Chinese language which is already dead hundreds of years ago became embedded in the genes of an eleven-year-old Caucasian American enabling him to speak the language is ridiculous.

The concept of 'racial memory' or 'memory transference through genes' cannot account for the apparent memories of former lives. Newton (2016b, p. 136) wrote,

> "*I want to provide more information about divisions of memory recall and DNA. There are people who have the belief that all memories are carried by DNA. In this way they derive comfort from what they consider to be a scientific position against reincarnation. Certainly, everyone has a perfect right not to believe in reincarnation for a number of personal reasons, religious and otherwise. But to say that all past life memory is actually genetic in origin, carried in our DNA cells from remote ancestors, is an argument that, for me, fails in several ways.*"

Also, these children are almost never descendants of the individuals they claim to be, usually belonging to another family in another town. Can the 'memory transference through genes' explain the intermission memories?

Pre-birth communications are authentic because they involve a 'prophecy' coupled with 'fulfilment' of test. These are not psychological projections, i.e., wishes and beliefs of the dreamers. Instead, these dreams and visions give us hints that discarnate entities sometimes desire to incarnate with a zest and craving for it, and often shows keen interest in the selection of a family for another incarnation.

Some skeptics say that the past-life identities are simply imaginary playmates that the children have called forth to keep them company. But according to Stevenson (1983b, p. 747) this argument is not valid because the incarnation cases differ markedly from cases of imaginary playmates. A child who has an imaginary playmate regards the playmate as living contemporaneously with himself and as being a different person. In contrast, children who claim to remember previous lives believe that they were another person – always a deceased one, not a living one – in another physical body, time and place. The children who remember past-lives identify themselves with that deceased person and believe themselves to be that same person, though in a new physical body.

Some critics say that the reincarnation cases are the result of two unconscious processes – confabulation and cryptomnesia. But several cases that I have discussed in this chapter do not support their argument.

Confabulation is a process where we fill in gaps in our memories with manufactured memories which appear to make sense. As far as the individual is concerned these are factual memories. Confabulation cannot be the explanation for many of the cases the researchers had investigated. In the solved cases, the past-life memories are verified, as I have shown in many case examples, and found to be true. These are certainly not manufactured memories. Stevenson's cases have repeatedly shown us that the identification with the previous person typically has a strong emotional component that cannot be explained by confabulation. One child felt such a strong desire to go to his former home that he refused to eat for three days until he was taken there. Some children run away from home to meet their past relatives. Many children revealed strong attachments to the property of the persons of whom they are speaking, to the point of asserting their ownership of it. Can 'manufactured memory" argument explain the strong emotional component in their past-life recalls?

Cryptomnesia is the recollection of past experiences, usually material or events from books, film or television, which make a lasting impression on our memory. These tend to be items with emotional impact or relate to material that is of personal interest. Although these become 'forgotten', at least on a conscious level, they will often emerge later as our own 'personal' memories or experiences. Can we explain xenoglossy cases as cryptomnesia? If cryptomnesia is the cause for passing memories from one life to another, then how is it possible that some people can speak and write lost and dead languages or speak in rare dialects? Can cryptomnesia explain the songs and dances performed by Swarnlata Mishra? At the age of five or six years she had performed unusual songs and dances in front of others which she had had no opportunity to learn in her present lifetime. How to explain the Uttara Huddar/ Sharada Chattopadhaya case? Uttara had never been to Bengal, had not learned its language, but she could not only speak the language fluently but displayed extraordinary knowledge of Bengali culture also.

Confabulation and cryptomnesia also cannot explain the unusual talents, unusual birthmarks and birth defects, and phobias that clearly have roots in the past-lives. What about the unusual games these children play with uncanny ability to manage it in the most practical manner? Stevenson (1983c, p. 24) wrote,

> "*If observers...assert that the case definitely has a normal explanation [such as, role-playing, loss of inhibition, dissociation, cryptomnesia, desire to please the hypnotist, subconscious projection and integration etc.,], ... they have the duty of showing the actual steps in the occurrence of this process. It is not enough to say how it might have happened*".

The critics are certainly in error. Secondly, can any of the critics' arguments explain the birthmark and birth defect cases? The stimulation of memories during the child's visits to the previous family or community seems better explained by mental associations than any other opinions.

One critic wrote that most of those who recall previous lives claim to have been important and powerful people, kings, queens, generals, etc., few were ever servants or scullery-maids. This is also not true. Most of those who remember past-lives had belonged to much lower stratum in the society. Stevenson (1987, p. 96) noted that many of those children resided in small towns or villages are born into relatively uneducated and impoverished families. Amongst Indian cases of Stevenson, two-thirds recalled lives in better conditions and one-third in similar or worse conditions. The earlier mentioned Swarnlata Mishra belonged to a sweeper class in her previous life and engaged in behaviors characteristic of the previous person's station in life. Earlier I had discussed about the unusual games the children play – how many children had played King Arthur, Queen Victoria, famous scientists like Einstein, Newton or President of USA? In the famous Virginia Tighe/Bridey Murphy case, we have noted that Bridey had a low status in the society; she most probably lived in a slum.

One guess is that the discarnate spirits are influencing these children by transmitting their terrestrial memories to them, i.e., possession cases. If that was the case, the children would have been influenced by several deceased personalities and hence would not have been able to stick to one previous life narration alone. Also, if previous life memories were of such origin, more than one child would be claiming the identity of a single discarnate personality. Also such entities are usually anxious to reveal their names and claim the credit. This had not happened so far.

One critic had pointed out that many of the claimants' report that in their past lives they lived in such mythical locations as Atlantis, or Lemuria – unknown lands never known to have existed. This argument has a flaw. No doubt, a few such cases were documented from the readings of Edgar Cayce. But it would be a mistake to conclude that such 'mythological' locations really did not exist in the past. Once in a while we are astonished to see what the archeologists have unearthed – what are "lands known never to have existed" today, may be tomorrow's "breaking news – archeologists have discovered a great civilization" on the daily newspaper. For hundreds of years the world refused to accept the ocean explorers' claim of the existence of a great southern continent. Today, despite of much bigotry of such all-knowing skeptics, Antarctica exists as a hard fact. People have documented several thousand accurate readings of Edgar Cayce. He really had access to paranormal knowledge that overcame the barrier of time. Atlantis, or Lemuria – the two 'mythological locations' of today are yet to be discovered like Antarctica.

When the skeptics could not discredit Stevenson and other dedicated researchers, they turned to the unsolved cases that they had investigated. As example, Edge (1986, p. 347) attempted to prove that unsolved cases were fantasies, and interpreted the similarities between solved and unsolved cases as throwing solved cases into doubt. He had an unclear reasoning. A case may remain unsolved for several reasons such as, unverifiable data, lack of significant information, the past-life location is far away etc. We cannot completely rule out fantasy, but it would be illogical to say that all unsolved cases are fantasy-related. Subjects of unsolved cases mentioned the name of the previous person significantly less often than did subjects of solved cases. Names are usually required to solve a case, this fact would certainly have contributed to their being unsolved (Cook et al., 1983a, p. 47). Some unsolved cases include verified statements, while other cases are demonstrably mixtures of fantasy and fact (Cook et al., 1983b, pp. 132-34). The majority of Stevenson's Asian cases are solved (Stevenson, 1983a, p. 191). Cook et al. (1983b, p. 117) showed that the proportion of solved cases varied by country – 92% in Thailand, 80% in Burma, 72% in India, but only 20% in the USA, the only Western country they considered. Hence we cannot assume that all the Stevenson's cases are fantasies.

Rogo (1985, pp. 77-79) and Wilson (1988, pp. 227-29) have portrayed Stevenson as unresponsive to criticism. However, a look at the literature shows that Stevenson had quite often responded to questions about his work and to interpretations of cases alternative to those he has put forward.

Stevenson has engaged in dialogue with most of his prominent critics from 1961 onwards till 1988 (his death), and these exchanges occurred in scholarly journals, as example, with Prof. C. T. K. Chari (published in 1961, 1962, 1973, 1986), L. E. Rhine (published in 1966, 1967), G. Murphy (published in 1973), R. Haynes (published in 1976, 1978, 1979), M. Grosso (published in 1979, 1980), C. T. Tart (published in 1980), R. K. Siegal (published in 1980, 1981), W. G. Roll (published in 1984), D. S. Rogo (published in 1985, 1986, 1987), Stevenson (1987) and I. Wilson (published in 1988). Though the exchanges occurred in scholarly journals, many of the critiques of Stevenson's work have been made in popular books, such as Rogo (1985) and Wilson (1982 and 1987). Stevenson did not consider criticisms of his work directly in his own books, but since he has addressed responsible criticism in the scholarly journal widely read and scrutinized by academic world, it is wrong to censure him for this.

D. S. Rogo also has charged that Stevenson has suppressed reports critical of his work. One of these is a "devastating" report that is said, on second-hand testimony, to have been prepared by Champe Ransom before he left Stevenson's employment as a research assistant (Rogo, 1985, p. 79). Stevenson has defended himself against the charge, which was recorded by Edwards (1987, pp. 46-53). Evidently in response to Edwards, Ransom (1987, p. 59) himself has now gone on record to say that Stevenson did not suppress this report and that "*I find it difficult to think that Stevenson would ever try to suppress any writing critical of his research.*"

On several occasions Stevenson's critics have crossed the limit of academic honesty to discredit him but failed miserably. After attacking

Stevenson, Rogo next attempted to discredit D. R. Barker, who along with S. K. Pasricha, had done notable research on reincarnation in India. Although Barker and Pasricha's sample is small, it is based on a systematic survey, and deserves special respect for that reason. Rogo (1985, p. 78) referred to unpublished reports by Barker, based on a conversation he thought he may have had (Rogo, 1986, p. 470) with Barker during a Parapsychological Association Convention. Stevenson explained that the disagreement with Barker stemmed not from written reports but from Stevenson's siding with Pasricha in a dispute she had with Barker over the sharing of data and the matter sorted out.

Another critic, Prof. C. T. K. Chari labels even strongly veridical past-life memory cases "fantasies". He referred one such case where a girl claimed to be the incarnation of the Goddess Kali or Durga. She had birthmarks resembling necklaces, bangles, and anklets worn by this goddess, and continued to speak "*with an oracular wisdom beyond her years*" till she was seven years old (Chari, 1981, pp. 127-28). The claimed identification and the birthmarks started fading by age seven. In my opinion, such a case is a combination of fantasy (claim of reincarnation of Goddess) and facts (oracular wisdom not expected in her age). Probably she was a Hindu godman in her previous life and her delusion had originated from that life. This is a possibility we cannot ignore. This case was not investigated in details and therefore we cannot come to a conclusion. But we can ask why it should cause us to question cases that on other grounds we have come to consider paranormal, where no other explanation except reincarnation is plausible. 'Fantasy' cannot be the blanket explanation for all the cases. At times, Chari (1978, p. 315) had abandoned his 'fantasy' hypothesis, and assigned a possible role to ESP, though he had also expressed doubt on his own opinion. On this point Stevenson (1987, pp. 154-55) argues that if ESP is a major factor in past-life memory cases, why the subjects almost never exhibit the faculty at other times? Subjects make error while narrating a past-life. Some subjects have difficulty recognizing persons and places that have changed substantially since the previous person's death. It means they are accessing information from memory not ESP. Hence, a simple ESP explanation is not logical. Also, ESP cannot explain unusual birthmarks, birth defects and behavioral memories.

Even if the strongly veridical past-life memory cases are disqualified as "fantasies", can they explain why cases so similar to each other have been reported by so many persons from so many places over such a length of time? Why the learned skeptics are silent on this issue? Sometimes skeptics' explanations are awfully awkward, and it creates more problems than it solves.

Reyna argues that the "laws of genetics" are ignored in interpreting past-life memory cases in terms of reincarnation, "*If there were no dependable laws of heredity.... A pregnant woman could never be certain just what she was likely to bear. If it were not for the control exercised by evolution and genetics ... many incongruous situations could and would arise*" (Reyna, 1973, p. 107). However Reyna's statement is confusing. No researcher of past-life memory cases had ever proposed reincarnation as an alternative to heredity. Reincarnation allows paranormal transfer of information, but without a physical body the law of heredity cannot manifest.

When some critics brought the issue that reincarnation cannot be shown to happen in controlled condition in a laboratory experiment, Stevenson (Kelly, 2013, p. 19) commented,

> "*The study of spontaneous cases of extrasensory perception sometimes needs defending against the disapproval of those who have come to equate science with the controlled conditions that laboratories can offer and naturalistic situations cannot. Here the first point to make is that some important phenomena, such as the weather, volcanoes, fossils, earthquakes, and meteorites, do not occur in laboratories under controlled conditions, and yet we study them with scientific methods. We do this because science is not a physical location where we obtain evidence, but instead a process for appraising evidence wherever we find it.*"

We cannot limit 'truth' to what could be proven by laboratory demonstration alone. Extensive research had been done over long time and by many people to identify and short list very convincing cases throughout the world that cannot be explained by any other known processes. Critics can take these final selected cases, carefully analyze them, and see the truth by themselves – the laboratory will be the whole world. Since ages the reincarnation theory has been proven by local people and by their own methods of verification. Here we are not professing on belief or faith but hard practical facts.

In spite of much rejection from critics, in some circles Stevenson is a scientific legend. His collection of cases, his meticulous documentation and cross-checking, his prodigious and scholarly publication have made him a hero to many people who would like respectable reasons to distrust the radical materialism of Western science. For his own part, Stevenson has reached this conclusion, "*I think a rational person, if he wants, can believe in reincarnation on the basis of evidence*" (Davis, 1989, p. 75). Unable to discredit Stevenson, some critics took a nasty way to ridicule him instead of facing him for an academic debate. First, they started sending mails and telephone calls to the President of the university where he was teaching protesting what he was doing. However, Stevenson did not give up; whether he got any mainstream respect or not, he continued his research, "*But by that time, I was convinced that there was really something substantial in what I was seeing, something that should be pursued no matter what the cost. So I devoted more and more time to the cases*" (Shroder, 1999). Before he retired, he had compiled enough solid, empirical evidence to prove that physical death is not the end.

Unable to debate him, the critics started taunting his wife in his absence. On his late wife Stevenson wrote, "*What was more distressing was that other people, instead of coming to me and saying, 'I'd like to see your data', would make cracks to her at cocktail parties in my absence, tease her, and I thought that was shameful...*" (Shroder, 1999). This shocking level of indecency is condemnable. Do they honestly wish to investigate the subject seriously? This is how things get messy.

The critics have strongly opposed the therapists who use hypnosis to elicit past-life memories to produce therapeutic effects. As example, Mills and Lynn (2000, p. 297) commented,

> "*There is no reason to believe that recall past lives has any salutary effect on present-day problems, although this issue has not been systematically investigated, In fact, it could be argued that the person's best interests are not served if he or she is treated with past-life regression therapy when there is an empirically validated treatment for that particular problem.*"

These overstated and misleading criticisms, however, are not an accurate representation of the facts. Some critics of past-life therapy commented that "*few of the past-life hypnotists have doctoral degrees in psychology or medicine*" do not accurately represent the facts (Venn, 1986, p. 410). This type of criticism simply is inappropriate in any academic field. Indeed, there is no shortage of famous professional psychotherapists with doctoral degrees, such as Ronald Jue, Hazel Denning, Roger Woolger, Edith Fiore, Chet Snow, Edward Reynolds, Thorwald Dethlefsen, and Ernest Pecci – to name a few of them, among others who have provided "systematic documentation and follow-up". Many of these had been published in scientific journals that demonstrate the therapeutic effects of past-life regression.

The simple fact is that no matter how the critics want to refute the reincarnation cases, it seems that reincarnation hypothesis always has the upper hand, and in the end, reincarnation comes to seem the most satisfactory interpretation of the cases as a group. It explains all the objections to survival brought in the name of logic. The reincarnation hypothesis, admittedly, is so far in good shape. All the critics have failed and the reincarnation researchers have records of many hundreds published and unpublished cases that are not only veridical but also solved. If I hear about a single case of reincarnation, I might dismiss it without a second thought. But when various distinct stories begin to show with remarkable similarities, when they begin to appear more and more frequently in my readings and conversations and, finally, when I can, myself, speak to people, hear their own personal stories about reincarnation and verify data for accuracy then the narratives become evidential. Whatever concrete evidence are required to support the reincarnation hypothesis are available today, thanks to Ian Stevenson and the new workers who joined the ranks.

Masses of evidence are available for those who honestly wish to investigate the subject seriously. Reincarnation is a scientifically proven fact, not a religious or metaphysical revelation – that's all. Researchers should not go beyond this firm and explicit conclusion.

Reincarnation is accepted by the court of law. Curtiss (1949, pp. 57-58) recorded the case of Monsur Atrash of the Jebel Druz (Syria). Monsur, soon after marriage was killed in a raid. Within an hour of his death a boy named Najib Abu Faray was born in the mountains of Lebanon hundreds of miles away. At the age of 20, Najib by sheer of chance visited the native place of Monsur, and exclaimed, "I must be in a dream! I have seen all these places before; they are more familiar than my native mountains". When he came to the village where Monsur had lived he recognized the village and walked through the queer twisting streets, straight to the house of Monsur. Then he went to a walled-up window, had the bricks torn out and found a bag of money he remembered having put there before he went on the raid in which he was killed. Later he went to some vineyards of his past family where there were disputed boundaries. He pointed out the boundaries he had laid down as Monsur. A court of law accepted them as correct. He gave sufficient proofs of his identity so that his past family members recognized him, and gave Najib, the reincarnated boy, ten camel-loads of grain as gift. This case is particularly important because a court of law, after full investigation, officially acknowledged reincarnation. No farther proof is necessary.

The present-day researchers are gaining support from scientists in other fields also. We are confronting a scientific phenomenon today. Today we want to know the "rules" by which reincarnation is governed. However, many questions still stand in the way of a general acceptance of reincarnation for integrating it with mainstream scientific beliefs. Next step of reincarnation research is, how the quantum consciousness moves from one physical body to another and at what point it enters the fetus.

7.10: Conclusion

"*The reincarnation of man is as simple and natural as the reincarnation of Nature in the Spring. And rebirth is no more a miracle than is birth.*"

Frank Homer Curtiss, MD

The reincarnation theory provides a comprehensive and intelligible framework in which all the quite dissimilar, seemingly unrelated, and apparently meaningless events of one's life make sense and are seen to have an inner structure. If there is sense and purpose in one's life and death, then reincarnation offers the farther idea that even seemingly senseless tragedies operate for a greater good and "*as a part of a larger plan, as a method of teaching ourselves some important truth or as a means of developing certain abilities*" (Roberts, 1970, p. 134), and "... *certain scriptural passages could only be explained in the light of reincarnation*" (Grof, 1988, p. 88). Curtiss (1949, pp. 10, 12) is more elaborate on this issue.

> "*The supreme test of any theory is: How completely does it explain the facts? Reincarnation explains apparently discordant and irreconcilable phenomena, the inequality of life, the apparent injustice of God, the great differences in personality, from the idiot to the child prodigy and the genius, and assures the certainty of future lives here on earth in which to correct our mistakes, right our wrongs and attain our cherished ambitions and ideals. This removes all fear of death as the certainty of the coming of spring removes the fear of winter.*"

> "*Aside from the fact that this doctrine most satisfactorily solves the problems and includes all the facts of our life here on Earth, how else do we know that the doctrine is true? First, there is the testimony of the ages. No doctrine or theory can survive critical examination and application from age to age if it is not founded on truth. Theories of science, religion and philosophy arise, flourish for a time, then pass away, but reincarnation eternally remains. In fact, it reaches back beyond recorded history. It is found in the most ancient writings of Egypt, Babylonia, India, Greece, China, Japan, even in Atlantis and Lemuria. Alexander found it among the Gymnosophists of India, Caesar among the Druids of Gaul, and Herodotus among the Egyptians and the Magi of Persia. It was also taught in the mystery schools of Eleusis, Baccus and Isis.*"

Theoretically, any past-life memory could be recollected by an experimental research method that would relax the individual sufficiently so that enough solid information could make itself known that could be checked against existing historical records and public documents. In spite of this, the reincarnation concept cannot be accommodated within the present scientific framework without a radical change. As Grof (2000, p. 163) put it,

> "*Denial of the possibility of reincarnation represents a rare instance of complete agreement between the Christian church and materialistic science. Therefore, in Western culture, acceptance and intellectual integration of a past life memory is a difficult task for either an atheist or a traditionally religious person*".

That change would have to accept that mind is an independent reality, which could exist without a brain, and which would be the vehicle for the transmission of memory from one brain (belonging to a deceased person) to another (the person who is claiming memories). Wheatley (1979, p. 118) calls it as "'minded' astral body."

Parapsychologist C. T. K. Chari states that reincarnation is not scientifically testable for two reasons. First, though some limited and testable hypotheses about ESP and PK are available, but "*no theory extensive enough to carry the load of survival speculation.* Second, mind-body dualisms, in all their previously proposed forms, "*are inadequate to survival research, as they would have to be totally rephrased to be compatible with the existence of psi capacities [which none had done yet]*". (Chari, 1978, pp. 314-15). However, Seth material (session 126) presents a logical framework within which reincarnation could logically operate.

> "*Every effect of any kind, experienced by the human being, exists as a series of electrical signals and codes that in themselves form a pattern that is an electrical pattern. They exist within the cells, or I should more properly say that the cells form about them. These electric coded signals then form electric counterparts of complete experience, as it has been felt by any given individual. The pattern is independent of the physical system, while residing within it. Each individual from birth on forms his own counterpart from built up, individual, continuous electric signals. At physical death his personality then exists in its complete form, and of course escapes the sort of ending that it would suffer if it were an integral part of the physical system. This electrical pattern is the personality with all the experiences of its earthly time. It then can join or partake of the inner self. Though the ego was adopted originally by the inner self, and was a product of physical heredity and environment, it does not die; but its existence is changed from physical reality into electrical reality. It is still individual. No individuality is lost, but it becomes a part of the inner self, and its experiences are added to the total experience of the many personalities that have composed the inner self*". (Roberts, 1998, p. 235)

The concept of reincarnation proves that human personality is not formed by genetics and environmental influences only, but the root is much... much deeper – "*Psychic genetics is more important than biological genetics in determining the character of our lives*" (Goldberg, 2004, p. 24). Deep within us a large treasure of wisdom is hidden which can be tapped by each and every one. If we consider reincarnation and the law of Karma together, we will understand that everyone has to be responsible for his or her own spiritual development, and the healing of his or her soul over many lifetimes. Together it's a profound issue because this is an essential part of the evolution of the Universe.

In sum, the reincarnation research of recent years, in the proper sense of the term, is scientific. Past-life recalls are normal, scientific and psychological facts. It is simply an extension or expansion of normal human soul's abilities, the evidence for the multidimensional nature of the human psyche and for abilities that lie within each individual, that are a part of our species heritage, and that more clearly define how the soul's abilities in life show themselves. The Law of Karma, i.e., the moral law of cause and effect, makes reincarnation into an automatic, almost mechanical process.

Chapter 8

The law of Karma

"*Life is a schooling ground. We reincarnate into the classroom of earthly existence with a certain curriculum of instruction. Those subjects which we have mastered earlier come easily; those we have failed will have to be repeated until they are mastered.*"

Adrian Finkelstein, famous past-life regression therapist

"*It knows not wrath nor pardon; utter true*
Its measures mete, its faultless balance weighs;
Times are as nought, tomorrow it will judge,
Or after many days".

Sir Edwin Arnold

In the society we come across many instances of unfair discrimination – virtuous persons undergoing endless suffering and pain while outlaws perpetually enjoying pleasurable lives, lazy people achieving great success while hardworking people meeting repeated failures, the wise suffering adversity while the fools living in prosperity, egoists held in high esteem while the righteous held in contempt, some die young while others age gracefully to old age and many more as if they are being punished by some 'higher power' for a great sin. We find some persons born with silver spoon in their mouths while fate seems to have chosen others for the constant objects of its most deadly blows. While some children born into families of extreme wealth with a myriad of doors swinging open to them by virtue of their class, there are beings who, from the moment of their birth to the hour of their death, utter only cries of suffering and despair.

Similarly, unprecedented natural calamities like famine, epidemics, tornadoes, flood, damage by lightning and earthquake and 'untimely death' are commonly known as predestination. What crime have they committed? They are here in spite of themselves, against their will. God would be unjust and wicked if he imposed so miserable an existence upon beings who have done nothing to incur it, and have not asked for it.

Such phenomena raise many questions and doubts about the role of fate in life. A scientific man would ask – why the world is full of injustices and inequalities? What is the relationship of virtuous and evil deeds with happiness and grief in life? Does destiny have a role to play in life? Does the human suffering and injustice occur by random chance? Some doubters may become very much perplexed by such phenomena and form opinions, such as a mistaken belief that the gain and loss being inevitability of fate and there is no necessity of personal effort, which are extremely dangerous for life.

The afterlife researchers have shown us with ample evidence that higher deities exist in the spirit world who express unconditional love to all souls. If there is no favoritism in the Universe, and all immortal souls have the same everlasting facilities for growth, then there must be rational and logical explanations of relationship between human deeds and destiny. There must be a universal divine law by which we can explain the events of good fortune and misfortune, happiness and suffering in human life.

From here comes the core understanding of the law of Karma. O'Flaherty (1980, p. xi) describes Karma as "*a theory of rebirth based on the moral quality of previous lives*", and Weber (1963, p. 145) presents Karma as "*the most complete formal solution of the problem of theodicy... Each individual forges his own destiny exclusively, and in the strictest sense of the word*". Reichenbach (1990, p. 2) explains it as,

> "*a special application of the law of universal causation, an application which uses the metaphysics of causation both to explain a moral phenomenon and to vindicate the moral order by applying universal justice to human moral actions.*"

The doctrine makes everything wonderfully clear – good actions lead to good results, and bad actions lead to bad results – a simple and exact explanation of evidential inequality as Leadbeater (1952, p. 6) commented, "*... the man makes his bed during earth life and afterwards he has to lie on it*" – perfect justice is done and nothing is ever lost. All good or bad things that we experience are our own creations and we are fully responsible for the consequences. It liberates us from the fantasies of both fear and hope. The belief "bribe of heaven and threat of hell" of the Western World does not exist. The present condition of each soul is due to its own progress, development, advancement, unfoldment, or the lack of the same. The soul being is its own fate and destiny; the enforcer of the Law upon itself, under the law of Karma.

The doctrine of Karma essentially maintains that when a person dies, a record of his actions (good and bad) is imprinted upon his soul. When that soul eventually reincarnates into another body, those actions, as well as their attendant thoughts, words, and desires, will then manifest in the newborn's genes and determine the quality and conditions of his life. Hence, the concept of Karma is inextricably interwoven with that of reincarnation and it is difficult to examine one without the other, for the two theories rely upon each other. According to Wilhelm Halbfass, the doctrine of Karma and its corollary of cyclic rebirth were "*fully established and almost universally accepted as a comprehensive world-view in classical and later Indian thought*" (Halbfass, 1980, p. 269). Reichenbach (1990, p. 13) speaks of the law of Karma as "*embedded in a body of philosophical and religious doctrines*". According to him, some consequences are manifested immediately or in this life, some in the next life, and some remotely. The effects of karmic actions can be accumulated. Karma is not fundamentally a fatalistic dogma.

Psychiatrist Stanislav Grof is one of the co-founders of transpersonal psychology movement. This is the branch of psychology that deals with the sense of identity or self that extends beyond (i.e., trans the individual) to encompass wider aspects of humankind, life, psyche, and cosmos. He had done extensive research on reincarnation and the law of Karma. According to him all past-life experiences are "Karmic experiences" (Grof, 1988, p. 41). Elsewhere Grof (2000, pp. 162-63) wrote,

> "*Past-life experiences can complicate life in several different ways. Before their content emerges fully into consciousness and reveals itself, one can be haunted in everyday life by strange emotions, physical feelings, and visions without knowing where these are coming from or what they mean. Experienced out of context, these experiences naturally appear incomprehensible and irrational... When the content of a karmic experience fully emerges into consciousness, it can suddenly provide an explanation for many otherwise incomprehensible aspects of one's daily life. Strange difficulties in relationships with certain people, unsubstantiated fears, and peculiar idiosyncrasies and attractions, as well as otherwise incomprehensible emotional and psychosomatic symptoms now seem to make sense as karmic carry-overs from a previous lifetime. The problems typically disappear when the karmic pattern in question is fully and consciously experienced.... Another kind of complication occurs when a particularly strong karmic experience starts emerging into consciousness in the middle of everyday activities and interferes with normal functioning. One might also feel compelled to act out some of the elements of the karmic pattern before it is fully experienced and understood or completed.... Fundamentalist Christians and those who have a strong investment in rationality and the traditional scientific perspective can be catapulted into a period of confusion when they are confronted with convincing personal experiences that seem to challenge their belief system.*"

Ruth Montgomery (1913-2001), a journalist by profession, had the gift of 'automatic writing' (trance typewriting) by which she could communicate with various deceased personalities. She was able to channel a great deal of information from the other side, specifically from her deceased friend, the famous spiritualist and medium, Arthur Ford (famous for revealing Houdini's secret code). Montgomery received amazing information regarding law of Karma, and the soul realm from the other side and documented these revelations in a series of books. Montgomery (1972, p. 46) wrote,

> "*The greater the obstacles in the physical body, the more opportunity for a soul to pay off karmic debts and achieve more spiritual growth. The hurdles are stepping-stones.... The reward is not in the physical form but in spiritual development, and the more hurdles that are overcome in a physical lifetime, the less often that soul will thereafter need to return to physical form to round off the rough spots in his character.*"

Karma is the reason why we reincarnate on the Earth plane. It is our actions (and inactions) that determine what our future fate will invariably be from one lifetime to another. Cooper (2007, pp. 27, 53) commented,

> "*The chief purpose of reincarnation is education. To this end we are born again and again on earth, not because of any external pressure, but because we, as souls, desire to grow.*"

> "*Reincarnation is not an endless process, and when we have learned the lessons taught in the World-School we return no more to physical incarnation unless we come back of our own accord to act as Teachers of humanity or as Helpers in the glorious plan of evolution.*"

The word "Karma" comes from the Sanskrit, and means action, work or deed (Sanskrit word 'kri' means 'to do'). Sometimes it is described as law of equilibrium, a law of spiritual dynamics, or the moral law of cause and effect (Smith, 1965, p. 76). All action is Karma because absolute inactivity means death, although traditionally it has most often been associated with the effects of our actions. The word Karma is now almost naturalized into English. From various case studies, it appears that Law of Karma is automatic in action, and that there is no possible escape from it. The absolute justice is manifested in its operations without a single grain of mercy or wrath.

8.1: Our karmic paths cross repeatedly through reincarnation

> "*Understanding the Law of Karma is enough to live wisely in the world.*"
> Jack Kornfield

> "*We here know each other through many many lives, some having been together at various stages in physical development, but all of us at one*

time or another crossing paths, here or there. As a consequence there's no such thing as a stranger here, which makes it easier for us to understand that we are all part of one another as well as of God."

Ruth Montgomery

There are karmic reasons behind the serious events involving relationships in our lives. A great number of experiences from many past lives negatively affect us in our present daily lives. Past-life regressions can exactly pinpoint the problem in a relationship because a skilled therapist by following the karmic thread reaches at the root of the trouble and find out how much karmic debt is yet to be repaid. First, I will discuss few simple examples from Goldberg (1982, pp. 57-58; 2004, p. 7), and then more complicated ones.

1. A middle-aged woman was treated for insomnia. She revealed a previous life as a male civil war sentry. Once he fell asleep at his post, and as a result enemy soldiers killed him and his fellow soldiers
2. An overweight man remembered a past-life when he starved to death
3. A man wondered why he was such an overprotective father. He remembered two past lives. In both the times he had deserted his family.
4. A workaholic in present life witnessed his family starving to death in Greece hundreds of years ago because he was not able to adequately provide for them. By overworking himself he was preventing that from ever happening again.
5. A woman suffering from frigidity in present life remembered a past life when she was rejected by her husband because she was raped. Her husband in the past life is also her husband in present life.
6. A man who was a celibate priest who always prayed for resistance to sexual urges during the Middle Ages is impotent at the present life.
7. A woman who saw her children die of scarlet fever in the 19th century and swore she would never have another child is barren in the 21st century.

All these are real life problems. The middle-aged woman, the overactive father, the priest and the workaholic – all of them are working out their Karma which has been put out for them; it is the only way. The frigid woman is repaying her husband for what he had done to her in a past life because the husband had incurred a karmic debt. Montgomery (1972, p. 63) wrote,

"*Accidents seldom exist, for the planning on this side takes care of nearly everything except sheer, monumental evil which grows rapidly in a bad man's soul and overpowers the original plan he had pledged to carry out.*"

Karma is not optional; it is spontaneous and enforces itself as indicative in the following short examples from Montgomery (1972, pp. 47, 48, 77, 147). This is their way of balancing the ledger.

1. A weak and trembling woman with palsy had a past life when she was a cruel soldier (male) in ancient Rome. He delighted in frightening others until they trembled with fear. He would turn wild beasts loose on tortured Christians to see them shake and tremble.
2. A very kind-hearted man did generous acts. He loved everyone, and in turn loved by others. But people were repulsed by a giant welt on his face and neck. What a pity, they thought that this kindly man has such a heavy cross to bear. In a past life he struck a child so roughly across the face and neck that the bones were scattered and the child died.
3. A soul reincarnated in such a body so weakened by malformation that it will not sustain life. Hence the soul withdraws itself after a brief struggle for life. In a previous life, the soul had ended the life of a new baby through neglect of its need.
4. Many people today who had devoted their lives to stop racism against black people were white slave traders in various past lives. They were intolerant towards the human rights of their black slaves and minions, and in present life they are in the forefront of the civil rights movement to repay their karmic debts.

In all the above they are "correcting" a wrong (a harm or an injustice) that has happened. The concept of right and wrong are not always same to different group of people. But within all of us is the innate knowledge that to deliberate harm another person, physically or mentally, is unethical. We have the power to reason and to know right from wrong. The next case (Newton, 2016a, pp. 230-46) explains this clearly.

A successful businessman, by the name Steve had two failed marriages. He was also an alcoholic and it seemed though he was financially well off, he was unhappy from his childhood because his mother disappeared after leaving him on the steps of a church in Texas within a week of his birth. After a few lonely and unhappy years in an orphanage, an older couple adopted him, but he was again unhappy with his foster parents as they were stern disciplinarians who seemed to disapprove of him all the time. His frustration was rooted in feelings of isolation and abandonment issues. He felt that he was losing control over his life.

Under hypnosis Steve recollected vivid memories of his babyhood with his mother. His mother was young and not married to his father because his father was already married. She was crying and her tears were falling on the baby's face. Before leaving the baby on the steps of the church she said,

"*I must leave you for your own good. I have no money to take care of you. My parents won't help us. I love you. I will always love you and hold you in my heart forever*". Next, he recollected his memory, how his foster parents were never satisfied with him, and how they made him feel guilty about everything by controlling and judging him continuously.

To find the root of the karmic issue, Newton took him to a previous life where the childhood trauma of his present life had originated. The source of the karmic debt between the mother and the abandoned baby was in a past-life thousands of years ago when Steve was a high priest of a tribe. He saw himself wearing a long, white robe and sandals with a stick in his hand with gold snakes on it as a symbol of his authority. Soon it was unfolded that he was a tribal leader located on the Arabian Peninsula near Red Sea around 2000 BC. This area was known as the Kingdom of Sheba (or Saba). Under deep hypnosis, Steve saw himself on the step of a temple passing death sentence on his own mother. As a high priest he had too much control over the daily lives of his people. The fault of his mother was that she had broken into the storage house and stole food to give to the people. Many people were hungry at that time of year, but as a high priest, he alone could order distribution. The high priest used the distribution of food as a means of control over his people, because he wanted them all to be loyal to him. Since his mother had violated his authority, he ordered her death by banging his stick on the stone steps. The mother of the high priest in a past-life is the mother of Steve in the present life. The karmic connection that was established in 2000 BC resulted in a disordered life between mother and son in the present life. The karmic payment that was due for about four thousand years was ultimately paid when the sacred bond between a mother and her baby was severed.

The enforcer of the law of Karma may take time in preparing an appropriate environment for dispensing just rewards and punishments, but every karmic debt must be paid in full, to the last penny. No compensation is made as answer to prayer to a higher source.

However, Steve's story does not end here. Under deep hypnotic trance, he remembered another life at Germany. In that life Steve was a high-ranking officer who neglected his family and was the object of scorn from his wife's influential parents. Steve had a strong desire to control others in that life, but at the same time, he had thoughts of escape by self-destruction. Because of this nature he had conflict with the society. He had a karmic lesson to learn – to overcome his selfish desire to control others at any cost and to resolve his disputes with others in the society. He had learned his lesson when during his childhood he was constantly ridiculed by his adoptive parents.

This case makes us pondering over a common issue. Though most of the biological parents are good and kind to their children, there are no shortage of cases where children are brought up in dysfunctional families with unresolved and hurtful memories of parents who should have offered love and protection but did not. Such children grow up thinking of themselves as victims.

Karmic issues of various people are involved in the relationship – "*a soul's desire to experience and advance through various social structures.*" (Goldberg, 2004, p. 8). Newton (2016a, p. 246) wrote,

> "*There is usually some karmic purpose for receiving pain or pleasure from someone close to us. Remember, along with learning our own lessons, we come to Earth to play a part in the drama of others' lessons as well*".

If we imagine life as a grand stage play where we have the lead roles as an actor, then whatever we do on the stage influences other minor characters. We have free will and the minor characters also have free will. So the script is not fixed. Their parts are altered by us and ours by them because the script changes while the play is in progress. Similarly, other souls who share the same stage with us as minor actors are also playing leading roles in another play, but on the same stage where we are playing supporting roles for them. Because of these complications, it is often said that 'Unfathomable is the mystery of Karma'. An acquaintance in one life will often appear repeatedly in future lifetimes. Goldberg (1982, p. 39) wrote,

> "*We do not just reincarnate individually. Rather as I have been suggesting, our own separate karmic cycles are intertwined with many others. For example, your parents may have been your children in a former life. Your wife may have been your brother or son, etc. This is not to say that karma involves any form of incest or other such moral judgment. It simply implies that our lessons are intermingled with the lessons of other entities. These lessons have an effect between entities and among others around them.*"

I wish to explain more. We connect with people on many levels for a multitude of karmic lessons in every earthly life. It's not just the Karma of one or two souls. Rather it's the Karma of each and every soul who interacts (including past several lives across several thousand years) with each other and set up major or minor karmic debts. Our lessons are intermingled with the lessons of other entities. In addition, there are karmic issues of our ancestors who are no more on Earth but left their karmic legacy (as example, if I inherit my late grandfather's ill-gotten wealth then as per law of Karma, I will incur negative Karma). Collectively, the whole thing can be called a tangled hierarchy. That's the reason the path of Karma is mysterious. But with mathematical certainty it always works in the right direction.

From Edgar Cayce's treasure of past-life readings we can come across many cases where karmic actions are prominently noticeable. Initially, Cayce himself had a hard time accepting what he was saying during the trance states. But he gradually understood the basis of reincarnation and Karma and how they help us comprehend the seemingly incomprehensible aspects of human life.

A woman of forty, suffered from certain allergies since childhood. Eating certain foods, mainly bread and cereal, made her sneeze heavily. Coming in physical contact with shoe leather and plastic glass gave her severe pains in her left side. Doctors could not cure her but a hypnotic treatment at the age of 25 gave her some relief. Cayce went deeper into the cause of her allergies. The reading said that in another life she was a chemist, and used many harmful chemicals to produce itching in others. In her present life Karma worked like a boomerang. Those same substances she used to inflict pain on others are now causing pain to her. In her past-life she had also used certain chemical substances that caused the breath itself to be poisonous to others. As a karmic consequence she now finds herself immediately poisoned in the presence of certain metals, plastics, odors and leathers. If these leathers are tanned with oak, they do not trouble her. If they are tanned with the very same things that she once used to hinder someone else, they cause problem.

A man with distressing digestive weakness from infancy came to Cayce for opinion. He was found to be a glutton in his past two lives. In both these lives he could not control his habit of overeating. In another reading of Cayce of a man having chronic anemia revealed that five incarnations back he was a ruthless conqueror in Peru and brutally caused a lot of bloodshed amongst the people he subdued. The Karmic reaction had taken over in having his own body struggling for blood. The past bloody slaughter of theirs now encompassed his own present state. The law of Karma awarded him a protracted form of educative justice throughout the present life. Probably he had already paid much of his karmic debt in past few lives already.

Souls reincarnate on Earth to work on their own shortcomings. Let us take the aforementioned Elizabeth/Stanley case from Newton's file. Elizabeth loved her husband, but Stanley left her alone and went to Africa. During 1919, at the age of 52, Elizabeth died of influenza with much loneliness and sorrow. This suffering had started a karmic issue between them and as a result they reincarnated again in an entirely different set up. These two souls reincarnated as Belinda (Elizabeth) and Stuart (Stanley) to resolve the karmic issue.

When Belinda met Newton, she was 47 and had never been married because she had strange feelings of abandonment and loss if she would enter in a marital relationship. She moved to California after a stormy breakup with Stuart about 20 years before. Belinda cared for Stuart but she had broken off their engagement after making a decision to change her life and to pursue a new career. She asked Stuart to come with her but he pleaded with Belinda to marry him and stay in the area where they had both grown up but she refused. Stuart was devastated by her leaving him. This is how the Karma manifested and the debt was paid with same treatment.

This is Karma – its blade cuts both ways. Stanley left Elizabeth in a swift, uncompromising and brutal way in the past life. As a result Stuart felt the emotional pain of rejection in present life. There is a karmic lesson for Belinda as well. Elizabeth did not understand what freedom meant for her husband. So, Belinda has carried the mental imprint (strange feelings of abandonment and loss in a marriage) of the past life into her life today for this realization. When she abandoned her lover, she understood what freedom means for her. In all possibility Elizabeth and Stanley are soulmates. Since the karmic debt is paid, it is likely they will assume a new role together and enter in a very successful relationship unless some other karmic issues in another life need to be resolved and a balance is made.

Spiritual regressionists and past-life therapists have investigated countless number of cases where love was tormented, deprived, cruel, deadly, heroic and unforgiving because of strict karmic challenges in one or more previous lives, but the couples are happily married in present life.

One very strong case where divine justice had prominently manifested itself is reported by Stevenson. A boy H. A. Wijeratne (born on 17 January 1947) from Uggalkaltota, a remote village of Ceylon claimed to have reincarnated in his own family as 'his' previous brother's son. In past life his name was Ratran Hami. At his birth, his parents noticed a marked deformity of his right chest and arm. In the right upper chest, there was a hollow area about two inches in diameter. The entire right arm and the fingers were underdeveloped in comparison with the rest of the body. In this condition, the child could only grasp a pen or pencil. His hand was almost useless for grasping or holding bigger or heavier objects.

His parents attributed his condition in a general way to some Karma in a past-life. As time would pass, their assumption would prove to be accurate when the child starts revealing a past-life of a murderer and sentenced to death. Wijeratne's father (Tileratne Hami) also noted certain resemblances to his deceased brother, Ratran Hami. The child was dark in complexion like Ratran Hami, while the other children in the family were rather fair. Other resemblances include noticeable facial features between Wijeratne and Ratran Hami.

When Wijeratne was between two-and-a-half years old he began walking around the house in a lonely way talking to himself. When his mother (Huratal Hami) paid attention to his monologues, she overheard him saying that his arm was deformed because he had murdered his wife in his previous life – "*He [Ratran Hami] had killed my wife by using my hand.*" (Stevenson, 1974b, p. 154). He mentioned a number of details connected with a crime of which his mother, until that time, had heard nothing (a tightly guarded family secret). When she asked her husband about the child's statements, he confirmed the accuracy of what the boy was saying. It was his younger brother, Ratran Hami, who had been executed for the murder of his wife, Podi Menike.

Wijeratne continued talking as if he was a cursed human being. Often in a remorseful lonely way to himself and at other times to persons who asked him about his arm, he narrated "*the details of the crime, arrest, and execution of Ratran Hami with a vividness and abundance of detail*". (Stevenson, 1974b, p. 149). During 1961, Stevenson interviewed Wijeratne, his parents, and many others, and obtained a certified transcript of the trial for murder of Ratran Hami. This document enabled Stevenson to ascertain certain dates and established facts.

Wijeratne's father was the older brother by about fifteen years of Ratran Hami. They were farmers in a small village at the time Ratran Hami murdered his wife, Podi Menike, with a 'kris' (Malay knife) because she refused to leave her parents' home and accompany him to his village. The murder occurred on October 14, 1927, Ratran Hami was tried in June, 1928, and executed in July, 1928. Few days before his death, Ratran Hami told his brother that he would return (means, he would be born again). Wijeratne remembered this incident, recognized and pointed out to his father the plank on which he (Ratran Hami) had sharpened the kris that was used to kill his wife and the orange tree under which the plank stood. The orange tree and the plank were in the same place as they had been two decades ago. He also showed other objects and their part in the murder. Wijeratne also confirmed that Ratran Hami had an unbearable temper. He also remembers with stunning details how he had been executed.

Stevenson (1974b, pp. 149-71) had thoroughly researched this case and included his findings in details in his book 'twenty cases suggestive of reincarnation'. He met Wijeratne several times during later years when he completed his school days and entered university. He had successfully undergone surgery to separate the fingers of the right hand that were webbed together. His hand healed well and he was able to make better use of it after the operation. Though his physical condition improved, he suffered from severe mental illness as a girl whom he loved passionately, rejected him.

There are strong paranormal connections linking three lives along karmic lines – Ratran Hami (the murderer), H. A. Wijeratne (the murderer reincarnated), and Podi Menike (the murdered). Wijeratne believed that the concave deformity of his own right chest was at the site of the fatal wound he (Ratran Hami) gave to his wife, and regarded the deformity as a just punishment for his behavior and fully as much so as his being hanged.

When Ratran Hami murdered his wife, a karmic debt was formed that must be paid in full either in present life or future lives. The debt was paid partially by the capital punishment he received. Rest of the bad 'residue' he carried forward in his present life as Wijeratne. Even as a child he understood the possible karmic origin of his deformities. How could a child, who belongs to a semi-literate poor family, have such an understanding and wise realization at the age of two or so? Throughout his present life, his physical deformity constantly reminded him of his crime committed decades ago in the past-life.

Wijeratne had an unbearable temper. It is reported that he had abused his first wife as well and she had died at a young age. As a result, in his present life he was so rejected by a girl he loved that he suffered from mental illness, and was admitted to a psychiatric hospital for almost a month. When we truly love others, we will experience being loved in return. On the other hand, if a person is more inclined to hate and abuse people then they too will ultimately be hated and abused, whether in the present life or in a subsequent one.

Karma does not dissolve without its various fruits being tasted and consumed. Ratran Hami / Wijeratne learned a lesson through the line of the law of Karma. On January 1969, he wrote a letter to Stevenson where he had expressed his new understanding.

> "*I carefully considered the assertion of what one should do if a wife behaved in an unseemly manner. I thought it is wise that as a primary step she should be made aware of her weakness and advised accordingly. These are common occurrences in society. If, however, a wife disregards [means misconduct by wives] her husband's advice it is wise to divorce her. Or else the sudden anger that can arise in a person can lead to* ***the destruction of many lives****. Thus, according to Buddha's teaching* ***if one's actions are guided by patience and wisdom it can lead to a happy life.***" (Stevenson, 1974b, p. 165)

Wijeratne's reference to "the destruction of many lives" needs specific understanding. This is what the enforcer of the law of Karma teaches us repeatedly but we ignore. If Ratran Hami had the wisdom then many sorrows would have been avoided. It is the 'fruits' of our past-lives that determine much of what our present circumstances will be. It means, the actions of the present will inevitably be accounted for in the future. In a very practical way, the human beings are all the sum totals of their past deeds – nothing happens by chance. Wijeratne's physical deformities and mental illness had an exact cause. Every occurrence has its cause from which it follows by necessity. Karma then is our best spiritual teacher. We spiritually learn and grow as our actions return to us to be resolved and dissolved. The karmic doctrine emphasizes the necessity to erase the debts and not to create new ones.

The law of Karma counts not only our actions but inactions also. Newton (2016b, p. 360) wrote,

> "*Karma does not only pertain to our deeds, it is internal as well, reflecting our thoughts, feelings and impulses – all relating to cause and effect. Karma is more than taking proper actions toward others, it is also having the intention to do so.*"

A grieving mother, whose eight-year-old daughter died, was put under deep hypnosis for regression. She recalled (Newton, 2016b, p. 382),

"I was a wealthy matron in London in the nineteenth century. I paid little attention to the suffering of the young waifs on the street around my townhouse. I callously disregarded their plight because they were not my children; to my mind they were the responsibility of their parents or the state and had nothing to do with me. I looked the other way even though I had plenty of money to support an orphanage and a safe house for young unwed mothers nearby. I knew these services were struggling to make ends meet and I did nothing."

She learnt her lesson in a hard way.

Karma is the ultimate affirmation of the free will of a self-aware soul. I had free will in each of my past-life and my past had determined my present. At present life I again have free will and my present life will determine my future life. Then whom should I blame for my miseries and whom should I thank for my fortunes when at every moment I am exercising my free will? At the best I can say that Karma sets up the situation, but not the choices I make about the situation. I 'pay forward' my 'reactive past'; if life is cruel, it is of our making here on this Earth. Our current life represents all past experiences both pleasant and unpleasant, and so we are the product of all our former choices. If an irresponsible motorcycle rider lived for speed and essentially got a high from the dangers of his obsession, then he had deliberately put himself in that position by using his free will. Hence, Karma and destiny are opposing forces. Karma was set in motion an unknown long time ago, and it will keep on going till the time a final balance is reached and no soul needs to reincarnate anymore. Perhaps my best efforts that I put in explaining the law of Karma in this chapter have its root in my past lives.

Souls generally prefer to reincarnate in places where they have been before. However, future life selections are not based on ethnicity or nationalism, or comfortable familiarity of culture they once lived, but more due to karmic choices. For this reason, many souls stay within family bloodlines. As example, a dying man is expected to come back as his own unborn grandchild for some unusual karmic circumstances. If two brothers had a close affinity for each other, and one were to die suddenly while still young, the soul of the dead sibling might want to return in the surviving sibling's child to restore this broken life connection to finish an important task. According to Newton (2016a, p. 219), most common of this type are the souls of young children who die soon after birth and then return to the same parents as the soul of their next baby. These tragic family events are all made in advance by the souls and their guides. They involve a maze of karmic issues. Here the child dies early for the parents to learn an important karmic lesson. Curtiss (1949, p. 32) wrote,

"Often the whole life of worldly-minded parents is changed to a more spiritual one after a short visit of a more advanced Soul as their child. The short incarnation was like the visit of an angel."

Newton (2016a, p. 219) had a case where a person remembered dying from a birth defect early in his last life. When Newton asked him the purpose of ending life when he was only a few days old, he replied that the lesson was not for him but for his parents (means, the person had no karmic issue but his parents had). This type of short life is called 'a filler life', i.e., when souls return for a short life to help someone else rather than work on their own issues, because there isn't time. Newton explains,

> "*In this case, the parents had abused and finally caused the death of another child when they were together in an earlier life. Although they were a loving young couple in the last life of my client, these parents evidently needed to experience the grief of having a child they desperately wanted taken away from them. Experiencing the anguish from this terrible loss gave the souls of these parents a deeper insight into the effects of severing a blood bond*".

Therefore, we can see that all lives are preplanned, and if the life ends unexpectedly, it has some plan behind it.

> "*Souls who become involved in these tragedies are not caught in the wrong place at the wrong time with a capricious God looking the other way. Every soul has a motive for the events in which it chooses to participate.*" (Newton, 2016a, p. 219)

To speed up their learning, some souls choose harsh situations voluntarily. One person under hypnosis commented that he chooses to live a short life of seven-year-old American-Indian boy because, "*I was looking for a short-burst lesson in humility and this life as a mistreated starving half-breed was enough*". This lesson was perhaps due from another past incarnation. Therefore, from karmic point of view a short-life is no way less significant than a long one. A person can live for hundred years but make little progress in his karmic path if he could not learn life lessons utilizing his physical body and exercising his free will.

Some souls are so eager and determined to make progress on their karmic path that they deliberately choose a handicapped body. Some of them prefer to live in extreme poverty or hardness. In a human body these souls devote to causes for the betterment of others, often at his own expense.

> "*These are souls so desperate to pay off karmic debts that are holding them back that they are willing even to undergo that torture in order to advance spiritually. Sometimes they are deliberately assigned to such afflicted bodies as a means of atonement for abuses committed in previous lives. Other times, if they are truly repentant of serious sins, they will voluntarily select such a body, but in most instances it is an assignment by higher forces who compassionately select that body for a soul so*

troubled and tortured by past misdeeds that he is incapable of making his own choice". (Montgomery, 1972, p. 46)

Hence, a poor, or hard life, or a handicapped person living in a damaged body does not necessarily have to involve a karmic debt they are paying off because of past-life responsibility for an injury to someone else.

"*When we see people who are victims of great adversity in life, this does not necessarily mean they were perpetrators of evil or wrongdoing of any kind in a former life. A soul with no such past associations might choose to suffer through a particular aspect of emotional pain to learn greater compassion and empathy for others by volunteering in advance for a life of travail.*" (Newton, 2016b, p. 104)

This is just another type of lesson where the soul is keeping his karmic path straight. After all, it is soul's destiny "*to search for truth in their experiences in order to gain wisdom.*" (Newton, 2016b, p. 44). By experiencing difficult lives at free will, they learn great life-lessons, that they should be sympathetic to the poor and not to exploit them, that they should help those who are facing hardship in life, that physically challenged people should not be ridiculed, but assisted. These lessons help the souls to make fewer mistakes in the forthcoming lives. These souls accumulate great positive Karma in every life on Earth and ultimately a time comes when they don't need to reincarnate again; they join the rank of guides and higher powers.

On the contrary there are many souls who don't wish to reincarnate because the spiritual environment is hard to leave and also due to past-life sufferings they remember, ultimately they have to come back to Earth in a physical form to pay karmic debts. These souls often lag behind because only through reincarnation the evolution of the souls can take place. The transition from imperfection to perfection is possible only when the soul had overcome many difficult body assignments during their task-oriented lives.

Hence, reincarnation is a purposeful action, not dependent on luck and chance. Newton (2016a, p. 202) wrote, "*Our karma of past deeds towards humanity and our mistakes and achievements have all been evaluated with an eye toward the best course of future endeavors.*" It is evident that older and much developed souls reincarnate less. Or, they incarnate in other worlds where life-form has great spiritual development. Spiritual regressionists have confirmed that there are different life-forms in many worlds other than our Earth. When a world dies, those entities with unfinished karmic issue move on to another world which has a suitable life-form for the kind of work they have been doing. Some life-forms are so advanced that they are purely mental world in a physical setup.

We have free will, and Karma works to develop our ability to handle free will responsibly. As example, Newton (2016a, p. 50) described a case where one person had terribly hurt a girl in one of his life. After returning to spirit world, his spirit guide had exclusively scrutinized his soul and he was again sent back to Earth very soon as a woman (i.e., reincarnated as a woman) amongst many cruel people around. As an abused woman itself, the soul understood its responsibility to realize the damage it had done to an innocent girl. The spirit guides are very strict with those who have been involved with cruelty. This is not a punishment but 'regeneration'.

Many of us have learnt hard lessons from broken relationships. There is nothing called 'true love'. It's a fantasy driven by an addiction to have love at any price. Hence the important thing is to forgive and move on in life to work out the Karma otherwise we will make the same mistakes over and over again. Newton (2016b, p. 285) wrote,

> "*Each life is a piece of fabric which makes up the whole tapestry of our existence. If a family member or friend is harsh and uncompromising, or perhaps weak and emotionally distant toward us in life, we are only seeing an external portion of the entire true character of that soul. Role assignments in life all have purpose.* ***If you grew up with a particularly difficult parent… ask yourself this question: What did I learn at the hands of this person that has given me wisdom I would not possess if he or she had never been in my life?***"

The better we understand it, the easier our lives will be. Karma works in a cycle where the negativity is balanced by positivity and the principle of forgiveness helps to speed up this process. If we understand Karma, we will much appreciate the grand design to life and afterlife. Newton (2016a, pp. 51-52) commented,

> "*The key to growth is understanding we are given the ability to make mid-course corrections in our life and having the courage to make necessary changes when what we are doing is not working for us. By conquering fear and taking risks, our karmic pattern adjusts to the effects of new choices. At the end of every life, rather than having a monster waiting to devour our souls, we serve as our most severe critic in front of teacher-guides. This is why karma is both just and merciful. With the help of our spiritual counselors and peers we decide on the proper mode of justice for our conduct.*"

Negative Karma is not permanent. A person who had displayed negative attitudes towards others can erase his negative Karma if he continuously makes an effort to change – "*... and the only way to erase the bad marks is to perform a kindly act for someone in need*". (Montgomery, 1972, p. 138). He can work it out during his many incarnated lives on Earth. Let me discuss one case (Newton, 2016a, pp. 224-29) to analyze the issue.

A tall and well-built woman enjoyed participating in outdoor sports despite being bothered all her life with recurring leg pains. She had visited many physicians but there was no cure. Ultimately, she tried past-life regression therapy for relief thinking that her problem might be rooted in the past. When she was put under deep hypnosis, she remembered two past-lives – one is that of a Viking called Leth around AD 800, who navigated with his band of invaders over long distances, sailing upriver and hiking through thick, virgin forests, pillaging settlements, killing mercilessly and raping women along the way. Leth was killed during a raid while looting a village. Another life she remembered was that of a six-year-old girl named Ashley living in New England in the year 1871. Ashley had a road accident by which she was physically handicapped. One of the heavy rear wheels of a fully loaded, horse-drawn carriage had rolled over her legs at the same point above both knees, crushing the bones. She was never able to stand or walk again, and with her crippled body she lived another 41 years, but the rest of her life she had a productive period as a writer and tutor of disadvantaged children.

Can we see the karmic justice in these two lives – a strong brutal man and a helpless crippled woman? As an invader, Leth had generated a lot of negative Karma that he had to pay in the next life in a pitiable condition of a woman. However Ashley had worked out her Karma as she put her crippled body to good use by assisting disadvantaged children. The physical lives of Leth and Ashley are examples of karmic compensation. Here one important point to note that even as a victim of karmic debt, Ashley was a beneficiary of circumstances and made progress along the path of Karma. This is the beauty of karmic justice. From many similar cases like this, it is found that in one life if the soul shows extreme behavior, in the next life this will be counterbalanced by an opposite choice to even-out development.

Self-discovery is an essential part of a soul's development. As example before a crisis arises on Earth (as example, a devastating war), many souls reincarnate on Earth only to take the opportunity to make changes for growth (Newton, 2016a, p. 52). The spirit guide is always ready to help, as long as the soul continues to try. But if the soul does not cooperate, everything comes to a standstill in its development. Montgomery (1972, pp. 64, 81) wrote,

> "*We learn, for instance, that the best way to advance is to love, for an unkind or openly hostile thought about another soul retards the progress to such a degree that sometimes more than one future lifetime is required to erase the blot from the record. Speak no evil. Think no evil. There is no evil except that which we create*... ***We are our own devils, with our thoughts and subsequent deeds.***"

> "*Growth, development, love, constructive action, and consideration for others are the keys to unlock the kingdom of heaven, and those who use force and anger to destroy, instead of love to rebuild, are earning dire consequences for themselves in this spirit life and in future incarnations.*"

Also when adversity strikes we should not sit back with a fatalistic attitude and not fight to improve the situation by making changes favorable to us. We have free will, as Newton (2016a, p. 213) wrote,

> "*During our lives all of us will experience opportunities for change which involve risk. These occasions may come at inconvenient times. We may not act upon them, but the challenge is there for us. The purpose of reincarnation is the exercise of free will. Without this ability, we would be impotent creatures indeed.*
>
> *Thus, karmic destiny means we are not just caught up in events over which we have no control. This also means we have karmic lessons and responsibilities. The law of cause and effect for our actions always exists, which is why this case did not want to make a mistake in choosing a life unsuited to him. But whatever happens to us in life, it is important we understand that our happiness or pain does not reflect either blessings or betrayal on the part of a God-oversoul, our guides, or life selection coordinators.* ***We are the masters of our destiny.***"

Karma is merely a process of evolution, of achieving greater levels of enlightenment. Goldberg (2004, p. 267) wrote that many people asked him to help them speed up their karmic cycles so that they won't have to reincarnate again. But only the individual can do that – "*They must be honest, truthful, and faithful to their own code of ethics. If they follow this simple advice, they are well on their way to the higher planes*". According to Goldberg (2004, p. 187), the soul guides give tremendous opportunities to the reincarnating souls to speed up their Karma.

> "*If you ignore these opportunities, then your life won't change much. You will stay on your average or below-average frequencies. However, if you follow the laws of karma, you will switch to a much more desirable frequency, which will not only assure you of a better life in this incarnation, but it will result in more positive future lifetimes. The choice, as always, is yours*".

Being homosexual or lesbian often carries a sexual stigma in our society. It presents a more difficult road in life. Though altered sexual preferences should be treated with same ethical standard, when that past-life of these people are regressed we can trace related events in their past which had started a karmic debt. There is spiritual divinity that cares for everyone irrespective of sexual preferences, belief and disbelief in god etc. The karmic justice is same for everyone.

Life is hard, but suicide is not an option because suicide by a physically healthy person is not a prearranged karmic option for anyone (Newton, 2016b, p. 235). The next case involves a 32-year-old married woman called Hester with masculine feelings who had easily manipulated men all her life because she felt incomplete as a woman. Under hypnosis, she experienced a series of male lives including a short-life as a prosecuting attorney called Ross Feldon during the 1880s. Ross had committed suicide at the age of thirty-three. Under hypnosis, Hester revealed that after her death (as Ross Feldon) her spirit guide was disappointed because Ross did not have the courage to face difficulties. In a serious relationship if the other partner is cruel and uncompromising, we are only seeing an external portion of the entire true character of that soul. Every adverse situation that we face in life has a meaning by which we possess new wisdom.

8.2: The beginning and end of the reincarnation and karmic cycle

> "*If death meant just leaving the stage long enough to change costumes and come back as a new character... Would you slow down? Or speed up? Or would you decide that your part in the play was done and leave the stage for good?*"
>
> Chuck Palahniuk

Spiritualists often wonder how, when and why the reincarnation and karmic cycle started, and when it is going to end. Spiritual regressionists have put forward many theories on this. Arthur Ford revealed through Ruth Montgomery that the souls have originated from another planet. Earth was a testing ground for them. But the souls had misused the human bodies, and as a result the karmic cycle started.

> "*The father [highly evolved souls from other planets] who conceived the earth phase for testing souls put no evil there, but the errant souls who eagerly inhabited bodies lusted, fought, and squabbled, hoping to enhance their own importance, thus establishing a force of evil...*". (Montgomery, 1972, p. 65).

So, the force of evil created by the migratory souls caused the Karma to begin. And since their negative Karma could not be worked out in one lifetime, these souls had to reincarnate once the physical body is worn out. Bruce Goldberg came to a similar conclusion. Some mysterious "Light" people, originating from other solar systems, are responsible for not only our evolutionary advancement, but for the karmic cycle itself. He calls them "Light" people because they are pure energy in the form of light. They don't possess any physical body.

> "*The 'light' people are sent to Earth from another galaxy to experience life in human bodies. Their goal is to assist us in our evolutionary development. When 'light' people leave their human bodies, they return to an examination room (although this is not a physical room as we know it). Their progress is evaluated by a group of monitors or Planners.*

> *If they do well, their vibrational rate is raised, but if they fail, it's reduced. These Planners are directed by Master Planners who communicate with them from the home planet many galaxies away*". (Goldberg, 2004, p. 124)

These "Light" people came to Earth to facilitate our evolution, and they inhabited the bodies of primitive humans, altered genetic coding and other biological processes to promote our development. These people could enter and leave the physical body any time by their will. The Planners trained them to perform certain functions and assist the human they are occupying in its intelligence and social functions. But sometimes these "Light" people got carried away with the physicality of the body and violated moral and ethereal codes (such as obsessions with sex, or murder or oppression), or merely refused to perform the functions for which they were trained. When this happened, the Planners punished these "Light" people.

> "*The mechanism of the origin of our karmic cycle now became clear. Advanced ETs from a distant galaxy in the form of light energy experimented with humans to aid us in our evolution. Many of these "light" people took advantage (or were overwhelmed) by our physicality and ran afoul with what the Master Planners had in store. The Planners, as supervisors to the progress of these "light" people, had the power to trap these light beings into our physical bodies and remove their memories so they would not be psychologically compromised as they began life as a human*". (Goldberg, 2004, p. 128).

So, this is how, the "light" people, while trapped in human bodies, represented the beginning of our karmic cycle. We are fortunate that these aliens tampered with our evolution. Probably our present level of technology might have been unattainable without their assistance.

This entire process of reincarnation and Karma will end when we will pay our karmic debts. At this phase we will fully understand and accept the universal oneness of all mankind and the laws which govern us by many reincarnations – "*The truth is that there is no such thing as race or color, but simply different souls which spring from the same source, God.*" (Montgomery, 1972, p. 166). Fears, prejudices, and judgments will completely disappear from our awareness as we evolve spiritually. The resulting expansion of this awareness will allow God to reveal the truth once and for all to us (Goldberg, 2004, p. 268). This is the ultimate truth.

> "*We not only were created in God's image but of the very stuff of God, so that in order to complete our cycle and return to Him, we must absorb the philosophy of the universe and come to understand its laws, so that* ***we never again will be out of harmony with the creation***". (Montgomery, 1972, p. 57)

Karmic cycles can be speed up if we are honest, truthful, and faithful to our own code of ethics. If we follow this simple advice, we are well on our way to stop the karmic cycle. The reward for this is ascension, and liberation of our soul from the wheel of birth and death and freedom from the karmic pull of the Earth. We are on the path to reunite with God. Goldberg (2004, p. 268) wrote,

"*Ascension removes you from the cycle of birth and death, and allows you to enter the heavenly words ("eternal now") to join God. You do have the option of remaining on these lower planes as a guide, but free of the discomforts you currently experience*".

Ascension is the true purpose of our incarnation on this planet. Once the subconscious is purified, it no longer needs Karma, or the 'karmic cycle'. The result is ascension and a return to God, and meld with God in perfect union. The spirit guides or angels are always helping us grow spiritually so our eventual ascension will be faster. Montgomery (1972, pp. 161-62) wrote,

"*Obviously we here are yet to experience that bliss, but there is a teaching here that when souls near that final perfection they once again review not only their past lives but every thought and concept and idea which has touched them, or they it, since the beginning of the life of all of us. This is during the sixth plane. They finally decide that no stone remains unturned that they have not repaid in some manner or thought or way, and that they therefore have atoned for misdeeds and are ready to join God. There is no conceit in this decision but a totally accurate assessment of life since the beginning. They then are drawn into the oneness of God in perfect peace.*"

It is the nature of the soul to experience all levels and conditions of God. Thus, the Earth experience is part of the soul's evolution into the greater consciousness of God.

8.3: Skeptic's views

"*If we see only what we know, how does anyone ever see anything new? The unknown...how do we ever get out of our box?*"

Anonymous

"*Science is a voyage of discovery, and as with all such voyages, you have to believe there is something meaningful out there to discover before you embark on it. And with every new scientific discovery made, that belief is confirmed*".

Paul Davies

Karma is a testable hypothesis, rather than as matters requiring dogmatic adherence. There's no scientific way to explain the law of Karma, nor to prove or disprove its existence because it involves the interaction of non-quantifiable parameters like consciousness, free will and motivation that are beyond the grasp of classical physics. That's the reason we can believe in this doctrine without even considering science. It stands firm on logic and reason and promotes ethical values in society, and therefore is worth believing in.

If the doctrine of Karma is unintelligible then by the same reason our entire legal system, which assigns responsibility to people for the decisions that they make, would be unintelligible. The entire moral and legal foundation of our civilization rests on the assumption that the personality generally controls and is, therefore, responsible for the behaviors of its body because it has the power within itself to create effects in the actual world. Similarly, the doctrine of Karma attached this responsibility with the immortal soul that carries the consequences of his action, and a form of reincarnation establishes a causal (karmic) connection between two successive personalities – it is rooted in logic.

There is another reason we can strongly believe this doctrine to be true. Newtonian physics confirms that inanimate objects obey laws for any interaction of any kind from the microscopic level to the macroscopic level. In fact, classical physics is all about the study and application of nature's laws. Not a single rain-drop falls from the sky except by law. Therefore, if laws govern all of nature, how can we claim that humans alone are the law-exempt odd man out? If classical physics cannot exactly explain human qualities, how can this doctrine be labeled as non-existent? Karma is the law of cause and effect in the moral dimension. Quantum physics had proven that consciousness is a self-experienced reality. Even skeptics who deny the existence of quantum consciousness are conscious beings because they deny – its attempted denial becomes its undeniable proof. If classical physics can explain interactions of objects with mathematical calculations, how can we label interaction of consciousness as unscientific? All we need is a new branch of science that can precisely discern, quantify and explain all the human qualities, and then we will be able to explain the doctrine of Karma with mathematical certainty.

Human quest for knowledge should not be checked and choked by such narrow-mindedness. Already quantum physics, though at its infancy, has supplanted classical physics in many fields. With farther development, the possibility is always open that there may exist many varieties of additional properties, qualities, and systems that govern consciousness in other dimensions, that would explain many things that classical physics cannot explain. The realm of scientific study is always open-ended.

8.4: Final conclusion

"*We are in reality, energy. As such, we cannot be destroyed. We cannot die. We simply appear to change bodies every 75 years or so.*"

Bruce Goldberg

"*In the spirit world nothing is insignificant. No act goes unrecorded.*"
Michael Duff Newton

"*The world is not to be narrowed till it will go into the understanding ..., but the understanding to be expanded and opened till it can take in the image of the world as it is in fact.*"
Sir Francis Bacon

The evidence presented in the previous chapters shows conclusively that there is overwhelming proof for the existence of the afterlife. The study of the afterlife belongs to the realm of psychic science.

If close-minded skeptics still refuse to investigate or rebut the voluminous available objective evidence, they should not make any valid comments about it. Skeptics discredit the proofs, first, by ignoring the evidence, second, by refusing to examine the evidence, and third, by insisting on overly stringent standards of evidence, which, if adopted, would render any experiential science impossible. They believe that they are 'scientific' but at some point, they cross the line between the reasonable demand for scientific evidence and the unreasonable (and unscientific) demand for logical proof. However, Champlain (2013, p. 95) had a fine observation regarding the skeptics.

"*I shared that I was writing a book with a heart surgeon recently who has spoken with thousands of people before undergoing heart surgery. Certainly there is fear of the unknown and people realize that they may lose their life during an operation.*

He told me that 100% of the time, whether a person is religious, irreligious, or atheist, the same three things are shared by all people, they feel love for their family and those they are closest to, they have sadness and regret for the things they have not said or done, ***they pray and have faith in an afterlife***".

Today the evidence for an afterlife is sufficiently strong and convincing. Finally, the weight of evidence begins to set in, and several mainstream scientists are ready to announce to the world that afterlife is a scientifically proven fact. And then it will become impossible for our culture to do business as usual. Goldberg (2004, p. 24) commented,

"*Skeptics, especially those who pride themselves on their rationalism, must come to terms with the fact that quantum physics and superstring theory are now accepted scientific paradigms. Concepts formerly ridiculed as "metaphysical" — multidimensionality, simultaneity, even reincarnation and Karma — now have a scientific foundation.*"

So far, we have discussed spirituality in the academy as something that religious faiths have told us, but not as something for which there could be empirical evidence. When serious discussions of spirituality will start, it would mark the beginning of the end of a self-centered culture whose driving forces have been greed, ambition and control on fellow human beings, and which measures success in terms of material possessions, wealth, reputation, prestige, power and social status. This is the reason the question of an afterlife has immense importance for the human beings. When we will grow in our ability to feel kindness and compassion towards all beings, and when we will understand that the purpose of life is love and knowledge, the atmosphere of 'taboo' that our culture has created will quickly disappear. With this, much discomfort and anxiety generated by the taboo will also disappear. That day is not far away.

CHAPTER 9

The spirit world

"For an Infinite God there must be an infinite home."

Minot J. Savage

"The Universe is a vast exhibition of intense activity, movement, and intelligence – a becoming through perpetual evolution. This consists of two systems – the natural or physical, and the psychic or spiritual world – and each of them is governed by its own laws, which are entirely different in their action. These two world-systems are perpetually acting and reacting on each other; the physical world being subservient to the spiritual world, and controlled by it. Furthermore, the inhabitants of the spirit world are merely human beings freed from the limitations imposed upon them by their physical bodies."

George Lindsay Johnson

In addition to the huge number of NDE and reincarnation cases, other experiences that suggest the existence of a mysterious and highly organized spirit world beyond our earthly comprehension include soul memories recovered under hypnosis. An expert hypnotist can open the gateway to the spirit world with a client by using his skills to reach and unlock the subject's memory of their existence in this mysterious place in between two successive physical lives. In other words, the client has the opportunity to actually see his immortality as a soul. Newton (2016a, p. 195) wrote,

"I should add that most people who are in deep hypnosis are able to see beyond an Earth reality of three-dimensional space, into alternate realities of timelessness. In the subconscious state, my subjects experience a chronology of time with their past and present lives which resembles

what they perceive when conscious. There is a change when I take them into superconsciousness and the spirit world. Here they see the now of time as one homogeneous unit of past, present, and future. Seconds in the spirit world seem to represent years on Earth. When their sessions are over, clients will often express surprise at how time in the spirit world is unified."

After spending decades on research on this fascinating subject many world-famous past-life therapists have constructed a working model of the spirit world structure. We call these master hypnotists as spiritual regressionists.

The astounding thing most regressionists find is that once subjects are regressed back into their soul state they all display a remarkable consistency in responding to questions about the spirit world. It does not matter if the subject was an atheist or deeply religious. There is extraordinary uniformity in their accounts as to their manner of spiritual travel, routes, and destinations, although what they see along the way is distinctive with each person. People even use the same words and graphic descriptions in colloquial language when discussing their lives as souls. Since the regressionists affirm each other's independent research findings, we cannot dismiss them as wishful thinking or something like 'a fertile mind working overtime' etc. Sometimes there are differences in narrative reporting between cases, but this is due more to the level of soul development than to variances in how each subject basically saw the spirit world.

When the spiritual regressionist initially brings a client into the spirit world, his visions are spontaneous, particularly as to spiritual order and his place in a community of soul life. No one sees the spirit world as confining. Most people are able to recall with great clarity about having freedom of movement and going to open spaces where souls of many learning levels gather in a very friendly atmosphere.

The details that I give in this chapter about this world 'between lives' is prepared after the spiritual regressionists have analyzed a high volume of cases. The validity and reliability of their findings are beyond doubt. After reading many such narratives about the spirit world, I have come to appreciate that the spirit world is highly organized, and there is a grand thoughtful design to life and afterlife. In fact, there is so much about the spirit world that often clients are unable to describe in earthly terms. This unseen world is so beautiful that sometimes a subject will even express disbelief at his own visions.

9.1: The experience of dying

"*We who must die demand a miracle. How could the Eternal do a temporal act, The Infinite become a finite fact? Nothing can save us that is possible. We who must die demand a miracle.*"

W. H. Auden

> *"Death can be our best friend. It helps us to become aware of the other worlds that are denied to us on the physical plane. Death actually assists us in finding genuine happiness."*
>
> Bruce Goldberg

In very deep hypnotic trance levels, many people remember death experiences from previous incarnations. These recollections give valuable insight into the process of dying. When there is an eminent danger ahead, such as an unavoidable accident which will devastate the physical body and there is no chance of surviving, the soul leaves the body a moment before actual death. In this way the soul emerges with their energy more intact. The transition from a physical life to soul life is rather peaceful. We are also not alone, isolated or unaided immediately following death. Unseen intelligent energy forces guide each of us throughout the transition. In a brief the dying experience is like this,

1. The person will hear all sorts of noises following death, such as buzzing sounds which is most commonly reported. Other sounds include, ringing, clicks, roars, banging noises, whistling and musical. He may see many different bright colors. This experience changes quickly to the next.
2. The person will have a floating sensation. Whatever physical discomforts and pain he had in his deathbed will slowly vanish. He will have an inner peace and quiet with complete absence of fear, and a strange feeling of 'timelessness'. Some people report telepathic communication from other departed souls telling them not to fear.
3. The soul is aware of the presence of a 'silver cord' which is attached to the back of the head of the astral body and connects the physical body. As long as this cord is unbroken, the person's physical body is still alive. Upon physical death this silver cord is broken. Many people who had an OBE also confirm seeing this silver cord.
4. Once the silver cord is broken the soul appears as a mass of self-conscious energy, but it may still display human characteristics. Souls often use their capacity to project former life forms. Newton (2016b, p. 2) wrote that just after death all souls encounter a "wispy cloudiness" around them, but it soon becomes clear, enabling them to look off into a great distance all-around.
5. The new astral body is subject to very different and strange physical laws. The astral body has the ability to do many things which the physical body cannot. For example, the astral body can move through solid walls and travel thousands of miles in a matter of second (nonlocality of consciousness). Some people regain complete knowledge of former lives and are able to read the minds of those who were involved in former lives.

6. Either the soul proceeds to soul world or remain earthbound. Earthbound souls are disturbed spirits commonly known as 'ghosts'. They hover around as their unfinished business is so overpowering that they do not want to leave Earth's astral plane. Only a small number of souls become ghosts, while majority of the souls are eager to move on to the spirit world. Ghosts are 'trapped' – a condition of mental obstruction rather than any material hindrance and often have unpleasant influences on other human lives. Since the free will of the souls is respected, our benevolent spirit guides allow the disturbed spirits to wander around lost, unhappy and alone.
7. Those souls who want to enter spirit world will experience what they 'expect' to experience. The thought can take many forms. If he has a strong belief in hell, or if he thinks that he is destined to hell due to his wrongdoings, the hell will often manifest itself temporarily. Fortunately, these experiences will disappear quickly, and the tunnel experience will start following the person's entry to the spirit world. Every soul has a designated place in the spirit world. Almost all the souls pass through a dense atmosphere of light around the astral plane of Earth. This light has patches of darkish gray but no impenetrable black zones (Newton, 2016b, p. 52). Then the souls quickly move into the bright light of the spirit world which is single ethereal space without zones or barriers around it.
8. The first person they see in the spirit world is their personal guide. The guide appears to people who are very religious as figures of their faith. But if the soulmate, or a former relative or close friend appears to the incoming soul, their regular guide might be absent from the scene. Soon before and after death, the guides are somewhere in close proximity, monitoring the incomer's arrival in their own way. The leadership of a guide is more parental than dictatorial.

Dying experience doesn't always follow the order I have described. Also, there may be time lags between each step. Sometimes the soul does not realise that he has passed into spirit, so he hovers around, wondering why no one seems to pay attention to him. Sometimes the soul thinks his new state to be figments of his own imagination (Montgomery, 1972, pp. 33, 118). When the person accepts the death state easily and quickly, the entire process becomes very smooth and peaceful. The expectations of a person what the death state is supposed to be that will affect the actual experience.

In the afterlife realm, the souls move from one place to another by mere thinking.

> "*There are no barriers, no barricades, no blocks to our free passage. The mind wills where we will be, and there we are. The net effect is to be as nearly Godlike as it is possible for mere souls to be.*

> *It's the thought that transports us, and since* ***all solid objects on the earth's surface are merely thought forms*** *[fully consistent with quantum physics that the world is made from wave functions, like water waves, sound waves etc., which has created the illusion that matter is made from particles!], we move through them.*" (Montgomery, 1972, pp. 27, 61)

A common misconception is that all souls become omniscient at death. There are adjustment periods and the duration of soul adjustment depends upon the circumstances of death, attachments of each soul to the memories of the life just ended, and level of advancement. When a young life ends suddenly, the soul may be bewildered and confused over leaving people they love. They are unprepared for death. The highly developed masters and teachers take the initial impact of a soul's frustration following an untimely death. These advanced entities have better knowledge about the soul maturity because they have close connections with the soul over a prolonged series of past lives.

9.2: The spiritual journey begins at deathbed

> "*We forfeit our body in death, but our eternal life energy unites with the force of a divine oversoul. Death is not darkness, but light.*"
>
> Michael Duff Newton

The homecoming welcome starts when the person is at deathbed. Often the discarnate souls (close friends, parents, relatives etc.) visit the dying person at his dreams or 'in person' (may be simultaneously seen by relatives and medical personnel) just to assure him that he is merely in a transition stage between two great phases of life, and to accompany him to the spirit world. Often, they convey some meaningful messages. The departing soul is anxious to get moving on the way home, as the sufferings on Earth do drain energy He experiences a gradual dulling of the physical senses. Sight, hearing and feeling grow dimmer and dimmer, and the "life" of the person seems as a flickering candle flame gradually approaching utter extinction. But, while the physical senses are growing dimmer, the psychical senses are growing wonderfully acute. The dying persons often manifest a consciousness of what is occurring in another room, or another place. In many cases, the dying person has been able to so strongly project his personality (crisis apparition) that friends and relatives at a distance have actually seen his form, and in some cases have been able to communicate with him (Ramacharaka, 1909, p. 28). His astral body gradually disengages itself from its physical counterpart.

However, the soul does not go directly to the soul plane. Below the soul plane there are various lower planes. According to Bruce Goldberg there are five lower planes (Goldberg, 1982, pp. 34-35). Our Karmic cycle is worked out in these five planes. The lowest of these planes is the Earth plane (physical plane) where we function with a physical body. The greatest amount of Karma is erased or added at this level. This is the most difficult level.

When the soul starts its afterlife adventure with an astral body, it experiences the ascent into the spirit world as "*rising through misty layers of translucent light*" (Newton, 2016b, p. 51). The intellectual abilities, thoughts, emotions, desires – all remain exactly intact at this moment. The soul generally does no longer feel hate, anger, envy, jealousy and the like, but they can feel sadness because of their karmic guilt for making very poor choices, especially when others were hurt by these actions. Some souls carry nostalgia for the good times in all their past physical lives.

The soul enters the astral plane, and from here a series of rising dimensions starts which blends into the spiritual. Some souls arrive in severely damaged condition. These are the souls who were contaminated by their physical bodies and became involved with intentional evil acts (Newton, 2016b, p. 3). The masters and guides always isolate these souls for rehabilitation and carefully evaluate the degrees of harm done to others from mischief to malevolence. Such souls can remain in a kind of suspension for many thousands of years (Montgomery, 1972, p. 17). These souls are not allowed to interact with other souls because they can damage the karmic development of the rather developed souls. However, no soul is looked down upon as having less value than any other soul.

9.3: The astral plane

"*I am hopeful my years of research into the life we lead as souls may assist survivors in recognizing that death only exchanges one reality for another in the long continuum of existence*".

Michael Duff Newton

In an out-of-body experience, the soul is hovering in this plane. This is the plane after which the tunnel experience starts. The ghosts, earthbound spirits and those souls that need to take an early rebirth to progress their karmic cycle lingers in this plane but we generally cannot see them.

The astral plane exists here on Earth but we are unaware of this plane. Some researchers suggest that though OBEs appear to be in space and time of waking life, there are always details out of place. It means that such experiences happen in those portions of the transphysical worlds that most closely approximate that of our daily lives. Hence those who belong to the astral plane can see all the activities on Earth, but from Earth plane we are not aware of their existence, except few gifted people, such as, mediums and psychics who can sense ghosts.

A soul can be a ghost or earthbound for various reasons, such as, sudden death (the soul is confused or bewildered by an unexpected change), unfinished business (money matters, to help out children), guilt (suicide victims), revenge (a murder victim), resentful (at the sight of others enjoying their old homes and possessions) etc. Certain souls can be so disturbed by an act of injustice against them in life that they won't leave astral plane after death until they gain some sort of resolution. Otherwise, the souls generally don't interfere with people on Earth and the privacy of the living are respected (Newton, 2016b, p. 45). Terrestrial angels also live in this plane to help the earthbound spirits.

At this plane some souls prefer seclusion. These are the entities who won't go to higher planes after death. We don't feel their presence as ghosts, because they simply don't want to be in contact with anyone. Some of them want to return as quickly as possible in a new body. It means, they want to reincarnate immediately after death instead of going back to the soul plane, receiving counseling from masters and guides, studying their karmic lessons and taking some part in the selection of a new body (Newton, 2016b, p. 65). Some of them are so habituated to their body that they don't want to give up their physical form for any length of time. Many of this type have been real frontline warriors on Earth. They want to maintain continuity with their physical life. Some of them are so unhappy that they won't even talk to their teachers because of the extent of their unhappiness. But eventually, most of them make the decision to ask for assistance when they come to the conclusion that they can't progress alone. A client under deep hypnosis informed Newton,

> "*It's any space they want to create for themselves. They design their own reality with memories of a physical life. Some souls live in nice places like a garden setting. Others – those who have harmed people, for instance – design terrible spaces for themselves like a prison, a room with no windows. In these spaces they box themselves in so they can't experience much light or make contact with anyone. It is self-imposed punishment.*" (Newton, 2016b, p. 66)

Occasionally the terrestrial angels give them a new body to reincarnate immediately. Some souls prefer seclusion for a good purpose. They carry a big burden of negative energy and they feel that some isolation is necessary out of concern for contaminating other souls with negative energy.

Sometimes a living being can hold back the dead, such as, obsessed lovers, bereaved family members etc. (Shrikhande, 2009, p. 88). Most souls who are eager to depart for the spirit world will not leave Earth's astral plane until they take some sort of action to comfort those in distress who care about them (Newton, 2016b, p. 14). Newton (2016b, p. 22) recorded the following strange experience of a recent widow whose husband, Clay, died of cancer. Clay loved big band dancing.

> "*One night after Clay's death, his widow, my wife and the rest of the support group were in a circle in the middle of this lady's living room floor talking about my theories of how souls reach back to comfort the people they love. The widow exclaimed in frustration, 'Why hasn't Clay made himself known in a way that would comfort me?' There was a moment of silence and suddenly a music box on top of a book shelf began*

to play Glenn Miller's song 'In the Mood'. From what I understand, there was a stunned silence followed by nervous laughter from the group. All the widow could say was, 'That music box hasn't been touched in two years!' It didn't matter. I think she got Clay's message."

Some evil entities who are barred from entering higher planes, continue with their evil intentions (Shrikhande, 2009, p. 88). Possibly, the distressing NDEs are caused by these evil entities that linger on astral plane. Though the terrestrial angels are always eager to assist us for our journey to the spirit world through the tunnel, these powerful evil beings may cause trouble to a few human souls. So, once we cross the tunnel and face the divine light there are no more 'sights' of hell.

Also, in astral plane, the soul can encounter some strange beings – "*odd, strange shapes, wispy or dense ... not human-looking*" (Newton, 2016b, p. 70). These non-human entities had no incarnation experiences on Earth; they are visitors from other planets like 'vacation trip'. They know that human beings are afraid of them, and most of them would like to dispel the fear, but they don't want to get entangled with people's lives in any major way by interfering in their karmic path. Some of them might be mischievous whom we colloquially refer as demons, but the most appropriate term is 'spirit parasites'.

"*They are not bad or evil, just clumsy, mischievous children.... Their amusements distract them. We consider them as naughty youngsters. These pranksters think Earth is their playground where they can engage in devilish behavior with susceptible, gullible people and scare the hell out of them. They have a hilarious time before they are caught by one of the Rovers (tracker guides) sent to recapture these truants.*" (Newton, 2016b, p. 72)

In my opinion, the astral plane is right here on our visible Earth and all-around us. Newton has the same opinion as he wrote (2016b, pp. 51-52),

"*All my research with subjects in a higher state of consciousness indicates to me that upon death we go directly from one astral plane around Earth through the gateway into the spirit world.... People in hypnosis report that within the astral plane surrounding Earth, alternate or coexistent realities are part of our physical world. Apparently, within these realities, non-material beings can be seen by some people in our physical reality.*"

To understand quantum gravity, we must accept that the Earth has more than three dimensions to explain the weak gravitational forces in comparison to the other fundamental forces of nature. The size of the undetected dimensions can be infinitely big. Shrikhande (2009, p. 34) wrote,

"*... some of the lower ones [astral plane] is in a constant state of flux, due to the rotation of the earth around its axis and also the revolution of*

> *the earth around the sun. The lowest and densest region of the astral plane is supposed to be partly on the surface of the earth and partly beneath it.... As one rises higher and higher on the astral plane matter becomes less dense...., the scenery more beautiful and beings more spiritually advanced.*"

There is continuous interaction between the astral plane and the physical Earth plane and both have many similar characteristics. Since matter in the astral plane exists with an additional higher dimension than matter in our physical world, a being from astral plane can materialize and dematerialize their form on Earth plane at will. This is a simple case of interdimensional travel – the being just enters in an undetected dimension and instantly becomes invisible to us. In this case, the new co-ordinates beyond three spatial dimensions must be physical and within mathematical structure. In fact, the extra-dimension hypothesis perfectly fits with mathematics, as example,

$X^2 + Y^2 = 1$ (circle – two dimensional)

$X^2 + Y^2 + Z^2 = 1$ (sphere – three dimensional)

$X^2 + Y^2 + Z^2 + W^2 = 1$ (hypersphere – four dimensional, 'W' denotes the extra dimension coordinate)

By this way we can mathematically and logically add any number of extra dimensions and define it with mathematical equations. We can also make pictures of three-dimensional shadows of four-dimensional objects. If the shadow of a three-dimensional object is two-dimensional, within the same argument the shadow of a four-dimensional object will be three dimensional. A client wrote to Newton,

> "*Working with you has made me realize that our reality is like a movie projector showing us images on a three-dimensional screen of sky, mountains, and seas. If a second projector, with its own imprint of alternating light frequencies and space-time sequences, was synchronized with the first, both realities could exist simultaneously with material and non-material entities in the same zone.*" (Newton, 2016b, p. 53)

The earth-bound souls, guiding angels, ghosts, nature spirits, evil entities etc., are capable of existing in different realities within the same astral plane surrounding Earth – indeed on Earth itself. Beyond the understanding of mainstream science, what we perceive as ghosts are three-dimensional "shadows" of the displaced souls living and moving in a four-dimensional space. Unless we expand our mental faculties, visualization of four-dimensional objects is almost impossible.

Newton (2016b, pp. 53-54) recorded the experience of a woman who claimed to have seen elves in her vineyard and talked to them. She described them as being about two feet high with pointed ears and wearing baggy pants.

When this news got out on a national TV show many people in her area thought she was crazy. However, the advice she received from the elves about what to use in her soil to increase the quantity and quality of grape production over that of the neighboring farms soon caused many of them to take her more seriously. She was invited to have her brainwaves tested. When her senses were stimulated it was found that portions of her brain were capable of a much higher energy output than normal. She was not crazy; the higher power brain activity helped her to look at the astral plane which is just within another one or two spatial dimensions apart. Newton had another client who also claimed to have such abilities. Under deep hypnotic trance she narrated,

> "*Fairy folk were here long before the rise of our civilizations and have never left. Most of us do not see them today, as in ancient times, because they are so old their density has become very light, while our Earth bodies still have heavy energy... While a rock has a 1-D (density), a tree would be a 2-D and our bodies are at the 3-D level. Thus, the beings of nature would be invisible with a transparency registering between 4-D and 6-D.*" (Newton, 2016b, pp. 53-54)

The Findhorn Garden experiment (Northeast Scotland, UK) that started during 1963 confirms the ancient wisdom about the existence of those beings. By working consciously with the spirits of nature (devas) and angels, the Findhorn staff was able to turn sandy soil swept by the winds into a lush garden and grow oversized vegetables.

The shape of extra dimensions may explain the complexities of particle physics. However, before we get too carried away, we should bear in mind that when the scientists will find a way to detect them in experiments, probably we will know better about the inhabitants of the astral plane.

9.4: The causal plane, mental plane and etheric plane

All these planes are infinitely beautiful, and filled with light, love, and truth. A person who had experienced an NDE had reached any of these planes. No soul floats around aimlessly by themselves after entering these planes because organized soul support groups exist and the group placement is determined by soul maturity level. Spaces are reserved for their own colony. Always, surveillance by a higher power is reported here.

The Akashic Records are kept in causal plane where a medium projects him- or herself to get information. The mental plane is the plane of pure intellect. In the etheric plane, truth and beauty are most important things (Goldberg, 1982, p. 35). However, some researchers believe that these three planes are symbolic and the spirit world is a single ethereal space without zones or barriers around it. The life-review and confronting the divine light are two most important features in these planes which are absent in the astral plane.

The soul gets helpful guidance from Masters and Guides. They are highly evolved entities who have finished their karmic cycles many centuries ago. "*Many of them need never reincarnate, because they not only fulfilled their destiny on earth but have contributed so much on this side that their missions are complete.*" (Montgomery, 1972, p. 56). But most of the souls are still far from perfect beings in the spirit world. The highly developed entities help less-developed souls to adjust to their death trauma and lead them to white light. After entering the white light, the soul reaches the next higher plane, i.e., the soul plane (Goldberg, 1982, p. 36). Since the soul always has a free will, the Masters and Guides will never force the soul to enter the white light. If souls want solitude, they can have it. If they don't want to advance in their assignments or don't want to reincarnate this too is honored – "*No one will force them to work, but neither will they grow or advance... No one is forced to return to physical form. If we so choose, we are permitted to remain here throughout eternity, although it is harder to advance*". (Montgomery, 1972, pp. 38, 149-50). Curtiss (1949, p. 34) had encountered an old Atlantean teacher in a séance who had refused to incarnate for over 20,000 years so that she might continue to give her teachings to humanity through various mediums all down through the ages.

These higher entities are nonjudgmental, but they will give a tremendous amount of help and advice in all important decisions. There are three reasons why a soul's free will is never challenged by the higher entities. First, the karmic issues cannot be justified unless there is free will. Second, if souls were forced to do what is right for them they would learn nothing from their mistakes, and lastly, by forcing an immature soul, the guide may accidently start his own karmic cycle. None can escape the law of Karma, not even the guide. If the soul is older and has experience from many former lives, it will enter the white light without hesitation following the advice of the guides to reach to the soul plane. But a young soul, or a child who has died, may be a little disoriented.

There is a common misconception that all souls are mixed into one great congregation of space in the spirit world. But this is not true; every individual soul has a designated place in the spirit world. Many clients confirm that the spirit world is 'limitless' – not restricted by space and time.

Akashic Records are Life Books, which are stored in symbolic libraries that are seen adjacent to other spiritual places in the spirit world. Every thought, word and deed from every lifetime in our past, along with every event in which we participated, are recorded in the Akashic record. "Akasha" is extremely ancient, predating all of Earth's languages, past and present. Every human soul on Earth or on another planet in this or any other solar system or Universe even countless light years away from Earth has an Akashic Record. The Lords of Karma have complete access to all Libraries of Akasha (Herzog, 2003, pp. 13, 17-footnote). Many people under deep hypnosis speak about being in research library settings soon after rejoining their soul groups where the souls can read their past lives in depth and karmic records, such as missed opportunities and their accountability for past actions in this spiritual library.

On Earth, a library represents a systematic collection of books arranged by subjects and names which provide information. Similarly, in the spirit world, the titles of spiritual Life Books have every soul's spiritual name on them. Some psychics claim they have privileged access to events of the future through Akashic Records and that by working exclusively with them they can divert their followers from catastrophe. One most common feature of these books is that these are three-dimensional illuminated viewing screens. Newton (2016b, p. 162) described,

> "*These records give the illusion of books with pages, but they are sheets of energy which vibrate and form live picture-patterns of events... All cosmic viewing screens are multidimensional, with coordinates to record spacetime avenues of occurrence. These are often referred to as timelines and they can be manipulated by thought scanning.*"

Events on any screen can be moved forward or backward. The soul can enter the screen in two ways, either as an observer with no influence on events, something like working with virtual reality, or as participants where they will assume roles in the action of the scene. They can even alter the reality from the original one.

9.5: The soul plane

> "*You'll not be in heaven if you're not leaning on the arm of someone you have helped.*"
>
> Edgar Cayce

On this plane, the earthliness of the soul changes completely. They don't grieve about their recent physical death, though some of them take longer to adjust than others. The teacher-guides review the special karmic issues of past several incarnations of the soul on Earth, particularly those souls who were involved with evil acts. Since there is a difference between wrongdoing with no premeditated desire to hurt someone and intentional evil, the teacher-guides carefully evaluate the degrees of harm to others from mischief to malevolence. In this plane, the soul feels the presence of teacher-guides everywhere although not always in a manifested form. Newton wrote,

> "*Those souls who have been associated with evil are taken to special centers which some clients call 'intensive care units'. Here, I am told, their energy is remodeled to make it whole again. Depending upon the nature of their transgressions, these souls could be rather quickly returned to Earth. They might well choose to serve as the victims of other's evil*

acts in the next life. Still, if their actions were prolonged and especially cruel over a number of lives, this would denote a pattern of wrongful behavior. Such souls could spend a long while in a solitary spiritual existence, possibly over a thousand Earth years. A guiding principle in the spirit world is that wrongdoing, intentional or unintentional, on the part of all souls will need to be redressed in some form in a future life. This is not considered punishment or even penance as much as an opportunity for karmic growth. There is no hell for souls, except perhaps on Earth." (Newton, 2016b, p. 3).

It means hell does not exist. The process of reincarnation starts at soul plane. The teacher-guides put much effort to explain the nature of reality to the soul and the soul's present purpose on this plane. The soul is asked to study, analyze and understand various events from many past lives and how they fit into the soul's karmic patterns. This is how the soul is prepared for its next life on Earth (Goldberg, 1982, p. 36). First, the soul is asked to select an era of time for the next life.

But the soul will always have a free will. The teacher-guide says, "*We are ready when you are*". (Newton, 2016b, p. 7). There is so much free will that if the soul does not want to leave Earth's astral plane after death for a variety of personal reasons, the guide will allow the soul to stay around until such time the soul wishes to go to a higher plane. At will, the soul is allowed to travel from the soul plane to any lower plane.

Above the teacher-guides there is a council of elders. These are also highly evolved souls a step or two above the teacher-guides. Members of the council talk to the soul about its mistakes in various past lives and what the soul can do to correct negative behavior in the next many lives (Newton, 2016b, p. 8). They don't moralize or pass judgment but simply advice and try to help as best they can. The souls always have free will to ignore their advice. This is the reason, in life we sometimes take decisions very poorly. The council of elders also receives advice from even higher entities. The higher entities receive advice from even more evolved sources (Goldberg, 1982, p. 40). The ultimate result is, of course, excellent guidance. With the help of these highly evolved spirit-guides, the soul becomes an expression of beauty, imagination and creativity. The consideration for the right body for the soul's next life begins so that the soul can develop his personality and character, and advance by repaying karmic debts.

The spirit world is a timeless and spaceless zone where the soul sees the 'now' of time as one homogeneous unit of past, present, and future. Seconds in the spirit world seem to represent years on Earth.

"*Time, of course, is different. There's no such thing as clock time here, for we are able to eliminate time as well as space, since we are able to will ourselves to be anywhere at any moment of earth time and are able*

> *to look ahead so far into what you call the future that this also transcends the earthly idea of time. For things are planned ahead – make no mistake. If earthlings realized how much of it is planned ahead, they would not struggle so strongly to avert certain catastrophies, as they view them.*
>
> *We are ageless, having existed since the beginning, and we are without end. Thus, we are here, and that is all there is to time*". (Montgomery, 1972, pp. 14, 65)

When their sessions are over, the souls will often express surprise at how time in the spirit world is unified (Newton, 2016a, p. 195). But some souls who are uncomfortable with timelessness will see the passage of time in a chronological fashion. However, this doesn't contradict the concept of oneness for past, present, and future because this is a created illusion. Newton (2016a, p. 195) wrote,

> "*the illusion of time progression is created and sustained for those souls coming to and from physical dimensions (who are used to such biological responses as aging), so they may more easily gauge their advancement. Thus, it makes sense to me when the quantum physicists hypothesize that time, rather than being an absolute of three phases, is only an expression of change.*"
>
> "*When my subjects speak of traveling as souls on lines which curve, I think of the space-time theories of those astrophysicists who believe light and motion are a union of time and space curving back on itself. They say if space is bent severely enough, time stops. Indeed, when listening to my clients talk about time zones and tunnels of passage into different dimensions, I think about the similarities here to current astronomical theories of physical space being warped, or twisted, into cosmic loops creating "mouths" of hyperspace and black holes which may lead out of our three-dimensional universe. Perhaps the space-time concepts of astrophysics and metaphysics are edging closer together.*"

Before reincarnation, the soul goes to a space where a number of future bodies are reviewed that might help the soul to grow spiritually. Many souls don't want to come back to Earth, but they have to reincarnate to resolve various karmic issues. Before reincarnation the soul gets a chance to look into the probable future. In some cases, the soul is given chances to actually test out different bodies before making a choice. The soul is also allowed to choose its parents, brothers, sisters and other family members so that all the major events in the forthcoming life can be planned. But there is a very important point in this choice. The soul does not have many options because not only of its own karmic cycle but the karmic cycles of the many significant people with which he would have deep interactions in the forthcoming life are involved (Goldberg, 1982, p. 38). This is a very complicated selection process because the others must also agree as they also have free will. The blade of Karma cuts both ways.

Some souls voluntarily select less than perfect bodies, abusive parents, and painful events. They do so to address karmic debts or to work on different aspects of a lesson they have had trouble with in the past – "*That which you gain from each difficult life, you gain for all eternity*" (Newton, 2016b, p. 216). Though most souls accept the bodies offered to them in the selection room but a soul can reject what is offered and even delay reincarnating. The soul can also ask to go to a physical planet other than Earth for a while (Newton, 2016b, p. 8). In some of these physical planets life is much harder than on Earth.

It means, we cannot blame others for a bad childhood, or a painful marriage, or extreme poverty etc. We also cannot blame God for any misfortune because we have chosen our destiny on Earth before birth. Hence if we ask a question, why life had 'cheated' me out of happiness, the answer is that we are directly responsible for our lives because we have chosen the environment.

Once the soul selects a body, it is time for the soul's return to Earth. While inside a body, the soul takes utter responsibility of the body. Newton (2016b, p. 79) wrote,

> "*Souls take their responsibility very seriously, even to the extent of being inside nonfunctional bodies. They are not materially trapped. For instance, a soul may inhabit a comatose host body for many years and not abandon it until death. These souls are able to roam freely across the land visiting other souls who might be making brief trips away from their bodies during normal sleep states. This is especially true of souls in the bodies of babies. Souls are very respectful of their host body assignments, even if they are bored. They leave a small portion of their energy so they can return quickly if needed*".

The soul does not take its full energy while occupying a new body on Earth. When a soul reviews its own future life from the spirit world the guides advice the soul about the energy requirements of the body it will occupy. But the decision of how much energy the soul should take is its own. Many souls want to leave as much behind as possible because they love their home and the activities going on there. Emotional and physical trauma drains our energy reserves. So, in the next life if the soul does not need to function in traumatic days, the soul does not prefer to take much of its energy.

The soul can reincarnate in more than one physical body and live parallel lives on Earth. There are motivations behind it. The souls who choose to split into two or more bodies within the same time frame on Earth want to accelerate their learning process. In that case, for example, the soul might leave up to 10% of its energy behind and place the rest in two or three bodies. Our guides allow us to live parallel lives because we have free will, but they advise against it. Most souls who try parallel lives do so only a time or two before giving it up. Souls don't wish to lead parallel lives unless they are extraordinarily ambitious. Also, souls generally don't incarnate as twins and live parallel lives. Dividing the energy to be in a family with the same genetics, parental influence, environment, society and so forth would be counterproductive because there is lack of diversity.

In most cases once a spiritual level is attained by the soul it stays there. Another important point to note is that neither IQ nor creative talent does necessarily increase with the spiritual growth of the soul. Low IQ or handicapped brain does not mean that the soul is inexperienced. The advancement of the soul also cannot be measured by the amount of power the soul has achieved on Earth. Rather the opposite is true; souls in a high state of advancement are often found in humble circumstances on Earth. By the same argument, people in the strata of influence in human society are by no means in a blissful state of soul maturity.

9.6: Reincarnation: temporary departure from the spirit world

The decision of the soul to take another trip on Earth is not easy. The spirit world is a world of total wisdom, where they exist in a blissful state of freedom whereas on the Earth, souls have to survive with the physical and mental demands of a human body surrounded by aggressive and competing humans. Many souls don't want to think about returning to Earth again, but sooner or later they feel the pull of having a physical expression for his identity when the wounds of past life are healed. The Masters and Guides, teacher guides, and sometimes the Council of Elders prepare us for the next life by evaluating our karmic debts accumulated of several past lives.

When the soul gives a final thought of living again, the process starts. The soul is given not many choices, such as place and time of life selection, body choice, parents' selection, etc. There can even be competition for certain bodies (Goldberg, 1982, p. 40). Montgomery (1972, p. 44) wrote,

> "*If there is an overly heavy competition for one particular vehicle (or mother as you term it) then the various qualifications are fitted into records here, which automatically select the proper soul to be assigned that particular mission.*"

Our spiritual guides only advise us as we have free will, and it is left to the soul alone to view how the soul might fit into certain environments in future time segments with full actions with color, light, sound and smell. The soul also chooses to 'work' with other souls whom the soul loves very much and who love the soul (Schwartz, 2007, p. 81). Some souls are simply loners who reincarnate without any great feeling for life. There are others who like to return when their contemporaries from some particular past historical time return again. Sometimes a number of souls reincarnate simultaneously into lives that will have a great deal of interaction. On Earth they will cross paths, sometimes very intensely with great involvements, and other times it will be just passing through each other's lives but leaving a great impact upon one another. There are karmic links.

However, those souls whose acts in host bodies are very heinous are not permitted to reincarnate. They are kept in a holding ground for examination. Then their old energy is rearranged and repaired with new purified energy. The remodeled soul is then kept under observation for some time and much care is taken with their next incarnations and the selections of bodies (Newton, 2016b, pp. 94, 95, 99, 100). Fortunately, there are not many souls like this. Though these souls make the same mistakes again and again they are not destroyed permanently. Their free will is also not compromised.

In rarest cases, the soul is not salvageable, i.e., the soul falls again and again into the same pattern. Since no soul can avoid karmic justice, these souls can incarnate only in a victim's body for a number of future lives. If a suitable body for reincarnation is not available, the guides disseminate their energy, i.e., their energy is diluted with much new energy (Newton, 2016b, p. 103). Many souls return back within past-lives family bloodlines because of unusual karmic circumstances that gives them no other choice but to come back within same family connection.

9.7: The ministry of angels

Angels are spiritual, intelligent, non-physical beings. Though the skepticism of present age has discouraged any belief in angels, afterlife researchers and spiritual regressionists have gathered enough evidence of the existence of the angels and their activities from NDE studies and hypnotic regression sessions. The credibility of these accounts is beyond question because they typically describe the same stages, by people who didn't know each other nor knew anything about NDEs. Some researchers even admitted working closely with angels and having learned much from them. Many artists and scientists confirm being guided by the angels. Trained mediums report frequent encounters with various angels. Children frequently see and talk to their guardian angel. All the angels have good sense of humor. It serves as remedy for people who take spiritual questions too seriously, to the point of forgetting to live their life.

Every soul has a guardian angel, which is a soul deity or an empathetic spirit assigned to protect the soul during the soul's presence on Earth as a human being and also when the soul is roaming in the spirit world. The guardian angel can be called upon for divine help during a crisis. During NDE, a person met his guardian angel as this,

> "*My spirit left the body, and I could see it lying under the derrick, and at that moment my guardian angel, my mother, and my sister Ann were*

beside me. My mother died January 31, 1918, and my sister at the age of four years." (Lundahl, 1982, p. 172)

We think of angels as white-robed figures with wings and a halo as the religious scriptures depict them. But these beings are surrounded by white light and may appear in robes, and they don't have wings. Some of them have finished their reincarnation and karmic cycle on Earth several thousand years ago, while others have never incarnated on Earth. But still they sometimes reincarnate as holy sages to guide the mankind. The spiritual guides and the angels are different though both serve the ministry of the eternal consciousness.

These entities have nonhuman characteristics and do not incarnate in human bodies, yet they interact with discarnate human spirits – and sometimes incarnate ones as well through thoughts and impressions, in other words through psi. Howard Storm, in his book, 'My Descent into Death: And the message of love which brought me back' wrote from his own experience that the angels had a bright opalescent glow (Storm, 2000, pp. 87-88). He had interacted with an angel who told him, "*We [angels] can appear to you in human form if you wish, or in any form you want so you will be comfortable with us.*" (Storm, 2000, p. 34). Since they can take many appearances, their identification varies with the NDEr's religious background. For example, a Hindu might identify the being as a prominent Hindu deity whereas a Christian person might identify the being as Christ.

An angel may briefly materialize to help someone in difficult circumstances, but in a way which would not have been possible for a human being. Sometimes they take the form of an animal also, but in whatever form they appear in front of a human being the encounters always contain an unusual or even supernatural element thus pointing to an intervention by an angel. These interventions are commonly known as miracles or spiritual healings. Sometimes we receive their help and guidance without even knowing that they are helping us. We think it as coincidence when we receive messages in the form of significant synchronicities.

There are two ranks of angels – celestial angels and terrestrial angels. From various case studies, it appears that celestial angels are in a higher position than their terrestrial counterpart.

The mysterious beings that many people had encountered during intermission period (discussed in chapter 7), such as, a man with long white hair, a Sadhu (a Hindu holy man or Saint), an old man dressed in white who offered the "fruit of forgetfulness", and god-like entity who made suggestions about their future parents or giving permission, are terrestrial angels. People have encountered these beings also while on their deathbed. The terrestrial angels are stationed on the Earth and astral plane. In the scriptures we can find descriptions of many kinds of earthly spiritual beings that are around us. With the industrial revolution, and now in this computer age, the existence of angels has been pushed aside in a little corner together with children's tales, fantasy land, and wishful thinking.

These beings are the elect or chosen emissaries of the higher guides and masters of the spirit world. Terrestrial angels seem to have less special powers or psychic abilities. But they are very powerful in what they do. They live in a state of immediate knowledge and are a source of happiness and exaltation. They live fully in the moment and in full concentration.

Sometimes the terrestrial angels guide dying people in their dreams and visions or trances to help the person acquiring a peaceful detachment at the end. They can disappear and reappear at will to a living human being, and they can come in a manner in which a person can talk with them and not even know it. Many of us have noticed the elderly talking to themselves a lot particularly when they are alone. They are preparing for separation at the other end with the help of their guiding angels without knowing.

These higher, caring entities have incredible ability to discern good from evil and their main purpose is to guide discarnate beings to the spirit world. But when some karmic issues are still not fulfilled because the person had died without completing his full lifespan, there is a need for that person to reincarnate at the earliest. These earth-bound angels help them to find a new body immediately so that the karmic cycle can continue and fulfill the requirements.

Some NDE researchers describe the angels as "Beings of light". Moody described the being of light as one of 15 elements in the NDE, and his first case of a childhood NDE, a nine-year-old boy described that a group of glowing angels without wings welcomed him with too much love (Lundahl, 1992, p. 49). Some NDErs confuse the being of light as a deceased family member (Sorensen and Willmore, 1988, p. 48). The angels have individual existence, in other words, a deceased family member and an angel are not one and the same entity, even though both may appear in a bright light. Whether an angel appears as a being of light or not depends on the circumstances of the occasion.

The celestial angels perform in the capacities of guide (leading and directing the soul through a death experience and simultaneously explaining the points of interest), messenger (to carry an important message to a person), or guard/protector.

In the following NDE case, the angel acted as a guide.

> "*It was between 10 and 11 o'clock that a visitor suddenly made his appearance in the room, and standing by the couch on which I lay, placed his hand on my head and asked if I was ready to go. I answered, 'Yes'; and just at that instant I seemed to stand upon the floor, my body lying on the bed. I looked around to see if my father could see us, but he seemed to have been too interested in reading to have noticed us. We started off on our journey through space, seemingly with the rapidity of*

lightning. I asked my guide who he was. He answered he was one of the guardian angels sent to bring the dead." (Heinerman, 1978, pp. 108-09)

Next NDE case, the angel acted as a messenger and reminder of promises and commitments.

"*I was nearing the bright light. Then I saw someone coming toward me, with many other people behind him. He was an angel who had come to get me. I don't know who he was, but he was someone who had always helped me. We had been familiar with one another for a very long time, and it would have been ridiculous to make an introduction at this point. I was excited and wanted to express my happiness at the relief I felt from the cares of the world, but I was told that I had made some promises and commitments and had been set apart to do some work before this world was. I had accepted a responsibility that would have a great missionary effect*". (Sorensen and Willmore, 1988, pp. 94-95)

Angels take the responsibility to escort the soul to the spirit world.

"*I found myself floating on the ceiling over the bed looking down at my unconscious body. I barely had time to realize the glorious strangeness of the situation – that I was me but not in my body – when I was joined by a radiant being bathed in a shimmering white glow. Like myself, this being flew but had no wings. I felt a reverent awe when I turned to him; this was no ordinary angel or spirit, but he had been sent to deliver me. Such love and gentleness emanated from his being that I felt that I was in the presence of the messiah.*

Whoever he was, his presence deepened my serenity and awakened a feeling of joy as I recognized my companion. Gently he took my hand and we flew right through the window. I felt no surprise at my ability to do this. In this wondrous presence, everything was as it should be.

Now, still hand in hand with the angel, I was led into the opening of the small, dark passageway.... Finally, I reached my destination. It was only when I emerged from the other end that I realized that I was no longer accompanied by the being who had brought me there. But I wasn't alone. There, before me, was the living presence of the Light." (Ring, 1991, p. 15)

Some angels also take the responsibility to guard or protect the NDEr.

"*...my spirit left the body; just how I cannot tell... my body was lying, lifeless, on the bed... I realized everything that was going on, and perceived that I was the same in the spirit as I had been in the body. While contemplating this new condition, something attracted my attention, and on turning around I beheld a personage, who said, 'You did not know that I was here'.*

I replied, 'No, but I see you are. Who are you?'

'I am your guardian angel; I have been following you constantly while on earth'.

I asked, 'What will you do now?'

He replied, 'I am to report your presence, and you will remain here until I return'.

He informed me, on returning, that we should wait there, as my sister desired to see me, but was busy just at that time. Presently she came". (Johnson, 1920, p. 451)

The above account confirms that the primary responsibility of a guardian angel is to protect the soul. When the soul completes the physical existence on Earth, the guardian angel often accompanies the soul to the spirit world.

9.8: Seeing living persons during NDE

In many NDE cases, people report meeting those people who are still alive on Earth. In a study conducted by Kelly (2001, pp. 239-40) of 274 NDE cases, 11 reported seeing living persons whom they recognized while 28 people saw dead persons. Hence, the doubt arises if these NDErs are actually hallucinating, otherwise how living persons can appear in their visions. Yes, this seems illogical but true. This curious phenomenon is known as 'Soul Duality' – the souls have the ability to divide their essence so they can be living on Earth with a physical body while leaving a significant amount of their total energy in the spirit world. This left-behind energy is an exact replica of the living person.

This part of energy that remains in the spirit world is dormant and it is waiting to be rejoined to the rest of the energy. However this energy, which is an exact duplicate while we incarnate, remains in a pure, uncontaminated state, it is still potent. Thus, it is possible for a soul to see anyone upon returning from a life even though the person may have died thirty Earth years before and reincarnated again.

The ability of a soul to unite with itself in the spirit world is a natural process of energy regeneration after physical death on Earth. Because of the nature of soul duality, the souls are quite capable of performing many tasks at once. There are few reasons why a soul does not carry its full energy while incarnating on Earth. First, the soul does not want total separation from the maker or source. They see the spirit world as true reality and Earth as an illusion created to teach us. Also, they love the beautiful spirit world and the activities going on there. Second, a part of the soul always remains in the spirit world to work on lessons and interacting with other souls (Newton, 2016b, p. 62). The education process for the growth of the soul continues in the other world also. The third reason is, if the soul takes 100% of its energy into a physical body during an incarnation, it would blow the circuits of the brain. A human brain cannot take a full charge of all a soul's energy into one human body. Apparently, this could happen with even the less potent, undeveloped souls (Newton, 2016b, p. 117). People at NDE see this dormant part of the reincarnating soul.

For some people soul duality is an uncomfortable idea because it is against all their preconceptions of a singular, individualized spirit. Newton wrote,

> "*the concept of soul duality perplexing, especially when faced with the further proposition that one soul may even be capable of living in different dimensions during the same relative time. What we must appreciate is, if our souls are all part of one great oversoul energy force which divides, or extends itself to create our souls, then why shouldn't the offspring of this intelligent soul energy have the same capacity to detach and then recombine?*" (Newton, 2016a, p. 155)

> "*The percentages of energy souls leave behind may vary but each particle of light is an exact duplicate of every other Self and replicates the whole identity. This phenomenon is analogous to the way light images are split and duplicated in a hologram. Yet there are differences with a hologram. If only a small percentage of a soul's energy is left behind in the spirit world, that particle of Self is more dormant because it is less concentrated. However, because this energy remains in a pure, uncontaminated state, it is still potent*". (Newton, 2016b, p. 116)

Since the part of the soul living in the spirit world is an exact duplicate of the other part (which has incarnated on Earth and living a physical life), the NDErs actually meets this left-behind part in their experiences. This is not a hallucination, but a real happening.

9.9: The highly evolved souls

The purpose of the Masters and Guides, Teacher-guides, Council of Elders is simply to help and advice the soul to our next lives. They are highly evolved complex entities who have completed their reincarnation cycles may be several thousand earth-years ago. The spirit world is a telepathic world where no subterfuge or deception can exist. The spirit guides know everything about the soul – its learning habits, strong and weak points, fears, willingness to learn etc.

The Elders have very kindly faces. They bring less matured and still reincarnating souls into the company of a warm, loving creative power. They are also very honest and truthful when they evaluate the soul's perceptions of the life it had just lived and how the soul could have done better with the talents and what it did that was beneficial. They are not judgmental; the soul can freely express frustrations and desires. They motivate, instill courage and help the soul to be aware of the continuity of life. Every individual soul has a personal spiritual guide. These guides are the essential parts of the fulfillment of the soul's destiny because these learned teachers may remain with the soul for thousands of earth-years to assist in the soul's spiritual growth before, during, and after countless incarnations on Earth and other physical worlds. They perfectly integrate with our permanent soul identity and keenly feel their responsibilities towards us as teachers. Newton (2016b, p. 204) wrote,

> "*The spirit world is a place of order and the Council of Elders exemplifies justice. They are not the ultimate source of divine authority, but they appear to represent the last station of beings responsible for souls still incarnating on Earth. These wise beings have great compassion for human weakness and they demonstrate infinite patience with our faults. We will be given many second chances in future lives. They won't be lives of easy karmic choices, otherwise we would learn nothing by coming to Earth. However, the risks of life and sanity on this planet are not designed to cause us any further pain after death.*"

The souls appear before their council at least once – either immediately arriving at the soul plane or before rebirth. Some souls meet the council at both times. The teacher-guides escort the souls in the chambers of these ascended masters, but don't play a large role at these hearings. They maintain silence, but if they think the soul is confused at any point during the proceedings, they interpret. In the first meeting, various important points in our karmic path are evaluated carefully without bitterness or finger-pointing. If there is a second visit, it is more relaxed with discussions centering around potential life choices, opportunities and expectations for the future. Our intent in life is of utmost importance at council meetings. The Elders know all about us before we appear (Newton, 2016b, p. 211). Though the soul can make same mistakes in several lifetimes, the Elders are never impatient with us. Newton wrote,

> "*The council just doesn't inquire into our most immediate past life. Lines of questioning follow across the sum of all our lives and cover the larger picture of our progress toward self-fulfillment. The Elders wish to explore if we are developing to our potential. ...the committee is carefully balanced by certain Elders whose character and background have some sort of common ground with the souls who come before them. ... [there is] a personal affinity... Individual Elders seem to identify with a soul's character, strengths and weaknesses, interests and purposes.*" (Newton, 2016b, p. 216)

In this spiritual court-room there is no deceitfulness but only brutal honesty because everyone communicates telepathically. There is no need for rules of evidence, witness, defense attorneys or juries. Compulsions, illusions and attachments are never taken as excuses by the souls for their conduct.

The most revered masters want to make sure that we totally understand the consequences of our actions, particularly toward others.

Above the soul plane there are many other higher planes occupied by the higher evolved souls, exalted beings, and the Lords of Karma (highly evolved cosmic beings who work as a group to adjudicate the cycles of individual Karma, group Karma, national Karma and world Karma, always seeking to apply the Law in the way that will give people the best opportunity to make spiritual progress). These beings form the government of God.

In this point, readers may ask one very relevant question. In the spirit world, how close can we come to God? There is no short answer for this question but still I will try. As long as a soul has karmic debts, it cannot enter higher planes above soul plane. And once the soul finishes its cycle of Karma, it does not need to reincarnate. This is the reason we don't know much about these higher planes that ultimately end at the God Plane – the one God or more than one God, or the eternal consciousness who had fine-tuned the cosmos so that life can evolve in many planets, including our Planet Earth.

At council meetings, for many advanced souls who are nearing the end of their regular incarnations, "*there is the overwhelming feeling of an even higher force which is simply called 'the Presence'. Many subjects state, 'This is as close to God as we get'.*" (Newton, 2016b, p. 243). This entity or entities whom we can call the 'Presence' have capabilities immensely superior to the council of elders. The Presence has infinite knowledge equated with a larger omnipotent and omnipresent energy force in the spirit world. Those advanced souls who speak about the 'Presence' always speak only few sentences. These Higher souls are more aware of us than we are of them, and they can live simultaneously (Montgomery, 1972, pp. 152, 161). Newton (2016b, p. 244) wrote,

> "*I do not actually see the Presence, but feel it as the ultimate energy. It is there for the council, but mostly for me. The Elders don't serve as intermediaries between myself and this Source of power.*"
>
> "*When I am in the council chamber the Presence oversees the Elders...*"
>
> "*It is... massive, but soft... powerful... yet gentle.*"
>
> "*The Presence is above and in back of the council. Only with difficulty can I look up at this power. I feel its sanctity so strongly that I don't think I should try to look at it directly during the council meeting.*"
>
> "*The council seems to acknowledge the Presence without being too deferential to it in such a way as to slow down the proceedings.*"
>
> "*The Presence represents a purity of energy which assists the council on my behalf. I believe that the council needs the help of the Presence because it has been so long since they themselves incarnated in biological form.*

The pure wisdom of this energy allows both the council and myself to see more clearly where we all should be going."

"*The brilliance and drawing power of the Presence is a calling ... an eagerness ...directed at everyone in the chamber for all of us to join it someday. It is like a parent waiting for us to grow up and unite with it in adult understanding.*"

"*When you stand in the council chamber and feel the Presence it is like a penetrating resonance in your mind. Even my master guide encounters the sense of bliss that I do. It is a fountainhead of love and understanding. When my time with the council is over and I leave the Presence ... there is such a yearning to go back and be close to it once more.*"

"*... full of a knowing presence which is everywhere for us and... alive!*"

Therefore, this is as close as possible we can know about the ultimate divinity. The 'Presence' is not one entity but many. The 'Presence' has no definite shape; the essence of the 'Presence' comes from everywhere. We don't know, if the 'Presence' is the ultimate deity of all Universes and all dimensions connecting these Universes, or only for the spirit world of earth-souls. The eternal consciousness, which existed before the Big Bang and will exist even after the Big Crunch will always remain a mystery. Arthur Ford revealed through Montgomery (1972, p. 31) that,

"*God is the core of the universe from which all else flows forth. He is truth and energy. He is matter and spirit, and all things of heaven and earth. He is eternity itself, wise and all-knowing, but whether we are aware of it or not, He is also the essence of our being, without which nothing would exist. It is His total harmony which melds together the universe and all therein and thereon, so that without His perfect Being the universe would instantly fall apart. God is! The eternal I Am... Without God there is nothing and no thing.... there is no life or being without Him. Thus,* ***we are as much a part of Him as He is of us,*** *and because we are imperfect in our reactions and behavioural pattern, we must strive enough onward through many earth cycles until we achieve sufficient perfection to rejoin God as cocreators.* ***It is the law, for no imperfect being will ever have the opportunity to become a part of the Godhead*** *which would not function properly if full of imperfections. It is the law, immutable. Thus our ceaseless attempts to return to the physical state in order to erase our rough edges and be able to fit into the Godhead as perfect segments of the whole.*"

This ultimate mysterious power is a tremendous force for good that knows no other than good. God is not only the total awareness, but also truth supreme, wisdom and all-knowing, and without Him there would be only chaotic blackness.

9.9.1: The religious and scientific views of higher dimensional beings

"The reality of the spirit world is not based on human reason. It is based on fact. It is what it is. The fact that it is invisible to the human eye does not make it any less real."

Dan Delzell

We often wonder how to perceive a higher-dimensional being from our three-dimensional reality since there is no visual imagery or verbal language constructs within our three-dimensional reality to fit other, higher-dimensional models. Hence first, I wish to take a step back to the second dimension, familiarizing ourselves with the reality there and then looking at the third dimension that we are already familiar with, we can begin to have an understanding of what the fourth and higher spatial dimension would mean to us.

For argument's sake, let us consider a two-dimensional being resided on the surface (plane) of the water in a pond (similar to Flatland, Edwin A. Abbott's celebrated novel that imagines two-dimensional beings living on a planar world that has only length and width). Sitting on the side, I am moving a sphere closer to the surface of the water. Initially, there would be intersection in the form of a point when the sphere first touched the water. The point would then turn into a circle, necessarily changing size as the sphere started to submerge beneath the surface of the water. So, a two-dimensional being will first see a point that took the form of a curved line which became bigger and bigger. When the sphere is half-submersed, the curved line was the biggest. Then the curved line became smaller and smaller and ultimately receded to a point and then completely vanished. He will see curved line, not the circle because he will never be able to view the whole circle at once though he can walk around the circle to understand its existence.

So, this is the best the two-dimensional creature will understand the three-dimensional sphere. The only way he can understand the total reality of the sphere in relation to his own dimension of existence is when he is taken out of the two-dimensional world so that the sphere could be viewed from all angles. If the creature is intelligent enough to receive and understand communication from the three-dimensional world, he will still have limited imagination of the greater reality. But he can never have a first-hand experience from his two-dimensional setting unless he gets assistance from the three-dimensional beings. Bewildered, the two-dimensional creature will not try to understand the sphere by using science and logic; he will rather give it a religious overtone. From his perspective a three-dimensional being has seemingly god-like powers, such as being able to remove objects from a house without going through the door, i.e., by moving them "up and across" the third dimension.

Now, all of this talk about the two-dimensional beings is really just an analogy. There are higher-dimensional beings, those possess exactly the qualities that I've described above, along with many others, and they are able to do such things to us. Hope, now it is more feasible for us to conceive four- and higher dimensional beings. A four-dimensional being would be capable of similar feats from our three-dimensional perspective. Suppose a higher being wants to pass a hyper-sphere (four-dimensional sphere) through our three-dimensional reality. We will see a small sphere appears from nowhere disobeying the physical laws of the three-dimensional plane and then grow seemingly on its own will. Once past the equator, the sphere begins to shrink again, until it disappears as the hyper-sphere leaves our three-dimensional space again. We will have no clue unless the higher beings want to explain the greater reality. Also, the higher beings must have complete understanding of our perceptions. If they do not understand how cause and effect works in our three-dimensional worldview, then though they may have totally benevolent intentions in their manipulation it will turn out to be highly freaky and startling to us.

A better understanding of higher-dimensional reality will solve many mysteries, such as UFOs (Unidentified Flying Objects) which physical science alone cannot explain. Do they belong to higher dimensions? When they move into our plane momentarily, they seem to appear out of nowhere. When they move back into another plane, they seem to disappear without a trace. People who encountered aliens have stated that these beings communicate through telepathy very similar to spirit world. Aliens are very much in tune with the psychic level of reality. Once again, this reinforces the truth that aliens are spiritual in nature. Are the aliens actually angels? People who have encountered aliens confirm that they are spiritual beings capable of taking on any form. They sometimes appear as reptilian forms, and small grey creatures with large heads at other times. But in their truest form, they are pure light beings with humanoid shape.

If we apply this dimensional analogy to quantum physics, there are many logic-defying facts, such as quantum entanglement and coexistence of super positioned probability waves (Quantum superposition: much like waves in classical physics, any two or more quantum states can be added together, i.e., 'superposed' and the result will be another valid quantum state) that we are still struggling to explain. The subatomic particles are interacting according to properties and interactions that we cannot fully conceive.

Is this an indicative of some higher dimensions (space and time) interacting with our own? We have seen in quantum entanglement that whatever option a photon takes, its twin would always make the other choice "instantaneously"– faster than the speed of light. Do the quantum particles actually follow the laws of higher dimensions including time dimension?

Let us take another hypothetical example. Suppose I am viewing a two-dimensional prison on a sheet of paper. Here a large circle, or square, or rectangle or, any closed shape would suffice, since it would cover the criminals 'all around', and they would be unable to escape. However, if a third-dimensional being wished to assist a criminal to escape, he could easily 'lift' the criminal right out of the jail. It would appear to the prison guard that the criminal just 'disappeared', and then 'reappeared' on the outside. This is known as teleportation or teletransportation (transfer of matter or energy from one point to another without traversing the physical space between them). Secondly, from a three-dimensional existence, I can watch all of them simultaneously – no one can hide from my sight. In this case I would be like god for them. A 'god' is said to be omniscient, and since I am on a higher dimension, I am also omniscient for a lower dimension creature. This is not an overstatement in any way.

Many people report that in their NDEs they have confronted one or more super-intelligence – the Divine Light (a godlike or angelic presence) which is a real and vivid sensory phenomenon. The Light Being seems to know **EVERYTHING** about the person. This is a Deity from religious point of view. However, from scientific point of view, this is a higher-dimensional (space and time) life-form. We, as three-dimensional beings, cannot fathom the depth of intelligence of this life-form. Since we cannot comprehend this life-form, the light being exists without the need of a name, identity, or definition – for a Hindu this is Lord Krishna, for a Christian this is Jesus Christ, for Buddhists it is Buddha and so on.

The entire spirit world and afterlife realm can be explained scientifically. Extradimensional beings or intelligences are not theoretical or fictional entity; they really exist in a dimension beyond our own. Countless number of NDE cases had already confirmed this. We don't need to search religious books; the science will explain everything. Since there is no harmony between scientific and religious ways of thought, religious understanding must not be placed on equal footing with scientific understanding.

Two-dimensional objects are bounded by one-dimensional lines and curves, and three-dimensional objects are bounded not by lines or curves, but by two-dimensional surfaces. By the same logic, in a four-dimensional world, the objects are bounded not by points, lines, or even surfaces, but volumes. Is our known Universe the three-dimensional surface of a four-dimensional hyper-sphere? We cannot even imagine what happens in fifth or in much higher spatial dimensions and time dimension. It would be rather difficult to realize this without applying dimensional analogy.

We can place our finger inside the two-dimensional object without touching the sides. Similarly, four-dimensional beings can easily put their finger inside a solid object without penetrating its sides. Higher dimensional life-form, therefore, would have tremendous powers beyond imagination – they can scan the entire Universe in a fraction of second, walk through walls, disappear and reappear at will, constantly change shape and colour, reach into the strongest steel vaults, and see through buildings. They would be omniscient, omnipotent, and omnipresent (all-knowing, all-powerful and all-present) – the qualities we attribute to God.

In other words, the 'supernatural' powers of a higher-dimensional life-form are actually the product of limited perception on our part. When our soul is trapped inside a physical body our brains are not set up to perceive (problem is with Biology rather than Physics) what we take to be natural – the higher dimensions. The human soul actually belongs to higher than three-dimensional reality. Hence, in an NDE state the person feels more powerful and more fulfilled (the blinds can see, all physical discomforts are gone etc.) than before. Seeming supernatural is one implication of higher dimensions that our brains can't perceive. To operate from the fourth and higher dimensions seems omniscient, omnipresent, and omnipotent as related to our known world. The NDEs are not a limitation of perception, rather it's how the greater reality works. The Council of Elders, the Lords of Karma, Masters and Guides, angels – all amounts to the same order of explanation.

9.10: Conclusion

"*Begin to see yourself as a soul with a body, rather than a body with a soul.*"

Wayne Dyer

"*People need to understand that the spiritual realm is their true home that they will return to, not a place that has to be earned.*"

Michael Duff Newton

"*This Heaven is more like Earth than you imagined, but still it is so very different – it is at once both familiar and fabulous. Everything is made of loving energy, most things seem to be somewhat conscious, and because nothing ever decays and night never falls, there is a permanent, timeless beauty to it all.*"

Roberta Grimes, author of 'The Fun of Dying'

The soul world is our real home. Arthur Yensen had an NDE after a car accident. In his NDE, he recalled having been there before to the point that he knew what would be there at the next curve.

"*Then I noticed that the landscape was gradually becoming familiar. It seemed as if I had been here before. I remembered what was on the other side of the mountains. Then with a sudden burst of joy,* ***I realized that this was my real home! Back on earth I had been a visitor, a misfit, and***

> ***a homesick stranger.*** *With a sigh of relief, I said to myself, Thank God I'm back again. This time I'll stay!*" (Linn et al., 2016, p. xx)

Another person remembered,

> "*He [a spiritual being] showed me a gate behind which I saw the same landscape. But now, with this gate in front,* ***it suddenly looked extremely familiar. I came to the startling conclusion: I've been here before. It felt like a homecoming after an arduous journey.*** *A state that led to complete peace of mind, a peace of mind I hadn't known for a long time. For me this was the highlight of the experience.*" (Van Lommel, 2010, p. 39)

One person who remembered his soul memories under hypnosis commented as follows,

> "*Coming to Earth is about traveling away from our home to a foreign land. Some things seem familiar but most are strange until we get used to them, especially conditions which are unforgiving.* ***Our real home is a place of absolute peace, total acceptance and complete love.*** *As souls separated from our home we can no longer assume these beautiful features will be present around us. On Earth we must learn to cope with intolerance, anger and sadness while searching for joy and love. We must not lose our integrity along the way, sacrificing goodness for survival and acquiring attitudes either superior or inferior to those around us. We know that living in an imperfect world will help us to appreciate the true meaning of perfection. We ask for courage and humility before our journey into another life. As we grow in awareness so will the quality of our existence. This is how we are tested. Passing this test is our destiny.*" (Newton, 2016b, p. 401)

The Earth like many other physical planets is a training ground for the souls to develop spiritually. Souls end their incarnations on Earth when they reach full maturity. Montgomery (1972, p. 154-55, 158) wrote,

> "*Many of the planets are occupied by spirit forms in various states of consciousness. Some are in higher and some in lower forms of consciousness than the earth dwellers, but because of various levels of development, some evolve more rapidly in certain vibratory planes than in others.... As we learn our lessons here in this intermediate state, we are given the choice of reincarnating or travelling onward to other realms of consciousness.... While these planets contain life forms, they are totally unrecognisable in terms of the life forms which inhabit earth in physical form*".

In my opinion the Earth as a training ground is continuously failing and a great number of souls who inhabit human bodies on Earth today are still in the early stages of spiritual development. I came to this conclusion after seeing so much hate, terror, misunderstanding, injustice, cruelty and violence amongst us.

The quantum soul defies Darwin's "natural selection" principle. In a materialistic world, natural selection was Darwin's attempt to provide atheism with its much-needed "creation" story. This theory asserts that organisms evolve to become more sophisticated because they experience chance mutations that result in favorable adaptations. Hence, those who are fit, strong, clever, self-seeking, and ruthless will be more likely to live and bear offsprings, perpetuating the adaptations they experience that made them more fit.

A supernatural higher power has no place in this system. The Harvard evolutionist Stephen Jay Gould has stressed that Darwin led us into a world where matter is everything and "*mind, spirit, and God as well, are just words that express the wondrous results of neuronal complexity*" (Gould, 1977, p. 13). But the evolution in spirituality actually discourages people to compete in the world. Darwin's mistake was that he could not conceive of an eternal existence of consciousness. That's why he did not realise that it is the consciousness that evolves, not the bodies. The winners are not fitter, stronger, more self-seeking and more ruthless. They are, in fact, willing to give up their own possessions, be transparent and honest, focus on others, and give without reservation. Hence more materialistic a person is, less is his understanding about spiritualism. The weakness becomes strength once we come out of a materialistic view.

The human race must operate from a place of peace, co-operation and understanding. We are all connected at the sub-atomic level and quantum physics states we are indestructible. This is our omnipresent connection to the Universe! Arthur Ford revealed through Montgomery (1972, pp. 12-13) that,

> "*There has never been a time when we were not, and we always will be, even though in constantly changing forms and stages, for we are as much God as God is a part of us.... For if each of us is God, then taken together we are God; and since it takes all of us to make a complete God, we know that another person is as necessary to us and to the common welfare as we ourselves. Therefore, it behooves each of us to concern ourselves mightily with others, for they are as necessary to us as our own arms and legs and eyes and ears.*
>
> *Each of us is incomplete without the totality of humanity, both living and dead. Don't forget that this all-for-one-and-one-for-all applies equally to the living and so-called dead, for it is the totality that makes us the whole of the Universal Spirit which we are wont to call God. The clergy may not like this concept, but....*".

Albert Schweitzer, an early biocentric thinker, believed that the most fundamental fact of human consciousness is the realization that 'I am life which wills to live, in the midst of life which wills to live' (Martin, 2007, p. 5), and that it is around this fact that ethics should be built. Van Lommel (2010, p. 35) recorded this statement of an NDEr.

> "*That very same moment, in a split second, I gained access to a wealth of knowledge, a complete knowing and understanding. All knowledge. Universal knowledge.* ***I understood the origins of the cosmos, how the universe works, and why people do what they do. Their positive actions, but also why they hurt one another, deliberately or not. Wars and natural disasters, everything has a purpose, a reason. It all makes sense.*** *I understood the past, the present, and the future. I saw evolution.* ***Everything and everyone evolves and develops together.*** *I saw and understood – without any judgment – the connection, the coherence, the logical and sometimes major consequences of every single act. I mean at every level and down to the smallest detail.... The way all kinds of mechanical, electrical, and electronic equipment, gadgets, and engines work. Everything. I knew and understood all about mathematics, electronics, physics, DNA, atoms and quantum physics....* ***I also saw where evolution is headed, what its ultimate goal is. I realized that this grand scheme not only includes me, but everything and everybody, every human being, every soul, every animal, every cell, the earth and every other planet, the universe, the cosmos, the Light. Everything is connected and everything is one.*** *'I see!' I thought happily. 'I get it. It's all so simple. So obvious. It all makes sense...'. No, I wasn't allowed to bring back the knowledge itself. Why, I don't know.... Perhaps we're not supposed to have such universal knowledge in the here and now, in our physical form. Perhaps we're here to learn. Perhaps there's another reason.*"

The core message in the above NDE statement is very clear, very loud, and very certain – our lives are deeply important to higher consciousness and to the existence of the Universe. There is a purpose to life on Earth, and therefore life is worth fighting for even when depression is at its peak and living seems unbearable.

> "*Go through life as an instrument of the Creator, asking noting for yourself except that for which you work in order to live comfortably. Forget about publicized alms and make yourself a well which will never run dry, because bubbling up from that well is love which, freely given, continuously pumps up more love to overflowing*". (Montgomery, 1972, p. 124).

> "*We grow, we live, we love, to return in endless cycles until at last we slough off the imperfection which we picked up along the way and are fit to become a part of God Himself.*" (Montgomery, 1972, pp. 133-34)

Richard Dawkins, the "intellectually fulfilled atheist", may not agree with me, but the hard fact is that today spiritualism is winning over materialism. Large number of people are becoming increasingly compassionate and other-centered though they live in a society which is utterly self-absorbed and materialistic. The spiritual growth is not the result of a genetic mutation. It is actually the result of the fact that we are spiritual beings having a physical experience, and our true natures are overpowering physical realm instincts as we reduce their influence over us. By defying Darwinian evolution, we are evolving toward spiritual maturity, not toward physical prowess that dominates through force and not toward intellectual self-centeredness that dominates through devious cleverness.

References

1. Agrillo, Christian (2011); Near-death experience: out-of-body and out-of-brain?, Review of General Psychology, vol. 15, issue 1.

2. Akolkar, V. V. (1992); The Search for Sharada: Report of a Case and Its Investigation. Journal of the American Society for Psychical Research, vol. 86, July issue, pp. 209-47.

3. Alexander, Eben (2012); Interview video recorded during the 11th annual International Bioethics Forum of the Bio-Pharmaceutical Technology Center Institute in Madison, Wisconsin, April 26, 2012.

4. Alfano, Sean (2005); Poll: Majority believe in ghosts, CBS News, on-line report. URL: http://www.cbsnews.com/stories/2005/10/29/opinion/polls/main994766.shtml, (last accessed July 29, 2019).

5. Almeder, Robert (1992); Death and Personal Survival, Rowman & Littlefield Publishers, Maryland, USA.

6. Almeder, Robert (1996); Recent responses to survival research. The Journal for Scientific Exploration, vol. 10, issue 4, pp. 495-517.

7. Almeder, Robert (1997); A Critique of Arguments Offered Against Reincarnation, Journal of Scientific Exploration, vol. 11, no. 4, pp. 499-526.

8. Almeder, Robert (2001); On reincarnation: A reply to Hales. Philosophia, vol. 28 (issues 1-4), pp. 347-358.

9. Alvarado, Carlos S. (1997); Mapping the characteristics of out-of-body experiences, Journal of the American Society for Psychical Research, vol. 91, pp.13-30.

10. Alvarado, Carlos S. (2000); Out-of-body experiences. In 'The Varieties of Anomalous Experience: Examining the Scientific Evidence', ed. By E. Cardena, S.J. Lynn, and S. Krippner, American Psychological Association, Washington D.C., pp. 183–218.

11. Alvarado, Carlos S. (2006a); Human Radiations: Concepts of Force in Mesmerism, Spiritualism and Psychical Research, Journal of the Society for Psychical Research, vol. 70, no. 884, pp. 138-162.

12. Alvarado, Carlos S. (2006b); Neglected Near-Death Phenomena, Journal of Near-Death studies, vol. 24, issue 3, Spring 2006.

13. Andrade, Hernani Guimaraes (1980); A case suggestive of reincarnation: Jacira and Ronaldo (Monograph no. 3), Brazilian Institute for Psychobiophysical Research, Sao Paolo.
14. Anonymous (1854); Curious psychological Phenomenon. American Phrenological Journal and Repository of Science, Literature and General Intelligence, vol. 19
15. Arcangel, Dianne (1997); Investigating the relationship between the Myers-Briggs Type Indicator and facilitated reunion experiences. Journal of the American Society for Psychical Research, vol. 91, issue 2.
16. Arcangel, Dianne (2005); Afterlife Encounters: Ordinary People, Extraordinary Experiences, Hampton Roads Publishing Company, Charlottesville, Virginia.
17. Ariel, Aurora Juliana (2010); Earth 2012: The Violet Age: A Return to Eden, the Regenesis that is Birthing a New World, Aeos, Inc, California.
18. Arnold, James (2008); Finally, All about God: Integrating Religion and Science, iUniverse, Lincoln, USA.
19. Atherton, Henry (1680); The resurrection proved: or, the life to come demonstrated being a strange but true relation of what happened to Mrs. Anna Atherton, T. Dawks, London.
20. Atwater, P. M. H. (1999); Children of the New Millennium: Children's Near-Death Experiences and the Evolution of Humankind, Three Rivers Press, New York.
21. Atwater, P. M.H. (1988); Coming Back to Life, Dodd, Mead & Co., New York.
22. Atwater, P. M. H. (2003); The New Children and Near-Death Experiences, Bear & Co., Rochester, Vermont, USA.
23. Atwater, P. M. H. (1994); Beyond the Light: What Isn't Being Said About Near-death Experience. Birch Lane Press, New York.
24. Atwater, P. M. H. (2007); The Big Book of Near-Death Experiences: The Ultimate Guide to What Happens When We Die, Hampton Roads, Charlottesville, Virginia.
25. Atwater, P. M. H. (2000); What the near-death experience reveals about consciousness, Talk given at the Transpersonal Psychiatrists Conference of the Netherlands on November 25, 2000.
26. Auerbach, Loyd (1993); Reincarnation, Channeling and Possession: A Parapsychologist's Handbook, Warner Books, New York.
27. Bailey, Lee W. and Yates, Jenny (1996); The Near-Death Experience: A Reader, Routledge, Abingdon, UK.
28. Ba Maw (1968); Breakthrough in Burma: memoirs of a revolution, 1939-1946, Yale University Press, New Haven, USA.
29. Banerjee, Rahul and Chakrabarti, Bikas K. (2008); Models of Brain and Mind: Physical, Computational and Psychological Approaches, Elsevier, Amsterdam, The Netherlands.
30. Bandler, Richard (1985); Using your brain – for a change, Real People Press, Moab, Utah, USA.
31. Barbato, Michael (2009); Reflections of a setting sun: Healing experiences around death (1st ed.), Griffin Press, Adelaide, Australia.

32. Barbato, Michael; Blunden, Cathy; Reid, Kerry; Irwin, Harvey; and Rodriquez, Paul (1999); Parapsychological phenomena near the time of death, Journal of Palliative Care, vol. 15, issue 2, pp. 30-37.
33. Barrett, William Fletcher (1926); Death-Bed Visions, Methuen, London.
34. Barrington, Mary Rose (1992); Palladino and the Invisible Man Who Never Was, Journal of the Society for Psychical Research, vol. 58, No. 828, pp. 324-40.
35. Barrington, Mary Rose (2011); Archive No. 74: Researches with The Medium Eva C. (Marthe Beraud), The Paranormal Review, Issue 54.
36. Barrow, John and Tipler, Frank (1986); The Anthropic Cosmological Principle, Oxford University Press.
37. Bauer, Dietrich; Hoffmeister, Max; and Goerg, Hartmut (2005); Children Who Communicate before They are Born: Conversations with Unborn Souls. Forest Row, Temple Lodge, UK.
38. Bender, Hans (1969); New developments in poltergeist research: Presidential address, Proceedings of the Parapsychological Association, vol. 6.
39. Bennett, Gillian (1999); Alas, poor ghost!: traditions of belief in story and discourse, Utah State University Press, Logan, Utah, USA.
40. Bennett, Gillian and Bennett, Kate Mary (2000); The presence of the dead: an empirical study, Mortality, vol. 5, no. 2.
41. Bernstein, Morey (1956); The search for Bridey Murphy, Doubleday, Garden City, New York.
42. Betty, Stafford L. (2006); Are they hallucinations or are they real? The spirituality of deathbed and near-death visions, Omega: Journal of Death & Dying, vol. 53 (issue 1-2), pp. 37-49.
43. Betty, Stafford L. (2005); The Growing Evidence for "Demonic Possession": What Should Psychiatry's Response be? Journal of Religion and Health, Vol. 44, No. 1, Spring 2005 issue.
44. Black, Joseph (2011); The Broadview Anthology of British Literature, Second Concise Edition, Broadview Press, Canada.
45. Blackmore, Susan Jane (1982); Beyond the body: An investigation of out-of-body experiences, Heinemann, London.
46. Blackmore, Susan Jane (1984); A postal survey of OBEs and other experiences. Journal of the Society for Physical Research, issue 52, pp. 225-244.
47. Blackmore, Susan Jane (2003); Consciousness: An Introduction, Oxford University Press.
48. Blackmore, Susan Jane (1993); Dying to Live, Prometheus, Buffalo, New York.
49. Blackmore, Susan Jane and Troscianko, Tom (1989); The Physiology of the Tunnel, Journal of Near-Death Studies, vol. 8, issue 1.
50. Blanke, Olaf and Dieguez, Sebastian (2009); Leaving Body and Life Behind: Out-of-Body and Near-Death Experience, S. Laureys and G. Tononi (Eds.) The Neurology of Consciousness, Elsevier Ltd.
51. Bletzer, June G. (1986); The donning international encyclopedic psychic dictionary, Whitford Press / Schiffer Publishing Ltd, West Chester, PA.

52. Boar, Roger and Blundell, Nigel (1991); The World's greatest Ghosts, The Hamlyn Publishing Group Ltd, London.
53. Bonenfant, Richard J. (2001); A child's encounter with the devil: An unusual near-death experience with both blissful and frightening elements, Journal of Near-Death Studies, vol. 20 (issue 2), Winter 2001, Human Sciences Press.
54. Botkin, Allan (2014); Induced After Death Communication: A Miraculous Therapy for Grief and Loss, Hampton Roads Publishing Inc, Charlottesville, Virginia.
55. Bourguignon, Erika (1976); Possession, Chandler & Sharp Series in Cross-cultural Themes, Chandler & Sharp Publishers. San Francisco.
56. Bowman, Carol (2001); Return from Heaven: Beloved Relatives Reincarnated within your Family, Harper Collins, New York.
57. Bozzano, Ernesto (1910); Des cas d'identification spirite. Annales des Sciences Psychiques, vol. 20, pp. 302–308.
58. Bozzano, Ernesto (1911); Considérations et hypothèses sur les phénomènes de 'bilocation.' Annales des Sciences Psychiques, vol. 21, pp. 65-72, 109-116, 143-152, 166-172.
59. Bozzano, Ernesto (1923); Phénomènes psychiques au moment de la mort, Éditions de la B.P.S. Paris.
60. Bozzano, Ernesto (1934); Les phénomènes de bilocation, Jean Meyer, Paris.
61. Bozzano, Ernesto (1938); Discarnate influences in human life, John M. Watkins. London.
62. Braude, Stephen (1991); The Limits of Influence, Routledge, London.
63. Braude, Stephen (2003); Immortal Remains: The Evidence for Life After Death, Rowman & Littlefield Publishers, Maryland, USA.
64. Brayne, Sue, Farnham, Chris; and Fenwick, Peter (2006); Deathbed Phenomena and their effect on the palliative care team: a pilot study, American Journal of Hospice and Palliative Medicine, vol. 23, issue 1, pp. 17-24.
65. Brayne, Sue; Lovelace, Hilary; and Fenwick, Peter (2008); End-of-life experiences and the dying process in a Gloucestershire nursing home as reported by nurses and care assistants. American Journal of Hospice and Palliative Medicine, vol. 25 (issue 3), pp. 195-206.
66. Brenda, J.; Dunne, B.; and Bisaha John P. (1979); Precognitive remote viewing in the Chicago area: A replication of the Stanford experiment. Journal of Parapsychology, vol. 43, March issue.
67. Bret P. T. (1939); Les metapsychoses: La metapsychorragic, la telepathic, la hantise, vol. 1, Introduction et la metapsychorragic fantasmale. J. B. Bailliere, Paris.
68. Brierre de Boismont, A. (2003); A history of dreams, visions, apparitions, ecstasy, magnetism and somnambulism, (Original work published 1855)
69. Briggs, Victoria Constance (2010); Encyclopedia of the Unseen World, Weiser Books, Sun Francisco.
70. Brittan Samuel Buron (1864); Man and his relations: Illustrating the influence of the mind on the body, W. A. Townsend, New York.

71. Broad, Charlie Dunbar (1962); Lectures on Psychical Research (Routledge Revivals): Incorporating the lectures given in Cambridge University in 1959 and 1960, Routledge & Kegan Paul Ltd.

72. Brown, Alan S. (2003); A review of the déjà vu experience. Psychological Bulletin, vol. 129 (issue 3), pp. 394-413.

73. Brown, David Jay and Tart, Charles (2009); Exploring the Near-Death Experience: An Interview with Charles Tart, PhD on December 16, 2009, maps bulletin, Vol. xx, issue 1.

74. Browne, Sylvia and Harrison, Lindsay (2000); Life on the Other Side, A Psychic's Tour of the Afterlife, DUTTON (the Penguin Group), USA.

75. Bryan, Ronald (2000); What Can Elementary Particles Tell Us About the World in Which We Live? Journal of Scientific Exploration, vol. 14, no. 2.

76. Buckland, Raymond (2005); The Spirit Book: The Encyclopedia of Clairvcyance, Channeling, and Spirit Communication, Visible Ink Press, Detroit, Michigan, USA.

77. Bufford, Rodger K. (1988); Counseling and the Demonic, Word Book Publishers, Dallas, Texas, USA.

78. Burke, John (2015); Imagine Heaven: Near-Death Experiences, God's Promises, and the Exhilarating Future That Awaits You, Baker Book House, Grand Rapids, Michigan, USA.

79. Burlingame, Michael (2008); Abraham Lincoln: A Life, Vol. 1, The John Hopkins University Press, Baltimore, USA.

80. Bush, Nancy Evens (2012); Dancing Past the Dark: Distressing Near-Death Experiences, Parson's Porch Books, Cleveland, Tennessee, USA.

81. Bush, Nancy Evens (1983); The near-death experience in children: Shades of the prison-house reopening. Anabiosis: The Journal of Near-Death Studies, vol. 3, issue 2, pp. 177-193.

82. Bush, Nancy Evans and Greyson, Bruce (2014); Distressing Near-Death Experiences: The Basics, Missouri Medicine, vol. 111, issue 5 (September/October).

83. Bush, Nancy Evans, and Greyson, Bruce (1992); Distressing Near-death Experiences, Psychiatry, vol. 55, February issue.

84. Cahagnet, Louis Alphonse (1850); The Celestial Telegraph. George Pierce, London. (originally published in French 1847-48).

85. Callanan, Maggie, and Kelley, Patricia (1993); Final Gifts: Understanding the Special Needs, Awareness, and Communications of the Dying. Poseidon Press New York.

86. Cameron, Brady (2007); The Abstract Man and the Reflective Reality, AuthorHouse. Bloomington, Indiana, USA.

87. Capra, Fritjof (1975); The Tao of Physics. Boulder, Shambhala, Colorado, USA.

88. Carman, E. M., and Carman, N. J. (2013); Cosmic Cradle: Spiritual Dimensions of Life before Birth (Rev. ed). North Atlantic Books, Berkeley, California.

89. Cattoi T.; Moreman, C.; Harcourt G. C. (2015); Death, Dying, and Mysticism: The Ecstasy of the End, Palgrave Macmillan, USA

90. Cavendish, Richard (1977); Visions of heaven and hell, Harmony Books, New York.

91. CBS News (1997); 48 Hours, 20 November 1997.

92. Chalmers, David J. (1995); Facing up to the problem of consciousness. Journal of Consciousness Studies, vol. 2, issue 3, pp. 200–219.

93. Champlain, Sandra (2013); We Don't Die: A skeptics Discovery of Life after Death, Imbue Press an imprint of Morgan James Publishing, New York.

94. Chari, Cadambur Tiruvenkatachari Krishnama (1978); Reincarnation research: Method and interpretation. In M. Ebon (Ed.), Signet Handbook of Parapsychology, pp. 313-24, NAL Books, New York.

95. Chari, Cadambur Tiruvenkatachari Krishnama (1981); A new look at reincarnation. Christian Parapsychologist, vol. 4, pp. 121-129.

96. Chopra, Deepak (1989); Quantum Healing: Exploring the Frontiers of Mind/Body Medicine, Bantam, New York.

97. Chopra, Deepak (1993); Ageless Body, Timeless Mind: The Quantum Alternative to Growing Old. Random House, New York.

98. Cobbe, Frances Power (1877); The Peak in Darien: The Riddle of Death. Little's Living Age (5th series), vol. 19.

99. Collingwood, Rick (2011); Go Deeper: Illusions Within Reality, Resonanz Recording International Pty Ltd, Queensland, Australia.

100. Collins, B. A. (1948); The Cheltenham Ghost, Psychic Press, London.

101. Collins, Francis S. (2007); The language of God: A scientist presents evidence for belief, Simon & Schuster, Africa House, London.

102. Collins, Pat (2006); Mind and Spirit: Psychology and Spirituality in Dialogue, Columbia University Press, New York.

103. Constable, George (1988); Phantom Encounters (Mysteries of the Unknown), Time Life Books Inc., Fairfax, Virginia.

104. Cook, E. F. W., Pasricha, S., Samararatne, G., U Win Maung, and Stevenson, I. (1983a); A review and analysis of "unsolved" cases of the reincarnation type: I. Introduction and illustrative case reports. Journal of the American Society for Psychical Research, vol. 77, pp. 45-62.

105. Cook, E. F. W., Pasricha, S., Samararatne, G., U Win Maung, and Stevenson, I. (1983b); A review and analysis of "unsolved" cases of the reincarnation type: II. Comparison of features of solved and unsolved cases. Journal of the American Society for Psychical Research, vol. 77, pp. 115-135.

106. Cook, E. F. W. (1986); Reincarnation among the Druses: An empirical study. Unpublished master's thesis, University of Virginia, Charlottesville, Virginia.

107. Cook, Emily Williams, and Delanoy, Deborah L. (1994); Research in Parapsychology 1991: Abstracts and Papers from the Thirty-Fourth Annual Convention of the Parapsychological Association, Scarecrow Press, Lanham, USA.

108. Cook, Emily Williams; Greyson, Bruce and Stevenson, Ian (1998); Do Any Near-Death Experiences Provide Evidence for the Survival of Human Personality after Death? Relevant Features and Illustrative Case Reports. Journal of Scientific Exploration, vol. 12, no. 3.

109. Cooper, Irving S. (2007); Reincarnation: A hope of the world, The Book Tree, San Diego, California (originally published 1927).

110. Corey, Michael Anthony, (1993); God and the New Cosmology: The Anthropic Design Argument, Rowman & Littlefield Publishers Inc. Maryland, USA.

111. Cornell, Tony (2002); Investigating the Paranormal, Helix Press, New York.

112. Council, J. R.; Smith, E. J. H.; Kaster-Bundgaard, J.; Glaude, B. A. (1997). Ethical evaluation of hypnosis research: A survey of investigators and their institutional review boards. American Journal of Clinical Hypnosis, vol. 39, issue 4, pp. 258-265.

113. Cox, Benjamin R. III (2009); The Science of Mediumship and the Evidence of Survival. Master's dissertation, Masters of Liberal Studies Theses. Paper 31 Rollins College, Hamilton Holt School, Winter Park, Florida.

114. Cressy, Judith (1994); The Near-Death Experience: Mysticism or Madness, Christopher Publishing House, Hanover, Massachusetts, USA.

115. Crookall, Robert (1966); The Study and Practice of Astral Projection, University Books, New Hyde Park, New York (Original work published 1960).

116. Crookall, Robert (1972); Case-Book of Astral Projection, University Books, pp. 545-746, Secaucus, New Jersey.

117. Crookall, Robert (1967); Events on the threshold of the afterlife: "Clues" as to "the greatest of all enigmas", Darshana International, Moradabad, India.

118. Crookall, Robert (1970); Out of the Body Experiences, Carol Publishing (edition 1992), New York.

119. Crowe, Catherine (1848); The night side of the Nature, or Ghosts and ghost seers (two volumes), T. C. Newby, London.

120. Crowther, Duane S. (2005); Life everlasting: A definitive study of life after death, Horizon Publishers, Cedar Fort, Springville, USA.

121. Cunningham, Paul F (2009); An Experimental Investigation of Past-Life Experiences, A research proposal document, August, 2009.

122. Curtis, Karla Baker (2011); Spirit Communications: Experiments with Mediums, Doctoral Dissertation, Holos University.

123. Curtiss, Homer Frank (1949); Reincarnation, Willing Publishing Company, San Gabriel, California.

124. Cutler, Robin R. (2007); A Soul on Trial: A Marine Corps Mystery at the Turn of the Twentieth Century, Rowman & Littlefield Publishers, Maryland, USA.

125. Davey, John L. (2007); Partners in God's Love, Xulon Press, USA.

126. Davies, Paul (1982); The Accidental Universe. Cambridge University Press, Cambridge.

127. Davies, Paul (1984); Superforce: The Search for a Grand Unified Theory of Nature, Simon & Schuster, New York.

128. Davies, Paul (1983); God and the New Physics, J.M. Dent & Sons, London.

129. Davies, Paul (1988); The Cosmic Blueprint: New Discoveries. In Nature's Creative Ability To Order Universe, Templeton Foundation Press, Pennsylvania, USA.

130. Davies, Douglas and Shaw, Alastair (1995); Reusing old graves: a report on popular British attitudes. Shaw and Sons, Crayford, London.

131. Davies, Douglas (1997); Death, ritual and belief: the rhetoric of funerary rites. Cassell, London.

132. Davis, John Jefferson (1987); The Design Argument, Cosmic 'Fine-tuning', and the Anthropic Principle, The International Journal of Philosophy of Religion, vol. 22, issue 3.

133. Davis, Stephen T. (1989); Death and Afterlife, Palgrave Macmillan, New York.

134. De, Sudipta Kumar (2016); Oceans and the future of the human race, genNEXT Publishers, New Delhi, India.

135. Deer, Patrick (2009); Culture in Camouflage: War, Empire, and Modern British Literature, Oxford University Press Inc, USA.

136. Delanne, Gabriel (1909); Les Apparitions Materialisees des vivants et des morts: Tome 1. Les fantomes des vivants [Materialised apparitions of the living and the dead: vol. 1. Phantasms of the Living], Librairie Spirite, Paris.

137. Dell'Olio, Andrew J. (2010); Do near-death experiences provide a rational basis for belief in life after death? Sophia, vol. 49, issue 1.

138. Dennett, Daniel (1991); Consciousness Explained, Little, Brown and Co. Boston.

139. Denning, Hazel M. (1996); True Hauntings, Llewellyn Publications, St Paul, Minnesota, USA.

140. Dernbach, Katherine Boris (2005); Spirits of the Hereafter: Death Funerary Possession, And the Afterlife in Chuuk, Micronesia. Ethnology, vol. 44 (issue 2), pp. 99-123.

141. Devinsky O.; Feldmann E.; Burrowes K.; and Bromfield E. (1989); Autoscopic phenomena with seizures. Archives of Neurology, vol. 46.

142. Deza, Michel Marie and Deza, Elena (2013); Encyclopedia of Distances, Springer, London.

143. Dillon, Charles Raymond (2001); They Came Back: Tales of Reincarnation, Ghosts, and Life after Death, Authors Choice Press, New York.

144. Dirac, Paul A. M. (1963); The Evolution of the Physicist's Picture of Nature, Scientific American, vol. 208, issue no. 5 (May 1963).

145. Dlin, B. M. (1980); The experience of surviving almost certain death. Adv Psychosom Med, vol. 10.

146. Doyle, Arthur Conan (2006); The History of Spiritualism (vol. 1), The Echo Library, Teddington, (original published in 1926).

147. Doyle, Arthur Conan (2008); The History of Spiritualism (vol. 2) Easyread Large Edition, (original published in 1926).

148. Drab, Kevin J. (1981); The tunnel experience: Reality or hallucination? Anabiosis: The Journal of Near-Death Studies, vol. 1, pp. 126-152.

149. Dreller, Larry (1997); Beginner's Guide to Mediumship. Samuel Weiser Inc. York Beach, Maine, USA.

150. Driesch, Hans Adolf Eduard (1951); Lebenserinnerungen, Ernst Reinhardt Munchen, Germany and Basel, Switzerland.

151. Ducasse, Curt John (1961); A critical examination of the belief in a life after death, Charles C. Thomas Publisher, Springfield, Illinois, USA.

152. Dunn, Earl V. and Smith, Jenice (1977); Ghosts: Their Appearance During Bereavement, Canadian Family Physician, October issue.

153. Ebon, Martin (1969); Reincarnation in the twentieth century, World Publishing Company, Cleveland, USA.

154. Edge, H. L. (1986); Survival and other philosophical questions, In H. L. Edge, R. L. Morris, J. H. Rush, and J. Palmer, Foundations of parapsychology, Routledge and Kegan Paul, London.

155. Edwards, Harry (1978); The Mediumship of Jack Webber, The Harry Edwards Spiritual Healing Sanctuary, Guildford, Surrey, England.

156. Edwards, Paul (1987); The case against reincarnation. Part 4. Free Inquiry, pp. 46-53.

157. Ehrenwald, Jan (1974); Out-of-body experiences and the denial of death. Journal of Nervous and Mental Disease, vol. 159, issue 4.

158. Eijck, Michiel van and Roth, Wolff-Michael (2013); Imagination of Science in Education: From Epics to Novelization, Springer science + media Dordrecht, London.

159. Eliot, Charles W. (Ed.) (1909); Letters by Pliny the Younger [W. Melmoth, trans. rev. by F.C.T. Bosanquet], The Harvard Classics, issue 9, P. F. Collier & Son, New York.

160. Erdelyi, M. H. (1994); Hypnotic hypermnesia: the empty set of hypermnesia. Int. J. Clin. Exp. Hypn. vol. 42.

161. Estrada, James and Newkirk, Willie (Jr.) (2013); God's Cops, XLIBRIS, Bloomington, USA.

162. Facco, Enrico (2012); Near-death experiences and hypnosis: two different phenomena with something in common, Contemporary Hypnosis and Integrative Therapy, vol. 29, pp. 284-297.

163. Facco, Enrico, and Agrillo, Christian (2012); Near-death-like experiences without life-threatening conditions or brain disorders: a hypothesis from a case report, Frontiers in Psychology, vol. 3.

164. Feather, Sally Rhine and Schmicker, Michael (2005); The Gift: ESP, the Extraordinary Experiences of Ordinary People, St. Martin's Press, New York.

165. Feifel, Herman (1959); The Meaning of Death, McGraw-Hill, New York.

166. Fenwick, Peter, and Fenwick, Elizabeth (1995); The truth in the light: An investigation of over 300 near-death experiences, Berkley Books, New York.

167. Fenwick, Peter, Lovelace, Hilary, and Brayne, Sue (2010); Comfort for the dying: five year retrospective and one year prospective studies of end of life experiences. Archives of Gerontology and Geriatrics, vol. 51 (issue 2), pp. 173-179.

168. Fenwick, Peter (2004); Dying: a spiritual experience as shown by Near Death Experiences and Deathbed Visions, public lecture.

169. Feilding, Everard (1963); Sittings with Eusapia Palladino & Other Studies, University Books, New Hyde Park, New York.

170. Fielding-Hall, Harold (1902); The soul of a people (4th ed.), Macmillan, London.

171. Finnegan, Ruth (2014); Communicating: The Multiple Modes of Human Communication, Rouledge, Abingdon, Oxon, UK.

172. Fisher, Joe (1986); The Case for Reincarnation, Grafton Books London.

173. Fisica, Societa Italiana di (2012); Il Nuovo Cimento Della Società Italiana Di Fisica, Nabu Press, Italy.

174. Flammarion, Camille (1900); L'inconnu: The Unknown, Harper and Brothers, New York.

175. Flammarion, Camille (1922); Death and its mystery: At the moment of death, (Latrobe Carroll translation), The Century Co., New York.

176. Flew, Antony (2008); There is a GOD: How the World's Most Notorious Atheist Changed His Mind, HarperOne, New York.

177. Flynn, Charles Peter (1986); After the Beyond: Human Transformation and the Near-Death Experience, Prentice Hall, Englewood Cliffs, New Jersey.

178. Fontana, David (1991); A Responsive Poltergeist: A Case from South Wales, Journal of the Society for Psychical Research, vol. 57, no. 823 (April), pp. 385-402.

179. Fontana, David (2005); Is There an Afterlife?, A Comprehensive Overview of the Evidence, iff books (John Hunt Publishing), UK.

180. Foy, Robin Peter (2008); Witnessing the Impossible, Torcal Publications, Diss, Norfolk, UK.

181. Frederick Copleston (1983); The history of philosophy, vol. 1, Seiid Jalal al-din Mojtabavi.

182. Fredriksson, Ingrid (2015); The Mysteries of Consciousness: Essays on Spacetime, Evolution and Well-Being, McFarland & Company, North Carolina, USA.

183. Freud, Sigmund (1950); Totem and Taboo, W.W. Norton & Company, New York.

184. Funk, Isaac Kaufmann (1907); The psychic riddle, Funk and Wagnails, New York.

185. Gabbard G. O. and Twemlow A. W (1984); With the eyes of the mind: An empirical analysis of out-of-body states. Praeger Scientific, New York.

186. Gallup, George, and Proctor, William (1982); Adventures in Immortality: A Look beyond the Threshold of Death, McGraw-Hill, New York.

187. Garrett, Eileen J. (1943); Awareness, Creative Age Press, New York.

188. Gauld, Alan (1982); Mediumship and Survival: A century of investigations. Heinemann, London.

189. Gauld, Alan and Cornell, A. D. (1979); Poltergeists, Routledge & Kegan Paul, Boston, Massachusetts, USA.

190. Geley, Gustave (2006); Clairvoyance and Materialisation: A Record of experiments, Kessinger Publishing LLC, Whitefish, Montana, USA (originally published 1927).

191. Geley, Gustave (1920); From the Unconscious to the Conscious, William Collins Sons and Co, Glasgow.

192. Gibson, E. P (1944); An examination of motivation as found in selected cases from 'Phantasms of the Living', Journal of the American Society for Psychical Research, vol. 38.

193. Gibson, Arvin S. (2006); They Saw Beyond Death: New insights on near-death experiences, Horizon Publishers & Distributors, Springville, Utah.

194. Glanvil, Joseph (1682); Saducismus Triumphatus, printed by Tho. Newcomb, for S. Lownds at his Shop by the Savoy Gate, London.

195. Glenconner, Pamela (1921); The Earthen vessel, John Lane Co., London.

196. Glick, Ira, Weiss; Robert Stuart and Parkes, Colin Murray (1974); The first year of bereavement. John Wiley, New York.

197. Goldberg, Bruce (1982); Past lives, Future lives, Ballantine Books, New York.

198. Goldberg, Bruce (2004); Past lives, future lives revealed, New Page Books, a division of The Career Press Inc. Franklin Lakes, Book-mart Press, New Jersey.

199. Gonzalez, Guillermo, and Richards, Jay Wesley (2004); The Privileged Planet: How Our Place in the Cosmos is Designed for Discovery, Regnery Publishing, Inc., Washington DC.

200. Goswami, Amit (1993); The Self-Aware Universe: How Consciousness Creates the Material World, G. P. Putnam's Sons, New York.

201. Goswami, Amit (2006); The Visionary Window: A Quantum Physicist's Guide to Enlightenment, Quest books, Chennai, India.

202. Goswami, Amit (2013); Physics of the soul: The Quantum Book of Living, Dying, Reincarnation, and Immortality, Hampton Roads Publishing Company Inc. Charlottesville, Virginia.

203. Gould, Stephen Jay (1977); Ever Since Darwin, W.W. Norton & Co., New York.

204. Goullart, Peter (1961); The Monastery of Jade Mountain, John Murray, London.

205. Govinda, Lama Anagarika (1974); Foundations of Tibetan Mysticism, Samuel Weiser, New York.

206. Govinda, Lama Anagarika (1988); The way of the white clouds, Shambhala, Boston.

207. Gravitz, Melvin A. (2002); The Search for Bridey Murphy: Implications for Modern Hypnosis, American Journal of Clinical Hypnosis, vol. 45, issue 1 (July).

208. Green, Celia Elizabeth (1968); Out-of-the-Body Experiences, Hamish Hamilton, London.

209. Green, David and Carrington, Hereward (2012); True Ghost Stories, DODO Publishing.

210. Grey, Margot (1985); Return from death: An exploration of the near-death experience, Arkana, London.

211. Greyson, Bruce (1983); The near-death experience scale: Construction, reliability, and validity, The Journal of Nervous and Mental Disease, vol. 185.

212. Greyson, Bruce (2007); Consistency of near-death experience accounts over two decades: Are reports embellished over time? Resuscitation, vol. 73.

213. Greyson, Bruce (1985); A Typology of Near-Death Experiences, American Journal of Psychiatry, vol. 142, issue 8.

214. Greyson, Bruce (2003); Incidence and correlates of near-death experiences in a cardiac care unit. Gen Hosp Psychiatry, vol. 25.

215. Greyson, Bruce (2010); Seeing Dead People Not Known to Have Died: "Peak in Darien" Experiences, Anthropology and Humanism, vol. 35, Issue 2, The American Anthropological Association.

216. Grof, Stanislav (1988); The adventure of self-discovery: Dimensions of consciousness and new perspectives in psychotherapy and inner exploration, State University of New York Press, Albany, New York.

217. Grof, Stanislav (1994); Books of the dead, Thames and Hudson, New York.

218. Grof, Stanislav (2000); Psychology of the future: Lessons from modern consciousness research, State University New York Press, Albany, New York.

219. Groothuis, Douglas (1995); Deceived by the Light, Harvest House Publishers, Irvine, California.

220. Gross, David (2005); Einstein and the search for unification, Current Science, vol. 89, no. 12, 25 December 2005 issue.

221. Grosso, Michael (2004); Experiencing the Next World Now, Paraview Pocket Books, New York.

222. Grottendieck W. G. (1906); A poltergeist case, Journal of the society for Psychical research, vol. 12.

223. Guiley, Rosemary Ellen (2010); Spirit Communications, Chelsea House Publishers, New York.

224. Gunaratna, V. F.; Rao, P. M.; Karunaratne, T. B.; Story, Francis; Jayatilleke, K.N.; Nanajivako, Bhikkhu; Khantipalo, Bhikkhu; Joshi, Lal Mani (2011); Collected Wheel Publications, vol. X, nos. 132–151, Buddhist Publication Society, Kandi, Sri Lanka.

225. Gurney E.; Myers F. W. H. and Podmore F. (1886); Phantasms of the living (two volumes), Trubner, London.

226. Gurney, E., and Myers, F. W. H. (1888-89); On apparitions occurring soon after death. Proceedings of the Society for Psychical Research, vol. 5, pp. 403-485.

227. Gustus, Sandie (2011); Less Incomplete: A Guide to Experiencing the Human Condition beyond the Physical Body, O-books, Alresford, UK.

228. Habermas, Gary R. and Moreland, J. P. (1992); Immortality: The other side of death, Thomas Nelson, Nashville, Tennessee, USA.

229. Habermas, Gary and Moreland, James Porter (2004); Beyond Death: Exploring the evidence for immortality, Wipf and Stock Publishers, Oregon, USA.

230. Hafele, Joseph C. and Keating, Richard E. (1972); Around-the-World Atomic Clocks: Predicted Relativistic Time Gains, Science, vol. 177.

231. Haig, Scott (2007); The brain: the power of hope. Time Magazine, vol. 169.

232. Halbfass, Wilhelm (1980); Karma, Apurva, and 'Natural' Causes: Observations on the Growth and Limits of the Theory of Samsara. In (ed.) O'Flaherty, Wendy Doniger, Karma and Rebirth in Classical Indian Traditions. University of California Press, Berkeley and Los Angeles.

233. Haldane, John Burdon Sanderson (1927); Possible worlds and other essays, Chatto & Windus, London.

234. Hall, Granville Stanley (1897); A study of fears, American Journal of Psychology, vol. 8.

235. Hallett, Elisabeth (2002); Stories of the Unborn Soul: The Mystery and Delight of Prebirth Communication. Writer's Club, San Jose, California.

236. Hamilton, T. Glen (1942); Intention and Survival: Psychical research studies and the bearing of intentional actions by trance personalities on the problem of human survival (reprinted 1977) Regency Press, London and Toronto.

237. Hannesson, Gudmundur (1924); Remarkable phenomena in Iceland, Journal A.S.P.R (JASPR), vol. 18.

238. Haraldsson, Erlendur (2009); Alleged Encounters with the Dead: The Importance of Violent Death in 337 new cases, The Journal of Parapsychology, vol. 73.

239. Haraldsson, Erlendur (1987); The Iyenger-Kirti case: An Apparitional Case of the Bystander Type, Journal of the Society for Psychical Research, vol. 54, no. 806.

240. Haraldsson, Erlendur (2000); Birthmarks and Claims of Previous-Life Memories, I. The case of Purnima Ekanayake, Journal of the Society for Psychical Research, vol. 64.1, no. 858.

241. Haraldsson, Erlendur (2008); Ian Stevenson's Contributions to the Study of Mediumship, Journal of Scientific Exploration, vol. 22, no. 1, pp. 64-72.

242. Haraldsson, Erlendur (2012); The Departed Among the Living: An Investigative Study of Afterlife Encounters, White Crow Books, Guildford, Surrey, England.

243. Harler, Courtney A. (2013); The Ogbanje in Little Bee by Chris Cleave, Master's Thesis Collection, Eastern Washington University, Cheney, Washington.

244. Harriger, Kelly Ryan (2009); God: An Unauthorized Biography, Exploring the Rational basis for faith, Xulon Press, USA.

245. Harrison, William (1879); Spirits before our eyes, W. H. Harrison, London.

246. Harrison, P. and Harrison, M. (1991); The children that time forgot, Berkley Books, New York (Original work published 1983 as Life before birth).

247. Hart, Hornell (1954); ESP projection: Spontaneous cases and the experimental methods, Journal of the American Society for Psychical Research, vol. 48.

248. Hart, Hornell (1967); Scientific survival research, International Journal of Parapsychology. vol. 9.

249. Hart Hornell and Hart E. B (1933); Visions and apparitions collectively and reciprocally perceived, Proceedings of the Society for Psychical Research, vol. 41.

250. Hart, Hornell (1959); The Enigma of Survival: The Case for and against an After Life, Springfield, Illinois, USA.

251. Hartley, Robert (2007); Helen Duncan: The Mystery Show Trial, HPR Publishing Limited, London.

252. Hastings, A.; Hutton, M.; Braud, W.; Bennett, C.; Berk, I.; Boynton, T.; Dawn, C.; Ferguson, E.; Goldman, A.; Greene, E.; Hewett, M.; Lind, V.; McLellan, K.; and Steinbach-Humphrey, S. (2002); Psychomanteum research: Experiences and effects on bereavement. Omega: Journal of Death & Dying, vol. 45, pp. 211-228.

253. Hastings, Arthur (1991); With the Tongues of Men and Angels: A Study of Channeling, Holt, Rinehart and Winston, Fort Worth, Texas, USA.

254. Hastings, Arthur (2012); Effects on bereavement using a restricted sensory environment (psychomanteum), The Journal of Transpersonal Psychology, vol. 44, no. 1.

255. Haught, John F. (2005); Science and scientism: the importance of a distinction. Zygon: Journal of Religion and Science, vol. 40, pp. 363-368.

256. Hawking, Stephen (1998); A brief history of time, Bantam Press, New York.

257. Heim, Albert (1892); Notizen über den Tod durch Absturz, Jahrbuch des Schweizer Alpenklub, (Experience of Dying from Falls, Yearbook of the Swiss Alpine Club), vol. 27.

258. Heinerman, J. (1978); Spirit world manifestations, Magazine Printing and Publishing, Salt Lake City, Utah, USA.

259. Henderson, Y. and Haggard, H. W. (1927); Noxious gases and the principles of respiration influencing their action, American Chemical Society, New York.

260. Henry, Jane (2005); Psychokinesis. In J. Henry (Ed.), Parapsychology: Research into exceptional experiences (pp. 125-137), Routledge, London.

261. Herzog, Roberta S. (2003); The Akashic Records: Your Soul's Journey through Time, Lux Light Associates Union, New Jersey.

262. Higgins, Joseph M. and Bergman, Chuck (2011); The Everything Guide to Evidence of the Afterlife: A Scientific Approach to proving the existence of life after death, Adams Media, Massachusetts, USA.

263. Hinze, Sara (2016); The Announcing Dream: Dreams and Visions of Children Waiting to be Born, Three Orchard Productions, Mesa, Arizona, USA.

264. Hodgson, Richard (1898); A further record of observation of certain phenomena of trance. Proceedings of the Society for Psychical Research, vol. 13, pp. 284-582.

265. Hodgson, Richard (1892); A Record of Observations of Certain Phenomena of Trance, Proceedings of the Society for Psychical Research, vol. 8.

266. Hoffman, Regina M. (1995); Disclosure Habits After Near-Death Experience: Influences, Obstacles, and Listeners Selection, Journal of Near-Death Studies, vol. 14, pp. 29-48.

267. Hogan, Craig (2008); Your eternal self, Greater Reality Publications.

268. Holden, Janice Miner, Bruce Greyson, and Debbie James (2009); The Handbook of Near-Death Experiences: Thirty Years of Investigation, Praeger–ABC-CLIO, Santa Barbara, California.

269. Holt, Henry (1914); On the Cosmic Relations, Houghton Mifflin Company, Boston, USA.

270. Holt, Henry (1919); The Cosmic Relations and Immortality, Volume 1, Houghton Mifflin Company, Boston, USA.

271. Home, Daniel Dunglas (1879); Lights and Shadows of Spiritualism, G. W. Carleton & Co. New York.

272. Horgan, John (1999); The Undiscovered Mind: How the Human Brain Defies Replication, Medication and Explanation, The Free Press, New York.

273. Houran, James and Lange, Rense (2001); Hauntings and Poltergeists: Multidisciplinary Perspectives, MacFarland and Company, Inc, Publishers, North Carolina, USA.

274. Howell, Michael J. (2008); Timothy's Titanic Scrapbook (a personal diary of author's grandfather).

275. Hoyle, Fred (1981); The Universe: Past and Present Reflections, Engineering and Science, November 1981 issue.

276. Htin Aung (1967); A History of Burma, Columbia University Press, New York.

277. Hudson, Thomson Jay (1901); A scientific demonstration of the future life, A. C. McClurg, Chicago.

278. Hugenot, Alan Ross (2016); The New Science of Consciousness Survival and the Metaparadigm Shift to a conscious universe, Dog Ear Publishing, Indianapolis, USA.

279. Hunter, Jack (2012); Contemporary Physical Mediumship: Is it Part of a Continuous Tradition? Paranthropology: Journal of Anthropological Approaches to the Paranormal, vol. 3, no. 1.

280. Hu'o'ng, Le Quang (1972); Histoires vietnamiennes de reincarnation. Message d'Extreme-Orient, vol. 2, issue 7, pp. 535-539.

281. Hyslop, James Hervey (1912); A review, a record and a discussion, Journal of the American Society for Psychical Research, vol. 6.

282. Hyslop, James Hervey (1915); Incidents, Journal of the American Society for Psychical Research, vol. 9, pp. 392-393.

283. Hyslop, James Hervey (1908); Psychical Research and the Resurrection. Small, Maynard & Company, Boston.

284. IFSR booklet (nd); Glimpses of the Beyond Experiences Pointing to Life After Death, Booklet prepared by International Foundation for Survival Research, Inc. San Rafael, California.

285. Iida, F. (2006); Twin soul: My fortunate journey, PHP Institute, Tokyo, Japan.

286. Imich, Alex (2007); My Life with Parapsychology: The Most Important Science. Journal of Spirituality and Paranormal Studies, vol. 30, issue 1, pp. 30-35.

287. Irmak, M. Kemal (2014); Schizophrenia or Possession? Journal of Religion and Health, vol. 53, pp. 773-777.

288. Irwin, Harvey J. (1985); Flight of mind: A psychological study of the out-of-body experience, Scarecrow Press, Metuchen, New Jersey.

289. Irwin, Harvey J. (1987); Out-of-body experiences in the blind, Journal of Near-Death Studies, vol. 6.

290. Irwin, Harvey J. (1999); Near-death experiences. In Irwin, H. J. (ed.) An Introduction to Parapsychology, 3rd Edition, McFarland, Jefferson & Company, North Carolina.

291. Irwin, Harvey J., and Bramwell, Barbara A. (1988); The devil in heaven: A near death Experience with both positive and negative facets. Journal of Near-Death Studies, vol. 7, pp. 38-43.

292. Isaacs, Craig T. (1987); The Possessive States Disorder: The Diagnosis of Demonic Possession, Pastoral Psychology, vol. 35, issue 4.

293. Jackson, Kathryn Patricia (2012); Giving up the ghost. Healers' perceptions of the perimortal process: a phenomenological study, PhD thesis, School of Health and Human Sciences, Southern Cross University, Lismore, New South Wales, Australia.

294. Jahn, Robert G. (2001); The challenge of consciousness. The Journal of Scientific Exploration, vol. 15, issue 4, pp. 443-457.

295. James, William (1978); Upon the knees of the gods. In M. Ebon (Ed.), The Signet Handbook of Parapsychology. NAL (New American Library) Penguin Inc., New York, pp. 43-53.

296. James, William (1986); Essays in Psychical Research, Harvard University Press, USA.

297. James, William (1902); The Varieties of Religious Experience: A Study in Human Nature, Longman, Green and Co., New York.

298. Jayatilleke, Kulatissa Nanda (2000); Facets of Buddhist Thought: Collected Essays, Buddhist Publication Society, Kandy, Sri Lanka.

299. Johnson, Alice (1899); Coincidences. Proceedings of the Society for Psychical Research, vol. 14.

300. Johnson, George Lindsay (1936); Does Man Survive?: The Great Problem of the Life Hereafter and the Evidence for Its Solution, Harper & Brothers, New York.

301. Johnson, P. E. (1920); A testimony, Relief Society Magazine, vol. 3, issue 8, August issue.

302. Jung C. G. (1998); Jung on Synchronicity and the Paranormal, Princeton University Press, New Jersey.

303. Jung-Stilling, Joachim Heinrich (1851); Theory of Pneumatology, J. S. Redfield, New York, (originally published in German, 1808).

304. Kaku, Michio (1994); Hyperspace, Oxford University Press, New York.

305. Kalish, R. A. and Reynolds, D. K. (1973); Phenomenological reality and post-death contact. Journal for the Scientific Study of Religion, issue 12.

306. Kalmus, Natalie M. (1949); Doorway to Another World. Coronet, vol. 25, issue 6.

307. Kampman, R. (1976); Hypnotically induced multiple personality: An experimental study, International Journal of Clinical and Experimental Hypnosis, 24, 215-227.

308. Karl, Jason (2007); An Illustrated History of the Haunted World, New Holland Publishers (UK) Ltd, Singapore.

309. Kean, Leslie (2017); Surviving Death: A Journalist Investigates Evidence for an Afterlife, Crown Publishing Group, New York.

310. Keen, Montague (2001); The Scole Investigation: A Study in Critical Analysis of Paranormal Physical Phenomena, Journal of Scientific Exploration, vol. 15, No. 2.

311. Keen, Montague (2003); Communicating with the Dead: The Evidence Ignored Why Paul Kurtz is Wrong. Journal of Scientific Exploration, vol. 17, no. 2, pp. 291-299.

312. Keil, H. H. J and Tucker, J. B (2000); An unusual birthmark case thought to be linked to a person who had previously died. Psychological Report, vol. 87.

313. Kelly, Emily Williams (2010); Some directions for mediumship research. Journal of Scientific Exploration, vol. 24, issue 2.

314. Kelly, Emily Williams (2013); Science, the Self, and Survival after Death: Selected Writings of Ian Stevenson, Rowman & Littlefield Publishers Inc. Maryland, UK.

315. Kelly, Emily Williams, Bruce Greyson, and Edward F. Kelly (2007); Unusual Experiences Near Death and Related Phenomena. In Irreducible Mind: Toward a Psychology for the 21st Century. Edward F. Kelly, Emily Williams Kelly, Adam Crabtree, Alan Gauld, Michael Grosso, and Bruce Greyson, Rowman and Littlefield, Lanham, Maryland, USA.

316. Kelly, Emily Williams, Greyson, Bruce, Stevenson, Ian (2010); Can experiences near death furnish evidence of life after death?, Omega, Journal of death and dying, vol. 40, issue 4.

317. Kelly, Williams Emily (2001); Near-death experiences with reports of meeting deceased people, Death Studies, vol. 25.

318. Kennedy, David (1973); A Venture in Immortality, Colin Smythe Ltd, UK.

319. Kerr. Christopher W.; Donnelly, James P.; Wright, Scott T.; Kuszczak, Sarah M.; Banas, Anne; Grant, Pei C.; Luczkiewicz, Debra L. (2014); End-of-Life Dreams and Visions: A Longitudinal Study of Hospice Patients' Experiences, Journal of Palliative Medicine, vol. 17, no. 3.

320. King, L. S. (1975); Reincarnation, Journal of the American Medical Association, vol. 234.

321. Kingsford, S. M. (1920); Psychical Research for the Plain Man, Kegan Paul, Trench & Co. Ltd. London.

322. Klimo, Jon (1987); Channeling: Investigations on Receiving Information from Paranormal Sources, Jeremy P. Tarcher Inc., Los Angeles.

323. Klinge, Brad; Klinge, Barry; and Passero, Kathy (2011); Chasing Ghosts, Texas Style: On the Road with Everyday Paranormal, Thomas Dunne Books, New York.

324. Knight, Zelda Gillian (1995); The healing power of the unconscious: How can we understand past life experiences in psychotherapy?, South African Journal of Psychology, vol. 25 (issue 2), pp. 90-98.

325. Komp, Diane M. (1992); A window to heaven: When children see life in death, Zondervan Publishing, Grand Rapids, Michigan, USA.

326. Kost, Paul F. (1965); Dangers of hypnosis. International Journal of Clinical and Experimental Hypnosis, vol. 13, issue 4.

327. Koteskey, Ronald C. (1979); Toward the Development of a Christian Psychology: Adjustment and Maladjustment, Journal of Psychology and Theology, vol. 7 (issue 3) (Fall 1979).

328. Krishnan, Armin (2017); Military Neuroscience and the Coming Age of Neurowarfare, Routledge, Abingdon, Oxon, UK.

329. Kubler-Ross, Elisabeth (1983); On Children and Death, Macmillan, New York.

330. Kurtz, Paul (2003); Are they Compatible, Editor, Science and Religion, Prometheus Books, Amherst, New York.

331. Lacy, Phillip H. De and Einarson, Benedict (1984); Plutarch's Moralia (volume 7), William Heinemann, London.

332. Lamont, Peter (2005); The First Psychic: The Peculiar Mystery of a Notorious Victorian Wizard, Abacus, London.

333. Landau, Lucian (1963); An Unusual Out-of-the-Body Experience, Journal of the Society for Psychical Research, vol. 42, no. 717.

334. Lanza, Robert (2009); Biocentrism: How Life and Consciousness are the Keys to Understanding the True Nature of the Universe, BenBella Books, Dallas, Texas.

335. Larusdottir, Elinborg (1946); Midillinn Hafsteinn Bjomsson (The Medium Hafsteinn Bjornsson) Nordri, Iceland.

336. Laureys, Steven and Tononi, Giulio (2009); The Neurology of Consciousness: Cognitive Neuroscience and Neuropathology, Elsevier Ltd, London.

337. Lawrence M., and Repede E. (2013); The Incidence of deathbed communications and their impact on the dying process. Am J Hosp Palliat Care, vol. 30, issue 7 (November).

338. Lazarus, Richard (1993); The Case Against Death, Warner Books, London.

339. Leadbeater, Charles Webster (1952); The life after death and how theosophy unveils it. The Theosophical Publishing House, Adyar, Madras, India.

340. Leane, Elizabeth (2007); Reading Popular Physics: Disciplinary Skirmishes and Textual Strategies, Ashgate Publishing Ltd, Aldershot, UK.

341. Leininger, Bruce; Leininger, Andrea; and Gross, Ken (2009); Soul Survivor: The Reincarnation of a World War II Fighter Pilot, Hay House, London.

342. Lenggenhager, Bigna; Smith S. T.; and Blanke Olaf (2006); Functional and neural mechanisms of embodiment: Importance of the vestibular system and the temporal parietal junction. Rev Neurosci, vol 17.

343. Leonard, Gladys Osborne (1931); My life in two worlds, Cassell & Company Ltd., London.

344. Leonard, Todd Jay (2005); Talking to the Other Side: a History of Modern Spiritualism And Mediumship, iUniverse, Inc., Lincoln, USA.

345. Leslie, John (1988); How to Draw Conclusions from a Fine-Tuned Cosmos. In Robert Russell, et al., eds., Physics, Philosophy and Theology: A Common Quest for Understanding. Vatican Observatory Press, Vatican City State.

346. Leslie, John (1989); Universes. Routledge, New York.

347. Leslie, John (2001); Infinite Minds: A Philosophical Cosmology, Clarendon Press, Oxford University Press, New York.

348. Lester, David (2003); Critics of near-death experiences as evidence for survival: A methodological note [Letter], Journal of Near-Death Studies, vol. 21, no. 4, (summer, 2003).

349. Leuba, James H. (1896); A Study in the Psychology of Religious Phenomena. American Journal of Psychology, vol. 7, issue 3.

350. Leveille, David E. (2014); Surviving Cancer: Not Somehow ... but Triumphantly, WestBow Press, Bloomington, Indiana, USA.

351. Lewis, James R. (2004); The Encyclopedic Sourcebook of New Age Religions, Prometheus Books, Amherst, New York.

352. Lief, Harold I. (1977); Commentary on Dr. Ian Stevenson's 'Research into the evidence of man's survival after death', Journal of Nervous and Mental Disease, 165, 171-173.

353. Linn, Sheila Fabricant; Linn, Dennis and Linn, Matthew (2016); The Gifts of Near-Death Experiences: You Don't Have to Die to Experience your true home, Hampton Roads Publishing Company Ltd., Charlottesville, Virginia.

354. Livio, Mario (2010); Is God a Mathematician?, Simon & Schuster Paperbacks, New York.

355. Lodge, Oliver (1916); Raymond or life and death, George H. Doran Company, New York.

356. Long, Jeffrey (2010); Evidence of the Afterlife: The science of near-death experiences, HarperOne, New York.

357. Ludden, Ken (2011); Mystic Apprentice 5: Psychic Skills LPE, Lulu, USA.

358. Ludden, Ken (2012); Mystic Apprentice, Master Volume, Lulu, USA.

359. Lundahl, Craig R. (1982); Near-death experiences of Mormons. In Lundahl, C. R. (Ed.), A collection of near-death research readings (pp. 165-179). Chicago, IL: Nelson-Hall.

360. Lundahl, Craig R. (1992); Angels in Near-Death Experiences, Journal of Near-Death Studies, vol. 11 (issue 1) Fall 1992.

361. Lundahl, Craig R. (2001); Prophetic Revelations in Near-Death Experiences, Journal of Near-Death Studies, vol. 19, issue 4 Summer 2001, Human Sciences Press Inc.

362. Lyons, Linda (2005); One-third of Americans believe dearly may not have departed. Gallup Survey. URL: http://www.gallup.com/poll/17275/OneThirdAmericans-Believe-Dearly-May-departed.aspx. (last accessed July 29, 2019).

363. MacKenzie, Andrew (1982); Hauntings and Apparitions, Heinemann, London.

364. MacNutt, Francis (1995); Deliverance from Evil Spirits, Chosen Books, Grand Rapids, Michigan, USA.

365. Madsen, Wayne (2012); The Manufacturing of a President, The CIA's Insertion of Barack H. Obama, Jr. into the White House, CreateSpace Independent Publishing Platform, North Charleston, USA.

366. Maher, Michaeleen C. (1992); The study of ghosts: A brief synopsis. In L. A. Henkel and G. R. Schmeidler (Eds.) Research in Parapsychology 1990 (pp. 137 – 138), Scarecrow Press, Metuchen, New Jersey.

367. Maksimonus (2009); "BBC: Pam Sees God. NDE Pam Reynolds. Amazing! Full Version!." Filmed [2002] Youtube video, 10:57. Posted on April 6, 2009, URL: www.youtube.com/watch?v=WNbdUEqDB-k (last accessed July 31, 2019).

368. Malia, Linda (2001); A Fresh Look at a Remarkable Document: Exorcism: The Report of a Commission Convened by the Bishop of Exeter. Anglican Theological Review, vol. 83 (issue 1), pp. 65-88.

369. Marris, Peter (1958); Widows and their Families, Routledge and Kegan Paul Ltd, London.

370. Marsh, Michael N. (2010); Out-of-Body and Near-Death Experiences: Brain-State Phenomena or Glimpses of Immortality? Oxford University Press, Oxford.

371. Marshal, Andrew (1815); The morbid anatomy of the brain in mania and hydrophobia, Longman, London.

372. Marshall, Paul (2019); The Shape of the Soul: What Mystical Experience Tells Us about Ourselves and reality, Rowman & Littlefield, Maryland, UK.

373. Martensen-Larsen, H. (1926); An der Pforte des Todes, Furche, Berlin, Germany.

374. Martin, Malachi (1992); Hostage to the Devil: The Possession and Exorcism of Five Americans, HarperSanFrancisco, New York.

375. Martin, Mike W (2007); Albert Schweitzer's Reverence for Life: Ethical Idealism and Self-Realization, Ashgate Publishing Ltd, Hampshire, UK.

376. Martin, Walter and Zacharias, Ravi (2003); The Kingdom of the Cults, Bethany House Publishers, Michigan, USA.

377. Masayuki, Ohkado and Akira, Ikegawa (2014); Children with Life-Between-Life Memories, Journal of Scientific Exploration, vol. 28, no. 3.

378. Mascaro, K. R. (2016a); Announcing dreams: Perceived communication with baby-to-be. Journal of Prenatal and Perinatal Psychology and Health, vol. 30 (issue 3), pp. 191-207.

379. Mascaro, K. R. (2016b); The effects of announcing dreams: An investigation of pregnant women's perceived communication with their unborn. International Journal of Dream Research, vol. 9 (issue 1), pp. 7-14.

380. Matlock, James G. and Giesler-Petersen, Iris (2016); Asian Versus Western Intermission Memories: Universal Features and Cultural Variations, Journal of Near Death Studies, vol. 35 (issue 1), Fall 2016.

381. Maxwell, Joseph (1920); Preface. In E. Bozzano, Les phénomènes de hantise (pp. v-xii), Félix Alcan, Paris.

382. Mazzarino-Willett April (2010); Deathbed phenomena: Its role in peaceful death and terminal restlessness, Am J Hospice Palliat Care, vol. 27, issue 2.

383. McClenon, James (1994); Wondrous Events. Foundations of Religious Beliefs, University of Pennsylvania Press, Philadelphia, USA.

384. McCue, Peter A. (2011); Apparitions on Scotland's A75, Phenomena Magazine, November 2011 issue, pp. 25-28.

385. Mead, George Robert Stow (1907); The vision of Aridaeus (volume III), Theosophical Publishing Society, London.

386. Melechi, Antonio (2008); Servants of the Supernatural: The Night Side of the Victorian Mind, William Heinemann, London.

387. Melton, Gordon J. (1978); "Spiritualism". Encyclopedia of American Religions, Volume 2, McGrath Publishing Company, Wilmington, North Carolina, USA.

388. Metzinger, Thomas (2005); Out-of-Body Experiences as the Origin of the Concept of a "Soul", Mind & Matter, vol. 3, issue 1.

389. Michell, John and Rickard Bob (2007); The Rough Guide to Unexplained Phenomena, Rough Guides Ltd, London.

390. Mills, Antonia C. (1988); Preliminary investigation of cases of the reincarnation type among the Beaver and Gitksan Indians. Anthropologica, vol. 30, pp. 23-59.

391. Mills, A., and Lynn, S. J. (2000); Past life experiences. In E. Cardeña, S. J. Lynn, & S. Krippner (Eds.), Varieties of anomalous experience: Examining the scientific evidence (pp. 283-313), American Psychological Association, Washington, DC.

392. Monk, Dorothy (1922); The process of dying witnessed by eight persons: Visible evidences of the spirit body. Light, issue 42.

393. Montgomery, Ruth (1972); A world beyond, Fawcett Crest, New York.

394. Moody, Raymond Á., and Perry, Paul (1993); Reunions. Villard Books, New York.

395. Moody, Raymond A. (1975); Life After Life, Mocking bird Books, Covington, Georgia.

396. Moody, Raymond A., and Perry, Paul (2010); Glimpses of Eternity: An investigation into shared death experiences, Guideposts, New York.

397. Moody, Raymond A. (1992); Family Reunions: Visionary Encounters with the Departed in a Modern-Day Psychomanteum, Journal of Near-Death Studies, vol. 11, issue 2 (Winter 1992).

398. Moody, Raymond Á., and Perry, Paul (1988); The Light Beyond, Bantam, NY.

399. Moody, Raymond A. (2012); Paranormal: My Life in Pursuit of the Afterlife, Random House Group Company, USA.

400. Moore, Carrie A. (2006); The unseen realm: Science is making room for near-death experiences beyond the world. Deseret Morning News, February 18, 2006 issue.

401. Moraldi, Luigi (1987); Nach dem Tode. Jenseitsvorstellungen von den Babyloniern bis zum Christentum, Benzinger, Köln, Germany.

402. Moreira-Almeida, Alexander and Santos, Franklin Santana (2012); Exploring Frontiers of the Mind-Brain Relationship, Springer, New York.

403. Moreland J. P, Meister Chad V., and Sweis, Khaldoun A. (2013); Debating Christian Theism, Oxford University Press, New York.

404. MORI (1998); Paranormal survey [Conducted for the Sun Newspaper], URL: http://www.ipsos-mori.com/researchpublications/researcharchive/poll.aspx?oItemId=2082. (last accessed July 31, 2019).

405. Morris, R. L., Harary, S. B., Janis, J., Hartwell, J., and Roll, W. G. (1978); Studies of communication during out-of-body experiences. Journal of the American Society for Psychical Research, vol. 72, pp. 1 - 24.

406. Morse, M., Castillo P, Venecia D, Milstein J, Tyler D. C. (1986); Childhood near-death experiences. Am J Dis Child, vol. 140 (issue 11), pp. 1110-1114.

407. Morse, Melvin (1992); Transformed by the Light, Ballantine Books, New York.

408. Morse, Melvin (1990); Closer to the Light: Learning from the Near-Death Experiences of Children, Random House, New York.

409. Morse, Melvin and Perry, Paul (1990): Closer to the Light: Learning from the Near-Death Experiences of Children. Villard, New York.

410. Morse, M.; Castillo, P.; Venecia, D.; Milstein, J.; and Tyler, D. C. (1986); Childhood near-death experiences, American Journal of Diseases of Children, 140, issue 11 (November), pp. 1110-14.

411. Morselli, Enrico Agostino (1908); Psicologia e 'Spiritismo:' Impressioni e note critiche sui fenomeni medianici di Eusapia Paladino (vol. 1), Fratelli Bocca, Turin, Italy.

412. Morton, R. C. (1892); Record of a haunted house. Proceedings of the Society for Psychical Research, issue 8, pp. 311-332.

413. Muldoon, Sylvan Joseph and Carrington, Hereward (1973); Projection of the Astral Body, Weiser Books, Boston.

414. Muldoon, Sylvan Joseph and Carrington, Hereward (1969); The Phenomena of Astral Projection, Rider, London (Original work published 1951).

415. Murdock, J. Z. (2014); Death of Heaven: 2014 (revised 2nd Edition), Zilyon Publishing.

416. Murray, Michael J. (1999); Reason for the Hope Within, William B. Eerdmans Publishing Company, Cambridge, UK.

417. Myers, William Henry Myers (1903); Human Personality and its Survival of Bodily Death (two volumes), Longmans, Green, London.

418. Myers, William Henry Myers (1892); On indications of continued terrene knowledge on the part of phantasms of the dead. Proceedings of the Society for Psychical Research, issue 8, pp. 170-252.

419. Myers, F. W. H; Lodge, O; Leaf, W.; James, W., (1890); A Record of Observations of Certain Phenomena of Trance, Proceedings of the Society for Psychical Research, vol. 6, pp. 436-659.

420. Myers, John, (1968); Voices From the Edge of Eternity, Revell-Spire, Old Tappan, New Jersey.

421. Nahm, Michael and Greyson, Bruce (2013); The death of Anna Katharina Ehmer: A Case study in Terminal Lucidity, OMEGA (Westport), vol. 68, issue 1.

422. Nahm, Michael (2009); Terminal Lucidity in People with Mental Illness and Other Mental Disability: An Overview and Implications for Possible Explanatory Models, Journal of Near-Death Studies, vol. 28 (issue 2), Winter 2009.

423. Nahm, Michael and Greyson, Bruce (2009); Terminal Lucidity in Patients With Chronic Schizophrenia and Dementia: A Survey of the Literature, The Journal of Nervous and Mental Disease, vol. 197, no. 12, December 2009.

424. Nahm, Michael; Greyson, Bruce; Kelly, Emily Williams; and Haraldsson, Erlendur (2011); Terminal lucidity: A review and a case collection, Archives of Gerontology and Geriatrics.

425. Natsis, Carol and Potter, Maryl (1995); Almanac of the Uncanny: Stories of the supernatural through the centuries, Reader's Digest (Australia) Pty Ltd, Sydney.

426. Nee, Watchman (1972); The Latent Power of the Soul, Christian Fellowship Publishers, Inc. New York.

427. Nelson, K. R., Mattingly M, Schmitt F. A. (2007); Out-of-body experience and arousal. Neurology, vol. 68.

428. Nelson, Lee (1988); Beyond the veil. Volume I, Cedar Fort, Orem, Utah, USA.

429. Neppe, Vernon M. (2010); Déjà vu: Origins and phenomenology: Implications of the four subtypes for future research. The Journal of Parapsychology, vol. 74 (issue 1), pp. 61-97.

430. Newton, Michael (2016a); Journey of Souls: New case studies of life between lives, Lllewellyn Publications, Woodbury, USA.

431. Newton, Michael (2016b); Destiny of Souls: New case studies of life between lives, Lllewellyn Publications, Woodbury, USA.

432. Nightline, (1991); Topics: Exorcism and possession, ABC News (April 5, 1991), Quote from Father James LeBar.

433. Nowatzki, N. R., and Kalischuk, Grant, R. (2009); Post-death encounters: Grieving, mourning, and healing. Omega: Journal of Death and Dying, vol. 59, issue 2.

434. Noyes, M. (1952); A true account of a beautiful passing. Light 72, 65.

435. Noyes, Russell and Kletti, Roy (1977); Depersonalisation in response to life-threatening danger. Comprehen Psychiatr, vol. 18, issue 4. (July-August).

436. Noyes, Russell and Slymen, Donald (1979); The subjective response to life-threatening danger. Omega, Journal of Death and Dying, vol. 9, no. 4 (1st Dec issue).

437. Oakley, Donald G. (2011); In Search of the Self, Eyrie Press, Fens, North Cambridgeshire UK.

438. O'Flaherty, Wendy Doniger (1980); Karma and Rebirth in Classical Indian Traditions. Berkeley and Los Angeles, University of California Press, Calif.

439. Ohkado, Masayuki and Greyson, Bruce (2014); A Comparative Analysis of Japanese and Western NDEs, Journal of Near-Death Studies, vol. 32, issue 4, (Summer).

440. Ohkado, Masayuki (2016); A same-family case of the reincarnation type in Japan. Journal of Scientific Exploration, vol. 30, pp. 524-536.

441. Orne, E. C.; Whitehouse, W. G.; Dinges, D. F. and Orne, M. T. (1996); Memory liabilities associated with hypnosis: does low hypnotizability confer immunity? International Journal Of Clinical & Experimental Hypnosis, vol. 44, pp. 354-69.

442. Osis, Karlis (1986); Characteristics of purposeful action in an apparition case. Journal of the American Society for Psychical Research, issue 80, pp. 175-193.

443. Osis, Karlis, and Haraldsson, Erlendur (1997); At the hour of our death: A new look at evidence for life after death (3rd ed.), Hastings House Book Publishers, Norwalk, Connecticut, USA.

444. Osis, Karlis, and McCormick, Donna (1980); Kinetic effects at the ostensible location of an out-of-body projection during perceptual testing. Journal of the American Society for Psychical Research, issue 74, pp. 319-29.

445. Osis, Karlis and Haraldsson, Erlendur (1977b); Deathbed Observations by Physicians and Nurses: A Cross-Cultural Survey, The Journal of the American Society for Physical Research, vol. 71, no. 3.

446. Osis, Karlis and Haraldsson, Erlendur (1977a); At the Hour of Death, Avon Books, New York.

447. Osty, Eugen (1930); La vision de soi, Revue matapsychique, no. 4.

448. Overman Dean L. (1997); A Case Against Accident and Self-Organization, Rowman & Littlefield Publishers Inc, Maryland, USA.

449. Owen, Robert Dale (1860); Footballs on the boundary of another world, J. B. Lippincott. Philadelphia.

450. Owens, J. E., Cook, E. W., and Stevenson, I. (1990); Features of 'near-death experience' in relation to whether or not patients were near death, Lancet, vol. 336,

451. Oyama T.; Jin, T and Yamaya R. (1980); Profound Analgesic Effects of B-Endorphin in man. The Lancet, Volume 315, Issue 8160 (19 January 1980), pp. 109-164.

452. Palmieri, Arianna; Calvo, Vincenzo; Kleinbub Johann. R.; Meconi, Federica; Marangoni, Matteo; Barilaro, Paolo; Broggio, Alice; Sambin, Marco and Sessa, Paola (2014); "Reality" of near-death-experience memories: evidence from a psychodynamic and electrophysiological integrated study, Frontiers in Human Neuroscience, Volume 8, Article 429.

453. Pam Reynolds (2003) in "The Day I Died," prod. Kate Broome (British Broadcasting Corporation, 5 February 2003), Bristol, England.

454. Parish, Robert (2004); All about reincarnation; Astrolog Publishing House Ltd, Israel.

455. Parnia, Sam; Waller, D. G.; Yeates, R. and Fenwick, P. (2001); A Qualitative and Quantitative Study of the Incidence, Features and Aetiology of Near-Death Experiences in Cardiac Arrest Survivors. Resuscitation, vol. 48 (2001), pp. 149-56.

456. Parry, Hugh (1992); Thelxis: Magic and Imagination in Greek Myth and Poetry, University Press of America, ýLanhamý, Maryland.

457. Pasricha, Satwant (1995); Near death experiences in south India: A systematic survey. Journal of Scientific Exploration, vol. 7, no. 2. Pp. 161-71.

458. Pasricha, S. K., Keil, J., Tucker, J. B., and Stevenson, I. (2005); Some bodily malformations attributed to previous lives. Journal of Scientific Exploration, 19, pp. 359-383.

459. Pearson, Patricia (2015); Opening Heaven's Door: What the Dying Are Trying to Say About Where They're going, Atria Paperback, New York.

460. Peck, Morgan Scott (1983); People of the Lie. Simon & Schuster, New York.

461. Peden, Creighton W. (2010); Empirical Tradition in American Liberal Religious Thought, 1860-1960, Peter Lang Publishing Inc, New York.

462. Pember, George Hawkins (1975); Earth's Earliest Ages and Their Connection with Modern Spiritualism and Theosophy, Kregel Publications, Grand Rapids, Michigan, USA.

463. Penrose, Roger (1989); The emperor's new mind: Concerning computers, minds, and the laws of physics, Oxford University Press, New York.

464. Perry, C. W., Laurence, J. R., D'Eon, J., and Tallant, B. (1988); Hypnotic age regression techniques in the elicitation of memories: Applied uses and abuses. In H. M. Pettinati (Ed.), Hypnosis and memory (pp. 128-154), Guilford Press, New York.

465. Perty, Josef Anton Maximilian (1861); Die mystischen Erscheinungen der menschlichen Natur, Winter'sche Verlagschandlung, Leipzig and Heidelberg, Germany.

466. Petersen, Lauren Hackworth (2006); The Freedman in Roman Art and Art History, Cambridge University Press, New York.

467. Peterson, Robert (2013); Out-of-Body Experiences: How to Have Them and What to Expect, Hampton Roads Publishing Company, Newburyport, Massachusetts, USA.

468. Pettinati, Helen M. (1988); Hypnosis and memory: Integrative summary and future directions. In H. M. Pettinati (Ed.), Hypnosis and memory (pp. 277-291), Guilford Press, New York.

469. Piccinini, G., and Rinaldi, G. M. (1990); I fantasmi dei morenti: Inchiesta su una credenza [Phantasms of the dying: Survey of a belief], IL Cardo, Viareggio, Italy.

470. Pickover, Clifford (2008); Archimedes to Hawking: Laws of Science and the Great Minds Behind Them, Oxford University Press, USA.

471. Podmore, Frank (1894); Apparitions and thought-transference. Walter Scott, London.

472. Podmore, Frank (1897); Studies in Psychical Research, Kegan Paul, Trench, Trubner & Co. Ltd, London.

473. Podmore, Frank (2011); The Naturalisation of the Supernatural, Cambridge University Press, New York (Originally published 1908).

474. Polidoro, Massimo (2001); Final Seance: The Strange Friendship Between Houdini and Conan Doyle, Prometheus Books, Amherst, New York.

475. Potts, Michael (2002); The evidential value of near-death experiences for belief in life after death, Journal of Near-Death Studies, vol. 20,

476. Prager, Dennis (2013); A Finely Tuned Universe, in The Schwarz Report, August 2013 issue, vol. 53, no. 8.

477. Prigogine, Ilya (1980); From Being to Becoming, W. H. Freeman and Co, San Francisco.

478. Prince, Walter F. (1921); Peculiar Experiences connected with noted persons, Journal of the American Society for Psychical Research, vol. 15, pp. 109-131.

479. Prince, Walter F. (1926); A Review of the Margery Mediumship, The American Journal of Psychology, vol.37, no. 3, pp. 43-441.

480. Pye, Michael and Dalley, Kirsten (2013); Ghosts, Specters, and Haunted Places, The Rosen Publishing Group Inc, New York.

481. Radin, D. I., & Roll, W. G. (1994); A radioactive ghost in a music hall. Proceedings of Presented Papers: The Parapsychological Association 37th Annual Convention (pp. 337 – 346), Parapsychological Association Inc, Durham, North Carolina, USA.

482. Ramacharaka, Yogi (1909); The Life Beyond Death, YOGeBooks (Roger L. Cole), Hollister, Missouri, USA.

483. Ramesh, Chidambaram (2014); Thought-forms and Hallucinations: Some curious effects of the holographic mind process, Notion Press, Chennai, India

484. Ramster, Peter (1994); Past lives and hypnosis. Australian Journal of Clinical Hypnotherapy and Hypnosis, vol. 15 (issue 2), pp. 67-91.

485. Ramster, Peter (1990); In Search of Lives Past, Somerset Publishing, Sydney, Australia.

486. Randall, Lisa (2007); The case for extra dimensions, Physics Today, (July 2007 issue), American Institute of Physics.

487. Rankawat, B. D. (1959); Study of spontaneous cases, Indian Journal of Parapsychology, vol. 1, pp. 76-80.

488. Ransom, Champe (1987); Letter to the editor, Free Inquiry, vol. 7, no. 4.

489. Rawat, K. S., and Rivas, T. (2007); Reincarnation: The scientific evidence is building, Writers, Vancouver, Canada.

490. Rawlings, Maurice (1978); Beyond Death's Door, Thomas Nelson, Nashville, Tennessee, USA.

491. Rees, W. Dewi (1971); The Hallucinations of Widowhood, British Medical Journal, vol. 4 (October issue), pp. 39-41.

492. Registrar's office (1851); Calendar of Queen's [afterw.] University college, Hodges and Smith, Dublin.

493. Reichenbach, Bruce R. (1990); The Law of Karma: A Philosophical Study, Macmillan, London.

494. Reyna, Ruth (1973); Reincarnation and Science, Sterling Publishers Private Ltd, New Delhi, India.

495. Rhine, Joseph Banks (1960); Incorporeal personal agency: The prospect of a scientific solution, Journal of Parapsychology, issue 24, pp. 279-309.

496. Rhine, Louisa E. (1968); Hidden Channels of the mind, William Sloane, New York (original work published in 1961).

497. Rhine, Louisa E. (1957); Hallucinatory psi experiences. II. The initiative of the percipient in hallucinations of the living, the dying, and the dead. Journal of Parapsychology, issue 21, pp. 13-46.

498. Rhine, Louisa E. (1981); The Invisible Picture: A Study of Psychic Experiences, McFarland & Company Inc. Jefferson, North Carolina.

499. Richardson, Robert D. (2006); William James: In the Maelstrom of American Modernism, A mariner book, Boston.

500. Richet, Charles (1922); Traite de metaphychique, Felix Alcan, Paris.

501. Richet, Charles (1923); Thirty Years of Psychical Research, Salzwasser Verlag, Paderborn, Germany.

502. Ring, Kenneth. (1984); Heading toward omega, William Morrow, New York.

503. Ring, Kenneth (1980); Life at Death: A Scientific Investigation of the Near-Death Experience, published by 'Coward, McCann & Geoghegan', New York.

504. Ring, Kenneth (1988); Prophetic Visions in 1988: A Critical Reappraisal, Journal of Near-Death Studies, vol. 7, issue 1 (Fall 2988), Human Sciences Press.

505. Ring, Kenneth (1991); Amazing Grace: The Near-Death Experience as a Compensatory Gift, Journal of Near-Death Studies, vol. 10, issue 1.

506. Ring, Kenneth (2000); Religious Wars in the NDE Movement: Some Personal Reflections on Michael Sabom's Light and Death, Journal of Near-Death Studies vol. 18, issue 4.

507. Ring, Kenneth and Cooper, Sharon (1997); Near-Death and Out-of-Body Experiences in the Blind: A Study of Apparent Eyeless Vision, Journal of Near-Death Studies, vol. 16, issue 2.

508. Ringger, P. (1958); Die Mystik im Irrsinn, Neue Wissenschaft, issue 8, pp. 217-220.

509. Rinpoche, Sogyal (1993); The Tibetan Book of Living and Dying, Harper, San Francisco.

510. Roberts, Glenn and Owen, John (1988); The Near-Death Experience. British Journal of Psychiatry, issue 153, pp. 607-617.

511. Roberts, Jane (1993); How to develop your ESP power: he First Published Encounter with Seth, Lifetime Books, Hollywood, Florida, USA (Original work published 1966).

512. Roberts, Jane (1970); The Seth material, Prentice-Hall, Englewood Cliffs, New Jersey.

513. Roberts, Jane (1998); The early sessions: Volume 3 of the Seth material. New Awareness Network. Manhasset, New York.

514. Roberts, Jane (2000); ESP Power, Frederick Fell Publishers Inc, Florida, USA.

515. Roberts, Jane (1972); Seth Speaks: The Eternal Validity of the Soul. Englewood Cliffs, Prentice-Hall, New Jersey, [Notes by Robert F. Butts; new edition co-published 1994 Amber-Allen/New World Library, Novato, California].

516. Roesermueller, Wilhelm Otto (1957); Um die Todesstunde, Nurnberg, Selbstverlag, Germany.

517. Rogers, Sandra (2009); Lessons From the Light: In-Sights From a Journey to the Other Side, Warner Books, New York, (first published May 01, 1995).

518. Rogo, D. Scott (1972); A psychic study of 'the music of the spheres' (NAD, volume II), University Books, Secaucus, New York.

519. Rogo, D. Scott (1985); The search for yesterday: A critical examination of the evidence for reincarnation. Englewood Cliffs, Prentice-Hall, New Jersey.

520. Rogo, D. Scott (1986); Correspondence, Journal of the Society for Psychical Research, vol. 53, pp. 468-471.

521. Roll, William G. (1977); Poltergeists, In Benjamin B. Wolman (ed.), Handbook of Parapsychology, Van Nostrand Reinhold, New York, pp. 382-413.

522. Roll, William G. (1991); Journey to the Grey Ghost, Fate, (May issue), pp. 55-61.

523. Roll, W. G., and Persinger, M. A. (2001); Investigations of poltergeists and haunts: A review and interpretation. In J. Houran and R. Lange (Eds.) Hauntings and Poltergeists: Multidisciplinary Perspectives, McFarland & Company Inc, Jefferson, North Carolina.

524. Roll, William G. (2006); A Discussion of the Evidence that Personal Consciousness Persists After Death with Special Reference to Poltergeist Phenomena, Australian Journal of Parapsychology, vol. 6, no. 1, pp. 5-20.

525. Rommer, Barbara (2000); Blessing in Disguise: Another Side of the Near-Death Experience, Llewellyn Publications, St. Paul, Minnesota, USA.

526. Rosen, Eliot Jay (1998); Experiencing the Soul: Before Birth, During Life, After Death, Hays House, Carlsbad, California.

527. Rosen, David H. (1975); Suicide survivors: A Follow-up Study of Persons Who Survived Jumping from the Golden Gate and San Francisco-Oakland Bay Bridges, The Western Journal of Medicine, vol. 122 (issue 4, April).

528. Rosen, Eliot Jay (2006), Experiencing the Soul Before Birth, During Life, After Death, Motilal Banarsidass Publishers Pvt. Ltd, New Delhi, India.

529. Ross, Huge Norman (1995); The Creator and the Cosmos: How the Greatest Scientific Discoveries of the Century Reveal God, NavPress Publishing Group.

530. Rossi, Ernest L. (1987); The collected papers of Milton H. Erickson on hypnosis, vol. 1. The nature of hypnosis and suggestion, Irvington Publishers, New York.

531. Roy, Archie (1996); Archives of the Mind, SNU Publications, Stanstead, Canada.

532. Runsheng Tu (2018); Quantum Mechanics' Return to Local Realism, Cambridge Scholar Publishing, Newcastle Upon Tyne, UK.

533. Rush, Benjamin (1812); Mental inquiries and observations upon diseases of the mind, Kimber & Richardson, Philadelphia, Pennsylvania, USA.

534. Ryals, Steve (2006); Drunk with Wonder: Awakening to the God Within, Rock Creek Press, Ukiah, USA.

535. Sabom, Michael (1998); Light and Death: One Doctor's Fascinating Account of Near-Death Experiences, Zondervan, Grand Rapids, Michigan, USA.

536. Sabom, Michael (1982); Recollections of death: A medical investigation, Corgi Books, GB.

537. Sagan, Carl (1996); The demon-haunted world: Science as a candle in the dark, Random House, New York.

538. Sahay, K. K. N. (1927); Reincarnation: Verified cases of rebirth after death, Gupta Publishers, Bareilly, India.

539. Sall, Mallard J. (1976); Demon Possession or Psychology? A Critical Differentiation, Journal of Psychology and Theology, vol. 4 (issue 4).

540. Sandberg, Anne (1977); Seeing the invisible, Logos International, Plainfield, New Jersey.

541. Sartori, Penny (2008); The Near-Death Experiences of Hospitalized Intensive Care Patients: A Five-Year Clinical Study, Edwin Mellen, Lewiston, UK.

542. Schmicker, Michael (2002); Best Evidence: 2nd Edition, Writers Club Press, Lincoln, USA.

543. Schnabel, Jim (1997); Remote Viewers: The Secret History of America's Psychic Spies, Dell, New York.

544. Schroeter-Kunhardt, M. (1993); A review of near death experiences, Journal of Scientific Exploration, vol. 7, no. 3.

545. Schubert, Gotthilf Heinrich von (1967); Ansichten von der Nachtseite der Naturwissenschaft, Wissenschaftliche Buchgesellschaft, Darmstadt, Germany (Original work published in 1808).

546. Schmidt, Helmut (1976); PK effect on pre-recorded targets, Journal of the American Society for Psychical Research, vol. 70, issue 3, pp. 267-92.

547. Schwarz, Berthold (1994); Presumed Paranormal Linkage of Rings, International Journal of Psychosomatics, vol. 41, nos. 1-4, pp. 95-99.

548. Schwartz, Gary (2002); The Afterlife Experiments: Breakthrough Scientific Evidence of Life After Death, Pocket Books, New York.

549. Schwartz, Robert (2007); Courageous Souls: Do We Plan Our Life Challenges Before Birth?, Whispering Winds Press.

550. Scoboria, A., Mazzoni, G., Kirsch, I., and Milling, L. S. (2002); Immediate and persisting effects of misleading questions and hypnosis on memory reports, Journal of Experimental Psychology, vol. 8, issue 1.

551. Serdahely, William J. (1990); Pediatric near-death experiences, Journal of Near-Death Studies, vol. 9, issue 1.

552. Sharma, Poonam, and Tucker, Jim B. (2004); Cases of the Reincarnation Type with Memories from the Intermission Between Lives, Journal of Near-Death Studies, Vol. 23, issue 2.

553. Sharp, Kimberly Clark (1995); After the Light: What I Discovered on the Other Side of Life That Can Change Your World, William and Morrow & Co. Inc. New York.

554. Sheehan, Marianne S (2011); Evidence from near-death experience for the existence of consciousness outside the brain, a dissertation submitted in May 2011 for the degree of Master of Arts in Liberal Studies, Graduate School-Camden Rutgers, The State University of New Jersey.

555. Shirley, Ralpp (1936); The problem of rebirth: An enquiry into the basis of the reincarnationist hypothesis, Rider, London.

556. Shor, Ronald E. (1979); A phenomenological method for the measurements of variables important to an understanding of the nature of hypnosis. In E. Fromm & R. E. Shor (Eds.), Hypnosis: Developments in research and new perspectives (pp. 105-138), Aldine New York.

557. Shorey, Paul (1946); Plato's republic, William Heinemann, London.

558. Shrikhande, Mehra (2009); Paranormal experiences: Beyond the realm of reasons, Unicorn Books, New Delhi, India.

559. Shroder, Tom (1999); Old Souls: The Scientific Evidence for Past Lives, Simon & Schuster, New York.

560. Sidgwick, Henry (1892); On the Evidence for Clairvoyance, Proceedings of the Society for Psychical Research, vol. 7, pp. 30-99.

561. Sidgwick, Eleanor Mildred (1885); Notes on the Evidence, Collected by the Society, for Phantasms of the Dead. Proceedings of the Society for Psychical Research, Vol. 3, pp. 69-150

562. Sidgwick, H (1894); Report on the census of hallucinations, Proceedings of the Society for Psychical Research, issue 10.

563. Sidgwick, H. (1882); Address by the president at the first general meeting. Proceedings of the Society for Psychical Research, 1, pp. 7–12.

564. Siegel, Ronald (1980); The Psychology of Life After Death, American Psychologist, vol. 35, no. 10.

565. Sitwell, Sacheverell (1988); Poltergeists: an introduction and examination followed by chosen instances, Dorset Press, New York.

566. Smedley, Jenny (2010); Soul Angels, Hay House, London.

567. Smith, Huston (1965); The Religions of Man, Harper & Row, New York.

568. Smith, Huston (1976); Forgotten Truth, Harper & Row, New York.

569. Smith, Huston (2012); The Huston Smith Reader, University of California Press, USA

570. Smith, Susy (1964); The mediumship of Mrs. Leonard, University Books, Hyde Park, New York.

571. Smith, Susy (2000); Life Is Forever: Evidence for Survival After Death, iUniverse, USA.

572. Smith, Leonard S. (2010); Religion and the Rise of History: Martin Luther and the Cultural Revolution in Germany 1760-1810, James Clarke and Co., Cambridge, UK.

573. Snell, Joy (1959); The Ministry of Angels: Here and Beyond, Citadel Press, New York, (original work published 1918).

574. Society for Psychical Research (2012); The Proceedings of the Society for Psychical Research, vol. 11, Nabu Press, Charleston, South Carolina, USA.

575. Solomon, Grant and Solomon, Jane (1999); The Scole Experiment, Scientific Evidence and Life After Death Piatkus London. New edition 2006 Campion London.

576. Somers, Jenny (2009); Holy Shift: A true story of a woman channeling God's Love, Jesus and Jenny, Tucson, Arizona, USA.

577. Sondermann, Margot and Janzen, Catherine (2011); Deathbed Phenomena: Real or Imagined? A power point presentation given by Catherine Palliative Consult Team at Alberta Health Services.

578. Sorensen, Michele R., and Willmore, David R. (1988); The journey beyond life, Family Affair, Orem, Utah.

579. Spanos, N. P.; Menary, E.; Gabora, N. J.; DuBreuil, S. C. and Dewhirst, B. (1991); Secondary identity enactments during hypnotic past-life regression: A sociocognitive perspective. Journal of Personality and Social Psychology, vol. 61, issue 2, 308-320.

580. Spencer, Christine (2011); Pathways to Peace: Understanding 'Death' and Embracing Life, Balboa Press, Bloomington, Indiana, USA.

581. Spencer, Jon and Spencer Anne (1998); Powers of the mind. Orion.

582. Stanford, Rex G. (1987); The out-of-body experience as an imaginal journey: The developmental perspective, Journal of Parapsychology, vol. 51, no. 2, pp. 136-155.

583. Stanley, John M. (1988); Gods, Ghosts, and Possession. In Zelliot, E. Berntsen, M. (eds), The Experience of Hinduism: Essays on Religion in Maharashtra (pp 26-59), SUNY Press, Albany, New York.

584. Stapp, Henry (1989); The quantum theory of consciousness, Paper presented at the interrelationship between mind and matter.

585. Starbuck, Edwin D. (1906); The Psychology of Religion: An Empirical Study of the Growth of Religious Consciousness. Walter Scott, New York.

586. Steiger, Brad (2003); Real Ghosts, Restless Spirits, and Haunted Places, Visible Ink Press, Canton, Michigan.

587. Steiger, Brad (1966); Strange Guests, Ace Books, New York.

588. Steiger, Brad and Steiger, Sherry Hansen (1995); Children of the Light: The Startling and Inspiring Truth About Children's Near-Death Experiences and How They Illuminate the Beyond, Signet-Penguin, New York.

589. Stevens, Winchester E. (1887); The Watseka Wonder, Religio-Philosophical Publishing House, Chicago.

590. Stevenson, Ian (2006); Half a career with the paranormal, Journal of Scientific Exploration, vol. 20, no. 1, pp. 13-21.

591. Stevenson, Ian (1965); New evidence on an important detail in the case of Abraham Florentine, Journal of the American Society for Psychical Research, vol. 59, pp. 47-55.

592. Stevenson, Ian (1972); Are poltergeists living or are they dead? The Journal of the American Society for Psychical Research, vol. 66, no. 3.

593. Stevenson, Ian (1973); Characteristics of cases of the reincarnation type in Ceylon, Contributions to Asian Studies, vol. 3, pp. 26-29.

594. Stevenson, Ian (1974b); Twenty cases suggestive of reincarnation (2nd ed.) University Press of Virginia, Charlottesville, Virginia.

595. Stevenson, Ian (1975); Cases of the reincarnation type. I: Ten cases in India. University Press of Virginia, Charlottesville, Virginia.

596. Stevenson, Ian (1977a); The explanatory value of the idea of reincarnation, Journal of Nervous and Mental Disease, vol. 164, no. 5, pp. 305-326.

597. Stevenson, Ian (1977b); Research into the evidence of man's survival after death. Journal of Nervous and Mental Disease, issue 165, pp. 152-170.

598. Stevenson, Ian (1986); Characteristics of cases of the reincarnation type among the Igbo of Nigeria. Journal of Asian and African Studies, issue 21, pp. 204-216.

599. Stevenson, Ian (1987); Children who remember previous lives: A question of reincarnation, University Press of Virginia, Charlottesville. Virginia.

600. Stevenson, Ian (1977b); The Southeast Asian interpretation of gender dysphoria: an illustrative case report, The Journal of nervous and mental disease, vol. 165, no. 3.

601. Stevenson, I., and Edelstein, S. J. (1982); The belief in reincarnation among the Igbo of southeastern Nigeria with particular reference to connections between the ogbanje (repeater babies) and sickle-cell anemia. In W. G. Roll, R. L. Morris, & R. A. White (Eds.), Research in parapsychology 1981 (pp. 178-179), Scarecrow Press, Metuchen, New Jersey.

602. Stevenson, I., and Pasricha, S. (1980); A preliminary report on an unusual case of the reincarnation type with xenoglossy. Journal of the American Society for Psychical Research, vol. 74, pp. 331-348.

603. Stevenson, Ian (1959); The Uncomfortable Facts About Extrasensory Perception. Harper's Magazine, issue 219.

604. Stevenson, Ian (1960); The Evidence for Survival from Claimed Memories of Former Incarnations, Part 1, Journal of the American Society for Psychical Research, vol. LIV (April, 1960), no. 2.

605. Stevenson, Ian (1970); A communicator unknown to medium and sitters. Journal of the American Society for Psychical Research, vol. 64.

606. Stevenson, Ian (1974a); Xenoglossy: A Review and Report of a Case, University Press of Virginia, Charlottesville, Virginia.

607. Stevenson, Ian (1976); A preliminary report on a new case of responsive xenoglossy: The case of Gretchen, Journal of the American Society for Psychical Research, issue. 70, pp. 65-77.

608. Stevenson, Ian (1980); Cases of the reincarnation type. Ill: Twelve cases in Lebanon and Turkey, University Press of Virginia, Charlottesville, Virginia.

609. Stevenson, Ian (1982); The contribution of apparitions to the evidence for survival. Journal of the American Society for Psychical Research, vol. 76, October issue, pp. 341-358.

610. Stevenson, Ian (1983a); Cases of the reincarnation type. IV: Twelve cases in Thailand and Burma, University Press of Virginia, Charlottesville, Virginia.

611. Stevenson, Ian (1983b); American children who claim to remember previous lives, Journal of Nervous and Mental Disease, vol. 171, issue 12.

612. Stevenson, Ian (1983c); Cryptomnesia and parapsychology. Journal of the Society for Psychical Research, 52, pp. 1-30.

613. Stevenson, Ian (2001); Children Who Remember Previous Lives: A Question of Reincarnation (rev. ed.), McFarland, Jefferson, North Carolina, USA.

614. Stevenson, Ian (1990); Phobias in Children Who Claim to Remember Previous Lives, Journal of Scientific Exploration, vol. 4, no. 2.

615. Stevenson, Ian (1993); Birthmarks and Birth Defects Corresponding to Wounds on Deceased Persons, Journal of Scientific Exploration, vol. 7, no. 4.

616. Stevenson, Ian (1994); A case of the psychotherapist's fallacy: Hypnotic regression to 'previous lives'. American Journal of Clinical Hypnosis, vol. 36, pp. 188-193.

617. Stevenson, Ian (1995); Six Modern Apparitional Experiences, Journal of Scientific Exploration, vol. 9, no. 3, pp. 351-366.

618. Stevenson, I., and Cook, E. W. (1995); Involuntary memories during severe physical illness or injury. Journal of Nervous and Mental Disease, vol. 183, pp. 452-58

619. Stevenson, Ian (1997a); Where reincarnation and biology intersect, Praeger Publishers, Westport, Connecticut, USA.

620. Stevenson, Ian (1997b); Reincarnation and biology: A contribution to the etiology of birthmarks and birth defects (2 vols.), Praeger Publishers, Westport, Connecticut, USA.

621. Stevenson, Ian (2000); Unusual Play in Young Children Who Claim to Remember Previous Lives, Journal of Scientific Exploration, vol. 14, no. 4.

622. Stevenson, Ian and Beloff, John (1980); An Analysis of Some Suspect Drop-in Communications, Journal of the Society for Psychical Research, vol. 50, issue 785.

623. Stevenson, Ian and Keil, Jurgen (2005); Children of Myanmar Who Behave like Japanese Soldiers: A Possible Third Element in Personality, Journal of Scientific Exploration, vol. 19, no. 2.

624. Stevenson, Ian (2003); European Cases of the Reincarnation Type, McFarland, Jefferson, North Carolina, USA.

625. Stevenson, Ian (1984); Unlearned language: New studies in xenoglossy, University Press of Virginia, Charlottesville, Virginia, USA.

626. Stevenson, Ian (1974c); Some questions related to cases of the reincarnation type, Journal of the American Society for Psychical Research, vol 68, pp. 395-416.

627. Stokes, Douglas M. (2007); The Conscious Mind and the Material World: On Psi, the Soul and the Self, McFarland & Company Inc., North Carolina, USA.

628. Storm, Howard (2000); My Descent into Death: And the message of love which brought me back, Clairview Books, Great Barrington, Massachusetts, USA.

629. Story, Francis (1975); Rebirth as Doctrine and Experience: Essays and Case Studies. Buddhist Publishing Society, Kandy, Sri Lanka.

630. Stritter, Paul (1930); Seelsorge an Geistesschwachen, In. P. Blau (Ed.), Seelsorge an den Erwachsenen (pp. 172-191), Bertelsmann, Gütersloh, Germany.

631. Suckling, Nigel (2006); Witches, Artists' and Photographers' Press Ltd, London.

632. Sudduth, Michael (2016); A Philosophical Critique of Empirical Arguments for Postmortem Survival, Palgrave Macmillan, New York.

633. Surya, G. W. (1921); Der Tod kein Ende, Peter Hofmann, Freiburg im Breisgau, Germany.

634. Sutherland, Cherie (1989); Psychic Phenomena Following Near-Death Experiences: An Australian Study, Journal of Near-Death Studies, vol. 8 (issue 2, Winter 1989).

635. Suzuki, H. (2005); Rinshitaiken: Inochi no hibiki [Near-death experience: Resonance of life]. Yamato Shobo, Tokyo, Japan.

636. Swaab, Dick Frans (2014); We Are Our Brains: From the Womb to Alzheimer's, Penguin Books, London.

637. Tabori, Paul (1972); Pioneers of the unseen, Taplinger Publishing Company, Incorporated, New York.

638. Tachibana, Takashi (2003); Shogen: Rinshi taiken [Testimonies of near-death experience]. Bungeishunju, Tokyo, Japan.

639. Tanner, Amy Eliza and Hall, Stanley (1994); Studies in Spiritism, Prometheus, Buffalo, New York (first published in 1910).

640. Tarazi, Linda (1990); An unusual case of hypnotic regression with some unexplained contents, Journal of the American Society for Psychical Research, 84, pp. 309-344.

641. Tart, Charles T. (1974); Out-of-the-body experiences. In E. D. Mitchell, & J. W. White (Eds.), Psychic Exploration: A challenge for science (pp. 349-373), G. P. Putnam's Sons, New York.

642. Taylor, Greg (2014); The Dying Light: Exploring the strange phenomenon of lights seen at the time of death, Darklore, vol. 8, Daily Grail Publishing (August 19, 2014 issue).

643. TenDam, Hans (1987); Exploring Reincarnation, Arkana Press, London.

644. Thalbourne, Michael A. (2003); A Glossary of Terms Used in Parapsychology, Puente Publications, Charlottesville, Virginia, USA.

645. Thomas, Charls Drayton (1922); Some new evidence for Human survival, William Collins Publisher, London.

646. Thomas, Randy (1982); Death Is at Your Door Are You Ready?, Shalom International Publishers, Oxted, Surrey, UK.

647. Thompson, Richard L. (2003); MAYA: The world as virtual reality, Govardhan Hill Publishing, Alachua, Florida.

648. Thonnard, M., Charland-Verville, V., Brédart, S., Dehon, H., Ledoux, D., Laureys, S., (2013); Characteristics of near-death experiences memories as compared to real and imagined events memories, PLoS ONE, vol. 8 (issue 3).

649. Tipler, Frank (1994); The Physics of Immortality, Doubleday, New York.

650. Tobacyk J. J and Mitchell T. P (1987); The out-of-body experience and personality adjustment. Journal of Nervous and Mental Disease, vol. 175, issue 6, pp. 367-370.

651. Treffert, Darold A. (2010); Islands of Genius: The Bountiful Mind of the Autistic, Acquired, and Sudden Savant, Jessica Kingsley Publishers, London.

652. Tucker, Jim B. (2005); Life before Life: A Scientific Investigation of Children's Memories of a Previous Life, St. Martin's Press, New York.

653. Turner, K. H. (1970); A South Yorkshire haunt, Journal of the Society for Psychical Research, vol. 45.

654. Turner, Alice R. (1993); The History of Hell., Harcourt Brace and Company, New York.

655. Twemlow, S. W, Gabbard G. O. and Jones, F. C (1982); The out-of-body experience: A phenomenological typology based on questionnaire responses, American Journal of Psychiatry, issue 139, pp. 450-455.

656. Tyrrell, George Nugent Merle (1953); Apparitions, Pantheon Books, New York.

657. Tyrrell, George Nugent Merle (1961); Science and Psychical Phenomena/ Apparitions. New Hyde Park, University Books, New York.

658. Underwood, Peter (1980); Gazetteer of Scottish Ghosts, Fontana/Collins, Glasgow.

659. Van Gelder, David W. (1987); A Case of Demon Possession, Journal of Pastoral Care, vol. 41 (issue 2), pp. 151-161.

660. Van Lommel, Pim (2004); About the Continuity of Our Consciousness. Advances in Experimental Medicine and Biology, issue 550.

661. Van Lommel, Pim (2006); Near-death experience, consciousness and the brain: A new concept about the continuity of our consciousness based on recent scientific research on near-death experience in survivors of cardiac arrest, World Futures, vol. 62, pp. 134-151.

662. Van Lommel, Pim (2011); Near-death experiences: the experience of the self as real and not as an illusion, Annals of the New York Academy of Sciences, issue 1234, Oct. 2011, pp. 19-28.

663. Van Lommel, Pim. (2010); Consciousness Beyond Life. The Science of the Near-Death Experience, HarperCollins Publishers, New York.

664. Van Lommel, Pim; Wees, Ruud van; Meyers, Vincent, Elfferich, Ingrid (2001); Near-death experience in survivors of cardiac arrest: a prospective study in the Netherlands, The Lancet, vol. 358, (Dec. 15, issue).

665. Varga, Josie (2009); Visits from Heaven, A.R.E Press, Virginia, USA.

666. Venn, Jonathan (1986); Hypnosis and the reincarnation hypothesis: A critical review and intensive case study. Journal of the American Society for Psychical Research, vol. 80, pp. 409-425.

667. Vintini, Leonardo (2013); Xenoglossy: Evidence of past lives?, Science & Beyond, September 12-18 issue, The Epoch Times.

668. Waelti Ernst (1983); Der dritte Kreis des Wissens, Ansata, Interlaken, Switzerland.

669. Wagstaff, G. F.; Brunas-Wagstaff, J.; Cole, J.; Knapton, L.; Winterbottom, J. and Crean, V. (2004); Facilitating memory with hypnosis, focused meditation, and eye closure, International Journal of Clinical & Experimental Hypnosis, vol. 52, issue 4.

670. Wainer, Howard (2016); Truth or Truthiness: Distinguishing Fact from Fiction by Learning to Think like a data scientist, Cambridge University Press, USA.

671. Ward, Paul Von (2008); The Soul Genome: Science and Reincarnation, Fenestra Books, Arizona, USA.

672. Wassilko-Serecki, Zoe (1926); Observations on Eleonore Zugun, Journal of the American Society for Psychical Research, vol. 20, issue. 10, pp. 593-603.

673. Watters, R. A. (1935); Sleep, Journal of the American Society for Psychical Research, issue 29, pp. 101-10.

674. Weaver, Richard F. (2008); We Are Our Ancestors, RoseDog Books, Pittsburgh, Pennsylvania, USA.

675. Weber, Max (1963); The Sociology of Religion (Ephraim Fischoff, translation), Beacon Press, Boston.

676. Weintraub, Sandra (1998); The Hidden Intelligence: Innovation Through Intuition, Butterworth-Heinemann, USA.

677. Wiese, Bill (2017), 23 Minutes in Hell, Charisma House, Florida, USA.

678. Weiss, Brian (1988); Many Lives, Many Masters, Simon & Schuster, New York.

679. Weiss, Brian (2004); Same Soul, Many Bodies, Free Press, Simon & Schuster Inc., New York.

680. Weiss, Eric M. (2012); The Long Trajectory: The Metaphysics of Reincarnation and Life After Death, iUniverse Inc, Bloomington.

681. Wells, Amber D. (1993); Reincarnation Beliefs Among Near Death Experiencers, Journal of Near-Death Studies, vol. 12 (issue 1 fall 1993).

682. Wenger, Susanne, and Chesi, Gert (1980); Ein Leben Mit den Gottern, Perlinger Verlags Ges. m.b.H, Austria.

683. West, Ann Frazier (2014); The Great Transition: Bridges to the Afterlife, Balboa Press, USA.

684. Wettach, George E. (2000); The near death experience as a product of isolated subcortical brain function. Journal of Near-Death Studies, vol. 19, pp. 71-90.

685. Wheatley, J. M. O. (1979); Reincarnation, “astral bodies,” and “psi-components”, Journal of the American Society for Psychical Research, vol. 73, pp. 109-122.

686. Whiteman, Joseph Hilary Michael (1965); Evidence of survival from “other-world” experiences, Journal of the American Society for Physical Research, vol. 59.

687. Whitmer, O. J. (1924); Mediumistic communications and physical phenomena, Journal of the American Society for Psychical Research, vol. 18.

688. Whitton, Joel and Fisher Joe (1987); Life Between Life, Grafton Books, London.

689. Wickland, Carl A. (1924); 30 Years Among the Dead, Llewellyn Publishers, California.

690. Widdison, H. A. (2002); Book review of Children of the new millennium, Harold Widdison responds [Letter], Journal of Near-Death Studies, issue 20, pp. 281-285.

691. Williams, Bryan; Ventola, Annalisa; and Wilson, Mike (2007); Magnetic Fields and Haunting Phenomena: A Basic Primer for Paranormal Enthusiasts, Haunting Blog.

692. Williams, Gary (1989); A Life Beyond Death, Robert Hale, London.

693. Williamson, Kay (1972); Igbo-English Dictionary: Based on the Onitsha Dialect, Ethiope Publishing Corporation, Benin City, Nigeria.

694. Willis, Judy (2007); Brain-friendly Strategies for the Inclusion Classroom, Association for Supervision & Curriculum Development, Alexandria, Virginia, USA.

695. Wills-Brandon, Carla (2007); One last hug before I go: The mystery and meaning of deathbed visions, Hastings House Book Publishers, New York.

696. Wilson, Colin (2000); After Life: An Investigation of the Evidence for Life After Death Llewellyn Publications, St. Paul, Minnesota, USA.

697. Wilson, Ian (1982); All in the mind: Reincarnation, hypnotic regression, stigmata, multiple personality, and other little understood powers of the mind, Doubleday, Garden City, New York, (Originally published 1981 as Mind out of time? by Gollancz, London).

698. Wilson, Ian (1987); The after death experience: The physics of the non-physical, William Morrow Publishing, New York.

699. Wilson, Ian (1988); Review of Children who remember previous lives by I. Stevenson. Journal of the Society for Psychical Research, vol. 55, pp. 227-229.

700. Windt, Jennifer M. (2015); Dreaming: A Conceptual Framework for Philosophy of Mind and Empirical Research, The MIT Press, Cambridge, London.

701. Winkelman, Michael (1986); Trance states: A theoretical model and cross-cultural analysis, Ethos, vol. 14, issue 2 (Summer), pp. 174-203.

702. Winsham, Willow (2016); Accused: British Witches throughout History, Pen & Sword Books Ltd, Barnsley, South Yorkshire, UK.

703. Wittneben, Wilhelm (1934); Erziehung, Behandlung und Pflege Geistesschwacher. Geisteskrankenpflege, issue 38, pp. 146-154.

704. Woerlee, Gerald M. (2013); Illusory Souls, CreateSpace Independent Publishing Platform, Scotts Valley, California, USA.

705. Woerlee, Gerald M. (2005); Mortal Minds: The Biology of Near-Death Experiences, Prometheus Books, Amherst, New York.

706. Woznicki, Andrew N. (2007); Transcendent Mystery in Man: A Global Approach to Ecumenism, Academcia Press, Bethesda, USA.

707. Wright, J. Edward (2000); The Early History of Heaven, Oxford University Press, New York.

708. Wright, Sylvia Hart (2002); When Spirits Come Calling: The open-minded skeptic's guide to after-death contacts, Blue Dolphin Publishing, Nevada City, California.

709. Wuppuluri, Shyam and Ghirardi, Giancarlo (2017); Space, Time and the Limits of Human Understanding, Springer International Publishing AG, Cham, Switzerland.

710. Xiong, Jesse Hong (2010); The Outline of Parapsychology, University Press of America Inc., Maryland, USA.

711. Yacobi, Ben G. (2013); The Human Dilemma Life Between Illusion and Reality, Journal of Philosophy of Life, vol. 3, no. 3.

712. Yogananda, Paramhansa (2007); Autobiography of a Yogi, Sterling Publishers Pvt. Ltd, New Delhi, India (originally published 1946).

713. Young, Robert (2015); Parapsychology: Ghosts and Hauntings, The office of Parapsychological Societies, Nottingham, UK.

714. Zaleski, Carol (1987); Otherworld Journeys: Accounts of Near-Death Experience in Medieval and Modern Times, Oxford University Press, New York.

715. Zaleski, Carol (1995); Death and Near-Death Today, in Death, Ecstasy, and Other-Worldly Journeys, (ed. John J. Collins and Michael Fishbane), State University of New York Press, Albany, New York.

716. Zap, Jonathan (2012); Crossing the Event Horizon: Human Metamorphosis and the Singularity Archetype, Steam Press, Colorado, USA.

717. Zollner, Johann (1976); Transcendental Physics, reprint of the 1888 edition, Arno Press, New York.